老虎

P9-CRO-416

A
Qui
C

ACT Quick Start Guide

WELCOME TO *ACT 2015 6 PRACTICE TESTS WITH 12 EXPERT VIDEO TUTORIALS!*

Congratulations on taking the first step to the ACT score you need! The Kaplan *ACT 2015 6 Practice Tests with 12 Expert Video Tutorials* has a wide range of features you'll use to prepare for Test Day.

In this Quick Start Guide, we'll walk you through everything you'll need to know to take advantage of the book, practice tests, DVD, and online resources. We'll help you prep smarter and score higher.

Kaplan's *ACT 2015 6 Practice Tests with 12 Expert Video Tutorials* gives you everything you need for Test Day. Follow this handy checklist to get your studying on track:

o **Register your online companion** for extra practice, Live Online classroom events, chapter-specific tutorial videos, sample essays for the Writing section, and more.

o **Set a score goal** based on the schools you're considering applying to. Review admissions information or contact admissions departments for a strong idea of what to aim for.

o **Take the online Diagnostic Quiz** to figure out your strong and weak areas.

o **Build your study plan** with practice hours, scheduled practice tests, and review time leading up to Test Day.

o **Review** English, Reading, Math, Science, and Writing concepts.

o **Practice, practice, practice** with our quizzes and full-length tests in the book and online.

o **Watch the included DVD** containing instruction and tips from elite Kaplan teachers.

YOUR *ACT 2015 6 PRACTICE TESTS WITH 12 EXPERT VIDEO TUTORIALS* BOOK

Kaplan's *ACT 2015 6 Practice Tests with 12 Expert Video Tutorials* is packed with resources to help you get ready for Test Day.

It has:

- A targeted review of key ACT terms and concepts

- Tips and strategies for each exam section and every question type

- Lots of test practice (including three full-length exams in the book and Three online)

TAKE ADVANTAGE OF KAPLAN EXCLUSIVES

These powerful tools will help you score higher on Test Day!

SMARTPOINTS™

Throughout the book, you will see Kaplan's SmartPoints. Because the ACT follows established patterns and tests predictable content every year (and because of Kaplan's decades of preparing students for the ACT), Kaplan is able to give you a section-by-section breakdown of which question types will earn you points. This will tell you where you should spend the most time prepping.

SmartPoints rank the skills and topics that are tested most often on the ACT. Build your score to 36 by focusing on the points you need to earn!

USING YOUR ACT ONLINE COMPANION

1. REGISTER YOUR ONLINE COMPANION

The online companion gives you access to even more test prep, including three full-length practice tests, Fast Fact videos, registration for Live Online events, a Diagnostic Quiz, fresh new quizzes every month, and more!

Register your online companion using these simple steps:

1. Go to kaptest.com/booksonline.

2. Follow the on-screen instructions. Please have a copy of your book available.

2. TAKE THE ONLINE DIAGNOSTIC QUIZ

The Diagnostic Quiz will help you to do the following:

- **Identify your strengths and weaknesses.** This will help you target your practice time so you can work on the SmartPoints that will get you to your goal.

- **Develop your ACT study plan.** Once you review the results of your Diagnostic Quiz, you will know where to spend time. Build your study plan based on your needs and schedule.

  - Check your answers carefully, noting how many questions you got right and wrong, how long it took you to answer each question, and how often you skipped questions.

  - Look for patterns. Were you stronger in some areas than others?

- **Know what to expect on Test Day.** The Diagnostic Quiz provides you with a sample of every question type, so you'll know what's waiting for you on Test Day.

- **Reinforce key skills and earn more points!**

3. GET TO KNOW THE ACT AND CREATE YOUR STUDY PLAN

Remember, your *ACT 2015 6 Practice Tests with 12 Expert Video Tutorials* program is designed to meet your individual needs.

WHAT DOES THAT MEAN?

- **You're in control.** Study how and when it works best for you.

- **You can customize your study.** We've made your ACT program interactive—you get to mix things up by jumping between the book and the online resources.

Take some time to familiarize yourself with the contents of your *ACT 2015 6 Practice Tests with 12 Expert Video Tutorials* book. It has all the tools you'll need to conquer the ACT.

4. JOIN A LIVE ONLINE SESSION

Kaplan's ACT Live Online sessions are interactive instructor-led ACT prep lessons that you can participate in from anywhere you can access the Internet.

ACT Live Online sessions are held in a state-of-the-art virtual classroom—actual lessons in real time, just like a physical classroom experience. Interact with your teacher and other classmates using audio, instant chat, whiteboard, polling, and screen-sharing functionality. And just like courses at Kaplan centers, ACT Live Online sessions are led by experienced Kaplan instructors.

TO REGISTER FOR AN ACT LIVE ONLINE EVENT:

1. Once you've signed in to your student home page, open your Syllabus.

2. In the Syllabus window, go to the "Live Online Registration" menu option.

3. Click on the link. A separate window will appear with registration instructions.

ACT Live Online events are scheduled to take place throughout 2014. Please check your online companion for dates and times!

Please note: Registration begins one month before the session date. Be sure to sign up early, since spaces are reserved on a first come, first served basis.

5. WATCH THE FAST FACT VIDEOS

In Fast Fact videos, Kaplan's highly rated ACT teachers explain and reinforce the most important concepts from each chapter.

Fast Fact videos can be accessed only through your online companion.

Here's how:

1. Once you've signed in to your student home page, open your Syllabus.

2. In the Syllabus window, go to the "Fast Fact Videos" menu option.

3. Click on the link for the video you'd like to see. A separate window will appear with your video.

Good luck!

TIPS FOR CUSTOMIZING YOUR STUDY PLAN

The most effective study plan will adapt to your individual needs. Here are some helpful tips:

o Map the strongest and weakest areas from your Diagnostic Quiz against the SmartPoints for each area. Make sure the areas you're studying are not only ones where you missed questions, but also where you can substantially raise your score. Some topics matter more than others!

o Review the Kaplan content for areas that need the most improvement before starting the quizzes. Kaplan's strategies and tips will help you see the largest increases on your quizzes and practice tests.

o Make a study calendar for yourself based on your commitments and availability. Don't just figure you'll study "when you have time"—you're too busy for that! Plan your schedule so you know when you *are* studying and when you're *not*.

o Use the six full-length practice tests as milestones—don't plan on saving them all for the final weeks. Test yourself periodically and chart your progress.

o As time permits, go back to the question types that you aced so you can keep the material sharp.

o Take time to practice your essay writing. Understanding the essay requirements and practicing your writing will help you deliver a great essay on Test Day.

o Using your practice tests and quizzes, reevaluate your strengths and weaknesses regularly. If they change, adjust your plan accordingly.

Related Titles for College-Bound Students

AP Biology

AP Calculus AB & BC

AP Chemistry

AP English Language & Composition

AP English Literature & Composition

AP Environmental Science

AP European History

AP Human Geography

AP Macroeconomics/Microeconomics

AP Physics B & C

AP Psychology

AP Statistics

AP U.S. Government & Politics

AP U.S. History

AP World History

ACT English and Reading Workbook

ACT Math and Science Workbook

ACT Strategies for Super Busy Students

SAT Strategies, Practice, and Review

SAT Premier

12 Practice Tests for the SAT

SAT 2400

SAT Critical Reading Workbook

SAT Math Workbook

SAT Writing Workbook

SAT Strategies for Super Busy Students

Frankenstein: A Kaplan SAT Score-Raising Classic

The Tales of Edgar Allan Poe: A Kaplan SAT Score-Raising Classic

Dr. Jekyll and Mr. Hyde: A Kaplan SAT Score-Raising Classic

The Scarlet Letter: A Kaplan SAT Score-Raising Classic

The War of the Worlds: A Kaplan SAT Score-Raising Classic

Wuthering Heights: A Kaplan SAT Score-Raising Classic

SAT Score-Raising Dictionary

SAT Subject Test: Biology E/M

SAT Subject Test: Chemistry

SAT Subject Test: Literature

SAT Subject Test: Mathematics Level 1

SAT Subject Test: Mathematics Level 2

SAT Subject Test: Physics

SAT Subject Test: Spanish

SAT Subject Test: U.S. History

SAT Subject Test: World History

ACT®
6 Practice Tests with 12 Expert Video Tutorials

© 2014 by Kaplan, Inc.

Published by Kaplan Publishing, a division of Kaplan, Inc.
395 Hudson St., 4th Floor
New York, NY 10014

Printed in the United States of America

10 9 8 7 6 5 4 3 2 1

ISBN-13: 978-1-61865-778-7

Kaplan Publishing books are available at special quantity discounts to use for sales promotions, employee premiums, or educational purposes. For more information or to order books, please call the Simon & Schuster special sales department at 866-506-1949.

Contents

ACT QUICK START GUIDE

WELCOME TO KAPLAN'S *ACT 2015 6 PRACTICE TESTS WITH 12 EXPERT VIDEO TUTORIALS*

PART ONE: ACT BASICS

CHAPTER 1: Introduction to the ACT 3

Four Keys to ACT Success 4

ACT FAQs 6

ACT Registration Overview 11

CHAPTER 2: The Subject Tests: A Preview 13

English 15

Math 16

Reading 17

Science 19

Writing 20

CHAPTER 3: Taking Control: Your ACT Mind-Set and the Top Ten Strategies .. 23

The ACT Mind-Set 24

Top Ten Strategies for Mastering the ACT 25

Take Control 32

Basic Strategy Reference Sheet 33

PART TWO: THE ACT TESTS

Unit 1: English 37

CHAPTER 4:   English Part 1: Inside the ACT English Test **39**

The Kaplan Method for ACT English 39

Quick Tips 40

Timing: Pacing and Approach 41

Scoring 42

SmartPoint Breakdown 42

Grammar and Punctuation Rules to Know 44

Summary 49

CHAPTER 5:   English Part 2: ACT English Strategy in Depth **51**

Overview 51

Sentence Sense—3 Points 52

Punctuation—5 Points 54

Verb Tenses—6 Points 56

Word Choice—5 Points 57

Wordiness—5 Points 63

Connections—7 Points 65

Writing Strategy—4 Points 67

Organization—1 Point 68

Summary 70

Unit 2: Math 71

CHAPTER 6:   Math Part 1: Inside the ACT Math Test **73**

The Kaplan Method for ACT Math 73

Quick Tips 75

Timing 76

Scoring 76

Point Builders 76

SmartPoint Breakdown 79

100 Key Math Concepts 81

Summary 113

CHAPTER 7:   Math Part 2: ACT Math Strategy In Depth **115**

Overview 115

Number Properties—2 Points 116

Operations—3 Points 119

Variable Manipulation—7 Points 124

Proportions and Probability—6 Points 130

Coordinate Geometry—6 Points 143

Plane Geometry—7 Points 147

Patterns, Logic, and Data—3 Points 166

Trigonometry—2 Points 171

Summary 174

Unit 3: Reading 177

CHAPTER 8:   Reading Part 1: Inside the ACT Reading Test **179**

The Kaplan Method for ACT Reading 179

Quick Tips 181

Timing: Pacing and Approach 182

Scoring 183

SmartPoint Breakdown 183

Method Breakdown 185

Summary 196

CHAPTER 9:   Reading Part 2: ACT Reading Strategy In Depth **197**

Overview 197

Details—12 Points 198

Vocab-In-Context—1 Point 200

Inference—8 Points 201

Function—6 Points 203

Writer's View—1 Point 204

Generalizations—8 Points 206

Summary 212

Unit 4: Science 213

CHAPTER 10: Science Part 1: Inside the ACT Science Test **215**

The Kaplan Method for ACT Science 215

Quick Tips 217

Timing: Pacing and Approach 218

Scoring 219

SmartPoint Breakdown 219

Method Breakdown 220

Summary 225

CHAPTER 11: Science Part 2: ACT Science Strategy In Depth **227**

Overview 227

Figure Interpretation—12 Points 228

Simple Question Strategies 229

Patterns—11 Points 233

Scientific Reasoning—13 Points 239

Summary 246

Unit 5: Writing 247

CHAPTER 12: Writing Part 1: Inside the ACT Writing Test **249**

The Kaplan Method for ACT Writing 249

Quick Tips 250

Timing 251

Scoring 252

Method Breakdown 252

Summary 257

CHAPTER 13: Writing Part 2: ACT Writing Strategy in Depth **259**

Overview 259

Paragraph by Paragraph 260

Putting It All Together 266

View from the Other Side: Getting Your Score and Grading Essays 271

Summary 279

CHAPTER 14: Last-Minute Tips **281**

PART THREE: PRACTICE TESTS AND EXPLANATIONS

Practice Test One **287**

How to Take These Practice Tests 287

Answers and Explanations 344

Practice Test Two **373**

Answers and Explanations 434

Practice Test Three **461**

Answers and Explanations 531

Compute Your Score **569**

Welcome to Kaplan's *ACT 2015 6 Practice Tests with 12 Expert Video Tutorials*

Are you ready to conquer the ACT?

Kaplan knows a high score on the ACT exam is important to you. A great score can help you stand out from the crowd when applying to colleges and can help you get the scholarships and financial aid to pay for it all.

Kaplan has more than 75 years of experience getting students ready for their exams. We've spent decades building a powerful arsenal of test-taking tools designed with *you* in mind, and the book you have in front of you contains everything you need to score higher on the ACT.

The 2015 edition of Kaplan's *ACT 2015 6 Practice Tests with 12 Expert Video Tutorials* includes proven ACT strategies, six realistic ACT practice tests (three in the book and three online), a DVD of elite Kaplan teachers providing instruction and tips, and in-depth reviews of every kind of question the ACT will throw at you. Kaplan's ACT tools work. Use them to your advantage, and get ready to score higher on the ACT!

LET'S GET STARTED!

Kaplan's *6 Practice Tests for the ACT* has everything you need to get ready for Test Day, but how you use this book is *your* choice. No one knows your test-prep needs and schedule better than you, so we've designed this book to put you in control of the type and amount of study that best suit your needs.

This book is designed to allow you to determine the path your test prep takes. Use it front to back, or jump around and focus on the test sections you need the most help with—it's your call.

In addition to all the great test prep inside the book, we've put a Diagnostic Quiz online to help you determine your test strengths and weaknesses and focus your study plan. This is a great place to get started.

TAKE THE ONLINE DIAGNOSTIC QUIZ

Taking the online Diagnostic Quiz is a great way to figure out where your ACT skills stand and how to structure your study time between now and Test Day. Take the Diagnostic Quiz and see what sections are your strongest and which will require the most prep.

Here's how to access your ACT Diagnostic Quiz online:

1. Go to kaptest.com/booksonline.

2. Follow the on-screen instructions. Please have a copy of your book available.

BUILD YOUR ACT STUDY PLAN

Okay, so you've taken the Diagnostic Quiz. Now what? Well, now that you have a good idea which test sections are your strongest and which need the most attention, you are ready to make the most of this book and build your study plan.

YOUR ACT STUDY PLAN—FIVE STEPS TO SUCCESS

1. Carefully go through the lessons in this book, paying close attention to the areas that focus on the test sections that were weakest on your Diagnostic Quiz.

2. Don't hesitate to review challenging concepts more than once. Doing well on the ACT is worth the extra study time!

3. Take time to practice your writing skills for the ACT essay. Use the strategies provided in this book to wow the essay graders on Test Day!

4. As you gain comfort with the various ACT question types and test material, dive into the full-length practice tests in the back of the book. Don't save all of them for the end— use them to measure your growth and build confidence. Test yourself under realistic

Test Day conditions and chart your progress. If your strengths and weaknesses change, adjust your study plan.

Let's get started!

PART ONE

ACT Basics

CHAPTER 1

Introduction to the ACT

Before you plunge into studying for the ACT, let's take a step back and look at the big picture. What's the ACT all about? What does it do for you? How can you prepare for it? What do you need to do to get a high score? This chapter will answer these questions and more.

First, you should think of the ACT as an opportunity, not a barrier. In fact, you should be glad that you're taking it. Really. The purpose of the ACT is to help you get into the college of your choice and get the scholarships you need to pay for it. And it's something you can control: a strong ACT score doesn't depend on how good your high school is, how many college alumni you know, how rich and famous your family is, or whether any of your teachers will swear in a letter of recommendation that you're the greatest scientific mind since Isaac Newton. No, your ACT score only depends on you.

> **✔ EXPERT TUTOR TIP**
>
> If you have two weeks or fewer to prep for the ACT, don't panic. The first thing you should do is become familiar with the test. This chapter is the place to start.

It's important that you take the test in the right spirit. Don't be timid in the face of the ACT or unfamiliar with what it's going to ask. You can and *must* take control of the test. This book will show you exactly how to do that.

FOUR KEYS TO ACT SUCCESS

There are four basic keys to achieving ACT success. Following any of these by itself will improve your score. Following all four together will get you to where you want to be.

1. LEARN THE TEST

The ACT is very predictable. The test makers are excellent at crafting the types of challenges that show what they're trying to see in your score. As a result, the same kinds of questions, testing the same skills and concepts, appear every time the ACT is given. This is to your considerable advantage.

Because the test specifications rarely change, you can learn in advance what to expect on every section. Just a little familiarity can make an enormous difference. Here are a few ways learning the test will boost your score:

- **You'll know the directions.** Why waste valuable time reading directions when you can have them down pat beforehand? You need every second during the test to answer questions and get points.

- **You'll know the difficulty range of questions.** Every question on the ACT is worth the same number of points, and the questions aren't in any order of difficulty. Knowing this, you can plan your approach to recognize the points you can earn quickly and move past the questions that will take too long until you can get back to them. Doing the questions in the order the ACT gives them to you isn't a strategy. Finding every last point you can get *is*.

- **You'll get extra points by guessing.** Unlike other standardized tests, the ACT has no wrong-answer penalty. Knowing how to apply that fact can boost your score significantly. You miss 100 percent of shots you don't take. So if you can't answer a question, guess.

- **You'll know how to write a high-scoring essay.** If you are taking the optional Writing test, learning how it is evaluated will help you get a top score.

We'll help you get a better understanding of the ACT in the next chapter, **The Subject Tests: A Preview.**

2. LEARN THE KAPLAN METHODS AND STRATEGIES

The ACT isn't like the exams you take in school. Most school exams test your memory for what you've just been taught. Instead, the ACT tests your problem-solving skills and how you use them, mostly on unfamiliar content. So instead of worrying about what you do or don't know, focus on learning the Kaplan problem-solving Methods and Strategies to earn you points!

Most ACT questions can be answered without perfect knowledge of the material being tested. Often, all you need to do to succeed on the ACT is to think strategically and creatively. We call this kind of strategic, creative frame of mind the ACT Mind-Set.

How do you put yourself into the ACT Mind-Set? You continually ask yourself questions such as: "What am I being asked? What does this mean? How can I put this into a form I can understand and use? How can I do this faster?" Once you develop some savvy test-taking skills, you'll find yourself capable of working out problems that, at first reading, might have seemed unsolvable. In fact, we'll show you how you can sometimes get right answers when you don't even understand the questions.

There are many, many specific strategies you can use to boost your score. Here are just a few things you'll learn:

- **You'll learn the peculiarities of the ACT format.** Except for the Writing test, the ACT is a multiple-choice test. The correct answer is *always* in front of you—you just have to identify it. We'll show you how to develop specific tactics for each question type to find the correct answer. Wrong answers often take predictable forms as well, so knowing how to recognize them can give you an important edge.

- **You'll learn a plan of attack for each subject test.** We'll show you useful and distinct ways of attacking each subject test. You'll learn the most common questions and content on each section so you know what will get you the most points. You'll learn how to do "question triage"—deciding which questions to do now and which to save for later. You'll learn the Kaplan Method—designed to get you points quickly and systematically—for each ACT subject test. You'll learn gridding techniques to avoid any answer sheet disasters.

- **You'll learn "unofficial" ways of getting right answers fast.** On the ACT, your score is based on whether you get the right answer, not how you decide which choice to select. That's different from most high school tests, which give credit for showing that you've done questions the "right" way (that is, the way you were taught to do them by your high school teacher). We'll show you how to find creative shortcuts—methods that will save you precious time and net you extra points.

3. LEARN THE TESTED MATERIAL

The ACT is designed to test skills and concepts learned in high school and needed for college. But familiarity with the test, coupled with effective test-taking strategies, will take you only so far. For your best score, you need to sharpen the skills and content knowledge that the ACT tests.

The good news is that most of the content on the ACT is covered by sophomore year at most high schools, with the majority of it even earlier than that. So you've probably already learned most of what the ACT expects you to know, but you may need to spend some time remembering or finding better ways to approach the information. That's partly what this book is for—to remind you of the knowledge you already have and to build and refine the specific skills you've developed so far. Here are just a few of the things we'll review:

- How to read graphs and tables efficiently for the Science section.

- The rules for grammar and punctuation (yes, there are consistent and absolute rules, and we'll tell you what they are).

- Math rules for triangles, probabilities, algebraic expressions, and more.

- The difference between generalizations and details, inference and summary, and how to make a passage map that saves you more time than it takes to make it.

- What goes into an excellent persuasive essay, what to leave out, and what to choose if you're running out of time.

4. PRACTICE, PRACTICE, PRACTICE

Practice creates confidence. On Test Day, you need to have the Kaplan Methods and Strategies and the tested concepts ready to go and be relaxed enough to let them all work. So reading and understanding the contents of this book are key, but there's one more step: you need to make the Kaplan Methods part of your everyday routine. The best way to do that is to practice as much as possible.

Test Day will bring its own challenges—you have to be up early to take a long test, in a room full of people you may or may not know, everyone in a state of anticipation and nervousness—and the anxiety is contagious! You'll be the one who doesn't let nerves take over and make you forget what you know about doing well. Your best ally is the confidence practice gives you.

Note: If you don't have time to practice with all of the sections of this book, you can (and should!) practice in the areas you feel weakest.

So here are your four keys to ACT success:

1. Learn the test.

2. Learn the strategies.

3. Learn the material tested.

4. Practice, practice, practice.

Follow these steps, and you'll find yourself just where you want to be: in full command of your ACT test-taking experience, ready to get your highest score. Count on it.

ACT FAQS

Here are some quick answers to the questions students ask most frequently about the ACT.

WHAT IS THE ACT?

As you know, the ACT is a standardized test. That means it tests predefined concepts in predictable ways and is administered to all students the same way. Each time the ACT is administered, it has the same number of questions per section, the same distribution of passages, the same timing, and the same average level of difficulty. You'll learn more about the tested concepts and the predictability of the ACT as you work with this book. For now, you should understand one thing: the more you know about how the test is written and structured, the more in control you'll feel on Test Day. You can only work on the Math section when the proctor announces, "You have the next 60 minutes to work on Section 2," but you don't necessarily need to work on the questions in any particular order. As you learn more about each section, you'll find your own way of approaching the questions with confidence and a plan for earning the most points possible. Your success begins with knowing exactly what to expect on the ACT.

So before anything else, take some time and get to know your test. Let's start with the basics.

The ACT is a three-hour exam (three and a half hours if you take the optional Writing test) taken mostly by high school juniors and seniors to gain admission to and scholarships for college. It is not an IQ test; it is a test of problem-solving skills—which means you can improve your performance by preparing for common question types.

Because the skills being tested and the format of the test are standardized, the universities get a straightforward and understandable way of comparing students, no matter their academic backgrounds and no matter how grade inflation affects grade point averages. So you can be sure that the admissions offices are going to take a serious look at your test scores.

To evaluate those skills, the ACT utilizes four subject tests: English, Math, Reading, and Science, as well as the optional Writing test. All of the subject tests are primarily designed to test skills rather than knowledge, though some knowledge is required—particularly in English and Math, which test your ability to quickly and accurately apply rules you've learned throughout your school years.

HOW IS THE ACT STRUCTURED?

- The ACT is about three hours long (three and a half with the Writing test). There will be a short break between the Math and Reading subject tests.

- It consists of a total of 215 scored multiple-choice questions and one optional essay.

- It is comprised of four subject tests and an optional Writing test:

    – English (45 minutes, 75 questions)

    – Math (60 minutes, 60 questions)

    – Reading (35 minutes, 40 questions)

    – Science (35 minutes, 40 questions)

    – Writing (30 minutes, 1 essay question)

HOW IS THE ACT SCORED?

The ACT is scored differently from most tests that you take at school. Your ACT score on a test section is not reported as the total number of questions you answered correctly, nor does it directly represent the percentage of questions you answered correctly. Instead, the test makers add up all of your correct answers in a section to get what's called your raw score. They then use a conversion chart, or scale, that matches up a particular raw score with what's called a scaled score. The scaled score is the number that gets reported as your score for that ACT subject test. For each version of the ACT administered, the test maker uses a unique conversion chart that equates a particular raw score with a particular scaled score.

ACT scaled scores range from 1 to 36. Nearly half of all test takers score within a much narrower range: 17–23. Tests and scores on different dates vary slightly, but the data below is based on a recent administration of the test and can be considered typical.

ACT Approximate Percentile Rank*	Scaled (or Composite) Score	Percentage of Questions Correct
99%	33	90%
90%	28	75%
74%	24	63%
49%	20	53%
28%	17	43%

*Percentage of ACT takers scoring at or below given score

Notice that to earn a score of 20 (the national average), you need to answer only about 53 percent of the questions correctly. On most tests, getting only a bit more than half the questions right would not be a passing grade, nor the average. Not so on the ACT. A score of 20 puts you in the middle range of test takers.

> ✔ **EXPERT TUTOR TIP**
>
> Just a few questions right or wrong on the ACT can make a big difference. Answering only five extra questions correctly on each subject test can move you from the bottom of the applicant pool into the middle or from the middle up to the top.

The score table includes two very strong scores: 28 and 33. Either score would impress almost any college admissions officer. A 28 would put you in the top 10 percent of the students who take the exam, and a 33 would put you in the top 1 percent. Even a 33 requires getting only about 90 percent of the questions right! So the best-scoring students will probably get at least a dozen questions wrong, but will still get the scores they need to get into college.

If you earn a score of 24, you'll be in about the 74th percentile. That means that you did as well as or better than 74 percent of the test takers—in other words, you're in the top quarter of people who took the ACT. That's a strong score, but notice that to earn this score, you need only about 63 percent of the questions correct. On most tests, a score of 63 percent is probably a D or lower. But on the ACT, it's about a B+.

HOW MANY ACT SCORES WILL YOU GET?

The ACT scaled score we've talked about so far is technically called the Composite score—when people say "I got ___ on the ACT," this is what they're talking about. While the Composite score is really important, you'll see a dozen or more different scores and subscores when you get your ACT results: the Composite score, four (or five) subject scores, and up to eight subscores. Though the subject scores can play a role in decisions or course placement at some schools, the subscores usually aren't as important as the Composite. So feel free to skim over the following chart if you aren't ready to look at subscores.

Here's the full battery of ACT scores (1–36) you'll receive:

English Score (1–36)	Usage/Mechanics subscore (1–18); Rhetorical Skills subscore (1–18)
Mathematics Score (1–36)	Pre-Algebra/Elementary Algebra subscore (1–18); Algebra/Coordinate Geometry subscore (1–18); Plane Geometry/Trigonometry subscore (1–18)
Reading Score (1–36)	Social Studies/Sciences subscore (1–18); Arts/Literature subscore (1–18)
Science Score (1–36)	There are no subscores in Science.
(Optional) Combined English-Writing Score (1–36)	There are no subscores for the Combined English-Writing score. This score does not count toward your Composite score, but colleges will see it.
(Optional) Writing Score (0–12)	There are no subscores in Writing.

HOW DO COLLEGES USE YOUR ACT SCORE?

The most important score is typically the Composite score (which is an unweighted average of the four major subject scores). This is the score used by most colleges and universities in the admissions and scholarship process. The subject scores and subscores may be used for advanced placement or occasionally for scholarships, but they are primarily used by college advisors to help students select majors and first-year courses.

Although many schools deny that they use benchmark scores as cutoffs, students have had mixed experiences, and it's well worth understanding the impact of all of your scores.

Highly competitive universities generally decline to accept students with any Composite scores below 22 or 23. For less competitive schools, the benchmark score may be lower than that; for some very selective schools, the cutoff may be higher.

To be clear, no school uses the ACT as an absolute or stand-alone bar to admission; for most applicants, though, a low ACT score can be decisive. As a rule, only students whose backgrounds are extremely unusual or who have overcome enormous disadvantages are accepted if their ACT scores are below the school's benchmark.

SHOULD YOU TAKE THE OPTIONAL WRITING TEST?

The ACT calls the Writing test optional, but you will want to find out whether either your high school (if you're taking the ACT as part of your school's curriculum) or the colleges you're applying to require it. If they do, it's not optional! A list of colleges requiring the test is maintained on the ACT website, www.act.org/aap/writing. If you are unsure about what schools you will apply to, you should plan to take the Writing test. However, testing will be available later if you decide not to take the Writing test and discover later that you need it. This book will give you strong guidance on achieving your best score on the Writing test.

HOW DO SCHOOLS USE THE OPTIONAL WRITING TEST?

The ACT Writing test may be used for either admissions or course placement purposes, and sometimes both. Students who take the Writing test will receive an English score, a Writing subscore, and a combined English-Writing score on a 1–36 scale. (The Combined English-Writing score is not averaged into the Composite score.) Copies of the essay (with the graders' comments) will be available online for downloading. Schools that do not require the Writing test will also receive the Combined English-Writing score for students who have taken the Writing test, unless the school specifically asks *not* to receive those results.

SHOULD YOU GUESS ON THE ACT?

The short answer? Yes! The long answer? Yes, always!

As you've seen, ACT scores are only based on the number of correct answers. But questions you leave blank and questions you answer incorrectly simply don't count for or against your score—unlike some standardized tests, the ACT doesn't have a wrong answer penalty. That's why you should *always* guess on every ACT question you can't answer, even if you don't have time to read it; you have a statistical likelihood of getting each question right just by answering! Though the questions vary enormously in difficulty, harder questions are worth exactly the same as easier ones. So it pays to mark the hardest questions to return to later and to guess on them, and spend your time gaining all the easier points you can find first.

CAN YOU RETAKE THE TEST?

You can take the ACT as many times as you like before it's time for your college applications to be done. If you take it more than once, you can select whichever test score you prefer to be sent to colleges when you apply. However, you can only take advantage of this option if, at the time you register for the test, you do not designate certain colleges to receive your scores automatically. Thus, if you are even possibly interested in taking the test more than once, it is crucial that you not designate any colleges when you register for the test. You can (for a small additional fee) have ACT scores sent to colleges at any time after the scores are reported.

So if you can afford the small extra fee to send the scores again, give yourself the freedom to retake the test (unless you're taking it under the wire and need your scores to reach your target schools ASAP). What this means, of course, is that even if you don't get the score you're looking for the first time, you can give yourself another chance without the schools of your choice seeing every score. The ACT is one of the few areas of your academic life in which you get a second chance. Still, keep in mind that your goal is to get your desired score as soon as possible by using your Kaplan Strategies and Methods. Once you get the score you're looking for, you can breathe a little easier about your college applications!

> ✔ **EXPERT TUTOR TIP**
>
> The ACT is offered many times per year, so plan your prep and testing around the date that will give you the most time to prepare. Consider activities, class tests, and personal plans when setting your prep and test schedule so you can give your preparation the attention it deserves.

ACT REGISTRATION OVERVIEW

- To get a registration packet, see your guidance counselor, or contact:

  ACT Student Services

  2727 Scott Boulevard, minizip 46

  P.O. Box 451

  Iowa City, IA 52243-0451

  Phone: (319) 337-1270

- You can also register online at www.actstudent.org.

- Students with disabilities or with other special circumstances can call (319) 337-1332.

- Go online: visit the test maker's website at www.act.org for the latest information on test registration, fees, and content.

- The basic fee at press time for the ACT is $36.50 without the Writing test and $52.50 with the Writing test in the United States. (For students testing outside the United States or Canada, the fee is $69.50 or $85.50 for the ACT with Writing test.) This price includes reports for you, your high school, and up to four college choices. There are additional fees for late registration, standby testing, changing test centers or test dates, and additional services and products.

- In the United States, the ACT is administered in September, October, December, February, April, and June. (The February date is not available in the state of New York.) In selected states, the ACT is also offered in late September. Register early to secure the time you want at the test center of your choice and to avoid late registration fees.

- You may take the ACT as often as you wish. Many students take it twice, once as a junior and again as a senior. There are no limitations on how many times you can take the ACT, but there are some restrictions on how often you can test or how late the schools you're applying to will accept your application.

- Be sure you take your test center admission ticket and acceptable identification with you to the test center. Acceptable forms of identification are a photo ID or a recently published photo with your full name printed. Unacceptable forms of identification are a birth certificate, Social Security card, or any other ID without photo. You will not be admitted without acceptable identification. Check the ACT website at the time of registration and shortly before your test to be sure you have the right documentation.

- Check with ACT, Inc., for all the latest information on the test. Every effort is made to keep the information in this book up-to-date, but changes may occur after the book is published.

- Go online (act.org) to make sure you know ALL the ACT regulations for Test Day. **Note:** Violation of the test rules, such as an alarm going off, a phone ringing in the test room, or use of a unapproved calculator may result in your dismissal from the room and your answer sheet not being scored.

You might be considering whether to take the ACT, the SAT, or both. For more information on the SAT, go to the College Board's website at www.collegeboard.com. While the SAT and ACT have similar purposes, their structure and content are different enough that many people prefer one over the other. Take a sample test of each to find out which will show you at your best for your applications.

THE PLAN EXAM

Students taking the ACT may also be aware of the PLAN® exam, a test offered to 10th-grade students that offers a preview of the format and content of the ACT. A student's success on this exam is often an accurate predictor of success on the ACT. The PLAN exam helps students decide which courses to take in their junior and senior years of high school. It helps them consider certain career paths prior to college, based on their strengths or weaknesses as indicated by their scores. To learn more, visit PLAN's website for student information at www.actstudent.org/plan.

CHAPTER 2

The Subject Tests: A Preview

Okay, now you've seen how the ACT is set up. But to really do well, you've got to know something about the ACT subject tests and how each breaks down into points:

Looking at each content area, you want to see a road to 36—a set of questions covering a predictable range of content, with a set number of points that will get you to your goal score on Test Day. The ACT has been very careful and successful in determining which types of questions do the best job of evaluating your overall score. Over the decades that Kaplan has studied this, we've been able to create a road map of your path to 36 points. We call the questions on this road map the *SmartPoints*.

SmartPoints are specific types of questions—like "Detail" in English or "Plane Geometry" in Math—that you can *know* will show up a certain number of times and make up a certain amount of your score on Test Day. What's the benefit of knowing this? You will have no doubt exactly where you *should* and *shouldn't* spend time studying. If you miss half of the questions about circles, it could lower your score up to 3 points. If you miss half of the questions about *sine-cosine-tangent*, it will bring your score down a maximum of 1 point. So which do you want to study?

Want to see how you get to 36 on each section? Here it is:

Point Value	English
7	Connections
6	Verb Tenses
5	Punctuation
5	Word Choice
5	Wordiness
4	Writing Strategy
3	Sentence Sense
1	Organization
36	Total

Point Value	Math
7	Plane Geometry
7	Variable Manipulation
6	Proportions and Probability
6	Coordinate Geometry
3	Operations
3	Patterns, Logic, and Data
2	Number Properties
2	Trigonometry
36	Total

Point Value	Reading
12	Detail
8	Inference
8	Generalization
6	Function
1	Vocab-in-Context
1	Writer's View
36	Total

Point Value	Science
13	Scientific Reasoning
12	Figure Interpretation
11	Patterns
36	Total

You'll be looking in depth at all of the questions as you move through this book, but it will all come back to these points. These are the points you'll be earning to get your score, and you'll be making choices as you go through your preparation about how to invest your time.

In addition to finding the best ways to answer questions, you'll also be studying how to approach each section of the test strategically. Remember: **The questions are not arranged in order of difficulty.** This should change your approach substantially—every question is another chance to raise your score, and you need to find every point you can get, wherever it is.

So here's a preview of the types of questions and strategies you'll see on each of the subject tests. After we look at the four required subject tests, we'll give you a preview of the optional Writing test. Let's get started.

ENGLISH

The English test lasts 45 minutes and includes 75 questions. That works out to about 30 seconds per question, but you'll learn in the English chapters to organize your time around whole passages, not individual questions.

You're not tested on spelling or vocabulary on the ACT—there are absolutely no spelling questions of any type, and you won't be asked to define any vocabulary words. Rather, the ACT is designed to test your understanding of the conventions of English—punctuation, grammar, sentence structure—and of rhetorical skills. Rhetorical skills consist of strategies like organizing the text and making sure it's consistently styled and concise. So you'll learn the "things to know" on the English test here, but keep in mind that it is mostly organized around following rules and identifying well-written language.

The average number of questions students get right is higher on the English section than on any other ACT subject area, but that also means there's a harder scoring scale on this section. To earn an average English subscore (a 20, say), you would have to get almost two-thirds of the questions right, while on the rest of the test you would need to get only about half of the questions right.

THE FORMAT

More than half of the English questions follow a standard format. A word, phrase, or sentence in a passage is underlined. You're given four choices: to leave the underlined portion alone (NO CHANGE, which is *always* the first choice) or to replace it with one of three alternatives.

A single question can test several kinds of writing errors. We find that about one-third of the English questions test your ability to write concisely (we call these Wordiness questions), about another third test for logic and sense (Word Choice and Sentence Sense questions), and the remaining one-third test hard-and-fast rules of grammar and punctuation. By recognizing which questions you do best on and which appear most often, you'll know which areas to study.

TO OMIT OR NOT TO OMIT

Some English questions offer, as one of the alternatives, the chance to completely omit the underlined portion.

On recent ACTs, when OMIT has appeared as a choice, it's been correct more than half of the time. Before choosing OMIT, however, read the passage text *without* the underlined portion to ensure that it is clear and correct that way.

NONSTANDARD-FORMAT QUESTIONS

Some ACT English questions—about 20 per test—don't follow the typical format of presenting you with an underlined portion and three possible revisions; they are referred to as Nonstandard-Format questions. Such questions may ask for the LEAST acceptable alternative to the underlined part, or which of the offered choices best accomplishes a specific goal, or whether to add or delete material, or how to rearrange the passage. For questions like these, it's important to read carefully! Because they often deal with the passage as a whole, many Nonstandard-Format questions occur at the end of a passage.

We think you'll like the English subject test. Picking the best way of saying something, identifying awkward phrases, and playing with the pieces of a passage can be fun. We'll cover strategies for the English question types in the English chapters.

MATH

The Math test is 60 minutes long and includes 60 questions. That works out to one minute per question, but you'll wind up using more time on some questions and less on others.

THE FORMAT

All of the Math questions have the same basic multiple-choice format, with a stand-alone question and five possible answers (unlike questions on the other subject tests, which have only four choices each).

The questions cover a wide range of math topics, from pre-algebra to plane geometry and even a little bit of trigonometry. More emphasis is placed on earlier-level math skills (variable manipulation, order of operations) and less on the higher-level math. This book contains the 100 Key Math Concepts for the ACT to help you review the math content you need.

READING AND DRAWING DIAGRAMS

About one-third of the Math questions either give you a diagram or describe a situation that should be diagrammed. For these questions, the diagrams are crucial—you don't get any points for solving questions in your head, so draw *everything* out.

> ✔ **EXPERT TUTOR TIP**
>
> In ACT Math questions, the choice "cannot be determined" is rare. When it does appear, it's rarely the right answer, and is almost always wrong in a question that comes with a diagram or for which you can draw one.

HOW TO APPROACH A STORY PROBLEM

About another third of the Math questions are story problems. A good way to comprehend—and resolve—a story problem is to think of a real situation like the one in the story. Translating into a situation you can imagine can be a lot easier than relating abstract numbers. Imagining an actual trip with miles and speeds and turns makes questions more approachable. (Note: We'll show you more about questions like these and alternative ways to answer them later on.)

> ✔ **PERFECT SCORE TIP**
>
> Don't let variables or abstract stories confuse you. When you see them, calm down and make them simpler by putting real numbers in for the variables. You'll learn more about this Picking Numbers Strategy in Math Workout 1.

GETTING THE CONCEPT

Finally, about one-third of ACT Math questions directly ask you to demonstrate your knowledge of specific math concepts.

These three types of Math questions, of course, will be discussed more fully in the Math chapters.

READING

The Reading test is 35 minutes long and includes 40 questions. It contains four passages, each followed by 10 questions. You should allow three minutes (or less) to read and mark up the passage. You will then have about 30 seconds per question.

THE FORMAT

There are four categories of reading passages: Prose Fiction, Social Science, Humanities, and Natural Science. You'll always get one passage in each category, always in that order. The passages are about 1,000 words each and are written at about the same difficulty level as college textbooks and readings. After each passage, you'll always find 10 questions.

> ✔ **PERFECT SCORE TIP**
>
> You do not have to do the passages in order. For example, if you always have trouble with Prose but are very good at Natural Science, do Natural Science first to make sure you don't run out of time to get those easy points. Develop a personal order that works for you, especially if you have trouble with time.

Three main Reading SmartPoints—Detail, Inference, and Generalization—account for 28 out of your 36 points. In other words, just getting those three topics right puts you in the 90th percentile! We'll dig into all three in the Reading chapters, but let's take a quick look at each now, since they make up so much of the test.

NAILING DOWN THE DETAILS

Detail questions ask about things stated explicitly in the passage. Your challenge is to find the exact place in the passage where the answer can be found and match the detail from the text in the passage with the correct answer (by locating either similar words or paraphrases). The other choices will try to tempt you by presenting facts from other parts of the passage, bringing in new information, or drawing conclusions that the passage doesn't directly support. But every question has exactly one right answer, and if you can find the specific reference, those points are yours!

> ✔ **PERFECT SCORE TIP**
>
> Remember, the scorers are not looking for your opinions or ideas about the passage. Base all your answers on what is explicitly written in the passage—not your own knowledge of the material.

The instructions will also encourage you to "refer to the passage." That's a good idea before you look at the answers—find the answer in the passage, predict in your own words what the answer will say, then find it in the answers provided. This will help you to avoid being tempted by wrong answers.

MAKING AN INFERENCE

Most Reading passages also include a large number of Inference questions, which require you to "read between the lines"—to conclude something that *must be true* based on what is in the passage, but is not directly stated.

Whereas Detail questions asked specifically about items in the text, Inference questions ask you to go a step beyond what's stated. Inference questions may seem like they're asking you to guess, but that's not how the ACT works! Some of the choices for Inference questions will be definitely false, and some may or may not be true, but the right answer is always something that MUST be true based on what is stated in the passage.

GETTING THE BIG PICTURE

Along with Detail and Inference questions, the Reading subject test also includes Generalization questions. Some Generalization questions ask about the passage as a whole, requiring you to find the purpose, tone, or structure of the passage. Others ask you to evaluate the writing.

Language like "the author's main point" or "the passage overall" tells you that you're looking at a Generalization question. To correctly answer these, you need to consider the points that are most important to the point of passage, and make sure your answer doesn't go far beyond the scope of the passage. Look for verbs like "argue," "show," "prove," or "describe"—passages that do one probably don't do another, so if you're looking at a passage that's just description, "argue" or "prove" might be key words to avoid.

You'll look at the four types of Reading passages and the question types they all have in common in the Reading chapters.

SCIENCE

The Science test is 35 minutes long and includes 40 questions. It has seven passages, each with five to seven questions. This breaks down to approximately 5 minutes per passage, including questions.

Good news: you don't have to be a scientist to succeed on the ACT Science test. All the test requires is common sense and careful reading skills (though a knowledge of standard scientific processes and procedures sure does help). You'll be given passages containing various kinds of scientific information—drawn from the fields of biology, chemistry, physics, geology, astronomy, and meteorology—which you'll have to familiarize yourself with and use as a basis for inferences.

THE FORMAT

On the Science test, the seven passages are broken down as follows:

- Three passages (each with approximately five questions) about tables and graphs

- Three passages (each with approximately six questions) about experiments

- One passage (with approximately seven questions) that presents opposing viewpoints on the same issue

ANALYZING DATA

Up to two-thirds of the questions on the Science test will require you to read data from graphs or tables. On easier questions, you need only identify and report the information on the charts. On harder questions, you will need to draw inferences or note patterns in the data.

Conducting Experiments

Other Science questions require that you understand the way experiments are designed and what they prove. For example, part of a passage might describe an experiment and ask you to understand what can be proved from each step, avoiding answers that aren't definitely true or related to other steps.

> ✔ **PERFECT SCORE TIP**
>
> Remember that like Reading, Science questions will never ask you to make inferences too far beyond what is given. Analyze the data, but DO NOT make unjustified conclusions.

THE PRINCIPLE OF THE THING

The remaining Science questions require you either to logically apply a principle or to identify ways of defending or attacking a principle. In some passages, the question will involve two scientists stating opposing views on the same subject, but this is not *always* the case.

We'll be showing you strategies for each kind of Science question in the three Science chapters.

WRITING

The Writing test is 30 minutes long and is comprised of one persuasive essay. You'll be given an issue on which you must take a position, supporting your point of view with arguments and evidence.

You don't have to be a great creative writer to succeed on the ACT Writing test, nor should you be concerned with being "right." Instead, you have to show that you can focus on an issue and argue your point of view in a coherent, direct way with concrete examples. Furthermore, the essay graders are not primarily concerned with your grammar and punctuation skills, as long as your points are clear. You are being tested on your ability to communicate in writing.

One of the biggest challenges of the Writing test is the time frame. With only 30 minutes to read about the issue, plan your response, draft the essay, and proofread it, you have to work quickly and efficiently. Coming up with a plan and sticking to it are key to succeeding on the Writing test.

THE FORMAT

The Writing test consists of one prompt that lays out the issue and gives directions for your response. There are no choices of topic; you have to respond to the topic that's there. Don't worry too much about not knowing anything about the issue you have to write about—test makers craft topics that will be relevant to high school students and about which they can be expected to have a point of view. And it isn't your point of view, even, that will earn you points, but your ability to clearly state and defend one.

WRITING TEST SKILLS

The graders realize that you're writing under time pressure, and they expect you to make some mistakes. **The content of your essay is not relevant; readers are not checking your facts, nor will they judge you on your opinions. They only want to see how well you can communicate a relevant, coherent point of view.**

The ACT identifies the following as the skills tested on the Writing test:

- **Stating a clear perspective on an issue.** This means directly answering the question in the prompt—picking a side.

- **Providing supporting evidence and logical reasoning.** This means offering relevant support for your opinion and building an argument based on concrete details and examples. Don't just "think" you're right. Be able to prove it.

- **Maintaining focus and organizing ideas logically.** You've got to be organized, avoid digressions, and tie all your ideas together in a sensible way.

- **Writing clearly.** This is the only skill addressing your ability to write directly, and it's limited to clarity.

CHAPTER 3

Taking Control: Your ACT Mind-Set and the Top Ten Strategies

Now that you have a better idea of the kind of questions you'll see on the ACT, it's time to start developing strategies for managing them. In other words, you have to start developing your ACT Mind-Set.

The ACT, as you've seen, isn't a normal test that requires you to rely almost exclusively on your memory of things you've learned. On a normal test, you'd see questions like this:

> The "golden spike," which joined the Union Pacific and Central Pacific Railroads, was driven in Ogden, Utah, in May 1869. Who was president of the United States at the time?

To answer this question, you have to resort to memory dredging. Either you know the answer is Ulysses S. Grant or else you don't. No matter how hard you think, you'll *never* be able to answer this question if you don't remember that fact.

But the ACT doesn't test your memory. The answer to every ACT question can be found on the test—the ACT tests your ability to find the right one. Theoretically, if you read carefully and understand the words and concepts the test uses, you can get any ACT question right.

Notice the difference between the previous regular test question and the following ACT-type question:

Example

1. What is the product of n and m^2, where n is an odd number and m is an even number?

    A. An odd number

    B. A multiple of 4

    C. A noninteger

    D. An irrational number

    E. The square of an integer

Aside from the obvious distinction (this question has choices, while the previous one does not), there's another difference: the ACT question tests your ability to understand a situation rather than your ability to remember a fact. Nobody expects you to know off the top of your head what the product of an odd number and the square of an even number is. But the ACT test makers do expect you to be able to roll up your sleeves and figure it out (as we'll do throughout this book).

THE ACT MIND-SET

Most students walk into ACT with the same mind-set they use for normal tests. With their brains on "memory mode," students often panic because they can't seem to "remember" enough to answer the questions. **But you know that's not how to get points. You get points for finding the right answer where it is on the page, not remembering it from before the test started.**

On the ACT, if you understand what a question is really asking, you can almost always answer it. For instance, take the previous math problem. You might have been thrown by the way it was phrased. "How can I solve this problem?" you may have asked yourself. "It doesn't even have numbers in it!"

But a prepared student isn't surprised by questions like this and knows how to solve them. This Kaplan book will show you a number of ways of solving every question, even if you aren't sure yet how to start. This chapter contains the top ten strategies you'll use to build your ACT Mind-Set!

✔ **EXPERT TUTOR TIP**

ACT questions are puzzles to solve. Don't think: "Can I remember?" Think: "Let me figure this thing out!"

By the way, the answer to the question is (B). Any odd number (n) times any even number (m or m^2) will be an even number, which eliminates (A), (C), and (D) immediately. But it won't necessarily be a perfect square, which eliminates (E). If you pick numbers, you'll see (B) is definitely right. More on that later!

Of course, this doesn't always mean the questions are easy. Many ACT questions are built on basic concepts but are tough to answer nonetheless. The previous problem, for instance, is difficult because it requires some thought to figure out what's being asked and some abstract thinking to deal with variables instead of numbers. This isn't only true in Math—it's the same for every part of the ACT.

The creative, take-control kind of thinking of the ACT Mind-Set is something that will help you on every ACT question you encounter. As you'll see, being in the ACT Mind-Set means reshaping the test-taking experience so that you are in the driver's seat.

It means:

- Answering questions **if** you want to (by guessing on high-difficulty questions rather than spending more time on them than they're worth)

- Answering questions **when** you want to (by skipping tough-but-doable questions and coming back to them after you've gotten all of the easy questions done)

- Answering questions **how** you want to (by using "unofficial" ways of getting correct answers quickly)

That's really what the ACT Mind-Set boils down to: taking control, being creative, and selecting specific questions to answer to get points as quickly and easily as you can.

What follows are the top ten strategies you need to do just that.

> 🛜 **GO ONLINE**
>
> With three full-length practice tests and more online, you'll get plenty of opportunities to practice the strategies in this chapter.

TOP TEN STRATEGIES FOR MASTERING THE ACT

1. TRIAGE THE QUESTIONS

In a hospital emergency room, the triage nurse is the person who evaluates each patient and decides who gets attention first and who should be treated later. You should do the same thing on the ACT. Every question is worth the same number of points, but they don't all take the same amount of time to solve. Your first job is to find the questions you can get quickly and easily, putting those points in the bank while you go back to work on the ones that will take longer.

Practicing triage is one of the most important ways of controlling your test-taking experience. Follow these steps to approach the test strategically:

- If the question looks comprehensible and reasonably doable, do it right away.

- If the question looks tough and time-consuming, but ultimately doable, skip it for now, circle the question number in your test booklet, and come back to it later. (Make sure to skip that line on your grid, too!)

- If the question looks impossible, forget about it. Guess and move on. *Never* to return unless you have gotten literally every other question right.

> ✔ **EXPERT TUTOR TIP**
>
> The key to question triage is to evaluate questions quickly. If you linger over these decisions, you will lose valuable time on Test Day.

This triage method will ensure that you spend the time needed to do all the quick and easy questions before getting bogged down with tougher ones. Doing the questions in the order they're listed isn't a strategy—it's not a good use of time to spend three minutes struggling on a hard question when you could move on to two or more others that you could answer correctly instead!

Answering easier questions first has another benefit: it gives you confidence to answer harder ones later. Doing problems in the order *you choose* rather than in the order imposed by the test gives you control.

YOUR TRIAGED PLAN OF ATTACK

For the English, Reading, and Science tests, the best plan of attack is to do each passage as a block, because the questions wind up being related to each other. Take a first pass through the questions, doing the easy ones, guessing on the impossible ones, and skipping any that look like they might cause trouble. Then make a second pass (a "cleanup pass"), and do those questions you think you can solve with some elbow grease. Keep an eye on your overall per-passage timing (which you'll learn about in the individual subject test chapters) so you don't spend so long on those elbow grease questions that you take away time from the next passage.

For Math, you use the same two-pass strategy, except you move through the whole subject test twice. Work through the doable questions first, then come back and attack the questions that look possible but tough or time-consuming. The questions are not in order of difficulty, and more importantly *you* will be better at some question types than others, so it's crucial you see every question.

No matter what subject test you're working on, **be extremely careful to grid your answers in the right place.** It's easy to misgrid when you're skipping around, so check your line numbers frequently. And of course, *make sure you have an answer gridded for* **every** *question by the time the subject test is over!*

2. PUT THE MATERIAL INTO A FORM YOU CAN UNDERSTAND AND USE

ACT questions are rarely presented in the simplest, most helpful way. In fact, your main job for many questions is to figure out what the question means so you can solve it. Since much of the material is presented in a puzzle form, one of your best strategies for taking control is to recast (reword) the material into a form you can handle better. While some methods will only apply to specific question types, many can help you on every section.

MARK UP YOUR TEST BOOKLET

This strategy should be employed on all four subject tests. In Reading and Science, you can reduce the amount of rereading you have to do by circling or underlining main ideas, important transitions, or other items you'll want to return to quickly. Make yourself a road map of the passage, labeling each paragraph so you understand how the ideas all fit together. That way, you'll also know— later, when you're doing the questions— where in the passage to find certain types of information you need.

> ✔ **EXPERT TUTOR TIP**
>
> Write all over your test booklet. Crossing out wrong answers eliminates confusion and helps you to see clearly which answer is correct. Underlining key points when reading passages helps you to determine the main idea.

In Math, you'll have a lot of figuring to do and diagrams to draw. Remember—you don't get extra points for solving the questions in your head, but you do stand to *lose* points if you make a mistake because you didn't write it out. And in English, you'll dramatically improve your chances of finding the right answer if you cross out wrong answers as you identify them.

REWORD THE QUESTIONS

You'll find that you also need to do some recasting of the *questions*. For instance, take a question from a Science passage that asks "According to Figure 1, at approximately what latitude would calculations using an estimated value at sea level of $g = 9.80$ m/sec^2 produce the least error?"

Ask yourself: "What does *produce the least error* mean?" We're looking for a solution, like in the Math section—a point on a graph. And we're looking for it in terms of latitude—a degree on the *x*-axis. So the question is really just asking, "At what latitude does 9.80 (*y*-axis) hit the curve?" Now that's a form of the question you can understand, and you can answer it by reading the chart.

DRAW DIAGRAMS

Often, what the Math section in particular is evaluating is whether you can translate information out of a question and into a diagram, and sometimes it's just easier to solve if you can visualize. For instance, take a look at the following math problem:

"Jason bought a painting with a frame 1 inch wide. If the dimensions of the outside of the frame are 5 inches by 7 inches, which of the following could be the length of one of the sides of the painting inside the frame?"

Looking at the question the first time, you might be tempted to either just picture it in your head or to subtract 1 from the outside dimensions and assume the inside dimensions are 4 by 6 (and pick choice (G)). Why isn't this the right answer? Take a look at a sketch of it to find out:

Subtracting 1 from 5 by 7 doesn't work because the frame goes all the way around—above and below the painting and to the right and left. So you actually need to subtract 1 from *each side*, much clearer when you look at it—if the outside dimensions are 5 by 7, the inside dimensions must be 3 by 5.

So remember: on the ACT, put everything into a form that you can understand and use.

3. IGNORE IRRELEVANT ISSUES

It's easy to waste time on ACT questions by considering irrelevant issues. Just because an issue looks interesting, or you're worried about something, doesn't make it important.

Questions like this usually contain distractions. Sometimes the distractions will fix something that doesn't need fixing, or will introduce information that may be interesting but doesn't actually apply. So we have to focus on the relevant issue: what is the question asking?

Remember, you've got limited time, so don't get caught up in issues that won't get you a point.

4. CHECK BACK

Remember, the ACT is not a test of your memory. It's an open-book test. All of the information you need is in the test itself, so don't be afraid to refer to it.

Many questions will contain reference to a specific line, table, graph, or experiment. *Always* refer back to the section referenced—that's what it's there for!

Common wrong answers may either refer to a fact in the passage that appears in the wrong section (providing a detail from paragraph 2 in a question that asks about paragraph 3) or refer to outside information you know or suspect to be true, but is not stated to in the passage.

Checking back is especially important in Reading and Science because of how many details the passages contain. Often, wrong answers will be misplaced details taken from different parts of the passage or things that don't answer the question properly but that might sound good to you if you aren't careful. By checking back in the passage, you can avoid choosing such tempting wrong choices.

There's another important lesson here: **don't pick a choice just because it contains key words you remember from the passage.** Many wrong choices are distortions—they use the right words but say the wrong things. Look for choices that contain the same ideas you find in the passage.

Remember: The best way to avoid choosing misplaced details and distortions is to refer to the passage.

5. ANSWER THE RIGHT QUESTION

This strategy is a natural extension of the last. As we said, **the ACT often includes among the wrong choices for a question the correct answer to a *different* question.** Under time pressure, it's easy to fall for one of these red herrings, thinking you know what's being asked for but finding something else.

A common form for this to take is a math question with multiple variables, asking for the solution to one of them, but providing the solution to others in the answer choices. If the question asks for *x* and you solve for *y*, you may have done the math right, but the answer still won't get any points.

Always check the question again before choosing your answer. In this case, by stopping short of solving all the way through, you might have fallen for three of the other choices. You're doing all the right work—get the right answer too, by answering the right question.

6. LOOK FOR THE HIDDEN ANSWER

On many ACT questions, the right answer is hidden or disguised in one way or another. For example, you might work out a problem and get 1.5 as your answer, but then find that 1.5 isn't among the choices. Then you notice that one choice reads $\frac{3}{2}$. You've found the hidden answer! It pays to think flexibly about numbers.

There's another way the ACT can hide answers. **Many ACT questions have more than one possible right solution, though only one correct choice is given. The ACT will hide that answer by offering one of the less obvious possible answers to a question.**

Keep in mind that though only one right choice for each question will be offered, that right answer may not be the one that occurs to you first. This can lead to second-guessing your work, when you should be looking for the answer you solved for. In this situation, a common mistake is to pick an answer that seems sort of like the answer you're looking for, even when you know it's wrong—it looks "close enough." Don't fall for it—if you know something is wrong, don't select it, and if you don't find your answer, don't assume you're wrong. Try to think of another right way to answer the question.

7. GUESS INTELLIGENTLY

An unanswered question is always wrong, but even a wild guess may be right. The odds are clear: if you have *no idea* and guess, you have a 20 to 25 percent chance (depending on the subject test) of getting the point. If you know at least one wrong answer, your odds go to 25 to 33 percent, and up from there. Your odds if you don't guess? Always 0 percent. *Always* guess on every ACT question you can't answer. Never leave a question blank.

You'll be doing two different kinds of guessing during your two sweeps through any subject test:

1. Blind guessing (which you do mostly on questions you deem too hard or time-consuming to spend time on at all)

2. Strategic guessing (which you do mostly on questions that you do some work on but don't get all the way through)

When you guess blindly, just choose any letter you feel like choosing. Don't fall for any rumors that there is a letter choice that appears most frequently. There's no validity to that—the answers are truly random. So just pick any letter.

When you guess in a strategic way, on the other hand, you've usually done enough work on a question to eliminate at least one or two choices. If you can eliminate any choices, you'll up the odds of guessing correctly.

Here are some fun facts about guessing: If you were to work on only half of the questions on the ACT but get them all right, then guess blindly on the other half of the questions, your composite ACT score would be around 23 (assuming you had a statistically reasonable success rate on your guesses). A 23 would put you in roughly the top quarter of all those who take the ACT. And all you had to do was answer half of the questions correctly.

On the other hand, if you were to hurry and work on all the questions but get only half of them right, you'd earn around a 19, which is below the 50th percentile.

How? Why are you better off answering half and getting them all right than answering all and getting only half right?

Here's the trick: The student who works carefully and answers half of the questions right and skips the others can still take guesses on the unanswered questions—and odds are this student will have enough correct guesses to move up four points, from a 19 to a 23. But the student who works too quickly, answers all the questions, and gets half wrong doesn't have the luxury of taking guesses.

In short, **guess if you can't figure out an answer for any question!**

8. BE CAREFUL WITH THE ANSWER GRID

Your ACT score is based on the answers you select on your answer grid. Even if you work out every question correctly, you won't get the score you earned if you misgrid your answers. So be careful! Don't disdain the process of filling in those little "bubbles" on the grid. Sure, it's mindless, but under time pressure, it's easy to lose control and make mistakes.

It's important to **develop a disciplined strategy for filling in the answer grid.** Many students gain speed by gridding in the answers in groups rather than one question at a time. Give it a try on one of your Kaplan practice tests, if you haven't before. What you should do is this: As you figure out each question in the test booklet, circle your answer. Then, transfer those answers to the answer grid in groups of five or more (until you get close to the end of the section, when you should start gridding answers one by one—you don't want to be caught with ungridded answers when time is called).

Gridding in groups like this cuts down on errors because you can focus on this one task and do it right. It can also save time you'd otherwise spend moving papers around, finding your place, and redirecting your mind. Answering ACT questions takes deep, hard thinking. Filling out answer grids is easy, but you have to be careful, especially if you do a lot of skipping around. Shifting between hard thinking and careful bookkeeping takes time and effort.

During the test, the proctor should warn you when you have about five minutes left on each subject test. But don't depend on proctors! **Rely on your own watch.** When there are five minutes left on a subject test, start gridding your answers one by one. With a minute or two left, start filling in everything you've left blank. Remember: Even one question left blank could cut your score.

9. USE THE LETTERS OF THE CHOICES TO STAY ON TRACK

One oddity about the ACT is that even-numbered questions have F, G, H, J (and, in Math, K) as choices, rather than A, B, C, D (and, again, E in Math). This might be confusing at first, but you can make it work for you. **A common mistake with the answer grid is to accidentally enter an answer one row up or down. On the ACT, that won't happen if you**

pay attention to the letter in the answer. If you're looking for an A and you see only F, G, H, J, and K, you'll know you're in the wrong row on the answer grid.

Another advantage of having answers F through K for even-numbered questions is that it makes you less nervous about patterns in the answers. It's common to start worrying if you've picked the same letter a few times in a row. Since the questions have different letters, this can't happen on the ACT. Of course, you could pick the first choice (A or F) for several questions in a row, but this shouldn't worry you. It's common for the answers in the same position to be correct three times in a row, and even four times in a row isn't unheard of. It's all a matter of random order, and sometimes that will look like an intentional pattern. It isn't.

10. KEEP TRACK OF TIME

During each subject test, you have to pace yourself. Trying to answer as many questions as possible until time is called isn't a strategy. On average, English, Reading, and Science questions should take about 30 seconds each, and Math questions should average less than one minute each (full details are available in each individual content area of this book). Remember to take into account the fact that you'll probably be taking two passes through the questions.

A great way to keep track is to set your watch to 12:00 at the beginning of each subject test so it will be easy to check your time. Again, don't rely on proctors, even if they promise that they will dutifully call out the time every 15 minutes. Take control of your own timing.

More basic questions should take less time, and harder ones will probably take more. In Math, for instance, you need to go much faster than one per minute during your first sweep. But at the end, you may spend two or three minutes on each of the harder problems you work out.

TAKE CONTROL

You are the master of the test-taking experience. A common thread in all ten strategies is that you should take control. That's Kaplan's ACT Mind-Set. Do the questions in the order you want and in the way you want. Don't get bogged down or agonize. Remember, you don't earn points for suffering, but you do earn points for moving on to the next question and getting it right.

THE ACT IS NOT SCHOOL

You have spent at least 11 years in school at this point. There, you learned some techniques that will not help you on the ACT. (Want two good examples? "Don't guess on a test" and "If you show your work on math problems, you'll get partial credit.") Many of these school-driven methods will actually work *against* you on the ACT.

Test Day is an exciting and stressful event. Don't approach it with a familiar school mind-set. Instead, practice using the ten strategies in this chapter so that you're rehearsed and confident for Test Day.

Just reading and understanding these strategies once before the test doesn't mean you'll do them effectively on Test Day. The ACT Mind-Set will work only if you use it, so practice!

As you practice, time yourself. Buy or borrow a digital watch, and get used to working with it so it doesn't beep at the wrong moment. Your cell phone will be turned off during the test, so you won't be able to use it as a timekeeper.

Practice the various sections of the test at home and take practice tests in single sittings to make sure you're comfortable and ready to get your highest score on Test Day.

> ### 🛜 GO ONLINE
>
> Before going on to the subject-specific workouts, take the online Diagnostic Quiz if you haven't already. You'll learn where to focus your study time.

BASIC STRATEGY REFERENCE SHEET

THE FOUR KEYS TO ACT SUCCESS

1. LEARN THE TEST

- Learn the directions before Test Day.

- Become familiar with all the subject tests.

- Get a sense of the range of difficulty of the questions.

2. LEARN THE KAPLAN METHODS AND STRATEGIES

- Develop a plan of attack for each subject test.

- Develop a guessing strategy that works for you.

- Find "unofficial" ways of finding answers fast.

3. LEARN THE MATERIAL TESTED

- Bone up on weak areas.

- Find out what is and isn't part of the ACT knowledge base.

- Use the ACT study resources section to review important Math and English concepts.

4. PRACTICE, PRACTICE, PRACTICE

THE TOP TEN STRATEGIES

1. Do question triage.

2. Put the material into a form you can understand and use.

3. Ignore irrelevant issues.

4. Check back.

5. Answer the right question.

6. Look for the hidden answer.

7. Guess intelligently.

8. Be careful with the answer grid.

9. Use the letters of the choices to stay on track.

10. Keep track of time.

PART TWO

The ACT Tests

UNIT 1: ENGLISH

The Basics:

45 Minutes

75 Questions

5 Passages

Pacing:

Pace your time by the passage as opposed to minutes per question.

Spend nine minutes per passage, including questions.

TEST DAY DIRECTIONS AND FORMAT

The directions on the English test illustrate why there's an advantage to knowing them beforehand—they're long, complicated, and if you learn them now, you'll already be racking up points while everyone else is reading the directions on Test Day. The directions on Test Day will look like this:

Directions: In the five passages that follow, certain words and phrases are underlined and numbered. In the right-hand column, you will find alternatives for the underlined parts. In most cases, you are to choose the one that best expresses the idea, makes the statement appropriate for standard written English, or is worded most consistently with the style and tone of the passage as a whole. If you think the original version is best, choose NO CHANGE. In some cases, you will find in the right-hand column a question about the underlined part. You are to choose the best answer to the question.

You will also find questions about a section of the passage or about the passage as a whole. These questions do not refer to an underlined portion of the passage, but rather are identified by a number or numbers in a box.

For each question, choose the alternative you consider best and fill in the corresponding oval on your answer grid. Read each passage through once before you answer the questions that accompany it. For many questions, you must read several sentences beyond the underlined portion to determine the answer. Be sure that you have read enough ahead each time you answer a question.

OUTSIDE KNOWLEDGE

There is some knowledge of grammar rules required. You will learn about all the grammar and punctuation questions the ACT has for you during this test's strategy review. You can find an all-in-one reference in the Grammar and Punctuation Rules to Know section on pages 44–49.

THE INSIDE SCOOP

The ACT is designed to test your understanding of the conventions of written English—punctuation, grammar, sentence structure—and of general rhetorical skills. (Rhetorical skills are more strategic concepts like organizing the text and making sure it's consistently styled and concise.)

The questions *do not* get harder as you proceed through the test.

SMARTPOINTS

Point Value	Topic	Basics Page	Details and Practice
7	Connections		
6	Verb Tenses		
5	Punctuation		
5	Word Choice		
5	Wordiness		
4	Writing Strategy		
3	Sentence Sense		
1	Organization		

CHAPTER 4

English Part 1: Inside the ACT English Test

As we introduced earlier, Kaplan has a dedicated method for every area of the ACT. Follow these steps to save yourself time, attack the questions strategically, and get your highest score!

THE KAPLAN METHOD FOR ACT ENGLISH

STEP 1: READ UNTIL YOU HAVE ENOUGH INFORMATION TO IDENTIFY THE ISSUE.

The instructions on the ACT will tell you to read the whole passage and then answer the questions about it, but remember: You get points for answering questions, not for reading passages. So to balance your time in favor of the questions, read the passage just as far as necessary to answer each question, and then answer them in turn. That being said, don't skip over sentences without questions in them—you'll need to understand the whole passage when you answer summary questions at the end. But for some questions, you'll only need to read a sentence to find the issue being tested. (Keep in mind, issues are not necessarily errors, because some sentences have no errors, and some English questions test your understanding of the passage as a whole.)

STEP 2: ELIMINATE CHOICES THAT DO NOT ADDRESS THE ISSUE.

Now that you've identified the issue that the question is testing, read through the answers to see which ones do not address the issue, and cross them out in your book (really do cross them out—this will help you keep track of which answers *can't* be right and will help you guess strategically if needed). Once you've eliminated any choices that don't fix the issue, if you aren't ready to answer, move on to Step 3.

STEP 3: PLUG IN THE REMAINING CHOICES TO SELECT THE MOST CORRECT, CONCISE, AND RELEVANT CHOICE.

Finally, try out the remaining choices by plugging them into the sentence or paragraph and seeing how they work. This may mean reading the questions without the underlined phrase to see if OMIT is the best choice. Remember: the best choice will always be *correct* (grammatically), *concise* (short and sweet), and *relevant* (makes sense with the rest of the passage). Make these three words the cornerstone of your decision-making in the English section. When in doubt, just remember *correct, concise, and relevant*.

QUICK TIPS

MIND-SET

- **When in doubt, take it out.** Make sure that everything is written as concisely as possible. If you think something doesn't belong in a sentence, it probably doesn't, so choose an answer that leaves it out. Between two grammatically correct and relevant choices, the shorter one will always be right. Not just better—*right*.

- **Make sure it makes sense.** When switching phrases in and out, it's easy to find grammar but lose logic. Consider sentence formation, making sure that you use complete sentences and not fragments, and that ideas relate logically. For an answer to be correct in ACT English, it must create a sentence that is logically *and* grammatically correct.

- **Trust your eyes and ears.** Mistakes in grammar often look or sound wrong —trust that instinct. Don't choose the answer that "sounds fancy," choose the one that sounds *right*. Review the Grammar and Punctuation Rules to Know on pages 44–49.

SPECIAL STRATEGIES

A few questions will require you to rearrange the words in a sentence, the sentences in a paragraph, or even the paragraphs in a passage. Others may ask questions about the meaning of all or part of the passage, or about its structure. Your approach to these questions should be:

1. **Determine your task.** What are you being asked to do?

2. **Consider the passage as a whole.** Read the sentences around the numbered question to get the big picture—you need to know the points made there. Most passages will have a well-defined theme, laid out in a logical way, so choose the answer that expresses the arrangement of elements that best continues the "flow" of the passage.

3. **Predict your answer.** As you'll see again in the Reading section, making a prediction should give you an idea of what the answer is before looking at the choices.

TIMING: PACING AND APPROACH

Set your watch to 12:00 at the beginning of the subject test. Here's roughly where you should be at the following checkpoints.

12:09 . . . . . One passage finished and answers gridded in

12:18 . . . . . Two passages finished and answers gridded in

12:27 . . . . . Three passages finished and answers gridded in

12:36 . . . . . Four passages finished and answers gridded in

12:45 . . . . . Five passages finished and answers for the entire section gridded in

Note that you should have at least looked at all 75 English questions and made sure you have at least a guess gridded in for every question when time is called.

Organized Approach: Because of the passage-based format, we recommend that you *not* skip around in the English subject test. Move straight from beginning to end, answering all of the questions as you go. Unlike some sections, in English you'll usually have at least a sense of what the right answer should be rather quickly. But remember, even the correct answer will start to sound wrong if you think about it too much!

WHEN YOU'RE RUNNING OUT OF TIME

If you have no time left to even read the last few questions, choose the shortest answer for each one. Remember that OMIT, when it appears, counts as the shortest answer. For questions not based on clarity, pick a letter of the day and just use that. No choice is more likely than any other, so pick one letter and use it for all questions you can't work on.

SCORING

Your performance on the English subject test will be averaged into your ACT Composite Score, weighted equally with your scores on the other three subject tests. You will also receive the following:

- English subject score (1 to 36) for the entire English subject test

- Usage/Mechanics subscore (1 to 18) for questions testing grammar, usage, punctuation, and sentence structure

- Rhetorical Skills subscore (1 to 18) for questions testing strategy, organization, and style

- Writing subscore (2 to 12) for the optional Writing test

- Combined English-Writing score (1 to 36) if you take the optional Writing test

SMARTPOINT BREAKDOWN

Here is a brief overview of what exactly to expect and how much of it you should be expecting.

CONNECTIONS—7 POINTS

Extremely Important

Connection questions test your ability to understand the relationship between ideas. You will have to decide whether the underlined connections words and phrases establish the proper transition. The two most common types of connections tested on the ACT are *cause and effect* (does one idea cause the next?) and *contrast* (are these ideas the same or different?). Other connections tested are *sequence* (did these ideas happen in an order?) and *emphasis* (does one idea exist to emphasize the other?). To find the best connection word or phrase for a question, you must read the non-underlined part of the passage carefully. Sometimes you only need to read the sentence that contains the underlined portion, but other times you need to go back and carefully read the sentence before it as well. Turn to page 65 for more information and practice with this question type, as well as a table of common connection words and phrases.

VERB TENSES—6 POINTS

Very Important

Verb Tense questions test appropriate tense usage in context. Consistency of usage is a priority, and the most commonly tested issue. Unless context makes it clear that more than one time frame is being discussed, verb tense usage should remain consistent in the sentence and with other verbs used in the passage. Turn to page 56 for more information and practice with this question type, as well as a table of commonly tested irregular verbs.

PUNCTUATION—5 POINTS

Important

Punctuation questions test usage of a limited number of punctuation rules. The list is very specific and predictable, so even if you don't think of punctuation as your strongest suit, you can still know which rules will be tested so you can get them right on Test Day! The tested forms of punctuation are: commas, dashes, colons, semicolons, periods, question marks, exclamation points, and apostrophes. Turn to page 54 for a breakdown of each form of punctuation and how it's tested, and refer to the Grammar and Punctuation Rules to Know on page 44 for all tested grammar rules.

WORD CHOICE—5 POINTS

Important

Word Choice questions are the broadest question type on the ACT English test, and they deal primarily with subject-verb agreement and pronoun agreement. They also relate to modifiers and idioms. Each is discussed in more detail on page 57.

WORDINESS—5 POINTS

Important

Wordiness questions test redundancy (saying the same thing twice) and verbosity (using more words than necessary). As you've seen, concise writing is highly valued on the ACT, making it part of the big three in the English Method. Sometimes, an answer on the ACT will be right simply because it's shorter without losing any information. OMIT (removing the underlined portion entirely) is always the shortest answer, and it is often the correct option, as long as it doesn't delete something the sentence needs. Turn to page 63 for a more thorough discussion of wordiness.

WRITING STRATEGY—4 POINTS

Somewhat Important

Writing Strategy questions ask about larger chunks of text, and they always appear with a question stem. These are some of the higher-difficulty questions on the English test and require you to understand the context of the passage. Specifically, these questions deal with tone, consistency, adding or deleting information, and purpose. Follow the Special

Strategies listed under Quick Tips. Refer to page 67 for a more thorough discussion of these strategies and Writing Strategy questions in general.

SENTENCE SENSE—3 POINTS

Somewhat Important

Sentence Sense questions test your ability to form proper clauses while fixing run-ons and fragments. Though this skill is not frequently tested directly, understanding independent clauses and dependent clauses is essential to many of the other SmartPoints that test knowledge of grammar, such as Verb Tenses, Punctuation, and Word Choice. Refer to page 52 for a detailed discussion, including everything you need to know for those more frequent question types. As usual, for all things grammar, refer to Grammar and Punctuation Rules to Know on page 44.

ORGANIZATION—1 POINT

Less Important

Organization questions test your understanding of logical sequence. These questions ask you to organize sentences within a paragraph or to organize paragraphs within the passage as a whole. Refer to page 68 for a thorough discussion.

GRAMMAR AND PUNCTUATION RULES TO KNOW

Here they are! Every rule commonly tested on the ACT follows. Go over these now, and refer back to them as often as needed. This is the outside knowledge you're expected to bring with you to Test Day. Get comfortable with each rule.

RULE 1: NUMBER AGREEMENT

The most tested agreement rule on the ACT is this: Singular nouns must match with singular verbs and pronouns, and plural nouns must match with plural verbs and pronouns. A common error in this area involves the use of the word *they*. It's plural, but in everyday speech, we often use it as singular.

WRONG:	"If a student won't study, they won't do well."
PROBLEM:	*A student* (singular) and *they* (plural) don't agree in number.
CORRECTION:	"If students won't study, they won't do well," or "If a student won't study, he or she won't do well."

RULE 2: PRONOUNS IN COMPOUNDS

Another common agreement or matching error concerns compounds, which are phrases that join two words with *and* or *or*.

WRONG:	"The fool gave the wrong tickets to Bob and I."
PROBLEM:	*I* can't be the object of the preposition *to*.
CORRECTION:	"The fool gave the wrong tickets to Bob and me."

Hint: Try dropping the rest of the compound (*Bob and*). "The fool gave the wrong tickets to I" should sound funny to you, which is your first hint it's a problem.

RULE 3: COMMAS OR DASHES AROUND PARENTHETICAL PHRASES

Parenthetical phrases must begin and end with the same punctuation mark. Such phrases can be recognized because, while they add information to a sentence, without them the sentence would still be complete. For instance: "Bob, on his way to the store, saw a large lizard in the street." If you dropped the phrase "on his way to the store," the sentence would still be complete. Thus, this phrase is parenthetical. It could be marked off with commas, parentheses, or dashes, but the same mark is needed at both ends of the phrase.

WRONG:	"Bob—on his way to the store, saw a lizard."
PROBLEM:	The parenthetical phrase starts with a dash but finishes with a comma.
CORRECTION:	"Bob, on his way to the store, saw a lizard."

RULE 4: RUN-ONS AND COMMA SPLICES

You can't combine two complete sentences into one with a comma (though you can with a semicolon or a comma plus a conjunction).

WRONG:	"Ed's a slacker, Sara isn't."
PROBLEM:	Two complete sentences are spliced together with a comma.
CORRECTION:	"Ed's a slacker, but Sara isn't," or "Ed's a slacker; Sara isn't," or "Ed, unlike Sara, is a slacker."

RULE 5: FRAGMENTS

This rule goes hand-in-hand with the previous one. **A sentence must contain at least one complete idea.** A fragment is writing that could be a subordinate part of a sentence but not a whole sentence itself.

WRONG:	"Emily listened to music. While she studied."
PROBLEM:	"She studied" would be a sentence, but *while* makes this a fragment.
CORRECTION:	"Emily listened to music while she studied."

RULE 6: *-ly* ENDINGS (ADVERBS AND ADJECTIVES)

The ACT expects you to understand the difference between adverbs (which often end in *-ly*) and adjectives. The two are similar because they're both modifiers—they modify, refer to, or describe another word or phrase in the sentence. Nouns and pronouns must be modified by adjectives, while verbs, adjectives, and adverbs themselves must be modified by adverbs.

WRONG:	"Anna is an extreme gifted child, and she speaks beautiful too."
PROBLEM:	*Extreme* and *beautiful* are adjectives, but they're supposed to modify an adjective (*gifted*) and a verb (*speaks*) here, so they should be adverbs.
CORRECTION:	"Anna is an extremely gifted child, and she speaks beautifully too."

RULE 7: *-er* AND *-est*, *More* AND *Most* (COMPARATIVES AND SUPERLATIVES)

Whenever you see the endings *-er* or *-est* or the words *more* or *most*, double-check to make sure they're used correctly. Words with *-er* or *more* are only used to compare exactly two things. If there are more than two things involved, use *-est* or *most*.

WRONG:	"Bob is the fastest of the two runners."
PROBLEM:	The comparison is between just two things, so *-est* is inappropriate.
CORRECTION:	"Bob is the faster of the two runners."

RULE 8: COMMONLY INVERTED WORDS

There are several word pairs that we commonly switch around in spoken English, even when it breaks grammatical rules. On the ACT, some of these will be tested, so you will want to know how to use them correctly. Note: Don't get bogged down with these; they will rarely be tested on more than one question total.

GOOD OR *WELL*

Good is an adjective (modifies a noun or pronoun); *well* is an adverb (modifies verbs, adjectives, adverbs).

WRONG:	"Joe did good on the ACT."
PROBLEM:	*Good* is an adjective, but here it's modifying a verb (*did*), so use an adverb.
CORRECTION:	"Joe did well on the ACT."

One exception: *well* can also be an adjective when it means "healthy." So "Joe was well again by the morning of the ACT" is correct.

LIE OR *LAY*

In short, *lie* is something a subject <u>does</u> ("I'm going to lie down for a while"), whereas *lay* is something a subject <u>does to an object</u> ("I'm going to lay the book down for a while.") A reliable way to test this is to replace the word with "put"—if you can ("I'm going to put the book down"), you can use *lay*. If you can't ("I'm going to put down for a while"), you need *lie*.

WHO OR WHOM

Your rule to never miss this question again: *who* goes where *he* goes; *whom* goes where *him* goes! If the answer to the question being asked is *he*, the form should be *who*. If the answer is *him*, the form should be *whom*.

WRONG:	"Always remember who you're speaking to."
PROBLEM:	*Who* is wrong. Ask: Speaking to who? Speaking to him, not to he. So it should be *whom*.
CORRECTION:	"Always remember whom you're speaking to."

Some students try to avoid the *who/whom* problem by using the word *which* instead. Don't. It's not nice to call people "whiches." Never use the word *which* (or *that*) for a person.

LESS OR FEWER

The word *less* is used only for uncountable things. When things can be counted, they are *fewer*.

WRONG:	"I have fewer water than I thought, so I can fill less buckets."
PROBLEM:	You can count buckets; you can't count water.
CORRECTION:	"I have less water than I thought, so I can fill fewer buckets."

BETWEEN OR AMONG

The word *between* is used only when there are exactly two things involved. When there are more than two things, or an unknown number of things, use *among*.

WRONG:	"I will walk among the two halves of the class, between the many students in class."
PROBLEM:	Use *between* for two things and *among* for more than two.
CORRECTION:	"I will walk between the two halves of the class, among the many students in class."

RULE 9: *Be* AND *Was* (FORMS OF THE VERB *To Be*)

The ACT tests the use of proper verb forms, especially of the verb *to be*. You must use the following forms. Memorize them if you have to:

Present Tense:	I *am*, we *are*, you *are*, they *are*, he/she/it *is*
Past Tense:	I *was*, we *were*, you *were*, they *were*, he/she/it *was*
Future Tense:	I/we/you/they/he/she/it *will be*
Perfect Tense:	I/we/you *have been*, he/she/it *has been*
Past Perfect:	I/we/you/he/she/it *had been*
Future Perfect:	I/we/you/he/she/it *will have been*

You can decide which form (*am, are, is, were, was, will be, have been, had been, will have been*) is correct by determining what the subject is and what the verb tense is. In many dialects, the words *be* and *was* are used instead of the special forms given. For example, many speakers might say, "They *be* going home" or "They *was* going home." On the ACT, the correct form is "They *are* (or *were*) going home."

RULE 10: PUNCTUATION

The ACT doesn't test uncommon rules of punctuation. However, it does expect you to know what punctuation marks mean and how they are commonly used. Here are some common punctuation marks and their uses:

Use a **comma** (,) or **commas** to do the following:

- Set off items in a list of three or more items

- Combine two independent clauses with a FANBOYS conjunction (For, And, Nor, But, Or, Yet, So)

- Set off an introductory phrase from the rest of the sentence

- Separate nonessential information (something that could be considered a parenthetical phrase) from the rest of the sentence

- **Note:** You may have learned different or even conflicting rules about whether to put a comma before the *and* in a list (known as the serial or Oxford comma), as in this example:

  "At the store, we need bread, juice**, and** eggs."

As opposed to:

  "At the store, we need bread, juice **and** eggs."

Different schools and publications have different rules, but the ACT *does* use the serial/ Oxford comma, so you should always be on the lookout for lists!

Use a **semicolon** (;) to do the following:

- Combine two independent clauses when a FANBOYS word is not present.
  "Emily studied for hours; she had a big test the next day."

- Separate items in a series or list if those items already include commas.
  "At the grocery store, George needed milk, eggs, and butter; Alice needed cereal, bread, and juice; and Dan needed apples, water, and ice cream."

Use a **colon** (:) to introduce or emphasize a short phrase, quotation, example, explanation, or list.

  "Peter needed to study three topics before Test Day: punctuation, transitions, and sentence structure."

  "One wild animal causes suburban pet-owners more stress than any other: the skunk."

Use a **dash** (—) or **dashes** to set off an explanatory or parenthetical phrase in a sentence.

Use an **apostrophe** (') to do the following:

- Indicate the possessive form of a noun (*not* a pronoun).

- Stand in for a missing letter or letters in a contraction.

SPECIAL RECOGNITION: *Its, It's, or Its'*

Because apostrophes are *not* used to create the possessive form of pronouns (you wouldn't say "it's his' book" or "it's her's car"), the word *its* follows very specific rules:

- *It's* means "It is" or "It has." That's it. There are no other uses for *it's*.

  "It's going to be a little bit before the movie starts."

  "It's been a while since last time we went to the movies."

- *Its* is the possessive form of *it*.

  "The car was safe in its spot when I came outside."

- *Its'* is not a word. Don't use it. Ever. You always mean one of the other forms.

SUMMARY

In this chapter, we went over the basic strategy and outside knowledge required to master the ACT English test.

Remember to read through the issue instead of skipping to it. Eliminate when you can, then use your ear and plug in the remaining choice or choices. Listen for what sounds right. Then decide on the answer that is the most *correct, concise, and relevant*.

Make sure the sentence makes sense, and when in doubt, take it out!

To master the ACT English test, combine these strategies with the outside knowledge listed in Grammar and Punctuation Rules to Know. Flag or highlight the rules you still struggle with, then use the following chapter to review the various question types.

In the next chapter, we'll dive further into each SmartPoint listed. After point-by-point explanations, you'll get to see what each question type looks like on its own and get a chance to practice on those examples. Remember, spend more time mastering question types that are tested more often to maximize your score!

CHAPTER 5

English Part 2: ACT English Strategy in Depth

OVERVIEW

Use this chapter to get familiar with all of the question types on the ACT English test. They are detailed and discussed fully in this chapter, and examples are provided for each type. To get a quick sense of what's to come, refer to the SmartPoint Breakdownon page 42. In the last chapter, they were discussed in order of Test Day value, with the more heavily tested SmartPoints listed first. That's generally how you should prioritize your prep time, especially if you are short on time or close to your goal score.

In this chapter, the SmartPoints are discussed in order of building *complexity*, as the knowledge for some question types contributes to other, more frequently tested SmartPoints. So if you have time and want to thoroughly work your English skill set, start at the beginning of the chapter and work your way through.

Enjoy your studies!

The following SmartPoints are shown in order of building complexity, SmartPoint by SmartPoint.

SENTENCE SENSE—3 POINTS

Complexity: Low. Based on grammar and punctuation rules. Relates to: All other grammar-based SmartPoints—Punctuation, Verb Tense, Word Choice, and Connections.

Before we discuss how the ACT tests sentence structure, you need to be comfortable with just a few grammatical terms.

A *sentence* is a group of words that contains these three parts: a subject, a predicate verb, and a complete thought. You will see about 18 questions about sentence structure on the ACT English test.

A sentence is made up of one or more clauses. A *clause* is a group of words that contains a subject and a verb. A clause *may* constitute a complete sentence, but it doesn't necessarily have to. If a clause can stand alone as a sentence, it's called an *independent clause.* If a clause cannot stand alone as a sentence, it's called a *dependent clause.* You will not need to directly identify dependent and independent clauses on Test Day, but you will need to recognize them so you can punctuate them correctly.

When you see words such as *because, that, if, whereas,* and *while* in an underlined part of an ACT English passage, sentence structure may be one of the issues tested by that problem. Remember, just because a group of words in an ACT passage starts with a capital letter and ends with a period, that doesn't necessarily mean it's a proper complete sentence. Be on the lookout for dependent clauses that aren't joined to independent clauses; these would be sentence fragments.

Another kind of sentence structure error is a *run-on sentence*. A run-on sentence contains two or more clauses that are incorrectly strung together. A well-formed sentence can have more than one clause, but the clauses must be joined properly.

RULES FOR CORRECTING RUN-ON SENTENCES

The ACT uses three primary fixes for breaking up run-on sentences. Here are the three ways to correctly combine two independent clauses in a single sentence:

1. Use a comma plus a FANBOYS conjunction (*For, And, Nor, But, Or, Yet, So*):

    My history teacher requires us to use at least two books in our research, **so** *I have to go to the library this weekend.*

2. Use a semicolon between the two clauses. After a semicolon, it is not correct to use a FANBOYS word, but it is acceptable to use a transitional word such as *however, moreover,* or *nevertheless*:

    *My history teacher requires us to use at least two books in our research**; therefore,** I have to go to the library this weekend.*

3. Change one of the independent clauses to a dependent clause by adding a word such as *although, because, despite,* or *since*:

    Because my history teacher requires us to use at least two books in our research, I have to go to the library this weekend.

(You will sometimes have the option to use a period to create multiple sentences, but often the ACT will ask you to properly fit multiple clauses into one sentence.)

VERBS WITH *-ING* RULE

Another common sentence structure rule you should be on the lookout for involves verbs ending with *-ing,* which can easily create sentence fragments. The verb form ending in *-ing* cannot be used without a helping verb, such as *is, was, has, had,* or *have been,* as the main verb in a clause. A helping verb does not show action by itself, but can "help" the main verb show action. Here's an example:

The monkey swinging from tree to tree is incorrect as a complete sentence, because *swinging* is used alone as the main verb. A helping verb is needed. Depending on the context, you might say something like *The monkey is swinging from tree to tree* or *The monkey had been swinging from tree to tree.*

PARALLEL STRUCTURE RULE

Items in a series, list, or compound must be parallel in form, meaning all items in a list must have the same "shape"—they must use the same tense, number, helping pronouns, or other structures. Review the examples in this chart:

Check for Parallelism if the Sentence Contains:	Example of Parallel Forms	Parallel Elements in Example
a list	Before you leave, you should **charge** your phone, **clean** your room, and **find** your keys.	Three verb phrases
a compound (words joined by *and* or *or*)	I don't like **swimming** or **hiking**.	Two *-ing* verb forms
an idiomatic phrase like *both…and* and *not only…but also*	It's necessary not only **to prepare thoroughly** but also **to listen carefully**.	Two verb phrases that start with *to*
a comparison	Your **homework** is just as important as your **participation** in class.	Two nouns
related nouns	**Students** who complete all of their homework **assignments** will be rewarded with higher **grades**.	Three plural nouns that are related in the sentence

PUNCTUATION—5 POINTS

Complexity: Low. Based on grammar and punctuation rules. Relates to: Sentence Sense.

Some of the easiest questions to recognize are Punctuation questions. When you look at the choices, you'll see that they all use the same or nearly the same words, but have different punctuation marks. One great thing about the ACT is that it tests a limited number of punctuation rules.

The questions test commas, dashes, colons, semicolons, periods, question marks, exclamation points, and apostrophes. Review the Grammar and Punctuation Rules to Know section (p. 44) for more details.

Comma usage is tested most frequently, followed by semicolon usage.

COMMA RULES

Use commas:

1. To separate introductory words from the main part of the sentence.

   Before you leave the house, you should make sure you've eaten a healthy breakfast.

2. To set off words or phrases that aren't essential to the sentence structure.

   Sonia, who will be playing the role of the lawyer, is a skilled actress.

3. To separate two independent clauses when they're joined by a FANBOYS word (*For, And, Nor, But, Or, Yet, So*).

   Many of my friends drink coffee, but I do not.

4. To separate items in a series.

Steps involved in a research paper include choosing a topic, conducting the research, writing a first draft, and doing at least one round of revisions.

These four examples are the only uses of the comma that the ACT tests. Learn to recognize when each rule should be applied, and keep in mind the following additional hint: You should avoid unnecessary commas. Sometimes your task on an ACT punctuation question is to remove commas that disturb the flow of a sentence.

SEMICOLON RULES

Use a semicolon to link two independent clauses that are *not* joined by a FANBOYS word.

I will be missing school to visit colleges; however, my teacher said I will not have to make up the Spanish quiz I will miss.

Certain words are frequently used to connect two independent clauses. These words are acceptable to use after a semicolon:

furthermore	moreover
however	nevertheless
in fact	therefore
indeed	thus

Do *not* use these words after a semicolon:

although	which
despite	where
whereas	that
who	

DASH RULES

Use dashes:

1. To indicate a break in thought.

You did see the movie—am I right about that?

2. To set off parenthetical information from the main part of a sentence.

Many people find that small necessary items—a wallet, a cell phone, a transit card—are unfortunately very easy to misplace.

APOSTROPHE RULES

Use an apostrophe:

1. To take the place of one or more missing letters in a contraction.

   You can't be late.

2. To show the possessive form of a noun.

   My sister's friends are coming to the party. (This is correct if you're using the singular form, one sister.)

   My sisters' teams both won games this weekend. (This is correct if you're using the plural form, two sisters who play on two separate teams.)

When a question is testing punctuation, think about how the various parts of each sentence relate to one another. Identify the types of clauses, the nonessential information, and the transition words around the underlined punctuation. Recall the rules about commas and semicolons and which words are acceptable with each to join two clauses.

VERB TENSES—6 POINTS

Complexity: Low-Medium. Based on grammar rules. Relates to: Sentence Sense, Word Choice.

You probably remember that a verb is a word that expresses an action (*draw, eat, walk*) or a word that expresses a state of being (*is, were, was*). Though there are many grammatical rules relating to verbs, there are really only three verb usage rules on the ACT:

1. A verb must agree with its subject.

2. A verb's tense must be logically consistent with time-related phrases in the sentence and other verbs used in the passage.

3. Some verbs can form the past tense in a way other than using *-ed*.

An easy way to know if you have to apply one of these rules is to get used to noticing underlined verbs in the ACT English test. When you notice an underlined verb, ask yourself these questions:

- What is the subject of this verb? Does the underlined verb agree with its grammatical subject?

- Does the tense of the underlined verb make sense in relation to other words in the sentence? Is the underlined verb consistent with other verb tenses used in nearby sentences and the passage as a whole?

- Does this verb form the past tense correctly? Does it sound right?

We'll talk more about subject-verb agreement under the next SmartPoint—Word Choice. For this SmartPoint, we'll focus on the second two questions to make sure we have the verb in the right tense.

Does the tense of the underlined verb make sense in relation to other words in the sentence? Is the underlined verb consistent with other verb tenses used in nearby sentences and the passage as a whole?

To determine if an underlined verb makes sense within its own sentence, watch for time-related phrases and non-underlined verbs.

It's a good idea to train your ear to listen for past-tense forms that are common errors—the following forms are never correct: *had did, had flied, had wrote, had took.* You don't need to memorize every verb that forms the past tense irregularly (that is, with a spelling other than simply adding *-ed),* but you should be aware that this type of error is sometimes tested on the ACT. Examine the following chart for a list of commonly tested irregular verbs.

Forms of the "Helping Verbs"		
	Present Tense	**Past Tense**
To be	am, are, is	was, were
To have	have, has	had

Examples of Verbs That Use an Irregular Past Tense		
Present	**Past**	**Past Participle (use with** *had, has,* **or** *have***)**
begin	began	begun
come	came	come
do	did	done
drive	drove	driven
know	knew	known
swim	swam	swum
take	took	taken

WORD CHOICE—5 POINTS

Complexity: Medium. Mostly based on grammar rules. Somewhat based on rhetorical skills. Relates to: Sentence Sense, Verb Tense.

Word Choice questions primarily test:

• Verbs (related to subject-verb agreement)

• Pronouns

They also test:

• Modifiers

• Idioms

We'll look at each one in turn.

VERBS

How to identify and use verbs in the correct tense is discussed in the Verb Tenses section. For Word Choice questions, the tested issue is subject-verb agreement.

Again, when you see a verb underlined, it is testing one of these three usage rules:

1. A verb must agree with its subject.

2. A verb's tense must be logically consistent with time-related phrases in the sentence and other verbs that are used in the passage.

3. Some verbs can form the past tense in a way other than using -ed.

Numbers 2 and 3 are discussed under Verb Tenses.

For rule number 1, ask yourself, *What is the subject of this verb? Does the underlined verb agree with its grammatical subject?*

One key thing to remember—and a common trap on the ACT—is that the noun immediately before the verb may not actually be the verb's subject. It may be, but placement is no guarantee.

In this example of incorrect subject-verb agreement, circle the subject and jot down the correction for the underlined verb in the space provided:

> Many of my friends, including everyone in the brass section of the band,
> <u>is</u> [_____]planning to come to my party.

Recall that the *subject* is who or what is doing the action the verb expresses. In the sentence, you should have circled the word *my friends,* the subject of this sentence. Detecting the incorrect subject-verb agreement here can be tricky because the subject is separated from the verb by several words—a whole dependent clause. As you work through English questions, both in your practice and on Test Day, circle the subject that goes with the underlined verb. Then read the subject and the verb without the words that appear between them. When you do this, you'll hear a mistake more easily. You wouldn't say, <u>*My friends is* planning to come.</u> You would make the correction: <u>*My friends are* planning to come.</u>

Use this chart to study the commonly tested subject-verb agreement rules:

Subject-Verb Agreement		
A verb must agree with its subject noun in person and number.	The noun closest to a verb may not be its subject.	Only the conjunction *and* forms a compound subject that requires a plural verb form.
A stamp sticks to an envelope. Stamps _____ to envelopes.	The chair with the cabriole legs is an antique. MP3 players, small portable devices that play digital audio files, _____ popular with many different demographic groups.	Either Kyle or Trisha is managing the crew. Kyle and Trisha _____ managing the crew. Neither Kyle nor Trisha _____ managing the crew.

The final verb area tested on the ACT is *active voice*. Determining whether or not a sentence is in active voice or *passive voice* requires you to relate subjects to verbs in the context of the sentence as a whole. While both active and passive voice can be grammatically correct, if you have to choose between them to find a right answer on the ACT, you should always select the active voice. You will notice as you practice and take the ACT that the active voice is also usually shorter.

Most sentences in English are worded in what we call the active voice. When a sentence is in the active voice, the subject of the sentence is the person or thing doing whatever action the verb expresses. On the other hand, when a sentence is in the passive voice, the subject of the verb is *receiving* the action instead of *doing* it. In other words, when an active sentence is written in the passive, the subject becomes an object. Some examples will make the difference clear. In the following sentences, the subjects are capitalized and the objects are underlined.

>   **Active Voice:**   My FAMILY packed the <u>car</u> carefully before we left for vacation.
>
>   **Passive Voice:** The CAR was packed carefully by my <u>family</u> before we left for vacation.
>
>   **Active Voice:**   My AUNT gave me a new <u>phone</u>.
>
>   **Passive Voice:** A new PHONE was given to me by my <u>aunt</u>.

The active voice puts the emphasis on the subject. Occasionally, a writer who wants to emphasize the object, rather than the subject, chooses to use the passive voice, but the active voice is desirable most of the time. Once in a while, you may come across an ACT question that tests whether you can recognize the difference, in which case understanding the difference can earn you more points. While the active voice is preferable if all other things are equal, there are some situations in which the passive voice is the only correct choice (the most common instance is in a sentence that begins with a modifying phrase), so don't automatically eliminate any answer choices in the passive voice, only be sure before selecting them that there isn't another choice that is active and correct.

PRONOUNS

A *pronoun* is a word that either takes the place of or refers to a noun or another pronoun. Train yourself to spot pronouns in the underlined portion of an ACT English passage, as pronouns can easily be confusing or refer to the wrong parts of the sentence.

Any pronoun can be described in terms of two things: case and number. Pronoun *case* refers to how the pronoun is used in a sentence—as a subject or an object. In the sentence *He will call you later,* the pronoun *He* acts as the subject, while the pronoun *you* acts as the object. A pronoun's *number* is either singular or plural. Most personal pronouns take a different form (that is, a different word is used) depending on whether they are used as the subject or object in a sentence and depending on whether they are singular or plural. The following table shows the personal pronouns for which you must consider both case and number.

	Singular	Plural
Subject	I, he, she, it,	we, they
Object	me, him, her, it	us, them

Generally, your ear tells you which form of a personal pronoun is correct. The ACT often makes a pronoun question trickier by using a personal pronoun in combination with *and.* You would never say **Him** *went to the store,* but on the ACT, you might see something like **Him and Jesse** *went to the store together.* By reading this sentence without the words *and Jesse,* your ear helps you determine that *Him* should be changed to *He* in this sentence.

Examples of correct pronoun usage as subjects and objects:

1. **We** must be respectful in this class, or the teacher will give *us* detention.

2. Kevin and **I** are going skating tonight.

3. The guests said **they** were thankful for the help that *we* volunteers provided.

4. Ginny told **me** there was no need to return the book to *her.*

5. Can you believe my parents said **they** will give *us* the car for the weekend?

Did you notice that the table of personal pronouns above doesn't include the pronoun *you?* The reason for this is that the pronoun *you* takes the same form whether it's used as the subject or object in a sentence. Here's an example:

> *You* must be respectful in the class, or the teacher will give *you* a detention.

However, the ACT does test the pronoun *you* in a different way—by using the word *one* in a sentence that also uses *you.* More about that now!

PRONOUN-SHIFT RULE

A pronoun that can serve a similar purpose as *you* is *one*. But the ACT will test this by making them interchangeable, which they are not. Avoid the *one-you* shift: do not shift between the words *one* and *you* in the same sentence or paragraph.

Here's how the *one-you* shift might look on the ACT:

> <u>When one is planning</u> for college, you need to keep many factors in mind.

Here, because the non-underlined part of the sentence uses the word *you*, the underlined part of the sentence should be corrected to *you are*. The sentence could also equalize this by saying *one needs to keep many factors in mind*, but because that section isn't underlined, that isn't an option.

WHICH/WHO/WHOM RULES

In addition to the personal pronouns and the *one-you* shift, another aspect of pronouns frequently tested on the ACT is the use of *who, whom,* and *which*. Fortunately, there are solid rules to learn for this as well!

Who and *whom* intimidate many people, but it's not hard to use them correctly if you think about how each word functions in its sentence or clause. Think about whether it is a subject or an object. Remember this rule: "*Who* goes where *he* goes, and *whom* goes where *him* goes." That is, if you can correctly substitute the pronoun *he* into a sentence, then *who* is correct, but if you can substitute *him* into a sentence, then *whom* is correct.

Which should be used entirely differently—it only applies to nonhuman nouns. So *Which restaurant did you pick?* is correct, while *I invited three friends, one of which has already accepted* is incorrect. Learn to apply these rules:

- Use *which* only to refer to things, never to refer to people.

- Use *who* in a sentence context where *he* or *she* would be correct.

- Use *whom* in a sentence context where *him* or *her* would be correct.

Modifiers and *Idioms* are less-frequently tested Word Choice issues.

MODIFIERS

A *modifier* is a word or phrase that describes or provides more information about another word. Two different parts of speech—adjectives and adverbs—function as modifiers. Let's look at the two modifier rules that are tested on the ACT.

SINGLE-WORD MODIFIER RULE

Most modifiers are single words that help explain or describe (modify) a simple idea. Commonly, these are adjectives and adverbs. An adjective must be used only to modify a noun or a pronoun. An adverb must be used only to modify a verb, an adjective, or another adverb.

MODIFYING PHRASE RULE

A *modifying phrase* should be placed as close as possible to the word it modifies. Specifically, when a sentence begins with a modifying phrase, the next noun or pronoun in the sentence *must* be the word that phrase logically modifies.

You can easily spot most introductory modifying phrases because they usually begin with a verb that ends in *-ed* or *-ing*. If you remember this, you'll have no trouble at all with introductory modifiers on the ACT.

If you notice that a sentence starts with a modifying phrase, you should next ask yourself who or what this phrase logically describes. Once you identify that, you'll find this type of question easy to get right! The key here is paying attention to the non-underlined context of the sentence and using it to determine the right answer.

COMPARATIVE AND SUPERLATIVE RULE

Another modifier issue tests the use of *comparative* and *superlative* adjectives, which are modifiers used to compare items—one thing is *bigger* or *faster* than another, or something is the *most* or *best* of something. These are common parts of speech and important to get right on the ACT. Generally, comparative adjectives end with *-er*, and superlative adjectives end in *-est*. You determine whether the comparative or superlative form of an adjective is correct by asking how many items are being compared.

Use the comparative form of an adjective (for example, *older* or *shorter*) when only two objects are being compared. Use the superlative form of an adjective (for example, *oldest* or *shortest)* when comparing three or more objects.

Because the ACT questions always have exactly one unambiguously correct answer, the context surrounding a comparative or superlative *must* always make it clear how many things are being compared.

IDIOMS

The final Word Choice issue tested on the ACT is idiomatic usage. An *idiom* is an expression that is conventionally phrased in a particular way, whether or not there's a firm rule to rely on. These are phrases you've simply heard so often you know how they should be. Idiomatic usage isn't heavily tested on the ACT.

Most often, correct idiomatic usage hinges on prepositions—for example, you would never say, "I'm traveling *at* school." You'd say, "I'm traveling *to* school."

Whenever you notice that the underlined portion of a sentence includes a preposition, think about how it sounds in context to make sure it's idiomatically correct—if your ear tells you something's wrong, it may well be.

Use the following chart to identify Idiom questions and correctly answer them:

Ask	Is a preposition underlined?	Is a verb form that starts with *to* or ends in *-ing* underlined?	Is part of a commonly tested idiomatic expression used somewhere in the sentence?	Does the sentence include the word *barely*, *hardly*, or *scarcely*?
Check	Determine if the preposition sounds appropriate with other words in the sentence.	Determine if the infinitive, participle, or gerund form is used appropriately.	Check for common idioms such as *either… or* and *neither… nor*.	Watch out for other negative words such as *no*, *none*, and *not* that would create a double negative.

Here are the most commonly tested prepositions and idioms on the ACT:

Prepositions	Commonly Tested Idiomatic Expressions	Words That Can't Be Paired with Negative Words
at *by* *for* *from* *of* *on* *to* *with*	*as…as* *between…and* *both…and* *either…or* *just as…so* *neither…nor* *not only…but also*	*barely* *hardly* *scarcely*

Sometimes, when you've eliminated two choices and are trying to choose the better one of the remaining two, thinking about correct idiomatic usage will help you select the correct answer.

WORDINESS—5 POINTS

Complexity: Moderate. Based on rhetorical skills. Relates to: None. This is a stand-alone SmartPoint.

Remember the big three words to focus on in the English section. Always use the Kaplan Method, and remember to choose your answer based on the choice that is the most *correct*, *concise*, and *relevant*.

The SmartPoints you've looked at so far all primarily relate to the *correct* part of the big three. They've been based in grammar rules and primarily test mechanics.

Word Choice starts to bridge the gap, as some questions have more to do with rhetorical skill than with making things technically correct, but Wordiness is the first SmartPoint you'll look at that falls entirely outside of grammar rules.

With these next SmartPoints, it's essential to keep the words *concise* and *relevant* in mind, in addition to making sure sentences are correct.

So it's time to get those rhetorical skills rolling. We'll start with the importance of being *concise* to master the Wordiness SmartPoint.

Keep this in mind: sometimes, one choice will be better than another *simply because it's shorter.*

This means that some questions will have more than one choice that is *grammatically correct*, but there is still only one answer the ACT will call *right*. It's easy to lose sight of this when you're working through grammar rules questions and all questions have choices that are cut and dry. Sometimes the grammatically correct answer isn't the only right one.

There are two types of Wordiness errors you can expect to see on the ACT: Redundancy and Verbosity.

REDUNDANCY

Redundancy means saying the same thing twice. This is usually not literally; it may be saying something one way and then repeating the meaning in different words. For example:

> My little brother worked hard on and put a lot of effort into building his sand castle.

What should catch your eye here is that *worked hard on* and *put a lot of effort into* mean pretty much the same thing. Once you've said one, you really don't need the other, so only one phrase should be used, not both.

Fortunately for you, many Redundancy questions come with a built-in clue that Wordiness is the tested issue: the "OMIT the underlined portion" choice. Whenever you see OMIT as a choice, always start by asking yourself: "Is the underlined portion truly necessary, and would anything valuable be lost if the underlined portion were taken out?" If the answers to these questions are "no," then you can confidently select OMIT as the right choice. You should note that when OMIT is offered as a choice, it always appears as the fourth choice. OMIT is the correct answer more than half of the time, so *when OMIT is present, always check that choice first!*

VERBOSITY

Verbosity means simply using more words than are necessary. Verbosity questions don't always include OMIT as a choice, so they are not as easy to spot, but you will often see a difference in the length of the choices. Verbosity results when a long, drawn-out expression is used in place of a shorter one. For example:

The student council held a meeting for the purpose of determining what would be the most profitable kind of event for fund-raising.Here's a more concise way to express the idea:

The student council met to determine the most profitable kind of fund-raising event.

Same idea, far shorter. There are many ways of expressing an idea simply, so you may see variations, but the key is to notice the wordy phrases that could be replaced with shorter alternatives. Remember: if there are multiple answers that explain the same idea and are grammatically correct, the shortest one will be right. The others will be wrong because they could be more concise.

CONNECTIONS—7 POINTS

Complexity: Medium-High. Based on rhetorical skills. Relates to: Sentence Sense.

Connections words and phrases are those that express a relationship between ideas. The two most common types of Connections tested on the ACT are Cause-and-Effect and Contrast Connections. Other Connections tested are Sequence and Emphasis. You should thoroughly familiarize yourself with the words and phrases in the following table. Spotting a Connections word on the ACT is a red flag that you need to think about logical relationships—whenever you see a Connections word underlined, you can expect that the other answer choices will also be various Connections words and phrases.

Connections Words and Phrases	
Connections that show addition, continuation, emphasis, or examples	additionally and for example for instance furthermore indeed in addition in fact likewise moreover
Connections that show cause and effect	as a result because consequently leading to since so therefore thus

Connections that show contrast	although but despite even though however nevertheless on the other hand rather though whereas while
Connections that show sequence	finally first if…then last later next second then

Let's look at an example of how Connections words and phrases are tested on the ACT.

1. Many of my friends enjoy team sports; <u>however,</u> I prefer individual activities such as running and yoga.

    A. NO CHANGE

    B. but

    C. therefore

    D. in addition

Whenever you notice that a Connections word or phrase is underlined, read carefully in the surrounding context to determine how the ideas are related. This sentence has two parts. The first is *many of my friends enjoy team sports*. The second is *I prefer individual activities*. Ask yourself how the two ideas are related. Because *team sports* are different from *individual activities,* the relationship is one of contrast. When you first read the sentence, it should sound logical because *however* is a contrast connection. Indeed, (A) is the best answer here. You can eliminate (C) and (D) because they do not express contrast. Choice (B) does express contrast, but it is not appropriate here because a semicolon is used between the two independent clauses, and a FANBOYS conjunction like *but* is incorrect after a semicolon.

Once you learn to recognize the various Connections words, you should have no trouble with Connections questions on the ACT. Just let the presence of any underlined Connections word remind you to consider the kind of logical relationship expressed in the sentence. Don't worry if a question includes more than one choice in the right category of connections. If that's the case, use your ear to determine which one is appropriate.

WRITING STRATEGY—4 POINTS

Complexity: High. Based on rhetorical skills. Relates to: None. This is a stand-alone SmartPoint.

The last two SmartPoints on the English test are the most complex (Writing Strategy and Organization). Each will always have a question stem (text between the question number and multiple-choice answers stating exactly what is being asked), and you'll need to read further for more information to properly answer these questions. Remember the first step of the Kaplan Method—read until you have enough information to identify the issue. For these two question types, you'll have to consider more of the passage, or the passage as whole, in order to understand the author's purpose and methods.

But fear not! Though these questions seem intimidating, there are effective strategies to deal with both. The big three for the English test—*correct*, *concise*, and *relevant*—still very much apply.

We'll start with the more common of the two—Writing Strategy.

Writing Strategy questions ask you to choose what kind of phrasing most effectively accomplishes a particular purpose. The most important thing you need to do is to *consider the question stem carefully!* This type of question can ask for a number of different answers, so when you read the question stem, think about what the particular question is asking for. When you focus clearly on what the question is asking, the best answer will usually stand out among the offered choices.

Writing Strategy questions for which you will *not* find a key phrase in the question stem are questions that ask about the effect of adding or deleting a certain phrase or sentence. For questions that ask about deletion, focus on the given phrase, asking yourself what effect it creates for you as a reader. Consider the example:

> The construction site was littered with debris. Scraps of wood, drywall, and various types of nails were scattered on the ground. Even large sheets of roofing materials, some still packaged as they came from the supplier, were lying against the unfinished exterior walls. [1]

1. The author is considering deleting the following sentence:

   Scraps of wood, drywall, and various types of nails were scattered on the ground.

   What would be lost if the author made this deletion?

   A. information about how long the building site had been unattended

   B. a description of what materials are needed in construction

   C. a suggestion about how to clean the site

   D. specific details that provide information about what the site looks like

To answer this question, consider the given sentence in the context of the passage. The previous sentence describes the site as *littered with debris*, and the sentence in question lists items that make up that debris. Because it offers specific details describing the debris, (D)

is the right answer. If you focus on the given sentence's relation to the sentences around it and how it adds to your understanding of the author's purpose, you shouldn't fall for the wrong answer traps.

Again, for Writing Strategy questions that ask about the effect of deleting information, *consider the context and determine how the information contributes to the writer's purpose.*

ORGANIZATION—1 POINT

Complexity: High. Based on rhetorical skills. Relates to: None. This is a stand-alone SmartPoint.

Organization questions test your understanding of logical sequence in a passage. It's easy to recognize an Organization question because it will involve sentences or paragraphs that are labeled with bracketed numbers in the passage. Some Organization questions ask you to rearrange the order of the sentences within the paragraph or the order of the paragraphs within the whole passage. Other Organization questions present a sentence to be *added* to the passage, and then ask you to determine the best location for the new sentence.

The important thing to keep in mind about Organization questions is that *they are based on logic.* The ACT won't present an Organization question unless there is a clearly discernible logical order to the particular paragraph or passage. Each question on the ACT can have only one possible correct answer, these included. Therefore, the way to succeed with an Organization question is first to recognize that it's testing logical sequence, and then search carefully in the passage for particular words and phrases that provide the key to the correct sequence.

Sometimes a passage is organized according to a rough outline structure. For example, in a passage on nutrition, you might find separate paragraphs that discuss proteins, carbohydrates, fats, and antioxidants. If you were asked where to add a sentence about the antioxidant potential of a particular fruit, you'd put it in the fourth paragraph—the one focusing on antioxidants. Remember to use your reading skills to help you find the best answer to a question like that.

Another organizational format is the chronological sequence. As you read through an English passage that includes an organization question, be alert for specific dates and time references, such as *in 1750* or *before the American Revolution.* Dates and time references can serve as key clues when you need to determine the best location to add new information.

Another format similar to the chronological one is the description of stages in a process. As you read, notice words such as *first, second, then, next, last,* and *finally.* These words serve as clues to help you keep track of sequencing and can be useful if you need to find the best spot in the passage to add information.

As you work on this ACT-like Organization question, underline key words that help you determine the logical sequence:

[1] If you're like most people, you may find that applying to college is a complicated process. [2] This in itself can be time-consuming; you need to search through guidebooks, learn about colleges from their websites, and talk to admissions officers at college fairs. [3] You also need to take standardized tests and continue to maintain your high school grade point average. [4] Then, by the fall of your senior year, you must actually start filling out applications and arranging to have supporting documentation sent to the colleges.

1. Upon reviewing the paragraph and realizing that some information has been left out, the writer composes the following sentence:

   > The first challenge is to narrow down a list of places you'd like to study.

   The most logical placement for this sentence would be:

   A. before sentence 1.
   B. after sentence 1.
   C. after sentence 2.
   D. after sentence 3.

Did you find any words to underline in the paragraph? The word *then* in sentence 4 is one indicator of sequence. The sentence to be added, which is stated in the question stem, also contains a sequence clue: *first*. This word indicates that the sentence should most likely be added somewhere near the beginning of the paragraph. To find the right place, plug the new sentence into the passage at the locations described by the answer choices, and think about how it sounds in each context. Notice that sentence 1 introduces the topic of the paragraph. Therefore, it wouldn't make sense to place the additional sentence before that. Read the new sentence *after* sentence 1, and continue reading sentence 2. The additional sentence fits perfectly here because sentence 2 lists several things that must be done in order to *narrow down a list of places*, as the new sentence introduces. You can quickly plug the sentence in at the other locations if you have time, but you should feel pretty confident that you've found the right answer in (B).

The *sentences* in that last passage were numbered. When you notice that a whole passage is presented with numbered paragraphs (the numbers will be in brackets, centered above each paragraph), be aware as you're working through the passage that the paragraphs may not be printed in the most logical order. The other possibility when a passage is printed with numbered paragraphs is that a question will ask where it is most appropriate to add extra information. If a question asks you to add a paragraph, the existing paragraphs will be printed in the most logical order, and you will not see a scrambled paragraphs question for this passage.

For an Organization question that asks you to determine the best ordering of paragraphs, there are several points you should consider. First, glance at each paragraph to determine its topic. You might want to make a brief note in the margin or circle a word or phrase in each paragraph to help you identify the main idea. Second, ask yourself which of the paragraphs sounds like it would make the best introduction to the passage. Third, ask yourself which paragraph sounds most like a concluding paragraph. Usually, simply identifying the most logical introductory and concluding paragraphs is enough to determine the best sequence for all the paragraphs. Sometimes you may have to consider the topics and relationships among the body paragraphs as well.

SUMMARY

In this chapter, we went over every SmartPoint and question type you will encounter on the ACT English test. Use this chapter for continued study and reference as you practice English passages and find the skills you need to focus on. Remember: SmartPoints can be organized into grammar-based and rhetorical skills categories.

Grammar-based SmartPoints are:

- Sentence Sense

- Punctuation

- Verb Tense

- Word Choice

Each of these SmartPoints is based on outside knowledge that can be found in the Grammar and Punctuation Rules to Know section on page 44.

The knowledge necessary to master these questions builds from one to the next. If you are struggling with any of these SmartPoints, you should spend more time studying the SmartPoints listed above it as well.

Word Choice has some questions that are based on Rhetorical Skills as well.

The primary *Rhetorical Skills* SmartPoints are:

- Wordiness

- Connections

- Writing Strategy

- Organization

These questions don't require any outside knowledge and don't build off of each other, but they are more complex and often require you to read and understand more of the passage. For these questions, the first step of the Kaplan Method—read until you have enough information—goes beyond the question itself. These Rhetorical Skills questions require you to read through the underlined portion, instead of simply skipping to the sentence with the underlined portion.

As always, when deciding on an answer in English, remember the big three: *correct, concise,* and *relevant*!

UNIT 2: MATH

The Basics:

60 Minutes

60 Questions

Pacing:

Pace your time per question.

Spend an average of 1 minute per question.

TEST DAY DIRECTIONS AND FORMAT

Here's what the Math directions will look like:

Directions: Solve each problem, choose the correct answer, and then fill in the corresponding oval on your answer document.

Do not linger over problems that take too much time. Solve as many as you can, then return to the others in the time you have left for this test.

You are permitted to use a calculator on this test. You may use your calculator for any problems you choose, but some of the problems may best be done without using a calculator.

Note: Unless otherwise noted, all of the following should be assumed:

1. Illustrative figures are NOT necessarily drawn to scale.

2. Geometric figures lie in a plane.

3. The word *line* indicates a straight line.

4. The word *average* indicates arithmetic mean.

As in the English section, when it comes to directions on the ACT, the golden rule is: Don't read anything on Test Day you already know! Familiarize yourself with everything now, and save yourself time later.

The Math directions don't really tell you much anyway. Of the four special notes at the end of the Math directions, #2, #3, and #4 almost go without saying. Note #1 is pretty important, though—while the rules "bend" a little bit when you have to guess, it's important to know that your eyes *don't* tell you what you need to know about figures; you really do have to do the math. What a figure *looks like* won't reliably get you the right answer.

OUTSIDE KNOWLEDGE

The ACT Math test thoroughly covers rules from a variety of common Math topics, mostly from courses students typically complete by the end of the 11th grade. The outside knowledge required is summed up at the end of this chapter in 100 Key Math Concepts on pages 81–113. The needed math "facts" are also addressed in the strategic discussion throughout this math unit.

THE INSIDE SCOOP

The ACT Math test is designed to measure problem-solving and logical reasoning primarily, but it does test basic computational skills. Covered topics are pre-algebra, algebra, coordinate geometry, plane geometry, and trigonometry.

Questions are not specifically arranged in order of difficulty, but the topics tested *do get more advanced* as you proceed through the test.

SMARTPOINTS

Point Value	Topic	Basics Page	Details and Practice
7	**Plane Geometry**		
7	**Variable Manipulation**		
6	**Proportions and Probability**		
6	**Coordinate Geometry**		
3	**Operations**		
3	**Patterns, Logic, and Data**		
2	**Number Properties**		
2	**Trigonometry**		

CHAPTER 6

Math Part 1: Inside the ACT Math Test

THE KAPLAN METHOD FOR ACT MATH

STEP 1: WHAT IS THE QUESTION?

First, focus on the *question stem* (the part before the answer choices), and make sure you understand the problem. ACT Math questions can have complicated phrasing, and if you don't know *precisely* what you're looking for, you aren't likely to find it. So first, locate the end goal—the objective—and circle it. Do you need to solve for *x*? Find an odd number? Maybe it's a story problem and you need to find how many adults were admitted to an exhibit, or the number of girls in a classroom. If it is a word problem and you get lost, break the question into pieces and make sure you come away with a clear understanding of what you're looking for. What is the end objective of your work? Again, *circle the question*, or objective as stated in the question stem, when you've found it.

STEP 2: WHAT INFORMATION AM I GIVEN?

Look through the question stem again, and *underline the pieces of information provided*. Ask yourself whether you have everything you'll need to solve the problem, or if there are intermediary steps you'll have to take. By underlining everything, you'll have a place to start, even if you're lost, as the ACT rarely provides information you don't need to solve the problem. Then, examine the format of the answer choices. This can help you determine your strategy. For example, you may think you need to solve for *x* in an equation, but then you see that all of the answers are given *in terms of x*, so you don't actually need to find *x*, just come up with a formula. Additionally, if you are given information in fractions and see answers in decimals, you'll know you need to convert from one to the other at some point.

STEP 3: WHAT CAN I DO WITH THE INFORMATION?

Now that you've gathered the information, time to solve the question. Decide on a plan of attack:

- **Straightforward math.** Do you know how to solve the problem using your math skills? Go for it!

- **Picking numbers.** Are there variables in the answer choices? If so, is there a way to pick some easy-to-use numbers you can plug in for the variable to help you get to the right answer? (This strategy is discussed in depth in the Point Builders section on page 77.)

- **Backsolving.** Are there numbers in the answer choices? What is the question asking for? Is there a way to use the answer choices to get to the right answer? (This strategy is also discussed in the Point Builders section on page 78.)

- **Guess strategically.** If you're really not sure, you can guess—you don't lose points for incorrect answers on the ACT. Try to eliminate as many incorrect choices as you can before guessing, and mark the question in your booklet so you can return to it at the end of the Math test and try again.

STEP 4: AM I FINISHED?

In Step 1, you circled the objective. Check what you circled now. Is that what you found? Have you fully answered the question? Some questions may require several steps, and you may miss the last step if you don't check before you select. The ACT will frequently offer tempting answer choices for students who don't recheck the question. For example, you may need to find the area of a circle and you've only determined the radius—and the radius might be an answer choice! Since you will have identified and marked the question in Step 1, double-checking that you're finished should take only a few seconds, and it can make a real difference on Test Day. If you're stuck, circle the problem in your test book and come back later—always get through the easy questions first.

QUICK TIPS

MIND-SET

- **The end justifies the means.** Your goal is to get as many points as possible, not to demonstrate how great you are at any particular math area, or to show all your work, or get all the "hard" questions—just to get points, plain and simple. That means getting as many correct answers as quickly as possible. If that means doing straightforward questions in a straightforward way, that's fine. But many questions can be solved faster by using Kaplan Methods, such as backsolving and picking numbers, and will make you both faster and more accurate. (Learn these strategies in the Point Builder section on page 76.)

- **Take time to save time.** It sounds paradoxical, but to go your fastest on the Math test, you sometimes have to slow down. Don't just dive in headlong, wildly crunching numbers or manipulating equations without first giving the problem some thought. Remember your priority is the whole section, not just this one question.

- **When in doubt, shake it up.** ACT Math questions are not always what they seem at first glance. Sometimes all you need is a new perspective to break through the disguise. Take a step back and look at the question another way.

SPECIAL STRATEGIES

We offer several recommendations for what to do when you get stuck. If after a few moments of thought you find you still can't come up with a reasonable way of doing the problem, try one of these techniques:

- **Restate.** When you get stuck, try looking at the problem from a different angle. Try rearranging the numbers, changing decimals to fractions, changing fractions to decimals, multiplying out numbers, factoring problems, redrawing a diagram, or doing anything that might help you to look at the problem a bit differently.

- **Remove the disguise.** Find out what the question is really asking—it might not be what the problem appears to ask at first. Find the objective and circle it, especially when you're confused.

- **Try eyeballing.** Even though the directions warn you that diagrams are "not necessarily" drawn to scale, eyeballing is a surprisingly effective guessing strategy. You won't be able to get specifics without doing the math, sometimes, but you will be able to rule some answers out, or get a better idea of what you're looking for.

TIMING

You have an average of 1 minute to spend per question. Ideally, you'll be able to spend significantly less time on easy questions so you can buy more time on the hard questions.

Spend about 45 minutes on your first pass through the Math subject test. Do the easier questions, guess on the questions you suspect aren't going to come to you no matter what, and mark the tough ones that you'll want to come back to. Spend the last 15 minutes picking up those questions you skipped on the first pass.

We recommend you grid your answers at the end of every page or two. In the last five minutes or so, start gridding your answers one by one. And make sure that you have an answer (even if it's a blind guess) gridded for every question by the time the test is over.

Don't worry if you have to guess on a lot of the Math questions. You can miss a lot of questions on the Math test and still get a great score. Remember that the average ACT test taker gets fewer than half of the Math questions right!

WHEN YOU'RE RUNNING OUT OF TIME

If at some point you realize you have more questions left than you have time for, be willing to skip around, looking for questions you understand right away. Pick your points, and concentrate on the questions you have the best chance of correctly answering. Just be sure to grid an answer—even if it's just a wild guess—for every question.

SCORING

Your performance on the Math subject test will be averaged into your ACT Composite Score, equally weighted with your scores on the other three major subject tests. You will also receive:

- Math subject score—from 1 to 36—for the entire Math subject test

- Pre-Algebra/Elementary Algebra subscore—from 1 to 18

- Intermediate Algebra/Coordinate Geometry subscore—from 1 to 18

- Plane Geometry/Trigonometry subscore—from 1 to 18

POINT BUILDERS

As we promised, there are many ways to view questions. Here are the top two ways to think outside the box about how to solve any given Math problem.

PICKING NUMBERS

This strategy relates to questions with variables. You can Pick Numbers to make abstract problems—ones that insist on dealing with variables rather than numbers—more concrete. **Use this problem when there are variables in the answer choices.** If there are variables in the answer choices, you won't have to solve for the variables, just determine how they would behave if they were real numbers. Thus, don't assume—pick a real number and see for yourself. Follow these guidelines:

Step 1: Pick a simple number to stand in for the variables, making sure it follows the rules listed in the question stem. Does the number have to be even or odd? Positive or negative? Be careful when using 0 and 1, as they behave differently than most other numbers, but always use easy-to-use numbers.

Step 2: Solve the question using the number you picked.

Step 3: Try out all the answer choices using the number you picked, eliminating those that give you a result you're not looking for.

Step 4: If more than one choice remains, pick a different set of numbers and repeat steps 1–3.

Let's try this strategy on the following problem.

1. If a is an odd integer and b is an even integer, which of the following must be odd?

    A. $2a + b$

    B. $a + 2b$

    C. ab

    D. a^2b

    E. ab^2

Rather than try to think this one through abstractly, it's easier to pick numbers for a and b. There are rules that predict the evenness or oddness of sums, differences, and products, but there's no need to memorize those rules.

Just say, for the time being, that $a = 3$ (remember, 1 can be used, but is not typically helpful) and $b = 2$. Plug those values into the answer choices, and there's a good chance only one choice will be odd:

    A. $2a + b = 2(3) + 2 = 8$

    B. $a + 2b = 3 + 2(2) = 9$

    C. $ab = (3)(2) = 6$

    D. $a^2b = (3)^2(2) = 18$

    E. $ab^2 = (3)(2)^2 = 12$

Choice (B) was the only odd one for $a = 3$ and $b = 2$, so it *must* be the one that's odd no matter *what* odd number a and even number b actually stand for. Even if you're not positive

(B) will always be right, you know for a fact that all the others are definitely wrong, which is just as good!

BACKSOLVING

Because you can know for certain that one of the answer choices is right (as opposed to a fill-in-the-blank test), with some ACT Math problems, it may actually be easier to try out each answer choice until you find the one that works, rather than attempt to solve the problem and then look among the choices for the answer. We call this approach Backsolving.

Try it out.

2. All 200 tickets were sold for a particular concert. Some tickets cost $10 apiece, and the others cost $5 apiece. If total ticket sales were $1,750, how many of the more expensive tickets were sold?

    F. 20
    G. 75
    H. 100
    J. 150
    K. 175

There are ways to solve this problem by setting up an equation or two, but if you're not comfortable with the algebraic approach to this one, why not just try out each answer choice? You know one of them will work.

Here's the next part you need to know: when Backsolving, *always start with the middle answer choice*. The numerical answer choices on the ACT are always in ascending order. If you solve for the one in the middle and it comes out too big, you can eliminate it *and the two larger numbers*, and same if it's too small. So trying **one** answer choice can eliminate **three** options.

So start with choice (H). If 100 tickets were sold for $10 each, then the other 100 have to have been sold for $5 each. 100 at $10 is $1,000, and 100 tickets at $5 is $500, for a total of $1,500—too small. There *must* have been more than 100 $10 tickets.

This is great news! If we know it's not (H), and we know (H) is too small, we can eliminate (F) and (G) as well. By solving for one value, we've eliminated three answer choices. Even if you had to stop and guess now, you'd be picking from two answers, not five! So, which answer do we try next? More good news—it doesn't actually matter. If you solve for (J) and it's wrong, the answer must be (K); you don't even have to solve for (K) to know that. So either remaining answer works equally well. That being the case, you should solve for whichever one looks easier, since it's just about doing the math. In this case, 150 looks a little bit easier to solve than 175, so we'll start with (J).

If 150 tickets went for $10, then the other 50 went for $5. So 150 tickets at $10 is $1,500, and 50 tickets at $5 is $250, for a total of $1,750—that's it! The answer is (J), no need to go any further.

Backsolving your way to the answer may not be a method you'd show your algebra teacher, but your algebra teacher won't be watching on Test Day. Remember, all that matters is right answers—it doesn't matter how you get them.

SMARTPOINT BREAKDOWN

Here is a brief overview of what exactly to expect and how much of it you should be expecting.

PLANE GEOMETRY—7 POINTS

Extremely Important

Plane Geometry questions test your ability to solve problems related to figures, angles, and lines. Triangles—specifically right triangles—and circles are the two most commonly tested shapes, but you can expect to see questions on a variety of polygons, complex 2-D and simple 3-D shapes. Fortunately, like the rest of the ACT Math test, the number of rules to remember is limited, and they only pertain to simple shapes. Turn to 100 Key Math Concepts on page 81 for a list of these rules. Otherwise, the test will ask you to break down complex figures into recognizable shapes and use problem-solving skills to transfer information throughout a figure. The next chapter has a thorough discussion of each of these concepts and strategies, as well as practice problems, on page 147.

VARIABLE MANIPULATION—7 POINTS

Extremely Important

Variable Manipulation questions extensively test your ability to solve for an unknown quantity given a wide range of information of varying complexity. The simplest questions are pulled from elementary algebra and require you to solve for a single variable. They build up to intermediate algebra, and ask you to solve simultaneous equations, equations involving absolute value, inequalities, or quadratic equations. The tested rules pull extensively from the operations and number properties SmartPoints, and can all be found in 100 Key Math Concepts on page 81. However, unlike those SmartPoints—which can be a simpler test of your knowledge of rules—variable manipulation questions involve applying those concepts with adept strategy and problem solving. For a more thorough discussion of these problems, strategies to deal with them, and samples to practice, refer to page 124.

PROPORTIONS AND PROBABILITY—6 POINTS

Very Important

Proportions and Probability questions test a number of key mathematical concepts that involve relating numbers, including percents, ratios, and averages, as well as distance, rate, and time, and of course, probability itself (the likelihood of an event taking place). Refer to 100 Key Math Concepts on page 81 for the three-part formulas essential for this SmartPoint. Memorizing and applying those are key to mastering this section. For more discussion and practice, refer to page 130.

COORDINATE GEOMETRY—6 POINTS

Very Important

Coordinate Geometry questions primarily test knowledge of equations and graphs of lines. The centers around an (x,y) coordinate plane. The Slope-Intercept formula is the most important equation to remember here, as most ACT Coordinate Geometry questions ask about properties of a single, straight line. Slope is paramount, as are the concepts of parallel and perpendicular lines. However, the test will also ask questions that require knowledge of the Midpoint and Distance formulas, quadratics and the associated parabolas, and occasionally the graphs of simple shapes such as triangles and circles. All formulas are listed in 100 Key Math Concepts on page 81 and discussed in detail with strategies on practice on page 143.

OPERATIONS—3 POINTS

Somewhat Important

Like Number Properties, Operations are not directly tested on many questions, but thorough knowledge of them is necessary for many question types, especially Variable Manipulation and Proportions and Probability. Tested operations include all parts of the PEMDAS order of operations (Parenthesis, Exponents, Multiplication, Division, Addition, and Subtraction). Complex Operation questions ask you to perform many of these functions in a single string of numbers. Rarer questions test basic knowledge of imaginary numbers, radicals, and logarithms. All rules for these are listed in 100 Key Math Concepts on page 81. For in-depth discussion and samples of this SmartPoint, refer to page 119.

PATTERNS, LOGIC, AND DATA—3 POINTS

Somewhat Important

Many of these questions don't even look like Math questions at first glance. They often involve pie charts, tables, matrices, and line and bar graphs that would be more at home on the Science subject test. Complex, infrequently tested areas are grouped under this SmartPoint, including Permutations and Combinations, Union and Intersection of Sets, Matrices, and Functions. Fear not, all you need to know is listed, as always, in 100 Key Math Concepts on page 81, and the vast majority of these problems can be solved by calmly identifying what is being asked of you, then using simple, step-by-step logic to get there. Thorough strategy discussion and practice can be found on page 166.

NUMBER PROPERTIES—2 POINTS

Somewhat Important

This is another fundamental SmartPoint, like Operations, that is not often tested directly, but forms a base of knowledge that contributes to a number of other question types, such as Variable Manipulation and Proportions and Probability. Number Properties questions ask you to understand the behavior of numbers, particularly evens and odds, and positives and negatives. These questions are ripe for picking numbers, discussed earlier in this chapter. It also tests properties of divisibility, such as factors, multiples, and prime numbers. As usual, refer to 100 Key Math Concepts on page 81 for a full list of rules and turn to page 116 for a detailed discussion of strategies for this question type.

TRIGONOMETRY—2 POINTS

Somewhat Important

The fact that the ACT tests Trigonometry scares a lot of test takers. Take a deep breath, because you're about to get good news. Trigonometry is very lightly tested and the questions are extremely predictable. Almost all questions center around sine, cosine, and tangent and some of the most common trigonometric functions. Also good to know: You should expect four trigonometry questions or fewer. Memorize the few rules listed in 100 Key Math Concepts on page 81 and practice them with the more in-depth strategy discussion on page 171 and you can master the Trigonometry portion of the ACT in no time.

100 KEY MATH CONCEPTS

Below is an extensive list of the most frequently tested rules of the ACT Math subject test. Look over this list now and as you review the following chapter, and if you're short on time before Test Day, this is a great place to cram. Otherwise, use this list in conjunction with the SmartPoint-by-SmartPoint discussion in the next chapter, in which the most commonly tested rules are discussed more thoroughly with sample problems similar to the ones you'll see on the ACT.

NUMBER PROPERTIES

1. UNDEFINED

On the ACT, when something is **divided by zero**, it is considered *undefined*. For example, the expression $\dfrac{a}{bc}$ is undefined if either b or c equals 0.

2. REAL/IMAGINARY

A real number is a number that has a **location on the number line**—positive, negative, whole numbers, fractions—all are considered real numbers. Imaginary numbers, on the other hand, are numbers that involve the square root of a negative number.

3. INTEGER/NONINTEGER

Integers are **whole numbers,** which means no fractions, decimals, or mixed numbers; they include both negative and positive numbers, as well as zero.

4. RATIONAL/IRRATIONAL

Any number that can be expressed as a fraction or a repeating decimal is a rational number. This includes numbers like 3, 2/5, −.1666 or .333. **Irrational numbers cannot be expressed precisely as a fraction or decimal.** For the purposes of the ACT, the most important **irrational numbers** are $\sqrt{2}, \sqrt{3}$, and π.

5. ADDING/SUBTRACTING SIGNED NUMBERS

To **add a positive and a negative,** subtract the negative number from the positive number. For instance, −9 + 1 is the same as 1 − 9. Alternately, you can find the difference between the two numbers, and then keep the original sign of the larger number. Again using the example −9 + 1, the difference between 1 and 9 is 8, and since 9 was the larger number, keep the negative sign, so −9 + 1 = −8.

Subtracting a negative number is the same as adding a positive. For example, think of 17 − (−21) as 17 + (+21).

To **add or subtract a string of positives and negatives,** add up all of the positive numbers, and add up all of the negative numbers. Then add those two sums together, keeping the sign of the greater sum. For instance, if you had the string 8 + 3 −12 + 4 − 6 − 5, combine the positives: 8 + 3 + 4 = 15. Combine the negatives: −12 + (− 6) + (−5) = −23. Now combine the two sums: 15 + (−23) = −8.

6. MULTIPLYING/DIVIDING SIGNED NUMBERS

Positives multiplied/divided with other positives are always positive. An even number of negative numbers, when multiplied or divided, will also be positive. However, if there is an odd number of negatives, the multiplication/division will be negative. For instance, (−2) × (−3) = 6, but (−2) × (−3) × (−4) = −24.

7. PEMDAS

When performing multiple operations, remember **PEMDAS,** which means start with anything inside **Parentheses** first, then deal with any **Exponents,** then all of the **Multiplication** and **Division** (left to right), and finally all of the **Addition** and **Subtraction** (left to right).

In the expression $9 - 2 \times (5 - 3)^2 + 6 \div 3$, begin with the parentheses: $(5 - 3) = 2$. Then do the exponent: $2^2 = 4$, so now the expression is: $9 - 2 \times 4 + 6 \div 3$. Next do the multiplication, $2 \times 4 = 8$, and division, $6 \div 3 = 2$, to get $9 - 8 + 2$. Finally, subtraction, $9 - 8 = 1$, and then the addition, $1 + 2$, which equals 3.

8. ABSOLUTE VALUE

The absolute value of something is its distance from zero on the number line, which is why absolute value is always positive. Treat absolute value signs a lot like **parentheses.** Do what's inside them first and then take the absolute value of the result. Don't take the absolute value of each piece between the bars before calculating. In order to calculate $|(-12) + 5 - (-4)| - |5 + (-10)|$, first do what's inside the bars to get: $|-3| - |-5|$, which is $3 - 5$, or -2.

9. COUNTING CONSECUTIVE INTEGERS

To find the number of consecutive integers between two values, **subtract the smallest from the largest and add 1.** So to find the number of consecutive integers from 13 through 31, subtract: $31 - 13 = 18$. Then add 1: $18 + 1 = 19$. There are 19 consecutive integers from 13 through 31.

DIVISIBILITY

10. FACTOR/MULTIPLE

A factor of an integer is any number that divides precisely into that integer (with no remainder.) The multiple of an integer is that integer times any number. In other words, factor × factor = multiple. All numbers are both factors and multiples of themselves. Six is a factor of 12, and 24 is a multiple of 12. Twelve is both a factor ($12 \div 12 = 1$) and a multiple ($12 \times 1 = 12$) of itself.

11. PRIME FACTORIZATION

A **prime number** is a positive integer that is divisible without a remainder by only 1 and itself. The number 2 is the smallest prime number and the only even prime number; 1 is not considered prime. To find the prime factorization of an integer, use a factor tree to keep breaking the integer up into factors until **all the factors are prime.** To find the prime factorization of 36, for example, you could begin by breaking it into 4×9:

$$36 = 4 \times 9 = 2 \times 2 \times 3 \times 3$$

12. RELATIVE PRIMES

Two integers are relative primes if they share no prime factors. To determine whether two integers are relative primes, break them both down to their prime factorizations. For example: 35 = 5 × 7, and 54 = 2 × 3 × 3 × 3. They have **no prime factors in common**, so 35 and 54 are relative primes.

13. COMMON MULTIPLE

You can always get a common multiple of two numbers by **multiplying** them, but unless the two numbers are relative primes, the product will not be the least common multiple—the smallest multiple both of those numbers divide into. For example, to find a common multiple for 12 and 15, you could just multiply: 12 × 15 = 180.

14. LEAST COMMON MULTIPLE (LCM)

To find the least common multiple, check out the **multiples of the larger number** until you find one that's **also a multiple of the smaller.**

To find the LCM of 12 and 15, begin by taking the multiples of 15: 1 × 15 = 15, which is not divisible by 12; 2 × 15 = 30, not divisible by 12; nor is 45, which is 3 × 15. But the next multiple of 15, 4 × 15 = 60, is divisible by 12, so it's the LCM.

15. GREATEST COMMON FACTOR (GCF)

The greatest common factor of two numbers is the highest number that divides precisely into each of them without a remainder. To find the greatest common factor, break down both numbers into their prime factorizations, and take **all the prime factors they have in common.** For example, take 36 and 48: 36 = 2 × 2 × 3 × 3, and 48 = 2 × 2 × 2 × 2 × 3. What they have in common is two 2s and one 3, so the GCF is 2 × 2 × 3 = 12.

16. EVEN/ODD

There are rules to predict whether a sum, difference, or product of an expression will be even or odd—"odd times even is even," for example—but there's no need to memorize them. **Pick numbers like 2 and 3 and see what happens.** Picking numbers is the easiest and most efficient way to deal with questions dealing with even/odd properties.

17. MULTIPLES OF 2 AND 4

An integer is divisible by 2 if the **last digit is even.** An integer is divisible by 4 if the **last two digits form a multiple of 4.** The last digit of 562 is 2, which is even, so 562 is a multiple of 2. The last two digits make 62, which is not divisible by 4, so 562 is not a multiple of 4. However, 4,928 is divisible by 4 because 28 is divisible by 4.

18. MULTIPLES OF 3 AND 9

An integer is divisible by 3 if the **sum of its digits is divisible by 3.** An integer is divisible by 9 if the **sum of its digits is divisible by 9.** Take the number 957—the sum of the digits is 9 + 5 + 7 = 21, and 21 is divisible by 3 but 21 is not divisible by 9, so 957 is divisible by 3 but not 9.

19. MULTIPLES OF 5 AND 10

An integer is divisible by 5 if the **last digit is 5 or 0.** An integer is divisible by 10 if the **last digit is 0.** The last digit of 665 is 5, so 665 is a multiple of 5 but not a multiple of 10.

20. REMAINDERS

The remainder is the number left over after division. If you divided 48 by 5, you'd first find the nearest multiple of 5 to 48, which is 45 (9 × 5). This means 5 goes into 48 nine times, but then there is still 3 left over, which makes the remainder 3.

FRACTIONS AND DECIMALS

21. REDUCING FRACTIONS

To reduce a fraction to lowest terms, **factor out and cancel** all factors the numerator and denominator have in common. For instance, if you had the fraction 28/36, you could reduce this fraction, because both 28 and 36 have a factor of 4 that can be taken out:

$$\frac{28}{36} = \frac{4 \times 7}{4 \times 9} = \frac{7}{9}$$

22. ADDING/SUBTRACTING FRACTIONS

To add or subtract fractions, first find a **common denominator,** and then add or subtract the numerators. Finding a common denominator often involves multiplying one or more of the fractions by a number so that the denominators come out the same:

$$\frac{2}{15} + \frac{3}{10} = \frac{4}{30} + \frac{9}{30} = \frac{4 \times 9}{30} = \frac{13}{30}$$

23. MULTIPLYING FRACTIONS

To multiply fractions, **multiply** straight across—numerator times numerator and denominator times denominator.

$$\frac{5}{7} \times \frac{3}{4} = \frac{5 \times 3}{7 \times 4} = \frac{15}{28}$$

24. DIVIDING FRACTIONS

To divide fractions, **invert** the fraction in the denominator and **multiply.**

$$\frac{1}{2} \div \frac{3}{5} = \frac{1}{2} \times \frac{5}{3} = \frac{1 \times 5}{2 \times 3} = \frac{5}{6}$$

25. CONVERTING A MIXED NUMBER TO AN IMPROPER FRACTION

To convert a mixed number, which is a whole number with a fraction, to an improper fraction, which is a fraction where the numerator is bigger than the denominator, **multiply** the whole number part by the denominator, then **add** the numerator. The result is the new numerator (over the same denominator). To convert $7\frac{1}{3}$ first multiply 7 by 3, then add 1, to get the new numerator of 22. Put that over the same denominator, 3, to get $\frac{22}{3}$.

26. CONVERTING AN IMPROPER FRACTION TO A MIXED NUMBER

To convert an improper fraction to a mixed number, **divide** the denominator into the numerator, and the remainder will be the numerator of the fraction part, with the same denominator. For example, to convert $\frac{108}{5}$, first divide 5 into 108, which yields 21 with a remainder of 3. Therefore, $\frac{108}{5} = 21\frac{3}{5}$.

27. RECIPROCAL

The reciprocal of a fraction is the inverse of that fraction. To find the reciprocal of a fraction, switch the numerator and the denominator. The reciprocal of $\frac{3}{7}$ is $\frac{7}{3}$. The reciprocal of 5 (or 5/1, because all whole numbers are over 1) is $\frac{1}{5}$. The product of reciprocals is always 1.

28. COMPARING FRACTIONS

One way to compare fractions is to manipulate them so they have a **common denominator.** For instance, to compare $\frac{3}{4}$ and $\frac{5}{7}$:

$\frac{3}{4} = \frac{21}{28}$ and $\frac{5}{7} = \frac{20}{28}$; $\frac{21}{28}$ is greater than $\frac{20}{28}$, so $\frac{3}{4}$ is greater than $\frac{5}{7}$.

Another way to compare fractions is to convert them both to **decimals.** $\frac{3}{4}$ converts to .75, and $\frac{5}{7}$ converts to approximately .714.

29. CONVERTING FRACTIONS TO DECIMALS

To convert a fraction to a decimal, **divide the numerator by the denominator.** To convert $\frac{5}{8}$, divide 5 by 8, yielding .625. Often, these numbers will start repeating, such as $\frac{1}{6}$. When 1 is divided by 6, the decimal starts repeating almost right away, so it can be written as $1.6\overline{6}$ (the line over the 66 means, 'repeating').

30. REPEATING DECIMAL

To find a particular digit in a repeating decimal, note the **number of digits in the cluster that repeats.** If there are two digits in that cluster, then every second digit is the same. If there are three digits in that cluster, then every third digit is the same. And so on. For example, the decimal equivalent of $\frac{1}{27}$ is .037037037…which is best written $.\overline{.037}$.

There are three digits in the repeating cluster, so every third digit is the same: 7. To find the 50th digit, look for the multiple of 3 just less than 50—that's 48. The 48th digit is 7, and with the 49th digit the pattern repeats with 0. So, the 50th digit is 3.

31. IDENTIFYING THE PARTS AND THE WHOLE

The key to solving most fraction and percent word problems is to identify the part and the whole. Usually, you'll find the **part** associated with the verb *is/are* and the **whole** associated with the word *of.* In the sentence, "Half of the boys are blonds," the whole is the boys ("*of* the boys"), and the part is the blonds ("*are* blonds"). Sometimes, the problem will give you just the parts: "The ratio of boys to girls is 2 to 3." In this case, we have a part:part relationship. To find the ratio of boys to the total, you would add the parts: 2 + 3 = 5, so the ratio of boys to total (part:whole) is 2 to 5.

PERCENTS

32. PERCENT FORMULA

In percent questions, whether you need to find the part, the whole, or the percent, use the same formula:

Part = Percent × Whole

When you use the formula, be sure to convert the percent into decimal form:

Example: What is 12% of 25?
Setup: Part = .12 × 25

Example: 15 is 3% of what number?
Setup: 15 = .03 × Whole

Example: 45 is what percent of 9?
Setup: 45 = Percent × 9

33. PERCENT INCREASE AND DECREASE

To increase a number by a percent, **add the percent to 100%,** convert to a decimal, and multiply. To increase 40 by 25%, add 25% to 100%, convert 125% to 1.25, and multiply by 40. $1.25 \times 40 = 50$. To decrease, just subtract the percent from 100%, convert to decimal, and multiply.

34. FINDING THE ORIGINAL WHOLE

To find the **original whole before a percent increase or decrease,** set up an equation with a variable in place of the original number. Say you have a 15% increase over an unknown original amount, say x, you would follow the same steps as always: 100% plus 15% is 115% percent, which is 1.15 when converted to decimal, and then multiply to the number, which in this case, is x, and you get $1.15x$, then set that equal to the 'new' amount.

Example: After a 5% increase, the population was 59,346. What was the population
                 before the increase?

Setup: $1.05x = 59{,}346$

35. COMBINED PERCENT INCREASE AND DECREASE

When there are multiple percent increases and/or decreases, and the question asks for the combined percent increase or decrease, the easiest and most effective strategy is to pick 100 for the original value and see what happens.

Example: A price went up 10% one year, and the new price went up 20% the next year.
                 What was the combined percent increase?

Setup: First year: $100 + (10\%\ \text{of}\ 100) = 110$. Second year: $110 + (20\%\ \text{of}\ 110) = 132$.
                 That's a combined 32% increase.

RATIOS, PROPORTIONS, AND RATES

36. SETTING UP A RATIO

To find a ratio, put the number associated with the word *of on top* (as the numerator) and the quantity associated with the word *to* **on the bottom** (as the denominator), and reduce. The ratio of 20 oranges to 12 apples is $\frac{20}{12}$, which reduces to $\frac{5}{3}$. Be sure to keep the parts in the same order—so if a second ratio of oranges to apples was given, the oranges should be on top, and the apples on the bottom.

37. PART-TO-PART AND PART-TO-WHOLE RATIOS

A part-to-part ratio can be turned into two part-to-whole ratios by putting **each number in the original ratio over the sum of the parts.** If the ratio of males to females is 1 to 2, then the males-to-people ratio is $\dfrac{1}{1+2} = \dfrac{1}{3}$ and the females-to-people ratio is $\dfrac{2}{1+2} = \dfrac{2}{3}$. Or, $\dfrac{2}{3}$ of all the people are female.

38. SOLVING A PROPORTION

A proportion is two fractions set equal to each other. To solve a proportion, **cross multiply:**

$$\frac{x}{5} = \frac{3}{4}$$
$$4x = 5(3)$$
$$x = \frac{15}{4} = 3.75$$

39. RATE

A rate is any "something per something"—days per week, miles per hour, dollars per gallon, etc. Pay close attention to the units of measurement, since often the rate is given in one measurement in the question, and a different measurement in the answer choices. This means you need to convert the rate to the other measurement before you solve the question.

Example: If snow is falling at the rate of one <u>foot</u> every four hours, how many <u>inches</u> of snow will fall in seven hours?

Setup:

$$\frac{1\,\text{foot}}{4\,\text{hours}} = \frac{x\,\text{inches}}{7\,\text{hours}}$$
$$\frac{12\,\text{inches}}{4\,\text{hours}} = \frac{x\,\text{inches}}{7\,\text{hours}}$$
$$4x = 12 \times 7$$
$$x = 21$$

40. AVERAGE RATE

Average rate is *not* simply the average of the rates. It's the average of the total amounts. The most common rate is speed—distance over time—and the most common question about average rates is average speed—total distance over total time.

$$\text{Average } A \text{ per } B = \frac{\text{Total } A}{\text{Total } B}$$
$$\text{Average speed} = \frac{\text{Total distance}}{\text{Total time}}$$

If the first 120 miles of a journey is at 40 mph and the next 120 miles at 60 mph, what is the average speed? **Don't just average the two speeds.** Instead, figure out the total distance and the total time. The total distance is 120 + 120 = 240 miles. The times are three hours for the first leg and two hours for the second leg, or five hours total. The average speed, then, is $\dfrac{240}{5} = 48$ miles per hour.

AVERAGES

41. AVERAGE FORMULA

To find the average of a set of numbers, **add them up and divide by the number of numbers.**

$$\text{Average} = \dfrac{\text{Sum of the terms}}{\text{Number of the terms}}$$

To find the average of the five numbers 12, 15, 23, 40, and 40, first add them: 12 + 15 + 23 + 40 + 40 = 130. Then divide the sum by 5: 130 ÷ 5 = 26.

42. AVERAGE OF EVENLY SPACED NUMBERS

When you have a set of evenly spaced numbers, such as 10 consecutive numbers, or all the odd numbers between 5 and 35, you can use a shortcut rather than the averages formula.

To find the average of evenly spaced numbers, just **average the smallest and the largest.**

The average of all the integers from 13 through 77 is the same as the average of 13 and 77: $\dfrac{13 + 77}{2} = \dfrac{90}{2} = 45$.

43. USING THE AVERAGE TO FIND THE SUM

Since the average is just the sum of the numbers divided by the number of numbers, it follows that:

$$\text{Sum} = (\text{Average}) \times (\text{Number of terms})$$

If the average of 10 numbers is 50, then they add up to 10 × 50, or 500.

44. FINDING THE MISSING NUMBER

To find a missing number when you're given the average, **use the sum.** If the average of four numbers is 7, then the sum of those four numbers is 4 × 7, or 28. Suppose that three of the numbers are 3, 5, and 8. These numbers add up to 16 of that 28, which leaves 12 for the fourth number.

POSSIBILITIES AND PROBABILITY

45. COUNTING THE POSSIBILITIES

The fundamental counting principle: If there are *m* **ways** one event can happen and *n* **ways** a second event can happen, then there are *m* × *n* **ways** for the two events to happen. For example, with 5 shirts and 7 pairs of pants to choose from, you can put together 5 × 7 = 35 different outfits.

46. PROBABILITY

Probability is always the number of desired outcomes divided by the number of possible outcomes. It can be expressed as a fraction, or sometimes, as a decimal.

$$\text{Probability} = \frac{\text{Favorable outcomes}}{\text{Total possible outcomes}}$$

If you have 12 shirts in a drawer and 9 of them are white, the probability of picking a white shirt at random is $\frac{9}{12} = \frac{3}{4}$. This probability can also be expressed as .75 or 75%.

POWERS AND ROOTS

47. MULTIPLYING AND DIVIDING POWERS

To multiply powers with the same base, **add the exponents:** $x^3 \times x^4 = x^{3+4} = x^7$.

To divide powers with the same base, **subtract the exponents:** $y^{13} \div y^8 = y^{13-8} = y^5$

48. RAISING POWERS TO POWERS

To raise a power to another power, **multiply the exponents:** $(x^3)^4 = x^{3*4} = x^{12}$

49. SIMPLIFYING SQUARE ROOTS

To simplify a square root, **factor out the perfect squares** under the radical, square root them, and put the result in front of the part left under the square root sign (the non-perfect-square factors):

$$\sqrt{12} = \sqrt{4 \times 3} = \sqrt{4} \times \sqrt{3} = 2\sqrt{3}$$

50. ADDING AND SUBTRACTING ROOTS

You can add or subtract radical expressions only if the part under the radicals is the same. In other words, treat it like a variable: just like 2x + 3x would equal 5x,

$$2\sqrt{3} + 3\sqrt{3} = 5\sqrt{3}$$

In other words, you can only add or subtract the numbers in front of the square root sign—the numbers under the sign stay the same.

51. MULTIPLYING AND DIVIDING ROOTS

You can distribute the square root sign over multiplication and division. The product of square roots is equal to the square root of the product:

$$\sqrt{3} \times \sqrt{5} = \sqrt{3 \times 5} = \sqrt{15}$$

The quotient of square roots is equal to the **square root of the quotient:**

$$\frac{\sqrt{6}}{\sqrt{3}} = \sqrt{\frac{6}{3}} = \sqrt{2}$$

ALGEBRAIC EXPRESSIONS

52. EVALUATING AN EXPRESSION

To evaluate an algebraic expression, **plug in** the given values for the unknowns and calculate according to PEMDAS. To find the value of $x^2 + 5x - 6$ when $x = -2$, plug in -2 for x:

$$(-2)^2 + 5(-2) - 6 = 4 - 10 - 6 = -12$$

53. ADDING AND SUBTRACTING MONOMIALS (COMBINING LIKE TERMS)

To combine like terms, **keep the variable part unchanged while adding or subtracting the coefficients (numbers):**

$$2a + 3a = (2 + 3)a = 5a$$

54. ADDING AND SUBTRACTING POLYNOMIALS

To add or subtract polynomials, **combine like terms:**

$$(3x^2 + 5x - 7) - (x^2 + 12) =$$
$$(3x^2 - x^2) + 5x + (-7 - 12) =$$
$$2x^2 + 5x - 19$$

55. MULTIPLYING MONOMIALS

To multiply monomials, **multiply the numbers and the variables separately:**

$$2a \times 3a = (2 \times 3)(a \times a) = 6a^2$$

56. MULTIPLYING BINOMIALS—FOIL

To multiply binomials, use **FOIL: First, Outer, Inner, Last:**

Example: $(x + 3)(x + 4)$

First multiply the **F**irst terms: $x \times x = x^2$.

Next the **O**uter terms: $x \times 4 = 4x$.

Then the **I**nner terms: $3 \times x = 3x$.

And finally the **L**ast terms: $3 \times 4 = 12$.

Then add and combine like terms: $x^2 + 4x + 3x + 12 = x^2 + 7x + 12$.

57. MULTIPLYING OTHER POLYNOMIALS

FOIL works only when you want to multiply two binomials (an expression with two terms.) If you want to multiply polynomials with more than two terms, make sure you **multiply each term in the first polynomial by each term in the second:**

$(x^2 + 3x + 4)(x + 5) =$

$x^2(x + 5) + 3x(x + 5) + 4(x + 5) =$

$x^3 + 5x^2 + 3x^2 + 15x + 4x + 20 =$

$x^3 + 8x^2 + 19x + 20$

FACTORING ALGEBRAIC EXPRESSIONS

58. FACTORING OUT A COMMON DIVISOR

A factor common to all terms of a polynomial can be **factored out.** All three terms in the polynomial $3x^3 + 12x^2 - 6x$ contain a factor of $3x$. Pulling out the common factor yields $3x(x^2 + 4x - 2)$. Remember that if you factor a term out completely, you are still left with 1: in the expression $6x^2 + 9x + 3$, you can factor a 3 out of everything. You're left with $3(2x^2 + 3x + 1)$.

59. FACTORING THE DIFFERENCE OF SQUARES

One of the test maker's favorite classic quadratics is the **difference of squares.**

$a^2 - b^2 = (a - b)(a + b)$

$x^2 - 9$, for example, factors to $(x - 3)(x + 3)$.

60. FACTORING THE SQUARE OF A BINOMIAL

There are two other classic quadratics that occur regularly on the ACT:

$a^2 + 2ab + b^2 = (a + b)^2$

$a^2 - 2ab + b^2 = (a - b)^2$

For example, $4x^2 + 12x + 9$ factors to $(2x + 3)^2$, and $n^2 - 10n + 25$ factors to $(n - 5)^2$. Recognizing a classic quadratic can save a lot of time on Test Day—be on the lookout for these patterns. (HINT: any time you have a quadratic and one of the numbers is a perfect square, you should check for one of these three patterns.)

61. FACTORING OTHER POLYNOMIALS—FOIL IN REVERSE

To factor a quadratic expression, **think about what binomials you could use FOIL on to get that quadratic expression.** To factor $x^2 - 5x + 6$, think about what **F**irst terms will produce x^2, what **L**ast terms will produce $+ 6$, and what **O**uter and **I**nner terms will produce $-5x$. If there is no number in front of the first term, you are looking for two numbers that add up to the middle term and multiply to the third term. So here, you'd want two numbers that add up to -5 and multiply to 6. (Pay attention to sign—negative vs. positive makes a big difference here!) The correct factors are $(x - 2)(x - 3)$.

62. SIMPLIFYING AN ALGEBRAIC FRACTION

Simplifying an algebraic fraction is a lot like simplifying a numerical fraction. The general idea is to **find factors common to the numerator and denominator and cancel them.** Thus, simplifying an algebraic fraction begins with factoring, which often involves reverse-FOIL.

To simplify $\dfrac{x^2 - x - 12}{x^2 - 9}$, first factor the numerator and denominator:

$$\frac{x^2 - x - 12}{x^2 - 9} = \frac{(x - 4)(x + 3)}{(x - 3)(x + 3)}$$

Canceling $x + 3$ from the numerator and denominator leaves you with $\dfrac{x - 4}{x - 3}$.

SOLVING EQUATIONS

63. SOLVING A LINEAR EQUATION

To solve an equation, **isolate the variable.** As long as you do the same thing to both sides of the equation, the equation is still balanced. To solve $5x - 12 = -2x + 9$, first get all the x terms on one side by adding $2x$ to both sides: $7x - 12 = 9$.

Then add 12 to both sides: $7x = 21$, then divide both sides by 7 to get: $x = 3$.

64. SOLVING "IN TERMS OF"

To solve an equation for one variable **in terms of** another means to **isolate the one variable that you are solving for on one side of the equation,** leaving an expression containing the other variable on the other side. To solve $3x - 10y = -5x + 6y$ for x in terms of y, isolate x:

$3x - 10y = -5x + 6y$

$3x + 5x = 6y + 10y$

$8x = 16y$

$x = 2y$

65. TRANSLATING FROM ENGLISH INTO ALGEBRA

To translate from English into algebra, look for the key words and work from left to right to turn phrases into algebraic expressions and sentences into equations. Be careful about order, especially when subtraction is called for.

Example: The charge for a phone call is r cents for the first 3 minutes and s cents for each minute thereafter. What is the cost, in cents, of a call lasting exactly t minutes? ($t > 3$)

Setup: The charge begins with r, and then something more is added, depending on the length of the call. The amount added is s times the number of minutes past 3 minutes. If the total number of minutes is t, then the number of minutes past 3 is $t - 3$. So the charge is $r + s(t - 3)$.

INTERMEDIATE ALGEBRA

66. SOLVING A QUADRATIC EQUATION

To solve a quadratic equation, put it in the form of $ax^2 + bx + c = 0$ - in other words, set it equal to 0. Then **factor** the left side (if you can), and set each factor equal to 0 separately to get the two solutions. To solve $x^2 + 12 = 7x$, first subtract 7x from both sides of the equation, which gives you $x^2 - 7x + 12 = 0$. Then use reverse-FOIL to factor the left side:

$(x - 3)(x - 4) = 0$

$x - 3 = 0$ or $x - 4 = 0$

$x = 3$ or 4

Sometimes the left side might not be obviously factorable. You can always use the **quadratic formula.** Just plug in the coefficients a, b, and c from $ax^2 + bx + c = 0$ into the formula:

$$\frac{-b \pm \sqrt{b^2 - 4ac}}{2a}$$

To solve $x^2 + 4x + 2 = 0$, plug $a = 1$, $b = 4$, and $c = 2$ into the formula:

$$x = \frac{-4 \pm \sqrt{4^2 - 4 \times 1 \times 2}}{2 \times 1}$$

$$= \frac{-4 \pm \sqrt{8}}{2} = -2 \pm \sqrt{2}$$

Whether you use reverse-FOIL or the quadratic equation, you will almost always get two solutions, or roots, to the equation.

67. SOLVING A SYSTEM OF EQUATIONS

You can solve for two variables only if you have two distinct equations. If you have one variable, you only need one equation, but if you have two variables, you need two distinct equations. Two forms of the same equation will not be adequate. If you have three variables, you need three distinct equations, and so on. **Combine the equations in such a way that one of the variables cancels out.** To solve the two equations $4x + 3y = 8$ and $x + y = 3$, multiply both sides of the second equation by –3 to get: $-3x - 3y = -9$. Now add the equations; the $3y$ and the $-3y$ cancel out, leaving $x = -1$:

$$
\begin{array}{rl}
4x + 3y &= 8 \\
+(-3x - 3y &= -9) \\
\hline
x \qquad\;\; &= -1
\end{array}
$$

Plug that back into either one of the original equations and you'll find that $y = 4$.

68. SOLVING AN EQUATION THAT INCLUDES ABSOLUTE VALUE SIGNS

To solve an equation that includes absolute value signs, **think about the two different cases**—one where what is inside the absolute value sign equals a positive number, and one where it equals a negative number. For example, to solve the equation $|x - 12| = 3$, think of it as two equations:

$x - 12 = 3$ or $x - 12 = -3$

$x = 15$ or 9

Just like with quadratic equations, equations with absolute value signs will have two possible solutions.

69. SOLVING AN INEQUALITY

Solving inequalities works just the same as solving equations—do the same thing to both sides, until the variable you are solving for is isolated—with one exception: When you **multiply or divide both sides by a negative number,** you must **reverse the inequality sign.** To solve $-5x + 7 < -3$, subtract 7 from both sides to get $-5x < -10$. Now divide both sides by –5, remembering to reverse the inequality sign: $x > 2$.

70. GRAPHING INEQUALITIES

To graph a range of values on a number line, use a thick, black line over the number line, and at the end(s) of the range, use a **solid circle** if the point *is* included or an **open circle** if the point is ***not* included.** The figure here shows the graph of $-3 < x \le 5$.

COORDINATE GEOMETRY

71. FINDING THE DISTANCE BETWEEN TWO POINTS

To find the distance between points, **use the Pythagorean theorem or special right triangles.** The difference between x_1 and x_2 is one leg and the difference between the y_1 and y_2 is the other leg.

In the figure above, to find the distance between the points P and Q, draw a right triangle where $\overline{PQ}$ is the hypotenuse, this makes a 3-4-5 right triangle, so $\overline{PQ} = 5$.

You can also use the **distance formula:**

$$d = \sqrt{(x_2 - x_1)^2 + (y_2 - y_1)^2}$$

For instance, to find the distance between $R(3, 6)$ and $S(5, -2)$:

$$d = \sqrt{(5 - 3)^2 + (-2 - 6)^2}$$
$$= \sqrt{(2)^2 + (-8)^2}$$
$$= \sqrt{68} = 2\sqrt{17}$$

72. USING TWO POINTS TO FIND THE SLOPE

In mathematics, the slope of a line is often called m.

$$\text{Slope} = m = \frac{\text{Change in } y}{\text{Change in } x} = \frac{\text{Rise}}{\text{Run}} = \frac{y_2 - y_1}{x_2 - x_1}$$

The slope of the line that contains the points

$A(2, 3)$ and $B(0, -1)$ is:

$$\frac{y_2 - y_1}{x_2 - x_1} = \frac{-1 - 3}{0 - 2} = \frac{-4}{-2} = 2$$

73. USING AN EQUATION TO FIND THE SLOPE

To find the slope of a line from an equation, put the equation into the **slope-intercept** form:

$$y = mx + b$$

Where the slope is m, and b is the y-intercept (the point where the line crosses the y-axis). To find the slope of the equation $3x + 2y = 4$, isolate y, so it's in slope-intercept form:

$$3x + 2y = 4$$

$$2y = -3x + 4$$

$$y = -\frac{3}{2}x + 2$$

The slope is $-\frac{3}{2}$.

74. USING AN EQUATION TO FIND AN INTERCEPT

To find the y-intercept, you can either put the equation into **$y = mx + b$ (slope-intercept)** form—in which case b is the y-intercept—or you can just plug $x = 0$ into the equation and solve for y. Since the y-intercept is the point where the line crosses the y-axis, which means $x = 0$. To find the x-intercept, plug $y = 0$ into the equation and solve for x.

75. EQUATION FOR A CIRCLE

The equation for a circle of radius r and centered at (h, k) is:

$$(x - h)^2 + (y - k)^2 = r^2$$

The figure below shows the graph of the equation

$$(x - 2)^2 + (y + 1)^2 = 25:$$

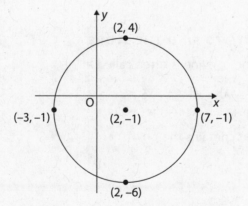

76. EQUATION FOR A PARABOLA

The graph of an equation in the form $y = ax^2 + bx + c$ is a parabola. The figure below shows the graph of seven pairs of numbers that satisfy the equation $y = x^2 - 4x + 3$:

77. EQUATION FOR AN ELLIPSE

The graph of an equation in the form

$$\frac{x^2}{a^2} = \frac{y^2}{b^2} = 1$$

is an ellipse, with $2a$ as the sum of the focal radii (the distance from each foci to the same point on the ellipse,) and with foci on the x-axis at $(0, -c)$ and $(0, c)$, where $c = \sqrt{a^2 - b^2}$. The following figure shows the graph of $\frac{x^2}{25} + \frac{y^2}{16} = 1$:

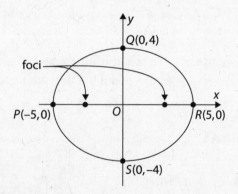

The foci are at $(-3, 0)$ and $(3, 0)$. $\overline{PR}$ is the **major axis,** and $\overline{QS}$ is the **minor axis.** This ellipse is symmetrical about both the x- and y-axes.

LINES AND ANGLES

78. INTERSECTING LINES

When two lines intersect, **adjacent angles are supplementary** (they make a line and add up to 180 degrees,) and **vertical angles** (angles across from each other) **are equal.**

In the figure above, the angles marked $a°$ and $b°$ are adjacent and supplementary, so $a + b = 180$. Furthermore, the angles marked $a°$ and 60° are vertical and equal, so $a = 60$.

79. PARALLEL LINES AND TRANSVERSALS

A line that cuts through two parallel lines is called a transversal. A transversal across parallel lines forms **four equal acute angles and four equal obtuse angles.**

Here, line 1 is parallel to line 2. Angles a, c, e, and g are obtuse, so they are all equal. Angles b, d, f, and h are acute, so they are all equal.

Furthermore, **any of the acute angles is supplementary to any of the obtuse angles.** Angles a and h are supplementary, as are b and e, c and f, and so on.

TRIANGLES—GENERAL

80. INTERIOR ANGLES OF A TRIANGLE

The three interior angles of any triangle **add up to 180°.**

In the figure above, $x + 50 + 100 = 180$, so $x = 30$.

81. EXTERIOR ANGLES OF A TRIANGLE

An exterior angle of a triangle is equal to the **sum of the remote interior angles**—that is, the two interior angles on the opposite side of the triangle.

In the figure shown here, the exterior angle labeled $x°$ is equal to the sum of the remote interior angles 50 and 100: $x = 50 + 100 = 150$

The three exterior angles of any triangle add up to 360°.

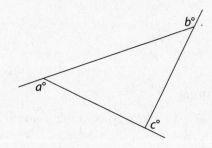

In the figure shown here, $a + b + c = 360$.

82. SIMILAR TRIANGLES

Similar triangles have the same shape: **corresponding angles are equal and corresponding sides are proportional.**

The triangles shown here are similar because they have the same angles. The 3 corresponds to the 4, and the 6 corresponds to the s.

83. AREA OF A TRIANGLE

Area of Triangle = $\dfrac{1}{2}$ (Base)(Height)

The height must be perpendicular to the base in order to use the area formula. This means if there isn't a right angle, you cannot find the height.

In the right triangle shown here, 4 is the height when the 7 is chosen as the base.

$$\text{Area} = \frac{1}{2}bh = \frac{1}{2}(7)(4) = 14$$

RIGHT TRIANGLES

84. PYTHAGOREAN THEOREM

For all right triangles (triangles with a 90 degree angle), where the hypotenuse is the side opposite the right angle:

$(\text{leg}_1)^2 + (\text{leg}_2)^2 = (\text{hypotenuse})^2$

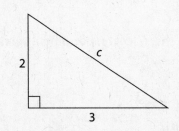

If one leg is 2 and the other leg is 3, then:

$$2^2 + 3^3 = c^2$$
$$c^2 = 4 + 9$$
$$c = \sqrt{13}$$

85. SPECIAL RIGHT TRIANGLES

3-4-5

If a right triangle's leg-to-leg ratio is 3:4 or if the leg-to-hypotenuse ratio is 3:5 or 4:5, then it's a 3-4-5 triangle, and you don't need to use the Pythagorean theorem to find the third side. Be on the lookout for multiples of this common pattern—a triangle with side lengths 6-8-10, for instance, is just a 3-4-5 times 2.

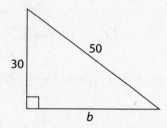

In the right triangle above, one leg is 30 and the hypotenuse is 50. This is 10 times 3-4-5. The other leg is 40.

5-12-13

If a right triangle's leg-to-leg ratio is 5:12 or if the leg-to-hypotenuse ratio is 5:13 or 12:13, then it's a 5-12-13 triangle, and you don't need to use the Pythagorean theorem to find the third side. Just figure out what multiple of 5-12-13 it is (get familiar with the first few multiples of 13, since they appear frequently as the length of the hypotenuse).

Here, one leg is 36 and the hypotenuse is 39. This is 3 times 5-12-13. The other leg is 15.

30°-60°-90°

There are also special right triangles based on angle measurement. The sides of a 30°-60°-90° triangle are in a ratio of $1 : \sqrt{3} : 2$. You don't need to use the Pythagorean theorem.

If the hypotenuse is 6, then the shorter leg is half that, or 3; and then the longer leg is equal to the short leg times

45°-45°-90°

The sides of a 45°-45°-90° triangle are in a ratio of $1 : 1 : \sqrt{2}$.

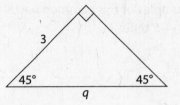

If one leg is 3, then the other leg is also 3, and the hypotenuse is equal to a leg times $\sqrt{2}$, or $3\sqrt{2}$.

OTHER POLYGONS

86. SPECIAL QUADRILATERALS

RECTANGLE

A rectangle is a **four-sided figure with four right angles.** Opposite sides are equal. Diagonals are equal.

Quadrilateral *ABCD* is shown to have three right angles. The fourth angle therefore also measures 90°, and *ABCD* is a rectangle. The perimeter of a rectangle is equal to the sum of the lengths of the four sides, which is equivalent to 2(length + width).

PARALLELOGRAM

A parallelogram has **two pairs of parallel sides.** Opposite sides are equal. Opposite angles are equal. Consecutive angles (angles adjacent to each other) add up to 180°.

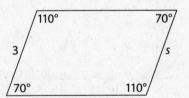

In this figure, *s* is the length of the side opposite the 3, so *s* = 3. The perimeter of a parallelogram is the sum of the lengths of all four sides.

SQUARE

A square is a **rectangle with four equal sides and four right angles.**

If *PQRS* is a square, all sides are the same length as *QR*. The perimeter of a square is equal to four times the length of one side.

TRAPEZOID

A **trapezoid** is a quadrilateral (a four-sided figure) with one pair of parallel sides and one pair of nonparallel sides.

In quadrilateral *EFGH*, sides $\overline{EF}$ and $\overline{GH}$ are parallel, while sides $\overline{EH}$ and $\overline{FG}$ are not parallel. *EFGH* is therefore a trapezoid.

87. AREAS OF SPECIAL QUADRILATERALS

Area of Rectangle = Length × Width
The area of a 7-by-3 rectangle is $7 \times 3 = 21$.

Area of Parallelogram = Base × Height
Just like with triangles, the base and the height must be perpendicular to each other, otherwise you cannot calculate the area of the parallelogram. The area of a parallelogram with a height of 4 and a base of 6 is $4 \times 6 = 24$.

Area of Square = (Side)^2

The area of a square with sides of length 5 is $5^2 = 25$.

$$\text{Area of Trapezoid} = \left(\frac{base_1 + base_2}{2} \right) \times \text{height}$$

Think of it as the average of the bases (the two parallel sides) times the height (the length perpendicular to the bases—not the side length).

In trapezoid *ABCD*, you can use side *AD* for the height, since it's already perpendicular to the bases. The average of the bases is $\frac{2 + 14}{2} = 8$, so the area is 5×8, or 40.

88. INTERIOR ANGLES OF A POLYGON

The sum of the measures of the interior angles of a polygon is (n – 2) × 180, where n is the number of sides.

Sum of the Angles = (n – 2) × 180 degrees

The eight angles of an octagon, for example, add up to (8 – 2) × 180 = 1,080.

A 'regular' shape on the ACT is a shape where all of the angles are the same and all of the side lengths are the same. To find **one angle of a regular polygon,** divide the sum of the angles by the number of angles (which is the same as the number of sides). The formula, therefore, is:

$$\text{Interior Angle} = \frac{(n - 2) \times 180}{n}$$

Angle A, and all of the other angles, of the regular octagon above measures $\frac{1,080}{8}$ = 135 degrees.

CIRCLES

89. CIRCUMFERENCE OF A CIRCLE

Circumference of a Circle = 2πr, where *r* is the radius of the circle (the distance from the center of the circle to the edge of the circle).

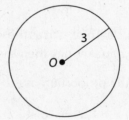

Here, the radius is 3, and so the circumference is 2π(3) = 6π.

90. LENGTH OF AN ARC

An **arc** is a piece of the circumference. Think of it like the crust on a slice of pizza. If *n* is the measure of the arc's central angle—the angle measure at the center of the circle, then the formula is:

Length of an Arc = $\frac{n}{360}$ (2πr), or the proportion of the 'slice' times the circumference of the circle.

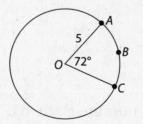

In the figure shown, the radius is 5 and the measure of the central angle is 72°. The arc length is $\frac{72}{360}$, or $\frac{1}{5}$ of the circumference:

$$\left(\frac{72}{360}\right)2\pi(5) = \left(\frac{1}{5}\right)10\pi = 2\pi$$

91. AREA OF A CIRCLE

Area of a Circle $= \pi r^2$

The area of the circle shown is $\pi(4)^2 = 16\pi$.

92. AREA OF A SECTOR

A **sector** is a piece of the area of a circle. Think of it as the whole slice of pizza (crust included!) If n is the measure of the sector's central angle, then the formula is:

Area of a Sector $= \dfrac{n}{360}(\pi r^2)$, or the proportion of the slice times the area of the circle.

In the figure shown, the radius is 6 and the measure of the sector's central angle is 30°. The sector has $\frac{30}{360}$, or $\frac{1}{12}$ of the area of the circle:

$$\left(\frac{30}{360}\right)(\pi)(6^2) = \left(\frac{1}{12}\right)(36\pi) = 3\pi$$

SOLIDS

93. SURFACE AREA OF A RECTANGULAR SOLID

The surface of a rectangular solid—a box, or a cube, for example—consists of three pairs of identical faces. To find the surface area, find the area of each face and add them up. If the length is l, the width is w, and the height is h, the formula is:

Surface Area $= 2lw + 2wh + 2lh$

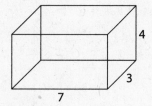

The surface area of the box shown is:

$2(7 \times 3) + 2(3 \times 4) + 2(7 \times 4) = 42 + 24 + 56 = 122$

94. VOLUME OF A RECTANGULAR SOLID

Volume of a Rectangular Solid = *lwh*, in other words, the area of the base times the height.

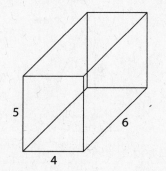

The volume of a 4-by-5-by-6 box is:

$4 \times 5 \times 6 = 120$

A cube is a rectangular solid with length, width, and height all equal. The volume formula if *e* is the length of an edge of the cube is:

Volume of a Cube = *e³*

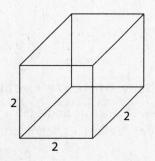

The volume of the cube above is $2^3 = 8$. It's still length times width times height, it's just that in a cube, those are all the same.

95. VOLUME OF OTHER SOLIDS

Volume of a Cylinder = *πr²h*, which is still just the area of the base, times the height.

The volume of a cylinder where $r = 2$ and $h = 5$ is $\pi(2^2)(5) = 20\pi$.

Volume of a Cone $= \dfrac{1}{3}\pi r^2 h$

The volume of a cone where $r = 3$ and $h = 6$ is:

$$\text{Volume} = \frac{1}{3}\pi(3)^2(6) = 18$$

$$\text{Volume of a Sphere} = \frac{4}{3}\pi r^3$$

If the radius of a sphere is 3, then:

$$\text{Volume} = \frac{4}{3}\pi(3)^3 = 36\pi$$

TRIGONOMETRY

96. SINE, COSINE, AND TANGENT OF ACUTE ANGLES

To find the sine, cosine, or tangent of an acute angle (an angle less than 90°), use SOHCAH-TOA, which is an abbreviation for the following definitions:

$$Sine = \frac{\text{Opposite}}{\text{Hypotenuse}}$$

$$Cosine = \frac{\text{Adjacent}}{\text{Hypotenuse}}$$

$$Tangent = \frac{\text{Opposite}}{\text{Adjacent}}$$

In the figure shown:

$$\sin A = \frac{8}{17}$$

$$\cos A = \frac{15}{17}$$

$$\tan A = \frac{8}{15}$$

97. COTANGENT, SECANT, AND COSECANT OF ACUTE ANGLES

Think of the cotangent, secant, and cosecant as the reciprocals of the SOHCAHTOA functions:

$$\text{Cotangent} = \frac{1}{\text{Tangent}} = \frac{\text{adjacent}}{\text{Opposite}}$$

$$\text{Secant} = \frac{1}{\text{Cosine}} = \frac{\text{Hypotenuse}}{\text{adjacent}}$$

$$\text{Cosecant} = \frac{1}{\text{Sine}} = \frac{\text{Hypotenuse}}{\text{Opposite}}$$

In the figure shown:

$$\cot D = \frac{2}{3}$$

$$\sec D = \frac{\sqrt{13}}{2}$$

$$\csc D = \frac{\sqrt{13}}{3}$$

98. TRIGONOMETRIC FUNCTIONS OF OTHER ANGLES

To find a trigonometric function of an angle greater than 90°, sketch a circle of radius 1 centered at the origin of the coordinate grid. Start from the point (1, 0) and rotate counter-clockwise until you hit the hypotenuse.

In the "unit circle" setup shown, the basic trigonometric functions are defined in terms of the coordinates a and b:

$\sin\theta = b$

$\cos\theta = a$

$\tan\theta = \dfrac{b}{a}$

Example: $\sin 210° = ?$

Setup: Sketch a 210° angle in the coordinate plane:

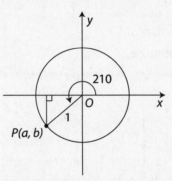

Because the triangle shown in this figure is a 30°-60°-90° right triangle (we know this because the x-axis is the first 180 degrees of our angle, which means there are 30° between the x-axis and the hypotenuse,) we can determine that the coordinates of point P are $-\dfrac{\sqrt{3}}{2}, -\dfrac{1}{2}$. The sine is therefore $-\dfrac{1}{2}$.

99. SIMPLIFYING TRIGONOMETRIC EXPRESSIONS

To simplify trigonometric expressions, use the inverse function definitions along with the fundamental trigonometric identity:

$\sin^2 x + \cos^2 x = 1$

Example: $\dfrac{\sin^2\theta + \cos^2\theta}{\cos\theta} = ?s$

Setup: The numerator equals 1, so:

$$\frac{\sin^2 \theta + \cos^2 \theta}{\cos \theta} = \frac{1}{\cos \theta} = \sec \theta$$

100. GRAPHING TRIGONOMETRIC FUNCTIONS

To graph trigonometric functions, use the x-axis for the angle and the y-axis for the value of the trigonometric function. Use special angles—0°, 30°, 45°, 60°, 90°, 120°, 135°, 150°, 180°, etc.—to plot key points.

This figure shows a portion of the graph of $y = \sin x$.

SUMMARY

In this chapter, we went over the basics of strategy and the pieces of outside knowledge required to master the ACT Math test.

Remember to circle the real question (what is the objective, the thing you're trying to find?), underline the givens (what info are you going to use to solve the problem?), then examine the format of the answer choices (numbers, decimals, variables, radicals?) before choosing a strategy to solve the problem. Problems often look more complex than they are. Feel free to get to the easy ones first, but don't completely skip a question simply because it looks scary. Do the math if you have it mastered, but remember Point Building strategies such as Picking Numbers and Backsolving. The more tools you have in your repertoire, and the more flexibly you're able to think about a problem, the more prepared you'll be for anything the ACT Math test can throw at you. After you have your answer, remember to check what you circled to be sure you answered the right question.

Think flexibly. You don't have to do problems the "right" way!

To master the ACT Math test, combine these strategies with the outside knowledge listed in 100 Key Math Concepts. Flag or highlight the rules you still struggle with, then use the following chapter to practice the various question types and the strategies you'll need to apply those rules to more complex problems.

Know the outside knowledge, know the test and the question types, and practice the strategies.

CHAPTER 7

Math Part 2: ACT Math Strategy In Depth

OVERVIEW

Use this chapter to become familiar with all of the question types on the ACT Math test. All question types are detailed and discussed fully, and examples are provided for each. To get a quick sense of what's to come, refer to the SmartPoint Breakdown in the previous chapter page 79. There, they are discussed in order of Test Day weight. The more heavily-tested SmartPoints are listed there first. That's also how you should prioritize your time, especially if you are short on it, or close to your goal score. However, the SmartPoints that follow are discussed in order of building complexity, as the knowledge for some areas not commonly tested contributes to other, more frequently tested SmartPoints. If you have time, and want to thoroughly work your Math skill set, start at the beginning and work your way through.

The following SmartPoints are shown in order of building complexity, SmartPoint by SmartPoint.

NUMBER PROPERTIES—2 POINTS

Complexity: Low. Relates to: Operations, Variable Manipulation, Proportions and Probability

Being comfortable with how numbers work can make your life easier on all sorts of math question types on the ACT.

Here are some essential rules and definitions to know:

- *Integers* **include 0 and negative whole numbers.** If a question says "x and y are integers," it's not ruling out numbers like 0 and –1.

- *Evens and odds* **include 0 and negative whole numbers.** Zero and –2 are even numbers; –1 is an odd number.

- *Prime numbers* **do not include 1.** The technical definition of a prime number is a positive integer with exactly two distinct positive integer factors. Two is prime because it has exactly two positive factors: 1 and 2. It is the smallest, and the only even, prime number. Four is not prime because it has three positive factors (1, 2, and 4)—too many! And 1 is not prime because it has only one positive factor (1)—too few!

- *Remainders* **are integers.** If a question asks for the remainder when 15 is divided by 2, don't say "15 divided by 2 is 7.5, so the remainder is .5." What you should say is: "15 divided by 2 is 7 with a remainder of 1."

- *The $\sqrt{}$ symbol represents the positive square root only.* The equation $x^2 = 9$ has two solutions: 3 and –3. But when you see, $\sqrt{9}$ it means positive 3 only.

Remind yourself about evens and odds, and positives and negatives, by filling out these charts (hint: Pick Numbers if you're stuck):

Know this about Odds and Evens on the ACT

Even × Even = Even Even × Odd = Even Odd × Odd = Odd	Even ± Even = Even Odd ± Odd = Even Even ± Odd = Odd
Even $^{\text{Positive Integer}}$ = Even Odd $^{\text{Positive Integer}}$ = Odd	

Know this about Positives and Negatives on the ACT

Positive × Positive = Positive Negative × Negative = Positive Positive × Negative = Negative	Subtracting a negative number is the same as adding a positive number
Negative $^{\text{Even Exponent}}$ = Positive	Positive Fraction $^{\text{Positive Integer}}$ = Smaller Positive Fraction
Negative $^{\text{Odd Exponent}}$ = Negative	Negative Fraction $^{\text{Positive Integer}}$ = Smaller Negative or Positive Fraction

Know that the Kaplan Method isn't intended to be a rigid procedure, but a set of guidelines that will keep you on track, moving quickly, and evading traps.

STEP 1: WHAT IS THE QUESTION?

Before you can begin to solve this problem, you have to figure out what it's asking. You'll need to know the meanings of *sum, product, consecutive, even*, and *integer*. Put the question stem into words you can understand. What the question stem is really saying here is that when you add up these five consecutive even integers, you get the same thing as when you multiply them.

STEP 2: WHAT INFORMATION AM I GIVEN?

We are not given any numbers in the problem, but we *are* told that we'll be working with consecutive even integers, and we *are* given five answer choices—five numbers that *could* be the final term of the five-even-number sequence. Because the question specifies *even* numbers, the difference between each integer in this series will be 2. And a quick glance at the answer choices tells us they are all positive. Good to know.

STEP 3: WHAT CAN I DO WITH THE INFORMATION?

How are we going to figure out what these five numbers are? We could set up an equation:

$$x + (x - 2) + (x - 4) + (x - 6) + (x - 8) = x(x - 2)(x - 4)(x - 6)(x - 8)$$

That would work. But you may well not have time to create and solve an equation like this! So if that wasn't the first option that came to mind, come up with a better way.

Let's stop and think logically about this one for a moment. When we think about sums and products, it's natural to think mostly of positive integers. With positive integers, we would generally expect the product to be *greater* than the sum. Multiplying makes bigger results than adding. But what about negative integers? Hmm. Well, the sum of five negatives is negative, and the product of five negatives is also negative. Generally the product will be "more negative" than the sum, so with negative integers, the product will be *less than* the sum.

So when will the product and sum be the same? How about right at the boundary of positive and negative—that is, around 0? That makes some sense. So try (A)—see if the five consecutive even integers with equal product and sum are: −4, −2, 0, 2, and 4.

$$(-4) \times (-2) \times 0 \times 2 \times 4 = (-4) + (-2) + 0 + 2 + 4$$

The product and sum are both 0. We've done it!

How to Backsolve: The question asks which is the greatest of the integers, so you have to start with the greatest answer choice: (E)—if you start with any other, even if it works you won't know if it's the *largest*. If the largest number is 20, then the other numbers must be 18, 16, 14, 12. Their sum is $20 + 18 + 16 + 14 + 12 = 80$. 20 times 18 is already 360, so we know that choice (K) is not correct and is WAY too big! Let's try one a good bit smaller, (C) 14. We want to add: $14 + 12 + 10 + 8 + 6 = 50$. Still too big, because 10 times 6 is already 60. So let's try 4, (A). $4 + 2 + 0 + (-2) + (-4) = 4 \times 2 \times 0 \times (-2) \times (-4) = 0$. It works!

The final area of Number Properties you'll need to be aware of is divisibility. Divisibility questions involve factors (including greatest common factor), multiples (including least common multiple), and primes (including prime factorization). All concepts are occasionally tested directly, but more often, a thorough understanding of each will help you navigate through more complex questions from different SmartPoints.

Let's review:

The **factors** of a number divide evenly into that number without a remainder. 2, 4, and 8 are **factors** of 16. Negative numbers and fractions don't count. Those are all of the factors of 8 that exist.

The **multiples** of a number can be divided by that number without a remainder. 4, 8, and 16 are **multiples** of 2, but there's a problem with listing all of them: The multiples of any number are infinite. They go on forever.

Thus, to keep factors and multiples straight, remember that there are *few factors and many multiples*.

Additionally, notice that 8 was listed twice. Every positive integer is both a factor and a multiple of itself.

To find all factors of a number, you can use a Factor T-Chart.

Finally, a **prime number** is an integer that only has itself and 1 as factors.

The first eight prime numbers are 2, 3, 5, 7, 11, 13, 17, and 19. 1 is not prime, and negatives cannot be prime.

The **prime factorization** of an integer is the number broken down into all prime factors. To find prime factorization, pick two factors of the integer (other than itself and 1) and keep finding factors of those integers until all are prime.

Here are the definitions of least common multiple and greatest common factor, which you can also find in 100 Key Math Concepts.

COMMON MULTIPLE

You can always get a common multiple of two numbers by **multiplying** them, but unless the two numbers are relative primes, the product will not be the least common multiple. For example, to find a common multiple for 12 and 15, you could just multiply: $12 \times 15 = 180$. But it's not necessarily the least common multiple (in fact, it's not).

LEAST COMMON MULTIPLE (LCM)

To find the least common multiple, check out the **multiples of the larger number** until you find one that's **also a multiple of the smaller.**

To find the LCM of 12 and 15, begin by taking the multiples of 15. 15 is not divisible by 12; 30 is not; nor is 45. But the next multiple of 15, 60, is divisible by 12, so that's the LCM.

GREATEST COMMON FACTOR (GCF)

To find the greatest common factor, break down both numbers into their prime factorizations, and take **all the prime factors they have in common.** $36 = 2 \times 2 \times 3 \times 3$, and $48 = 2 \times 2 \times 2 \times 2 \times 3$. What they have in common is two 2s and one 3, so the GCF is $2 \times 2 \times 3 = 12$.

OPERATIONS—3 POINTS

Complexity: Low. Relates to: Number Properties, Variable Manipulation, Proportions and Probability

There aren't many questions on the ACT that ask you to simply multiply or divide, but being adept at both is important throughout for answering larger questions.

We'll start by reviewing the Order of Operations, and what it means; then we'll tackle each of the more complex areas of the SmartPoints—Radicals, Imaginary Numbers, and Logarithms.

PEMDAS = Please Excuse My Dear Aunt Sally: This mnemonic will help you remember the order of operations.

P = Parentheses

E = Exponents

M = Multiplication

D = Division

A = Addition

S = Subtraction

Multiplication and division are ordered from left to right.

Addition and subtraction are ordered from left to right.

Example: $30 - 5 \times 4 + (7 - 3)^2 \div 8$

First, perform any operations within parentheses.

$30 - 5 \times 4 + 4^2 \div 8$

(If the expression has parentheses within parentheses, work from the innermost out.)

Next, raise to any powers indicated by exponents: $30 - 5 \times 4 + 16 \div 8$.

Then, do all multiplication and division from left to right: $30 - 20 + 2$.

Finally, do all addition and subtraction from left to right: $10 + 2 = 12$.

WORKING WITH EXPONENTS

The most challenging element of those basic operations is exponents. The ACT tests exponents in a variety of ways. By remembering a few simple rules, you can make your life much easier when dealing with exponents. You'll also be well on your way to understanding more advanced concepts, like radicals and logarithms.

Here are those rules:

In the term $3x^2$, 3 is the coefficient, x is the base, and 2 is the exponent. The exponent refers to the number of times the base is a factor of the expression—the number of times the base is multiplied by itself. For example, 4^3 has 3 factors of 4, or $4^3 = 4 \times 4 \times 4$—it's multiplied by itself 3 times.

An integer times itself is the **square** of that integer. ($y \times y$ is the square of y, or y^2)

An integer times itself twice is the **cube** of that integer. ($4 \times 4 \times 4$ is the cube of 4, or 4^3)

To multiply two terms with the same base, keep the base and add the exponents.

$m^4 \times m^7 = m^{4+7} = m^{11}$

EXAMPLE:

$2^2 \times 2^3 = (2 \times 2)(2 \times 2 \times 2)$ or $2^2 \times 2^3 = 2^{2+3}$

$= (2 \times 2 \times 2 \times 2 \times 2)$ $= 2^5$

$= 2^5$

To divide two terms with the same base, keep the base and subtract the exponent of the denominator from the exponent of the numerator.

$d^{10} \div d^7 = d^{10-7} = d^3$

EXAMPLE:

$$4^4 \div 4^2 = \frac{4 \times 4 \times 4 \times 4}{4 \times 4}$$

$$= \frac{4 \times 4}{1} \qquad \text{or} \qquad \begin{aligned} 4^4 \div 4^2 &= 4^{4-2} \\ &= 4^2 \end{aligned}$$

$$= 4^2$$

To raise a power to another power, multiply the exponents.

$$(p^5)^3 = p^{5 \times 3} = p^{15}$$

EXAMPLE:

$$(3^2)^4 = (3 \times 3)^4$$

$$= (3 \times 3)(3 \times 3)(3 \times 3)(3 \times 3) \qquad \text{or} \qquad (3^2)^4 = 3^{2 \times 4}$$

$$= 3^8 \qquad\qquad\qquad\qquad\qquad = 3^8$$

Any nonzero number raised to the zero power is equal to 1. $a^0 = 1$ as long as $a \neq 0$. 0^0 is undefined.

To evaluate a negative exponent, take the reciprocal of the base and change the sign of the exponent.

$$a^{-n} = \frac{1}{a^n} \text{ or } \left(\frac{1}{a}\right)^n$$

EXAMPLE:

$$2^{-3} = \left(\frac{1}{2}\right)^3 = \frac{1}{2^3} = \frac{1}{8}$$

A fractional exponent indicates a **root**.

$(a)^{\frac{1}{n}} = \sqrt[n]{a}$ (Read "the nth root of a." If no "n" is present, the radical sign means a square root.)

EXAMPLE:

$8^{1/3} =$ the cube root of $8 = 2$

WORKING WITH RADICALS

To reverse the process of taking a number to a certain power, via an exponent, you would take the same root of that number, via a radical.

For example, $2^2 = 4$. To reverse this process, we'd take the square root of 4, $\sqrt{4} = 2$.

A radical implies that you're taking the square root of a number, as opposed to the cube root or above. You'll need to be able to work with and simplify radicals on Test Day.

When it comes to the four basic arithmetic operations, we treat radicals in much the same way we would treat variables.

Addition and subtraction: Only like radicals can be added to or subtracted from one another.

EXAMPLE:

$$2\sqrt{3} + 4\sqrt{2} - \sqrt{2} - 3\sqrt{3} = \left(4\sqrt{2} - \sqrt{2}\right) + \left(2\sqrt{3} - 3\sqrt{3}\right) \text{ Note: } \sqrt{2} = 1\sqrt{2}$$
$$= 3\sqrt{2} + \left(-\sqrt{3}\right)$$
$$= 3\sqrt{2} - \sqrt{3}$$

Multiplication and division: To multiply or divide one radical by another, multiply or divide the numbers outside the radical signs separately from the numbers inside the radical signs, much like you would with coefficients and variables.

EXAMPLE:

$$\left(6\sqrt{3}\right) \times \left(2\sqrt{5}\right) = (6 \times 2)\left(\sqrt{3} \times \sqrt{5}\right) = 12\sqrt{3 \times 5} = 12\sqrt{15}$$

EXAMPLE:

$$12\sqrt{15} \div 2\sqrt{5} = (12 \div 2)\left(\sqrt{15} \div \sqrt{5}\right) = 6\left(\frac{\sqrt{15}}{\sqrt{5}}\right) = 6\sqrt{3}$$

EXAMPLE:

$$\frac{4\sqrt{18}}{2\sqrt{6}} = \left(\frac{4}{2}\right)\left(\frac{\sqrt{18}}{\sqrt{6}}\right) = 2\left(\sqrt{\frac{18}{6}}\right) = 2\sqrt{3}$$

If the number inside the radical is a multiple of a perfect square, the expression can be simplified by factoring out the perfect square.

EXAMPLE:

$$\sqrt{72} = \sqrt{(36 \times 2)} = \sqrt{36} \times \sqrt{2} = 6\sqrt{2}$$

The last two concepts to discuss under the Operations SmartPoint also relate to exponents, but are very lightly tested. Logarithms are a shortcut for exponents, similar to the way multiplication is a shortcut for addition. And Imaginary Numbers use exponents to create negative numbers where normally they would not.

Think of logarithms as a way of rearranging a number with a power. $2^3 = 8$ is the same thing as $\log_2 8 = 3$.

The base number, 2, becomes the base of the log, and remains the first number listed. The other two switch places.

Try it the other way—remember the base stays the first number listed, and the other two switch places.

$Log_5\ 25 = 2$

_____

In standard form, that's $5^2 = 25$.

And that's it. The ACT simply tests your basic knowledge of what logarithms are.

Though imaginary numbers seem scary, the tested rules on the ACT are just as simple as the ones tested for logarithms.

An **imaginary number** is a number that gives a *negative* result when squared.

So, by definition, $i^2 = -1$.

There are only four values of i you might need to remember.

$i = \sqrt{(-1)}$

$i^2 = -1$

$i^3 = -i$

$i^4 = 1$

Because i to the 4th is 1, i^5 cycles back to the beginning, and is the same as i to the first. $i^6 = i^2$, $i^7 = i^3$, and $i^8 = i^4 = 1$. We're back to 1 again, thus, i^9 starts the process all over, and i cycles through the same four values over and over and over again.

So, then, what is i^{77} ?

Should you count every 4, or is there a quicker way?

Try *dividing* by 4.

You'll get 19.25, or 19 with a remainder of 1. Thus, i^{77} is the same as i to the first, just i.

A complex number can seem scary on the ACT, but this problem defines it for you, so treat it like you would any other variable that you plug numbers into. In this problem, the key is swapping every i^2 with a -1. Begin by simplifying the first term in the expression:

$(i + 1)^2 = (i + 1)(i + 1) = i^2 + 2i + 1$
$= -1 + 2i + 1 = 2i$

Multiplying this by the second term gets you $2i\ (i - 1) = 2i^2 - 2i = 2(-1) - 2i = -2 - 2i$

That's the same as (K).

VARIABLE MANIPULATION—7 POINTS

Complexity: Low-Medium. Relates to: Number Properties, Operations

Variable Manipulation questions ask you to put together what you know about number properties and operations to solve for an unknown value, also known as a *variable*.

In Variable Manipulation questions' simplest forms, keep in mind the order of operations (PEMDAS) and the golden rule of equations:

Whatever you do to one side of the equation, you must do to the other.

To solve for a variable, simply go in the reverse order of PEMDAS, performing the opposite of the operations you see, until the variable is alone on one side of the equation (isolated). The number on the other side will be your answer.

Here's an example. Make sure you have the basics of the process down, then we'll dive into the many wrinkles the ACT will throw at you to see how adept you are at problem solving with variables.

$$2x + 7 = 13$$

Again, we reverse the order of PEMDAS and perform the opposite of the operations we see. The variable has been multiplied by 2 with 7 added to it.

Addition comes first, and the opposite of that function is subtraction.

Subtract 7 from both sides.

Now, our equation is

$$2x = 6.$$

Let's deal with the multiplication. The opposite of that function is division.

Divide both sides by 2, and you have your answer.

$$x = 3.$$

Remind yourself how you would use the opposite of the shown functions in the following situations.

i. $x + 3 = \dfrac{5}{2}$

ii. $3x = 7$

iii. $x^2 = 9$

iv. $\dfrac{x}{7} = 8$

v. $1\dfrac{1}{5} = x - 2$

Keep in mind that like terms can be combined:

$4x + 2x$ can be simplified to $6x$

However, terms can only be simplified if they are raised to the same power: and use the same variable

$4x^2 + 2x$ cannot be simplified.

$4x + 2y$ cannot be simplified

Now let's look some algebraic terminology, and build to the first examples of complex variable manipulation: polynomials and quadratic equations.

Terms: A *term* is a numerical constant or the product (or quotient) of a numerical constant and one or more variables. Examples of terms are $3x$, $4x2yz$, and $2a/c$.

All of the laws of arithmetic operations, such as the commutative, associative, and distributive laws, are applicable to polynomials as well.

Commutative law: $2x + 5y = 5y + 2x$
$5a \times 3b = 3b \times 5a = 15ab$

Associative law: $(2x + 3x) + 5x = 2x + (3x + 5x) = 10x$
$4s \times (7j \times 2p) = (4s \times 7j) \times 2p = 56sjp$

Distributive law: $3a(2b - 5c) = (3a \times 2b) - (3a \times 5c) = 6ab - 15ac$

Note: The product of two binomials can be calculated by applying the distributive law twice.

EXAMPLE:

$(x + 5)(x - 2) = x(x - 2) + 5(x - 2)$
$= x \times x - x \times 2 + 5 \times x - 5 \times 2$
$= x^2 - 2x + 5x - 10$
$= x^2 + 3x - 10$

A simple mnemonic for this is **F**irst **O**uter **I**nner **L**ast, or **FOIL**.

Factoring Algebraic Expressions

Factoring a polynomial means expressing it as a product of two or more simpler expressions.

Common monomial factor: When there is a monomial factor common to every term in the polynomial, it can be factored out by using the distributive law.

Example: $2a + 6ac = 2a(1 + 3c)$ ($2a$ is the greatest common factor of $2a$ and $6ac$)

Difference of two perfect squares: The difference of two squares can be factored into a product: $a^2 - b^2 = (a - b)(a + b)$.

Example: $9x^2 - 1 = (3x)^2 - (1)^2 = (3x + 1)(3x - 1)$

Polynomials of the form $a^2 + 2ab + b^2$: Any polynomial of this form is equivalent to the square of a binomial. Notice that $(a + b)^2 = a^2 + 2ab + b^2$ (try FOIL).

Factoring such a polynomial is just reversing this procedure.

Example: $x^2 + 6x + 9 = (x)^2 + 2(x)(3) + (3)^2 = (x + 3)^2$

Polynomials of the form $a^2 - 2ab + b^2$: Any polynomial of this form is equivalent to the square of a binomial as well. Here, though, the binomial is the difference of two terms: $(a - b) = a^2 - 2ab + b^2$.

Example: $x^2 - 4x + 4 = (x)^2 - 2(x)(2) + (2)^2 = (x - 2)^2$

Polynomials of the form $ax^2 + bx + c$: Polynomials of this form can nearly always be factored into a product of two binomials. The product of the first term in each binomial must equal the first term of the polynomial. The product of the last terms of the binomials must equal the third term of the polynomial. The sum of the remaining products must equal the second term of the polynomial. Factoring can be thought of as the FOIL method backward.

Example: $x^2 - 3x + 2$

We can factor this into two binomials, each containing an x term. Start by writing down what we know.

$$x^2 - 3x + 2 = (x + ...)(x + ...)$$

We need to fill in the missing term to the right of each binomial. The **product** of the two missing terms will be the last term in the polynomial: 2. The **sum** of the two missing terms will be the coefficient of the second term of the polynomial: −3. Try the possible factors of 2 until we get a pair that adds up to −3. There are two possibilities: 1 and 2, or −1 and −2. Since $(-1) + (-2) = -3$, we can fill −1 and −2 into the empty spaces.

Thus, $x^2 - 3x + 2 = (x - 1)(x - 2)$.

Note: Using FOIL on a factored polynomial is a great way to check your work.

To solve an equation with a polynomial, set it equal to 0, factor it into binomials, then set each of those equal to 0 and solve.

Example: $x^2 - 3x + 2 = 0$

To find the solutions, or roots, start by doing what we did earlier in this chapter– factor it. We can factor $x^2 - 3x + 2$ into $(x - 2)(x - 1)$, making our quadratic equation $(x - 2)(x - 1) = 0$.

We now have an equation where the product of two binomials equals 0. This can only be the case when at least one of the terms is 0. Therefore, to find the roots, we just need to set the two binomials equal to 0 and solve for x. In other words, either $x - 2 = 0$ or $x - 1 = 0$

(or both). Solving for x, we get $x = 2$ or $x = 1$. To check the math, plug 1 and 2 back into the original equation and make sure that both variables satisfy the equation.

$$2^2 - 3(2) + 2 = 0 \qquad\qquad 1^2 - 3(1) + 2 = 0$$
$$4 - 6 + 2 = 0 \qquad\qquad 1 - 3 + 2 = 0$$
$$0 = 0 \qquad\qquad\qquad\quad 0 = 0$$

The other commonly tested area of variable manipulation involves **simultaneous equations.**

Sometimes a problem on the ACT will involve an equation with more than one variable. In general, if you want to find numerical values for all of your variables, you will need as many **distinct** equations as you have variables. Two equations are distinct if neither simplifies into the other.

$x^2 + 2xy + 5y^2 = 5$ and $3x^2 + 6xy + 15y^2 = 15$ are *not* distinct since multiplying the first equation by 3 results in the second.

If we had one equation with two variables, such as $x - y = 7$, there are an infinite number of solution sets because each unique value of x has a different corresponding value for y. If $x = 8$, $y = 1$ (since $8 - 1 = 7$). If $x = 12$, $y = 5$ (since $12 - 5 = 7$). And so forth.

If we are given two distinct equations with two variables, we can combine them to get a unique solution set. This is known as a **system of equations**. There are two ways to do this:

Method I: Combination

Combination involves subtracting a multiple, positive or negative, of one equation from the other. The idea is to choose a multiple such that all but one of the variables is eliminated, solve for that variable, then plug that variable back into the other equation for the *other* variable if necessary.

Example: If $3a + 2b = 12$ and $5a + 4b = 23$, what is the value of a?

1. Start by lining up the equations, one under the other.

    $3a + 2b = 12$
    $5a + 4b = 23$

2. Multiply the top equation by 2, to get $4b$ in both.

    $6a + 4b = 24$
    $5a + 4b = 23$

3. Subtract to eliminate the b term.

    $$\begin{array}{r} 6a + 4b = 24 \\ -(5a + 4b = 23) \\ \hline a = 1 \end{array}$$

Method II: Substitution

Substitution involves solving for one of the variables in terms of the other in one equation, then substituting that value back into the other equation.

Example: Solve for m and n when $m = 4n + 2$ and $3m + 2n = 16$.

1.   We have m in terms of n so substitute $4n + 2$ for m in the second equation.

$$3(4n + 2) + 2n = 16$$
$$12n + 6 + 2n = 16$$

2.   Solve for n.

$$14n = 10$$
$$n = \frac{10}{14} = \frac{5}{7}$$

3.   Substitute $\frac{5}{7}$ for n in the first equation to solve for m.

$$m = 4n + 2$$
$$m = 4\left(\frac{5}{7}\right) + 2$$
$$= \frac{20}{7} + \frac{14}{7}$$
$$\frac{34}{7}$$

The ACT will have many questions involving systems of equations. Some will even be disguised as an entirely different question type. By being adept at Combination or Substitution, you can remove the disguise and efficiently find the answer.

1.   What are the (x, y) coordinates of the point of intersection of the line representing the equation $5x + 2y = 4$ and the line representing the equation $x - 2y = 8$?

A. $(2, 3)$

B. $(-2, 3)$

C. $(2, -3)$

D. $(-3, 2)$

E. $(3, -2)$

This may look like a coordinate geometry question, but do you really have to graph the lines to find the point of intersection? Remember, the ACT is looking for creative thinkers, not just calculators! Think about it for a moment—what's the special significance of the point of intersection, the one point that the two lines have in common? That's the one point whose coordinates will satisfy *both* equations.

So what we realize now is that this is not a coordinate geometry question at all, but a system-of-equations question. All it's really asking you to do is solve the pair of equations for x and y. The question has nothing to do with slopes, intercepts, axes, or quadrants. It's a pure algebra question in disguise.

Now that we know we're looking at a system of equations, we can solve the problem using combination and substitution. We'll go through combination, but if you can find the same answer using substitution if you prefer.

The first equation has $a + 2y$, and the second equation has $a - 2y$. If we just add the equations, the y terms cancel:

$$5x + 2y = 4$$
$$x - 2y = 8$$
$$6x = 12$$

If $6x = 12$, then $x = 2$. Plug that back into either of the original equations, and you'll find that $y = -3$. The point of intersection is $(2, -3)$, and the answer is (H).

The last (and less common) wrinkles the ACT will test with Variable Manipulation questions are inequalities and absolute values.

INEQUALITIES

Inequality symbols:

> greater than
< less than
≥ greater than or equal to
≤ less than or equal to

Example: $x > 4$ means all numbers greater than 4.

Example: $x < 0$ means all numbers less than zero (the negative numbers).

Example: $x > -2$ means x can be -2 or any number greater than -2.

Example: $x \leq \frac{1}{2}$ means x can be $\frac{1}{2}$ or any number less than $\frac{1}{2}$.

Solving inequalities: Inequalities behave the same way as normal equations with one exception: **Multiplying or dividing by a negative number reverses the inequality's direction.**

Example: $-1(-3x < 2) = 3x > -2$

Example: Solve for x and represent the solution set on a number line: $3 - \frac{x}{4} \geq 2$

1. Multiply both sides by 4.

2. Subtract 12 from both sides.

3. Divide both sides by -1 and change the direction of the sign. $x \leq 4$

Note: The solution set to an inequality is not a single value but a range of possible values. Here, the values include 4 and all numbers below 4.

Now, let's discuss the final concept tested under Variable Manipulation: **absolute value**.

ABSOLUTE VALUE

The absolute value of a number is its distance from 0 on a number line. Thus, because distance cannot be negative, absolute value is always positive or 0.

KNOW THIS ABOUT ABSOLUTE VALUE ON THE ACT

The absolute value of a number is its _____ from zero on the number line.

Because distance cannot be negative, absolute value is always _____.

Number	Absolute Value
7	
−7	
	8
	n

If you don't remember how to work with absolute values in an equation, remember those Point Builders. You don't need to know the "right" way to get to an answer to solve the problem.

PROPORTIONS AND PROBABILITY—6 POINTS

Complexity: Medium. Relates to: Number Properties, Operations

Proportions and Probability questions involve using what you know about numbers to relate them to each other and find a missing piece.

You'll need to know how to form and calculate percents and ratios (and decimals and fractions along with them). Then, you'll need to apply that knowledge to three-part formulas to find averages, distance/rate/time, and probability.

Let's start by reviewing how to work with fractions, and how that translates to finding percents.

FRACTIONS

In the fraction $\dfrac{4}{5}$

4 ← numerator

— ← fraction bar (means "divided by")

5 ← denominator

Equivalent Fractions: The value of a number is unchanged if you multiply the number by 1. In a fraction, multiplying the numerator and denominator by the same nonzero number is the same as multiplying the fraction by 1: The fraction is unchanged. Similarly, dividing the top and bottom by the same nonzero number leaves the fraction unchanged.

EXAMPLE:

$$\frac{1}{2} = \frac{1 \times 2}{2 \times 2} = \frac{2}{4}$$

$$\frac{5}{10} = \frac{5 \div 5}{10 \div 5} = \frac{1}{2}$$

Canceling and Reducing: Generally speaking, when you work with fractions on the ACT, you'll need to put them in **lowest terms**. This means the numerator and the denominator are not divisible by any common integer greater than 1. The fraction $\dfrac{1}{2}$ is in lowest terms, but the fraction $\dfrac{3}{6}$ is not, since 3 and 6 are both divisible by 3. The method we use to take such a fraction and put it in lowest terms is called **reducing**. That simply means to divide out any common multiples from both the numerator and denominator. This process is also commonly called **canceling**.

Example: Reduce $\dfrac{15}{35}$ to lowest terms.

First, determine the largest common factor of the numerator and denominator. Then, divide the top and bottom by that number to reduce.

$$\frac{15}{35} = \frac{3 \times 5}{7 \times 5} = \frac{3 \times 5 \div 5}{7 \times 5 \div 5} = \frac{3}{7}$$

Addition and Subtraction: We can't add or subtract two fractions directly unless they have the same denominator. Therefore, before adding (or subtracting), we must find a common denominator. A common denominator is just a **common multiple** of all the denominators of the fractions. The **least common denominator** is the **least common multiple** (the smallest positive number that is a multiple of all the terms).

EXAMPLE:

$\dfrac{3}{5} + \dfrac{2}{3} - \dfrac{1}{2}$. Denominators are 5, 3, 2.

LCM = 5 × 3 × 2 = 30 = LCD

Multiply the numerator and denominator of each fraction by the value that raises its respective denominator to the LCD.

$$\left(\frac{3}{5}\times\frac{6}{6}\right)+\left(\frac{2}{3}\times\frac{10}{10}\right)-\left(\frac{1}{2}\times\frac{15}{15}\right)$$

$$=\frac{18}{30}+\frac{20}{30}-\frac{15}{30}$$

Combine the numerators by adding or subtracting and keep the LCD as the denominator.

$$=\frac{18+20-15}{30}=\frac{23}{30}$$

Multiplication: We can easily combine fractions by multiplication by multiplying straight across the numerators to get a combined numerator then multiplying across the denominators to get a combined denominator, and finally simplifying as usual. However, we can also make it easier by canceling like terms (with shared factors) diagonally and vertically first.

Example: $\dfrac{10}{9}\times\dfrac{3}{4}\times\dfrac{8}{15}$

First, reduce (cancel) diagonally and vertically.

$$\frac{^{2}\cancel{10}}{_{3}\cancel{9}}\times\frac{^{1}\cancel{3}}{_{1}\cancel{4}}\times\frac{\cancel{8}^{2}}{\cancel{15}_{3}}$$

Then, multiply numerators and denominators. $\dfrac{2\times1\times2}{3\times1\times3}=\dfrac{4}{9}$

Division: Dividing is the same as multiplying by the **reciprocal** of the divisor. To get the reciprocal of a fraction, invert the numerator and the denominator. The reciprocal of the fraction $\dfrac{3}{7}$ is $\dfrac{7}{3}$.

Example: $\dfrac{4}{3}\div\dfrac{4}{9}$

To divide, invert the second term (the divisor), and then multiply as above.

$$\frac{4}{3}\div\frac{4}{9}=\frac{4}{3}\times\frac{9}{4}=\frac{^{1}\cancel{4}}{_{1}\cancel{3}}\times\frac{\cancel{9}^{3}}{\cancel{4}_{1}}=\frac{1\times3}{1\times1}=3$$

PERCENTS

Percents are one of the most commonly used mathematical relationships and are quite popular on the ACT. *Percent* is just another word for *hundredth*. For example, 27% (27 percent) means:

27 hundredths

$$\frac{27}{100}$$

0.27

27 out of every 100 things

27 parts out of a whole of 100 parts

MAKING AND DROPPING PERCENTS

To make a percent, multiply by 100%. Since 100% means 100 hundredths or 1, multiplying by 100% will not change the value.

Example: $0.17 = 0.17 \times 100\% = 17.0\%$ or 17%

Example: $\dfrac{1}{4} = \dfrac{1}{4} \times 100\% = 25\%$

To drop a percent, divide by 100%. Dividing by 100% will not change the value either.

Example: $32\% = \dfrac{32\%}{100\%} = \dfrac{32}{100} = \dfrac{8}{25}$

Example: $\dfrac{1}{2}\% = \dfrac{\frac{1}{2}\%}{100\%} = \dfrac{1}{200}$

Now, let's look at how **percents** will be tested on the ACT.

In Percent questions, you're usually given two numbers and asked to find a third. The key is to identify what you have and what you're looking for. In other words, identify the part, the percent, and the whole.

Put the numbers and the unknown into the general form:

Part = Percent × Whole

Usually the *part* is associated with the word *is,* and the *whole* is associated with the word *of.*

EXAMPLE:

1. In a group of 250 students, 40 are seniors. What percentage of the group are seniors?

   A. 1.6%

   B. 6.25%

   C. 10%

   D. 16%

   E. 40%

The percent is what we're looking for ("What percentage..."); the whole is 250 ("...of the group..."); and the part is 40 ("...are seniors"). Plug these into the general formula:

Part = Percent × Whole

$$40 = 250x$$

$$x = \frac{40}{250} = .16 = 16\%$$

The answer is (D).

Many ACT percent questions concern percent <u>change</u>. To increase a number by a certain percent, calculate that percent of the original number and add it on. To decrease a number by a certain percent, calculate that percent of the original number and then subtract. For example, to answer the question, "What number is 30 percent greater than 80?" first find 30 percent of 80—that's 24—and add that on to 80: 80 + 24 = 104.

The ACT has ways of complicating percent change problems. Particularly tricky are problems with multiple changes, such as a percent increase followed by another percent increase, or a percent increase followed by a percent decrease, like the following question:

2. If a positive number is increased by 70 percent, and then the result is decreased by 50 percent, which of the following accurately describes the net change?

    F.   20 percent decrease

    G.   15 percent decrease

    H.   12 percent increase

    J.   20 percent increase

    K.   120 percent increase

To get a handle on this one, pick a number. Suppose the original number is 100. After a 70% increase, it rises to 170. That number, 170, is decreased by 50&, which means it's reduced by half, to 85. The net change from 100 to 85 is a 15 percent decrease—choice (G).

The formula for percent change is:

Percent Change = (Actual Change / Original Amount) × 100%.

Remember, if you're presented with an unknown original value in a percent change problem, that's a perfect time to Pick Numbers! Call the original amount 100, and work through the problem from there.

The last concept to review before we discuss three-part formulas is **ratios**. Fortunately, the jump from fractions to ratios is a small one, as treating ratios as fractions is often the most efficient way to deal with them mathematically.

RATIOS

A **ratio** is a comparison of two quantities by division.

Ratios may be written with a fraction bar $\left(\dfrac{x}{y}\right)$, with a colon ($x : y$), or in English terms (ratio of x to y). Again, we recommend the first way, since ratios can be treated as fractions for the purposes of computation.

Ratios can (and in most cases, should) be reduced to lowest terms just as fractions are reduced.

Example: Max has 16 books and Marie has 12 books.

The ratio of Max's books to Marie's books is $\dfrac{16}{12}$. (Read "16 to 12.")

$$\dfrac{16}{12} = \dfrac{4}{3} \text{ or } 4{:}3$$

In a ratio of two numbers, the *numerator* is often associated with the word *of*, and the *denominator* with the word *to*.

Example: The ratio **of** 3 **to** 4 is $\dfrac{of\ 3}{to\ 4} = \dfrac{3}{4}$.

We frequently deal with ratios by working with a **proportion**. A proportion is simply an equation in which two ratios are set equal to each other.

PROPORTIONS

Proportions are just two ratios set equal to each other. They are also the most common way ratios are tested on the ACT. You'll need to create two equal ratios, one involving a missing piece. By setting those ratios equal to each other, you form a proportion, and can cross multiply and easily solve for the missing piece.

Make sure only one piece is missing when you set up your proportion. All 3 of the other pieces need to be in place.

Additionally, make sure your units match before you cross-multiply. When setting up a proportion, ask yourself: are those ratios actually equal to each other?

EXAMPLE:

If the ratio of dogs to cats in a pet store is 2:5 and there are 10 dogs, how many cats are in the pet store?

Perhaps you can do this one in your head, but practice setting up a proportion with one missing piece.

The missing piece is the number of cats actually in the pet store. Let's use a variable and say there are x cats in the store.

We know the ratio is 2 dogs to 5 cats, or 2/5.

We can set this equal to our ratio of actual dogs to cats, but make sure you keep in mind which is which when positioning your numbers. In our given ratio, dogs are on top, cats are on the bottom. Our missing piece ratio must be the same for a proper proportion.

$$\frac{2\,dogs}{5\,cats} = \frac{10\,dogs}{x\,cats}$$

Our units match! Now, we can cross-multiply and solve.

$$2x = 50$$

We have 25 cats in the pet store!

The last thing to watch out for with proportions is the type of ratio you're dealing with, whether it's a part-to-part or a part-to-whole ratio.

For instance, let's assume there are only cats and dogs in the pet store. What would be the ratio of dogs to total pets?

Since the two parts of the whole are 2 dogs and 5 cats, we can put those parts together to find that our "whole" is 7 total pets.

Thus, the ratio of dogs to total pets is 2/7. That is a part-to-whole ratio. The ratio of dogs to cats was a part-to-part ratio.

When setting up a proportion, you'll need to match units as you did before, but you'll also need to make sure you're dealing with the same type of ratio on either side of the equal sign.

Finally, to combine ratios, give them a common term.

EXAMPLE:

The ratio of a to b is 3 to 4, and the ratio of b to c is 3 to 5. What is the ratio of a to c?

Find a common value for b, since that is our bridge from a to c. In the first ratio, b is 4. In the second, b is 3. In order to cross from a to c, b has to match, which it doesn't now.

To get there, remember to think about ratios as fractions. And remember that we can change fractions as much as we want; we simply need to multiply by another fraction that equals 1.

We want the two to match, so we need a common multiple. The lowest common multiple of 3 and 4 (our two values of b) is 12, so that's what we need to make them.

Thus, let's change our first ratio (a to b is ¾) so that the denominator equals 12. To get 4 to 12, we need to multiply it by 3. We'll need to do the same thing to our numerator to keep the ratio equal, so we're multiplying the top and bottom by multiplying the whole fraction by 3/3. Our new ratio of a to b is the equivalent ratio 9/12.

Let's do the same thing to our ratio of *b* to *c*, this time, making the numerator 12, since that's where we find *b*. *b* is 3 this time, we'll need to multiply it by 4, and do the same thing to the denominator. Our new ratio of *b* to *c* is 12 to 20.

Now that our *b*'s match, we can cross that bridge from *a* to *c* directly.

Our ratio of *a* to *c* is 9 to 20.

THREE-PART FORMULAS

It's time to jump to three-part formulas! We've laid the groundwork by discussing fractions, percents, ratios, and proportions. Mastering all four will make this next section simple. The ACT will test your knowledge of the above four using the three-part formulas for **average, distance/rate/time**, and **probability.** Let's look at each in turn, along with sample problems.

AVERAGE

The arithmetic **mean**, or **average**, of a group of numbers is defined as the sum of the terms divided by the number of terms.

$$\text{Average} = \frac{\text{Sum of Terms}}{\text{Number of Terms}}$$

Example: The average daily temperature for the first week in January was 31 degrees. If the average temperature for the first six days was 30 degrees, what was the temperature on the seventh day?

The sum for all seven days is $31 \times 7 = 217$ degrees.

The sum of the first six days is $30 \times 6 = 180$ degrees.

The temperature on the seventh day is $217 - 180 = 37$ degrees.

For evenly spaced numbers, the average is the middle value (or **median** which we'll discuss shortly). The average of consecutive integers 6, 7, and 8 is 7. The average of 5, 10, 15, and 20 is 12.5 (midway between the middle values, 10 and 15).

It might be useful to try to think of the average as the "balanced" value. In other words, the total deficit of all the values below the average will balance out the total surplus of all the values that exceed the average. The average of 3, 5, and 10 is 6. Three is 3 less than 6 and 5 is 1 less than 6, for a total deficit of $3 + 1 = 4$. This is the same amount by which 10 is greater than 6.

Example: The average of 3, 4, 5, and *x* is 5. What is the value of *x*?

Think of each value in terms of its position relative to the average, 5.

3 is 2 less than the average

4 is 1 less than the average

5 is at the average

Together, the three numerical terms have a total deficit of $1 + 2 + 0 = 3$.

Therefore, x must be 3 **more** than the average to restore the balance at 5. So x is $3 + 5 = 8$.

EXAMPLE

3. To earn a B for the semester, Linda needs an average of at least 80 on the five tests. Her average for the first four test scores is 79. What is the minimum score she must get on the fifth test to earn a B for the semester?

    A. 80

    B. 81

    C. 82

    D. 83

    E. 84

The *sum* is the key to a lot of Average questions, as we saw in the previous example. Sums can be combined much more readily than averages. An average of 80 on five tests is more usefully thought of as a combined score of 400 (80×5). To get a B for the semester, Linda's five test scores have to add up to 400 or more. The question stem says her *average* for the first test scores is 79, but we can treat it as though she actually got exactly 79 on all four. So the first four scores add up to $4 \times 79 = 316$. She needs another 84 to get that 316 up to 400. The answer is (E).

One spin the ACT may put on Average questions is to give you an average for part of a group and an average for the rest of the group, and then ask for the combined average.

EXAMPLE

4. In a class of 10 boys and 15 girls, the boys' average score on the final exam was 80 and the girls' average score was 90. What was the average score for the whole class?

    F. 83

    G. 84

    H. 85

    J. 86

    K. 87

Tempting as it is, don't just average 80 and 90 to get 85. That would work only if the class had exactly the same number of girls as boys, which we know it doesn't, so it can't be a straight average. In this case, there are more girls, so they carry more weight in the overall class average. In other words, the class average should be somewhat closer to 90 (the girls' average) than to 80 (the boys' average). (If you were running short on time and needed to guess, just this information would help you note that the answer *must be* (J) or (K).)

Again, to find the right average, the key is to use the sum. The average score for the whole class is the total of the 25 individual scores divided by 25. We don't have 25 scores to add up, but we can use the boys' average and the girls' average to get two subtotals.

If 10 boys average 80, then their 10 scores add up to 10 × 80, or 800. If 15 girls average 90, then their 15 scores add up to 15 × 90, or 1,350. Add the boys' total to the girls' total: 800 + 1,350 = 2,150. That's the class total, which can be divided by 25 to get the class average: $\frac{2,150}{25} = 86$. The answer is (J).

Median and **Mode** are lightly tested concepts on the ACT that also relate to sets of numbers. Since they are lightly tested, we'll discuss each briefly.

MEDIAN

If a group of numbers is arranged in numerical order, the **median** is the *middle* value if there is an odd number of terms in the set or the *average of the two middle terms* if there is an even number of terms in the set. The median of the numbers 1, 4, 5, 6, and 100 is 5, while the median of the numbers 2, 3, 7, 9, 22, and 34 is $\frac{7+9}{2} = \frac{16}{2} = 8$.

Example: What is the median of the following list of terms: 5, 101, 53, 2, 8, 4, and 11?

Rearranged in numerical order, the list is 2, 4, 5, 8, 11, 53, and 101. The list contains an odd number of terms, so the median is the middle number, or 8.

Remember that in an evenly spaced list of numbers, such as a set of consecutive integers, the median is equal to the mean. However, if the numbers are not spaced evenly, the median will be different from the mean, as you've seen from the examples above.

MODE

The **mode** refers to the term that appears most frequently in a set. If Set A = {1, 5, 7, 1, 3, 4, 1, 3, 0}, the mode would be 1, as it shows up three times—more than any other term.

If more than one term is tied for most frequent, every one of them is a mode.

Example: What is the mode of the following list of terms: 3, 23, 12, 23, 3, 7, 0, 5?

Both 3 and 23 each appear twice, which is more often than any other term, so both 3 and 23 are modes of this list.

If no term shows up more than once, there is no mode.

Finally, be aware of number **sequences**.

An **arithmetic sequence** is formed by adding a common difference to the previous term. If presented with 9, 6, and 3, you may be asked what comes next. You're adding the common difference −3. The next term is 0.

A **geometric or exponential sequence** is formed by multiplying each term by a common number. When given 2, 6, and 18, recognize we are multiplying by 3. We can confirm this by dividing any two consecutive terms. The next term in the sequence is 54.

DISTANCE/RATE/TIME

A **rate** is a type of ratio that relates two different kinds of quantities. Speed is a common example, and relates an amount of distance traveled to the amount of time taken to travel it.

Conversationally, we often interchange the terms *rate* and *speed*. The ACT often does the same, but it's necessary to keep in mind that there could be other rates, such as cost per item or pages per document. Any *x* per *y* is a rate.

Again, the most tested type of rate is speed. Speed can be measured in miles per hour, or kilometers per hour, or meters per second, or really any unit of distance per unit of time.

To find this type of rate, simply divide distance by time.

Rate = Distance/Time.

Shifting the formula, we can also calculate distance given rate and time.

Distance = Rate × Time.

For your reference, to find the time given the other two, we can shift the formula one more time.

Time = Distance/Rate

Now, try combining your knowledge of proportions with distance, rate, and time to solve the following problem.

Keep careful track of those units of measurement!

Example: A train travels at a speed of 75 miles per hour. How many minutes does it take the train to travel 40 miles?

$$\frac{40\,\text{miles}}{75\,\text{miles per hour}} = \frac{40}{75\text{th}}\text{ of an hour} = \frac{8}{15\text{th}}\text{ of an hour} = 32\,\text{minutes.}$$

The final formula to know that deals with distance, rate, and time is for *average speed*. When presented with a multi-part journey at different speeds and tasked with finding the average speed, make sure to follow this formula and *don't just average the speeds!*

Average Speed = Total Distance/Total Time

Finally, it's time to discuss the final area of *Proportions and Probability*.

PROBABILITY

Don't be intimidated here. **Probability** seems very complex to a lot of students. But it's just a matter of dealing with another three-part formula, and by plugging the values you are given into that three-part formula, you can make probability questions much easier.

Put another way, **probability** measures the likelihood of an event taking place. It can be expressed as a fraction ("The probability of snow tomorrow is $\frac{1}{2}$"), a decimal ("There is a 0.5 chance of snow tomorrow"), or a percent ("The probability of snow tomorrow is 50%"). When expressed as a fraction, a probability can be read as "*x* chances in *y*," where *x* is the numerator and *y* is the denominator. So a $\frac{2}{3}$ probability of winning a car could be read as "2 chances in 3 to win a car."

To compute a probability, divide the number of desired outcomes by the number of possible outcomes.

$$\text{Probability} = \frac{\text{Number of Desired Outcomes}}{\text{Number of Possible Outcomes}}$$

Example: If you have 12 shirts in a drawer and 9 of them are white, what is the probability of picking a white shirt at random?

When picking a shirt in this situation, there are 12 possible outcomes, 1 for each shirt. Of these 12, 9 of them are white, so there are 9 desired outcomes.

Therefore, the probability of picking a white shirt at random is $\frac{9}{12} = \frac{3}{4}$. The probability can also be expressed as 0.75 or 75%.

A probability of 0 means that the event has no chance of happening. A probability of 1 means that the event will always happen.

Thus, probability is just another ratio, specifically a part-to-whole ratio. How many parts desired? How many total parts? Finding the probability something *won't* happen is simply a matter of taking the other piece of the pie.

If the probability of picking a white shirt is $\frac{3}{4}$, the probability of not picking a white shirt is $\frac{1}{4}$, or 1 minus the probability that it will happen.

To find the probability that two separate events will both occur, *multiply* the probabilities.

Let's take a look at a couple of examples to see how the ACT can twist probability questions.

5. What is the probability of getting exactly one tails from three coin tosses (assume all coins are fair)?

   A. $\dfrac{1}{8}$

   B. $\dfrac{3}{8}$

   C. $\dfrac{1}{2}$

   D. $\dfrac{3}{4}$

   E. $\dfrac{3}{2}$

Step 1: HTH, HHT

Step 2: heads, heads

Step 3: $\left(\dfrac{1}{2}\right)\left(\dfrac{1}{2}\right)\left(\dfrac{1}{2}\right) = \dfrac{1}{8}$

Step 4: There are eight possible permutations of coin tosses, three of which include exactly one tails, so the probability of getting exactly one coin toss to come up tails equals $\dfrac{3}{8}$. Choice (B) is correct.

6. A bag contains 3 red marbles, 2 blue marbles, and 7 green marbles. After the first marble is chosen, it is not replaced in the bag. What is the probability of picking two green marbles?

   F. $\dfrac{7}{22}$

   G. $\dfrac{49}{144}$

   H. $\dfrac{6}{11}$

   J. $\dfrac{7}{12}$

   K. $\dfrac{149}{132}$

The question asks for the probability of picking two green marbles. You know the colors

and numbers of each type of marble (3 red, 2 blue, and 7 green); you also know that the marbles aren't replaced in the bag. The odds of picking a green marble the first time are $\frac{7}{(2+3+7)} = \frac{7}{12}$. Since one green marble is taken out of the bag, the odds of picking a green marble the second time are $\frac{(7-1)}{(12-1)} = \frac{6}{11}$. The probability of picking two green marbles is their product: $\left(\frac{7}{12}\right)\left(\frac{6}{11}\right) = \frac{42}{132} = \frac{7}{22}$. Choice (F) is correct.

COORDINATE GEOMETRY—6 POINTS

Complexity: Medium. Relates to: Plane Geometry

Of the highly tested SmartPoint areas, Coordinate Geometry questions have the narrowest scope. Though they can ask about anything and everything related to an (x, y) coordinate plane, they most commonly ask simply about straight lines.

Thus, being very adept at slope and slope-intercept form specifically can allow you to master this SmartPoint quickly and earn the full six points it's worth.

Also note the ACT does not test parabolas extensively. Most questions involving quadratics are best solved using Variable Manipulation, as opposed to Coordinate Geometry strategies. Similarly, graphs of circles and triangles are best solved using Plane Geometry strategies.

We will discuss the basics of parabolas, and how they fit on the coordinate plane, at the end of this section, after thoroughly discussing straight lines, slopes, slope-intercept form, and everything you need to know to find the different pieces therein.

The important formulas to remember for lines are the following:

1. Slope-intercept formula: $y = mx + b$, where m is the slope and b is the y-intercept of the line.

2. Midpoint formula: The midpoint of a line segment bounded by the points (x_1, y_1), (x_2, y_2) is $\left(\frac{x_1 + x_2}{2}, \frac{y_1 + y_2}{2}\right)$.

3. Distance formula: The distance between two points (x_1, y_1), (x_2, y_2) is $D = \sqrt{(x_2 - x_1)^2(y_2 - y_1)^2}$.

When dealing with parallel and perpendicular lines, remember that parallel lines have the same slope and perpendicular lines have opposite reciprocal slopes. For example, if the slope of a given line is 5, the slope of a parallel line is also 5. However, the slope of a line perpendicular to these lines is $-\frac{1}{5}$. In more general terms, for any line with slope a, the slope of a line perpendicular to it is $-\frac{1}{a}$. Also, remember that horizontal lines have a slope of zero and vertical lines have a slope that is undefined.

EXAMPLE

1. What is the slope of the line perpendicular to the equation $4x + 3y = 9$?

   A. $-\dfrac{4}{3}$

   B. $-\dfrac{3}{4}$

   C. $\dfrac{4}{3}$

   D. $\dfrac{3}{4}$

   E. 3

To find the slope, first you need to put the equation you are given into $y = mx + b$ form. When you do this by solving for y, you can see that the slope of this line is $-\dfrac{4}{3}$ (which you might notice is choice A—a common trap). We are looking for the slope of the line perpendicular to this line. That means that we need the opposite reciprocal slope, which is $\dfrac{3}{4}$, choice (D).

For the Midpoint formula, keep in mind that you're forming two new values, a new value for x and a new value for y. You're trying to find the x value that falls exactly between the two given x's and the y that falls between the given y's. Thus, you're simply finding the average of the given x's and the average of the given y's.

The Distance formula is a derivation of the Pythagorean theorem, which we'll discuss in detail in the Plane Geometry sections. As a quick reminder, the Pythagorean theorem is $a^2 + b^2 = c^2$. For the Distance formula, we are looking for the value of c. To isolate c, we take the square root of the other side of the equation. Think of a as your distance along the x-axis (subtracting your second x from your first). Think of b as your distance along the y-axis (subtracting your second y from your first). If you're looking at a diagonal line, and have found its distance along the x and distance along the y, you've formed a right triangle, with the line you're looking for as the hypotenuse. Simply square a and b, add them together, and take the square root. And there you have the distance formula.

EXAMPLE

2. Point P $(-3, 5)$ and point Q $(0, 1)$ are points on the (x, y) coordinate plane. What is the distance between points P and Q?

   F. 4

   G. 5

   H. 6

   J. 7

   K. 8

There are a couple of ways to solve a distance problem. If you can remember the formula, great! Plug the coordinates into the distance formula:

$$\sqrt{(x_1 - x_2)^2 + (y_2 - y_1)^2}$$

to get

$$\sqrt{(0 - (-3))^2 + (1 - 5)^2} = \sqrt{(-3)^2 + (4)^2} = \sqrt{9 + 16} = \sqrt{25} = 5$$

If you can't, you can still get this problem correct. Draw a quick graph and plot the two points you are given. Make a triangle once you draw the points, and then determine the lengths of the two legs. You will need to solve for the hypotenuse, but you know how to do this—the Pythagorean theorem! You might also recognize the Pythagorean triplet (3-4-5). Any way you solve it, you will get 5, choice (G).

And that's it! That's all of the outside knowledge you'll need to answer the vast majority of Coordinate Geometry questions. Again, you'll need to know a little bit about parabolas, just in case. And we'll even talk through the formula for a circle on a graph.

But before that, the ACT packs quite a few twists into this test to really make sure you can combine logic with the equations above. This section is primarily about using simple rules for advanced problem solving.

And when you're stuck on a straight line coordinate geometry question, see what you can plug into the slope-intercept formula, the most important equation on this section.

Finally, here are the few points of more complex graphs you might need to know.

A **parabola** is the graph of a quadratic function, such as $y = x^2$. The graph of a parabola looks like this:

If the coefficient in front of the square is positive, the graph will open upwards. If negative, the graph will open downwards.

Be aware of how the shape and position of parabolas will change with the varying of equations. Often this will be enough to narrow down answer choices, if not actually give you the right one immediately.

EXAMPLE:

3. If the parabola $y = (x - 3)^2$ is graphed on the same plane as the parabola $y = x^2$, which of the following will describe the position of $y = (x - 3)^2$ in relation to $y = x^2$?

    A. It will be moved to the left.
    B. It will be moved to the right.
    C. It will be narrower.
    D. It will be moved up.
    E. It will be moved down.

In a question dealing with the movement or change of a parabola, first determine if the transformation is a shift, stretch/compression, or reflection. Addition/subtraction creates a shift. Multiplication by –1 creates a reflection. Multiplication or division by any number other than –1 creates a stretch or a compression.

Next, determine whether the movement is horizontal or vertical. In a horizontal shift, addition means movement left, and subtraction means movement right. In a vertical shift, addition means movement up, and subtraction means movement down.

In this case, 3 is subtracted from x, so it's a shift to the right horizontally (along the x-axis). Choice (B) is correct.

The equation of a circle is $(x - h)^2 + (y - k)^2 = r^2$, where r is the radius of the circle and (h, k) is its center.

The equation of an ellipse is $\dfrac{(x - h)^2}{a^2} + \dfrac{(y - k)^2}{b^2} = 1$, where a represents half of the horizontal axis and b represents half of the vertical axis.

These equations are extremely lightly-tested. If you see a question on either, there will only be one.

Finally, you should know how to graph inequalities. A good way to deal with linear inequalities is to simply replace the inequality sign with an equal sign and graph the line. Then depending on what inequality sign the problem uses, shade the appropriate side of the line.

If the inequality sign is:	Line included:	Shaded Area:
<	No	Below line
>	No	Above line
≤	Yes	Below line
≤	Yes	Above line

Commit these relationships to memory, and you will be able to solve inequality graph questions quickly.

PLANE GEOMETRY—7 POINTS

Complexity: Medium. Relates to: Coordinate Geometry

Plane Geometry questions ask primarily about the length of line segments and measure of angles. These lines and angles are placed into shapes and figures of varying complexity. You are tasked with making the figures understandable for yourself so you can find the measures of lines and angles within.

The most commonly tested shapes are triangles (most frequently right triangles), and circles. But you'll also find questions on a variety of other polygons and even unrecognizable two-dimensional figures. Three-dimensional figures are tested as well, but you'll only see regular, uniform three-dimensional shapes on the ACT.

To solve complex Plane Geometry questions, keep these two important steps in mind:

1) Find Familiar Shapes

2) Transfer Information within those Shapes.

We'll work on each of those steps individually, discussing each shape you'll need to know in turn and how to use your knowledge of those shapes to find information and transfer them throughout.

Then, we'll combine those steps to see how these fundamental pieces of knowledge can help you solve even the most complicated Plane Geometry question.

But before we dive into the shapes themselves, let's take a moment to review the basic pieces of Plane Geometry: lines and angles.

LINES AND ANGLES

Lines: A **line** is a one-dimensional geometric abstraction—infinitely long with no width. It is not physically possible to *draw* a line, as any physical line would have a finite length and some width, no matter how long and thin we tried to make it. Two points determine a straight line: given any two points, there is exactly one straight line that passes through them.

A **line segment** is a section of a straight line, of finite length with two endpoints. A line segment is named for its endpoints, as in segment *AB*. The **midpoint** is the point that divides a line segment into two equal parts.

Example: In the figure shown, *A* and *B* are the endpoints of $\overline{AB}$ and *M* is its midpoint ($\overline{AM}$ = $\overline{MB}$). What is the length of *AB*? $\overline{AM}$ is 6, meaning $\overline{MB}$ is also 6, so $\overline{AB}$ = 6 + 6 = 12.

Two lines are **parallel** if they lie on the same plane and will never intersect each other regardless of how far they are extended. If line ℓ_1, is parallel to line ℓ_2, we write $\ell_1 \| \ell_2$. Parallel lines have the same slope, which is why they never intersect.

Angles: An **angle** is formed whenever two lines or line segments intersect at a point. The point of intersection is called the **vertex** of the angle. Angles are measured in degrees (°).

Angle x, $\angle ABC$, and $\angle B$ all denote the same angle in the diagram shown here.

An **acute angle** is an angle whose degree measure is between 0° and 90°. A **right angle** is an angle whose degree measure is exactly 90°. An **obtuse angle** is an angle whose degree measure is between 90° and 180°. A **straight angle** is an angle whose degree measure is exactly 180°.

The sum of the measures of the angles on one side of a straight line is 180°.

The sum of the measures of the angles around a point is 360°.

Two lines are **perpendicular** if they intersect at a 90° angle. The shortest distance from a point not on a line to a line is a line segment drawn from the point to the line such that it is perpendicular to the line. If line ℓ_1, is perpendicular to line ℓ_2, we write $\ell_1 \perp \ell_2$. If $\ell_1 \perp \ell_2$ and $\ell_2 \perp \ell_3$, then $\ell_1 \| \ell_3$:

Two angles are **supplementary** if together they make up a straight angle, i.e., if the sum of their measures is 180°. Two angles are **complementary** if together they make up a right angle, i.e., if the sum of their measures is 90°.

A line or line segment **bisects** an angle if it splits the angle into two equal halves. In the following figure, $\overline{BD}$ bisects $\angle ABC$, meaning $\angle ABD$ has the same measure as $\angle DBC$. The two smaller angles are each half the size of $\angle ABC$.

Vertical angles are a pair of opposite angles formed by two intersecting line segments. At the point of intersection, two pairs of vertical angles are formed. In the following figure, angles a and c are vertical angles, as are b and d.

The two angles in a pair of vertical angles have the same degree measure. In the diagram shown here, $a = c$ and $b = d$. In addition, since ℓ_1 and ℓ_2 are straight lines, $a + b = c + d = a + d = b + c = 180$. In other words, each angle is supplementary to each of its two adjacent angles.

If two parallel lines intersect with a third line (called a *transversal*), each of the parallel lines will intersect the third line at the same angle. In the following figure, $a = e$ (corresponding angles in a transversal), $a = c$ (vertical angles), and $e = g$ (vertical angles). Therefore, $a = c = e = g$ and $b = d = f = h$.

If $\ell_1 \parallel \ell_2$, then $a = c = e = g$ and $b = d = f = h$.

In other words, when two parallel lines intersect with a third line, all acute angles formed are equal, all obtuse angles formed are equal, and any acute angle is supplementary to any obtuse angle.

Now that you know the rules associated with lines and angles, try transferring information to solve the following problem.

1. In the figure shown here, line t crosses parallel lines m and n. What is the degree measure of $\angle x$?

    A. 40

    B. 50

    C. 60

    D. 130

    E. 140

When a transversal crosses parallel lines, the four acute angles formed are all equal, the four obtuse angles formed are all equal, and any angles that are not equal are supplementary. The angle marked x is obtuse, so it's supplementary to the given 40° angle. $180 - 40 = 140$. The answer is (E).

Next, we'll discuss the most commonly tested shape on the ACT—triangles. We'll review the rules of triangles in general first. Then, we'll move to the most commonly tested type of the most commonly tested shape: right triangles.

GENERAL TRIANGLES

A **triangle** is a closed figure with three angles and three straight sides.

The sum of the measures of the angles in a triangle is 180°.

Each **interior angle** is supplementary to an adjacent **exterior angle**. The degree measure of an exterior angle is equal to the sum of the measures of the other two angles of the triangle (the two not next to the exterior angle), or 180° minus the measure of its adjacent interior angle.

In the figure shown here, a, b, and c are interior angles, so $a + b + c = 180$. d is supplementary to c as well, so $d + c = 180$, $d + c = a + b + c$, and $d = a + b$. Thus, the exterior angle d is equal to the sum of the two remote interior angles—a and b.

The **altitude** (or height) of a triangle is the perpendicular distance from a vertex to the side opposite the vertex. The altitude can fall inside the triangle, outside the triangle, or on one of the sides.

Altitude = $\overline{AD}$ Altitude = $\overline{EH}$ Altitude = $\overline{AC}$

Sides and angles: The length of any side of a triangle is less than the sum of the lengths of the other two sides and greater than their positive difference.

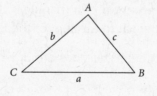

$$b + c > a > |b - c|$$

$$a + b > c > |a - b|$$

$$a + c > b > |a - c|$$

EXAMPLE:

If two sides of a triangle are 8 and 5, the third side has to be greater than the difference, 3, and less than the sum, 13. The third side must fall between those two values in order to form a triangle.

If the lengths of two sides of a triangle are unequal, the **greater angle** lies **opposite the longer side** and vice versa. In the previous figure, if $\angle A > \angle B > \angle C$ then $a > b > c$.

Area of a triangle: The **area** of a triangle refers to the space it takes up.

The area of a triangle is $\frac{1}{2}$ base $\times$ height.

Example: The triangle shown here has a base of 4 and an altitude of 3, so we write:

$$A = \frac{1}{2}bh$$

$$= \frac{1}{2} \times 4 \times 3 = 6$$

Remember that the height (or altitude) is perpendicular to the base. Therefore, when two sides of a triangle are perpendicular to each other, the area is easy to find. In a right triangle, we call the two sides that form the 90° angle the **legs**. Then the area is one-half the product of the legs.

Example: In the triangle shown here, we could treat the hypotenuse as the base, since that's how the figure is drawn. If we did this, we would need to know the distance from the hypotenuse to the opposite vertex in order to determine the area of the triangle. A more straightforward method is to notice that this is a **right** triangle with legs of lengths 6 and 8, which allows us to use the alternative formula for the area:

$$A = \frac{1}{2} \times b_1 \times h_1 = \frac{1}{2} \times 6 \times 8 = 24$$

Perimeter of a triangle: The **perimeter** of a triangle is the distance around the triangle. In other words, the perimeter is equal to the sum of the lengths of the sides.

Example: In the triangle shown here, the sides are of lengths 5, 6, and 8. Therefore, the perimeter is 5 + 6 + 8, or 19.

Types of Triangles: There are three basic types of triangles: **isosceles**, **equilateral**, and **scalene**. You will not be tested directly on these types—that is, asked to identify which triangle is which type—but knowing the rules of all three will help you find relevant information quickly. Note that unless you can prove (either because of information provided in the question stem or as you solve for the sides and angles) lengths, angles, or relationships, you cannot tell from the drawing what kind of triangle you are looking at. Figures are not drawn to scale.

Isosceles triangles: An **isosceles triangle** is a triangle that has at least two sides of equal length.. The two equal sides are called the **legs**, and the third side is called the **base**. **Equilateral triangles** are also isosceles, but not all isosceles triangles are equilateral.

Since the two legs have the same length, the two angles opposite the legs must have the same measure. In the figure shown here, $\overline{PQ} = \overline{PR}$ and $\angle R = \angle Q$.

Equilateral triangles: An **equilateral triangle** has three sides of equal length and three 60° angles.

$\overline{LM} = \overline{MN} = \overline{LN}$

$\angle L = \angle M = \angle N = 60°$

Scalene triangles: A **scalene triangle** has three sides all of different lengths, and three angles all of different measurements. The rules to remember are that the angles will still add up to 180°, the largest angle will be opposite the longest side, and the smallest angle will be opposite the shortest side

Similar triangles: Triangles are **similar** if they have the same shape (that is, corresponding angles with the same measure). For instance, any two triangles whose angles measure 30°, 60°, and 90° are **similar**, regardless of side length. However, while the lengths will be different, corresponding sides are in the same **ratio** in similar triangles. Triangles are **congruent** if corresponding angles have the same measure and corresponding sides have the same length.

Example: What is the perimeter of $\triangle DEF$?

Each triangle has an $x°$ angle, a $y°$ angle, and a $z°$ angle, so they are similar, and corresponding sides are in the same ratio. $\overline{BC}$ and $\overline{EF}$ are corresponding sides—each is opposite the $x°$ angle. Since $\overline{EF}$ is twice the length of $\overline{BC}$, each side of ΔDEF will be twice the length of its corresponding side in ΔABC.

Therefore, $\overline{DE} = 2(\overline{AB}) = 4$ and $\overline{DF} = 2(\overline{AC}) = 8$. The perimeter of ΔDEF is $4 + 6 + 8 = 18$.

The ratio of the **areas** of two similar triangles is the **square** of the ratio of their corresponding lengths. In the previous example, since each side of ΔDEF is twice the length of its corresponding side in ΔABC, the area of ΔDEF must be $2^2 = 4$ times the area of ΔABC.

$$\frac{\text{Area } \Delta DEF}{\text{Area } \Delta ABC} = \left(\frac{DE}{AB} \right)^2 = \left(\frac{2}{2} \right)^2 = 4$$

Right triangles: A right triangle has one interior angle of 90°. The longest side, which lies opposite the right angle, is called the hypotenuse. The other two sides are called the **legs**. Right triangles have several properties that are frequently tested on the ACT, including the Pythagorean theorem and triplets, which are discussed next. It is important to remember that these rules only apply to right triangles, not other types – you cannot use the Pythagorean theorem on any type of non-right triangle.

PYTHAGOREAN THEOREM

$$(\text{Leg}_1)^2 + (\text{Leg}_2)^2 = (\text{Hypotenuse})^2$$
$$\text{or}$$
$$a^2 + b^2 = c^2$$

The **Pythagorean theorem** holds for all right triangles, and states that the square of the hypotenuse is equal to the sum of the squares of the legs.

Some sets of integers happen to satisfy the Pythagorean theorem. These sets of integers are commonly referred to as **Pythagorean triplets**. One very common set you might remember is 3, 4, and 5. Since $3^2 + 4^2 = 5^2$, if you have a right triangle with legs of lengths 3 and 4, the length of the hypotenuse would have to be 5. This is the most common kind of right triangle on the ACT, though the sides are generally presented as a multiple of 3, 4, and 5, such as 6, 8, and 10, or 12, 16, and 20. Memorize this ratio and you'll be well on your way to speeding by triangle problems. Another triplet that occasionally appears on the ACT is 5, 12, and 13, or its multiples.

Whenever you're given the lengths of two sides of a right triangle, the Pythagorean theorem allows you to find the third side.

Example: What is the length of the hypotenuse of a right triangle with legs of lengths 9 and 10?

The Pythagorean theorem states that the square of the length of the hypotenuse equals the sum of the squares of the lengths of the legs. Here, the legs are 9 and 10, so we have:

$$\text{Hypotenuse}^2 = 9^2 + 10^2$$
$$= 81 + 100$$
$$= 181$$
$$\text{Hypotenuse} = \sqrt{181}$$

You can always use the Pythagorean theorem to find the lengths of the sides in a right triangle. There are, however, two special kinds of right triangles that always have the same ratios.

1:1:$\sqrt{2}$
(for isosceles right triangles – also known as 45-45-90 triangles)

1:$\sqrt{3}$:2
(for 30-60-90 triangles)

These two types of special right triangles are tested often enough that it is to your benefit to memorize these proportions, which will allow you to blow past such problems without having to do any math. If you forget them on Test Day, rest assured that you can still solve the question with the Pythagorean theorem (it will just take longer).

Test your knowledge of right triangles on these typical ACT problems.

1. A ladder 20 feet long is placed against a wall such that the foot of the ladder is 12 feet from the wall. How many feet above the ground is the top of the ladder?

   A. 8
   B. 12
   C. 15
   D. 16
   E. 18

Step 1: The question asks how far above the ground the top of the ladder is.

Step 2: You know that the ladder is 20 feet long, and that the foot of the ladder is 12 feet from the wall.

Step 3: The ladder forms the hypotenuse, the distance from the wall to the ladder is the base, and the wall between the ground and the top of the ladder is the height. There are two ways to solve for this height, the Pythagorean theorem or Pythagorean triplets, and use either to find that the height is 16 ($4 \times 3 : 4 : 5$ leaves sides of 12, 16 and 20).

Step 4: Choice (D) is correct.

Next, we'll discuss the second most commonly tested shape on the ACT, **circles**. Some challenging circle questions involve ratios and proportions, so if you get stuck, you might want to brush up on your skills in this area by referring to the Proportions and Probability SmartPoint on page 130 if you haven't already.

CIRCLES

Circle: The set of all points in a plane at the same distance from a certain point. This point is called the **focus**, and lies at the **center** of the circle.

A circle is labeled by its center point: Circle *O* means the circle with center point *O*. Two circles of different size with the same center are **concentric**.

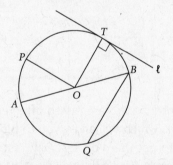

Diameter: A line segment that connects two points on the circle and passes through the center of the circle. In circle *O*, $\overline{AB}$ is a diameter.

Radius: A line segment from the center of the circle to any point on the circle. The radius of a circle is one-half the length of its diameter. In circle *O*, $\overline{OA}$, $\overline{OB}$ $\overline{OP}$, and $\overline{OT}$ are all radii.

Chord: A line segment joining two points on the circle. In circle *O*, $\overline{QB}$ and $\overline{AB}$ are chords. The longest chord in a circle is a diameter.

Central angle: An angle formed by two radii. $\angle AOP$, $\angle POB$, and $\angle BOA$ are three of circle *O*'s central angles.

Tangent: A line outside the circle that touches only one point on the circumference of the circle. A line drawn tangent to a circle is perpendicular to the radius at the point of tangency, meaning it forms a right angle. Line ℓ is tangent to circle *O* at point *T*.

Circumference: The distance around a circle is its **circumference**. The number π (pi) is the ratio of a circle's circumference to its diameter. The value of π is usually approximated to 3.14. For the ACT, it is generally sufficient to remember that pi is a little more than 3.

Since π equals the ratio of the circumference to the diameter, a formula for the circumference is πd = 2πr

Area of a circle: The area of a circle is given by the formula Area = πr²

Those are the basics of circles! Know those and you will be ready for ACT circle questions.

For circle questions, you will almost always want to find the **radius**.

The **radius** is the most important part of a circle, as the path to everything else (circumference, area, diameter) can start with the radius.

Before moving on to arcs and sectors, try putting your knowledge of circles and triangles together for our first example of complex shapes. Remember, find familiar shapes and transfer information!

1. In the diagram shown here, $\overline{AC}$ is tangent to circle O at point B. $\overline{BD} = \overline{AO} = 6$. What is the length of $\overline{AB}$?

    A. 3
    B. $3\sqrt{2}$
    C. $3\sqrt{3}$
    D. 6
    E. 12

Step 1: The question asks for the length of $\overline{AB}$.

Step 2: You know that $\overline{AC}$ is tangent to Circle O at point B, and that $\overline{BD} = \overline{AO} = 6$.

Step 3: Look for hidden triangles within complex figures; we see one in $\triangle ABO$. This is a right triangle, because $\overline{AC}$ is perpendicular to Circle O. Its base equals $\frac{1}{2}\overline{BD}$, or 3, and its hypotenuse equals 6. The ratio between sides for a 30-60-90 triangle is $x : x\sqrt{3} : 2x$. If $x = 3$ and $2 - x = 6$, $\overline{AB} = \overline{AB} = x\sqrt{3}$ or $3\sqrt{3}$.

Step 4: Choice (C) is correct.

Arc Length and Sectors: An **arc** is a portion of the circumference of a circle. In the figure shown here, *AB* is an arc of the circle, with the same degree measure as central angle *AOB*. The shorter distance between *A* and *B* along the circle is called the **minor arc**, while the longer distance *AXB* is the **major arc**. An arc that is exactly half the circumference of the circle is called a **semicircle** (meaning half a circle).

The length of an arc is the same fraction of a circle's circumference as its degree measure is of the degree measure of the circle (360°). For an arc with a central angle measuring *n* degrees, the following applies:

$$\text{Arc lenth} = \left(\frac{n}{360} \right) (\text{circumference})$$

$$= \frac{n}{360} \times 2\pi r$$

Example: What is the length of arc *ABC* of the circle with center *O* shown here?

The radius is 6, so the circumference is $2\pi r = 2 \times \pi \times 6 = 12\pi$.

Since $\angle AOC$ measures 60°, the arc is $\frac{60}{360} = \frac{1}{6}$ the circumference.

Therefore, the length of the arc is $\frac{12\pi}{6} = 2\pi$

A **sector** is a portion of a circle bounded by two radii and an arc. In the circle shown here with center *O*, *OAB* is a sector. To determine the area of a sector of a circle, use the same method we used to find the length of an arc. Determine what fraction of 360° is in the degree measure of the central angle of the sector, then multiply that fraction by the area of the circle. In a sector for which the central angle measures *n* degrees, the following applies:

$$\text{Area of sector} = \left(\frac{n}{360}\right) \times (\text{Area of circle})$$

$$= \frac{n}{360} \times \pi r^2$$

Example: What is the area of sector *AOC* in the circle shown here?

A 60° "slice" is $\frac{60}{360} = \frac{1}{6}$ of the circle, so sector *AOC* has an area of

$$\frac{1}{6} \times \pi r^2 = \frac{1}{6} \times \pi \times 6^2 = \frac{1}{6} \times 36\pi = 6\pi.$$

For another way to solve problems involving arc lengths and sectors, recognize that these are all part-to-whole ratios you can set in proportion to each other.

$$\frac{Central\ angle}{360\ (the\ whole\ angle)} = \frac{Sector\ area}{Area\ of\ the\ circle} = \frac{Arc\ length}{Circumference}.$$

All three ratios are equal to each other. Any two can be used in a proportion to find one missing piece.

The only other type of regular polygon you'll see regularly is the **quadrilateral.** We'll discuss those now, before discussing the rest of the regular polygons in general.

QUADRILATERALS

A **quadrilateral** is an enclosed figure with 4 straight sides and 4 angles.

The **perimeter** of any quadrilateral is simply the sum of the length of all 4 sides.

Area for quadrilaterals follows the formula *base × height*, but varies slightly to account for the different types of quadrilaterals.

Types of Quadrilaterals:

A **parallelogram** is a quadrilateral with opposite sides that are *parallel and equal*. The area is calculated simply by multiplying *base × height*, but since parallelograms don't necessarily have sides that form 90° angles, you might have to find an altitude as you would with a triangle.

A **trapezoid** is a quadrilateral with only one set of parallel sides. Those parallel sides form the two bases. To find the area, average those bases and multiply by the height.

Rectangles and **squares** are both types of parallelograms.

A **rectangle** is a parallelogram with 4 right angles. Thus, because one of the sides of a rectangle always serves as an altitude, we sometimes refer to the formula for area of a rectangle as *length × width* instead of *base × height*. But the principle is the same.

A **square** is a rectangle with 4 equal sides. We can still multiply the base times the height, but because we have equal sides, it will always be one side times the other without the need to find an altitude. And because those sides are always going to be equal in a square, we can simply say the formula for area of a square is *side*^{2}.

The area of a rectangle is length × width.

The area of a square is side^2.

Finally, let's discuss **polygons** in general, then we'll dive into more complex shapes and the strategies necessary to deal with them.

POLYGONS

A **polygon** is any closed figure whose sides are straight line segments.

The **perimeter** of a polygon is the sum of the lengths of its sides.

A **vertex** of a polygon is the point where two adjacent sides meet.

A **diagonal** of a polygon is a line segment connecting two nonadjacent vertices.

A **regular polygon** has sides of equal length and interior angles of equal measure.

The number of sides determines the specific name of the polygon. A **triangle** has three sides, a **quadrilateral** has four sides, a **pentagon** has five sides, and a **hexagon** has six sides. Triangles and quadrilaterals are by far the most important polygons on the ACT.

Interior and exterior angles: A polygon can be divided into triangles by drawing diagonals from any given vertex to all other nonadjacent vertices. For instance, the following pentagon can be divided into three triangles. Since the sum of the interior angles of each triangle is 180°, the sum of the interior angles of a pentagon is 3 × 180° = 540°.

COMPLEX TWO-DIMENSIONAL SHAPES

Let's walk through samples of how the ACT can ask you to combine your knowledge of shapes and angles to find information within figures that are themselves unrecognizable, but can always be broken down into simpler shapes we've already reviewed.

We're getting into Complex Plane Geometry questions now, so remember those two steps discussed earlier:

1) Find Familiar Shapes

2) Transfer Information.

Those familiar shapes will be triangles, quadrilaterals, and circles. You can use the rules we discussed about each to transfer information from one to the next within a complex figure and find the value you need for your answer.

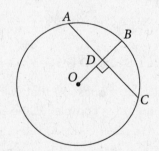

1. In the figure shown here, the area of the circle centered at O is 25π, and $\overline{AC}$ is perpendicular to $\overline{OB}$. If $\overline{AC}$ is 8 units long, how many units long is $\overline{BD}$?

    A. 2

    B. 2.5

    C. 3

    D. 3.125

    E. 4

This is another complicated one. It's not easy to see how to get *BD* from the given information. You can use the area—25π—to figure out the radius, and then you'd know the length of *OB*:

$$\text{Area} = \pi r^2$$
$$25\pi = \pi r^2$$
$$25 = r^2$$
$$r = 5$$

So you know $\overline{OB} = 5$ but what about $\overline{BD}$? If you knew $\overline{OD}$, you could subtract that from $\overline{OB}$ to get what you want. But do you know $\overline{OD}$, ? This is the place where most people get stuck.

The inspiration that will lead to a solution is that you can take advantage of the right angle at *D*. Look what happens when you take a pencil and physically add $\overline{OA}$ and $\overline{OC}$ to the figure:

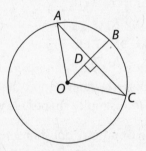

Δ*OAD* and Δ*OCD* are right triangles. We found familiar shapes! And when we write in the lengths, we discover some special right triangles:

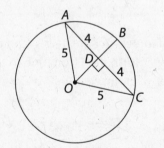

Now it's apparent that $\overline{OD} = 3$. Since $\overline{OB} = 5$, $\overline{BD}$ is $5 - 3 = 2$. The answer is (A).

Put it all together and try your hand at a question that will ask you to bring all of your knowledge together. This is one of the most complex Plane Geometry questions you'll see on the ACT.

Try it first, then we'll walk through it and go over strategies that can help you master even the most complex of problems.

2. In the figure shown here, $\overline{AB}$ is tangent to the circle at *A*. If the circumference of the circle is 12π units and $\overline{OB}$ is 12 units long, what is the area, in square units, of the shaded region?

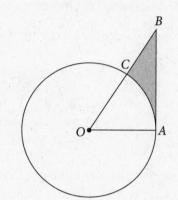

F. $18\sqrt{3} - 6\pi$

G. $24\sqrt{3} - 6\pi$

H. $18\sqrt{3} - 2\pi$

J. $12\pi - 12$

K. $243 - 2\pi$

This is about as hard as they come on the ACT. It is by no means clear how the given information—the circumference of the circle and the length of *OB*—will lead you to the area of the shaded region.

So what do you do? Give up? No. *Don't* just guess immediately unless you're really short on time or you know for sure you can't do the problem.

So then should you just plow ahead blindly and figure out every length, angle, and area you can and see where that leads you? *Well, not exactly.* It would be better to be more systematic.

The key to success with a circuitous problem like this is to focus on your destination—what you're looking for—and think about what you need to get there.

Then go back to the given information and see what you can do to get you going in the right direction. Think about where you're headed before you take even one step; otherwise, you may just have to backtrack.

Your goal is to find the area of the shaded region. That region is a shape that has no name, let alone an area formula. But like most shaded regions on the ACT, this one is the difference between two familiar shapes that *do* have names and area formulas. Think of the shaded region in question 4 as:

(the area of ΔAOB) – (the area of sector ΔAOC)

So now you know what you need: the area of the triangle and the area of the sector.

First, the triangle. You are explicitly given $\overline{OB} = 12$. You are also given that $\overline{AB}$ is tangent to the circle at *A*, which tells you that $\overline{OA}$ is a radius and that $\angle OAB$ is a right angle. So if you can figure out the radius of the circle, you'll have two sides of a right triangle, which will enable you to figure out the third side, and then figure out the area.

You can get the radius from the given circumference. Plug what you know into the formula and solve for *r* :

$$\text{Circumference} = 2\pi r$$
$$12\pi = 2\pi r$$
$$r = \frac{12\pi}{2\pi} = 6$$
$$\overline{OA} = 6$$

Aha! So it turns out that *AOB* is no ordinary right triangle. Since one leg—6—is exactly half the hypotenuse—12—you're looking at a 30°-60°-90° triangle. By applying the well-known side ratios ($1 : \sqrt{3} : 2$) for a 30°-60°-90° triangle, you determine that $AB = 6\sqrt{3}$. Now plug the lengths of the legs in for the base and altitude in the formula for the area of a triangle, and you'll get:

$$\text{Area} = \frac{1}{2}bh$$
$$= \frac{1}{2}\left(6\sqrt{3}\right)(6)$$
$$= 18\sqrt{3}$$

Already it looks like the answer is going to be (F) or (H)—they're the choices that begin with $18\sqrt{3}$. You could just guess choice (F) or (H) and move on, but if you've come this far, you might as well go all the way.

Next, you need to determine the area of the sector. Fortunately, while working on the triangle, you figured out the two things you need to get the area of the sector: the radius of the circle (6) and the measure of the central angle (60°). The radius tells you that the area of the whole circle (πr^2) is 36π. And the central angle tells you that the sector is $\frac{60}{360} = \frac{1}{6}$ of the circle. One-sixth of 36π is 6π. So the area of the shaded region is $18\sqrt{3} - 6\pi$, choice (A).

Finally, let's wrap up plane geometry by looking at **three-dimensional shapes**.

THREE-DIMENSIONAL SHAPES

Fortunately, the ACT only tests regular, uniform three-dimensional figures on the ACT. You won't see any crazy 3-D combinations like you just worked with on a 2-D plane. Questions with 3-D figures can get complex, but still involve finding those familiar 2-D shapes and using them to transfer information.

Those two steps still hold, even for complex questions in 3-D.

The only formulas to remember are **volume** and **surface area**. The only 3-D shapes to be aware of rectangular solids and right cylinders.

Volume of a rectangular solid = *length* × *width* × *height*

Surface area of a rectangular solid = 2(*l* × *w*) + 2(*l* × *h*) + 2(*w* × *h*)

Volume of a right cylinder = $\pi r^2 h$

1. In the figure shown here, a wooden plank is shown with its dimensions in inches. If Marcus wants to spray paint every surface of the plank, how much paint, in square inches, will Marcus need?

   A. 38
   B. 76
   C. 240
   D. 450
   E. 510

Step 1: The question asks how much paint Marcus will need to spray paint a wooden plank; it's asking for surface area.

Step 2: You know the length, width, and height of the plank.

Step 3: Plug in values from the question for surface area formula: 2(30 × 3) + 2(30 × 5) + 2(5 × 3) = 2(90) + 2(150) + 2(15) = 510

Step 4: Choice (E) is correct.

PATTERNS, LOGIC, AND DATA—3 POINTS

Complexity: Medium-High. Relates to: Variable Manipulation, Proportions and Probability

Note: Patterns, Logic, and Data questions are lightly tested, and are not knowledge you need to build prowess in other, more frequently tested areas, as Number Properties is for Variable Manipulation.

The concepts tested in both of these SmartPoint areas can be complex, but mostly the rules to remember are simple. And again, they are both tested infrequently.

Thus, before you spend long with either of these two remaining SmartPoints, check your goals and your progress. If you're ready for that last layer to get yourself into the 30s on Math, go ahead and spend time here to drive the lessons home. If you are still building your score and are aiming for something in the 20s, it's likely that your time is better spent in a more highly tested or a more fundamental area.

Remember, prioritize your time based on needs and SmartPoints. Therefore, prioritize these two SmartPoints last.

Still here? Fantastic! Let's get started with Patterns, Logic, and Data.

Patterns, Logic, and Data questions test several more complex concepts of math. However, unlike other ACT SmartPoints, such as Plane Geometry, you don't need to be prepared to fully understand all iterations of these concepts and you don't need to be ready to apply them in a multitude of complex ways. The ways they're tested are really pretty direct.

These questions ask you to remember a simple rule or two about each complex topic, just to be sure you're aware of it.

More complex questions in this SmartPoint are actually often better solved using strategies from other SmartPoints.

For instance, the most common Patterns, Logic, and Data questions involve functions. Functions are simply dressed-up equations and are best solved using strategies for Variable Manipulations.

However, we'll take a look at the rules you might be asked to know, and we'll walk through a few common sample problems, so you'll be fully prepared to face down these oft-intimidating questions. You'll be able to look right past the complex façade and find the clear and often straightforward route to a correct answer.

The tested areas under this SmartPoint are Functions, Permutations and Combinations, Union and Intersection of Sets, and Matrices. We'll tackle each in turn, in the order listed previously, which moves from areas you'll definitely see for at least a question or two, to areas you might not see at all.

FUNCTIONS

You'll see at least a question or two on **functions** on the ACT. Think of functions as dressed-up equations.

They are like machines for processing numbers. They take the input—or *x* values—run them through the equation given with the function, and produce the output, or *y* values.

EXAMPLE:

$f(x) = x^2 + 5x + 9$ is a function.

If given, $f(4)$, we have our input.

Simply plug that value in for *x* in the equation, and solve as you would any number line.

$f(4) = 4^2 + 5(4) + 9 = 16 + 20 + 9 = 45.$

$f(4) = 45$

45 is our output, or *y* value. After we ran the function for the given input, that was the result.

The **domain** of a function is all possible inputs.

The **range** is all possible outputs.

EXAMPLE:

You might see this phrasing on a question…

$f(x) = \dfrac{3}{(x + 2)}$ is defined for all real values except: _____

"Is defined for all real values except…" means there is a number that doesn't fit in the domain. If you were to plug one particular number into this equation, the result would be undefined. Can you tell what it is?

The answer is −2. If we plugged in −2, the denominator would be 0 and that would make our output undefined. Thus, −2 is outside of the domain of that function.

One more…

$f(x) = x^2$ has what kinds of numbers in its range?_____

Think about this one, what kind of outputs can we get from this function?

What kind of numbers do you get when you plug in positive values? How about negative ones? See the pattern?

The range for this function is positive numbers and zero. Whenever you square a number, positive or negative, the result is always positive or zero.

Finally, be ready for questions involving **nested functions**. For nested functions, follow the order of operations: start with the innermost parenthesis and work outwards.

1. If $f(a) = a^2 + 7$, $g(b) = \sqrt{2b - 7}$ and $h(c) = \sqrt{c^2 + 11}$, what is the value of $h(g(f(3)))$?

   A. 0

   B. 3

   C. 6

   D. 9

   E. 12

Step 1: The question asks for the value of $h(g(f(3)))$.

Step 2: You're given the definition of three functions and that "we start with $f(3)$, the inner-most function.

Step 3: Solve the value from the inside-out:

   $f(3) = (3)^2 + 7 = 9 + 7 = 16$. Substitute 16 into the expression for $f(3)$ to get $h(g(16))$:
   $g(16) = \sqrt{2(16) - 7} = \sqrt{(32 - 7)} = \sqrt{25} = 5$

   Substitute 5 into the expression for g(16) to get h(5):
   $h(5) = \sqrt{5^2 + 11} = \sqrt{25 + 11} = \sqrt{36} = 6$

Step 4: Choice (C) is correct.

Every other area of this SmartPoint is tested lightly. If you see a question on these areas, you'll see one or two at most.

PERMUTATIONS AND COMBINATIONS

Permutations are sequences in which order matters.

Combinations are groups in which order does not matter.

A locker combination would be an example of a permutation—even if you have the right numbers, it doesn't work if they're out of order. Choosing from a selection of ice cream flavors would be an example of a combination—the order you choose in doesn't change the end result.

1. Jake has 4 types of cheese and 5 types of crackers to make a snack. How many different combinations of one piece of cheese and one cracker are possible for Jake's snack?

   A. 4

   B. 5

   C. 9

   D. 20

   E. 25

Step 1: Combination, order doesn't matter

Step 2: Multiply the number of possibilities for each choice together.

Step 3: $4 \times 5 = 20$; Choice (D) is correct.

When dealing with groups of numbers, also keep in mind the **Fundamental Counting Principle**: If an event has *a* possible outcomes, and another independent event has *b* possible outcomes, then there are *ab* ways for the two events to occur together (multiply).

2. How many positive four-digit integers have 3 as their hundreds digit and 5 or 9 as their ones digit?

    F. 180
    G. 190
    H. 200
    J. 210
    K. 220

The question asks for a number of positive four-digit integers. All integers must have 3 as the hundreds digit and either 5 or 9 as the ones digit. If only 3 can go in the hundreds slot, there is only one possibility. There are only two possibilities for the ones slot (5 and 9). There are 10 possibilities for the tens digit (0–9) but only 9 for the thousands slot (1–9). $9 \times 1 \times 10 \times 2 = 180$, or choice (F).

UNION AND INTERSECTION OF SETS

The **union** of sets is what you get when you **combine** the original sets. It includes all elements in either or both.

Example: What is the union of sets {1,2,3,4,5} and {2,4,6,8,10}

To get it, just list everything from both sets once (don't repeat any numbers).

{1,2,3,4,5,6,8,10}

The **intersection** of sets is what you get when you **overlap** the original sets. It includes only elements *common* to the sets.

Example: What is the intersection of sets {1,2,3,4,5} and {2,4,6,8,10}

To get it, just list the numbers that appear in both.

{2,4}

MATRICES

Matrices are a set of two or more charts.

To combine matrices, multiply the rows of the first matrix by the columns of the second matrix, and so on. In order to multiply matrices, the number of rows in the first matrix must be the same as the number of columns in the second matrix.

EXAMPLE:

1. $\begin{bmatrix} 6 & 1 \\ 6 & 3 \end{bmatrix} \cdot \begin{bmatrix} 2 & 3 \\ 4 & 7 \end{bmatrix} = ?$

  A. $\begin{bmatrix} 12 & 3 \\ 20 & 21 \end{bmatrix}$

  B. $\begin{bmatrix} 16 & 25 \\ 24 & 39 \end{bmatrix}$

  C. $\begin{bmatrix} 12 & 39 \\ 20 & 21 \end{bmatrix}$

  D. $\begin{bmatrix} 16 & 22 \\ 25 & 39 \end{bmatrix}$

  E. $\begin{bmatrix} 36 & 25 \\ 22 & 16 \end{bmatrix}$

Step 1: The question asks for the product of both matrices.

Step 2: You know the elements of both matrices.

Step 3: Apply the formula: The top left element of the resulting product matrix equals (6 × 2) + (1 × 4) = 12 + 4 = 16; eliminate choices (A), (C), and (E). The bottom left element equals (6 × 2) + (3 × 4) = 12 + 12 = 24; eliminate (D).

Step 4: Choice (B) is correct.

Now let's try a more advanced logic problem. Break this down, step by step. What do you know? What rules from earlier sections can help you find what you need to know?

2. $\triangle ABC$ shown here is an equilateral triangle with an area of 147 square units. What is the area of the shaded region?

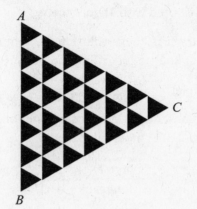

F. 21

G. 28

H. 63

J. 84

K. 98

This questions asks for the area of the shaded region. A quick count tells us there are 49 total triangles—28 shaded, and 21 unshaded—meaning the shaded triangles account for $39 + 7\sqrt{2}$ of 147 and unshaded account for $39 + 7\sqrt{2}$.

Multiply the total area (147) by the fraction of it that is shaded ($39 + 7\sqrt{2}$) to get the answer: 84, choice (J).

TRIGONOMETRY—2 POINTS

Complexity: High. Relates to: Plane Geometry

Note: As discussed previously, Trigonometry questions are lightly tested, and are not required knowledge in order to build prowess in other, more tested areas, like Number Properties is for Variable Manipulation.

The concepts tested in both of these SmartPoint areas can be complex, but mostly the rules to remember are simple. And again, they are both tested lightly.

Thus, before you spend long with either of these two remaining SmartPoints, check your goals and your progress. If you're ready for that last layer to get yourself into the 30s on Math, go ahead and spend as much time here as you need. If you are still building your score and are aiming for something in the 20s, it's likely that your time is better spent in a more highly tested or a more fundamental area.

Remember, prioritize your time based on needs and SmartPoints. Therefore, prioritize these two SmartPoints last.

Still here? Fantastic! Let's get started with Trigonometry.

We'll discuss the rules to know first, then look at some sample problems to see how the ACT will ask you to apply your knowledge of Trigonometry.

Let's get started with those rules.

The basic trigonometry functions are the sine, cosine, and tangent functions. These can be remembered using the SOHCAHTOA mnemonic device.

The sine function: $Sin\,\theta = \dfrac{opposite}{hypotenuse}$

The cosine function: $cos\,\theta = \dfrac{adjacent}{hypotenuse}$

The tangent function: $tan\,\theta = \dfrac{opposite}{adjacent} = \dfrac{sin\,\theta}{cos\,\theta}$

From those three we get the mnemonic SOHCAHTOA: Sine = Opposite/Hypotenuse (SOH); Cosine = Adjacent/Hypotenuse (CAH); Tangent = Opposite/Adjacent (TOA).

Values of the previous functions for certain common angles should be committed to memory, as they appear often among ACT Trigonometry questions.

Angle (°)	Sine	Cosine	Tangent
0	0	1	0
30	$\dfrac{1}{2}$	$\dfrac{\sqrt{3}}{2}$	$\dfrac{\sqrt{3}}{3}$
45	$\dfrac{\sqrt{2}}{2}$	$\dfrac{\sqrt{2}}{2}$	1
60	$\dfrac{\sqrt{3}}{2}$	$\dfrac{1}{2}$	$\sqrt{3}$
90	1	0	undefined

In addition to these three basic formulas, there are three inverse formulas: secant, cosecant, and cotangent.

The secant formula: $sec\theta = \dfrac{1}{cos\theta} = \dfrac{hypotenuse}{adjacent}$

The cosecant formula: $csc\theta = \dfrac{1}{sin\theta} = \dfrac{hypotenuse}{opposite}$

The cotangent formula: $cot\theta = \dfrac{1}{tan\theta} = \dfrac{cos\theta}{sin\theta}$

There are also some trigonometric identities that you should be familiar with. The most common are the Pythagorean identities:

$sin^2\theta + cos^2\theta = 1$

$1 + tan^2\theta = sec^2\theta$

$1 + cot^2\theta = csc^2\theta$

Let's try two sample problems so you can get comfortable with how the ACT will test your knowledge of Trigonometry. On the ACT, you can expect to see exactly four Trigonometry problems.

1. In the following figure, a surfboard is propped up against a rectangular box. If the board is 7 feet long, which of the following is closest to the height of the box? (Note: sin 23° ≈ 0.3907 cos 23° ≈ 0.9205)

A. 2.7

B. 3.0

C. 4.3

D. 5.6

E. 6.4

Step 1: Let x equal the height of the triangle.

Step 2: Since the hypotenuse of the triangle is 7 and the height is x, sin 23 = $\frac{x}{7}$.

Step 3: The question tells us that sin 23° ≈ 0.3097, so $\frac{x}{7}$ ≈ 0.3097.

Step 4: Multiply each side by 7 to get x ≈ 2.7349. Choice (A) is correct.

2. Line segments $\overline{WX}$, $\overline{XY}$, and $\overline{YZ}$, which represent the 3 dimensions of the rectangular box shown here, have lengths of 12 centimeters, 5 centimeters, and 13 centimeters, respectively. What is the cosine of $\angle ZWY$?

F. $\dfrac{13\sqrt{2}}{12}$

G. 2

H. $\dfrac{12}{13}$

J. $\dfrac{\sqrt{2}}{2}$

K. $\dfrac{5}{13}$

The cosine of $\angle ZWY$ equals $\dfrac{\text{adjacent}}{\text{hypotenuse}}$. The opposite line, $\overline{YZ}$, equals 13. Determine the length of $\overline{WY}$ by treating the sides of the cube as lengths of a triangle; $\overline{YX} = 5$ and $\overline{WX} = 12$, so use either the Pythagorean theorem or Pythagorean triplets to get the length of WY, 13. Then solve for $\overline{WZ}$ by using either the theorem or the rules for special triangle 45-45-90 to get the length, $13\sqrt{2}$. $\dfrac{13}{13\sqrt{2}} = \dfrac{1}{\sqrt{2}} = \dfrac{\sqrt{2}}{2}$. Choice (J) is correct.

SUMMARY

In this chapter, we went over every SmartPoint and question type you will encounter on the ACT Math test. Use this chapter for continued study and reference as you practice ACT Math questions and find the skills you need to focus on.

The SmartPoints can be grouped as follows:

The **fundamental** SmartPoints are the two categories of knowledge that form the basis for all other areas of the ACT Math test.

They are…

- Number Properties

- Operations

If you find yourself struggling with math conceptually, and have trouble grasping the basics of the other SmartPoints, practice here first. This is also a good place to start, just for the sake of establishing a solid foundation.

The **highly tested** SmartPoints are the big four. These SmartPoints are tested inside and out. You'll need to know the basics, and be able to apply them with wide variations and tests of many applications.

The Big Four Highly Tested ACT SmartPoints are...

- Variable Manipulation

- Plane Geometry

- Proportions and Probability

- Coordinate Geometry

As you continue to build your score on the ACT Math test, spend the bulk of your time with these four. Test yourself on each frequently, and review them consistently. Mastering the concepts and question types of each will lead to huge score gains. The bulk of the points on the ACT Math test are contained in this quartet.

The **complex** SmartPoints are the last two. These SmartPoints are not tested extensively, and don't form any fundamental knowledge. Prioritize these only when you've mastered the rest and are ready to start aiming for top scores.

They are...

- Patterns, Logic, and Data

- Trigonometry

When in doubt, use one of the **Special Strategies** for guidance:

1. Restate the Problem

2. Remove the Disguise

3. Try Eyeballing

When you're ready, complete one of your Practice Tests, then come back to this chapter to polish the skills you need. Good luck!

UNIT 3: READING

The Basics:

35 Minutes

40 Questions

4 Passages

Pacing:

Pace your time per passage as opposed to per question.

Plan to spend a little over eight minutes per passage, including reading and answering the questions. The exact pacing is eight minutes and 45 seconds per passage.

TEST DAY DIRECTIONS AND FORMAT

Here's what the Reading directions will say on Test Day:

Directions: There are four passages in this test. Each passage is followed by several questions. After reading a passage, choose the best answer to each question and fill in the corresponding oval on your answer document. You may refer to the passages as often as necessary.

OUTSIDE KNOWLEDGE

No outside knowledge is required. The answers to every question can be found in the passage.

THE INSIDE SCOOP

The ACT Reading test always has the same four passage types in the same order. You can expect to see—in order—Prose Fiction, Social Science, Humanities, and Natural Science passages. Each passage is about 1,000 words in length (or a pair of two shorter passages that add up to about 1,000 words) and written at the same level of complexity as typical college textbooks and readings.

The nonfiction passages (Social Science, Humanities, and Natural Science) are written with a clear purpose that you are expected to understand. You'll also need to comprehend specific facts relayed in these essays and the use of structure.

The Prose Fiction passage asks you to focus more on the thoughts, feelings, and motivations of fictional characters, even when these are not explicitly stated in the passage.

The questions *do not* get harder as you proceed through the test.

SMARTPOINTS

Point Value	Topic	Basics Page	Details and Practice
12	**Detail**		
8	**Inference**		
8	**Generalization**		
6	**Function**		
1	**Vocab-in-Context**		
1	**Writer's View**		

CHAPTER 8

Reading Part 1: Inside the ACT Reading Test

THE KAPLAN METHOD FOR ACT READING

STEP 1: ACTIVELY READ THE PASSAGE, TAKING NOTES AS YOU GO.

Active reading is the process of asking yourself questions while reading. It's faster than a careful, full read, and slightly slower than a skim. The idea is to quickly get a sense of the big picture of the passage. What's the gist? What's the author's purpose? Remember you're not reading this for fun—you're going to be asked questions about this content, so be ahead of the game by asking yourself what you're reading while you read. Don't get bogged down in the details—you can come back to those if the questions call for it. The passage isn't going anywhere, it's an open-book test. Here are some questions to ask yourself: Why did the author write this paragraph? How does it contribute to the purpose of the passage as a whole?

Next, take brief notes next to each paragraph on what you find from your questioning process. Again, details don't matter at this stage. This isn't meant to be a full outline, but a road map of the passage to guide you once you get to the questions. Find the *purpose* of each paragraph, then jot it in the margins in 3–5 words to create your *Passage Map*. Stick to that word limit, and think of these notes as labels to remind you of what each paragraph contains, to help you find information when you get to the questions. Focus on getting the purpose and themes down, as they are much harder to locate on a quick search.

STEP 2: EXAMINE THE QUESTION STEM, LOOKING FOR CLUES.

Analyze what the question stem is asking. What type of question is this? Most questions use typical phrasing to let you know if they're asking for details, or a purpose, or an inference. Refer to the particular SmartPoints—breaking down each question type—in Reading Part 2 for examples of these phrases. Now, think about the question stem without looking at the answer choices. Be disciplined; avoid the trap of misleading answers by not looking at any answers until you're fully ready. First, look for line references. If the question stem has one, great! Do your research by looking back at that part of the passage, *even if you feel like you remember it*. Remember to check your map for the big picture of the paragraph and read around the line to collect any details you need. If there is no line reference, that passage map will be invaluable—use it to help you locate what you need. Don't rely on your memory here; you don't get extra points for answering without double-checking. If the question is asking for details, locate those in the passage using the line reference or your map. If the question is asking for bigger-picture information, use the map you've created containing this information.

STEP 3: PREDICT THE ANSWER AND SELECT THE CHOICE THAT BEST MATCHES YOUR PREDICTION.

Don't look yet. Now that you've completed your research, you can save yourself time and avoid the temptation of wrong answer choices by forming a prediction of the answer before you peek at the given answer choices. Based on your work in Step 2, state in your own words what you think the answer will be. You'll do so by focusing your attention on the words in the passage. This will help you avoid tempting wrong answers that have less to do with the passage, and tempting wrong answers that present other details from the passage that are unrelated to this particular question. Finally, by having a prediction in your head, you'll be able to simply look for an answer choice that matches, instead of having to read and analyze all four choices equally. Evaluating each answer can be a very time-consuming practice on the ACT Reading test, and by predicting, you'll greatly increase your efficiency.

Predict before you peek!

Note: This method is a huge part of increasing your score on Test Day, but it will take some practice to master it and make it the extremely effective test-taking tool it can be. Thus, we'll discuss it further and give you a chance to practice in the Method Breakdown section, later in this chapter on page 185.

QUICK TIPS

MIND-SET

- **Know where the passage is going.** Read the passages actively, and pay attention to structural clues and key words and sentences to predict and evaluate what the passage is "doing." The easiest way to do this is to create a passage map.

- **Conquer the questions.** Look up the answers directly in the passage; don't be tempted by the choices or your memory.

- **Start with your strengths.** There's no reason to tackle these passages in the order given. Which subject interests you the most? Do you want to do that one first, or last? Do you prefer fiction? Science stuff? Passages about people? Get yourself on a roll by starting with the passage that is easiest for you to build confidence and bank your time.

SPECIAL STRATEGIES

THE PROSE FICTION PASSAGE

Pay attention to the characters, especially the main character, and who gets the most (or best) lines. Read between the lines to determine unspoken emotions and attitudes. Ask yourself:

- **Who are these people?** What are they like? How do the characters relate to each other?

- **What is their state of mind?** Are they angry, sad, reflective, excited?

- **What's going on?** What's happening on the surface? What's happening beneath the surface?

- **What is the author's attitude toward the characters?** What words indicate a particular tone? Do any phrases suggest the author is either approving of or critical of one of the characters?

NONFICTION PASSAGES

- **Don't be thrown by unfamiliar vocabulary or topics.** The Natural Science passage may take you into strange territory, but remember: this is the Reading test, not the Science test. Everything you need to know will be covered in the passages. If you find a difficult term, odds are the definition will be given to you in context (or else it simply might not matter what the word means). You can get most questions right even if you don't fully understand the passage. Remember, you can find all the answers in the passage.

TIMING: PACING AND APPROACH

Take a few seconds at the beginning of the subject test to flip through the four passages, gauging the difficulty of each. Start with the one that best suits your strengths and interests.

Treat each passage and its questions as a block. You have just under nine minutes per block. Spend the first three minutes on your active reading and passage mapping. Use the remaining time researching and answering the questions. Within each block, feel free to skip around and answer the easy questions first. Just make sure to keep track of time so you get to all the questions.

Set your watch to 12:00 at the beginning of the subject test. Although you should go faster if you can, here's roughly where you should be at the following checkpoints:

12:09. . . . . One passage finished and answers gridded in

12:18. . . . . Two passages finished and answers gridded in

12:27. . . . . Three passages finished and answers gridded in

12:35. . . . . Four passages finished and answers for entire section gridded in

Take about 30 seconds (average) per question. Some questions take more time than others (ones with Roman numerals in them and ones that have EXCEPT are examples—these will take longer either to research or to work through and eliminate). So remember, if you feel the need to spend a lot of time to get the right answer, don't. Either guess, or skip and come back. (Don't forget to do come back, though.)

Don't panic if you can't finish all four passages. Make sure you do a good job on at least three passages—and remember to grid answers (even if they're blind guesses) for all questions by the end. You can get in the mid to high 20s just by doing a great job on three passages. Even if you try all four passages, you probably won't really work on all 40 questions. For many questions, you'll have to guess. Just make sure you guess on the tough ones and actually work on the easy ones!

WHEN YOU'RE RUNNING OUT OF TIME

If you have less than five minutes left for the last passage, do the following:

1. **Look for questions with specific line references and do them.**

2. **Refer to the cited location in the passage and answer the question as best you can, based on what you see there.**

3. **Make sure you have gridded-in an answer for every question before time is called.**

SCORING

Your performance on the Reading subject test will be averaged into your ACT Composite Score, weighted equally with your scores on the other three subject tests. You will also receive:

- Reading subject score (1 to 36) for the entire Reading subject test

- Social Science/Sciences subscore (1 to 18) based on your performance on the nonfiction passages drawn from Social Studies and Natural Sciences

- Arts/Literature subscore (1 to 18) based on your performance on the nonfiction passage (drawn from the Humanities) and on the Prose Fiction passage

SMARTPOINT BREAKDOWN

Here is a brief overview of what exactly to expect and how much of it you should be expecting.

DETAIL QUESTIONS—12 POINTS

Extremely Important

Detail questions will ask you about specific points in the passage. These questions are very straightforward; you won't have to draw a conclusion or make an interpretation, just locate the particular detail in the passage and match it to an answer choice. Sometimes the correct answer choice even uses virtually the same wording found in the passage. At other times, the correct answer is a paraphrase of the wording from the passage. For further discussion on detail questions, and the question stem clues that you're dealing with a detail question, turn to page 183.

INFERENCE QUESTIONS—8 POINTS

Very Important

Inference questions ask you to read between the lines—you'll need to take the next logical step to discover what is implied or suggested by the author. Though you will have to draw a conclusion not directly stated in the passage, be careful not to assume that these questions are a matter of opinion. You will not have to make a wild guess; the correct answer will be logically necessary based on what is stated in the passage, and can best be answered by sticking close to the explicit meaning in the text. Turn to page 201 for discussion and practice with Inference questions, as well as the question stem clues used for this question type.

GENERALIZATION QUESTIONS—8 POINTS

Very Important

Generalization questions ask you to draw conclusions based on larger portions of or the whole passage. You'll need to understand the big picture, as the scope can include whole paragraphs, all of the beginning, middle, or end, or even the passage in its entirety. Make sure to keep the overall purpose of the passage in mind to answer these questions. Your passage map will be extremely helpful here, showing you how parts of the passage relate to other parts. For further discussion on these questions and the phrases in the question stems that indicate them, turn to page 206.

FUNCTION QUESTIONS—6 POINTS

Important

Function questions ask you to understand the purpose of an essay's structure or order. Specifically, you'll need to interpret why the author used a particular word, phrase, or detail in the passage. Look for the logical flow of a piece to find the correct answer. How does the part referenced fit into that flow? Is it a transition? Does it establish a relationship, such as cause and effect or contrast? You'll need to keep in mind the author's overall purpose to properly answer these questions. Turn to page 203 for more discussion on strategies for this question type, and the question stem hints associated with it.

VOCAB-IN-CONTEXT QUESTIONS—1 POINT

Less Important

Vocab-in-Context questions ask you to interpret the meaning of a specific word or phrase used in the passage. As implied in the name of the question type, you won't need to bring any outside knowledge of dictionary definitions to answer these questions. In fact, on the ACT they don't often ask about the bigger words you might not recognize. Instead, these questions focus on commonly used words with multiple meanings. You'll have to use the passage to decipher which meaning of the word is most appropriate to the passage. So don't think of these as "Vocab" questions, but as "Context" questions. Page 200 has more strategy discussion for this question type, and the typical question stems associated with Vocab-in-Context questions.

WRITER'S VIEW QUESTIONS—1 POINT

Less Important

Writer's View questions ask you to interpret the intentions or opinions of the author. Because this is often explicit in the nonfiction passages, these questions are mostly found after the

Prose Fiction passage. You'll need to take the author's perspective to determine the general attitude felt toward a character or event. Be careful not to confuse what the *characters* think about each other with what the *author* thinks. For strategies to deal with this question type, and question stem hints associated with Writer's View questions, turn to page 204.

METHOD BREAKDOWN

Active reading and **passage mapping**, the parts that form Step 1 of the Kaplan Method for ACT Reading, are essential techniques to practice to become a master of the Reading test. This method can earn you a great score increase all by itself if you can use it effectively.

Thus, without any outside knowledge to review, we'll use this section to really dive into the Kaplan method.

We'll thoroughly touch on the pieces of Step 1 mentioned: active reading and passage mapping. You'll be able to see exactly how to use this step of the method to full effect. Then, we'll see how it makes the next two steps of the method (answering the questions) that much easier.

Finally, you'll get a chance to practice it all, before we move on to Reading Part 2 and the details on the specific SmartPoints.

Let's get started!

ACTIVE READING

Read *actively* to quickly get a sense of the purpose or main idea of the passage and see how everything fits together to support that main idea. You read *actively* by continually asking yourself questions about what you're reading, trying to get behind the purpose and choices of the passage and the author, rather than focusing on details that may or may not be asked about. Look for the general outline of the passage—determine how it's structured. Don't worry about the details. You'll come back for those later. You're not reading slowly and carefully, and you're also not skimming. You're searching for the purpose and the main idea. The process is more like a treasure hunt than a typical read.

Fast, active reading, of course, requires more mental energy than slow, passive reading, but it pays off. Those who dwell on details—who passively let the passage reveal itself at its own pace—are sure to run out of time. Don't be that kind of reader! Make the passage reveal itself to you on *your* schedule, by skimming the passage with an eye to structure rather than detail. Look for key words that tell you what the author is doing so you can save yourself time. For instance, read "example" sentences very quickly, just glancing over the words. When an author says "for example," you know that what follows is an example of a general point. Do you need to understand that specific example? Maybe, maybe not. If you do, you can come back and read it when you're attacking the questions. If you *don't* need to know the example for any of the questions, great! You haven't wasted much time on something that won't get you a point.

You actually do this kind of "reading" all the time, and not just when you're reading a book or newspaper. When you watch TV or see a movie, for instance, you can often figure out much of what's going to happen in advance. You see the bad guys run out of a bank with bags of money in their hands, and you can guess that the next thing they'll do is get into a car and drive away in excess of the speed limit. You see a character in an old sitcom bragging to his friends about how great a driver he is, and you know that he's bound to get into a fender bender before the next commercial. **This ability to know where something is going is very valuable. Use it on the ACT.**

To help you know where an author is going, pay careful attention to structural clues. Words like *but, nevertheless*, and *moreover* help you get a sense of where a piece of writing is going. Look for signal phrases (like *clearly, as a result,* or *no one can deny that*) to determine the logic of the passage. These are the same words and phrases described under the Connections SmartPoint in the English test. When you spot these words in a passage, underline them. They provide important clues about the author's purpose and the structure of the passage. Refer to the following table for a list of these words and the type of connections they build:

KEY WORDS THAT INDICATE CAUSE AND EFFECT AND CONTRAST

Cause and Effect	Contrast
as a result	but
as shown by	claims (may suggest that a "claim" isn't)
because	difference
consequently	however
evidence shows	in contrast
for this reason	nevertheless
it follows that	on the other hand
so	some…others
therefore	whereas
thus	while

Of course, the words in the table don't form an exhaustive list, but they do give you an idea of the kinds of words to pay attention to when you need to determine the logical flow and notice what contrasts the writer presents. One thing to notice is that these words are not subject-specific. This is precisely why connections words and phrases are so important. They show up repeatedly in all three nonfiction ACT passages, no matter what topic the passage discusses. You can't predict the exact content of the passages you'll see on Test Day, but you can be certain that cause-and-effect and contrast words and phrases will be present and crucial to your understanding of the passage.

Finding how the pieces fit together is a big step. Use key words to help you spot the structure and the purpose more quickly. Focus on the main idea. How do these puzzle pieces connect? What picture forms when you put them together? The details, remember, you can come back for later, when you're doing the questions. **What's important in reading the passage is getting a sense of how those details fit together to express the point or points of the passage.**

PASSAGE MAPPING

As you actively read, it's important to take notes in the margins. When first trying this, students often figure it will take extra time—obviously reading *and writing things down* takes longer than just reading alone. But having notes saves you far more time when answering questions than it takes during the reading time. Try it out and see! You should organize your notes by paragraph, and write 3–5 words on the purpose of each. Use the active reading process and those transition words to help you find this purpose quickly.

You may be wondering, wouldn't it be quicker simply to underline a few words in the passage? Underlining is possibly a little quicker, but there's a danger involved—if you read through a paragraph thinking you'll underline what's important, you may find yourself underlining too many details. On the other hand, when you read each paragraph with the goal of determining the author's purpose for that paragraph, there's a certain discipline involved. The mental processing required to decide on a note to jot down in the margin is more likely to help you develop a good overall understanding of the passage. Writing a quick note in your own words in the margin is a more active approach than simply underlining words that are already there.

So find the purpose, and write it down. Give yourself a visual guide to the passage while keeping your brain active. You'll understand it better and more quickly this way. You'll also have reference points to what information is where in the passage when you get to the questions, and need to look back to find those details.

Find how the pieces fit, and label those pieces.

Here are some examples of what the purpose of the paragraphs might be:

TYPES OF PURPOSE:

State the Thesis

Establish the Tone

Provide a Supporting Argument

Provide Evidence

Give an Opinion

Provide a Counter-argument

Give the Backstory or History

That is by no means a comprehensive list, but is a guide to common types of purpose you might find. Note that you should never just write "establish the tone" if you've discovered that to be the purpose of a paragraph. It may well be the purpose, but you should write in your map what that tone actually is—scholarly, personal, humorous, angry, whatever you find it to be. Similarly, what is the opinion or thesis you've spotted? Look for these categories, jot down what it is that fits into them.

TWO PARTS, ONE STEP

Active Reading and Passage Mapping actually go hand-in-hand, both part of the same process. Here's a step-by-step guide summarizing how to effectively go about Step 1 of the Kaplan Method for ACT Reading:

1. Focus on the big picture. Note the purpose of each paragraph, and don't get bogged down in details.

2. Pay close attention to the first and last paragraphs. They often give great clues for determining the purpose of the passage as a whole.

3. Notice phrasing that indicates an example, such as *an illustration of, for example, for instance, this can be seen when,* or *to illustrate.* Remember that the example is a detail, but the general statement or principle it's illustrating is more general and could be a main idea.

4. Ask yourself questions as you read:

   a. What is the writer's purpose? Is he merely describing and explaining, or does he try to persuade the reader? Notice whether the writer is taking a side on an issue.

   b. What is the tone of the passage? Do you notice any phrasing that is approving, critical, or sarcastic?

   c. What is the internal logic of the passage? Do you notice features of a chronological structure or an outline structure or some of each?

5. Read for contrast, noting when the writer points out differences and contradictions. Pay attention to connection words and phrases that show contrast, such as *although, appears, but, despite, even though, however, in spite of, on the other hand, though,* and *yet.*

6. Notice where and when the writer states an opinion.

7. Notice where and when the writer makes an argument. What point is the evidence supporting? Notice words that direct the flow of an argument such as *as a result, because, consequently, resulting in, therefore,* or *thus.*

TRY IT OUT!

Now that you know how to read actively and create a passage map, put those skills together on an ACT Reading passage. Afterwards, we'll review what your notes could have been. Keep in mind that our suggestions are just a guide. If yours are slightly different, but you still found the purpose, fantastic!

PASSAGE I

By the tenth century most of northern Europe was divided into farming units known as manors…

Line
(5) Almost always a manor comprised four parts: arable, meadow, waste, and the village area itself. The arable was of course the land which grew the crops on which the inhabitants of the manor subsisted. To maintain fertility and keep down weeds it
(10) was necessary to fallow a part of the cultivated land each year. It was, therefore, usual (though not universal) to divide the arable into three fields. One such field was planted with winter grain, a second with spring
(15) grain, and the third left fallow; the following year, the fallow field would be planted with winter grain, the field in which winter grain had been raised was planted with spring grain, and the third field left fallow.
(20) By following such a rotation, the cycle was completed every three years. Since the fallow field had to be plowed twice in the year in order to keep down the weeds, and the others had to be plowed once, work for the
(25) plow teams extended almost throughout the year. Plowing stopped only at times when all hands were needed to bring in the harvest, or when the soil was too wet to be plowed, or was frozen. The amount
(30) of land that could be tilled was fixed fairly definitely by the number of plows and plow teams that the manor could muster; and official documents sometimes estimated the wealth and value of a manor in terms of the
(35) number of plows it possessed.

The three great fields lay open, without fences, but were subdivided into numerous small strips (often one acre in size, i.e., the amount of one day's plowing) which
(40) individual peasants "owned." The strips belonging to any one individual were scattered through the three fields in different parts, perhaps in order to assure that each peasant would have strips plowed
(45) early and late, in fertile and infertile parts of the arable land.

Custom severely restricted the individual's rights over his land. The time for plowing and planting was fixed by custom
(50) and each peasant had to conform, since he needed his neighbor's help to plow his strips and they needed his. Uniform cropping was imperative, since on a given day the village animals were turned into the fields to graze
(55) after the harvest had been gathered, and if some individual planted a crop which did not ripen as early as that of his neighbors, he had no means of defending his field from the hungry animals. If his crop ripened
(60) sooner, on the other hand, it could not be garnered without trampling neighboring fields. Moreover, the very idea of innovation was lacking: men did what custom prescribed, cooperated in the plowing and
(65) to some extent in the harvesting, and for many generations did not dream of trying to change.

The meadow was almost as important as the arable for the economy of the village.
(70) Hay from the meadow supported the indispensable draught animals through the winter. The idea that hay might be sown did not occur to men in medieval times; consequently they were compelled to rely on
(75) natural meadows alone. One result was that in many manors, shortage of winter fodder

for the plow teams was a constant danger. It was common practice to feed oxen on leaves picked from trees, and on straw from the (80) grain harvest; but despite such supplements the draught animals often nearly starved in winter. In some cases, oxen actually had to be carried out from their winter stalls to spring pastures until some of their strength (85) was recovered and plowing could begin. Thus on many manors, meadow land was even more valuable than the arable and was divided into much smaller strips (often the width of a scythe stroke).

(90)   The waste provided summer pasture for various animals of the manor: pigs, geese, cattle, and sheep. The animals of the whole manor normally grazed together under the watchful eyes of some young children or (95) other attendants who could keep them from wandering too far afield, and bring them back to the village at night. The waste also was the source of wood for fuel and for building purposes, and helped to supplement (100) the food supply with such things as nuts, berries, honey, and rabbits…

The fourth segment of the manor was the village itself, usually located in the center of the arable near a source of (105) drinking water, and perhaps along a road or path or footpath leading to the outside world. The cottages of medieval peasants were extremely humble, usually consisting of a single room, with earthen floor (110) and thatched roof. Around each cottage normally lay a small garden in which various vegetables and sometimes fruit trees were planted. In the village streets, chickens, ducks, and dogs picked up a precarious (115) living.

STEP 1: ACTIVELY READ THE PASSAGE, TAKING NOTES AS YOU GO.

Here's a sample Passage Map. Yours might be similar, but remember, differences are fine as long as you found the purpose for yourself.

Paragraph 1: Intro to Manors

Paragraph 2: Describe Arable, part of manor with crops. Seasonal planting cycles

Paragraph 3: Arable divided into 3 great fields, divided into strips.

Paragraph 4: Custom confined freedoms, limited innovation

Paragraph 5: Describe Meadow. Source of hay for animals, run short in the winter

Paragraph 6: Describe Waste. Summer pasture, source of wood.

Paragraph 7: Describe Village. Near water with small cottages.

How close were you? Did you remember to help yourself find the purpose of each paragraph by underlining transition words?

Now, get ready. It's time to use that map on the next steps of the method, to help you start earning those points.

STEP 2: EXAMINE THE QUESTION STEM, LOOKING FOR CLUES

Approaching the Reading questions requires self-discipline. Most test takers have an almost irresistible urge to immediately jump to the answer choices to see what "looks okay." That's not a good idea. Don't peek at the answer choices—there are too many ways to be led astray by tempting "almost" answers.

Read the question stem to identify what the test is asking. Which of the following is it about?

- A detail (what happened)

- The passage as a whole (the big idea)

- An inference (reading between the lines)

- A specific word or phrase used in the passage

Analyzing what the question stem is asking is very important, because the ACT will offer you choices that don't answer the question at hand. It is easy to get the right answer—if you know what you are looking for.

How do you know what you're looking for? There will be clues in the question stem. These clues could be as straightforward as a line reference or as vague as the phrase "as stated in the passage." In both cases, though, you know that you'll be able to find the answer in the passage.

This is where your notes come in handy.

On most questions, you won't be able to remember exactly what the passage said about the matter in question. That's okay. In fact, even if you do think you remember, don't trust your memory. Instead refer to the passage and your passage map. Your notes are all waiting to help you find the answers to the 10 questions, and to help you find the right spot in the passage.

STEP 3: PREDICT THE ANSWER AND SELECT THE CHOICE THAT BEST MATCHES YOUR PREDICTION

It's extremely important in Reading to **make a habit of answering the question in your own words** (based on your checking of the passage) *before* looking at the answer choices. Predict before you peek. Most students waste enormous amounts of time thinking about answer choices in Reading. If you do that, you'll **never** finish, and you'll get so confused you'll probably get more questions wrong.

Once you have an answer in your head based on what you've read, and have rechecked in the passage, match it to one of the answer choices. Avoid trying to see if they "look right." You wouldn't answer "1.5" on the Math test if you knew the answer was "2." 1.5 isn't "almost" 2. Don't settle for "almost" answers on the Reading test either.

Practice Steps 2 and 3. Use the following question stems to find the information you need and form a prediction.

The questions will then be repeated with the answer choices, but get in the habit of researching and predicting before you look.

QUESTIONS

1. The description of the near starvation of the oxen (lines 82–85) serves to:
   _____
   _____

2. According to the passage, the fact that the peasants' individual strips of land were unfenced subdivisions of larger fields required each peasant to:
   _____
   _____

3. According to the second paragraph (lines 4–35), the fallow part of the arable had to be plowed a total of how many times in any given calendar year?
   _____

4. The passage suggests that the practice of peasants owning strips "scattered through the three fields in different parts" (lines 42–43) was instituted in order to:
   _____
   _____

5. On the basis of the information in the passage, it may be inferred that people in medieval times did not think of sowing hay because:
   _____
   _____

6. As it is used in line 61, the word *garnered* means:
   _____
   _____

7. According to the passage, if one of the arable's three great fields were left fallow one year, it would be:
   _____
   _____

8. Which of the following conclusions is suggested by the fourth paragraph (lines 47–67)?
   _____
   _____

9. According to the passage, a manor's value might be judged according to the number of its plows because:
   _____
   _____

10. According to the passage, summer pasture for a manor's geese would be provided:
    _____
    _____

1. The description of the near starvation of the oxen (lines 82–85) serves to:

   A. demonstrate how difficult life on the manor was in tenth century northern Europe.

   B. showcase how important work animals were to medieval manors.

   C. emphasize how important natural meadows were to feeding the work animals.

   D. explain why uniform cropping was a critical practice that ensured survival on the medieval manor.

2. According to the passage, the fact that the peasants' individual strips of land were un-fenced subdivisions of larger fields required each peasant to:

   F. follow a fixed planting schedule so as to be able to harvest crops at the same time as the other peasants.

   G. harvest crops independently of his neighbors.

   H. limit the size of strips to what could be plowed in a single day.

   J. maintain small garden plots in order to provide his family with enough food.

3. According to the second paragraph (lines 4–35), the fallow part of the arable had to be plowed a total of how many times in any given calendar year?

   A. One

   B. Two

   C. Four

   D. Six

4. The passage suggests that the practice of peasants owning strips "scattered through the three fields in different parts" (lines 42–43) was instituted in order to:

   F. divide resources fairly evenly.

   G. preserve the wealth of elite landowners.

   H. protect the three fields from overuse.

   J. force neighbors to work only their own lands.

5. On the basis of the information in the passage, it may be inferred that people in medieval times did not think of sowing hay because:

   A. hay sowing had not been done in the past.

   B. the need for more hay was not great enough to warrant the extra work.

   C. northern Europeans did not yet have the necessary farming techniques for successful hay cultivation.

   D. the tight schedule of cultivating the arable meant that the peasants had no time to cultivate extra crops.

6. As it is used in line 61, the word *garnered* means:

   F. planted.

   G. watered.

   H. gathered.

   J. plowed.

7. According to the passage, if one of the arable's three great fields were left fallow one year, it would be:

   A. left fallow for two more years in succession.

   B. planted the next year with winter grain only.

   C. planted the next year with spring grain only.

   D. planted with either winter or spring grain the next year.

8. Which of the following conclusions is suggested by the fourth paragraph (lines 47–67)?

    I. An individual was free to cultivate his own land in any way he wished.

    II. The manor was run according to tradition.

    III. Successful farming required cooperative methods.

F. I and II only

G. I and III only

H. II and III only

J. I, II, and III

9. According to the passage, a manor's value might be judged according to the number of its plows because:

A. the more plows a manor had, the less land had to be left fallow.

B. plows, while not in themselves valuable, symbolized great wealth.

C. manors with sufficient plows could continue plowing throughout the year.

D. the number of plows a manor owned determined how much land could be cultivated.

10. According to the passage, summer pasture for a manor's geese would be provided:

F. next to cottages, within the village.

G. on the fallow field of the arable.

H. on the communal ground of the waste.

J. on the whole of the meadow.

Now, take a look at the answers to see how you did.

KEY TO PASSAGE I

(NONFICTION—SOCIAL STUDIES)

	Answer	Refer to	Type	Comments
1.	C	Lines 68–89	Function	The entire paragraph supports this claim.
2.	F	Lines 52–59	Detail	"Uniform cropping was imperative…"
3.	B	Lines 21–23	Detail	Don't confuse fallow with planted fields.
4.	F	Lines 43–46	Inference	Every peasant got some fertile and some infertile land—inferably, to be fair to each
5.	A	Lines 62–67, 72–75	Inference	No line reference, so you had to have a sense of the structure to find this.
6.	H	Lines 59–62	Vocab-in-Context	Use context. The crop is ripe, so it must be ready to be gathered.
7.	B	Lines 13–19	Detail	No line reference; otherwise, no problem.
8.	H	Lines 47–67	Inference	I: lines 47–52 say the opposite II: lines 48–52 III: lines 52–62 Statement I is false, so that means (F), (G), and (J) are wrong. That means (H) must be the answer.
9.	D	Lines 33–35	Detail	No line reference; number of plows = amount of land.
10.	H	Lines 90–92	Detail	Whole paragraph devoted to describing waste.

Get comfortable with this method. It might slow you down at first, but with time, it will make you a master of the ACT Reading test. Keep at it!

SUMMARY

In this chapter, we talked about the overall strategy necessary to master the ACT Reading test.

You learned how to **actively read** by asking questions as you go and focusing on the big picture. You learned how to **passage map** by finding the purpose and labeling each paragraph with 3–5 word notations. Remember to use transition words to help you put the pieces together.

After your map is complete, examine the question stem, then find the information you need in the passage. If it's a Detail question, the answer will be waiting for you. Use a line reference or your map to help you locate it. If it's not, use your passage map to help you get the broad sense of purpose necessary to draw whatever conclusion you need. Finally, predict the answer to save time and avoid traps. Only then should you look at the answer choices.

Practice this method. Then, keep practicing it. By learning how to actively read effectively, and passage map efficiently, you'll be able to maintain the speed necessary on the ACT Reading passages while still understanding what you need to earn points when you get to the questions.

Keep practicing, and work on the individual question types in the next chapter to help you refine your approach and get the score you covet.

CHAPTER 9

Reading Part 2: ACT Reading Strategy In Depth

OVERVIEW

Use this chapter to get familiar with all of the question types on the ACT Reading test. They are detailed and discussed fully, with examples provided for each. On the Reading test, each question type has certain key phrases repeated in the question stems. We'll review those phrases to help you easily recognize what type of question you're dealing with. Then use the samples to master the specific strategies for each question type. To get a quick sense of what's to come, refer to the SmartPoint Breakdown in the previous chapter (page 183). There, they are discussed in order of Test Day weight. The more heavily tested SmartPoints are listed there first. That's also how you should prioritize your time, especially if you are short on time or close to your goal score. However, the SmartPoints in this chapter are discussed in order of building complexity. We'll discuss the less complex questions first, as the knowledge necessary for those often builds to the conclusions you'll need to draw for more complex questions. If you have time, and want to thoroughly exercise your Reading skill set, start at the beginning and work your way through.

The following SmartPoints are shown in order of building complexity, SmartPoint by SmartPoint.

DETAILS—12 POINTS

Complexity: Low. Can be directly drawn from the passage without the need for interpretation or drawing conclusions.

A *detail* is a specific piece of information.

Detail questions will ask you about individual pieces of the passage. They are designed to test your basic understanding of what you read and ability to find information within the passage. This is far and away the biggest SmartPoint on the ACT Reading test, but remember you don't need to read for or memorize details; they're not going anywhere, as the ACT is an open-book test. Get a basic understanding as you read, to take care of that aspect of the question. As for the primary part of these questions—recalling specific information from the passage—don't rely on your memory! You won't need to map for details or remember them. When you notice a Detail question, just look up the answer in the passage.

But how do you know you're looking at a Detail question? Look for these phrases in the question stem:

Question Stem Indicators

- *As stated in the passage…*

- *According to the author…*

- *According to the passage…*

- *The passage states that…*

- *The writer states that…*

- *All of the following are cited in the passage EXCEPT…*

What all of these phrases have in common is that they refer you back to the passage, and they ask about something that is stated directly, rather than something that is implied.

STRATEGY

Although Detail questions are easy to answer when you know where in the passage to look, it can be challenging to locate the part of the passage that contains the answer. Therefore, it's important to take good notes for your passage map. Again, passage map notes should not include specific details but instead should note the location of details. For example, if a paragraph discusses the career of an artist, don't take notes about specific paintings and critical reactions. Instead, write a short note that describes the general purpose of the paragraph, such as *early career—critics admired*.

Each ACT Reading passage includes many details, but the test presents only 10 questions for each passage. Knowing this means many of the details in each passage will not be relevant to any of the questions. You simply won't need to know them all. So *focus on the big picture* as you read. Do *not* try to guess which details will show up in the questions.

Counterintuitive as it may seem, the best way to score points on Detail questions is by not getting too wrapped up in the details on your first read-through of the passage.

If you're attacking the questions and have difficulty locating a particular detail, don't sweat it. Just circle the question number in your test booklet and make an initial guess. If you have time before the section ends, you can come back to the circled question. Remember you don't have to answer every single question correctly to get a good score. This is especially important to keep in mind for Detail questions. Do your best, but don't obsess. No single question is worth more of your time than any other is.

Two important points to keep in mind:

1. There is one right answer, but there will be other tempting answers. Don't be tempted by "almost" answers. Find the *right* one.

2. "Refer to the passage" in the Reading directions is good advice, since you're not trying to memorize. Predict before you peek! That is, predict in your own words, or by pointing to a specific phrase in the passage, what you think the answer will be before you look at the choices provided.

Then, finish these questions off by matching the detail from the text in the passage with the correct answer. Locate either similar words or paraphrasing.

Note: Many wrong choices will be designed to trip you up by including details from other parts of the passage or by using the same wording as the passage while distorting the meaning. Questions on the ACT Reading test are written to have three wrong answers and *only* one right answer. Some answer choices may appear to be half-right, half-wrong; remember, if an answer choice has *anything* wrong with it, it is not the correct answer! Look for the one choice that is *flawless*.

Typical wrong answer choices on this question type are:

Misused Details: This is the most common wrong answer on Detail questions. It will tempt you by pulling information directly from the passage. However, that information will not answer this particular question. Use Step 2 before you peek to predict and find the information that *does* answer the question. Your prediction won't match misused details, so you'll be able to avoid this trap.

Distortions: This answer choice uses a detail with a twist. It almost matches what's in the passage, but it changes the details a little bit by combining two of them in an inaccurate way, or combining a detail in the passage with something else entirely. Thus, the almost-right details become distorted into something entirely wrong. Again, by researching in Step 2 and predicting, you'll have an idea of what is right before you peek at the choices, and you'll be much less likely to fall for the misleading wording of distorted choices.

Don't worry about identifying wrong answer choices. You're not there to decide whether a wrong answer is a distortion or a misused detail. Your job is to find the right answer. It just helps to be aware of how the ACT will attempt to lead you away from that answer.

VOCAB-IN-CONTEXT—1 POINT

Complexity: Low. You'll need to make a light interpretation to determine meaning.

As the question type implies, *Vocab-In-Context* questions ask about a word or phrase, but asks about it *as it's used in context*. Your task is to deduce the meaning of that word or phrase as it pertains to the surrounding passage. Thus, to properly answer these questions, you must use the context of the passage.

This question type is infrequent. You'll probably only see between 1 and 3 on Test Day. However, they are easy to spot and usually easy to answer quickly once you know the strategies. Because of this, always look for Vocab-In-Context questions and try to answer them. If you have to guess on any question, guess on a harder question that would take you more time to answer. Make use of any Vocab-In-Context questions you find in order to rack up a few easy points quickly.

So how do you recognize Vocab-In-Context questions? The clues here are simple to spot.

Question Stem Indicators

Phrases indicating meaning or definitions, such as…

- …*most nearly means*…

- …*can most closely be defined as*…

A leading phrase such as…

- *As it is used in the passage,…refers to…*

The word or phrase is always printed in italics, and a line reference is always provided.

STRATEGY

1. Look back to the line referenced by the question stem, and pretend the word you're looking to define is actually a blank in the sentence.

2. Read the sentence and look for clues to help you determine what word or phrase would make sense in the blank. Use that word or phrase as your prediction for this question.

3. Look at the answer choices and choose the one closest to your prediction.

Here are some more points to help you with Vocab-In-Context questions:

- Do *not* skip the prediction step! Words used for Vocab-In-Context questions are often chosen because they have more than one meaning. The most common or first meaning that comes to mind is not necessarily the appropriate meaning in the context of the passage. As its name suggests, Vocab-In-Context questions rely on the context of words as used in *this* passage.

- Occasionally, predicting is tough: You may not find any clues within the sentence where the word is used. If that's the case, look at the sentences before and after it. In nearly every case, one of these sentences contains specific clue words to let you predict the meaning of the "blank."

- Connections words and phrases are often the key to making your prediction. Pay particular attention to words such as *yet, but,* and *however.* These contrast clues may tell you that your prediction should be the opposite of another word that's used in the sentence.

Again, the words most frequently tested in this type are common words with multiple meanings, not complex or rare words. Thus, your task is much more about finding context from the passage as opposed to figuring out the definition of a word.

Typical wrong answer choices for this question are other definitions for the tested word.

The most common definition is usually wrong, but it will be among the answer choices. Avoid this trap by using the context of the passage and predicting!

INFERENCE—8 POINTS

Complexity: Medium. You will need to make conclusions about a small part of the passage.

An *inference* is an unstated conclusion reached by the evidence of stated information. An inference is something that **must** be true, based on what is stated. Not just **can** or **might** be true, but **must**.

Inference questions are the next logical step from Detail questions. Detail questions just ask you to find or know small pieces of information. Inference questions take those same small pieces of the passage, but ask you to know what they logically must mean. The idea is to test your ability to read between the lines.

You'll be able to recognize that you're dealing with Inference questions from the following question stem indicators:

Question Stem Indicators

- *It may be inferred from lines…*

- *The author implies…*

- *The phrase…suggests…*

- *The author suggests…*

- *It is most reasonable to infer…*

- *…most directly supports the conclusion…*

Infer, imply, suggest, and *conclude* are key words to look for.

STRATEGY

You may be tempted to think that such questions are a matter of opinion, that *anything* could be implied, but this is not the case. Although it's true that Inference questions, unlike Detail questions, ask you to draw a conclusion that's not directly stated in the passage, the correct answer to an Inference question will not be a huge logical step away from what is stated in the passage. In other words, to answer an Inference question correctly, do not go too far beyond what's in the passage. The best answer to an Inference question, like the best answer to all ACT Reading questions, is strongly grounded in the words of the passage.

Inference questions refer to a small, localized part of the passage. Read that part of the passage, and come up with a prediction based on what is stated there.

Your passage map will help you determine the overall purpose. Which piece of the purpose is the author putting into place with the line in question?

Remember, the answer is a small step from what is directly stated. It's a conclusion based on the overall themes you've already found. An inference isn't an opinion and it doesn't have to be a guess.

In fact, wrong answer choices are commonly extreme. They are usually headed in the right direction, but are worded in a way that goes too far. These are the kinds of words and phrases that appear frequently in *extreme* answer traps:

• *absolutely*	• *largest*
• *always*	• *never*
• *all*	• *no*
• *best*	• *none*
• *certainly*	• *smallest*
• *ever*	• *worst*
• *in every case*	• *without a doubt*

An answer choice that contains words or phrases like those listed is not *necessarily* the wrong answer. However, if an answer choice does contain extreme language, you should consider it a trap unless the extreme language is also used in the passage. Ask: "Is this thing really 'always' or 'never' the case? Literally?" Occasionally it might be, but more often the passage says "This thing sometimes happens" and the extreme answer choice is "This always happens."

The other common wrong answer type on Inference questions is **out-of-scope** answers.

Out-of-Scope traps go beyond what is stated in the passage. The *scope* of a passage refers to what information is covered in the passage. A passage that touches on a large topic has a scope that is broad. A passage that treats a smaller topic in greater depth and detail has a scope that is narrow. Because the correct answer to an ACT Reading question is always based on what is in the passage, you should pay close attention to the scope of the passage when you're considering answer choices and looking for the one that best matches your prediction. If an answer asks you to guess about something the passage doesn't even talk about, that answer is probably **out-of-scope**.

Again, don't worry about identifying what kind of wrong answers the choices are. Just be aware that both typical wrong answer choices are designed to lure you further away from the written text than you should go. The correct answer will be close to what is stated in the passage; it's simply the next step from a detail, a small conclusion combining information with meaning.

FUNCTION—6 POINTS

Complexity: Medium. You will need to make conclusions about a small-to-medium part of the passage.

Function questions task you with understanding the role of certain elements of a passage. They'll ask you why the author used a particular word, sentence, detail, quote, paragraph, or punctuation. These questions test your ability to interpret how the different pieces of a passage fit together. Types of connections, such as cause-and-effect, sequence, or contrast are important here.

You can recognize these questions from the following clues in the question stems:

Question Stem Indicators

- *The phrase...serves to...*

- *...is meant to...*

- *The author does...in order to...*

Notice that each indicates the idea of finding a purpose.

STRATEGY

To answer these questions, put yourself in the author's place. You make similar decisions when writing your own essays. Why would you use a particular example? Why would you include this paragraph?

Was the piece in question providing evidence or a transition? Was it establishing a relationship?

Refer to your passage map to find the answer. Focus on the big picture for that particular piece, and ask yourself how it fits into the surrounding pieces.

This question is the most like putting together the pieces of a jigsaw puzzle. Again, since you write essays yourself, it will be a puzzle you're familiar with.

Remember those connection words from English, and what type of relationship they build. Here they are again for your reference:

Connections Words and Phrases	
Connections that show addition, continuation, emphasis, or examples	additionally and for example for instance furthermore indeed in addition in fact likewise moreover
Connections that show cause and effect	as a result because consequently leading to since so therefore thus

Common wrong answer choices will be **out-of-scope,** discussed with Inference and Generalization questions (page 202), and **distortions,** discussed with Detail questions (page 199).

WRITER'S VIEW—1 POINT

Complexity: Medium-High. You will need to make conclusions about a small-to-large part of the passage.

Writer's View questions ask about something in the passage from the point of view of the writer (or possibly, in the case of a prose fiction passage, the narrator). Writer's View questions refer directly to *the author, the writer, the narrator,* or *the point of view.* The ACT is testing to make sure you can understand tone and intent. Much like on Function questions, recognize that the author uses a certain order or phrasing for a reason. Function questions ask you what an element does for the passage in relation to the surrounding pieces, whereas Writer's View questions ask you to interpret those pieces to conclude what the author is thinking. What was the intention of writing a particular piece or paragraph? What tone was the author using? All of this leads up to finding the opinion that the author holds.

Look for the following phrasing to indicate a Writer's View question.

Question Stem Indicators

- *The author would most likely agree that*

- *The view of the narrator regarding…appears to be*

- *The author's view of…is*

- *The writer's attitude toward*

- *From the point of view of…*

- *The author's approach to…*

Notice that each indicates the writer, and an opinion or point of view.

STRATEGY

Two things you should keep in mind in answering a Writer's View question are:

1. **Keep straight who says what.** If the passage describes multiple viewpoints, make sure you know which viewpoint the author supports or agrees with.

2. **Pay attention to the tone of the passage.** Even a single word such as *fortunately, unfortunately,* or *regrettably* can be a big clue in helping you determine the author's view.

Remember, you should be looking for the "why," or the purpose, in your passage maps. That should lead you to the correct answer.

In prose fiction, when the thesis is obscured, look for opinions expressed both in dialogue and character framing and narration to help you determine which side the author is on, if more than one character is strongly expressing opinions.

Here's an opinion not in dialogue:

> Carl had changed, Alexandra felt, much less
> than one might have expected. He had not become
> a self-satisfied city man. There was still something
> *Line* homely and wayward and personal about him. Even
> (5) his clothes were unconventional. He seemed to shrink
> into himself as he used to do, as if he were afraid of
> being hurt.

Alexandra is giving her opinion of Carl. It's more likely the author is on her side, as dialogue adds an extra layer, dissociating the author from the opinion, like when Carl gives his counterpoint later.

> Her visitor winced and paused. "You see," he
> said, "measured by your standards here, I'm a
> failure. I couldn't buy even one of your cornfields.
> *Line* I've enjoyed many things in New York, but I've got
> (5) nothing to show for it."

Both give opinions, but the author distances herself from Carl by letting Carl speak his own mind in dialogue. The author is closer to Alexandra, since they express opinions together without the need for dialogue.

An example of character framing here is the author referring to Carl as "Her visitor." Again, the author is taking Alexandra's perspective by looking at Carl (the visitor) through Alexandra's eyes.

The most common wrong answer choice for Writer's View questions will hold the wrong opinion or intent (perhaps the opinion of a different character or an opposing opinion given to provide the counter-argument). This is a **contradiction** trap.

Also, watch out of **extremes,** as discussed with Inference questions (page 202).

GENERALIZATIONS—8 POINTS

Complexity: High. You will need to make conclusions about large parts of the passage or the passage as a whole.

Generalization questions ask about large pieces of the passage, and task you with putting it all together to draw a supported conclusion. Hopefully, you've actively read and made a map aimed at the big picture—the overall purpose and themes of the passage. This heavily weighted question type will draw upon that global information. These questions are designed to test your grasp of the meaning and tone of the passage as a whole.

They rarely include line references, and can ask about a paragraph, a couple of paragraphs, the entirety of the beginning, middle, or end, and even the passage as a whole.

You can know you're dealing with a generalization question from the following question stem clues:

Question Stem Indicators

- *The primary purpose of the passage is to…*

- *The main point of the…paragraph is to…*

The question stems will point to a main idea or purpose, and will often end in "to," meaning the first word of the answer choices will be a verb.

STRATEGY

Actively read and take notes in your passage map. That step of the method is extremely important here. Read for the big picture, asking questions about why this passage is being written and how the pieces are fitting together. Practice the method. If you have this down, you'll be well on your way to mastering this complex question type.

Examine the first and last paragraphs. How the passage starts and ends can give you a quick idea of its overall scope and main idea.

If you're stuck, complete other questions with smaller scope first. The Detail questions and Inference questions might help you understand the overall purpose if you missed it on your read through, while making sure you get those points in time.

Also do look at the italicized words preceding the passage. Introductory information can give you vital and quick background information.

Remember that Generalization questions usually end in "to…," thus the answer choices often begin with a verb. Pay careful attention to this verb and make sure it matches the overall tone of the passage.

Common wrong answer types are **distortions** (page 199) and **out-of-scope** answers (page 202).

Be careful not to assume that the main idea of a single paragraph is the main idea of the passage as a whole. This is a common distortion in Generalization questions. Wrong answer choices might also mix in some wrong information with some right information to lead you astray. Predict to avoid this trap.

Now, make sure your passage mapping skill is still fresh and try out these Generalization questions.

EXAMPLE

With the spread of industry, the exodus of people from the countryside, and the resultant transformation of the urban landscape, city-dwellers of the
Line twentieth century have found themselves living in an
(5) increasingly colorless environment. Veiled in soot, towns and suburbs have lapsed into grimy taciturnity as an all-pervading drabness has overcome our great, sprawling urban complexes.

Improving the quality of life in the city is one
(10) of the primary objectives of street art. Color can help to save, rehabilitate, or otherwise give new life to neighborhoods and other urban sites doomed to demolition, dereliction, or anonymity. The aim is to provide the city-dweller with the opportunity
(15) to participate in the rebirth of a more human environment. By its very nature as communal space, the street lends itself to collective creativity that, in turn, leads to an enhanced sense of community pride and well-being.

1. The main idea of the passage is that:

    A. bold colors and street art positively affect urban environments.

    B. modern cities have been ruined by the use of drab colors.

    C. scholars have misunderstood the canons of Greek and Roman architecture.

    D. urban sites should be saved from demolition, dereliction, and anonymity.

- Choice (A): Correct; the main idea relates to the importance of color and public murals to cities.

- Choice (B): Extreme; nothing in the passage supports the idea that modern cities have been *ruined* by drab colors.

- Choice (C): Misused Detail; the author suggests this, but it's too small a point to be the main idea.

- Choice (D): Misused Detail; the author suggests this, but it's too small a point to be the main idea.

PASSAGE TYPES

Even the different passage types on Reading bring different challenges. We'll start by looking at those passage types and the challenges they bring.

PROSE FICTION—THE FIRST PASSAGE

The Prose Fiction passage is taken from a novel or short story. Because the Prose Fiction passage is centered on character's thoughts, moods, behaviors, and relationships, it's quite different from the three nonfiction passages.

One aspect of the Prose Fiction passage that can be challenging is that you must infer much of the meaning. Typically, fiction writers don't come right out and make explicit statements. They tend to *show* rather than *tell*. Thus, your ability to understand a prose passage hinges largely on your ability to make appropriate inferences. If you find this challenging, think about watching a movie. The writer and director don't often tell you what to think. Instead, they show you a situation. The music, lighting, and camera angles all affect how you interpret what the characters say and do. Obviously, a piece of literature doesn't use music and cinematography to impart meaning. Nonetheless, a prose passage may be easier for you to understand if you try to visualize it as a movie. Trying to visualize the characters as if they were on film, and not just as words on a page, can help you develop a fuller understanding of the prose passage.

The questions you need to keep in mind on Prose Fiction during your active reading process are different from the questions that help you understand a nonfiction passage. Ask yourself:

- Who are the characters?

- What do details about a character help you understand about that person? The ways the character looks, moves, and speaks can give you important clues.

- What are the characters' emotions, motivations, or opinions? These aspects can help you start to look at the "why" of the characters.

- How are the characters related? You can think of this first in a literal way: Are they friends, relatives, acquaintances, or strangers meeting for the first time? You can also think of this in a more psychological way, asking what connects them: Are they accepting and approving of each other, or are they tied together by negative emotions?

- What is the overall tone of the passage? Is the mood upbeat and joyful or serious and reflective? Do any words create a sense of tension, drama, or excitement?

- What contrasts does the passage present? Is one character portrayed as being different from another in personality, background, or values?

Often the ACT Prose passage focuses on only a few main characters, but it may include several minor characters as well. As you read through the Prose passage, one of the most important things you must do is develop your understanding of the main characters. If you come across a character that seems more minor, you can underline the name, but don't get distracted by giving equal attention to all the characters. Focus on the most important ones.

SOCIAL STUDIES—THE SECOND PASSAGE

The Social Studies or Social Sciences passage can cover a wide range of topics, including history, anthropology, archaeology, education, psychology, political science, biography, business, geography, sociology, or economics. Because Social Science is a nonfiction passage, remember to apply the usual method of active reading and passage mapping. Look for the connections words that illustrate the logical progression of the passage. Then, find the purpose and focus on the big picture. Topics you might see in a Social Science passage include:

- A reinterpretation of the traditional understanding of an historical event

- A discussion of several scholars who've done work in the field and similarities and differences in their viewpoints

- A presentation of one scholar's view on a topic and argument explaining why the writer agrees or disagrees with that view

- An explanation of a concept or idea and why it's important in the field of study

- A discussion of the causes of a historical event

- An overview of the work of an important person in the field

This list is merely representative; it certainly doesn't include everything you might find in a Social Science passage. No matter what the topic, your task while actively reading is to grasp the author's purpose for writing.

HUMANITIES—THE THIRD PASSAGE

The Humanities passage broadly relates to human creativity. The visual arts, such as drawing, painting, and sculpture, commonly fall into this category, as do many other areas, such as literature, theatre, music, dance, philosophy, language, communications, film, literary criticism, radio, television, and architecture. As you read the Humanities selection, you should apply all of the active reading questions that you'd use for any nonfiction selection. Some examples of topics that you might be likely to find in a Humanities passage include:

- A discussion of the style of one or more artists, and characteristics of the artist's work that make it noteworthy or unique

- A discussion relating to the development of a particular art form, what the origin of the form was, and how it changed over time as different artists used it

- A critical assessment of the work of a particular artist, how the artist's work was received in his own lifetime, and whether scholars in the field have maintained that view or come to a different view

- A chronological tracing of a particular artist's work over time, what the characteristics of the artist's early work were, what periods or stages scholars use to categorize the artist's work, and whether the work of a particular period is valued more highly than work from other periods

Again, this list is not exhaustive. Notice, however, that the outline form and the chronological structure appear in some way in each example. Even though you can't predict the topic you'll see in the Humanities passage, and you may find yourself on Test Day facing a topic you have little familiarity with, you don't need to be intimidated. The practice you've completed with the method will serve you well, and you'll find even an unknown topic will provide the structural clues and purpose you're well able to find.

NATURAL SCIENCE—THE FOURTH PASSAGE

The Natural Science passage could cover any number of technical sciences, including botany, zoology, natural history, biology, chemistry, earth sciences, physics, anatomy, astronomy, ecology, geology, medicine, meteorology, microbiology, physiology, and technology. Don't worry if a science passage includes technical terms that you aren't familiar with—this is a Reading test, not a Science test. If you need to understand a technical term to answer a question correctly, the term will be explained in the passage. Some examples of the way a topic might be treated in an ACT Natural Science Reading passage include:

- A concept is introduced and several different understandings of it are presented (Remember to keep straight who says what.)

- A historical view of a scientific concept is contrasted with a contemporary view

- Several different ways of investigating a particular phenomenon are discussed

- A first-person narrative discusses personal experience investigating a scientific concern

- A detached presentation of facts discusses what is known in a particular field

- A description of the current understanding of a concept is discussed, and suggestions of what researchers might investigate next are presented

While a science passage may seem challenging if you don't know much about the particular topic, you should be particularly careful with passages that address topics you *are* familiar with. If you've just studied a particular group of elements in your chemistry class and you find a passage that discusses those elements, your first read-through of the passage will go pretty quickly and comfortably because you've had some previous exposure to the material. When you attack the questions, however, you'll be tempted to rely on your previous knowledge, which is *not* a good approach. The correct answer is always based on something that's stated in the passage—outside knowledge is never tested in this section. So even when you're familiar with a topic (in fact, *especially* when you're familiar with it), it's important to read the question stem carefully and make sure that your prediction is grounded in the passage itself.

If you're unfamiliar with the topic, and it feels like a foreign language, fear not. This isn't the Science test. Everything you need to know is there in front of you. When reading, just avoid getting bogged down by details you don't understand. Find the big picture, and move on. If you get the gist, you can figure out the confusing details later, and only if they ask you to.

SUMMARY

In this chapter, we went over every SmartPoint and question type you will encounter on the ACT Reading test. We then discussed all passage types in their Test Day order. Use this chapter for continued study and reference as you practice Reading passages and find the skills you need to focus on.

Remember to practice the method first and foremost. If you're comfortable with active reading and can quickly find and map the purpose, you'll be ready for anything the ACT can throw at you. Then, research and predict to avoid traps.

For the questions themselves, remember to stick as closely as possible to what's stated in the passage. Most wrong answer choices will twist things from the passage or provide information outside of the scope of the text. Detail questions will usually have a directly stated answer. Find it and be ready for a paraphrase. But even the other question types, those requiring more and more inferences and conclusions based on larger and larger pieces of text, will still be rooted in what's written. The answer is in the passage. Find it and state it in your own words.

Don't be afraid to skip around. Start with your strongest passage to conserve time and ease into the section. You can even skip around within the questions for a passage—if you can't find an answer, it's still perfectly OK to guess on this section. No question is worth an abundance of your time.

However, with practice at passage mapping, your time searching will mostly be fairly short. With that and active reading, you'll become an ACT Reading master!

UNIT 4: SCIENCE

The Basics:

35 Minutes

40 Questions

7 Passages

Pacing:

Pace your time per passage as opposed to per question.

Spend roughly five minutes on each passage, going through the text, charts, and graphs, and answering the questions.

TEST DAY DIRECTIONS AND FORMAT

Here's what the Science directions will say on Test Day:

> **Directions:** There are seven passages in this test. Each passage is followed by several questions. After reading a passage, choose the best answer to each question and fill in the corresponding oval on your answer document. You may refer to the passages as often as necessary. You are NOT permitted to use a calculator on this test.

OUTSIDE KNOWLEDGE

You don't need to be a scientist to ace this section of the ACT, which primarily tests your ability to read and understand, not call on background knowledge. It helps to have a basic understanding of scientific terms and concepts, but you won't have to rely on any outside knowledge to answer the questions. Just like Reading, the answers are always in the passage.

THE INSIDE SCOOP

The purpose of the Science test is to test your scientific reasoning skills, as opposed to your ability to remember information from your high school science classes.

The seven passages are drawn from four basic areas of science—biology, chemistry, earth and space sciences, and physics. Expect one to two passages on each subject, but again, you're not expected to bring outside knowledge of these areas of science to the test.

You'll see three types of passages:

- *Data Representations* will simply show you data, occasionally with a brief passage beforehand to introduce the charts and graphs. No experiments or theories are involved. Expect three passages with five questions each.

- *Research Summary* passages will describe experiments and show you charts and graphs of the results. You'll need to interpret the data and understand the scientific method employed. Expect three passages with six questions each.

- *Conflicting Viewpoints* will describe a phenomenon, then two or more scientists will offer opinions on the cause of that phenomenon. You'll need to understand the conflicting opinions and the evidence associated with each. Expect one passage with seven questions.

The questions *do not* get harder as you proceed through the Science test.

SMARTPOINTS

Point Value	Topic	Basics Page	Details and Practice
13	**Scientific Reasoning**		
12	**Figure Interpretation**		
11	**Patterns**		

CHAPTER 10

Science Part 1: Inside the ACT Science Test

THE KAPLAN METHOD FOR ACT SCIENCE

On the Science test, the Kaplan Method varies depending on the passage type. Below is the basic method for all sections, but refer to the Method Breakdown on page 220 later in this chapter for an in-depth discussion of how to apply and alter these strategies to the various passage types.

STEP 1: MAP THE PASSAGE, IDENTIFYING AND MARKING THE PURPOSE, METHOD, AND RESULTS OF THE EXPERIMENT.

Overview the text, searching for the Purpose, Method, and Results. Don't get bogged down in the details; you can give everything else a quick read and come back later if the question requires it. Simply find the Purpose and Method within the text, take a moment to understand each, then get an overview of the Results.

Underline the Purpose. The Purpose is the "why" of the experiment. What were the researchers trying to learn, to do, to prove? Look for the infinitive form of the verb in the first paragraph to help you find this quickly. Examples: The Scientists are trying,…"To Determine," "To Calculate," "To Discover"…etc.

Bracket the Method. This is the "how" of the experiment. What did the researchers actually do? This is separate from the Purpose—they didn't "try to learn ___," they "heated the mixture," etc. It usually involves changing one variable while keeping the others constant, and describes how they are setting up their processes to answer the question outlined in the Purpose. For the first experiment, look for what you could see them doing. The Method won't be thinking or calculating; it will involve physically putting things in place. For any experiments past the first, focus on what is changing. What's different each time?

Star the Results. These are usually listed in charts and graphs, but may be in paragraph form. A high percentage of the questions on the ACT Science test will come from analyzing the data. Thus, move quickly through the text, understanding the Purpose and Method, so you can spend a little time analyzing the Results in Step 2.

STEP 2: SCAN FIGURES, IDENTIFYING VARIABLES AND PATTERNS.

Here's where you can analyze the data. This shouldn't be a long process, but by giving each chart and graph an overview as you go, focusing on a few key things, you'll be better prepared to find answers quickly once you get to the questions.

Scan Figures. This is the overview step. Get a sense of what is being represented by looking at the labels of charts, the axes of graphs, and the variables and how they change.

Indentify Variables. Now, dive into the variables. How do they relate to the experiment? Look specifically for independent variables and dependent variables. Which are the scientists changing themselves (independent) and how does that affect the one(s) they are observing (dependent)? If scientists wanted to see whether temperature affected how fast a student could read, the temperature would be the independent variable, and the speed of the student would be the dependent. Note: On a coordinate graph, the independent variable will often appear on the x-axis; the dependent will appear on the y.

Patterns. Finally, get a sense for how the different parts of the graph vary in relation to each other. Specifically, look at the independent and dependent variables (or other important variables) and determine if they vary directly or inversely. (Direct variation is where they both increase or decrease together. Inverse variation is where as one increases, the other decreases.)

STEP 3: FIND SUPPORT FOR THE ANSWER IN THE PASSAGE.

Always refer back to the passage before looking at the choices and selecting one. Make sure you read charts and graphs accurately and that you do not confuse different kinds of units. It helps to answer the question in your own words. Form a prediction of what you think the answer will be. Don't rely too much on your knowledge of science. Match your answer with one of the choices.

QUICK TIPS

MIND-SET

- **Look for patterns.** Usually, the exact data contained in Science passages is not as important as the *changes* in the data are. Look for extremes (maximums and minimums), critical points (points of change), and variation (direct and inverse).

- **Know your direction.** There are two kinds of scientific reasoning—general-to-specific and specific-to-general. *Always* be aware of when scientists are inferring a specific case from a general rule and when they are using specific data to form a (general) hypothesis.

- **Refer, don't remember.** Don't even think of trying to remember data. As with the Reading test, there is always more data than could possibly be asked about. The data is **always** there, right on the page, for you to refer to when needed.

SPECIAL STRATEGIES

READING TABLES AND GRAPHS

When reading tables and graphs, you should ask yourself:

- What does the figure show?

- What are the units of measurement?

- What is the pattern in the data?

EXPERIMENTS

Remember how experiments work. There is typically (though not always) a control group (a group in which the results are known and not changing) plus an experimental group or groups. In a well-designed experiment, the only difference between the groups will be a variation in the factor that's being tested. Ask yourself:

- What's the factor that's being varied intentionally (the independent variable)?

- What's the factor that changes as a result (the dependent variable)?

- What's the control group, if any?

- What do the results show? What differences exist between the results for one group and those for another?

CONFLICTING VIEWPOINTS PASSAGE

Spend a little more time than usual on the pre-reading step of the Conflicting Viewpoints passage. Focus on the two points of view—what are the scientists arguing about? What do they agree on, if anything? What do they differ on? Identify the following for each scientist:

- **Basic theory statement** (usually the first sentence of Scientist 1, and in the middle for Scientist 2)

- **Major pieces of data behind the theory** (keeping in mind whether each supports the scientist's own theory or weakens the opposing scientist's theory)

TIMING: PACING AND APPROACH

Some Science passages are a lot harder than others, and they're not arranged in order of difficulty, so you might want to **take a few seconds at the beginning of the subject test to page through the passages, gauging the difficulty of each one.** You may wish to skip an entire passage if it seems very difficult (but remember that a very difficult passage may have very easy questions).

As in Reading, treat each passage and its questions as a block. Get the easy questions on the first pass through and save the tougher ones for the second pass. Any questions that look like they will take far too long to answer, if at all, take an educated guess.

Set your watch to 12:00 at the beginning of the subject test. Although you should go faster if you can, here's where you should be at the following checkpoints:

12:05. . . . . One passage finished and answers gridded in

12:10. . . . . Two passages finished and answers gridded in

12:15. . . . . Three passages finished and answers gridded in

12:20. . . . . Four passages finished and answers gridded in

12:25. . . . . Five passages finished and answers gridded in

12:30. . . . . Six passages finished and answers gridded in

12:35. . . . . Seven passages finished and answers for the entire section gridded in

Don't spend time agonizing over specific questions. Avoid thinking long and hard about the answer choices. If you've spent a minute or so on a question and don't seem to be making any headway, make your best guess and move on.

Don't panic if you can't finish all seven passages, but try to do a good job on at least five of them. Make sure you remember to grid answers (even if they're blind guesses) for all questions by the end of the test.

WHEN YOU'RE RUNNING OUT OF TIME

If you have less than three minutes left for the last passage, do the following:

1. **Look for questions that refer to specific experiments or to specific graphs or tables.**

2. **Refer to the cited location in the passage and answer the question as best you can, based on what you see there.**

3. **Make sure you have gridded in an answer for every question before time is called.**

SCORING

Your performance on the Science subject test will be averaged into your ACT Composite score, weighted equally with your scores on the other three major subject tests. You will also receive:

- A Science subject score—from 1 to 36—for the entire Science subject test

Unlike the other three subject scores, the Science score is not divided into subscores.

SMARTPOINT BREAKDOWN

SCIENTIFIC REASONING—13 POINTS

Extremely Important

Scientific Reasoning questions ask you to think like a scientist. These are the conclusion- and inference-based questions on the ACT Science test. This SmartPoint is the reason you need to gather information from the passages and can't just skip to the charts and graphs. This is also the primary question type of the Conflicting Viewpoints passage. These questions task you with understanding the way experiments are designed and what they prove. You might even have to take the next step and figure out what the scientists should do next. They might also ask you to either logically apply a principle or identify ways of defending or attacking a principle. For a discussion of the different questions that fit into this category, and strategies for dealing with each, turn to page 239.

FIGURE INTERPRETATION—12 POINTS

Extremely Important

Figure Interpretation questions task you with locating data. These are data-based questions on which you don't need to draw a conclusion. Simply examine the charts and graphs carefully, and you'll find the answer you need. On the more difficult Figure Interpretation questions, the data necessary to answer the question can be hidden within complex charts and graphs. Still, with a diligent search, you'll be able to find the answer. For a strategy discussion of this question type, and how to efficiently search for your answer in both simple and complex figures, turn to page 228.

PATTERNS—11 POINTS

Extremely Important

Patterns questions ask you to interpret trends in data. These are data-based questions on which you'll need to draw conclusions or make inferences. Most commonly, you'll need to describe the relationships between variables. Do they vary directly or inversely? You may need to find this pattern within a chart or graph containing a multitude of data. More difficult questions will ask you to describe what would happen to new data points, or determine how a new variable would behave. Just like in Reading, the answer to any questions that involve an inference will be a small step from the data you can see, and will follow the pattern established. Always assume the patterns you can see won't change drastically. Refer to page 233 for strategies to isolate variables and find patterns even amidst complex data, and how to use existing data to find what would happen next.

METHOD BREAKDOWN

Because the passage types on Science are so different from each other, both in terms of how they are structured and what information you'll need to know to answer the questions, the method for Science is the most fluid of all Kaplan Methods.

With every other Kaplan Method, you should use one set of practices to efficiently work through the entire section. With the Kaplan Method for ACT Science, you'll gain efficiency by varying your approach to each passage type.

We'll use this section to take a closer look at the different passages, and how you can approach each to effectively answer their typical questions.

RESEARCH SUMMARY

Three passages. Six questions each.

Use the standard method, discussed earlier in this chapter (page 215).

This is the only passage type on which both the information in the text and the information in the data are likely to be equally important. All three of the SmartPoints can be tested here.

Step 1: The passage starts with text giving explanatory background and describing the overall process. The **Purpose** can usually be found at the end of this first paragraph. Underline it when you find it. Remember to look for the infinitive form of the verb to find it quickly (to determine, to calculate, to discover, to study).

Then, you'll usually have a paragraph dedicated to each of the different experiments the scientists perform to achieve their purpose. In the first such paragraph, look for the **Method** and bracket it. Here, focus on the steps of the process you could see the scientists do. In the paragraphs describing each subsequent method or experiment, focus on what's changing. What are they doing differently this time?

With Research Summaries, perform a quick read of the text. You don't need to be thorough. Find the Purpose and Method, take an extra moment to be sure you understand those two aspects of the process, and move on. Refer to the surrounding text as you need to in order to help you understand the Purpose and Method and you'll be ready for any Scientific Reasoning questions with this passage.

Step 2: After the text, the passage will usually contain charts and graphs relaying the results. Go through the usual process of Step 2 of the Kaplan Method with these charts and graphs to prepare yourself for any Figure Interpretation or Pattern questions.

Scan the figures to give yourself a sense of the results. Were the scientists aiming for something in particular in their purpose? Did they achieve it?

Identify the independent and dependent variables. What variable were they changing themselves? What variable changed as a result? When in doubt, the independent variable will be on the *x*-axis and the dependent variable will be on the *y*-axis.

Finally, look for patterns, especially between the independent and dependent variables, but if there are other variables present, get a quick sense for how those vary as well.

Step 3: Support your answer. Predict for any questions that involve conclusions. Don't rely on your memory! You can expect all three question types here, so be ready to find data, interpret patterns, and draw conclusions based on the process of the scientists.

DATA REPRESENTATION

Three passages. Five questions each.

Skip straight to Step 2 of the Kaplan Method discussed earlier in this chapter (page 216).

Only the information in the data is important in these passages. If there is text, it will simply be a description of the data on display in the charts and graphs.

The two tested SmartPoints are *Figure Interpretation* and *Patterns*. *Scientific Reasoning* does not appear on this passage type.

Skim the text, if there is any, to simply get a sense of the data to come. Remember, if it does throw in a question regarding a detail from the text, you can always go back and look.

But your time is better spent looking over the data on this particular passage type.

Suppose you saw the following graph in a Science passage:

Air Temperature at Various
Altitudes at Test Site #3

Scan the figure and ask, "What does this figure show? What are the units of measurement?" Well, the graph shows air temperature at various altitudes at Test Site #3—the title tells us that. The temperature is measured in °C (degrees Celsius), on the y-axis. We can assume the km above sea level is the independent variable, and the air temperature is dependent; when we look for patterns, we notice they vary inversely. As km above sea level increases, air temperature decreases.

Then you'll just move on! You don't need to focus on what the specifics are until a *question* asks you. Until it's going to earn you points, it just doesn't matter!

However, there are going to be questions like "What is the temperature at 2 km above sea level?" To answer, find 2 km on the x-axis. Draw a line straight up until you intersect the line. Then draw a straight line from this point to the y-axis. Use your pencil—the graphs are often pretty small, and eyeballing won't always give you an accurate enough estimate. Here, you can see that the temperature at 2 km is about 5°.

Data will also appear in the form of tables. Suppose you come across this in a passage:

| Concentration of *E. Coli* in Cooling Pool B ||
DISTANCE FROM EFFLUENT PIPE 3	1,000s OF *E. COLI* PER CENTILITER
0 m	0.4
5 m	5.6
10 m	27.6
15 m	14.0
20 m	7.5

Again, you'll scan to identify what the figure shows and the units of measurement (percent doesn't have units, time is in seconds). This time, don't linger on independent and dependent variables. It's not as important when there isn't an experiment. Do a quick check for patterns. You'll notice the distance increases constantly, but concentration goes up, and then down; there isn't a regular pattern. And that's okay! Sometimes, the variables won't have a clear relationship. Get a sense for how each one changes throughout, and move on. More specific analysis can wait until it'll earn you points.

For your reference, the fact that distance is listed on the left, and has consistent intervals of five, means it is likely the independent variable, meaning that concentration would be the dependent. Just consider how an experiment would be done—you're much more able to take concentration measurements every 5 meters than to measure distances according to *E. coli* concentration.

The questions on this table might ask "Five meters from Effluent Pipe 3, how many thousands of *E. coli* are found per centiliter of water?" To answer, find 5 in the "Distance" column (the row of boxes on the far left, running down). Follow the 5 m row over to the "1,000s of *E. Coli*" column. The value in that box is 0.4. There are 0.4 thousands per centiliter.

You might also be asked to identify trends in the data in a table. You'll be ready, since you've already noticed how the *E. coli* values change as you go down the distance column. They go up from 0.4 to 27.6, and then they start to go down.

These skills form the basics of graph and table reading. More complex questions will build from these fundamental skills, and we'll discuss them in detail under the corresponding SmartPoints in the next chapter.

CONFLICTING VIEWPOINTS

One passage. Seven questions each.

Employ a different method for this unique Science passage:

The Kaplan Method for Conflicting Viewpoints Passages

1. **Read the introductory text and the first author's viewpoint,** then answer the questions that ask *only about the first author's viewpoint.*

2. **Read the second author's viewpoint,** then answer questions that ask *only about the second author's viewpoint.*

3. **Answer the questions that refer to both authors' viewpoints.**[*]

Focus on the opinions of each scientist as you read and <u>underline the opinions</u> when you find them. The opinion of the first scientist will often be in the first or second sentence. The opinion of the second scientist will often be in the middle of the paragraph. The second scientist will often start by refuting the first, then transition to his or her unique opinion. With more than two scientists, look in the first or second sentence for each.

(When there are three or more author viewpoints, you'll read each viewpoint and answer the related questions before you answer the questions that relate to multiple viewpoints.)

This passage has a heavy focus on *Scientific Reasoning* questions. It's the only passage you'll want to take the time to read carefully.

Notice, though, that you'll take the unique approach of only reading one scientist at a time, then answering the questions that relate to him or her, as opposed to just reading straight through as you're used to. This approach keeps each scientist's points fresh in your mind, and keeps you from confusing their viewpoints. Practice this intermittent approach plenty, so it becomes a habit for this passage type by Test Day.

Structure: Each *Conflicting Viewpoints* passage is structured in generally the same way. There is an opening paragraph (or two) that explains some background information about a particular phenomenon. Generally, the opening paragraph is a statement of fact. It often supplies you with a few definitions of key terms.

Next, a scientist will offer one opinion on or possible explanation for the phenomenon. A second scientist will then offer a different opinion on or explanation for the phenomenon. Sometimes, a third or fourth scientist weighs in.

Each scientist will offer different evidence to support his or her viewpoint. Usually, these viewpoints will contradict each other. That's okay. Your job isn't to decide who is right and who is wrong, but to recognize each viewpoint and understand how each scientist uses evidence to support a viewpoint.

Questions: The questions following a *Conflicting Viewpoints* passage test your ability to follow a scientist's line of reasoning. They might ask you why a scientist included a particular detail in his or her argument or to apply a line of reasoning to a different situation. They might ask you to predict, based on what's written, what a scientist might think about a related topic.

Questions might also introduce new information and ask whether the new information weakens or strengthens one or both of the arguments. They might ask you to identify points of agreement between the two scientists (hint: look for answer choices drawn from the opening text). Conversely, a question might ask you to identify a point of disagreement.

Finally, some questions will test your reading comprehension, with phrasing like, "According to the passage, polypeptide molecules are…" or "The passage indicates that…" These questions are similar to those on the Reading test, and you'll handle them just as you would a Reading question: by going back to the passage to find your answer.

The most important thing to remember as you're taking the ACT Science test is that *answering questions*, not reading the passage, earns you points. Even though you should carefully read the *Conflicting Viewpoints* passage, it's still important to avoid getting caught up in the complex details.

Always spend your time on the questions, on every type of Science passage. That's where the payoff is.

SUMMARY

In this chapter, we talked about all of the strategy basics you need to master the ACT Science test.

Remember to vary your approach to tackle each passage type as efficiently as possible.

For Research Summaries, quickly read the text, looking for the Purpose and Method. Analyze the charts and graphs to find the independent and dependent variables and the patterns relating the two.

For Data Representation, skim the text and skip Step 1 of the Kaplan Method. Spend longer diving into the charts and graphs. Identify the variables when you can, and look for patterns.

For Conflicting Viewpoints, change it up entirely. Read the text carefully, underlining the opinions of the scientists when you find them. Read the introduction and Scientist 1, then answer the questions about Scientist 1 only. Then, read each subsequent scientist and do the same. Finally, answer the questions about more than one scientist last.

For all passage types, support your answers by looking back at the text, charts, and graphs. Don't rely on your memory, and don't get bogged down in the details.

Learn to recognize each passage type quickly. Keep practicing the various methods so you can handle each in stride on Test Day with maximum efficiency.

As always, the points come from the questions. Refer to the next chapter for a detailed discussion of each question type.

The Science test can be very intimidating, but its complexity only disguises a Reading test with scientific words. Know what to expect, know what information to look for to help yourself get to the questions quickly, and you can master the ACT Science test.

CHAPTER 11

Science Part 2: ACT Science Strategy In Depth

OVERVIEW

Use this chapter to get familiar with all of the question types on the ACT Science test. They are detailed and discussed fully, and examples are provided for each. To get a quick sense of what's to come, refer to the SmartPoint Breakdown in the previous chapter (page 219). In that chapter, they are discussed in order of Test Day weight. The more heavily tested SmartPoints are listed there first. That's also how you should prioritize your time, especially if you are short on it, or close to your goal score. However, the SmartPoints in this chapter are discussed in order of building complexity. The knowledge necessary for simpler questions often builds to the conclusions you'll need to draw for the complex ones. Each individual Science SmartPoint can also vary in complexity, and we'll work from simple to complex within all three SmartPoint categories, as we do the same from SmartPoint to SmartPoint. If you have time, and want to thoroughly work your Science skill set, start at the beginning and work your way all the way through.

The following SmartPoints are shown in order of building complexity, SmartPoint by SmartPoint.

FIGURE INTERPRETATION—12 POINTS

Complexity: Low-Medium. The information needed can be found explicitly in the charts and graphs.

Figures on the ACT Science test are charts or graphs designed to present data. *Figure Interpretation* questions task you with studying these diagrams to locate a particular piece of information. And that's it. These questions simply test your ability to carefully read and locate data on a figure. No interpretation or conclusions are necessary. They can be complex, by nature of intricate charts and graphs that are more difficult to read, but by cutting through the distracting information, the correct answer to every Figure Interpretation question will still be right there waiting for you. The most advanced thinking you'll need to do with this question type is comparing a few numbers from least to greatest, or combining a few to find sums or differences. Basically, you'll need to locate more than one piece of data and perform simple numerical evaluations.

That said, the ACT will throw complex charts and graphs at you. Thus, a few strategies for finding data efficiently will help.

Let's start by reviewing a few basic science terms. Again, the ACT Science test doesn't task you with remembering everything from your high school science classes. The answers can always be found in the passage. But by remembering a few basic terms and science processes, you can be more familiar with what you're seeing, and navigate the charts and graphs more easily.

BASIC SCIENCE TERMINOLOGY

The ACT most often uses the International System of Units (SI), which includes meters (m), kilograms (kg), seconds (s), ampere (A), Kelvin (K), mole (mol), as well as liters (L). However, it's not impossible that you'll see feet (ft), pounds (lb), degrees Celsius (°C), or even Fahrenheit (°F). You should be comfortable using derivatives of these units as well—milliliters (mL) and grams (g), for example. In most cases, all you'll need is to understand that these are units of measurements, but in some cases you might need to know which is larger than which.

You should know what it means to create a *solution* (a mixture in which a *solute* is dissolved into a *solvent*) and to *dilute* (thin or weaken). You should understand terms such as *density* (mass per unit volume) and *force* (that which causes a mass to accelerate).

This is by no means an exhaustive list of terms you may encounter, but it represents the general level of terminology you should be comfortable with. More specific terms and pieces of equipment (such as a *bomb calorimeter*) will generally be explained within the text.

SIMPLE QUESTION STRATEGIES

FINDING BASIC INFORMATION IN THE PASSAGE

This is the basic skill tested in Figure Interpretation questions. Your pencil is the key. If a question asks you to find a point on a graph, for example, draw a line up from the *x*-axis and over to the *y*-axis. You can even use a second pencil to keep your lines straight. Often, the graphs are printed pretty small, and eyeballing just isn't accurate enough.

When you find the right piece of data in a table, circle it as a visual aid. The wrong answer choices usually include the values just above or below the correct one, and it's very easy for your eyes to accidentally skip up or down a row in a table.

COMPARING AND COMBINING DATA

You might be asked to combine or compare data from two or more simple presentations. These questions will involve finding more than one data point, and using your basic math skills to combine or compare.

To compare data, circle all of the relevant points in the graph or table. This will help you to focus on only what's asked and exclude any possible distractions. Most often, questions of this type will ask you to order from least to greatest (or vice versa). For example, you may be shown a table that lists the viscosity of several liquids, and asked to order them from most to least viscous.

Other questions will ask you to combine data. Usually, this just means adding or subtracting the numbers. These questions will often ask you to find the difference between two data points.

Remember that on a first read, some questions (like some figures) will appear pretty complicated. Remind yourself that complicated questions are really just questions that ask you to put together a few simple steps. Take the question one step at a time, and you'll find that getting the answer is much easier than it first appeared.

Now, try out some simple Figure Interpretation questions. Then, we'll increase the complexity.

Example

Table 1		
Date	**Nitrate concentration (mg/L)**	**Phosphate concentration (mg/L)**
Dormitory 1		
June 1	19.1	8.3
June 2	17.7	6.6
June 3	18.5	9.2
June 4	19.1	9.0
June 5	22.5	7.9
Dormitory 2		
June 1	23.9	9.8
June 2	26.4	10.1
June 3	23.1	10.8
June 4	22.7	9.5
June 5	19.5	8.6

Table 2			
Date	**Suspended sediment concentration (mg/L)**	**Nitrate concentration (mg/L)**	**Phosphate concentration (mg/L)**
Stream 1			
June 1	33.5	35.5	7.1
June 2	42.0	33.4	9.3
June 3	512.9	36.8	52.6
June 4	1,668.2	62.4	102.9
June 5	687.5	57.0	55.7
Stream 2			
June 1	12.3	11.3	6.7
June 2	18.4	26.5	12.9
June 3	24.1	29.7	26.8
June 4	19.2	21.3	16.4
June 5	12.3	12.5	9.2

1. According to the data in Table 1, on which date was the nitrate concentration from Dormitory 2 the highest?

   A. June 1

   B. June 2

   C. June 3

   D. June 4

2. According to the data in Table 2, on which date were nitrate concentrations from Stream 2 the highest?

   F. June 1

   G. June 2

   H. June 3

   J. June 4

Question 1

- Read "Step 3" on p. 216. Then read the question stem.

- Where in the passage should you look for an answer? *Table 1*

- Where in Table 1 should we look? *Dormitory 2, Nitrate concentration column*

- On which date was the nitrate concentration highest? *on June 2*

- Which answer choice matches? Choice (B).

Question 2

- Where in the passage should you look for an answer? *Table 2*

- Where in Table 2 should you look? *Stream 2, nitrate concentration column*

- On which date was the nitrate concentration highest? *on June 3.*

- Which answer choice matches? Choice (H).

LOCATING DATA WITHIN COMPLEX PRESENTATIONS

Nothing is more intimidating than a science chart with lots of lines heading in all different directions, except for maybe a chart with lots of lines and a few random Greek letters. But keep your cool! The ACT doesn't expect that you have your Ph.D. The complex charts and graphs might look scary, but remind yourself that they're designed to be comprehensible to high school students just like you. In other words, they *look* complicated, but in fact are just going to ask you to find a few points on them.

As you read the passage containing the complex figure for the first time, skim the paragraph preceding the figure for an explanation of what it shows. Read the axis labels and any legend or key accompanying the figure so you know what you're looking at, but then stop there.

When a question asks you specifically about the complex figure, the key is to focus only on the relevant information and block out everything else that's going on. Often, complex figures are only complex because they show how more than one variable behaves at a time. Use your pencil to trace only the curve that applies to the question at hand, and you'll find that the figure often isn't really as complex as it first appeared.

COMPARING AND COMBINING DATA FROM COMPLEX PRESENTATIONS

Comparing and combining data from complex presentations isn't any more difficult than comparing and combining data from simple presentations. What's harder is *finding* the appropriate data in the midst of a complex presentation.

A complex presentation or figure usually involves the presence of lots of variables in one giant table, a bizarre-looking graph with three or more lines, at least one of which is zigzagging, and some kind of strange units, especially angstroms (Å) (that's 0.1 nanometer, usually used for wavelength). But finding data on a line about angstroms is no harder than finding data on a line about Fahrenheit. It's just a different word.

To find the right data in a complex presentation, use the same skills you would on any other Figure Interpretation question: Look to the axes to find units (which can point you to the correct variable), and use your pencil to highlight only the appropriate data. Then focus on the precise calculation the question stem is asking for. Sometimes you'll need to figure out which piece of data is bigger, or rank the data from least to greatest. Sometimes you'll have to add or subtract values. The actual calculations you make will be very simple. Calculators aren't allowed on the Science test, and you'll never need one.

The skills for all Figure Interpretation questions are the same, and they're fundamental. Keep calm when looking at complex figures, and use your pencil so that you don't get lost. Make sure to find exactly what the question stem is asking for, and you'll master this SmartPoint.

Try using your pencil to navigate these more complex charts and graphs.

Example

Directions: First, read and map the passage, identifying and marking the Purpose, Method, and Results of the experiment.

The survival of plant life depends heavily on the availability of nitrogen in the environment. Although about 72% of Earth's atmosphere consists of N^2 gas, this form of nitrogen is inaccessible to plants, since a plant cell is incapable of breaking the triple bond between the two nitrogen atoms. Certain bacteria in soil, however, are capable of processing N^2 into ammonia (NH^4), a form of nitrogen that plants can utilize. This process is called *nitrogen fixation*. Plant roots extract nitrogen in the form of ammonia from the soil and release back into the soil various forms of nitrogen as metabolic byproducts. After a plant dies, it also releases various forms of nitrogen as it decays. Figure 1 shows how the concentration of ammonia in the soil affects the growth rate of a certain bean plant.

Figure 1

1. According to Figure 1, the minimum ammonia concentration that allows for a maximum bean plant growth rate is approximately:

    A. 2 ppm.

    B. 3 ppm.

    C. 5 ppm.

    D. 7 ppm.

Step 1: Scan the figure, identifying variables and patterns. *Step 2:* The figure compares the growth of the bean plant and the ammonia concentration. The question asks at what concentration of ammonia does the maximum bean plant growth occur? *Step 3:* Locate the maximum plant growth, which is at 10 cm. This growth occurs when the ammonia concentration is 5 ppm. Choice (C) is the correct answer.

PATTERNS—11 POINTS

Complexity: Low-Medium to High-Medium. The information needed can be interpreted and inferred from the charts and graphs.

Patterns questions ask you to bring your analytical skills to charts and graphs. Figure Interpretation questions simply require you to find information. Patterns questions will ask you to find data and then relate it to other information, or take a new piece of information and insert it where it belongs. To answer them correctly, you'll need to find trends in the data. First, you need to be aware of the increases and decreases of any single variable, and then you'll have to decipher whether other variables increase or decrease in the same way, the opposite way, or in an unrelated way. By finding these trends, you can draw conclusions as to what the experiment found, and you'll be able to insert new data just by discovering how it fits with the trend.

Let's review the basic skills of Patterns questions.

DETERMINING THE RELATIONSHIP BETWEEN TWO VARIABLES

Determining the relationship between two variables means observing how one variable changes in response to another. A scientist studying the relationship between the number of cars on the highway and the number of accidents, for example, will record the number of cars she counts in one hour along with the number of accidents. Then she'll list her results in a table, with the number of cars in one column and the number of accidents in another. Or perhaps she'll graph them, with the number of cars on the x-axis and the number of accidents on the y-axis. Suppose these are her results:

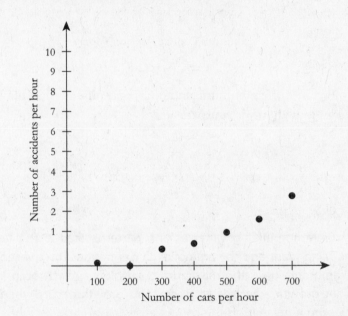

Your job is to understand by looking at the graph how the number of accidents changes with the number of cars. In this example, you can see that as the number of cars increases, the number of accidents increases. That's it! You might notice slight variations—the curve dips slightly from 100 to 200, and seems to increase more quickly at the end (curve instead of straight line), but these are minor variations that certainly don't change the overall trend. You now have the basic process of comparing variables and finding patterns!

You'll also need to keep an eye out for Critical Points.

CRITICAL POINTS

To find out how critical points can help you evaluate data, take a look at the graph representing the concentration of E. coli (a common type of bacterium) in Cooling Pool B.

Concentration of E. *coli* in Cooling Pool B

Notice how the concentration is low very near Effluent Pipe 3. From there, it rises until about 10 meters away from the pipe, then it falls again, tapering off as you get farther from the pipe. There's a critical point, then, right around 10 meters from Effluent Pipe 3. Somehow, that vicinity is most conducive to the growth of *E. coli*. As you move closer to or farther away from that point, the concentration falls off. So, in looking to explain the data, you'd want to focus on that location—10 meters from the pipe. What is it about that location that's so special? What makes it the hot new place for *E. coli* to see and be seen?

Now, see if you can find the relationships in this figure:

Hours of Sunlight	Air Temperature (Fahrenheit)		
	Chamber 1	**Chamber 2**	**Chamber 3**
2	73.23	75.67	78.87
4	71.23	75.79	79.78
6	69.23	74.76	81.34
8	67.23	79.87	82.12
10	65.23	80.65	83.06

What happens in Chamber 1? What do you think the temperature is going to be after 12 hours of sunlight? Do you notice the pattern? The temperature goes down by 2 degrees for every 2 hours of sunlight. The temperature is going to be 63.23 degrees.

As the number of hours of sunlight increases, what happens to the temperature in Chamber 2? When you look at the data, there doesn't appear to be a relationship. This is a valid answer.

Based on the data, what do you think the temperature will be after one hour of sunlight in Chamber 3? Well, as the number of hours of sunlight increase, the temperature in the chamber increases. So if you had to predict what would happen after only one hour of sunlight, then according to the table, it is going to be less than 78.87 degrees.

Now, let's make things slightly more complex, then we'll dive into some examples.

UNDERSTANDING THE RELATIONSHIP BETWEEN VARIABLES IN A COMPLEX DATA PRESENTATION

Understanding the relationship between variables will remain a primary skill in passages with complex data presentations. The basic methods are the same as those discussed with simpler question strategies, but you'll have to focus harder to zero in on the variables you need and ignore the ones you don't.

Work methodically. Locate one variable at a time (check the axes of a graph or the left-most column and top row of a table for your variables). If you can't find them, look for the appropriate units: If a question asks for temperature, look for °C or °F.

When you find your variables, ask yourself how one changes as the other increases or decreases. Then match your answer to the choices. Again, these complex questions often reduce to a series of a few simple steps. Take them one step at a time, and you'll find getting the answer is far easier than it looks!

INTERPOLATING POINTS

Interpolation simply means "reading between." So "Interpolating Points" just means "figuring out what happens *between* data points"—some questions will ask you to approximate values in between those actually shown in the passage. Again, this is a lot easier than it sounds.

Suppose, for example, a passage contains a table—say, one that lists distance in multiples of 10 cm in one column and corresponding intensity in the other—and you're asked to find the intensity at 15 cm. Your job would be to look for the values of intensity at 10 cm and 20 cm and make a guess halfway in between those. Easy!

If you're looking at a graph, the task is similar. Look for the values just below and above the point in question, and make a guess somewhere in the middle. Then simply match your guess to the answer choices.

TRANSLATING INFORMATION INTO A TABLE, GRAPH, OR DIAGRAM

Occasionally, a question will ask you to generate your own graph, table, or diagram. This sounds difficult, but these are usually easy if you know how to find patterns. That's because a) the graphs are usually very straightforward, and b) you don't actually have to generate them. You just have to pick the correct plot out of four choices.

To identify the correct plot, first check the general trend of the data by looking at the slope of the curve or the values in the table. Is the data you're looking for increasing, decreasing, or staying the same? Match the shape you're looking for to the answer choices.

If more than one choice remains after you check the trends, check individual values. If the information in the passage indicates that the data should have a specific value at a given point, look for the choice that contains that point. It shouldn't take more than a few seconds to backtrack your way to the correct answer.

IDENTIFYING AND USING COMPLEX RELATIONSHIPS BETWEEN VARIABLES

Even extremely complex questions regarding intricate charts and graphs will often come down to the same basic skill of relating variables that you've developed throughout this SmartPoint. Remember, these relationships are often pretty straightforward, and that will be true even in the most difficult of passages. As one variable increases by a constant amount, the other increases or decreases by a constant amount. Occasionally, the relationship will be more complex; as one variable doubles, for example, the other will quadruple. This is known as an *exponential* relationship, and is the most common sort of complex relationship on the ACT Science test.

If you suspect a complex relationship between variables, be sure to look at more than one data point. For example, if doubling the quantity of a solution quadruples the reaction time, check to see what tripling the quantity does (it should multiply the reaction time by nine). Take those extra few seconds to make sure you're seeing what you think you're seeing, but only get into this level of detailed analysis if the question asks you to. The basic relationship might be enough.

Mostly, you'll be tasked with using this complex relationship, as opposed to identifying exactly what it is. Nail down the relationship between the two variables, and use that to predict what will happen next.

EXTRAPOLATING FROM DATA

Extrapolating from data means predicting the value of a data point that falls beyond the range given. The rule here is to assume the data trends continue as indicated by the table or graph. If you see a line graphed as straight from 1 to 100 on the *x*-axis, assume it continues to be straight. If it's a curve that's beginning to level off at the top, assume that leveling trend continues. If a table shows a variable steadily increasing, you can safely assume that subsequent values not shown on the table continue to increase.

NEW RESULTS

Other questions will ask you to predict the results of a hypothetical new trial or experiment. The key in these is to identify *which* patterns and trends apply to the question at hand. The question stem will give you clues to figure out where you need to look.

You might see a question that asks you to do the reverse; that is, instead of asking what results come from new conditions, it'll ask which conditions would yield new results. The method for answering is the same: Identify the relevant experiment that manipulates the variable in question, find the trend in the data, and use that trend to identify the conditions that will give you the desired result.

The bottom line with additional trials and experiments questions is that the answer is in the passage. Additional trials and experiments must conform to the data you've already been given. Be wary of answer choices that stray too far from the passage.

Now, try putting your skills at understanding variables and relationships together on this more complex Patterns question.

Example

A high school physics class wished to determine the best way of calculating D, a snowmobile's total braking distance. They defined D as the total distance a snowmobile requires to stop from the moment the driver first sees a "stop" signal until the snowmobile comes to a complete stop.

The class used two methods. In Method 1, S is the distance traveled before the driver could begin the braking process when a driver reaction time of 0.8 sec was assumed, and T is the average distance traveled after the brakes were applied. Method 2 assumes that D is simply the initial speed in ft/sec times 2 sec. Table 1 shows the results of both methods with various initial speeds.

Table 1					
Initial speed (mi/hr)	**Initial speed (ft/sec)**	**Method 1**			**Method 2**
		S (ft)	T (ft)	D (ft)	D (ft)
25	37	30	28	58	74
35	51	41	75	116	102
45	66	53	144	197	132
55	81	65	245	310	162

The class then plotted the D they calculated through Method 1 and the D they calculated through Method 2. The results are shown in Figure 1.

Figure 1

1. According to Figure 1, if a snowmobile is traveling at an initial speed of 75 mi/hr, what will its *D* be according to Method 2?

    A. Less than 100 ft

    B. Between 105 and 200 ft

    C. Between 205 and 300 ft

    D. Greater than 300 ft

Apply Step 2 of the Kaplan Method and take a few seconds to examine the figure. *Step 2:* Table 1 shows the snowmobile's initial speed. The columns under Method 1 show the distance traveled by the snowmobile driver from when he saw the stop signal to when he actually reacted and began stopping; the distance required to actually stop; and the total required braking distance from the start of the signal. The column under Method 2 shows a total stopping distance, assuming stopping distance is simply twice the initial speed in ft/sec. Initial speed is given in units of both mi/hr and ft/sec. Every other measurement is given in ft.

Figure 1 shows a plot of initial speed versus stopping distance for Method 1 and Method 2. The units of the *x*-axis are mi/hr, and the *y*-axis is in feet.

Continue the straight line that represents Method 2 to 75 mi/hr or use Table 1 to estimate *D*. The straight line from Figure 1, if extended, gives *D* of about 225 feet, or (H). Looking at Table 1, each 10 mi/hr increase in initial speed increases *D* by about 30 ft. So an initial speed of 75 mi/hr would have a *D* that's about 60 feet greater than the *D* at 55 mi/hr, or about 222 feet, also (C).

SCIENTIFIC REASONING—13 POINTS

Complexity: Medium to High. The information needed can be inferred and concluded from the text of the passages.

Scientific Reasoning questions are the only ones that really require you to use the text. You'll almost never see these questions in Data Representation passages. They form about a third of Research Summary questions, and they are the most common questions on Conflicting Viewpoints passages.

In Research Summary passages, you'll be asked to understand the hypothesis being tested, how it's being tested, and whether or not the scientists reached the goals they were seeking. In other words, you need a good grasp of the Purpose and Method, and how they affect the Results. You might also be asked to conclude what the scientists should do next.

In Conflicting Viewpoints passages, you'll be asked to understand all viewpoints, how they could be strengthened or weakened, and their similarities and difference. You might also be asked how the viewpoints can be strengthened or weakened by new evidence.

UNDERSTANDING HYPOTHESES

While you'll likely never be asked to directly identify the hypothesis for an experiment, the ACT does test your understanding of hypotheses in general. So what is a hypothesis? It's the scientists' guess at the answer to the question they're asking (which is the Purpose you've already identified). Understand that a hypothesis is not a *statement of fact,* but rather one possible explanation for a phenomenon. "The sky is blue" is not a hypothesis. Scientist 1 saying "The sky is blue because of the salinity of evaporation off the oceans" and Scientist 2 saying "The sky appears blue not because of the salinity of the oceans, but because of the speed of Earth's rotation" is a pair of conflicting hypotheses.

Usually, the ACT makes it pretty clear when they're giving you a hypothesis, so you don't have to worry about ever coming up with one on your own. You'll see dead giveaways when you're dealing with a hypothesis question, like "If Scientist 1's hypothesis is correct..." You do need to understand how to support or weaken that hypothesis or how to further test it.

Supporting a hypothesis means backing it up with more information that fits the hypothesis. Weakening it means finding information that contradicts the hypothesis. To further test a hypothesis, you'll need to ask yourself what else you need to know to confirm or disprove this guess.

SELECTING HYPOTHESES, CONCLUSIONS, OR PREDICTIONS FROM THE DATA

Occasionally, you'll be asked to identify valid hypotheses or conclusions based on what is written in the passage. Your job is never more complicated than distinguishing the correct choice from among three choices that *must* be wrong.

To answer these questions, first go back to the passage. Find where it discusses the information in the question stem, and see if you can predict the answer. If you can, great. If you can't, then see if you can identify the fatal flaw in each of the incorrect answer choices. Often, these flaws will be pretty obvious: some choices might reference information that has absolutely nothing to do with the passage; some might reference an unrelated detail from another part of the passage; still others might reverse the correct relationship.

UNDERSTANDING THE TOOLS IN A SIMPLE EXPERIMENT

The opening paragraph or experiment descriptions of Research Summary passages might contain a complex-looking diagram, like this one:

In other words, some of the Experimental Setup diagrams will look pretty unfamiliar and complicated. Don't let that worry you! Treat a figure like this as you would any other figure on the ACT: Summarize the gist of it, and then move on. You can look at it in more detail when you come to a question that relates to it.

Other tools involved in a simple experiment are the same tools you've used in your high school science labs. Remember, the ACT assumes you've taken at least two years of science, and that usually includes a certain amount of lab work. You should be familiar with what it means to measure temperature, measure quantities of liquids, record masses, record physical observations, and carry out many of the other routine tasks required by a high school science lab.

UNDERSTANDING A SIMPLE EXPERIMENTAL DESIGN

Remember to look for the Method on Research Summary passages. Ask yourself, "How did they set up their experiment? Which were the variables that the researchers changed? Which variables changed in response? What did the researchers record in their results?"

Remember that experiments on the ACT, while they may look complicated at first glance, are usually very straightforward. Some basic equipment will be set up and a few trials will be run. Only a handful of variables will be manipulated. The passages usually look much harder at first glance than they really are.

IDENTIFYING A CONTROL IN AN EXPERIMENT

Remember to find the independent and dependent variables as you proceed through Step 2 of the Kaplan Method. Sometimes, which variable is which will be made clear by the

Purpose in Step 1. These will provide valuable hints to how and why the researchers did what they did. As a quick reminder: **Independent variables** are the variables deliberately manipulated by researchers; the ones researchers control. **Dependent variables** are those that are observed to change in response to the independent variables.

When researchers are trying to figure out the effects of the independent variables they're studying, they'll want to weed out effects caused by other variables they're not thinking of or measuring—the humidity of the room for a chemistry experiment, the amount of rainfall this year for an outdoor biology experiment, or any other factor that's not in their control or on their radar.

To do this, they'll usually run what's called a *control*. Think of this as a "blank" experiment of sorts; the experiment run without any of the independent variables in it at all. For example, if researchers are measuring how three patches of sunflowers grow when they're fed three different kinds of nutrient solutions, they may plant a fourth patch of sunflowers fed only water. The water-fed patch would be the experiment's control.

IDENTIFYING SIMILARITIES AND DIFFERENCES BETWEEN EXPERIMENTS

Questions asking you to identify the similarities and differences between experiments are a guarantee on the ACT, but luckily, finding the answer is straightforward. You may have already located this information using the Method. Usually, it's printed in the paragraph below the *Experiment 1, 2,* or *3* headings. Often, you'll see an explanation of Experiment 2 along the lines of "Scientists repeated Experiment 1, but brought the temperature of the solution to 25°C." Then, looking at the description of Experiment 1, you'll find that the scientists ran that experiment at 15°C.

You should also look quickly at the results the scientists achieved with each experiment. These are almost always printed in tables in Research Summaries passages, and the tables are usually pretty small (the biggest tables are found in Data Representation passages). Column 1 usually contains the independent variables and column 2 the dependent variables. If the first columns of the two tables match, you'll know that the researchers ran basically the same experiment again, with one minor difference. If the first columns are different, you'll know that the researchers varied more than just the temperature at which the experiment was run.

ADDITIONAL TRIALS AND EXPERIMENTS

The Research Summaries passages on the ACT might contain questions asking you to take the experiments one step further, by identifying trials or experiments that would give researchers more information. To answer these questions correctly, you'll have to build on the skills listed earlier: You must understand how experiments are set up and recognize the independent and dependent variables.

The secret to answering questions about new trials or experiments is to determine, from the question stem, exactly what the researchers need to know that they don't already. Then all you have to do is identify which answer choice addresses just this variable, while keeping the others constant. Watch out for answer choices that identify variables already explored in previous trials or experiments—they're there to confuse you by looking familiar. Also avoid answer choices that stray too far from the topic; don't be drawn to answer choices that look confusing and complicated.

NEW INFORMATION

Sometimes, the questions following a Research Summaries passage will introduce new information. That information might come in the form of text in the question stem or a new table or graph. Your job with these questions is to figure out how this new information relates to what's already stated in the passage and find an answer choice that works with both the passage and the new information.

Questions with new information can be confusing on first read. One strategy is to save these questions for last. That gives you a chance to become more familiar with the information in the passage before you try to integrate additional data.

UNDERSTANDING THE VIEWPOINTS

Some of the questions that accompany a Conflicting Viewpoints passage will simply test your ability to identify key issues or assumptions in each individual viewpoint. They're typically rather straightforward and reliably contain wrong answer choices that draw from other authors' viewpoints to trick you. That's why it's important to follow the Kaplan Method for Conflicting Viewpoints passages.

Remember, this Kaplan Method is completely different from the other two. Here it is again as a reminder:

THE KAPLAN METHOD FOR CONFLICTING VIEWPOINTS PASSAGES

1. Read the introductory text and the first author's viewpoint, then answer the questions that ask only about the first author's viewpoint.

2. Read the second author's viewpoint, then answer the questions that ask only about the second author's viewpoint.

3. Answer the questions that refer to both authors' viewpoints.

This Kaplan Method will require that you skip around in the questions. That's fine. There's no rule saying you have to answer the questions in the order in which they appear. And you'll find that it's much, much easier to deal with Conflicting Viewpoints passages when you minimize your opportunities to confuse the two (or three, or four) viewpoints.

IDENTIFYING SIMILARITIES AND DIFFERENCES BETWEEN VIEWPOINTS

You might see questions that ask you to identify a point on which the authors agree or a point on which they disagree. Remember to underline each author's main point as you're reading. Then when it's time to identify similarities and differences, you'll have the essence of their viewpoints highlighted.

Answer these questions immediately after you answer all the questions that deal with just one viewpoint at a time. Questions that ask you to identify similarities or differences are typically among the easier questions in the passage, so they're great for giving you a chance to make sure you have the subtleties of each viewpoint nailed down.

SUPPORTING AND WEAKENING VIEWPOINTS

It's common to see at least one question asking you to identify whether information supports or weakens the view of one or both authors. Typically, these questions will introduce new information or data, and your job will be to determine whether the data supports or weakens a viewpoint.

Information supports a viewpoint if it offers data that makes the viewpoint even more likely to be true. Conversely, information weakens a viewpoint if it contradicts some part of it. The information doesn't have to prove a viewpoint to be true in order to support it, and it doesn't have to prove it false to weaken it. You're simply supposed to judge whether the information adds to or detracts from any part of the viewpoint.

MORE ON STRENGTHENING AND WEAKENING VIEWPOINTS

Some complex questions might introduce new information, then ask you *why* the new information supports or weakens a viewpoint.

Questions that introduce new information sometimes look really confusing. The information might look overly complex or appear at first to have nothing to do with the rest of the passage. Remember that the questions don't rely on any outside knowledge, so you *do* have the information you need to answer them. Break these questions down into a series of simple steps, and always start by making sure you understand each viewpoint. Remember that information supports a viewpoint if it makes it more likely to be true and weakens it if it makes the viewpoint less likely to be true.

MAKING PREDICTIONS BASED ON VIEWPOINTS

Questions that ask you to make predictions based on the viewpoints are particularly common with the more technical passages. These questions often require you to apply a viewpoint to a specific process, or a hypothetical situation, and make a prediction about the outcome. For example, one recent ACT Conflicting Viewpoints passage presented four viewpoints about gene replication in bacteria. The questions accompanying this passage were focused almost exclusively on predicting the order in which the genes would be copied according to each viewpoint.

Confusion is the biggest source of error in these situations. Make sure you minimize potential confusion by reading one viewpoint at a time, and then answering the questions that apply to just that viewpoint.

HYPOTHESES, CONCLUSIONS, AND PREDICTIONS SUPPORTED BY TWO VIEWPOINTS

Another complicated question type will ask you to find hypotheses, conclusions, and predictions that are supported by two or more viewpoints or pieces of information. Again, your job is to find an answer choice that is compatible with both viewpoints or with one viewpoint and some additional information. Make sure you understand exactly what each viewpoint states, or how the viewpoint in question relates to the additional information in the question stem, before you answer the question. A big source of error on the ACT Science test is moving to the answer choices before you know what you're looking for. Make sure you have a guess in mind before reading the answer choices. For questions that ask "which of the following," it's generally quicker to evaluate the answer choices without making a guess, but you need to be certain that you know how to tell whether each choice is correct before you start.

GENERAL COMPLEX QUESTIONS

Sometimes, the ACT makes a question complex by veering far from what is directly stated in the passage. They might do this by introducing seemingly unrelated concepts, asking you to make a prediction or draw a conclusion that feels abstract, or asking you to apply a scientist's reasoning to an entirely new situation.

Complex questions ARE answerable. Start by making sure you understand exactly what the author is saying. Reread the relevant parts of the passage and summarize the main idea in your own words. Then go straight to the answer choices. Three will contain fatal flaws—look for these. The most common kind of wrong answer choice uses ideas drawn from the wrong parts of the passage (for example, ideas in the opening information or another author's viewpoint). Also, look out for answer choices that use just the right words but actually state the exact opposite of what is true, answer choices that use key words from the passage but aren't relevant to the question at hand (these are always tempting because they *look* so good), and answer choices that are outside of the scope of the passage. An answer choice doesn't have to be one you'd come up with on your own to be correct—it just has to be true according to the passage.

Finally, remember that you do have a time limit. Don't spend too much time on any one question. Guess, circle it in your test booklet, and come back for another look if you have time when you finish the section.

SUMMARY

In this chapter, we went over every SmartPoint on the ACT Science test, and the strategies to use for each at their various complexities.

We also saw how the SmartPoints fit into the three different passage types; you had a chance to use the distinct methods for each passage type discussed in the previous chapter, and the strategies for each question type within those passages.

Use this chapter for continued study and reference as you practice Science passages and find the skills you need to focus on.

Remember, don't get bogged down in the details and don't let complexity scare you. All of the information you need to answer the questions can be found in the passage. You can even answer most of the questions without a clear understanding of meaning. Carefully search the data for Figure Interpretation questions, relate variables for Pattern questions, and think like a scientist for the sake of Scientific Reasoning.

Continue to rehearse the Kaplan Methods. Being able to quickly recognize what passage type you're dealing with, then diving in with the appropriate strategy to find the information you need, is an important skill. Use the Practice Tests, when you're ready, to practice each Kaplan Method again. Refer back to this chapter and the previous chapter as often as necessary. Build these habits now to increase your efficiency on Test Day.

Use the strategies to find the info you need and nothing more. Get to the questions. Research your answer and earn points to master the ACT Science test!

UNIT 5: WRITING

The Basics:

30 Minutes

1 Prompt

Pacing:

Take 5 minutes to read the prompt and create a plan. Spend 23 minutes producing the essay. Spend 2 minutes proofreading.

TEST DAY DIRECTIONS AND FORMAT

This is a test of your writing skills. You will have thirty (30) minutes to write an essay in English. Before you begin planning and writing your essay, read the writing prompt carefully to understand exactly what you are being asked to do. Your essay will be evaluated on the evidence it provides of your ability to express judgments by taking a position on the issue in the writing prompt; to maintain a focus on the topic throughout the essay; to develop a position by using logical reasoning and by supporting your ideas; to organize ideas in a logical way; and to use language clearly and effectively according to the conventions of standard written English.

You may use the unlined pages in this test booklet to plan your essay. These pages will not be scored. *You must write your essay in pencil on the lined pages in the answer folder.* Your writing on those lined pages will be scored. You may not need all the lined pages, but to ensure you have enough room to finish, do NOT skip lines. You may write corrections or additions neatly between the lines of your essay, but do NOT write in the margins of the lined pages. *Illegible essays cannot be scored, so you must write (or print) clearly.*

If you finish before time is called, you may review your work. Lay your pencil down immediately when time is called.

OUTSIDE KNOWLEDGE

No outside knowledge is required.

THE INSIDE SCOOP

This is an optional part of the ACT, as far as your registration is concerned. Whether or not it is truly optional depends on whether your high school or the colleges you're applying to require it. If they do, it isn't optional! If you're not sure what schools you're applying to, or whether they require it, consider it mandatory—far better to have it and not need it than need it and not have it. Either way, it's an area which, with some advance practice and planning, you can get a high score on, so you should be prepare to take it with confidence.

The ACT Writing test is designed to gauge your ability to compose a clear and logical argument, and effectively present it in written form.

The essay prompt will present a relatable issue. You must take a point of view on that issue, state it clearly, support your point with clear and relevant examples, and provide a clear and coherent overall argument, preferably including a discussion of the opposing point of view.

The essay is *argument-based*, not *fact-based*. That is, you're being tested on what you can effectively argue, not what you know about the topic. Does this mean facts aren't relevant? Yes and no—you will not be scored based on whether your facts are *true* or not, but you will be scored based on whether the facts you use are effectively utilized. In other words, if in an essay about being active in your community you attribute the quote "Ask not what your country can do for you; ask what you can do for your country" to Abraham Lincoln, you will be factually wrong, but you will be using an effective piece of evidence anyway. So you will get "credit" for effective use of information, even though that was said by John F. Kennedy.

SMARTPOINTS

As there is only one prompt for the Writing Test, there are no SmartPoints. All strategies apply to the whole section.

CHAPTER 12

Writing Part 1: Inside the ACT Writing Test

THE KAPLAN METHOD FOR ACT WRITING

STEP 1: PROMPT

Read about the issue, and be sure you understand clearly what the core argument is. You cannot get a high score without clearly responding to the "this side or that side" issue. Pick a position on it. There is no right or wrong answer, but you also do not have to pick the side you agree with. You should take the side you can *best defend*, whether that's "your" side or not. Be aware that **both** sides can be effectively defended; there's no "easy" or "right" side.

STEP 2: PLAN

Take up to five minutes to plan your essay before you write. Most students skip this step on Test Day! Take this time to plan so you know what you're trying to accomplish and can give your best first draft. In this time, create your thesis. You already decided upon a stance, now compose an early sentence that states your position clearly. Then, focus on what kinds of reasoning and examples you can use to support your position. If you find you have more examples for a position different from the one you thought you would take, *change your position*. Finally, narrow it down. You won't have time to make every point. Choose the best two to three supporting points you have. You'll use one in each body paragraph. And decide upon two good pieces of evidence to use with each supporting piece. The strongest arguments will not just be hypothetical positions, but will be backed up with real-world evidence.

STEP 3: PRODUCE

Write your draft, sticking closely to your plan. You should aim to have four well-developed paragraphs with topic sentences and supporting details. Three to five paragraphs are generally fine as well, but four is a healthy number to aim for, as it gives you the space you need to develop an argument, without needing to stretch. You're not scored on a specific number of words or paragraphs, but on the strength of what you do put down. So it's much better to have four great paragraphs then rush and write five quick ones. Be very sure to include an introductory paragraph stating your position and a concluding paragraph—without those two framing paragraphs, you're missing fundamental ingredients of an essay. If possible, address a counter-argument as well; this is a highly effective and mature type of writing. Acknowledging that there is another side, and it is understandable why it is appealing, but here is why it is wrong, is far more impactful than either pretending there isn't another side or that it's clearly foolish. Remember, it isn't—and the essay-graders will have seen both sides argued effectively. So if you don't respect the other side, it just shows that you haven't thought about it, not that the other side is wrong. And do write neatly—words that cannot be read cannot be scored.

STEP 4: PROOFREAD

Always leave yourself the last couple of minutes to review your work—the time spent will definitely pay off. Very few of us can avoid the occasional confused sentence or omitted word when we write under pressure, and a missed word can make a huge difference to a sentence. Again, the grader can only score what they read, not what you might mean. So always quickly review your essay to be sure your ideas are clearly stated. Also, by leaving yourself this two-minute buffer at the end of your work, you'll avoid having to rush your conclusion. Remember, that's the last thing your essay grader will read, and you want to go out strong.

QUICK TIPS

MIND-SET

- **Don't wait until Test Day to think of examples you can use to support your ideas.** Regardless of what question is raised in the prompt, you will draw your support from the things you know best and are most comfortable writing about—things that you can describe in concrete detail. Think about important times in your life, people who have inspired you, experiences that define you. You will be able to bring many of these in regardless of the specific topic.

- **Refresh your memory about school subjects, current events, personal experiences, and activities—anything.** By doing so, you strengthen mental connections to those ideas and details—that will make it easier to connect to the right examples on Test Day. Again, the importance here is knowing that real-world evidence is far more powerful than hypothetical stances. Saying "This is right because I believe it" will never be as strong as saying "This is right—look at all this evidence."

SPECIAL STRATEGIES

You must be very focused in order to write a complete, coherent essay in 30 minutes. During the planning stage, you may want to use the two following strategies to get organized:

1. **Draw a "T" and list your argument on either side of it** (your stance on one side and your arguments addressing the other side on the other). This method will help you decide if you have enough to back up your stance. You may find you need to take the opposite point of view! It will also make it much easier to address a counter-argument, if you know what the counter-arguments are, and already have your rebuttals prepared.

2. **Then, list the topic of each paragraph** you plan to write, noting the segments of the argument that you want to make. Remember, you don't have time to make every point. Choose the best ones to support your thesis.

Stick to the plan as you write the essay. Don't change the plan in midstream if another idea suddenly comes to you; it might derail the essay. Keep your focus on the issue and don't digress.

Make the structure of your essay very easy for the reader to see. Have an introductory paragraph, two middle paragraphs, each focused on one supporting point with evidence, and a concluding paragraph.

Write neatly. Again, graders can only score what they can read, so illegible writing will affect your score. If your handwriting is a problem, print.

TIMING

With only 30 minutes, efficient use of time is critical. Divide your time as follows:

5–6 minutes—Read the prompt and plan your essay.

22–23 minutes—Draft your essay, sticking to the plan.

2 minutes—Proofread and correct any errors.

WHEN YOU'RE RUNNING OUT OF TIME

Unfortunately, you won't be able to guess on the last few questions when you're running out of time, as you would on the other tests. Thus, practice the timing carefully to avoid losing coherence because of time. If you do start running out of time, leave out one of your example paragraphs and go straight to the concluding paragraph. The conclusion is a necessary component of an essay, and its exclusion or short-changing will cost you more than a strong body paragraph will gain you. Even when you're rushed, still try to allow one to two minutes to proofread for errors that affect clarity.

SCORING

Two trained readers read and score each of your essays on a scale of 1–6; those scores are added together to arrive at your Writing subscore (from 2–12). Essays can get a zero if they are left blank, entirely off-topic, or illegible. If there's a difference of more than a point between the two readers' scores (for example: one grader gives you a 3 and the other a 5), your essay will be read by a third reader. Readers evaluate the essays *holistically*, judging the overall quality of each, not assigning separate scores for specific elements like grammar or organization.

A combined English-Writing score will also be recorded. Two-thirds of this score is based on your English score and one-third is based on your Writing subscore. The combined English-Writing score does not count toward your Composite score.

Statistically speaking, there will be few essays that score 12 out of 12. If each grader gives your essay a 4 or 5 (making your subscore 8 or 10), that will place you at the upper range of those taking the exam.

METHOD BREAKDOWN

STEP 1: PROMPT

The ACT Writing prompt usually relates to a topic that is familiar to high school students. It will outline an issue that teenagers are likely to have an opinion on. In most cases, the subject will be something fairly innocuous, like whether to use videos in classroom instruction, but if by chance the prompt describes a situation you feel strongly about, be sure to still present your argument in a careful, thoughtful manner. Do NOT write an overly emotional response. You are being gauged on the strength of your argument, not the strength of your feelings.

Here's an example of a typical ACT Writing prompt:

> In many high schools, the administration provides guidelines for the publication of student newspapers. These guidelines often determine which topics can and cannot be discussed in the newspaper and prohibit use of language that the administration deems inappropriate. Many administrators and teachers feel that these restrictions enable them to provide a safe learning environment for students. Others feel that any restriction on the student newspaper is a violation of freedom of speech. In your opinion, should high schools place restrictions on student newspapers?
>
> In your essay, take a position on this question. You may write about either one of the two points of view given, or you many present a different point of view on this question. Use specific reasons and examples to support your position.

As you read, be sure you understand the argument clearly. In this case, the argument is "Should high schools place restrictions on student newspapers—yes or no?" You know you have the right question in this case because it is stated clearly in the prompt, but it may not always be. If the question is not stated this clearly, make sure you get to a point where you can take one side or the other, but not both. As in this case—you can say "Yes, high schools should place restrictions on student newspapers," or "No, they shouldn't." You cannot argue both.

STEP 2: PLAN

Take five or six minutes to build a plan before you write. This step is critical—a successful plan leads directly to a high-scoring essay. Focus on what kinds of reasoning and examples you can use to support your position.

Note: If you find you have more examples for a position different from the one you thought you would take originally, *change your position*.

There is no single way to plan an essay. As mentioned, one method is to draw a large "T" on the page and align examples and ideas on either side of the line. This will take a few minutes, but can easily be done in the five minutes you have set aside for planning, and will make the actual production *much* faster and smoother. You might have the following notes on the prompt we started with in Step 1:

Newspapers in School	
safe learning environment (more control)	freedom of speech (less control)
can have faculty advisor monitor coverage to make sure issues are clearly, fairly, and *tastefully* presented administration can get its side heard promotes safe discussion, improves student morale, avoids protests	add coverage of state, local elections, & discussion of school issues imp't to students help prepare students to be adults who know how to think and to vote air debates about student rights ex. dress code ex. off-campus lunch privileges students have rights and should be acknowledged.

Conclusion: Everyone benefits from freedom of speech in a school newspaper.

Information banks: Don't wait until Test Day to think of examples you can use to support your ideas. Regardless of what question is raised in the prompt, you will draw your support from the things you know best and are most comfortable writing about—things you know a fair amount of concrete detail about.

Refresh your memory about your favorite or most memorable books, school subjects, historical events, personal experiences, activities—anything. By doing so, you strengthen mental connections to those ideas and details—that will make it easier to connect to the right examples on Test Day.

Structure your essay: Plan a clear introduction, a distinct middle section, and a strong conclusion. **Choose your best examples, decide in what order you'll handle them, and plan your paragraphs.**

With that in mind:

- Use an effective *hook* to bring the reader in.

- Use regular *transitions* to provide the "glue" that holds your ideas together.

- End with a *bang* to make your essay memorable.

Using a "hook" means avoiding an essay that opens (as thousands of other essays will): "In my opinion, … because …" Your opinion is not compelling to a reader who has graded hundreds of essays on the same subject. Make it something more exciting than that!

Using the "T" model presented earlier, you might use the following sentence:

A student newspaper should help students learn to think and express themselves.

A "bang" means a closing that ties the three example paragraphs together. A good choice can be a clear, succinct statement of your thesis in the essay or a vivid example that's right on point.

To conclude the planned "T" essay, you might finish with:

> *Both students and the administration would benefit from a school newspaper that covers a broad array of topics.*

In summary, a good plan:

- Responds to the prompt

- Has an introduction

- Has strong examples, usually one per paragraph

- Has a strong conclusion

STEP 3: PRODUCE

You are not graded directly on word count, but graders know that filling out a thorough argument takes time and space—it will be hard to present all the elements of a strong argument in few words or only a couple of paragraphs. So don't think about your *number of words*, think about the *strength of your arguments.*

Organization counts. Graders are far more able to follow—and be compelled by—your argument if they can see its distinct ingredients. **Use one paragraph for your introduction, one for each example or line of reasoning, and one for your conclusion so your essay will be easy for readers to follow.**

Write neatly. Graders may give you a zero if your essay is impossible to read. If your handwriting is a problem, print.

Stick with the plan. Resist any urge to introduce new ideas—no matter how good you think they are—or to digress from the central focus or organization of each paragraph.

Use topic sentences. Each paragraph should be organized around a topic sentence that you should finish in your mind before you start to write. These may begin:

- *One example…*

- *Another example…*

- *Therefore, we can conclude…*

You don't have to write it this way in the essay, but completing these sentences in your mind ensures that you focus on the idea that organizes each paragraph.

Choose words carefully. Use vocabulary you know well. Inserting new or fancy words that you have learned recently often sticks out. The result of unfamiliar words in an essay is the opposite of what you want: awkward, confusing thoughts. Instead of impressing the graders, you have obscured your points. Two more points here:

1. **Avoid using / excessively.** You are absolutely allowed to use personal examples ("At my school, we had this issue just last year, and I was very involved in the discussion…"),

but avoid using your opinions or beliefs *as evidence* ("I really think…" "I believe…" "In my opinion…"). You give your argument weak ground when they're founded on your thoughts, not what you can prove.

2. **Avoid slang.** Your tone should be personal and natural, but academic. This is a school paper. Abbreviations such as you might use in text messaging, online, or in personal e-mails are not appropriate here—at best, they're unprofessional, and at worst the grader won't know what you're talking about.

Use transitions. Think about the relationship between ideas as you write, and spell them out clearly. This makes it easy for the readers to follow your reasoning, and they'll appreciate it. **Use key words from the prompt as well as the kinds of words you've learned about in Reading that indicate contrast, opinion, relative importance, and support.**

Don't sweat the small stuff. Do not obsess over every little thing. If you cannot remember how to spell a word, do your best and just **keep going.** Even the top-scoring essays can have minor errors. The essay readers understand that you are writing first drafts and have no time for research or revision.

STEP 4: PROOFREAD

Always leave yourself two or three minutes to review your work—the time spent will definitely pay off. Very few of us can avoid the occasional confused sentence or omitted word when we write under pressure. Quickly review your essay to be sure your ideas are clearly stated.

> ✔ **EXPERT TUTOR TIP**
>
> Use a caret ∧ or an asterisk * to insert a word or words. Write a backward P or H to create a new paragraph, and cross words out with one line. Don't make a mess!

Don't hesitate to make corrections on your essay—these are timed first drafts, not term papers. But keep it clear: use a single line through deletions and an asterisk to mark where text should be inserted.

In this proofreading time, remind yourself **you don't have time to revise substantially**. This isn't the time for inserting new paragraphs, radically changing your tone, or (worst yet) changing your mind. Use your practice essays to learn the types of mistakes you tend to make, and look for them.

COMMON ERRORS

- Omitted words
- Sentence fragments
- Misplaced modifiers

- Misused words—especially homonyms like *their* for *there* or *they're*

- Spelling errors

COMMON STYLE PROBLEMS
- Choppy sentences (combine some)

- Too many long, complex sentences (break some up)

- Too many stuffy-sounding words (replace some with simple words)

- Too many simple words (add a few college-level words)

SUMMARY

In this chapter, we went over the basics of strategy necessary to write a high-scoring essay on the ACT Writing test.

Remember, the idea is to write an argumentative essay. Take a distinct stance, then support your argument with a clear logical flow of points and evidence. Make sure to plan! You can get a good score on the ACT Writing test just by having clear points and proper structure. Know what points you are going to make beforehand to avoid having an essay that sounds like a stream of consciousness. And use a new paragraph to start a new point.

The ideal structure: Put your thesis and a hook into your first paragraph. Have two body paragraphs, each with a distinct supporting point and evidence, at least one of which should address the counter-argument. Restate your thesis and wrap up your argument with a concluding paragraph. Make sure you don't bring up any new points in the conclusion. Just wrap things up neatly.

Leave yourself a couple of minutes to proofread. It'll also help you to have that time as a buffer, in case you run long. That way you won't have to cut your conclusion short.

In the next chapter, we'll go over each piece of the essay in detail, and how to craft those pieces to maximize your score.

Work on the sections you most need, whether it's crafting a compelling hook for your introduction or a clear thesis, or whether it's using well-developed evidence to drive a body paragraph home.

Put the pieces together at the end of these Writing chapters by completing a sample essay test and reviewing your strengths and weaknesses.

Keep an eye on where you're going. Take a side and be clear, create a plan and follow through, and support, and you're already well on your way to mastering the ACT Writing test.

CHAPTER 13

Writing Part 2: ACT Writing Strategy in Depth

OVERVIEW

Use this chapter to get familiar with how to form the proper pieces of an essay for the ACT Writing test.

We'll go over each in turn, paragraph-by-paragraph.

For the Introduction paragraph, we'll discuss how to create a thesis (the most important sentence of your essay) and how to draw the reader in with a hook.

For the Body paragraphs, we'll discuss further how to craft good supporting points, then create specific evidence to back those up. Finally, we'll look at the proper way to handle a counter-argument.

For the Conclusion, we'll discuss how to properly restate your thesis and bring the essay to a close.

Finally, we'll discuss essays holistically. Essays are graded holistically, meaning that they are looked at for a general impression as opposed to whether or not they contain specific pieces. We'll discuss how the pieces should fit together and how to make them flow to maximize your score potential.

PARAGRAPH BY PARAGRAPH

THE INTRODUCTION

You've likely been writing essays for as long as you've been in school, and may have had multiple teachers tell you at various points the "one right way" to write an essay. If you've come to suspect there may not really be "one right way," you're in good company. What good essays do have in common, however, is a set of ingredients. Some of these ingredients are optional and vary based on individual taste, but some are necessary to have something resembling an academic essay.

Think about a sandwich. You can have any kind of bread and any kind of fillings you like, but if you don't have a piece of bread on each side and something in the middle, you don't have a sandwich. In a formal essay like this, the Introduction and Conclusion are your bread, and your Body paragraphs are your filling. What will you put in, what will it look like, what will it do, all these things are yours to decide. But without those ingredients, you don't have a sandwich.

Your Introduction paragraph needs to fulfill certain roles. It must:

- Introduce the argument. By the end of the first paragraph, a person who has just picked up your essay should know what is being discussed and what the main arguments are.

- Establish your side of the argument. We'll talk more about your **Thesis Statement** soon, but do know this is where it goes. You may have heard before that your thesis should be the first line of the first paragraph, or the last line of the first paragraph, or the first line of the second paragraph, or any other location, but rest assured that it should just be *somewhere* in the first paragraph. Readers should go into the second paragraph (the first Body paragraph) knowing which side you're on.

- Set the tone for the essay. While your essay should be academic, there is still a lot of wiggle room in exactly what this means. Will your essay be fierce and uncompromising? Gentle but persuasive? Personal and humorous? Whatever tone comes most naturally to you, use that, but make sure to keep it consistent throughout the essay. Sudden changes of voice will distract readers.

Your Introduction paragraph *may* also introduce your arguments. A sentence explaining what evidence you are going to use to prove your point, if it fits naturally with the shape of the Introduction, can be beneficial. If it doesn't seem natural or necessary, this can be omitted and put in the Body paragraphs themselves.

If you've included these items, you have an Introduction! The Thesis and Hook are the most important pieces of this paragraph, and will draw readers into your argument fully, so let's dig into those further.

THE THESIS STATEMENT

Before you can create a thesis, you need to understand the issue. Start with Step 1 and read the prompt. To help you focus on the topic, it's a good idea to underline key words in the prompt as you read. Key words are the nouns and verbs that form the backbone of the prompt. These are words that you'll need to use in your essay to help you stay focused on your topic.

After reading the prompt, you move to Step 2, making your plan. You should create a brief written plan before you start writing your essay, but you don't need to do this immediately after reading the prompt. Take a minute to think about the question posed in the prompt. Do you have an immediate and strong reaction to it? Sometimes, you'll know right away how you feel about the question, and ideas and examples will pop into your head even as you're reading the prompt. At other times, though, you might be a little less certain. Perhaps both sides of the issue seem equally valid to you, and you can think of reasons to support both. In this case, don't spend too long deliberating. Remember, the questions posed in ACT prompts are chosen precisely because two reasonable people might have very legitimate reasons for supporting opposite views. Your essay score is not affected by which viewpoint you choose to defend.

Therefore, don't spend too much time deliberating over which side of the issue to support. Choose one viewpoint and jot down a list of evidence you can use to support that viewpoint. If you feel the opposite argument has validity, that's great, because you'll find it easy to think of a counter-argument. (You can read more about that in the sections that follow.) Once you've chosen a viewpoint, you need to formulate a good *thesis statement*. A thesis statement is a clear, simple sentence that describes the position you will support in your essay. Let's consider what a good thesis statement should look like. A strong thesis statement:

- answers the question in the prompt;

- leaves no doubt about where you stand on the issue; and

- doesn't necessarily contain reasons but does set the stage for your presentation of evidence that will follow.

WRITING EXERCISE 1

Suppose your essay prompt asks whether or not administrators should abolish the honor roll at your school. Consider each of the following sentences and put an asterisk next to the ones you think would make a good thesis sentence:

1. _____ I've always felt bad because I don't usually make the honor roll.

2. _____ The honor roll serves several educational purposes.

3. _____ Our school should continue to publish an honor roll.

4. _____ The honor roll actually distracts students from learning well.

5. _____ The honor roll unfairly rewards students with natural academic ability.

6. _____ We should maintain the honor roll because it continues to serve a useful purpose.

7. _____ While I do think students should be recognized for their academic successes, I think the honor roll as we know it should be discontinued.

8. _____ Teachers tend to give better grades to students they know have already been on the honor roll.

Sentences 3, 6, and 7 are the most appropriate thesis sentences. Sentences 1, 2, 4, 5, and 8 all discuss the honor roll, but they don't state a position relating to the question in the prompt. These sentences might be appropriate as part of your argument in the essay, but they can't take the place of a thesis statement.

DEMONSTRATING UNDERSTANDING OF COMPLEXITY

One thing an ACT essay grader expects to find in a top-scoring essay is an indication that the writer understands the complexity of the question in the prompt. The strongest ACT essays not only effectively argue a position, but also illustrate an understanding of the ramifications of that position. Two excellent ways to give your essay a broad context are to use the introduction to discuss the background of the question and to include a counter-argument and response to it later in the essay.

BODY PARAGRAPHS

Your essay should have 1 to 3 Body paragraphs between the Introduction and Conclusion. Each of these focuses on a different element of the main argument, whether the element is an example, a separate issue within the argument, or another way of looking at an issue. Each must serve to push the argument along. If there is a clear sequence between the points ("First this happens, then this happens, then this happens") the paragraphs should follow that sequence. If there isn't a definite relationship between the points ("Here's one example, here's another, here's another"), they can be in any order. You should, however, make sure to prioritize the strongest arguments to make sure they get written before time is called.

SUPPORTING POINTS

During your planning time, you should quickly brainstorm as many supporting points— reasons you're right, examples you can bring in—as possible. But then which to use? The strongest supporting points will:

• Clearly relate to the argument, not just be comparable ("limiting freedom of speech in school newspapers leaves students less prepared to form their own opinions" as opposed to "limiting freedom of speech is like telling people they can't go to their own church").

- Relate to real-world examples, not just hypothetical ("when District 58 required all student publications to submit work to administration for approval, student involvement in publications plummeted, and within two years all student-run newspapers in the district were closed because of lack of volunteers," not "if students have to submit their stories to administration, no one's going to want to do them").

- Treat counter-arguments seriously, but do refute their points. Don't be dismissive of them ("People who think administrators should review student newspapers are just totally wrong"), but make especially sure to not agree with them ("People who think administrators should monitor student newspapers have a point. Actually, they might be right."). Acknowledge that particular counter-arguments exist, and may even be appealing, but show why they're wrong.

Not all supporting points will satisfy all these criteria, but all should meet at least one of them, and the strongest essays will utilize all of these supporting types.

EVIDENCE

Now that you know what an appropriate thesis statement is, let's consider what your evidence should look like. The use of *evidence* (real-world examples) is highly effective, as it takes the argument off the page and grounds it in real issues. Consider these two points from our discussion of Supporting Points:

"When District 58 required all student publications to submit work to administration for approval, student involvement in publications plummeted, and within two years all student-run newspapers in the district were closed because of lack of volunteers."

"If students have to submit their stories to administration, no one's going to want to do them."

The first point is far stronger, not just because it's more developed (it explains both the consequence and the reason behind the consequence) but because it carries its own refutation of the counter-argument. To the second point, an opposing arguer can respond "Well, how do you know? Isn't that just your guess, or your opinion?" There is no refuting the real-world example, because it is not a guess.

The most important thing to remember in selecting evidence is that it should be specific and relevant to your topic. You should identify your examples and reasons in brief written notes in the plan step, but you'll actually flesh out your evidence in the produce step. That's when it's important to focus on developing your evidence specifically. A problem many unprepared students have with the ACT essay is not making evidence specific. Working under time pressure, many students don't plan evidence well, and they wind up talking in generalities instead of presenting specific evidence that supports a thesis. With practice, you can avoid this common flaw.

Because your ACT essay is an argument, you should take time during the planning step to reflect on the best way to organize your material. An essay that has a clear organization will be easy to follow and more likely to persuade the reader that you know what you're talking about and have good reasons for taking your position. The few minutes you spend in planning are crucial to organization. While you don't have to preplan every word you write, you should plan the key elements of your argument. If you know the topic of each paragraph, you're off to a good start.

Prepare solid examples to use by reading newspapers, staying informed about current events (local, national, and world), and read opinion articles and blogs. Doing so in the weeks leading up to Test Day will both provide you with a wealth of real-world examples and expose you to strong writing examples.

Try the following exercise to work on generating specific evidence.

WRITING EXERCISE 2

Suppose you want to support the viewpoint that students' cell phones should be turned off during school hours. Consider each of these sentences, and indicate whether it provides evidence that specifically supports your viewpoint:

1. _____ These days everybody has a cell phone.

2. _____ Ringing cell phones cause distractions in the classroom.

3. _____ The school makes too many rules that are unfair to students.

4. _____ Students who are texting in class are not learning the material the teacher is presenting.

5. _____ Pretty much everyone would agree with me that it's impossible to live without a cell phone.

6. _____ Teachers decide what we study, assign homework, and determine grades, but it's obvious that they should not tell us to turn off our phones during school time.

7. _____ Focused attention is necessary for learning, and having cell phones turned on compromises students' ability to focus.

8. _____ It's amazing how many things I can do with my tiny cell phone.

9. _____ The use of cell phones in the classroom, even for silent functions, can be annoying and distracting to other students.

10. _____ Using cell phones in the classroom takes students' attention away from the lesson and is therefore rude to teachers.

Did you notice that not every sentence that contains the words *cell phone* necessarily provides evidence supporting the argument? Only sentences 2, 4, 7, 9, and 10 present specific reasons supporting the argument that cell phones should be turned off in school. Notice that a couple of others use broad generalizations that aren't specific and relevant to the position. Be wary of using words such as *everybody* (sentence 1) and *everyone would agree with me* (sentence 5). You should also avoid a phrase like *it's obvious that* (sentence 6) because such wording assumes the reader sees your point. Your task in this essay is not to take the reader's agreement for granted but rather to use evidence that inspires agreement.

INFORMATION BANKS

Don't wait until Test Day to think about what subjects you can draw on for your examples to create animated and engaging essays. Examples can be drawn from anywhere: your life experience, a story you saw on the news, etc. So prepare yourself by refreshing your memory about your favorite subjects—collect examples that can be used for a variety of topics.

Don't hesitate to use your examples broadly. If the topic is about school, that doesn't mean you have to use school-based examples. It's better to write about things that you are comfortable with and know a lot about—but be sure to make it clear how they are relevant to the topic

THE COUNTER-ARGUMENT

Including a counter-argument in your essay is another good way to illustrate your understanding of the complexity of the issue. A counter-argument is an objection that someone might bring up about your argument. While you need to support your own position strongly, describing an objection that someone might make to it illustrates that you have the capacity to see both sides of the issue. Strongly supporting your own argument doesn't preclude acknowledging that someone on the other side may disagree with you for a particular reason. Discussing a counter-argument, acknowledging its validity, and then proceeding to give your response to it actually strengthens your own argument. You can bring up a counter-argument in either the middle or closer to the end of your essay. Effectively responding to an objection can be a part of your concluding paragraph.

And there you have the pieces of an excellent body paragraph! Before you move on, make sure to wrap up.

You'll want to have an evidence sandwich. In other words, you don't just want to jump into or out of your specific example. You take care of the one side of this with your topic sentence. This gives the reader an idea of the main point and what the evidence is supporting.

End your paragraph by coming back to the paragraph's topic sentence and evidence. Remind the reader what your evidence proved, wrap up the point, and move on.

CONCLUSION

Throughout this chapter and the last, we've discussed the importance of leaving time to write a strong conclusion. Remember: without a conclusion, you don't have a full formal essay, and your score will reflect that. Your conclusion serves multiple purposes:

- It ties all of your body paragraphs together ("Considering all of these arguments together…").

- It reminds the reader of the centrality of your argument ("Ultimately, we must remember the most important part…").

- It allows you to include a counter-argument if you have not yet done so ("Even with all these points, some will say…").

- It provides a chance to leave a lasting impression with a strong close ("We cannot overlook the importance of this issue…").

The tone and structure of your Conclusion will vary, but consider the opportunity you have, and make sure your Conclusion does all of the following:

- Restates your thesis, not word-for-word, but reiterates it to keep it clear in the reader's mind.

- Summarizes your points. Again, don't repeat them all, but reference them to reinforce their strength and relationship to your thesis.

- Wraps up the argument. By this point in the essay, you should be writing with the assumption that your reader agrees with you. Close with clear language about the rightness and importance of your argument.

PUTTING IT ALL TOGETHER

LANGUAGE

In your practice for the ACT English test, you're learning rules and principles to help you make the best choices about wording in the English passages. It's important that you keep these rules and principles in mind for the ACT Writing test as well. Remember that the last step of the Kaplan Method for ACT Writing is to proofread. If you spend an adequate amount of time on the prompt, plan, and produce steps, you'll have only a few minutes to proofread. Let's give some attention to the best ways to use this time effectively.

BE CAREFUL WITH PRONOUNS!

When you're writing under pressure, as you are on the ACT, it's easy to make some grammatical mistakes that affect the logic of your essay. The use of pronouns is an area that many students have trouble with. If you train yourself to pay attention to pronouns and think about what's involved in using them correctly, it will be easier to catch pronoun problems and correct them even when you're proofreading quickly. Everything you know about pronouns that you apply to the English test also holds true for the Writing test. Refresh yourself on the guidelines described here.

PRONOUN REFERENCE RULE

A pronoun refers to a noun or another pronoun. Do not use a pronoun if the sentence it's in or the sentence before it doesn't contain a word for the pronoun to refer logically to.

PRONOUN NUMBER RULE

A pronoun must agree in number with the noun or pronoun it refers to. Do not use a plural pronoun to refer to a singular noun.

PRONOUN SHIFT RULE

Do not switch between the words *one* and *you* in a given context.

AVOID SLANG AND CLICHÉS

Although some slang words and expressions are acceptable in ordinary conversation, you should avoid slang in your ACT essay. The purpose of the essay is to present a logical argument based on reasoning and evidence, and the language you choose should reflect the seriousness of the task. As you practice, become sensitive to the tone of various expressions. If you think something is slang or too informal, ask yourself if there's a more appropriate phrasing.

Like slang, clichéd language is best avoided in your ACT essay. A cliché is a worn-out, overused expression. Your essay should show that you're taking a fresh and thoughtful approach to the question posed, and the overuse of clichés undercuts the serious and thoughtful attention you bring to your argument.

USE CORRECT AND VARIED SENTENCE STRUCTURE

Sentence structure is tested directly on the ACT English test, but it's also very important for the essay you produce on the Writing test. To apply the principles of correct sentence structure in your essay, think about how you combine groups of words into sentences. You can avoid sentence fragments by making sure that each sentence includes a subject and a verb and expresses a complete thought. You can avoid run-ons by making sure that ideas are joined with proper punctuation and connections (transitions) words.

AVOID UNNECESSARY REPETITION

When you're writing an essay under very tight time constraints, as you must on the ACT, it's easy to find yourself using the same words and phrases frequently. Such repetition can detract from the effectiveness of your essay. You need to stay focused on the topic, that's true. However, if you use the same words and phrases repeatedly, it's a sign that you may not be developing your ideas thoroughly. Thus, the first remedy for needless repetition comes in the planning stage: Make sure you've reflected carefully about your viewpoint. To earn a high score, you must go beyond the ideas offered in the prompt; you must expand upon your own position with reasoning and evidence. Thinking through your plan and writing brief notes in the test booklet helps to ensure that you'll develop your ideas adequately during the production step. It can also help if you think of some synonyms for key words and phrases that are important to the topic.

SCORING

Step	A High-Scoring Essay	A Low-Scoring Essay
Prompt	clearly develops a position on the prompt	does not clearly state a position
Plan	supports with concrete, relevant examples	is general, repetitious, or overly simplistic
Produce	maintains clear focus and organization	digresses or has weak organization
Proofread	shows competent use of language	contains errors that reduce clarity

Kaplan has found this approach useful in our many years of experience with hundreds of sample essay statements on a wide range of tests. Let's look at what the test makers tell you about how the essays are scored.

To score a 4, you must:

- Answer the question

- Support ideas with examples

- Show logical thought and organization

- Avoid major or frequent errors that make your writing unclear

Organization and clarity are key to an above-average essay. If the reader can't follow your train of thought—if ideas aren't clearly organized or if grammatical errors, misspellings, and incorrect word choices make your writing unclear—you can't do well.

To score a 5, all you have to add to a 4 is:

- Address the topic in depth

In other words, offer more examples and details. The test graders love specific examples, and the more concrete your examples are, the more they clarify your thinking and keep you focused.

To score a 6, all you have to add to a 5 is:

- Make transitions smoother and show variety in syntax and vocabulary

Use words from the prompt to tie paragraphs together, rather than relying exclusively on connectors like *however* and *therefore*. Vary your sentence structure, sometimes using simple sentences and other times using compound and complex ones. Adding a few college-level vocabulary words will also boost your score.

Scoring the essay	In your essay, you must...	Your essay will not be affected by...
• The essay is scored by two readers, who each assign a score between 0 and 6. • The scores are added together to generate a final essay score that is between 0 and 12. • The essay is scored holistically. • Your ACT essay score is *not* included as part of your ACT Composite score. When you take this optional Writing test, you receive an additional score called the "Combined English/Writing Score," which is a combination of your section score in English and the essay score. The Combined English and Writing Score is between 1 and 36.	• answer the assignment question! • show an understanding of the issue. • show an understanding of the complexity of the issue. • have a distinct introduction and conclusion. • use effective organization. • have effective development of ideas. • maintain sustained focus. • demonstrate effective language use. • use effective transitions. • not have errors that detract from clarity and readability.	• which point of view you choose to defend • factual errors • a few minor spelling or grammatical errors

What does it mean for an essay to be scored holistically?

Your essay is scored *holistically*. That means it is based on the reader's overall impression of your writing skill, not a tally of points you got "right" or "wrong."

What is a rubric?

To maintain consistency in grading, though, graders do use a *rubric*. This is a general breakdown of the types of skill levels they can expect to see at particular score levels. A rubric very similar to the official one is provided here. Familiarize yourself with the types of things graders are looking for so you can give the essay your best!

6	5	4
PROMPT		
• Shows a *clear* understanding of the prompt • Displays *insightful* critical thinking skills • *Maintains focus on the prompt*	• Shows a *reasonably* clear understanding of the prompt • Displays *strong* critical thinking skills • *Maintains focus on the prompt*	• Shows *some* understanding of the prompt • Displays *competent* critical thinking skills • *Generally maintains focus on the prompt*
SUPPORT AND ORGANIZATION		
• Is developed *specifically* and *logically* • Uses examples that are *relevant* and *well developed* • Is *clearly* organized • Presents ideas *logically* • Uses transitions *effectively*	• Shows *generally specific* and *logical* development • Uses examples that are *generally relevant* and *well developed* • Is *generally clearly* organized • Presents ideas *logically* • *Generally* uses transitions *effectively*	• Is developed *adequately* • Uses examples that are *adequate* • Is *generally clearly* organized • *Generally* presents ideas *logically* • Uses transitions *sporadically*
LANGUAGE		
• Displays *good* use of language • Uses vocabulary that is *appropriate* and *varied* • Uses *varied* sentence structure • Has *few* if *any* errors • Has *no errors that distract* from clarity or readability	• Displays *competent* use of language • Uses vocabulary that is *appropriate* and *sometimes varied* • Uses *somewhat varied* sentence structure • Has *few* errors • Has errors that *rarely distract* from clarity or readability	• Displays *adequate* use of language • Uses vocabulary that is *somewhat appropriate* and *sometimes varied* • Uses *somewhat varied* sentence structure • Has *some* errors • Has errors that *may distract* from readability but *do not impact* clarity

3	2	1
PROMPT		
• Shows *some* understanding of the prompt • Shows *developing* critical thinking skills • May display *inconsistent* focus on the prompt	• Shows a *vague* or *limited* understanding of the prompt • Displays *weak* critical thinking skills • *Maintains poor* focus on the prompt	• Shows *little* or *no* understanding of the prompt • Displays critical thinking skills that are *fundamentally lacking* • *Generally fails to maintain* focus on the prompt
SUPPORT AND ORGANIZATION		
• Development *may be inconsistent* • Uses examples that *may be irrelevant* and/or *inadequate* • Shows *limited* organization • *May not* present ideas *logically* • May use *limited* transitions	• Shows *seriously limited* development • Uses examples that *may be irrelevant* and/or *insufficient* • Is *poorly* organized • *Does not* present ideas *logically* • Displays *weak* use of transitions	• Is developed *poorly* • Uses examples that are *limited* or *nonexistent* • Is *poorly* organized • *Does not* present ideas logically • *Does not* use transitions *effectively*
LANGUAGE		
• Displays *limited* use of language • Uses vocabulary that is *developing* but *inconsistent* • Uses sentence structure that *lacks variety* • May have *numerous* error • Has errors that *may distract* from readability and *may impact* clarity	• Displays *little facility* with language • Uses vocabulary that is *limited* and *occasionally incorrect* • Uses sentence structure that *displays frequent problems* • Has *numerous* errors • Has errors that *sometimes distract* from clarity or readability	• Displays *no facility* with language • Uses vocabulary with *little* or *no mastery* • Uses sentence structure that is *severely flawed* • Has errors that are *pervasive* • Has errors that *distract* from readability and *significantly impact* clarity

VIEW FROM THE OTHER SIDE: GETTING YOUR SCORE AND GRADING ESSAYS

GETTING YOUR SCORE

We've referenced the idea a few times that your essay score is *holistic*—that is, that it reflects the grader's overall impression of your writing skill, rather than a strict equation of "right" and "wrong" answers. There is not, for example, an automatic point deduction for a misspelled word, or a misused punctuation mark. However, an essay riddled with poor punctuation and spelling will be harder for a grader to give a high score. Still, there are elements essay graders consistently look for as hallmarks of strong writing. The grading criteria include:

- Does the author answer the question?

- Is the author's position clearly stated?

- Does the body of the essay support and develop the position taken?

- Are there at least two supporting paragraphs?

- Is the relevance of each supporting paragraph clear?

- Does the writer address the other side of the argument?

- Is the essay organized, with a clear introduction, middle, and end?

- Does the author start a new paragraph for each new idea?

- Is each sentence in a paragraph relevant to the point made in that paragraph?

- Are transitions clear?

- Is the essay easy to read? Is it engaging?

- Are sentences varied?

- Is vocabulary used effectively? Is college-level vocabulary used?

While a perfect essay will address all of these points, a strong essay that gets a 4 or 5 from each grader will have to do fairly well at most all the points. An essay that misses any of them completely or does multiple of them at a very low level will have a hard time getting a high score, and the more basic the requirement, the more it affects your score. For example, while an otherwise-strong essay that has only basic transitions can still do well, an essay that doesn't directly answer the question cannot score higher than a 2 from each grader.

GRADING ESSAYS

Let's look at some sample essays based on the "newspaper" prompt we've seen. Evaluate each essay against the points we've discussed, and give it a score.

SAMPLE ESSAY 1

In many high schools, the administration has provided guidelines for the publication of student newspapers. These guidelines often determine which topics can and cannot be discussed in the newspaper, and prohibit what the administration deems inappropriate language. Many administrators and teachers feel that these restrictions enable them to provide a safe, appropriate learning environment for students. Others feel that any restriction on the student newspaper is a violation of freedom of speech. In my opinion, students should be free to write on any topic.

Firstly, restrictions will not stop certain topics being talked about. Students will always discuss topics that they are interested in. Second, students are more aware of what is or is not appropriate than the administration might think. A newspaper is there to tell news and students will therefore write about the news.

Finally and most importantly, a right such as freedom of speech should not be checked at the school door. Students not being able to cognizant and value rights such as these if they are not taught their importance in school. So high schools should not place restrictions on student newspapers.

Score:_____ /6

It should have been fairly easy to see that this isn't a strong essay. This essay would get a score of 2 or 3 out of 6. The author does state a clear opinion, but half of the essay is a direct copy of the prompt—the graders will notice this and those sentences won't help the score. The time and space spent just quoting the prompt was completely wasted—it earned the writer zero points.

The rest of the essay is organized and uses transition words (*firstly* and *finally).* The author states her thesis, follows with three supporting reasons, and then a conclusion. However, none of this is discussed fully enough—no concrete details or examples are given. In the second paragraph, for instance, the author should have added an example demonstrating that students are aware of what is appropriate or an example of topics that students will discuss in the paper.

The language is understandable, but there are significant errors affecting clarity. For instance, the second sentence of paragraph 3 is a fragment—there is no verb. Some vocabulary words are used without a clear understanding of their meaning: In paragraph 3, "not being able to cognizant" is incorrect; perhaps the student meant "not being able to understand."

This essay looks like the writer couldn't think of good ideas, waited too long to start writing, and had to write in a hurry.

Let's try another essay. Read quickly and select a score before reading our evaluation.

SAMPLE ESSAY 2

Many high schools place restrictions on appropriate topics and language for student newspapers. Many people disagree with these restrictions. While arguments can be made for either side, I believe that newspapers, as part of the school, should be placed under guidelines of the school.

First, a high school necessarily has stricter rules than normal society. These rules are not in place to punish students. They protect them and providing a suitable learning environment. In this way, when students leave high school they will have grown from children to adults, ready to succeed in the larger world. For example, the strict time schedule, with exactly three or four minutes given between classes, prepares students for strict schedules in the broader world.

Second, students interested in journalism should have instruction in how to write and publish newspaper articles. A student newspaper, which for obvious reasons has limited scope, is a perfect laboratory for students to experiment with journalistic writing. The administration and faculty dedicated to the newspaper can guide students in choosing appropriate topics, such as student elections. Then they can write articles on politics in the future. Imagine a student whose high school teacher taught the proper techniques for reporting on the race for student council president, joining a major news organization and reporting on the United States Presidential election.

Lastly, students may not realize the harm which their writing may cause. In my school, a student discovered a teacher's affair and "reported" on it in a story on the student's TV network, before the school could interfere. The teacher's career was destroyed and his marriage fell apart. Perhaps he deserved it, but student television should not have been the vehicle that ruined his life. The student reporter felt terribly in the end, as she had not thought through the consequences of her story. The same consequences could occur in a student newspaper that was restricted by no guidelines from the school.

Therefore, while many people argue that freedom of speech is a right too precious to give up, it is more important to provide guidelines for young people.

Score:_____ /6

Okay, now how do you want to score this essay?

This sample exceeds the basic requirements and would earn a 4 or 5.

This essay addresses the assignment. The writer's position is clear, and the personal example in the fourth paragraph provides good support. The organization is good, and the author uses transition words. Each paragraph discusses a different aspect of the writer's argument. Let's look at why it doesn't rate a 6.

Some of the support isn't explained enough. The second paragraph, for example, doesn't show the connection between strict schedules and restrictions on newspaper reporting—the subject of the essay; those ideas are comparable, but not directly related. The idea, in paragraph 3, of a student growing up to be a presidential reporter is interesting, but it doesn't particularly address the idea of restrictions, so doesn't earn points. The final paragraph doesn't tie back to the main argument about newspapers; it only generally mentions "guidelines for young people."

The author's writing is good, but unexceptional. There are a few examples of complex sentences. For example, in paragraph 3: "A student newspaper, which for obvious reasons has limited scope, is a perfect laboratory for students to experiment with journalistic writing." The essay includes grammar mistakes, however, such as in paragraph 2: "They protect them and providing a suitable learning environment." In paragraph 3, the sentence "Then they can write articles on politics in the future" includes the ambiguous *they*, which could refer to the administration and teachers or the students.

Let's look at another essay. Read it quickly and decide how you would score it.

SAMPLE ESSAY 3

School administrations and teachers who support restrictions believe that these restrictions are needed to form an appropriate learning environment. But I agree with those who oppose such restrictions because they violate freedom of speech and these limits impede student progress and success after high school.

Despite the true need for rules in high schools, newspapers should be exempt. Students need discipline in the form of detention for misbehavior or demerits for poor study, but the student newspaper should not be a part of that system. Rather, it should mimic "real world" journalism.

Student editors, usually seniors aged seventeen or eighteen, are well aware of the overall environment in which they publish, and understand what is or is not appropriate. High school should give students practice at being cognizant of the larger arena in which they act. The few negative incidents that free press will admittedly cause will teach students that in life, one must take responsibility for one's actions.

Therefore, the argument for freedom of speech in student newspapers advances substantial educational goals for students, as well as our unalienable right of freedom of speech. This right, however, is paramount. The American public school is an extension of the American government and community, and censorship is inconsistent with American democracy. Again, students need to be prepared for the world they will live in; depriving them of rights that are promoted in the greater community prepares students poorly for life after high school.

Finally, censoring information in the student newspaper will not remove the subject from student discussion. Rather, it will remove a balanced, informative viewpoint, and often make the "inappropriate" action more desirable and "cool." Placing restrictions on student newspapers would be a serious mistake that would hinder students from learning what it is to participate in a free society.

Score:_____ /6

This essay is pretty good—it would earn a 4. The position is clearly stated, and some supporting reasoning is given.

However, the reasoning is too general and the writing is too ordinary to earn the top score. Let's see how it could be improved.

TURNING A 4 INTO A 6

The essay plunges right into the two points of view offered in the prompt. It could be improved by introducing the issue with a general statement, like:

> Many students, parents, and school administrators are debating the proper role of student newspapers. Should their language and content be restricted?

In the last sentence of the first paragraph, the writer introduces some additional reasoning *not* included in the prompt. That's excellent, but it would be better to make it clear where the position from the prompt ends and the author's position begins, perhaps like this:

> But I agree with those who oppose such restrictions because they violate freedom of speech. I would further argue that these limits impede student progress and success after high school.

The second paragraph is relevant and organized—it covers one of the two positions offered in the prompt. But it would be better if the writer tied this argument more clearly to something specific in the prompt, perhaps with an opening sentence using language from the prompt, like:

> Some people claim that high school students need strict guidelines in order to prepare for life after school.

Moreover, at the end of the paragraph, the reference to mimicking "real world" journalism would be improved by telling the reader what "real world" journalism is:

> Rather, it should mimic "real world" journalism, which strives to provide valid, balanced reporting on events important to the public, or in this case, the student body.

The third paragraph addresses the view in the prompt that students can cause harm by printing inappropriate articles. Again, it should be made clearer what part of the prompt this paragraph is responding to, with a first sentence like:

> Others believe that students may cause unintended harm with newspaper articles written on controversial subjects.

Paragraph four is pretty good, as is. It states clearly what the author considers the most important argument. The fifth paragraph raises good arguments, but leaves them undeveloped. It would be best to provide an example of what type of story would help promote "balanced, informative" discussion to counteract "inappropriate, cool" actions, like:

> For instance, a reporter for my high school paper researched and wrote an in-depth story on the increasing drug problem among students. The administration quickly intervened and stopped the story, declaring that drugs were an inappropriate topic for student discussion. This story, however, would have focused discussion on a crucial issue for students, so

that they can make the right choice when offered drugs or when they see friends using drugs. Unfortunately, this is a situation most students will face, and they need to be prepared. Suppressing the story made drugs seem even more rebellious and mysterious and most importantly did not give students facts with which they could prepare.

This makes it clear why the writer saved this argument for the last—an important, detailed example.

Finally, since this writer offers a fair number of supporting ideas, it would also be a good idea to add some transitions that establish the relative importance of those ideas. For example, in the third paragraph:

First of all, student editors, usually seniors aged seventeen or eighteen, are well aware of the overall environment in which they publish, and understand what is or is not appropriate. But even more importantly, high school should give students practice at being cognizant of the larger arena in which they act.

Here's how this essay would look with the improvements we've suggested.

Many students, parents, and school administrators are debating the proper role of student newspapers. Should their language and content be restricted? School administrations and teachers who support restrictions believe that these restrictions are needed to form an appropriate learning environment. But I agree with those who oppose such restrictions because they violate freedom of speech. I would further argue that these limits impede student progress and success after high school.

Some people claim that high school students need strict guidelines in order to prepare for life after school. Despite the true need for rules in high schools, newspapers should be exempt. Students need discipline in the form of detention for misbehavior or demerits for poor study, but the student newspaper should not be a part of that system. Rather, it should mimic "real world" journalism, which strives to provide valid, balanced reporting on events important to the public, or in this case the student body.

Others believe that students may cause unintended harm with newspaper articles written on controversial subjects. I think that is laughable. First of all, student editors, usually seniors aged seventeen or eighteen, are well aware of the overall environment in which they publish, and understand what is or is not appropriate. But even more importantly, high school should give students practice at being cognizant of the larger arena in which they act. The few negative incidents that free press will admittedly cause will teach students that in life, one must take responsibility for one's actions.

Therefore, the argument for freedom of speech in student newspapers advances substantial educational goals for students, as well as our unalienable right of freedom of speech. This right, however, is paramount. The American public school is an extension of the

American government and community, and censorship is inconsistent with American democracy. Again, students need to be prepared for the world they will live in; depriving them of rights that are promoted in the greater community prepares students poorly for life after high school.

Finally, censoring information in the student newspaper will not remove the subject from student discussion. Rather, it will remove a balanced, informative viewpoint, and often make the "inappropriate" action more desirable and "cool." For instance, a reporter for my high school paper researched and wrote an in-depth story on the increasing drug problem among students. The administration quickly intervened and stopped the story, declaring that drugs were an inappropriate topic for student discussion. This story, however, would have focused discussion on a crucial issue for students so that they can make the right choice when offered drugs or when they see friends using drugs. Unfortunately, this is a situation most students will face, and they need to be prepared. Suppressing the story made drugs seem even more rebellious and mysterious and most importantly did not give students facts with which they could prepare.

Placing restrictions on student newspapers would be a serious mistake that would hinder students from learning what it is to participate in a free society.

This is now a 6 essay. It addresses the task both fully and concretely. It addresses both sides of the argument, refutes two opposing arguments, and then moves to the bulk of the author's own reasoning. The first paragraph introduces all the lines of reasoning that will be used, demonstrating to the reader that the writer knew right from the start where this essay was headed. The development of ideas is clear and logical and the paragraphs reflect this organization.

The author shows a high level of skill with language. The transitions between paragraphs are clear and guide the reader through the reasoning. The sentence structure varies throughout the passage and is at times complex.

So what did we do to our 4 to make it a 6?

- We added examples and detail.

- We varied sentence structure and added stronger vocabulary (*strives, intervened, suppressing*).

- While length alone doesn't make a 6, we've added detail to our original essay.

- The conclusion, rather than being lost in the fifth paragraph, is now a strong, independent statement that concisely sums up the writer's point of view.

SUMMARY

In this chapter, we went over all of the necessary pieces of a great essay for the ACT Writing test. Use this chapter to work on the individual pieces.

Then, we saw how those pieces are put together into an overall essay and you had a chance to work on some general skills.

Finally, you learned the details of how an essay is scored, and had a chance to put that into practice and score some essays yourself.

Use this knowledge as you practice your essay on your Practice Tests. Time yourself accurately, and score your essays honestly. That will help you find which aspects you need to continue to work on.

Remember to keep developing your information banks. The more specific examples and personal stories you're ready to use to drive your points home, the better. Create your evidence sandwich and counter those arguments to make compelling body paragraphs.

Set a context and clarify your main argument in your introduction and conclusion.

Continue to practice. And if you're unable to fairly assess yourself, get a second opinion. Have someone else help you by reading your essay and assessing how clear it is.

Refine the pieces and practice the flow. Soon enough, you'll be able to master the ACT Writing test.

CHAPTER 14

Last-Minute Tips

Is it starting to feel like your whole life is a buildup to the ACT? You've known about it for years, you've worried about it for months, and now you've spent at least a few hours in solid preparation for it. As Test Day gets closer, you may find your anxiety is on the rise. Don't worry. After the preparation you've received from this book, you're in good shape for Test Day.

To calm any pretest jitters you may have (and assuming you've left yourself at least some breathing time before your ACT), let's go over a few last-minute strategies for the few days before and after Test Day.

> ✔ **EXPERT TUTOR TIP**
>
> If it is close to the ACT and you know there is one specific subject test you are not prepared for, do as many practice questions from that test as possible. Practice really does bring you closer to perfection.

THREE DAYS BEFORE THE TEST

- If you haven't already done so, take one of the full-length Practice Tests in this book under timed conditions. This book comes with eight practice tests—four in the back of the book, four online. If you have already worked through all the tests from the book, try an actual published ACT (your guidance counselor might have one). You can also find practice questions on the official ACT website at www.actstudent.org.

- Try to use all of the techniques and tips you've learned in this book. Take control. Approach the test strategically and confidently.

WARNING: Don't take any more practice ACTs within 48 hours before the test! Doing so will probably exhaust you, hurting your scoring potential on the actual test! You wouldn't run a marathon the day before the real thing, would you?

TWO DAYS BEFORE THE TEST

- **Go over the results of your Practice Test.** Don't worry too much about your score or whether you got a specific question right or wrong. Remember—the Practice Test doesn't count. But do examine your performance on specific questions with an eye to how you might get through each one more quickly and with greater accuracy on the actual test to come.

- **After reviewing your test, identify which topics have the most points left for you to earn.** Review the pages that deal most with those topics and do more practice questions.

- **This is the last study day—review a couple of the more difficult principles we've covered, do a few more practice problems, and call it quits.** It doesn't pay to make yourself crazy right before the test. You've prepared. You'll do well.

THE DAY BEFORE THE TEST

- **Don't study.**

- **Do find something stimulating to do.** Do a puzzle, read a good book, exercise, go for a walk. Don't just sit around or do something brainless (TV marathon, etc.); do things that will make you feel good and energized. Of course, don't work so hard that you can't get up the next day!

- **Get together an "ACT survival kit" containing the following items:**

  – Watch (preferably digital)

  – At least three sharpened No. 2 pencils and pencil sharpener

  – Two erasers

  – Photo ID card (if you're not taking the test at your high school, make sure your ID is official)

  – An approved calculator

  – Your admission ticket

  – Snack and a bottle of water—there's a break, and you'll probably get hungry

  – Confidence!

> ✔ **EXPERT TUTOR TIP**
>
> Make sure you prepare the things you will need the day before. It is not worth getting stressed the morning of because you cannot find your calculator or pencils.

- **Know exactly where you're going and how you're getting there.** It's a good idea to visit your test center sometime before Test Day so you know what to expect on the big day.

- **Get a good night's sleep.** Go to bed early and allow for some extra time to get ready in the morning. Make sure your rest schedule is roughly in line with your usual sleep pattern. If you normally go to bed at 10, don't go to bed at 7 the night before Test Day. That will just confuse your body and disrupt your rest.

THE MORNING OF THE TEST

- **Eat breakfast.** Protein is brain food, but don't eat anything too heavy or greasy. Don't drink a lot of coffee if you're not used to it; bathroom breaks cut into your time, and too much caffeine—or any other kind of stimulant—is a bad idea for your blood sugar and sustained energy (the test is four hours long, including breaks and hearing the proctoring instructions). Like sleep, get what your body needs, but don't deviate too far from your usual. If you normally have a small breakfast, add some protein and enough to keep yourself full, but don't turn it into a lumberjack breakfast that will make you ill.

- **Dress in layers** so that you can adjust to the temperature of the test room.

- **Read something.** Warm up your brain with a newspaper or a magazine. Don't let the ACT be the first thing you read that day.

- **Be sure to get there early.** Allow yourself extra time for traffic, mass-transit delays, and any other possible problems.

- **If you can, go to the test with a friend** (even if he or she isn't taking the test). It's nice to have somebody supporting you right up to the last minute.

DURING THE TEST

- **Don't get rattled.** If you find your confidence slipping, remind yourself how well you've prepared. You've followed the keys to ACT success, and you have practiced. You know the test; you know the strategies; you know the material tested. You're in great shape, as long as you relax! Take a step back and re-approach the question.

- **Even if something goes really wrong, don't panic.** If the test booklet is defective— two pages are stuck together or the ink has run—try to stay calm. Raise your hand, and tell the proctor you need a new book. If you accidentally mis-grid your answer page or put the answers in the wrong section, again, don't panic. Raise your hand, and tell the proctor. He or she might be able to arrange for you to re-grid your test after it's over, when it won't cost you any time.

Good luck! With all of your practice and Kaplan's strategies under your belt, we know you'll do great on the ACT.

AFTER THE TEST

Once the test is over, put it out of your mind. If you don't plan to take the ACT again, shelve this book and start thinking about more interesting things.

You might walk out of the ACT thinking that you could have done better. This is a normal reaction. Lots of people—even the highest scorers—feel that way. You tend to remember the questions that stumped you, not the many that you knew. If you're really concerned, call Kaplan for advice. Also call us if you had any problems with your test experience—a proctor who called time early, a testing room whose temperature hovered just below freezing. We'll do everything we can to make sure that your rights as a test taker are preserved!

However, we're positive you performed well and scored your best on the exam because you followed our ACT Personalized Strategies and practiced with your 8 Practice Tests. Be confident that you were prepared, and celebrate in the fact that the ACT is a distant memory.

If you want more help or just want to know more about the ACT, college admissions, or Kaplan prep courses for the ACT, give us a call at 1-800-KAP-TEST or visit us at www.kaptest.com. We're here to answer your questions and to help you in any way we can. Also, be sure to return one last time to your online syllabus and complete our survey. We're only as good as our successful students!

Congratulations on all you've accomplished. You're ready for your highest score, and to show colleges you're the student they should accept for admission. We're excited for you, so get excited for your new opportunities as well, and let us know how you do!

Practice Tests and Explanations

Practice Test One

HOW TO TAKE THESE PRACTICE TESTS

These three Practice Tests are Kaplan-created tests, similar to the actual ACT. Before taking a Practice Test, find a quiet room where you can work uninterrupted for three and a half hours. Make sure you have a comfortable desk, your calculator, and several No. 2 pencils. Use the answer sheet to record your answers. Once you start a Practice Test, don't stop until you've finished. Remember: You can review any questions within a subject test, but you may not jump from one subject test to another.

You'll find the answers and explanations to the test questions immediately following each test.

ACT Practice Test One
ANSWER SHEET

ENGLISH TEST

1. Ⓐ Ⓑ Ⓒ Ⓓ	11. Ⓐ Ⓑ Ⓒ Ⓓ	21. Ⓐ Ⓑ Ⓒ Ⓓ	31. Ⓐ Ⓑ Ⓒ Ⓓ	41. Ⓐ Ⓑ Ⓒ Ⓓ	51. Ⓐ Ⓑ Ⓒ Ⓓ	61. Ⓐ Ⓑ Ⓒ Ⓓ	71. Ⓐ Ⓑ Ⓒ Ⓓ
2. Ⓕ Ⓖ Ⓗ Ⓙ	12. Ⓕ Ⓖ Ⓗ Ⓙ	22. Ⓕ Ⓖ Ⓗ Ⓙ	32. Ⓕ Ⓖ Ⓗ Ⓙ	42. Ⓕ Ⓖ Ⓗ Ⓙ	52. Ⓕ Ⓖ Ⓗ Ⓙ	62. Ⓕ Ⓖ Ⓗ Ⓙ	72. Ⓕ Ⓖ Ⓗ Ⓙ
3. Ⓐ Ⓑ Ⓒ Ⓓ	13. Ⓐ Ⓑ Ⓒ Ⓓ	23. Ⓐ Ⓑ Ⓒ Ⓓ	33. Ⓐ Ⓑ Ⓒ Ⓓ	43. Ⓐ Ⓑ Ⓒ Ⓓ	53. Ⓐ Ⓑ Ⓒ Ⓓ	63. Ⓐ Ⓑ Ⓒ Ⓓ	73. Ⓐ Ⓑ Ⓒ Ⓓ
4. Ⓕ Ⓖ Ⓗ Ⓙ	14. Ⓕ Ⓖ Ⓗ Ⓙ	24. Ⓕ Ⓖ Ⓗ Ⓙ	34. Ⓕ Ⓖ Ⓗ Ⓙ	44. Ⓕ Ⓖ Ⓗ Ⓙ	54. Ⓕ Ⓖ Ⓗ Ⓙ	64. Ⓕ Ⓖ Ⓗ Ⓙ	74. Ⓕ Ⓖ Ⓗ Ⓙ
5. Ⓐ Ⓑ Ⓒ Ⓓ	15. Ⓐ Ⓑ Ⓒ Ⓓ	25. Ⓐ Ⓑ Ⓒ Ⓓ	35. Ⓐ Ⓑ Ⓒ Ⓓ	45. Ⓐ Ⓑ Ⓒ Ⓓ	55. Ⓐ Ⓑ Ⓒ Ⓓ	65. Ⓐ Ⓑ Ⓒ Ⓓ	75. Ⓐ Ⓑ Ⓒ Ⓓ
6. Ⓕ Ⓖ Ⓗ Ⓙ	16. Ⓕ Ⓖ Ⓗ Ⓙ	26. Ⓕ Ⓖ Ⓗ Ⓙ	36. Ⓕ Ⓖ Ⓗ Ⓙ	46. Ⓕ Ⓖ Ⓗ Ⓙ	56. Ⓕ Ⓖ Ⓗ Ⓙ	66. Ⓕ Ⓖ Ⓗ Ⓙ	
7. Ⓐ Ⓑ Ⓒ Ⓓ	17. Ⓐ Ⓑ Ⓒ Ⓓ	27. Ⓐ Ⓑ Ⓒ Ⓓ	37. Ⓐ Ⓑ Ⓒ Ⓓ	47. Ⓐ Ⓑ Ⓒ Ⓓ	57. Ⓐ Ⓑ Ⓒ Ⓓ	67. Ⓐ Ⓑ Ⓒ Ⓓ	
8. Ⓕ Ⓖ Ⓗ Ⓙ	18. Ⓕ Ⓖ Ⓗ Ⓙ	28. Ⓕ Ⓖ Ⓗ Ⓙ	38. Ⓕ Ⓖ Ⓗ Ⓙ	48. Ⓕ Ⓖ Ⓗ Ⓙ	58. Ⓕ Ⓖ Ⓗ Ⓙ	68. Ⓕ Ⓖ Ⓗ Ⓙ	
9. Ⓐ Ⓑ Ⓒ Ⓓ	19. Ⓐ Ⓑ Ⓒ Ⓓ	29. Ⓐ Ⓑ Ⓒ Ⓓ	39. Ⓐ Ⓑ Ⓒ Ⓓ	49. Ⓐ Ⓑ Ⓒ Ⓓ	59. Ⓐ Ⓑ Ⓒ Ⓓ	69. Ⓐ Ⓑ Ⓒ Ⓓ	
10. Ⓕ Ⓖ Ⓗ Ⓙ	20. Ⓕ Ⓖ Ⓗ Ⓙ	30. Ⓕ Ⓖ Ⓗ Ⓙ	40. Ⓕ Ⓖ Ⓗ Ⓙ	50. Ⓕ Ⓖ Ⓗ Ⓙ	60. Ⓕ Ⓖ Ⓗ Ⓙ	70. Ⓕ Ⓖ Ⓗ Ⓙ	

MATH TEST

1. Ⓐ Ⓑ Ⓒ Ⓓ Ⓔ	11. Ⓐ Ⓑ Ⓒ Ⓓ Ⓔ	21. Ⓐ Ⓑ Ⓒ Ⓓ Ⓔ	31. Ⓐ Ⓑ Ⓒ Ⓓ Ⓔ	41. Ⓐ Ⓑ Ⓒ Ⓓ Ⓔ	51. Ⓐ Ⓑ Ⓒ Ⓓ Ⓔ
2. Ⓐ Ⓑ Ⓒ Ⓓ Ⓔ	12. Ⓕ Ⓖ Ⓗ Ⓙ Ⓚ	22. Ⓕ Ⓖ Ⓗ Ⓙ Ⓚ	32. Ⓕ Ⓖ Ⓗ Ⓙ Ⓚ	42. Ⓕ Ⓖ Ⓗ Ⓙ Ⓚ	52. Ⓕ Ⓖ Ⓗ Ⓙ Ⓚ
3. Ⓐ Ⓑ Ⓒ Ⓓ Ⓔ	13. Ⓐ Ⓑ Ⓒ Ⓓ Ⓔ	23. Ⓐ Ⓑ Ⓒ Ⓓ Ⓔ	33. Ⓐ Ⓑ Ⓒ Ⓓ Ⓔ	43. Ⓐ Ⓑ Ⓒ Ⓓ Ⓔ	53. Ⓐ Ⓑ Ⓒ Ⓓ Ⓔ
4. Ⓕ Ⓖ Ⓗ Ⓙ Ⓚ	14. Ⓕ Ⓖ Ⓗ Ⓙ Ⓚ	24. Ⓕ Ⓖ Ⓗ Ⓙ Ⓚ	34. Ⓕ Ⓖ Ⓗ Ⓙ Ⓚ	44. Ⓕ Ⓖ Ⓗ Ⓙ Ⓚ	54. Ⓕ Ⓖ Ⓗ Ⓙ Ⓚ
5. Ⓐ Ⓑ Ⓒ Ⓓ Ⓔ	15. Ⓐ Ⓑ Ⓒ Ⓓ Ⓔ	25. Ⓐ Ⓑ Ⓒ Ⓓ Ⓔ	35. Ⓐ Ⓑ Ⓒ Ⓓ Ⓔ	45. Ⓐ Ⓑ Ⓒ Ⓓ Ⓔ	55. Ⓐ Ⓑ Ⓒ Ⓓ Ⓔ
6. Ⓕ Ⓖ Ⓗ Ⓙ Ⓚ	16. Ⓕ Ⓖ Ⓗ Ⓙ Ⓚ	26. Ⓕ Ⓖ Ⓗ Ⓙ Ⓚ	36. Ⓕ Ⓖ Ⓗ Ⓙ Ⓚ	46. Ⓕ Ⓖ Ⓗ Ⓙ Ⓚ	56. Ⓕ Ⓖ Ⓗ Ⓙ Ⓚ
7. Ⓐ Ⓑ Ⓒ Ⓓ Ⓔ	17. Ⓐ Ⓑ Ⓒ Ⓓ Ⓔ	27. Ⓐ Ⓑ Ⓒ Ⓓ Ⓔ	37. Ⓐ Ⓑ Ⓒ Ⓓ Ⓔ	47. Ⓐ Ⓑ Ⓒ Ⓓ Ⓔ	57. Ⓐ Ⓑ Ⓒ Ⓓ Ⓔ
8. Ⓕ Ⓖ Ⓗ Ⓙ Ⓚ	18. Ⓕ Ⓖ Ⓗ Ⓙ Ⓚ	28. Ⓕ Ⓖ Ⓗ Ⓙ Ⓚ	38. Ⓕ Ⓖ Ⓗ Ⓙ Ⓚ	48. Ⓕ Ⓖ Ⓗ Ⓙ Ⓚ	58. Ⓕ Ⓖ Ⓗ Ⓙ Ⓚ
9. Ⓐ Ⓑ Ⓒ Ⓓ Ⓔ	19. Ⓐ Ⓑ Ⓒ Ⓓ Ⓔ	29. Ⓐ Ⓑ Ⓒ Ⓓ Ⓔ	39. Ⓐ Ⓑ Ⓒ Ⓓ Ⓔ	49. Ⓐ Ⓑ Ⓒ Ⓓ Ⓔ	59. Ⓐ Ⓑ Ⓒ Ⓓ Ⓔ
10. Ⓕ Ⓖ Ⓗ Ⓙ Ⓚ	20. Ⓕ Ⓖ Ⓗ Ⓙ Ⓚ	30. Ⓕ Ⓖ Ⓗ Ⓙ Ⓚ	40. Ⓕ Ⓖ Ⓗ Ⓙ Ⓚ	50. Ⓕ Ⓖ Ⓗ Ⓙ Ⓚ	60. Ⓕ Ⓖ Ⓗ Ⓙ Ⓚ

READING TEST

1. Ⓐ Ⓑ Ⓒ Ⓓ	6. Ⓕ Ⓖ Ⓗ Ⓙ	11. Ⓐ Ⓑ Ⓒ Ⓓ	16. Ⓕ Ⓖ Ⓗ Ⓙ	21. Ⓐ Ⓑ Ⓒ Ⓓ	26. Ⓕ Ⓖ Ⓗ Ⓙ	31. Ⓐ Ⓑ Ⓒ Ⓓ	36. Ⓕ Ⓖ Ⓗ Ⓙ
2. Ⓕ Ⓖ Ⓗ Ⓙ	7. Ⓐ Ⓑ Ⓒ Ⓓ	12. Ⓕ Ⓖ Ⓗ Ⓙ	17. Ⓐ Ⓑ Ⓒ Ⓓ	22. Ⓕ Ⓖ Ⓗ Ⓙ	27. Ⓐ Ⓑ Ⓒ Ⓓ	32. Ⓕ Ⓖ Ⓗ Ⓙ	37. Ⓐ Ⓑ Ⓒ Ⓓ
3. Ⓐ Ⓑ Ⓒ Ⓓ	8. Ⓕ Ⓖ Ⓗ Ⓙ	13. Ⓐ Ⓑ Ⓒ Ⓓ	18. Ⓕ Ⓖ Ⓗ Ⓙ	23. Ⓐ Ⓑ Ⓒ Ⓓ	28. Ⓕ Ⓖ Ⓗ Ⓙ	33. Ⓐ Ⓑ Ⓒ Ⓓ	38. Ⓕ Ⓖ Ⓗ Ⓙ
4. Ⓕ Ⓖ Ⓗ Ⓙ	9. Ⓐ Ⓑ Ⓒ Ⓓ	14. Ⓕ Ⓖ Ⓗ Ⓙ	19. Ⓐ Ⓑ Ⓒ Ⓓ	24. Ⓕ Ⓖ Ⓗ Ⓙ	29. Ⓐ Ⓑ Ⓒ Ⓓ	34. Ⓕ Ⓖ Ⓗ Ⓙ	39. Ⓐ Ⓑ Ⓒ Ⓓ
5. Ⓐ Ⓑ Ⓒ Ⓓ	10. Ⓕ Ⓖ Ⓗ Ⓙ	15. Ⓐ Ⓑ Ⓒ Ⓓ	20. Ⓕ Ⓖ Ⓗ Ⓙ	25. Ⓐ Ⓑ Ⓒ Ⓓ	30. Ⓕ Ⓖ Ⓗ Ⓙ	35. Ⓐ Ⓑ Ⓒ Ⓓ	40. Ⓕ Ⓖ Ⓗ Ⓙ

SCIENCE TEST

1. Ⓐ Ⓑ Ⓒ Ⓓ	6. Ⓕ Ⓖ Ⓗ Ⓙ	11. Ⓐ Ⓑ Ⓒ Ⓓ	16. Ⓕ Ⓖ Ⓗ Ⓙ	21. Ⓐ Ⓑ Ⓒ Ⓓ	26. Ⓕ Ⓖ Ⓗ Ⓙ	31. Ⓐ Ⓑ Ⓒ Ⓓ	36. Ⓕ Ⓖ Ⓗ Ⓙ
2. Ⓕ Ⓖ Ⓗ Ⓙ	7. Ⓐ Ⓑ Ⓒ Ⓓ	12. Ⓕ Ⓖ Ⓗ Ⓙ	17. Ⓐ Ⓑ Ⓒ Ⓓ	22. Ⓕ Ⓖ Ⓗ Ⓙ	27. Ⓐ Ⓑ Ⓒ Ⓓ	32. Ⓕ Ⓖ Ⓗ Ⓙ	37. Ⓐ Ⓑ Ⓒ Ⓓ
3. Ⓐ Ⓑ Ⓒ Ⓓ	8. Ⓕ Ⓖ Ⓗ Ⓙ	13. Ⓐ Ⓑ Ⓒ Ⓓ	18. Ⓕ Ⓖ Ⓗ Ⓙ	23. Ⓐ Ⓑ Ⓒ Ⓓ	28. Ⓕ Ⓖ Ⓗ Ⓙ	33. Ⓐ Ⓑ Ⓒ Ⓓ	38. Ⓕ Ⓖ Ⓗ Ⓙ
4. Ⓕ Ⓖ Ⓗ Ⓙ	9. Ⓐ Ⓑ Ⓒ Ⓓ	14. Ⓕ Ⓖ Ⓗ Ⓙ	19. Ⓐ Ⓑ Ⓒ Ⓓ	24. Ⓕ Ⓖ Ⓗ Ⓙ	29. Ⓐ Ⓑ Ⓒ Ⓓ	34. Ⓕ Ⓖ Ⓗ Ⓙ	39. Ⓐ Ⓑ Ⓒ Ⓓ
5. Ⓐ Ⓑ Ⓒ Ⓓ	10. Ⓕ Ⓖ Ⓗ Ⓙ	15. Ⓐ Ⓑ Ⓒ Ⓓ	20. Ⓕ Ⓖ Ⓗ Ⓙ	25. Ⓐ Ⓑ Ⓒ Ⓓ	30. Ⓕ Ⓖ Ⓗ Ⓙ	35. Ⓐ Ⓑ Ⓒ Ⓓ	40. Ⓕ Ⓖ Ⓗ Ⓙ

ENGLISH TEST

45 Minutes—75 Questions

Directions: In the following five passages, certain words and phrases are underlined and numbered. In the right-hand column are alternatives for each underlined portion. Select the one that best conveys the idea, creates the most grammatically correct sentence, or is the most consistent with the style and tone of the passage. If you decide that the original version is best, select NO CHANGE. You may also find questions that ask about the entire passage or a section of the passage. These questions will correspond to small numbered boxes in the text. For these questions, decide which choice best accomplishes the purpose set out in the question stem. After you've selected the best choice, fill in the corresponding oval in your Answer Grid. For some questions, you'll need to read the context in order to answer correctly. Be sure to read until you have enough information to determine the correct answer choice.

You will also find questions about a section of the passage or about the passage as a whole. These questions do not refer to an underlined portion of the passage, but rather are identified by a number or numbers in a box.

For each question, choose the alternative you consider best and fill in the corresponding oval on your answer document. Read each passage through once before you begin to answer the questions that accompany it. For many of the questions, you must read several sentences beyond the question to determine the answer. Be sure that you have read enough ahead each time you choose an alternative.

PASSAGE I

ORIGINS OF URBAN LEGENDS

[1]

Since primitive times, societies have <u>created, and told</u> legends. Even before the development of written language, cultures would orally pass down these popular stories.

1. A. NO CHANGE
   B. created then subsequently told
   C. created and told
   D. created, and told original

[2]

2 These stories served the dual purpose of entertaining audiences and of transmitting values and beliefs from generation to generation.

2. Suppose that the author wants to insert a sentence here to describe the different kinds of oral stories told by these societies. Which of the following sentences would best serve that purpose?

F.   These myths and tales varied in substance, from the humorous to the heroic.

G.   These myths and tales were often recited by paid storytellers.

H.   Unfortunately, no recording of the original myths and tales exists.

J.   Sometimes it took several evenings for the full story to be recited.

<u>Indeed</u> today we have many more permanent ways of
   3
handing down our beliefs to future generations, we continue to create and tell legends. In our technological society, a new form of folktale has emerged:

3. A.   NO CHANGE
   B.   However,
   C.   Indeed,
   D.   Although

<u>the</u> urban legend.
   4

4. F.   NO CHANGE
   G.   it is called the
   H.   it being the
   J.   known as the

[3]

Urban legends are stories we all have heard; they are supposed to have really happened, but are never <u>verifiable however.</u> It seems that the people involved can
   5
never be found. Researchers of the urban legend call the elusive participant in such supposed "real-life" events a FOAF—a Friend of a Friend.

5. A.   NO CHANGE
   B.   verifiable, however.
   C.   verifiable, furthermore.
   D.   verifiable.

[4]

Urban legends have some characteristic features. They are often humorous in nature with a surprise

GO ON TO THE NEXT PAGE →

ending and a conclusion. One such legend is the tale of
the hunter who was returning home from an unsuccess-
ful hunting trip. On his way home, he accidentally hit
and killed a deer on a deserted highway. Even though
he knew it was illegal, he decided to keep the deer,
and he loads it in the back of his station wagon. As the
hunter continued driving, the deer,

he was only temporarily knocked unconscious by the
car, woke up and began thrashing around. The hunter
panicked, stopped the car, ran to the ditch, and watched
the enraged deer destroy his car.

[5]

One legend involves alligators in the sewer systems
of major metropolitan areas. According to the story, before alligators were a protected species, people vacation-
ing in Florida purchased baby alligators to take home as
souvenirs.

Between 1930 and 1940, nearly a million alligators in
Florida were killed for the value of their skin, used to
make expensive leather products such as boots and wal-
lets. After the novelty of having a pet alligator wore off,
many people flushed their baby souvenirs down toilets.
Legend has it that the baby alligators found a perfect
growing and breeding environment in city sewer systems, where they thrive to this day on the ample supply
of rats.

6. F. NO CHANGE
    G. ending.
    H. ending, which is a conclusion.
    J. ending or conclusion.

7. A. NO CHANGE
    B. loaded it in
    C. is loading it in
    D. had loaded it in

8. F. NO CHANGE
    G. which being
    H. that is
    J. which was

9. A. NO CHANGE
    B. species; people
    C. species. People
    D. species people

10. F. NO CHANGE
    G. Because their skin is used to make
        expensive leather products such as boots
        and wallets, nearly a million alligators
        in Florida were killed between 1930 and
        1940.
    H. Killed between 1930 and 1940, the
        skin of nearly a million alligators from
        Florida was used to make expensive
        leather products such as boots and
        wallets.
    J. OMIT the underlined portion.

GO ON TO THE NEXT PAGE

[6]

In addition to urban legends that are told from friend to friend, a growing number of urban legends are passed along through the Internet and email. One of the more popular stories <u>are about</u> a woman who
₁₁
was unwittingly charged $100 for a cookie recipe she requested at an upscale restaurant. To get her money's worth, this

<u>woman supposed</u> copied the recipe for the delicious
₁₂
cookies and forwarded it via email to everyone she knew.

[7]

Although today's technology enhances our ability to tell and retell urban legends, the Internet can also serve as a monitor of urban legends. <u>Dedicated to commonly</u>
₁₃
<u>told urban legends, research is done by many websites.</u>
₁₃
According to those websites, most legends, including the ones told here, have no basis in reality.

11. A. NO CHANGE
    B. would be about
    C. is about
    D. is dealing with

12. F. NO CHANGE
    G. woman supposedly
    H. women supposedly
    J. women supposed to

13. A. NO CHANGE
    B. Many websites are dedicated to researching the validity of commonly told urban legends.
    C. Researching the validity of commonly told urban legends, many websites are dedicated.
    D. OMIT the underlined portion.

GO ON TO THE NEXT PAGE

Questions 14–15 ask about the preceding passage as a whole.

14. The author wants to insert the following sentence:

> Other urban legends seem to be designed to instill fear.

What would be the most logical placement for this sentence?

F. After the last sentence of paragraph 3

G. After the second sentence of paragraph 4

H. Before the first sentence of paragraph 5

J. After the last sentence of paragraph 6

15. Suppose that the author had been assigned to write an essay comparing the purposes and topics of myths and legends in primitive societies and in our modern society. Would this essay fulfill that assignment?

A. Yes, because the essay describes myths and legends from primitive societies and modern society.

B. Yes, because the essay provides explanations of possible purposes and topics for myths and legends from primitive societies and modern society.

C. No, because the essay does not provide enough information about the topics of the myths and legends in primitive societies to make a valid comparison.

D. No, because the essay doesn't provide any information on the myths and legends of primitive societies.

PASSAGE II

HENRY DAVID THOREAU: A SUCCESSFUL LIFE

What does it mean to be successful? <u>Do one</u> measure
                                        16
success by money? If I told you about a

man: working as a teacher, a land surveyor, and a
    17
factory worker (never holding any of these jobs for more
than a few years), would that man sound like a success
to you? If I told you that he spent

16. F. NO CHANGE
     G. Does we
     H. Does one
     J. Did you

17. A. NO CHANGE
     B. man who worked
     C. man and worked
     D. man, which working

GO ON TO THE NEXT PAGE

two solitary years living alone in a small cabin that he
18
built for himself and that he spent those years looking at

plants and writing in a diary—would you think of him

as a celebrity or an important figure? What if I told you

that

he rarely ventured far from the town where he was born,
19
that he was thrown in jail for refusing to pay his taxes,

and that he died at the age of forty-five? Do any of these

facts seem to point to a man whose life should be stud-

ied and emulated?

You may already know about this man. You may

even have read some of his writings. His name was:
20
Henry David Thoreau, and he was, in addition to the
20
jobs listed above, a poet, an essayist, a naturalist, and a

social critic. Although the facts listed about him may

not seem to add up to much, he was, in fact a tremen-
21
dously influential person. Along with writers such as

Ralph Waldo Emerson, Mark Twain, and Walt Whit-

man, Thoreau helped to create the first literature and

philosophy that most people identify as unique Ameri-
22
can.

In 1845, Thoreau built a cabin. Near Walden Pond
23
and remained there for more than two years, living

alone, fending for himself, and observing the nature

around him. He kept scrupulous notes in his diary,

notes that he later distilled into his most famous work

titled *Walden*.

18. F. NO CHANGE
G. two years living alone
H. two solitary years all by himself
J. a couple of lonely years living in solitude

19. A. NO CHANGE
B. he is rarely venturing
C. he has rare ventures
D. this person was to venture rarely

20. F. NO CHANGE
G. was Henry David Thoreau and he
H. was: Henry David Thoreau; and he
J. was Henry David Thoreau, and he

21. A. NO CHANGE
B. was, in fact, a
C. was in fact a
D. was in fact, a

22. F. NO CHANGE
G. uniquely
H. uniqueness
J. the most unique

23. A. NO CHANGE
B. cabin. On
C. cabin, by
D. cabin near

GO ON TO THE NEXT PAGE

Walden is read by many literature students today.
                                                24
    [1] To protest slavery, Thoreau refused to pay his taxes in 1846. [2] Thoreau was a firm believer in the abolition of slavery, and he objected to the practice's extension into the new territories of the West. [3] For this act of rebellion, he was thrown in the Concord jail. 25

    Thoreau used his writing to spread his message of resistance and activism; he published an essay entitled
                                              26
Civil Disobedience (also known as *Resistance to Civil Government*). In it, Thoreau laid out his argument for refusing to obey unjust laws.

    Although Thoreau's life was very brief, his works
                                              27
and his ideas continue to touch and influence people. Students all over the country—all over the world—continue to read his essays and hear his unique voice, urging them to lead lives of principle, individuality, and freedom. 28 To be able to live out the ideas that burn in

the heart of a person—surely that is the meaning of
                29
success.

24. F. NO CHANGE
    G. This book is read by many literature students today.
    H. Today, many literature students read *Walden*.
    J. OMIT the underlined portion.

25. What is the most logical order of sentences in this paragraph?
    A. NO CHANGE
    B. 3, 2, 1
    C. 2, 1, 3
    D. 3, 1, 2

26. F. NO CHANGE
    G. activism, he published:
    H. activism, he published
    J. activism, he published,

27. A. NO CHANGE
    B. he's
    C. their
    D. those

28. The purpose of this paragraph is to:
    F. explain why Thoreau was put in jail.
    G. prove a point about people's conception of success.
    H. suggest that Thoreau may be misunderstood.
    J. discuss Thoreau's importance in today's world.

29. A. NO CHANGE
    B. one's heart
    C. the heart and soul of a person
    D. through the heart of a person

GO ON TO THE NEXT PAGE ⟶

Question 30 asks about the preceding passage as a whole.

30. By including questions throughout the entire first paragraph, the author allows the reader to:

F. answer each question as the passage proceeds.

G. think about the meaning of success.

H. assess the quality of Thoreau's work.

J. form an opinion about greed in modern society.

PASSAGE III

THE SLOTH: SLOW BUT NOT SLOTHFUL

[1]

More than half of the world's <u>currently living plant</u> and
                                            31
animal species live in tropical rain forests. Four square

miles of a Central American rain forest can be home

to up to 1,500 different species of flowering plants, 700

species of trees, 400 species of birds, and 125 species of

mammals. Of these mammals, the sloth is one of the

most unusual.

[2]

Unlike most mammals, the sloth is usually upside

down. A sloth does just about everything upside down,

including sleeping, eating, mating, and giving birth.

<u>Its' unique</u> anatomy allows the sloth to spend most of
      32
the time hanging from one tree branch or another, high

in the canopy of a rain forest tree. About the size of a

large domestic <u>cat, the</u> sloth hangs from its unusually
                   33
long limbs and long hooklike claws.

31. A. NO CHANGE
    B. currently existing plant
    C. living plant
    D. plant

32. F. NO CHANGE
    G. It's unique
    H. Its unique
    J. Its uniquely

33. A. NO CHANGE
    B. cat; the
    C. cat. The
    D. cat, but the

GO ON TO THE NEXT PAGE ⟶

Specially designed for limbs, the sloth's muscles seem to
cling to things.
34

[3]

In fact, a sloth's limbs are so specific adapted to
35
upside-down life that a sloth is essentially incapable

of walking on the ground. Instead, they must crawl or
36
drag itself with its massive claws. This makes it easy to

see why the sloth rarely leaves its home in the trees.

Because it can not move swiftly on the ground, the sloth
37
is an excellent swimmer.

[4]

38 A sloth can hang upside down and, without

34. F. NO CHANGE
   G. The sloth's muscles seem to cling to
      things for specially designed limbs.
   H. The muscles in a sloth's limbs seem to
      be specially designed for clinging to
      things.
   J. OMIT the underlined portion.

35. A. NO CHANGE
   B. so specific and
   C. so specified
   D. so specifically

36. F. NO CHANGE
   G. Instead, it
   H. However, they
   J. In addition, it

37. A. NO CHANGE
   B. Despite
   C. Similarly,
   D. Though

38. The author wants to insert a sentence here
   to help connect paragraph 3 and paragraph
   4. Which of the following sentences would
   best serve that purpose?
   F. Of course, many other animals are also
      excellent swimmers.
   G. Another unique characteristic of the
      sloth is its flexibility.
   H. In addition to swimming, the sloth is
      an incredible climber.
   J. Flexibility is a trait that helps the sloth
      survive.

GO ON TO THE NEXT PAGE

moving the rest of its <u>body turn</u> its face 180 degrees so
       39

that it <u>was looking</u> at the ground. A sloth can rotate
         40
its forelimbs in all directions, so it can easily reach the

leaves that make up its diet. The sloth can also roll itself

up into a ball in order to <u>protect and defend itself from</u>
                              41

predators. <u>The howler monkey, another inhabitant of</u>
                               42
<u>the rain forest, is not as flexible as the sloth.</u>
                42

[5]

The best defense a sloth has from predators such as

jaguars and large snakes, though, is its camouflage. Dur-

ing the rainy season, a sloth's thick brown or gray fur is

usually covered with a coat of blue-green <u>algae. Which</u>
                                              43
helps it blend in with its forest surroundings. Another

type of camouflage is the sloth's incredibly slow move-

ment: it often moves less than 100 feet during a 24-hour

period.

[6]

It is this slow movement that earned the sloth its

name. *Sloth* is also a word for laziness or an aversion to

work. But even though it sleeps an average of 15 hours a

day, the sloth isn't necessarily lazy. It just moves, upside

39. A. NO CHANGE
    B. body turns
    C. body, it has the capability of turning
    D. body, turn

40. F. NO CHANGE
    G. had been looking
    H. will have the ability to be looking
    J. can look

41. A. NO CHANGE
    B. protect itself and defend itself from
    C. protect itself so it won't be harmed by
    D. protect itself from

42. F. NO CHANGE
    G. Another inhabitant of the rain forest,
       the howler monkey, is not as flexible as
       the sloth.
    H. Not as flexible as the sloth is the howler
       monkey, another inhabitant of the rain
       forest.
    J. OMIT the underlined portion.

43. A. NO CHANGE
    B. algae, which
    C. algae, being that it
    D. algae

GO ON TO THE NEXT PAGE →

down, at its own slow pace through its world of rain

forest trees. 44

44. The author is considering deleting the last sentence of paragraph 6. This change would:

   F. diminish the amount of information provided about the habits of the sloth.

   G. make the ending of the passage more abrupt.

   H. emphasize the slothful nature of the sloth.

   J. make the tone of the essay more consistent.

Question 45 asks about the preceding passage as a whole.

45. The author wants to insert the following description:

   An observer could easily be tricked into thinking that a sloth was just a pile of decaying leaves.

   What would be the most appropriate placement for this sentence?

   A. After the last sentence of paragraph 1

   B. After the third sentence of paragraph 2

   C. Before the last sentence of paragraph 5

   D. Before the first sentence of paragraph 6

GO ON TO THE NEXT PAGE

PASSAGE IV

FIRES IN YELLOWSTONE

During the summer of 1988, I watched Yellowstone
National Park go up in flames. In June, <u>fires ignited</u>
₄₆
<u>by lightning</u> had been allowed to burn unsuppressed
₄₆
because park officials expected that the usual summer
rains would douse the flames. However, the rains never
<u>will have come</u>. A plentiful fuel supply of fallen logs and
₄₇
pine needles was available, and winds of up to 100 mph
whipped the spreading fires along and carried red-hot
embers to other areas, creating new fires. By the time
park officials succumbed to the pressure of public opinion and <u>decide</u> to try to extinguish the
₄₈

<u>flames. It's</u> too late. The situation remained out of con-
₄₉
trol in spite of the efforts of 9,000 firefighters who were
using state-of-the-art equipment. By September, more
than 720,000 acres of Yellowstone had been affected by
fire. <u>Nature was only able to curb the destruction</u>; the
₅₀
smoke did not begin to clear until the first snow arrived
on September 11.

<u>Being that I was</u> an ecologist who has studied
₅₁
forests for 20 years, I knew that this was not nearly
the tragedy it seemed to be. Large fires are, after

46. F. NO CHANGE
    G. fires having been ignited by lightning
    H. fires, the kind ignited by lightning,
    J. fires ignited and started by lightning

47. A. NO CHANGE
    B. came
    C. were coming
    D. have come

48. F. NO CHANGE
    G. are deciding
    H. decided
    J. OMIT the underlined portion.

49. A. NO CHANGE
    B. flames, it's
    C. flames, it was
    D. flames; it was

50. F. NO CHANGE
    G. Only curbing the destruction by able nature
    H. Only nature was able to curb the destruction
    J. Nature was able to curb only the destruction

51. A. NO CHANGE
    B. Being that I am
    C. I'm
    D. As

GO ON TO THE NEXT PAGE ⇒

all, necessary <u>in order that the continued health in</u>
<u>the forest ecosystem be maintained.</u> Fires thin out
52
overcrowded areas and allow the sun to reach species of

plants stunted by shade. Ash fertilizes the soil, and fire

smoke kills forest bacteria. In the case of the lodgepole

pine, fire is essential to reproduction: the <u>pines' cone</u>
53
open only when exposed to temperatures greater than

112 degrees.

The fires in Yellowstone did result in some loss of

wildlife, but overall, the region's animals proved to be

fire-tolerant and fire-adaptive. <u>However,</u> large ani-
54
mals

such as bison were often seen <u>grazing, and</u> bedding
55
down in meadows near burning forests. Also, the fire

posed little threat to the members of any endangered

animal species in the park.

My confidence in the natural resilience of the forest

has been borne out in the years since the fires ravaged

Yellowstone. <u>Judged from recent pictures of the park</u>
56

the forest was not destroyed; <u>it</u> was rejuvenated.
57

52. F. NO CHANGE
    G. for the continued health of the forest
        ecosystem to be maintained.
    H. in order to continue the maintenance of
        the health of the forest ecosystem.
    J. for the continued health of the forest
        ecosystem.

53. A. NO CHANGE
    B. pines cones'
    C. pine's cones
    D. pine's cone

54. F. NO CHANGE
    G. Clearly,
    H. In fact,
    J. Instead,

55. A. NO CHANGE
    B. grazing; and bedding
    C. grazing: and bedding
    D. grazing and bedding

56. F. NO CHANGE
    G. Recent pictures of the park show that
    H. Judging by the recent pictures of the
        park,
    J. As judged according to pictures taken
        of the park recently,

57. A. NO CHANGE
    B. they
    C. the fires
    D. I

GO ON TO THE NEXT PAGE ⟶

Questions 58–59 ask about the preceding passage as a whole.

58. The writer is considering inserting the following true statement after the first sentence of the second paragraph:

> Many more acres of forest burned in Alaska in 1988 than in Yellowstone Park.

Would this addition be appropriate for the essay?

F. Yes, the statement would add important information about the effects of large-scale forest fires.

G. Yes, the statement would provide an informative contrast to the Yellowstone fire.

H. No, the statement would not provide any additional information about the effect of the 1988 fire in Yellowstone.

J. No, the statement would undermine the author's position as an authority on the subject of forest fires.

59. Suppose that the writer wishes to provide additional support for the claim that the fire posed little threat to the members of any endangered animal species in the park. Which of the following additions would be most effective?

A. A list of the endangered animals known to inhabit the park

B. A discussion of the particular vulnerability of endangered species of birds to forest fires

C. An explanation of the relative infrequency of such an extensive series of forest fires

D. A summary of reports of biologists who monitored the activity of endangered species in the park during the fire

PASSAGE V

MY FIRST WHITE-WATER RAFTING TRIP

[1]

White-water rafting <u>being</u> a favorite pastime of mine
60
for several years. I have drifted down many challenging

North American rivers, including the Snake, the Green,

and the <u>Salmon, and there are many other rivers in</u>
61
<u>America as well.</u> I have spent some of my best moments
61
in dangerous rapids, yet nothing has matched the thrill

60. F. NO CHANGE
G. have been
H. has been
J. was

61. A. NO CHANGE
B. Salmon, just three of many rivers existing in North America.
C. Salmon; many other rivers exist in North America.
D. Salmon.

GO ON TO THE NEXT PAGE

I experienced facing my <u>first rapids, on the Deschutes</u>
                                    62
<u>River.</u>
62

[2]

My father and I spent the morning floating down a calm and peaceful stretch of the Deschutes in his wooden MacKenzie river boat. This trip <u>it being</u> the
                                        63
wooden boat's first time down rapids, as well as mine.

<u>Rapids are rated according to a uniform scale of relative</u>
                                    64
<u>difficulty.</u>
64

[3]

<u>Roaring, I was in the boat approaching Whitehorse</u>
                    65
<u>Rapids.</u> I felt much like a novice skier peering down her
65
first steep slope: I was scared, but even more excited.

The water <u>churned and covering me</u> with a refreshing
                        66
spray. My father, towards the stern, controlled the oars. The carefree expression he usually wore on the river had

been replaced <u>and instead he adopted</u> a look of intense
                        67
concentration as he maneuvered around boulders dotting our path. To release tension, we began to holler

62. **F.** NO CHANGE
    G. first: rapids on the Deschutes River.
    H. first rapids; on the Deschutes River.
    J. first rapids on the Deschutes River.

63. **A.** NO CHANGE
    B. it happened that it was
    C. was
    D. being

64. **F.** NO CHANGE
    G. Rated according to a uniform scale, rapids are relatively difficult.
    H. (Rapids are rated according to a uniform scale of relative difficulty.)
    J. OMIT the underlined portion.

65. **A.** NO CHANGE
    B. It roared, and the boat and I approached Whitehorse Rapids.
    C. While the roaring boat was approaching Whitehorse Rapids, I could hear the water.
    D. I could hear the water roar as we approached Whitehorse Rapids.

66. **F.** NO CHANGE
    G. churned, and covering me
    H. churning and covering me
    J. churned, covering me

67. **A.** NO CHANGE
    B. with
    C. by another countenance altogether:
    D. instead with another expression;

GO ON TO THE NEXT PAGE ▷

like kids on a roller coaster, our voices echoing <u>across</u>
                                                        68
the water as we lurched violently about.

68. F. NO CHANGE
    G. throughout
    H. around
    J. from

[4]

Suddenly we came to a jarring halt <u>and we stopped</u>;
                                          69
the left side of the bow was wedged on a large rock. A

whirlpool whirled around us; if we capsized, we would

be sucked into the undertow. Instinctively, I threw all

of my weight towards the right side of the tilting boat.

Luckily, <u>it was</u> just enough force to dislodge us, and
           70
we continued on down for about 10 more minutes of

spectacular rapids.

69. A. NO CHANGE
    B. which stopped us
    C. and stopped
    D. OMIT the underlined portion.

70. F. NO CHANGE
    G. it's
    H. it is
    J. its

[5]

Later that day, we went through Buckskin Mary

Rapids and Boxcar Rapids. When we pulled up on the

bank that evening, we saw that the boat had received its

first scar: <u>that scar was a</u> small hole on the upper bow
               71
from the boulder we had wrestled with. In the years to

come, we went down many rapids and the boat

<u>receiving many</u> bruises, but Whitehorse is the most
    72

71. A. NO CHANGE
    B. that was a
    C. which was a
    D. a

72. F. NO CHANGE
    G. received many
    H. received much
    J. receives many

GO ON TO THE NEXT PAGE

memorable rapids of all. 73

73. Which of the following concluding sentences would most effectively emphasize the final point made in this paragraph while retaining the style and tone of the narrative as a whole?

A. The brutal calamities that it presented the unwary rafter were more than offset by its beguiling excitement.

B. Perhaps it is true that your first close encounter with white water is your most intense.

C. Or, if not the most memorable, then at least a very memorable one!

D. Call me crazy or weird if you want, but white-water rafting is the sport for me.

Questions 74–75 ask about the preceding passage as a whole.

74. The writer has been assigned to write an essay that focuses on the techniques of white-water rafting. Would this essay meet the requirements of that assignment?

F. No, because the essay's main focus is on a particular experience, not on techniques.

G. No, because the essay mostly deals with the relationship between father and daughter.

H. Yes, because specific rafting techniques are the essay's main focus.

J. Yes, because it presents a dramatic story of a day of white-water rafting.

75. Suppose that the writer wants to add the following sentence to the essay:

It was such a peaceful summer day that it was hard to believe dangerous rapids awaited us downstream.

What would be the most logical placement of this sentence?

A. After the last sentence of paragraph 1

B. After the last sentence of paragraph 2

C. Before the first sentence of paragraph 4

D. After the last sentence of paragraph 4

MATH TEST

60 Minutes—60 Questions

Directions: Solve each problem, choose the correct answer, and then fill in the corresponding oval on your answer document.

Do not linger over problems that take too much time. Solve as many as you can, then return to the others in the time you have left for this test.

You are permitted to use a calculator on this test. You may use your calculator for any problems you choose, but some of the problems may best be done without using a calculator.

1. In a recent survey, 14 people found their mayor to be "very competent." This number is exactly 20% of the people surveyed. How many people were surveyed?

   A. 28
   B. 35
   C. 56
   D. 70
   E. 84

2. A train traveled at a rate of 90 miles per hour for x hours, and then at a rate of 60 miles per hour for y hours. Which expression represents the train's average rate in miles per hour for the entire distance traveled?

   F. $\dfrac{540}{xy}$

   G. $\dfrac{90}{x} \times \dfrac{60}{y}$

   H. $\dfrac{90}{x} + \dfrac{60}{y}$

   J. $\dfrac{90x + 60y}{x + y}$

   K. $\dfrac{150}{x + y}$

3. In a certain string ensemble, the ratio of men to women is 5:3. If there are a total of 24 people in the ensemble, how many women are there?

   A. 8
   B. 9
   C. 10
   D. 11
   E. 12

4. If $x \neq 0$, and $x^2 - 3x = 6x$, then $x = ?$

   F. -9
   G. -3
   H. $\sqrt{3}$
   J. 3
   K. 9

GO ON TO THE NEXT PAGE

5. The two overlapping circles below form three regions, as shown:

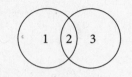

What is the maximum number of regions that can be formed by three overlapping circles?

A. 5

B. 6

C. 7

D. 8

E. 9

6. If $x^2 + 6x + 8 = 4 + 10x$, then x equals which of the following?

F. −2

G. −1

H. 0

J. 1

K. 2

7. Nine less than the number c is the same as the number d, and d less than twice c is 20. Which two equations could be used to determine the value of c and d?

A. $d - 9 = c$
    $d - 2c = 20$

B. $c - 9 = d$
    $2c - d = 20$

C. $c - 9 = d$
    $d - 2c = 20$

D. $9 - c = d$
    $2c - d = 20$

E. $9 - c = d$
    $2cd = 20$

8. An ice cream parlor offers five flavors of ice cream and four different toppings (sprinkles, hot fudge, whipped cream, and butterscotch). There is a special offer that includes one flavor of ice cream and one topping, served in a cup, sugar cone, or waffle cone. How many ways are there to order ice cream with the special offer?

F. 4

G. 5

H. 12

J. 23

K. 60

9. At a recent audition for a school play, 1 out of 3 students who auditioned were asked to come to a second audition. After the second audition, 75% of those asked to the second audition were offered parts. If 18 students were offered parts, how many students went to the first audition?

A. 18

B. 24

C. 48

D. 56

E. 72

10. One number is 5 times another number, and their sum is −60. What is the lesser of the two numbers?

F. −5

G. −10

H. −12

J. −48

K. −50

GO ON TO THE NEXT PAGE

11. In the following figure, which is composed of equilateral triangles, what is the greatest number of parallelograms that can be found?

   A. 6

   B. 9

   C. 12

   D. 15

   E. 18

12. The circle in the following figure is inscribed in a square with a perimeter of 16 inches. What is the area of the shaded region?

   F. 4π

   G. $16 - 2\pi$

   H. $16 - 4\pi$

   J. $8 - 2\pi$

   K. $8 - 4\pi$

13. How many positive integers less than 50 are multiples of 4 but *not* multiples of 6?

   A. 4

   B. 6

   C. 8

   D. 10

   E. 12

14. What is the value of $f(3)$ where $f(x) = (8 - 3x)(x^2 - 2x - 15)$?

   F. -30

   G. -18

   H. 12

   J. 24

   K. 30

15. A class contains five juniors and five seniors. If one member of the class is assigned at random to present a paper on a certain subject, and another member of the class is randomly assigned to assist him, what is the probability that both will be juniors?

   A. $\dfrac{1}{10}$

   B. $\dfrac{1}{5}$

   C. $\dfrac{2}{9}$

   D. $\dfrac{2}{5}$

   E. $\dfrac{1}{2}$

16. In triangle XYZ shown, $\overline{XS}$ and $\overline{SZ}$ are 3 and 12 units, respectively. If the area of triangle XYZ is 45 square units, how many units long is altitude $\overline{YS}$?

   F. 3

   G. 6

   H. 9

   J. 12

   K. 15

GO ON TO THE NEXT PAGE ⟩

17. At which y-coordinate does the line described by the equation $6y - 3x = 18$ intersect the y-axis?

   A. 2

   B. 3

   C. 6

   D. 9

   E. 18

18. If $x^2 - y^2 = 12$ and $x - y = 4$, what is the value of $x^2 + 2xy + y^2$?

   F. 3

   G. 8

   H. 9

   J. 12

   K. 16

19. What is the area in square units of the following figure?

   A. 147

   B. 108.5

   C. 91

   D. 60.5

   E. $39 + 7\sqrt{2}$

20. A carpenter is cutting wood to make a new bookcase with a board that is 12 feet long. If the carpenter cuts off three pieces, each of which is 17 inches long, how many inches long is the remaining fourth and final board? (A foot contains 12 inches.)

   F. 36

   G. 51

   H. 93

   J. 108

   K. 144

21. If $x^2 - 4x - 6 = 6$, what are the possible values for x?

   A. 4, 12

   B. −6, 2

   C. −6, −2

   D. 6, 2

   E. 6, −2

22. If −3 is a solution for the equation $x^2 + kx - 15 = 0$, what is the value of k?

   F. 5

   G. 2

   H. −2

   J. −5

   K. Cannot be determined from the information given.

23. If the lengths of all three sides of a triangle are integers, and one side is 7 inches long, what is the smallest possible perimeter of the triangle, in inches?

   A. 9

   B. 10

   C. 12

   D. 15

   E. 18

GO ON TO THE NEXT PAGE

24. If $0° < \theta < 90°$ and $\sin \theta = \dfrac{\sqrt{11}}{2\sqrt{3}}$, then $\cos \theta = ?$

    F. $\dfrac{1}{2\sqrt{3}}$

    G. $\dfrac{1}{\sqrt{11}}$

    H. $\dfrac{2}{\sqrt{3}}$

    J. $\dfrac{2\sqrt{3}}{\sqrt{11}}$

    K. $\dfrac{11}{2\sqrt{3}}$

25. Which of the following expressions is equivalent to $\dfrac{\sqrt{3+x}}{\sqrt{3-x}}$ for all x such that $-3 < x < 3$?

    A. $\dfrac{3-x}{3+x}$

    B. $\dfrac{3+x}{3-x}$

    C. $\dfrac{-3\sqrt{3+x}}{\sqrt{3-x}}$

    D. $\dfrac{\sqrt{9-x^2}}{3-x}$

    E. $\dfrac{x^2-9}{3+x}$

26. In a certain cookie jar containing only macaroons and gingersnaps, the ratio of macaroons to gingersnaps is 2 to 5. Which of the following could be the total number of cookies in the cookie jar?

    F. 24

    G. 35

    H. 39

    J. 48

    K. 52

27. What is the sum of $\dfrac{3}{16}$ and .175?

    A. .3165

    B. .3500

    C. .3625

    D. .3750

    E. .3875

28. What is the maximum possible area, in square inches, of a rectangle with a perimeter of 20 inches?

    F. 15

    G. 20

    H. 25

    J. 30

    K. 40

29. $\dfrac{\dfrac{3}{2}+\dfrac{7}{4}}{\left(\dfrac{15}{3}-\dfrac{3}{4}\right)-\left(\dfrac{4+3}{-4+3}\right)} = ?$

    A. $\dfrac{3}{8}$

    B. $\dfrac{2}{5}$

    C. $\dfrac{9}{13}$

    D. $\dfrac{5}{2}$

    E. $\dfrac{8}{3}$

30. If $x - 15 = 7 - 5(x - 4)$, then $x = ?$

    F. 0

    G. 2

    H. 4

    J. 5

    K. 7

GO ON TO THE NEXT PAGE

31. The following sketch shows the dimensions of a flower garden. What is the area of this garden in square meters?

9 meters

9 meters

13 meters

A. 31

B. 85

C. 99

D. 101

E. 117

32. What is the slope of the line described by the equation $6y - 3x = 18$?

F. -2

G. $-\dfrac{1}{2}$

H. $\dfrac{1}{2}$

J. 2

K. 3

33. Line m passes through the point $(4, 3)$ in the standard (x, y) coordinate plane and is perpendicular to the line described by the equation $y = -\dfrac{4}{5}x + 6$. Which of the following equations describes line m?

A. $y = \dfrac{5}{4}x - 2$

B. $y = -\dfrac{5}{4}x + 6$

C. $y = -\dfrac{4}{5}x - 2$

D. $y = -\dfrac{4}{5}x + 2$

E. $y = -\dfrac{5}{4}x - 2$

34. Line t in the standard (x, y) coordinate plane has a y-intercept of -3 and is parallel to the line having the equation $3x - 5y = 4$. Which of the following is an equation for line t?

F. $y = -\dfrac{3}{5}x + 3$

G. $y = -\dfrac{5}{3}x - 3$

H. $y = \dfrac{3}{5}x + 3$

J. $y = \dfrac{5}{3}x + 3$

K. $y = \dfrac{3}{5}x - 3$

35. If $y = mx + b$, which of the following equations expresses x in terms of y, m, and b?

A. $x = \dfrac{y - b}{m}$

B. $x = \dfrac{b - y}{m}$

C. $x = \dfrac{y + b}{m}$

D. $x = \dfrac{y}{m} - bx$

E. $x = \dfrac{y}{m} + b$

GO ON TO THE NEXT PAGE ⟩

36. In the following figure, $\overline{AB} = 20$, $\overline{BC} = 15$, and $\angle ADB$ and $\angle ABC$ are right angles. What is the length of $\overline{AD}$?

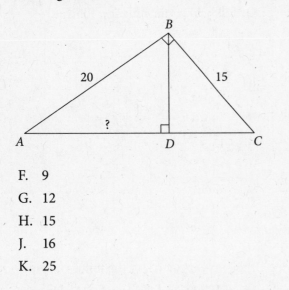

   F. 9
   G. 12
   H. 15
   J. 16
   K. 25

37. In the standard (x, y) coordinate plane shown in the figure, points A and B lie on line m, and point C lies below it. The coordinates of points A, B, and C are $(0, 5)$, $(5, 5)$, and $(3, 3)$, respectively. What is the shortest possible distance from point C to a point on line m?

   A. 2
   B. $2\sqrt{2}$
   C. 3
   D. $\sqrt{13}$
   E. 5

38. For all $x \neq 8$, $\dfrac{x^2 - 11x + 24}{8 - x} = ?$

   F. $8 - x$
   G. $3 - x$
   H. $x - 3$
   J. $x - 8$
   K. $x - 11$

39. Points A and B lie in the standard (x, y) coordinate plane. The (x, y) coordinates of A are $(2, 1)$ and the (x, y) coordinates of B are $(-2, -2)$. What is the distance from A to B?

   A. $3\sqrt{2}$
   B. $3\sqrt{3}$
   C. 5
   D. 6
   E. 7

40. In the following figure, $\overline{AB}$ and $\overline{CD}$ are both tangent to the circle as shown, and $ABCD$ is a rectangle with side lengths $2x$ and $5x$ as shown. What is the area of the shaded region?

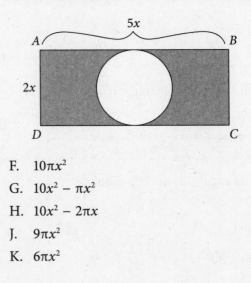

   F. $10\pi x^2$
   G. $10x^2 - \pi x^2$
   H. $10x^2 - 2\pi x$
   J. $9\pi x^2$
   K. $6\pi x^2$

GO ON TO THE NEXT PAGE

41. If $0° < \theta < 90°$ and $\cos \theta = \dfrac{5\sqrt{2}}{8}$, then $\tan \theta = ?$

    A. $\dfrac{5}{\sqrt{7}}$

    B. $\dfrac{\sqrt{7}}{5}$

    C. $\dfrac{\sqrt{14}}{8}$

    D. $\dfrac{8}{\sqrt{14}}$

    E. $\dfrac{8}{5\sqrt{2}}$

42. Consider fractions of the form $\dfrac{7}{n}$, where n is an integer. How many integer values of n make this fraction greater than .5 and less than .8?

    F. 3

    G. 4

    H. 5

    J. 6

    K. 7

43. The circumference of circle X is 12π and the circumference of circle Y is 8π. What is the greatest possible distance between two points, one of which lies on the circumference of circle X and one of which lies on the circumference of circle Y?

    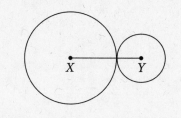

    A. 6

    B. 10

    C. 20

    D. 10π

    E. 20π

44. $\sqrt{(x^2 + 4)^2} - (x + 2)(x - 2) = ?$

    F. $2x^2$

    G. $x^2 - 8$

    H. $2(x - 2)$

    J. 0

    K. 8

45. If $s = -3$, then $s^3 + 2s^2 + 2s = ?$

    A. -15

    B. -10

    C. -5

    D. 5

    E. 33

46. How many different numbers are solutions for the equation $2x + 6 = (x + 5)(x + 3)$?

    F. 0

    G. 1

    H. 2

    J. 3

    K. Infinitely many

47. In square $ABCD$ shown, $\overline{AC} = 8$. What is the perimeter of $ABCD$?

    A. $4\sqrt{2}$

    B. 8

    C. $8\sqrt{2}$

    D. 16

    E. $16\sqrt{2}$

GO ON TO THE NEXT PAGE

48. The front surface of a fence panel is shown here with the lengths labeled representing inches. The panel is symmetrical along its center vertical axis. What is the surface area of the front surface of the panel in square inches?

F. 144

G. 132

H. 120

J. 80

K. $64 + 6\sqrt{5}$

49. In the following figure, O is the center of the circle, and C, D, and E are points on the circumference of the circle. If $\angle OCD$ measures 70° and $\angle OED$ measures 45°, what is the measure of $\angle CDE$?

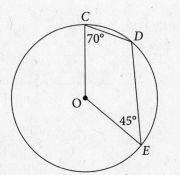

A. 25°

B. 45°

C. 70°

D. 90°

E. 115°

50. Which of the following systems of equations does NOT have a solution?

F. $x + 3y = 19$
   $3x + y = 6$

G. $x + 3y = 19$
   $x - 3y = 13$

H. $x - 3y = 19$
   $3x - y = 7$

J. $x - 3y = 19$
   $3x + y = 6$

K. $x + 3y = 6$
   $3x + 9y = 7$

51. What is the 46th digit to the right of the decimal point in the decimal equivalent of $\frac{1}{7}$?

A. 1

B. 2

C. 4

D. 7

E. 8

52. Which of the following inequalities is equivalent to $-2 - 4x \le -6x$?

F. $x \ge -2$

G. $x \ge 1$

H. $x \ge 2$

J. $x \le -1$

K. $x \le 1$

GO ON TO THE NEXT PAGE

53. If $x > 0$ and $y > 0$, $\dfrac{\sqrt{x}}{x} + \dfrac{\sqrt{y}}{y}$ is equivalent to which of the following?

   A. $\dfrac{2}{xy}$

   B. $\dfrac{\sqrt{x} + \sqrt{y}}{\sqrt{xy}}$

   C. $\dfrac{x + y}{xy}$

   D. $\dfrac{\sqrt{x} + \sqrt{y}}{\sqrt{x + y}}$

   E. $\dfrac{x + y}{\sqrt{xy}}$

54. In the following diagram, $\overline{CD}$, $\overline{BE}$, and $\overline{AF}$ are all parallel and are intersected by two transversals as shown. What is the length of $\overline{EF}$?

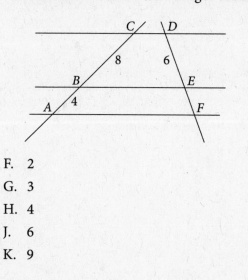

   F. 2

   G. 3

   H. 4

   J. 6

   K. 9

55. What is the area, in square units, of the square whose vertices are located at the (x, y) coordinate points indicated in the following figure?

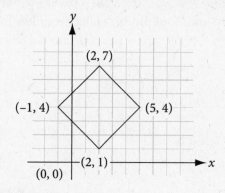

   A. 9

   B. 12

   C. 16

   D. 18

   E. 24

56. Compared to the graph of $y = \cos \theta$, the graph of $y = 2 \cos \theta$ has:

   F. twice the period and the same amplitude.

   G. half the period and the same amplitude.

   H. twice the period and half the amplitude.

   J. half the amplitude and the same period.

   K. twice the amplitude and the same period.

GO ON TO THE NEXT PAGE

57. Brandy has a collection of comic books. If she adds 15 to the number of comic books in her collection and multiplies the sum by 3, the result will be 65 less than 4 times the number of comic books in her collection. How many comic books are in her collection?

    A. 50
    B. 85
    C. 110
    D. 145
    E. 175

58. One empty cylinder has three times the height and twice the diameter of another empty cylinder. How many fillings of the smaller cylinder would be equivalent to one filling of the larger cylinder?

    (Note: The volume of a cylinder of radius r and height h is $\pi r^2 h$.)

    F. 6
    G. $6\sqrt{2}$
    H. 12
    J. 18
    K. 24

59. What is the perimeter of a 30°-60°-90° triangle with a long leg of 12 inches?

    A. $5\sqrt{3}+12$
    B. $4\sqrt{3}+18$
    C. $8\sqrt{3}+18$
    D. $12\sqrt{3}+12$
    E. $12\sqrt{3}+18$

60. A baseball team scores an average of x points in its first n games and then scores y points in its next and final game of the season. Which of the following represents the team's average score for the entire season?

    F. $x+\dfrac{y}{n}$

    G. $x+\dfrac{y}{n+1}$

    H. $\dfrac{x+ny}{n+1}$

    J. $\dfrac{nx+y}{n+1}$

    K. $\dfrac{n(x+y)}{n+1}$

READING TEST

35 Minutes—40 Questions

Directions: There are four passages in this test. Each passage is followed by several questions. After reading a passage, choose the best answer to each question and fill in the corresponding oval on your answer document. You may refer to the passages as often as necessary.

PASSAGE I

PROSE FICTION

This passage is adapted from the novel Emma *by Jane Austen. It was originally published in 1815.*

Emma Woodhouse, handsome, clever, and rich, with a comfortable home and happy disposition, seemed to unite some of the
Line best blessings of existence. She had lived
(5) nearly twenty-one years in the world with very little to distress or vex her. She was the youngest of the two daughters of a most affectionate, indulgent father, and had, in consequence of her sister's marriage, been
(10) mistress of his house from a very early period. Her mother had died too long ago for her to have more than an indistinct remembrance of her caresses, and her place had been taken by an excellent governess
(15) who had fallen little short of a mother in affection.

Sixteen years had Miss Taylor been in Mr. Woodhouse's family, less as a governess than a friend, very fond of both daughters,
(20) but particularly of Emma. Between them it was more the intimacy of sisters. Even before Miss Taylor had ceased to hold the nominal office of governess, the mildness of her temper had hardly allowed her
(25) to impose any restraint. The shadow of authority being now long passed away, they had been living together as friend and friend very mutually attached, and Emma doing just what she liked, highly esteeming Miss
(30) Taylor's judgment, but directed chiefly by her own. The real evils, indeed, of Emma's situation were the power of having rather

too much her own way, and a disposition to think a little too well of herself; these were
(35) the disadvantages which threatened alloy to her many enjoyments. The danger, however, was at present so unperceived, that they did not by any means rank as misfortunes with her.

(40) Sorrow came—a gentle sorrow—but not at all in the shape of any disagreeable consciousness. Miss Taylor married. It was Miss Taylor's loss which first brought grief. It was on the wedding-day of this beloved
(45) friend that Emma first sat in mournful thought of any continuance. The wedding over, and the bride-people gone, she and her father were left to dine together, with no prospect of a third to cheer a long evening.
(50) Her father composed himself to sleep after dinner, as usual, and she had then only to sit and think of what she had lost.

The marriage had every promise of happiness for her friend. Mr. Weston was
(55) a man of unexceptionable character, easy fortune, suitable age, and pleasant manners. There was some satisfaction in considering with what self-denying, generous friendship she had always wished and promoted the
(60) match, but it was a black morning's work for her. The want of Miss Taylor would be felt every hour of every day. She recalled her past kindness—the kindness, the affection of sixteen years—how she had taught her
(65) and how she had played with her from five years old—how she had devoted all her

GO ON TO THE NEXT PAGE ⟶

powers to attach and amuse her in health—
and how she had nursed her through the
various illnesses of childhood. A large
(70) debt of gratitude was owing here, but the
intercourse of he last seven years, the equal
footing and perfect unreserve which had
soon followed Isabella's marriage, on their
being left to each other, was yet a dearer,
(75) tenderer recollection. She had been a friend
and companion such as few possessed:
intelligent, well-informed, useful, gentle,
knowing all the ways of the family, interested
in all its concerns, and peculiarly
(80) interested in her, in every pleasure, every
scheme of hers—one to whom she could
speak every thought as it arose, and who
had such an affection for her as could never
find fault.
(85) How was she to bear the change? It was
true that her friend was going only half a
mile from them, but Emma was aware that
great must be the difference between a Mrs.
Weston, only half a mile from them, and
(90) a Miss Taylor in the house. With all her
advantages, natural and domestic, she was
now in great danger of suffering from intellectual
solitude.

1. According to the passage, what are the great-
    est disadvantages facing Emma?

    A. Her father is not a stimulating conversa-
        tionalist, and she is bored.

    B. She is lonely and afraid that Mrs.
        Weston will not have a happy marriage.

    C. She is used to having her way too much,
        and she thinks too highly of herself.

    D. She misses the companionship of her
        mother, her sister, and Miss Taylor.

2. The name of Emma's sister is:

    F. Mrs. Weston.

    G. Isabella.

    H. Miss Taylor.

    J. Mrs. Woodhouse.

3. As described in the passage, Emma's relation-
    ship with Miss Taylor can be characterized as:

    A. similar to a mother-daughter relation-
        ship.

    B. similar to the relationship of sisters or
        best friends.

    C. weaker than Emma's relationship with
        her sister.

    D. stronger than Miss Taylor's relationship
        with her new husband.

4. As used in line 33, *disposition* can most closely
    be defined as:

    F. a tendency.

    G. control.

    H. placement.

    J. transfer.

5. Which of the following are included in
    Emma's memories of her relationship with
    Miss Taylor?

        I. Miss Taylor taking care of Emma
            during childhood illnesses

       II. Miss Taylor entertaining Emma

      III. Miss Taylor teaching her mathemat-
            ics

       IV. Miss Taylor scolding her for being
            selfish

    A. I, III, and IV only

    B. I and III only

    C. II, III, and IV only

    D. I and II only

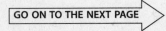 GO ON TO THE NEXT PAGE

6. It is most reasonable to infer from Emma's realization that "great must be the difference between a Mrs. Weston, only half a mile from them, and a Miss Taylor in the house" (lines 88–90) that:

   F. Miss Taylor will no longer be a part of Emma's life.

   G. Emma is happy about the marriage because now she will have more freedom.

   H. Emma regrets that her relationship with Miss Taylor will change.

   J. Emma believes that her relationship with Miss Taylor will become stronger.

7. Based on the passage, Emma could best be described as:

   A. sweet and naïve.

   B. self-centered and naïve.

   C. self-centered and headstrong.

   D. unappreciative and bitter.

8. The passage suggests that the quality Emma values most in a friend is:

   F. charisma.

   G. devotion.

   H. honesty.

   J. intelligence.

9. How does Emma view Mr. Weston?

   A. She thinks that he is an excellent match, and it required considerable self-sacrifice not to pursue him herself.

   B. She considers him to be a respectable if somewhat average match for her friend.

   C. She sees him as an intruder who has carried away her best friend in "a black morning's work" (line 60).

   D. She believes he is an indulgent, easily swayed man, reminiscent of her father.

10. From the passage, it can be inferred that Emma is accustomed to:

    F. behaving according to the wishes of her affectionate father.

    G. taking the advice of Miss Taylor when faced with deciding upon a course of action.

    H. doing as she pleases without permission from her father or governess.

    J. abiding by strict rules governing her behavior.

PASSAGE II

SOCIAL SCIENCE

This passage discusses different aspects of memory from a psychological perspective.

Learning and its result, memory, are processes by which we retain acquired information, emotions, and impressions
Line that can influence our behavior. At the
(5) psychological level, memory is not a single process. Sensory memory, the first of three main systems of memory, describes the momentary lingering of perceptual information as it is initially sensed and briefly
(10) recorded. When an image strikes the eyes, it lingers in the visual system for an instant while the image is interpreted, and is quickly overwritten by new information. In the visual system this is called *iconic memory*, in
(15) the auditory system it is *echoic memory*, and in reference to touch it is *haptic memory*.

If sensory information is processed, it can move into the second main system of memory, working memory. This was once
(20) known as short-term memory (and that term is still popularly used). But working memory is viewed as a more accurate term, since this system not only stores information for short periods of time, but also enables the use
(25) and manipulation of information processed

GO ON TO THE NEXT PAGE ▷

there. However, only a limited number of
items can be held in working memory (the
average for most people is seven), and decay
of the memory occurs rapidly, although
(30) it can be held longer if the information
is mentally or vocally repeated. Unless
we make a conscious effort to retain it, a
working memory may disappear forever.

Long-term memory is the most comprehensive
(35) of the three, with apparently
infinite capacity. Memories recorded in
long-term memory are never lost, although
at times there may be difficulty accessing
them. There are three independent categories
(40) of long-term memory which interact
extensively: *episodic* involves personal
memories and details of daily life, and
is closely identified with its time and
place; *semantic* contains facts and general
(45) knowledge that are not tied to when or how
they were learned; and *procedural* retains
skills used to perform certain activities that
eventually may not require conscious effort.

Although the main systems of memory
(50) are widely accepted, controversy continues
about memory formation and retrieval. It
was once believed that for a memory to
enter long-term memory it must first be
held in working memory. However, this idea
(55) has been challenged by an alternate theory
suggesting that sensory memories can be
directly entered into long-term memory
through a pathway that runs parallel to,
rather than in series with, working memory.
(60) Memories therefore can register simultaneously
in both systems.

Likewise, all agree that the retrieval of
long-term memories is facilitated by repetition,
but there is no agreement about the
(65) accuracy of these memories. For many
years, the scientific community viewed
human memory as similar to computer
memory, with the mind recording each
detail just as it was presented. However,
(70) there is a growing consensus that our
memory is sometimes flawed. An inference

or assumption made by an individual when
a memory is created may later be recalled
as fact, or the mind may fill in details that
(75) were originally missing. Moreover, when
we try to recall a particular memory, an
unrelated memory may alter it through a
process called interference. There is even
evidence that an entirely false memory can
(80) be incorporated as a memory indistinguishable
from true memories. Although for most
purposes these discrepancies are harmless,
concerns regarding the accuracy of human
memory challenge the reliability of eyewitness
(85) testimony.

11. The main purpose of the passage is to:

  A. describe the main memory systems and
     why they are increasingly controversial.

  B. describe the main memory systems and
     some views of memory formation and
     retrieval.

  C. demonstrate that early ideas about
     memory formation and retrieval were
     incorrect.

  D. demonstrate that theories about the
     main memory systems are incorrect.

12. Based on information in the passage, which of
    the following would be recalled from semantic
    long-term memory?

  F. Ballet steps

  G. A childhood birthday

  H. Multiplication tables

  J. Riding a bicycle

GO ON TO THE NEXT PAGE ⟶

13. It can be reasonably inferred from the passage that, if a man in a car accident is unable to remember details of his life and family, but does remember how to perform his job, his:

   A. episodic memories have been lost.

   B. episodic memories have become inaccessible.

   C. procedural memories have been lost.

   D. procedural memories have become inaccessible.

14. The fact that the scientific community once viewed human memory as similar to computer memory is mentioned in the last paragraph in order to:

   F. illustrate that memory is now viewed as complex rather than mechanical.

   G. explain that memory is now viewed as an exact record of events.

   H. illustrate that memory is always inaccurate.

   J. explain that memories are formed the same way computers encode data.

15. A person reads, "The baseball hit the window," and when asked to recall the sentence, remembers, "The baseball broke the window." According to the passage, this is probably an example of:

   A. interference altering a memory.

   B. a memory that became inaccessible.

   C. a reader's assumption altering a memory.

   D. a completely false memory being created.

16. According to the passage, all the following are examples of episodic memory EXCEPT:

   F. the meal you ate last night.

   G. the name of an old classmate.

   H. the year your class won a trophy.

   J. the face of a stranger passed on the street.

17. Based on information in the passage, the term *short-term memory* was most likely replaced with *working memory* in order to:

   A. refute the idea that memories in this category degrade quickly.

   B. emphasize that memories in this category can be manipulated.

   C. show that memories in this category become long-term memories.

   D. demonstrate that echoic memories are held in the visual system.

18. As it is used in the passage, the word *iconic* (line 14) most nearly means relating to:

   F. something sacred.

   G. a symbolic representation.

   H. visual sensory memory.

   J. a picture that represents a computer command.

19. According to the passage, most of the scientific community now agrees that:

   A. there are really four main categories of memory, not three.

   B. memories held in long-term memory remain forever.

   C. memories must be held in working memory before long-term memory.

   D. repetition does not affect the duration of memory.

20. According to the passage, which of the following is a characteristic of working memory?

   F. A slight echo in the ear

   G. Quick replacement by new sensory information

   H. Rapid forgetting

   J. Infinite capacity

GO ON TO THE NEXT PAGE

PASSAGE III

HUMANITIES

This passage is excerpted from A History of Women Artists, *© 1975 by Hugo Munsterberg; Clarkson N. Potter (a division of Random House, Inc.), publisher. Reprinted by permission of the author's family.*

There can be little doubt that women artists have been most prominent in photography and that they have made their greatest
Line contribution in this field. One reason for
(5) this is not difficult to ascertain. As several historians of photography have pointed out, photography, being a new medium outside the traditional academic framework, was wide open to women and offered them
(10) opportunities that the older fields did not....

All these observations apply to the first woman to have achieved eminence in photography, and that is Julia Margaret Cameron...Born in 1815 in Calcutta into an
(15) upper-middle-class family and married to Charles Hay Cameron, a distinguished jurist and member of the Supreme Court of India, Julia Cameron was well-known as a brilliant conversationalist and a woman of personality
(20) and intellect who was unconventional to the point of eccentricity. Although the mother of six children, she adopted several more and still found time to be active in social causes and literary activities. After
(25) the Camerons settled in England in 1848 at Freshwater Bay on the Isle of Wight, she became the center of an artistic and literary circle that included such notable figures as the poet Alfred Lord Tennyson and the
(30) painter George Frederick Watts. Pursuing numerous activities and taking care of her large family, Mrs. Cameron might have been remembered as still another rather remarkable and colorful Victorian lady had it not
(35) been for the fact that, in 1863, her daughter presented her with photographic equipment, thinking her mother might enjoy taking pictures of her family and friends. Although

forty-eight years old, Mrs. Cameron took
(40) up this new hobby with enormous enthusiasm and dedication. She was a complete beginner, but within a very few years she developed into one of the greatest photographers of her period and a giant in the
(45) history of photography. She worked ceaselessly as long as daylight lasted and mastered the technical processes of photography, at that time far more cumbersome than today, turning her coal house into a darkroom
(50) and her chicken house into a studio. To her, photography was a "divine art," and in it she found her vocation. In 1864, she wrote triumphantly under one of her photographs, "My First Success," and from then until her
(55) death in Ceylon in 1874, she devoted herself wholly to this art.

Working in a large format (her portrait studies are usually about 11 inches by 14 inches) and requiring a long exposure
(60) (on the average five minutes), she produced a large body of work that stands up as one of the notable artistic achievements of the Victorian period. The English art critic Roger Fry believed that her portraits were
(65) likely to outlive the works of artists who were her contemporaries. Her friend Watts, then a very celebrated portrait painter, inscribed on one of her photographs, "I wish I could paint such a picture as this."...Her
(70) work was widely exhibited, and she received gold, silver, and bronze medals in England, America, Germany, and Austria. No other female artist of the nineteenth century achieved such acclaim, and no other woman
(75) photographer has ever enjoyed such success.

Her work falls into two main categories on which her contemporaries and people today differ sharply. Victorian critics were particularly impressed by her allegorical
(80) pictures, many of them based on the poems

GO ON TO THE NEXT PAGE →

of her friend and neighbor Tennyson…
Contemporary taste much prefers her
portraits and finds her narrative scenes
sentimental and sometimes in bad taste. Yet,
(85) not only Julia Cameron, but also the painters
of that time loved to depict subjects such as
The Five Foolish Virgins or *Pray God, Bring
Father Safely Home*. Still, today her fame
rests upon her portraits for, as she herself
(90) said, she was intent upon representing not
only the outer likeness but also the inner
greatness of the people she portrayed.
Working with the utmost dedication, she
produced photographs of such eminent
(95) Victorians as Tennyson, Browning, Carlyle,
Trollope, Longfellow, Watts, Darwin, Ellen
Terry, Sir John Herschel, who was a close
friend of hers, and Mrs. Duckworth, the
mother of Virginia Woolf.

21. Which of the following conclusions can be
reasonably drawn from the passage's discussion of Julia Margaret Cameron?

   A. She was a traditional homemaker until
   she discovered photography.

   B. Her work holds a significant place in
   the history of photography.

   C. She was unable to achieve in her
   lifetime the artistic recognition she
   deserved.

   D. Her eccentricity has kept her from being
   taken seriously by modern critics of
   photography.

22. According to the passage, Cameron is most
respected by modern critics for her:

   F. portraits.

   G. allegorical pictures.

   H. use of a large format.

   J. service in recording the faces of so
   many twentieth century figures.

23. The author uses which of the following methods to develop the second paragraph (lines
11–56)?

   A. A series of anecdotes depicting
   Cameron's energy and unconventionality

   B. A presentation of factual data demonstrating Cameron's importance in the
   history of photography

   C. A description of the author's personal
   acquaintance with Cameron

   D. A chronological account of Cameron's
   background and artistic growth

24. As it is used in the passage, *cumbersome* (line
48) most closely means:

   F. difficult to manage.

   G. expensive.

   H. intense.

   J. enjoyable.

25. When the author says that Cameron had
found "her vocation" (line 52), his main point
is that photography:

   A. offered Cameron an escape from the
   confines of conventional social life.

   B. became the main interest of her life.

   C. became her primary source of income.

   D. provided her with a way to express her
   religious beliefs.

26. The main point of the third paragraph is that
Cameron:

   F. achieved great artistic success during
   her lifetime.

   G. is the greatest photographer who ever
   lived.

   H. was considered a more important artist
   during her lifetime than she is now.

   J. revolutionized photographic methods in
   the Victorian era.

GO ON TO THE NEXT PAGE

27. According to the passage, the art of photography offered women artists more opportunities than did other art forms because it:

    A. did not require expensive materials.

    B. allowed the artist to use family and friends for subject matter.

    C. was nontraditional.

    D. required little artistic skill.

28. *The Five Foolish Virgins* and *Pray God, Bring Father Safely Home* are examples of:

    F. portraits of celebrated Victorians.

    G. allegorical subjects of the sort that were popular during the Victorian era.

    H. photographs in which Cameron sought to show a subject's outer likeness and inner greatness.

    J. photographs by Cameron that were scoffed at by her contemporaries.

29. According to the passage, which of the following opinions of Cameron's work was held by Victorian critics but is NOT held by modern critics?

    A. Photographs should be based on poems.

    B. Her portraits are too sentimental.

    C. Narrative scenes are often in bad taste.

    D. Her allegorical pictures are her best work.

30. The author's treatment of Cameron's development as a photographer can best be described as:

    F. admiring.

    G. condescending.

    H. neutral.

    J. defensive.

PASSAGE IV

NATURAL SCIENCE

This passage discusses aspects of the harbor seal's sensory systems.

The harbor seal, *Phoca vitulina*, lives amphibiously along the northern Atlantic and Pacific coasts. This extraordinary
Line
(5) mammal, which does most of its fishing at night when visibility is low and in places where noise levels are high, has developed several unique adaptations that have sharpened its acoustic and visual acuity. The need for such adaptations has been
(10) compounded by the varying behavior of sound and light in each of the two habitats of the harbor seal—land and water.

    While the seal is on land, its ear operates much like the human ear, with sound waves
(15) traveling through air and entering the inner ear through the auditory canal. The directions from which sounds originate are distinguishable because the sound waves arrive at each inner ear at different times.
(20) In water, however, where sound waves travel faster than they do in air, the ability of the brain to differentiate arrival times between each ear is severely reduced. Yet it is crucial for the seal to be able to pinpoint the exact
(25) origins of sound in order to locate both its offspring and its prey. Therefore, the seal has developed an extremely sensitive quadraphonic hearing system, composed of a specialized band of tissue that extends
(30) down from the ear to the inner ear. In water, sound is conducted to the seal's inner ear by this special band of tissue, making it possible for the seal to identify the exact origins of sounds.

(35)   The eye of the seal is also uniquely adapted to operate in both air and water. The human eye, adapted to function primarily in air, is equipped with a cornea, which aids in the refraction and focusing
(40) of light onto the retina. As a result, when

GO ON TO THE NEXT PAGE ⟹

a human eye is submerged in water, light
rays are further refracted and the image is
blurry. The seal's cornea, however, refracts
light as water does. Therefore, in water, light
(45) rays are transmitted by the cornea without
distortion, and are clearly focused on the
retina. In air, however, the cornea is astigmatic,
resulting in a distortion of incoming
light rays. The seal compensates for this by
(50) having a stenopaic pupil, which constricts
into a vertical slit. Since the astigmatism is
most pronounced in the horizontal plane of
the eye, the vertical pupil serves to minimize
its effect on the seal's vision.

(55)   Since the harbor seal hunts for food
under conditions of low visibility, some
scientists believe it has echolocation systems
akin to those of bats, porpoises, and
dolphins. This kind of natural radar involves
(60) the emission of high frequency sound pulses
that reflect off obstacles such as predators,
prey, or natural barriers. The reflections
are received as sensory signals by the brain,
which processes them into an image. The
(65) animal, blinded by unfavorable lighting
conditions, is thus able to perceive its
surroundings. Such echolocation by harbor
seals is suggested by the fact that they emit
"clicks," high frequency sounds produced in
(70) short, fast bursts that occur mostly at night,
when visibility is low.

     Finally, there is speculation that the
seal's whiskers, or vibrissae, which are
unusually well developed and highly
(75) sensitive to vibrations, act as additional
sensory receptors. Scientists speculate that
the vibrissae may sense wave disturbances
produced by nearby moving fish, allowing
the seal to home in on and capture prey.

31. The harbor seal's eye compensates for the dis-
    tortion of light rays on land by means of its:

    A. vibrissae.

    B. cornea.

    C. stenopaic pupil.

    D. echolocation.

32. The passage implies that a harbor seal's vision
    is:

    F. inferior to a human's vision in the
        water, but superior to it on land.

    G. superior to a human's vision in the
        water, but inferior to it on land.

    H. inferior to a human's vision both in the
        water and on land.

    J. equivalent to a human's vision both in
        the water and on land.

33. According to the passage, scientists think
    vibrissae help harbor seals to catch prey by:

    A. improving underwater vision.

    B. sensing vibrations in the air.

    C. camouflaging predator seals.

    D. detecting underwater movement.

34. According to the passage, the speed of sound
    in water is:

    F. faster than the speed of sound in air.

    G. slower than the speed of sound in air.

    H. the same as the speed of sound in air.

    J. unable to be determined exactly.

GO ON TO THE NEXT PAGE ⟩

35. According to the passage, which of the following have contributed to the harbor seal's need to adapt its visual and acoustic senses?

    I.   Night hunting

    II. The need to operate in two habitats

    III. A noisy environment

A. I and II only

B. II and III only

C. I and III only

D. I, II, and III

36. Which of the following claims expresses the writer's opinion and not a fact?

F. The human eye is adapted to function primarily in air.

G. When the seal is on land, its ear operates like a human ear.

H. The "clicks" emitted by the harbor seal mean it uses echolocation.

J. The need for adaptation is increased if an animal lives in two habitats.

37. The passage suggests that the harbor seal lives in:

A. cold ocean waters with accessible coasts.

B. all areas with abundant fish populations.

C. most island and coastal regions.

D. warm coastlines with exceptionally clear waters.

38. According to the passage, a special band of tissue extending from the ear to the inner ear enables the harbor seal to:

F. make its distinctive "clicking" sounds.

G. find prey by echolocation.

H. breathe underwater.

J. determine where a sound originated.

39. The author compares harbor seal sensory organs to human sensory organs primarily in order to:

A. point out similarities among mammals.

B. explain how the seal's sensory organs function.

C. prove that seals are more adaptively successful than humans.

D. prove that humans are better adapted to their environment than seals.

40. According to the passage, one way in which seals differ from humans is:

F. that sound waves enter the inner ear through the auditory canal.

G. the degree of refraction of light by their corneas.

H. they focus light rays on the retina.

J. they have adapted to live in a certain environment.

SCIENCE TEST

35 Minutes—40 Questions

Directions: There are seven passages in this test. Each passage is followed by several questions. After reading a passage, choose the best answer to each question and fill in the corresponding oval on your answer document. You may refer to the passages as often as necessary. You are NOT permitted to use a calculator on this test.

PASSAGE I

The following table contains some physical properties of common optical materials. The refractive index of a material is a measure of the amount by which light is bent upon entering the material. The transmittance range is the range of wavelengths over which the material is transparent.

Table 1

Physical Properties of Optical Materials				
Material	Refractive index for light of 0.589 µm	Transmittance range (µm)	Useful range for prisms (µm)	Chemical resistance
Lithium fluoride	1.39	0.12–6	2.7–5.5	Poor
Calcium fluoride	1.43	0.12–12	5–9.4	Good
Sodium chloride	1.54	0.3–17	8–16	Poor
Quartz	1.54	0.20–3.3	0.20–2.7	Excellent
Potassium bromide	1.56	0.3–29	15–28	Poor
Flint glass*	1.66	0.35–2.2	0.35–2	Excellent
Cesium iodide	1.79	0.3–70	15–55	Poor

*Flint glass is lead oxide doped quartz.

1. According to the table, which material(s) will transmit light at 25 µm?

   A. Potassium bromide only
   B. Potassium bromide and cesium iodide
   C. Lithium fluoride and cesium iodide
   D. Lithium fluoride and flint glass

2. A scientist hypothesizes that any material with poor chemical resistance would have a transmittance range wider than 10 µm. The properties of which of the following materials contradicts this hypothesis?

   F. Lithium fluoride
   G. Flint glass
   H. Cesium iodide
   J. Quartz

GO ON TO THE NEXT PAGE

3. When light travels from one medium to another, total internal reflection can occur if the first medium has a higher refractive index than the second. Total internal reflection could occur if light were traveling from:

   A. lithium fluoride to flint glass.
   B. potassium bromide to cesium iodide.
   C. quartz to potassium bromide.
   D. flint glass to calcium fluoride.

4. Based on the information in the table, how is the transmittance range related to the useful prism range?

   F. The transmittance range is always narrower than the useful prism range.
   G. The transmittance range is narrower than or equal to the useful prism range.
   H. The transmittance range increases as the useful prism range decreases.
   J. The transmittance range is wider than and includes within it the useful prism range.

5. The addition of lead oxide to pure quartz has the effect of:

   A. decreasing the transmittance range and the refractive index.
   B. decreasing the transmittance range and increasing the refractive index.
   C. increasing the transmittance range and the useful prism range.
   D. increasing the transmittance range and decreasing the useful prism range.

GO ON TO THE NEXT PAGE

PASSAGE II

Osmosis is the diffusion of a solvent (often water) across a semipermeable membrane from the side of the membrane with a lower concentration of dissolved material to the side with a higher concentration of dissolved material. The result of osmosis is an equilibrium—an even distribution—on both sides of the membrane. In order to prevent osmosis, external pressure must be applied to the side with the higher concentration of dissolved material. *Osmotic pressure* is the external pressure required to prevent osmosis. The apparatus shown was used to measure osmotic pressure in the following experiments.

EXPERIMENT 1

Aqueous (water-based) solutions containing different concentrations of sucrose were placed in the closed side of the apparatus. The open side was filled with water. The sucrose solutions also contained a blue dye that binds to the sucrose. The osmotic pressure created by the piston was measured for each solution at various temperatures. The results are given in Table 1.

Table 1

Concentration of sucrose solution (mol/L)	Temperature (K)	Osmotic pressure (atm)
1.00	298.0	24.47
0.50	298.0	12.23
0.10	298.0	2.45
0.05	298.0	1.22
1.00	348.0	28.57
0.50	348.0	14.29
0.10	348.0	2.86
0.05	348.0	1.43

EXPERIMENT 2

Sucrose solutions of four different organic solvents were investigated in the same manner as in Experiment 1 with all trials at 298 K. The results are shown in Table 2.

Table 2

Solvent	Concentration of sucrose solution (mol/L)	Osmotic pressure (atm)
Ethanol	0.50	12.23
Ethanol	0.10	2.45
Acetone	0.50	12.23
Acetone	0.10	2.45
Diethyl ether	0.50	12.23
Diethyl ether	0.10	2.45
Methanol	0.50	12.23
Methanol	0.10	2.45

6. According to the experimental results, osmotic pressure is dependent upon the:

   F. solvent and temperature only.

   G. solvent and concentration only.

   H. temperature and concentration only.

   J. solvent, temperature, and concentration.

GO ON TO THE NEXT PAGE

7. According to Experiment 2, if methanol was used as a solvent, what pressure must be applied to a 0.5 mol/L solution of sucrose at 298 K to prevent osmosis?

   A. 1.23 atm

   B. 2.45 atm

   C. 12.23 atm

   D. 24.46 atm

8. A 0.10 mol/L aqueous sucrose solution is separated from an equal volume of pure water by a semipermeable membrane. If the solution is at a pressure of 1 atm and a temperature of 298 K:

   F. water will diffuse across the semipermeable membrane from the sucrose solution side to the pure water side.

   G. water will diffuse across the semipermeable membrane from the pure water side to the sucrose solution side.

   H. water will not diffuse across the semipermeable membrane.

   J. water will diffuse across the semipermeable membrane, but the direction of diffusion cannot be determined.

9. In Experiment 1, the scientists investigated the effect of:

   A. solvent and concentration on osmotic pressure.

   B. volume and temperature on osmotic pressure.

   C. concentration and temperature on osmotic pressure.

   D. temperature on atmospheric pressure.

10. Which of the following conclusions can be drawn from the experimental results?

    I. Osmotic pressure is independent of the solvent used.

    II. Osmotic pressure is only dependent upon the temperature of the system.

    III. Osmosis occurs only when the osmotic pressure is exceeded.

    F. I only

    G. III only

    H. I and II only

    J. I and III only

11. What was the most likely purpose of the dye placed in the sucrose solutions in Experiments 1 and 2?

    A. The dye showed when osmosis was completed.

    B. The dye showed the presence of ions in the solutions.

    C. The dye was used to make the experiment more colorful.

    D. The dye was used to make the onset of osmosis visible.

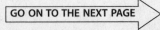 GO ON TO THE NEXT PAGE

PASSAGE III

A chemist investigating the influence of molecular weight and structure on the boiling point (transition from liquid to gaseous state) of different compounds recorded the data in the following tables. Two types of compounds were investigated: organic carbon compounds (shown in Table 1) and inorganic compounds (shown in Table 2).

Table 1

Straight-Chain Hydrocarbons		
Molecular formula	Molar weight* (g/mol)	Boiling point (°C)
CH_4	16	−162
C_2H_6	30	−88
C_3H_8	44	−42
C_4H_{10}	58	0
C_5H_{12}	72	36
C_8H_{18}	114	126
$C_{20}H_{42}$	282	345

*Molar weight is the weight of one mole, or an *Avogadro's Number* of molecules ($\approx 6 \times 10^{23}$), in grams.

Table 2

Other Substances (Polar and Non-Polar)		
Molecular formula	Molar weight (g/mol)	Boiling point (°C)
N_2*	28	−196
SiH_4*	32	−112
GeH_4*	77	−90
Br_2*	160	59
CO**	28	−192
PH_3**	34	−85
AsH_3**	78	−55
ICl**	162	97

*Non-Polar: molecule's charge is evenly distributed.

**Polar: molecule's negative and positive charges are partially separated.

12. Which of the following straight-chain hydrocarbons would NOT be a gas at room temperature?

    F. C_2H_6
    G. C_3H_8
    H. C_4H_{10}
    J. C_5H_{12}

13. Which of the following conclusions is supported by the observed results?

    I. Boiling point varies directly with molecular weight.
    II. Boiling point varies inversely with molecular weight.
    III. Boiling point is affected by molecular structure.

    A. I only
    B. II only
    C. I and III only
    D. II and III only

14. Based on the data in Table 1, the boiling point of the straight-chain hydrocarbon C_6H_{14} (molecular weight 86 g/mol) is most likely:

    F. 30°C.
    G. 70°C.
    H. 130°C.
    J. impossible to predict.

15. Based on the data in Table 2, as molecular weight increases, the difference between the boiling points of polar and non-polar substances of similar molecular weight:

    A. increases.
    B. decreases.
    C. remains constant.
    D. varies randomly.

GO ON TO THE NEXT PAGE

16. A polar substance with a boiling point of 0°C is likely to have a molar weight closest to which of the following:

F. 58

G. 80

H. 108

J. 132

PASSAGE IV

A series of experiments was performed to study the environmental factors affecting the size and number of leaves on the *Cycas* plant.

EXPERIMENT 1

Five groups of 25 *Cycas* seedlings, all from 2–3 cm tall, were allowed to grow for 3 months, each group at a different humidity level. All of the groups were kept at 75°F and received 9 hours of sunlight a day. The average leaf lengths, widths, and densities are given in Table 1.

Table 1

% Humidity	Average length (cm)	Average width (cm)	Average density* (leaves/cm)
15	5.6	1.6	0.13
35	7.1	1.8	0.25
55	9.8	2.0	0.56
75	14.6	2.6	0.61
95	7.5	1.7	0.52

*Number of leaves per 1 cm of plant stalk

EXPERIMENT 2

Five new groups of 25 seedlings, all from 2–3 cm tall, were allowed to grow for three months, each group receiving different amounts of sunlight at a constant humidity of 55%. All other conditions were the same as in Experiment 1. The results are listed in Table 2.

Table 2

Sunlight (hrs/day)	Average length (cm)	Average width (cm)	Average density* (leaves/cm)
0	5.3	1.5	0.32
3	12.4	2.4	0.59
6	11.2	2.0	0.56
9	8.4	1.8	0.26
12	7.7	1.7	0.19

*Number of leaves per 1 cm of plant stalk

EXPERIMENT 3

Five new groups of 25 seedlings, all from 2–3 cm tall, were allowed to grow at a constant humidity of 55% for three months at different daytime and nighttime temperatures. All other conditions were the same as in Experiment 1. The results are shown in Table 3.

Table 3

Day/night temperature (°F)	Average length (cm)	Average width (cm)	Average density* (leaves/cm)
85/85	6.8	1.5	0.28
85/65	12.3	2.1	0.53
65/85	8.1	1.7	0.33
75/75	7.1	1.9	0.45
65/65	8.3	1.7	0.39

*Number of leaves per 1 cm of plant stalk

17. Which of the following conclusions can be made based on the results of Experiment 2 alone?

A. The seedlings do not require long daily periods of sunlight to grow.

B. The average leaf density is independent of the humidity the seedlings receive.

C. The seedlings need more water at night than during the day.

D. The average length of the leaves increases as the amount of sunlight increases.

GO ON TO THE NEXT PAGE ⟶

18. Seedlings grown at a 40% humidity level under the same conditions as in Experiment 1 would have average leaf widths closest to:

    F. 1.6 cm.
    G. 1.9 cm.
    H. 2.2 cm.
    J. 2.5 cm.

19. According to the experimental results, under which set of conditions would a *Cycas* seedling be most likely to produce the largest leaves?

    A. 95% humidity and 3 hours of sunlight
    B. 75% humidity and 3 hours of sunlight
    C. 95% humidity and 6 hours of sunlight
    D. 75% humidity and 6 hours of sunlight

20. Which variable remained constant throughout all of the experiments?

    F. The number of seedling groups
    G. The percent of humidity
    H. The daytime temperature
    J. The nighttime temperature

21. It was assumed in the design of the three experiments that all of the *Cycas* seedlings were:

    A. more than 5 cm tall.
    B. equally capable of germinating.
    C. equally capable of producing flowers.
    D. equally capable of further growth.

22. As a continuation of the three experiments listed, it would be most appropriate to next investigate:

    F. how many leaves over 6.0 cm long there are on each plant.
    G. which animals consume *Cycas* seedlings.
    H. how the mineral content of the soil affects the leaf size and density.
    J. what time of year the seedlings have the darkest coloring.

PASSAGE V

The resistance (R) of a conductor is the extent to which it opposes the flow of electricity. Resistance depends not only on the conductor's resistivity (ρ), but also on the conductor's length (L) and cross-sectional area (A). The resistivity of a conductor is a physical property of the material that varies with temperature.

A research team designing a new appliance was researching the best type of wire to use in a particular circuit. The most important consideration was the wire's resistance. The team studied the resistance of wires made from four metals—gold (Au), aluminum (Al), tungsten (W), and iron (Fe). Two lengths and two gauges (diameters) of each type of wire were tested at 20°C. The results are recorded in the following table.

10-gauge wire
A = 5.26 mm²

16-gauge wire
A = 1.31 mm²

2.59 mm

1.29 mm

Note: area of circle = πr^2

GO ON TO THE NEXT PAGE ▷

Table 1

Material	Resistivity (mV–cm)	Length (cm)	Cross-sectional area (mm²)	Resistance (mV)
Au	2.44	1.0	5.26	46.4
Au	2.44	1.0	1.31	186.0
Au	2.44	2.0	5.26	92.8
Au	2.44	2.0	1.31	372.0
Al	2.83	1.0	5.26	53.8
Al	2.83	1.0	1.31	216.0
Al	2.83	2.0	5.26	107.6
Al	2.83	2.0	1.31	432.0
W	5.51	1.0	5.26	105.0
W	5.51	1.0	1.31	421.0
W	5.51	2.0	5.26	210.0
W	5.51	2.0	1.31	842.0
Fe	10.00	1.0	5.26	190.0
Fe	10.00	1.0	1.31	764.0
Fe	10.00	2.0	5.26	380.0
Fe	10.00	2.0	1.31	1,528.0

23. Of the wires tested, resistance increases for any given material as which parameter is decreased?

    A. Length

    B. Cross-sectional area

    C. Resistivity

    D. Gauge

24. Given the data in the table, which of the following best expresses resistance in terms of resistivity (ρ), cross-sectional area (A), and length (L)?

    F. $\dfrac{\rho^A}{L}$

    G. $\dfrac{\rho^L}{A}$

    H. ρAL

    J. $\dfrac{AL}{\rho}$

25. Which of the following wires would have the highest resistance?

    A. A 1-cm aluminum wire with a cross-sectional area of 0.33 mm²

    B. A 2-cm aluminum wire with a cross-sectional area of 0.33 mm²

    C. A 1-cm tungsten wire with a cross-sectional area of 0.33 mm²

    D. A 2-cm tungsten wire with a cross-sectional area of 0.33 mm²

26. According to the information given, which of the following statements is (are) correct?

    I. 10-gauge wire has a larger diameter than 16-gauge wire.

    II. Gold has a higher resistivity than tungsten.

    III. Aluminum conducts electricity better than iron.

    F. I only

    G. II only

    H. III only

    J. I and III only

GO ON TO THE NEXT PAGE

27. Which of the following graphs best represents the relationship between the resistivity of a tungsten wire and its length?

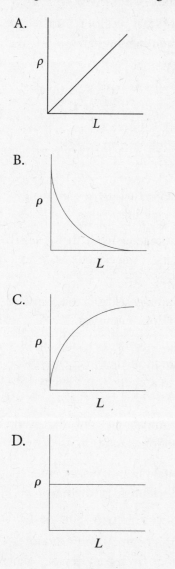

A.

B.

C.

D.

PASSAGE VI

How does evolution occur? Two views are presented here.

SCIENTIST 1

Evolution occurs by natural selection. Random mutations are continually occurring in a species as it propagates. A number of these mutations result in traits that help the species adapt to environmental changes. Because these mutant traits are advantageous, the members of the species who possess them tend to survive and pass on their genes more often than those who do not have these traits. Therefore, the percentage of the population with an advantageous trait increases over time. Long necks evolved in giraffes by natural selection. The ancestors of giraffes had necks of various sizes; however, their average neck length was much shorter than the average neck length of modern-day giraffes. Since the food supply was limited, the individuals with necks on the long range of the spectrum had access to more food (the leaves of trees) and therefore were more likely to survive and pass on their traits than individuals with shorter necks. Therefore, the proportion of the individuals with long necks is slightly greater in each subsequent generation.

SCIENTIST 2

Evolution occurs by the inheritance of acquired characteristics. Characteristics that are acquired by an individual member of a species during its lifetime are passed on to its offspring. Therefore, each generation's traits are partially accounted for by all the changes that occurred in the individuals of the previous generation. This includes changes that occurred as a result of accidents, changes in the environment, overuse of muscles, etc. The evolution of long necks of giraffes is an example. Ancestors of giraffes had short necks and consequently had to stretch their necks to reach the leaves of trees that were their main source of food.

GO ON TO THE NEXT PAGE

This repeated stretching of their necks caused them to elongate slightly. This trait was passed on, so that the individuals of the next generation had slightly longer necks. Each subsequent generation also stretched their necks to feed; therefore, each generation had slightly longer necks than the previous generation.

28. Both scientists agree that:

    F. the environment affects evolution.

    G. the individuals of a generation have identical traits.

    H. acquired characteristics are inherited.

    J. random mutations occur.

29. How would the two hypotheses be affected if it were found that all of the offspring of an individual with a missing leg due to an accident were born with a missing leg?

    A. It would support Scientist 1's hypothesis, because it is an example of random mutations occurring within a species.

    B. It would refute Scientist 1's hypothesis, because it is an example of random mutations occurring within a species.

    C. It would support Scientist 2's hypothesis, because it is an example of an acquired characteristic being passed on to the next generation.

    D. It would support Scientist 2's hypothesis, because it is an example of random mutations occurring within a species.

30. Which of the following characteristics can be inherited according to Scientist 2?

    I.   Fur color

    II. Bodily scars resulting from a fight with another animal

    III. Poor vision

    F. I only

    G. II only

    H. I and III only

    J. I, II, and III

31. Scientist 1 believes that the evolution of the long neck of the giraffe:

    A. is an advantageous trait that resulted from overuse of neck muscles over many generations.

    B. is an advantageous trait that resulted from a random mutation.

    C. is an advantageous trait that resulted from a mutation that occurred in response to a change in the environment.

    D. is a disadvantageous trait that resulted from a random mutation.

32. The fundamental point of disagreement between the two scientists is whether:

    F. giraffes' ancestors had short necks.

    G. evolved traits come from random mutations or from the previous generation.

    H. the environment affects the evolution of a species.

    J. the extinction of a species could be the result of random mutations.

GO ON TO THE NEXT PAGE ⟩

33. Suppose evidence was found that suggested that before the discovery of fire, human skin lacked the nerve endings necessary to detect extreme heat. Which of the following pieces of information, if true, would most seriously weaken the hypothesis of Scientist 2?

   A. Human skin is capable of generating nerve endings with new functions during life.

   B. The total number of nerve endings in the skin of a human is determined at birth and remains constant until death.

   C. An excess of nerve endings that are sensitive to extreme heat is a relatively common human mutation.

   D. No evidence exists to suggest that an excess of nerve endings that are sensitive to heat could be acquired through mutation.

34. The average height of a full-grown person today is significantly greater than was the average height of a full-grown person 1,000 years ago. If it was proven that the increase in average height was due only to evolutionary changes, how would Scientist 1 most likely explain this increase?

   F. People genetically prone to growing taller have been more likely to produce offspring over the last 1,000 years.

   G. Over the last 1,000 years, improvements in nutrition and medicine have led to greater average growth over a person's lifetime, and this growth has been passed from one generation to the next.

   H. Increased height is not a trait that can be acquired through mutation.

   J. Measurements of average height were less accurate 1,000 years ago than they are today.

PASSAGE VII

Bovine spongiform encephalopathy (BSE) is caused by the spread of a misfolded protein that eventually kills infected cattle. BSE is diagnosed postmortem from the diseased cavities that appear in brain tissue and is associated with the use in cattle feed of ground-up meat from scrapie-infected sheep. A series of experiments was performed to determine the mode of transmission of BSE. The results are given in the table below.

EXPERIMENT 1

Sixty healthy cows were divided into two equal groups. Group A's feed included meat from scrapie-free sheep; and Group B's feed included meat from scrapie-infected sheep. Eighteen months later, the two groups were slaughtered and their brains examined for BSE cavities.

EXPERIMENT 2

Researchers injected ground-up sheep brains directly into the brains of two groups of 30 healthy cows. The cows in Group C received brains from scrapie-free sheep. The cows in Group D received brains from scrapie-infected sheep. Eighteen months later, both groups were slaughtered and their brains examined for diseased cavities.

Table 1

Group	Mode of transmission	Scrapie present	Number of cows infected with BSE*
A	feed	no	1
B	feed	yes	12
C	injection	no	0
D	injection	yes	3

*As determined visually by presence/absence of spongiform encephalopathy

GO ON TO THE NEXT PAGE ▷

35. Which of the following hypotheses was investigated in Experiment 1?

    A. The injection of scrapie-infected sheep brains into cows' brains causes BSE.

    B. The ingestion of wild grasses causes BSE.

    C. The ingestion of scrapie-infected sheep meat causes scrapie.

    D. The ingestion of scrapie-infected sheep meat causes BSE.

36. What is the purpose of Experiment 2?

    F. To determine whether BSE can be transmitted by injection

    G. To determine whether BSE can be transmitted by ingestion

    H. To determine whether ingestion or injection is the primary mode of BSE transmission

    J. To determine the healthiest diet for cows

37. Which of the following assumptions is made by the researchers in Experiments 1 and 2?

    A. Cows do not suffer from scrapie.

    B. A year and a half is a sufficient amount of time for BSE to develop in a cow.

    C. Cows and sheep suffer from the same diseases.

    D. Cows that eat scrapie-free sheep meat will not develop BSE.

38. A researcher wishes to determine whether BSE can be transmitted through scrapie-infected goats. Which of the following experiments would best test this?

    F. Repeating Experiment 1, using a mixture of sheep and goat meat in Group C's feed

    G. Repeating Experiments 1 and 2, replacing sheep with healthy goats

    H. Repeating Experiments 1 and 2, replacing healthy sheep with healthy goats and scrapie-infected sheep with scrapie-infected goats

    J. Repeating Experiment 2, replacing healthy cows with healthy goats

39. What is the control group in Experiment 1?

    A. Group A

    B. Group B

    C. Group C

    D. Group D

40. Which of the following conclusions is (are) supported by the experiments?

    I. Cows that are exposed to scrapie-infected sheep are more likely to develop BSE than cows that are not.

    II. BSE is only transmitted by eating scrapie-infected sheep meat.

    III. A cow that eats scrapie-infected sheep meat is more likely to develop BSE than a cow that is injected with scrapie-infected sheep brains.

    F. II only

    G. III only

    H. I and III only

    J. II and III only

WRITING TEST

30 Minutes—1 Question

Directions: This is a test of your writing skills. You will have thirty (30) minutes to write an essay in English. Before you begin planning and writing your essay, read the writing prompt carefully to understand exactly what you are being asked to do. Your essay will be evaluated on the evidence it provides of your ability to express judgments by taking a position on the issue in the writing prompt; to maintain a focus on the topic throughout the essay; to develop a position by using logical reasoning and by supporting your ideas; to organize ideas in a logical way; and to use language clearly and effectively according to the conventions of standard written English. You may use the unlined pages in this test booklet to plan your essay. These pages will not be scored. *You must write your essay in pencil on the lined pages in the answer folder.* Your writing on those lined pages will be scored. You may not need all the lined pages, but to ensure you have enough room to finish, do NOT skip lines. You may write corrections or additions neatly between the lines of your essay, but do NOT write in the margins of the lined pages. *Illegible essays cannot be scored, so you must write (or print) clearly.*

If you finish before time is called, you may review your work. Lay your pencil down immediately when time is called.

DO NOT OPEN THIS BOOKLET UNTIL TOLD TO DO SO.

ACT WRITING TEST PROMPT

While some high schools offer art and music courses to their students, these courses are not always mandatory. Some teachers, students, and parents think that schools should emphasize traditional academic subjects like math and science, as those skills will help the students more in the future when they join the workforce. Others feel that requiring all high school students to take classes in music or the visual arts would teach equally valuable skills that the students may not learn otherwise and would also help them do better in traditional academic subject areas. In your opinion, should art or music classes be mandatory for all high school students?

In your essay, take a position on this question. You may write about either one of the two points of view given, or you may present a different point of view on this question. Use specific reasons and examples to support your position.

Use this space to *plan* your essay. Your work here will not be graded. Write your essay on the lined pages that follow.

_____

_____

_____

_____

_____

_____

_____

_____

_____

_____

_____

_____

_____

_____

_____

_____

_____

_____

_____

_____

_____

_____

_____

_____

_____

Practice Test One
ANSWER KEY

ENGLISH TEST

1. C	11. C	21. B	31. D	41. D	51. D	61. D	70. F
2. F	12. G	22. G	32. H	42. J	52. J	62. J	71. D
3. D	13. B	23. D	33. A	43. B	53. C	63. C	72. G
4. F	14. H	24. J	34. H	44. G	54. H	64. J	73. B
5. D	15. C	25. C	35. D	45. C	55. D	65. D	74. F
6. G	16. H	26. F	36. G	46. F	56. G	66. J	75. B
7. B	17. B	27. A	37. D	47. B	57. A	67. B	
8. J	18. G	28. J	38. G	48. H	58. H	68. F	
9. A	19. A	29. B	39. D	49. C	59. D	69. D	
10. J	20. J	30. G	40. J	50. H	60. H		

MATH TEST

1. D	9. E	17. B	25. D	33. A	41. B	49. E	57. C
2. J	10. K	18. H	26. G	34. K	42. H	50. K	58. H
3. D	11. D	19. D	27. C	35. A	43. C	51. E	59. D
4. K	12. H	20. H	28. H	36. J	44. K	52. K	60. J
5. C	13. C	21. E	29. B	37. A	45. A	53. B	
6. K	14. H	22. H	30. K	38. G	46. G	54. G	
7. B	15. C	23. D	31. C	39. C	47. E	55. D	
8. K	16. G	24. F	32. H	40. G	48. G	56. K	

READING TEST

1. C	6. H	11. B	16. J	21. B	26. F	31. C	36. H
2. G	7. C	12. H	17. B	22. F	27. C	32. G	37. A
3. B	8. G	13. B	18. H	23. D	28. G	33. D	38. J
4. F	9. B	14. F	19. B	24. F	29. D	34. F	39. B
5. D	10. H	15. C	20. H	25. B	30. F	35. D	40. G

SCIENCE TEST

1. B	6. H	11. D	16. H	21. D	26. J	31. B	36. F
2. F	7. C	12. J	17. A	22. H	27. D	32. G	37. B
3. D	8. G	13. C	18. G	23. B	28. F	33. B	38. H
4. J	9. C	14. G	19. B	24. G	29. C	34. F	39. A
5. B	10. F	15. A	20. F	25. D	30. J	35. D	40. G

ANSWERS AND EXPLANATIONS

ENGLISH TEST

PASSAGE I

1. C
Punctuation
Choice (C) is the most correct and concise answer choice. Choice (A) uses an unnecessary comma. Choice (B) is unnecessarily wordy. Choice (D) is redundant—if the societies created the legends, there is no need to describe the legends as original.

2. F
Writing Strategy
The question stem gives an important clue to the best answer: The purpose of the inserted sentence is "to describe the different kinds" of stories. Choice (F) is the only choice that does this. Choice (G) explains how the stories were told. Choice (H) explains why more is not known about the stories. Choice (J) describes the length of some stories.

3. D
Connections
Answer choices (A), (B), and (C) create run-on sentences. Choice (D) describes a relationship that makes sense between our "many more permanent ways of handing down our beliefs" and the fact that "we continue to create and tell legends." It also creates a complete sentence.

4. F
Verb Tenses
Choices (H) and (J) are ungrammatical after a colon. Choices (G), (H), and (J) are unnecessarily wordy.

5. D
Wordiness
Choices (A), (B), and (C) are redundant or unnecessarily wordy. Because the contrasting word *but* is

already used, *however* is repetitive and should be eliminated.

6. G
Wordiness
Choices (F), (H), and (J) are all redundant. The word *conclusion* is unnecessary because the word *ending* has already been used.

7. B
Verb Tenses
Choice (B) is the only choice that stays consistent with the verb tense established by *knew* and *decided*.

8. J
Verb Tenses
Choice (F) creates a run-on sentence and also makes it seem that the hunter, not the deer, "was only temporarily knocked unconscious by the car." Choices (G) and (H) use incorrect verb tenses.

9. A
Punctuation
Choice (B) is incorrect because the words preceding the semicolon could not be a complete sentence on their own. Choice (C) would create a sentence fragment. Choice (D) would create a run-on sentence.

10. J
Wordiness
Regardless of the sequence of the words, the information provided in (F), (G), and (H) is irrelevant to the passage's topic of urban legends.

11. C
Verb Tenses
The subject of the sentence is *One*, so the verb must be singular. Choices (B) and (D) use incorrect verb tenses.

12. G
Word Choice
Choice (F) creates a sentence that does not make sense. Choices (H) and (J) use the plural *women* instead of the singular *woman*.

13. B
Sentence Sense
Choice (B) most clearly expresses the idea that several websites research "the validity of commonly told urban legends." Because this information is relevant to the topic of urban legends, "OMIT the underlined portion" is not the best answer.

14. H
Writing Strategy
Paragraph 4 describes an urban legend that is "humorous in nature." Paragraph 5 describes a rather frightening legend: alligators living underneath the city in the sewer system. The sentence "Other urban legends seem to be designed to instill fear" is an appropriate topic sentence for paragraph 5, and it also serves as a needed transition between paragraph 4 and paragraph 5.

15. C
Writing Strategy
Although the third and fourth sentences of paragraph 1 provide *some* general information about the purpose and topics of the myths and legends of primitive societies, no specifics are given. This makes (C) the best answer.

PASSAGE II

16. H
Verb Tenses
Correct choices here could be *do you* or *does one*. The latter appears as an answer choice.

17. B
Punctuation
Choice (A) incorrectly uses a colon. Choices (C) and (D) are grammatically incorrect.

18. G
Wordiness
Solitary and *alone* are redundant in the same sentence. Choices (H) and (J) also have redundancy.

19. A
Word Choice
The underlined portion is clearest the way it is written.

20. J
Punctuation
The colon is incorrect, so eliminate (F) and (H). Because it is a compound sentence, a comma is needed before *and*.

21. B
Sentence Sense
In fact is nonessential—it should be set off by commas.

22. G
Word Choice
American (an adjective) is the word being modified. Therefore, the adverb form of *unique* is needed.

23. D
Sentence Sense
"Near Walden Pond…" is a long sentence fragment. The best way to fix the error is to simply combine the sentences by eliminating the period.

24. J
Sentence Sense
This paragraph and the ones that immediately follow outline Thoreau's life. His influence on the people of today is not discussed until the end of the essay. Therefore, the underlined sentence does not belong.

25. C
Organization
Sentence 3 logically follows sentence 1. Choice (C) is the only choice that lists this correct order.

26. F
Punctuation
There is one independent clause on each side of the semicolon, so the sentence is punctuated correctly. Choice (G) needs *and* after the comma to be correct. Choices (H) and (J) create run-on sentences.

27. A
Word Choice
A possessive pronoun is needed because the works belong to Thoreau. Eliminate (B) and (D). Choice (C) relates to more than one person, so it is incorrect as well.

28. J
Writing Strategy
This paragraph discusses Thoreau's impact on modern society; only (J) expresses the correct topic.

29. B
Wordiness
Choices (A), (C), and (D) are excessively wordy.

30. G
Writing Strategy
The use of questions forces the reader to think about the answers. Choice (F) is too literal, and (J) is too broad for the topic of the essay. Choice (H) is incorrect because the author establishes the quality of Thoreau's work.

PASSAGE III

31. D
Wordiness
Because the word *live* is used later in the sentence, (A), (B), and (C) contain redundant information.

32. H
Word Choice
In this sentence, the *its* must be possessive because the *unique anatomy* belongs to the sloth. The word describing *anatomy* must be an adjective, not an adverb.

33. A
Punctuation
The comma is correctly used in choice A to separate the nonessential descriptive phrase "about the size of a large domestic cat" from the rest of the sentence.

34. H
Sentence Sense
The information about the sloth's limbs is relevant to the topic, so it should not be omitted. Choice (H) clearly and directly expresses how the sloth's muscles are designed for clinging to things.

35. D
Word Choice
Adapted needs to be modified by an adverb, so (D) is the best choice.

36. G
Connections
Instead describes the right relationship between the two sentences. The pronouns must be consistent, and since *its* is already used in the sentence, (G) is the best choice.

37. D
Connections
(D) is the only choice that correctly describes the relationship between the sloth's inability to "move swiftly on the ground" and its ability to swim.

38. G
Writing Strategy
Choice (G) connects the sloth's unique characteristics discussed in paragraph 3 with the description of its flexibility in paragraph 4.

39. D
Punctuation

Choice (D) correctly uses the second comma necessary to separate the phrase "without moving the rest of its body" from the rest of the sentence. Choice (C) can be eliminated because it is unnecessarily wordy.

40. J
Verb Tenses

Choice (J) is the only choice that contains a verb tense consistent with the sentence.

41. D
Wordiness

Choices (A), (B), and (C) contain redundant information.

42. J
Wordiness

This information about the howler monkey is irrelevant to the topic of the passage.

43. B
Sentence Sense

Choice (A) creates a sentence fragment. Choice (C) is unnecessarily wordy and awkward. Choice (D) creates a run-on sentence.

44. G
Writing Strategy

The last sentence aptly concludes the entire passage, and removing it would make the ending more abrupt.

45. C
Organization

The description of the sloth's *camouflage* is in paragraph 5.

PASSAGE IV

46. F
Verb Tenses

The underlined portion is best left as is. The other answer choices make the sentence unnecessarily wordy.

47. B
Verb Tenses

The verb tense must agree with the tense that has been established up to this point. The passage is in the past tense, so (B) is correct.

48. H
Verb Tenses

Like the answer to the previous question, the simple past tense is correct.

49. C
Verb Tenses

Choice (A) creates a sentence fragment and uses an incorrect verb tense. Choice (B) also uses the wrong verb tense. Choice (D) incorrectly uses a semicolon, as the words preceding the semicolon do not constitute an independent clause.

50. H
Sentence Sense

In the context of the rest of the passage, only (H) makes sense. The firefighters' attempts to extinguish the flames failed; *only* nature could stop the fire with the first snowfall.

51. D
Wordiness

Choices (A) and (B) are unnecessarily wordy and awkward. Choice (C) creates a run-on sentence.

52. J
Wordiness

All of the other answer choices are unnecessarily wordy and/or repetitive.

53. C
Verb Tenses

From the plural verb *open*, you can determine that the best answer will contain *cones*. This makes (C) the only possible answer, as the apostrophe is incorrectly used in (B).

54. H
Connections

This is the only choice that makes sense in the context of the passage. The sighting of the large animals near burning forests is used as evidence that the animals of the region were "fire-tolerant and fire-adaptive."

55. D
Punctuation

The comma in (A) is unnecessary because the sentence has a list of only two examples, not three. The semicolon in (B) is incorrectly used because "and bedding down" does not begin an independent clause. The colon in (C) is incorrectly used because it is not being used to introduce or emphasize information.

56. G
Sentence Sense

The problem with "judging from recent pictures of the park" is that the phrase is modifying *forest*, and a forest obviously can't judge anything. The phrase would have been correct if the sentence read "judging from the recent pictures of the park, I think that the forest was not destroyed." In this case, the phrase modifies *I*, the author, who is capable of judging. Choice (G) takes care of the problem by rewriting the sentence so that the modifying phrase is gone.

57. A
Word Choice

The pronoun refers to *forest*.

58. H
Writing Strategy

The introduction of information about fires in Alaska is unwarranted, so (F) and (G) can be eliminated. Choice (J) is incorrect because the additional information would actually uphold the author's position as an authority.

59. D
Writing Strategy

The reports mentioned in (D) directly substantiate the author's claims much more than any of the other answer choices.

PASSAGE V

60. H
Verb Tenses

Choice (F) creates a sentence fragment, and (G) incorrectly uses a plural verb with a singular subject. The verb tense of the paragraph makes (H) a better choice than (J).

61. D
Wordiness

The final part of the sentence, "…and there are many other rivers in America as well," is completely irrelevant to the rest of the sentence and the paragraph, in which the author discusses white-water rafting and the rivers she's rafted.

62. J
Punctuation

Choice (F) is wrong because *rapids* is essential information and should not be set off by commas. Choice (G) is wrong because what follows the colon is not an explanation. Choice (H) is incorrect because what follows the semicolon cannot stand alone as a sentence.

63. C
Wordiness

Choices (A) and (D) create sentence fragments, and (B) is extremely awkward.

64. J
Wordiness
This sentence is irrelevant to the topic of the passage.

65. D
Word Choice
This sentence makes it sound as though the author were roaring, not the rapids; *roaring* is a misplaced modifier. Choice (B) doesn't fix the problem because the reader has no idea what *it* refers to. Choice (C) has *the boat* roaring. Choice (D) is the clearest choice.

66. J
Sentence Sense
The word *cover* must either be in past tense, or the structure of the sentence must change. Choice (J) does the latter.

67. B
Wordiness
Choice (B) is the simplest, most concise way of expressing the idea. Replacing "and instead he adopted" with "with" makes the sentence much less awkward.

68. F
Word Choice
Choices (G) and (J) make it sound as though the author were in the water. Choice (F) expresses the idea more accurately than (H) does.

69. D
Wordiness
The phrase "and we stopped" is redundant because "we came to a jarring halt" says the same thing much more expressively. Omit the underlined portion.

70. F
Word Choice
It was is fine here because the author is telling her story in the past tense. Choices (G) and (H) are the

present tense, and (J) incorrectly introduces the possessive form.

71. D
Wordiness
The other answer choices are unnecessarily wordy; the simplest choice, (D), is the best.

72. G
Verb Tenses
The participle *receiving* has to be changed into a verb in the past tense, *received*, in order to be consistent with *went*. Choice (G) is correct as opposed to (H) because the number of bruises something has can be counted, which necessitates *many bruises*, not *much bruises*.

73. B
Writing Strategy
Choice (A) wouldn't work as a concluding sentence because its style and tone are off; nowhere in the passage does the writer use language such as "brutal calamities" and "beguiling excitement." Also, the writer and her father were not "unwary rafters." Choice (C) contradicts the writer's main theme that nothing was as memorable as her first ride through the rapids. The tone in (D), "call me crazy or weird…," is much different from the writer's. Choice (B) is the choice that closely matches the author's style and tone while restating the main theme of the passage.

74. F
Writing Strategy
This essay relates a personal experience of the writer: her first time rafting down the rapids. There is very little mention of the techniques of whitewater rafting, so the essay would not meet the requirements of the assignment. Choice (G) is wrong because the essay does not focus on the relationship between father and daughter, but on their first rafting experience together.

75. B
Organization

The sentence foreshadows things to come, so it must appear toward the beginning of the essay. That eliminates (C) and (D). The second paragraph is about the peaceful setting, so (B) is the most sensible answer.

MATH TEST

Answer explanations for the Math test refer to 100 Key Math Concepts for the ACT, found inside Part 1.

1. D
Proportions and Probability

Key Math Concepts for the ACT, #32. You know that 14 people are 20% of the total, and you need to find 100% of the total. You could set up an equation, or you could multiply 14 by 5, since 100% is 5 times as much as 20%. The number of people surveyed is 14×5, or 70.

2. J
Proportions and Probability

Key Math Concepts for the ACT, #41. One safe way to answer this question is by Picking Numbers. For instance, if you let $x = 2$ and $y = 3$, the train would have traveled $90 \times 2 + 60 \times 3 = 360$ miles in 5 hours, or $\frac{360}{5} = 72$ miles per hour. If you then plug $x = 2$ and $y = 3$ into the answer choices, it's clear that the correct answer is (J). No other answer choice equals 72 when $x = 2$ and $y = 3$.

3. D
Proportions and Probability

Key Math Concepts for the ACT, #38. If the ratio of men to women is 5:3, then the ratio of women to the total is $3:3 + 5 = 3:8$. Since you know the total

number of string players is 24, you can set up the equation $\frac{3}{8} = \frac{x}{24}$ to find that $x = 9$. Also, without setting up the proportion, you could note that the total number of players is 3 times the ratio total, so the number of women will be 3 times the part of the ratio that represents women.

4. K
Variable Manipulation

Key Math Concepts for the ACT, #52. In a pinch, you could Backsolve on this question, but this one is fairly easy to solve algebraically:

$$x^2 - 3x = 6$$
$$x^2 = 9x$$

Now you can divide both sides by x because $x \neq 0$:

$$\frac{x^2}{x} = \frac{9x}{x}$$
$$x = 9$$

5. C
Patterns, Logic, and Data

With visual perception problems such as this one, the key is to play around with possibilities as you try to draw a solution. Eventually, you should be able to come up with a picture like this:

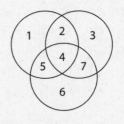

6. K
Variable Manipulation

Key Math Concepts for the ACT, #52. This problem could be solved algebraically, but look at the answer choices. They are all simple numbers, making this a great opportunity for Backsolving. Begin with choice (H).

Plugging in 0, you get:

$$(0)^2 + 6(0) + 8 = 4 + 10(0)$$

$$8 = 4$$

Since 8 does not equal 4, you know this isn't the correct answer. But it is difficult to know which answer to try next. Should you aim higher or lower? If you're unsure of which direction to go, just try whatever looks easiest. Choice (J), 1, looks like a good candidate:

$$(1)^2 + 6(1) + 8 = 4 + 10(1)$$

$$1 + 6 + 8 = 4 + 10$$

$$15 = 14$$

So (J) doesn't work either, but it looks like the numbers are getting closer, so you're going in the right direction. Try (K) just to be sure.

$$(2)^2 + 6(2) + 8 = 4 + 10(2)$$

$$4 + 12 + 8 = 4 + 20$$

$$24 = 24$$

Choice (K) is the correct answer.

7. B
Variable Manipulation

Key Math Concepts for the ACT, #65. Translate piece by piece:

"Nine less than c" indicates subtraction: $c - 9$.

"Nine less than c is the same as the number d": $c - 9 = d$. There's one equation.

"d less than" also indicates subtraction: $- d$.

"d less than twice c is 20": $2c - d = 20$. There's the second equation.

Choice (B) matches what we found.

8. K
Proportions and Probability

Key Math Concepts for the ACT, #45. To determine the total number of possible arrangements on a question like this one, simply determine the number of possibilities for each component, and then multiply them together. There are three ways of serving the ice cream, five flavors, and four toppings. Therefore, there are $3 \times 5 \times 4 = 60$ ways to order ice cream, and (K) is correct.

9. E
Proportions and Probability

Key Math Concepts for the ACT, #37. Backsolving is a great technique to use for this problem. Start with (C). The director asked 1 out of 3 students to come to the second audition and $\frac{1}{3}$ of 48 is 16, so 16 students were invited to a second audition. Then 75% of 16, which is $\frac{3}{4}(16) = 12$ students were offered parts. The question states that 18 students were offered parts, so you already know that (C) is too small. (You can also, thus, eliminate (A) and (B).) Since the director invited $\frac{1}{3}$ of the students to a second audition, the number of students at the first audition must be divisible by 3. (You can't have a fraction of a student.) That eliminates (D), which leaves only (E).

10. K
Variable Manipulation
Key Math Concepts for the ACT, #6. Begin by translating the English into math: $x + 5x = -60$, $6x = -60$, so $x = -10$, and the two numbers are -10 and -50. Thus, the lesser number is -50.

By the way, this is where most people mess up. They forget that the lesser of two negative numbers is the negative number with the larger absolute value (since *less* means *to the left of* on the number line):

11. D
Patterns, Logic, and Data
Key Math Concepts for the ACT, #86. You're looking for the total number of parallelograms that can be found among the triangles, and parallelograms could be formed two ways from these triangles, either from two adjacent triangles or from four adjacent triangles, like so:

Begin by looking for the smaller parallelograms. If you look for parallelograms leaning in the same direction as the one we drew, you'll find three. But there are two other possible orientations for the smaller parallelogram; it could be flipped horizontally, or it could be rotated 90 degrees so that one triangle sits atop the other in the form of a diamond; both of these orientations also have three parallelograms, for a total of nine smaller parallelograms.

Now look for larger parallelograms. Perhaps the easiest way to count these is to look along the sides of the larger composite triangle. You should be able to spot two of the larger parallelograms along each side, one originating at each vertex, for a total of six larger parallelograms.

Thus, there are a total of $9 + 6 = 15$ parallelograms in all.

12. H
Plane Geometry
Key Math Concepts for the ACT, #87, #91. The square has a perimeter of 16 inches, so each side of the square is 4 inches; the area of the square is, therefore, 16 square inches. If the side of the square is 4 inches, then the diameter of the circle is also 4 inches. The radius of the circle is then 2 inches. The area of the circle is 4π square inches. The area of the shaded region is then $16 - 4\pi$ square inches.

13. C
Number Properties
Key Math Concepts for the ACT, #10. The safest strategy is simply to list out the possibilities. It's also helpful to realize that multiples of both 4 and 6 are multiples of 12 (the least common multiple between the two), so skip over all multiples of 12:

4, 8, ~~12~~, 16, 20, ~~24~~, 28, 32, ~~36~~, 40, 44, ~~48~~

So there are 8 in all.

14. H
Variable Manipulation
Key Math Concepts for the ACT, #52. Don't be intimidated by the expression $f(x)$. In this case, you should just plug in the number that appears in the parentheses for the x in the expression they have given you.

So, if $f(x) = (8 - 3x)(x^2 - 2x - 15)$, $f(3) = [8 - 3(3)][(3)^2 - 2(3) - 15]$.

Once you get to this point, just remember PEMDAS.

$[8 - 3(3)][(3)^2 - 2(3) - 15] = (8 - 9)(9 - 6 - 15) = (-1)(-12) = 12$, choice (H).

15. C
Proportions and Probability
Key Math Concepts for the ACT, #46. A class contains five juniors and five seniors. If one member of the

class is assigned at random to present a paper on a certain subject, and another member of the class is randomly assigned to assist him, then:

The probability that the first student picked will be a

$$\text{junior} = \frac{\text{\# of juniors}}{\text{Total \# of students}} = \frac{5}{10} = \frac{1}{2}.$$

The probability that the second student picked will be a junior, given that the first student picked was a

$$\text{junior} = \frac{\text{\# of juniors remaining}}{\text{Total \# of students remaining}}.$$

So the probability that both students will be

$$\text{juniors} = \frac{1}{2} \times \frac{4}{9} = \frac{2}{9}.$$

16. G
Plane Geometry

Key Math Concepts for the ACT, #83. Since the formula to find the area of a triangle is $\frac{1}{2}$(base)(height), you can plug in the base and area to find the height. You know that the area of this triangle is 45 units and that the base is $3 + 12 = 15$. Let x be the length of altitude $\overline{YS}$. Plug these into the area formula to get $45 = \frac{15x}{2}$. Solve for x to get $x = 6$.

17. B
Coordinate Geometry

Key Math Concepts for the ACT, #74. The y-coordinate is the point on which the x value is zero, so plug $x = 0$ into the equation:

$$6y - 3(0) = 18$$

$$6y = 18$$

$$y = 3$$

18. H
Variable Manipulation

Key Math Concepts for the ACT, #67. This question involves common quadratics, so the key is to write

these quadratic expressions in their other forms. For instance, $x^2 - y^2 = 12$, so $(x + y)(x - y) = 12$. Since $x - y = 4$, $(x + y)(4) = 12$, so $x + y = 3$. Finally, $x^2 + 2xy + y^2 = (x + y)^2 = (3)^2 = 9$.

19. D
Plane Geometry

Key Math Concepts for the ACT, #87, #83. This shape must be divided into three simple shapes. By drawing downward two perpendicular line segments from the endpoints of the side which is 10 units long, you are left with a 3×10 rectangle, a triangle with a base of 4 and a height of 3, and a triangle with a base of 7 and a hypotenuse of $7\sqrt{2}$. The rectangle has an area of $3 \times 10 = 30$ square units. The smaller triangle has an area of $\frac{4 \times 3}{2} = 6$ square units. The larger triangle is a 45°-45°-90° triangle, so the height must be 7. Therefore, it has an area of $\frac{7 \times 7}{2} = 24.5$ square units. The entire shape has an area of $6 + 30 + 24.5 = 60.5$ square units.

20. H
Operations

Key Math Concepts for the ACT, #65. Although Backsolving is certainly possible with this problem, it's probably quicker to solve with arithmetic. The board is 12 feet long, which means it is $12 \times 12 = 144$ inches. The carpenter cuts off $3 \times 17 = 51$ inches. That leaves $144 - 51 = 93$ inches.

21. E
Variable Manipulation

Key Math Concepts for the ACT, #66. To answer this question, begin by setting the right side of the equation equal to zero:

$$x^2 - 4x - 6 = 6$$

$$x^2 - 4x - 12 = 0$$

Now use reverse-FOIL to factor the left side of the equation:

$$(x - 6)(x + 2) = 0$$

Thus, either $x - 6 = 0$ or $x + 2 = 0$, so $x = 6$ or -2.

22. H
Variable Manipulation

Key Math Concepts for the ACT, #66. Here's another question that tests your understanding of FOIL, but you have to be careful. The question states that -3 is a possible solution for the equation $x^2 + kx - 15 = 0$, so in its factored form, one set of parentheses with a factor inside must be $(x + 3)$. Since the last term in the equation in its expanded form is -15, that means that the entire factored equation must read $(x + 3)(x - 5) = 0$, which in its expanded form is $x^2 - 2x - 15 = 0$. Thus, $k = -2$.

23. D
Plane Geometry

To solve this problem, you need to understand the triangle inequality theorem, which states: The sum of the lengths of any two sides of a triangle is always greater than the length of the third side. Therefore, the other sides of this triangle must add up to more than 7. You know from the problem that every side must be an integer. That means that the sides must add up to at least 8 inches (4 inches and 4 inches, or 7 inches and 1 inch, for example). The smallest possible perimeter is $7 + 8 = 15$.

24. F
Trigonometry

Key Math Concepts for the ACT, #96. It's time to use SOHCAHTOA, and drawing a triangle might help as well. If the sine of θ (opposite side over hypotenuse) is $\dfrac{\sqrt{11}}{2\sqrt{3}}$, then one of the legs of the right triangle is $\sqrt{11}$, and the hypotenuse is $2\sqrt{3}$. Now apply the

Pythagorean theorem to come up with the other (adjacent) leg: $\left(\sqrt{11}\right)^2 + (n)^2 = \left(2\sqrt{3}\right)^2$, so $11 + n^2 = 12$, which means that $n^2 = 1$, and $n = 1$. Thus, cosine (adjacent side over hypotenuse) θ is $\dfrac{1}{2\sqrt{3}}$.

25. D
Operations

Key Math Concepts for the ACT, #49. Take a quick look at the answer choices before simplifying an expression like this one. Notice that none of these choices contain a radical sign in their denominators. So when you simplify the expression, try to eliminate that radical sign. Your calculations should look something like this:

$$\frac{\sqrt{3 + x}}{\sqrt{3 - x}} \times \frac{\sqrt{3 - x}}{\sqrt{3 - x}} = \frac{\sqrt{(3 + x)(3 - x)}}{\sqrt{(3 - x)^2}} =$$

$$\frac{\sqrt{9 - 3x + 3x - x^2}}{3 - x} = \frac{\sqrt{9 - x^2}}{3 - x}$$

So choice D is correct.

26. G
Proportions and Probability

Key Math Concepts for the ACT, #37. If the ratio of the parts is 2:5, then the ratio total is $2 + 5 = 7$. Thus, the actual total number of cookies must be a multiple of 7. The only choice that's a multiple of 7 is (G), 35.

27. C
Number Properties

Key Math Concepts for the ACT, #29. This question is a great opportunity to use your calculator.

Notice that all your choices are decimals. In order to solve, convert $\dfrac{3}{16}$ into a decimal and add that to .175. $\dfrac{3}{16} = .1875$, so the sum equals $.1875 + .175 = .3625$. So choice (C) is correct.

28. H
Plane Geometry
Key Math Concepts for the ACT, #87. Remember that if you are given a perimeter for a rectangle, the rectangle with the greatest area for that perimeter will be a square. So we are looking for the area of a square with a perimeter of 20. The perimeter of a square equals $4s$, where s is the length of one side of the square. If $4s = 20$, then $s = 5$. The area of the square equals $s^2 = 5^2 = 25$, (H).

29. B
Operations
Key Math Concepts for the ACT, #22, #23, #24. Be careful on this one. You can't start plugging numbers into your calculator without paying attention to the order of operations. This one is best solved on your own.

$$\frac{\dfrac{3}{2}+\dfrac{7}{4}}{\left(\dfrac{15}{8}-\dfrac{3}{4}\right)-\left(\dfrac{4+3}{-4+3}\right)}=$$

$$\frac{\dfrac{3}{2}+\dfrac{7}{4}}{\left(\dfrac{9}{8}\right)-\left(\dfrac{7}{-1}\right)}=\frac{\dfrac{13}{4}}{\dfrac{65}{8}}=\frac{13}{4}\times\frac{8}{65}=\frac{2}{5}$$

30. K
Variable Manipulation
Key Math Concepts for the ACT, #63. You could solve this algebraically for x as follows:

$$x - 15 = 7 - 5(x - 4)$$
$$x - 15 = 7 - 5x + 20$$
$$x - 15 = -5x + 27$$
$$6x = 42$$
$$x = 7$$

Remember also that if you are ever stuck, you can try to Backsolve with the answer choices. Here, if you try them all out, only 7 works:

$$7 - 15 = 7 - 5(7 - 4)$$
$$-8 = 7 - 5(3)$$
$$-8 = 7 - 15$$
$$-8 = -8$$

31. C
Plane Geometry
Key Math Concepts for the ACT, #87, #83. Break strange figures like this one up into shapes that are more familiar and easier to handle. In this case, the quadrilateral can be split into a square and a right triangle. The square is 9×9, so the area of that part of the figure is 81 square meters. The right triangle has a height of 9 and a base of 4, so the area of the triangle would be

$$\frac{1}{2}bh = \frac{1}{2}(4 \times 9) = \frac{1}{2}(36) = 18$$

square meters. So the total area of the figure is (81 + 18) square meters = 99 square meters, (C).

32. H
Coordinate Geometry
Key Math Concepts for the ACT, #73. The easiest way to solve this question is to put it in the form $y = mx + b$, in which case m equals the slope. In other words, you want to isolate y:

$$6y - 3x = 18$$
$$6y = 3x + 18$$
$$y = \frac{3x + 18}{6}$$
$$y = \frac{1}{2}x + 3$$

So the slope equals $\frac{1}{2}$.

33. A
Coordinate Geometry

To answer this question, you have to know that

perpendicular lines on the standard (x,y) coordinate plane have slopes that are negative reciprocals of each other. In other words, the line described by the equation $y = -\frac{4}{5}x + 6$ has a slope of $-\frac{4}{5}$, so a line perpendicular to it has a slope of $\frac{5}{4}$. This eliminates all choices but A. However, if you want to double-check, you can plug the coordinates you're given (4,3) into the equation found in choice (A).

$$3 = \frac{5}{4}(4) - 2$$
$$3 = 5 - 2$$
$$3 = 3$$

34. K
Coordinate Geometry

Key Math Concepts for the ACT, #73. Since the problem gives you the y-intercept, it is easy to look at the answer choices and rule out (F), (H), and (J). Put the equation from the question in slope-intercept form to find its slope:

$$3x - 5y = 4$$
$$-5y = -3x + 4$$
$$y = \frac{-3x + 4}{-5}$$
$$y = \frac{3}{5}x - \frac{4}{5}$$

Since line t is parallel, it has the same slope. This matches choice (K).

35. A
Variable Manipulation

Key Math Concepts for the ACT, #63. To solve for x in the equation $y = mx + b$, isolate x on one side of the equation. Begin by subtracting b from both sides. You will be left with $y - b = mx$. Then divide both sides by m, and you will be left with $x = \frac{y - b}{m}$, choice (A).

36. J
Plane Geometry

Key Math Concepts for the ACT, #85. In this figure, there are many right triangles and many similar triangles. If you know to be on the lookout for 3-4-5 triangles, it should be easy to spot that triangle ABC has sides of 15-20-25, so $\overline{AC}$ is 25. Now turn your attention to triangle ABD. Since it's a right triangle that shares $\angle BAC$ with triangle ABC, it too must be a 3-4-5 triangle. So if the hypotenuse is 20, the shorter leg $(\overline{BD})$ must have a length of 12, and the longer leg $(\overline{AD})$ must have a length of 16.

37. A
Coordinate Geometry

The shortest distance to line m will be a line perpendicular to m. So the distance will be the difference between the y-coordinates of point C and the nearest point on line m. Since every point on m has a y-coordinate of 5, and point C has a y-coordinate of 3, the difference is 2.

38. G
Variable Manipulation

While you could try factoring the numerator, you'll find that you can't easily cancel out the denominator by doing so. Perhaps the easiest approach here is to Pick Numbers. Pick a simple number such as $x = 2$. Thus,

$$\frac{x^2 - 11x + 24}{8 - x} = \frac{(2)^2 - 11(2) + 24}{6} =$$
$$\frac{4 - 22 + 24}{6} = \frac{6}{6} = 1.$$

So 1 is your target number. When you plug $x = 2$ into the choices, the only choice that gives you 1 is (G).

39. C
Coordinate Geometry

Key Math Concepts for the ACT, #71.

The textbook method for this problem would be to use the distance formula but that's time-consuming. Instead, it may help you to draw a picture. Draw a right triangle into the coordinate plane as we've done. Note that the distance between the two points represents the hypotenuse of the triangle. The legs of the triangle have lengths of 3 and 4, so the distance between the two points must be 5, (C).

40. G
Plane Geometry

Key Math Concepts for the ACT, #87, #91. To find the area of the shaded region, you must subtract the area of the circle from the area of the rectangle. Since the sides of the rectangle are $2x$ and $5x$, it has an area of $2x \times 5x = 10x^2$. By examining the diagram, you can see that the circle has a diameter of $2x$, so it has a radius of x. Its area is, therefore, πx^2. The shaded region, therefore, has an area of $10x^2 - \pi x^2$.

41. B
Trigonometry

Key Math Concepts for the ACT, #96. Since you are not given a diagram for this problem, it's best to draw a quick sketch of a right triangle to help keep the sides separate in your mind. Mark one of the acute angles θ. Since $\cos \theta = \dfrac{5\sqrt{2}}{8}$, mark the adja-

cent side $5\sqrt{2}$ and the hypotenuse as 8. (Remember SOHCAHTOA.) Use the Pythagorean theorem to find that the side opposite θ is $\sqrt{14}$. The problem asks you to find $\tan \theta$. Tangent $= \dfrac{\text{opposite}}{\text{adjacent}}$, so $\tan \theta = \dfrac{\sqrt{14}}{5\sqrt{2}}$, which can be simplified to $\dfrac{\sqrt{7}}{5}$.

42. H
Proportions and Probability

This question is one where your calculator can come in handy. Divide 7 by integer values for n, and look for values between .5 and .8. Begin by looking for the integer values of n where $\dfrac{7}{n}$ is greater than .5. If $n = 14$, then $\dfrac{7}{n} = .5$, so n must be less than 14. Work through values of n until you get to the point where $\dfrac{7}{n} \geq .8$. When $n = 9$, $\dfrac{7}{n} = .778$, but when $n = 8$, $\dfrac{7}{n} = .875$. So the integer values that work in this case are $n = 9, 10, 11, 12,$ and 13. Five integer values work, so (H) is correct.

43. C
Plane Geometry

The points are as far apart as possible when separated by a diameter of X and a diameter of Y.

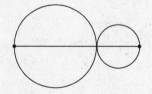

The circumference of a circle is $\pi \times$ (diameter), so the diameter of circle X is 12, and the diameter of circle Y is 8. The greatest possible distance between points then is $12 + 8 = 20$.

44. K
Variable Manipulation

Key Math Concepts for the ACT, #54. Begin by getting rid of the square root sign. If $y \geq 0$, then $\sqrt{y^2} = y$, so $\sqrt{(x^2 + 4)^2} = x^2 + 4$. $(x + 2)(x - 2) = x^2 - 4$, so you now have $(x^2 + 4) - (x^2 - 4) = ?$ Get rid of the parentheses, and you have $x^2 + 4 - x^2 + 4 = x^2 - x^2 + 4 + 4 = 8$.

45. A
Variable Manipulation

Key Math Concepts for the ACT, #52. Here, you need to substitute -3 for s and solve. That gives you the expression $(-3)^3 + 2(-3)^2 + 2(-3)$, which equals $-27 + 18 - 6$, or -15. If you missed this problem, you probably made a mistake with the signs of the numbers.

46. G
Variable Manipulation

Key Math Concepts for the ACT, #56. Be careful on this one. Begin by simplifying the equation by FOILing one side:

$$2x + 6 = (x + 5)(x + 3)$$

$$2x + 6 = x^2 + 8x + 15$$

Then get the right side of the equation to equal zero: $x^2 + 6x + 9 = 0$.

The left side of this equation is the perfect square $(x + 3)^2$, so $(x + 3)^2 = 0$, which has only one solution, $x = -3$. Choice (G) is correct.

47. E
Pythagorean Theorem

Key Math Concepts for the ACT, #84. The textbook method for this would be to use the Pythagorean theorem to find the length of a side and then multiply that by 4, but there's an easier way: eyeball it! The perimeter is greater than $\overline{AC}$, so you can get rid of (A) and (B). It appears to be quite a bit greater than $\overline{AC}$, more than twice as great, so (C) and (D) are out as well. That only leaves (E).

If you wanted to solve this the conventional way, since the perimeter is the sum of the lengths of all the sides of the square, you need to find the length of the square's sides. Let the length of each of the square's sides be x. $\overline{AC}$ divides the square into two right triangles, so we can apply the Pythagorean theorem: $\overline{AB}^2 + \overline{BC}^2 = \overline{AC}^2$. Since $\overline{AB}$ and $\overline{BC}$ are sides of the square, they have the same length. We can write that as $x^2 + x^2 = \overline{AC}^2$. $\overline{AC} = 8$, so $2x^2 = 8^2$, $2x^2 = 64$, $x^2 = 32$,

$$x = \sqrt{32} = \sqrt{16 \times 2} = 4\sqrt{2}.$$

So each side of the square is $4\sqrt{2}$, and the perimeter of the square is $4 \times 4\sqrt{2} = 16\sqrt{2}$.

48. G
Plane Geometry

Key Math Concepts for the ACT, #87, #83. To find the area of this complex shape, you could divide it into two simple shapes by drawing a line 30 inches up, parallel to the horizontal base. This leaves you with a 4×30 rectangle and a triangle with height of 6 and a base of 4. The rectangle has an area of $4 \times 30 = 120$ square inches, and the triangle has an area of $\dfrac{4 \times 6}{2} = 12$ square inches. That makes a total of $120 + 12 = 132$ square inches.

49. E
Plane Geometry

Key Math Concepts for the ACT, #80. Triangles are the secret to solving this one. Drawing $\overline{OD}$ divides quadrilateral $OCDE$ into two triangles, OCD and ODE. Both triangles are isosceles because $\overline{OC}$, $\overline{OD}$, and $\overline{OE}$ are all radii of circle O. Angles ODC and OCD have equal measures, since they're opposite equal sides, so $\angle ODC$ measures 70°. Similarly, $\angle ODE$ measures 45°. Together, angles ODC and ODE make up $\angle CDE$, so its measure is 70° + 45° = 115°.

50. K
Coordinate Geometry

Key Math Concepts for the ACT, #67. Remember that lines intersect at the point that is a solution to both equations. So equations with no common solution don't intersect—they have the same slope and are parallel. To solve this problem, search through the answer choices to find the pair of equations representing lines with the same slope. If you write the equations in (K) in slope-intercept form, you'll get

$$y = -\frac{1}{3}x + 2, y = -\frac{1}{3}x + \frac{7}{9},$$

so the slope is clearly the same for both equations.

51. E
Number Properties

Key Math Concepts for the ACT, #30. To solve a repeating decimal question, begin by determining the pattern of the decimal on your calculator. $\frac{1}{7} = 0.142857142857\ldots$, so you know that this fraction repeats every 6 decimal places. Since we are looking for the 46th decimal place, we need to determine where in the six-term pattern we would be at the 46th place. Divide 46 by 6, and look for the remainder. The remainder in this case is 4, so we are looking for the 4th term in the sequence, which is 8, (E).

52. K
Variable Manipulation

Key Math Concepts for the ACT, #69. Remember that you treat an inequality exactly like an equality, except that you need to flip the sign when you multiply or divide by a negative number. In this problem, you start with the inequality $-2 - 4x \leq -6x$. Add $4x$ to both sides to get $-2 \leq -2x$. Divide by -2 and flip the sign to get $1 \geq x$, which matches choice (K).

53. B
Operations

Key Math Concepts for the ACT, #22. For this problem, it would probably be easiest to Pick Numbers. Since you will be taking the square root of the numbers, it's easiest to pick perfect squares, like 4 and 9:

$$\frac{\sqrt{4}}{4} + \frac{\sqrt{9}}{9} = \frac{2}{4} + \frac{3}{9} = \frac{1}{2} + \frac{1}{3} = \frac{5}{6}$$

When you plug 4 and 9 into the answer choices, only (B) gives you $\frac{5}{6}$.

54. G
Plane Geometry

Key Math Concepts for the ACT, #79. When transversals intersect parallel lines, corresponding line segments on the transversals are proportional. In other words, $\frac{\overline{DE}}{\overline{CB}} = \frac{\overline{EF}}{\overline{BA}}$. Thus, $\frac{6}{8} = \frac{\overline{EF}}{4}$, so $EF = 3$.

55. D
Coordinate Geometry

Key Math Concepts for the ACT, #83. Divide the square into two right triangles by drawing the diagonal from (2,7) to (2,1). Remember that the area of each triangle is half its base times its height. Treat the diagonal as the base of a triangle. Its length is the distance from (2,7) to (2,1). Since the x-coordinates are the same, that distance is simply the difference between the y-coordinates, $7 - 1$, or 6. The diagonal bisects the square, so the height of the triangle is half the distance from (−1,4) to (5,4). We already know that a diagonal of this square is 6, so half the distance is 3. Therefore, the base and height of either triangle are 6 and 3, so the area of each triangle is $\dfrac{6 \times 3}{2}$, or 9 square units. The square is made up of two such triangles and so has twice the area, or 18 square units.

Alternatively, you could use the Distance Formula to find the length of one side and square that side to find the area.

56. K
Trigonometry

Key Math Concepts for the ACT, #100. Compared to the graph of $y = \cos \theta$, the graph of $y = 2\cos \theta$ would have twice the amplitude and the same period, choice K. Here you are doubling y, which represents the vertical coordinates, but the θ coordinates stay the same. The amplitude of a trigonometric equation refers to how high or low the curve moves from the horizontal axis. The period refers to the distance required to complete a single wave along the horizontal axis.

57. C
Variable Manipulation

Key Math Concepts for the ACT, #65. To solve this problem with algebra, you need to translate each phrase into mathematics. Translated, the problem is $3(x + 15) = 4x - 65$. Solve for x to get 110. Alternatively, you could Backsolve starting with the middle value:

$$3(110 + 15) = 4(110) - 65$$

$$3(125) = 440 - 65$$

$$75 = 75$$

Since the two sides are equal, choice (C) is correct.

58. H
Proportions and Probability

Key Math Concepts for the ACT, #36. You're given the formula for the volume of a cylinder in the equation so you can find the volume of both cylinders described. That turns this into a ratio problem where you're comparing the volumes of both cylinders.

Pick Numbers to make this question more concrete and plug them into this volume formula. Let's say the smaller cylinder has a height of 1 and a radius of 1 (diameter of 2), for a volume of $\pi(1)^2 \times 1 = \pi$. The larger cylinder would then have a height of 3 and a radius of 2 (diameter of 4), for a volume of $\pi(2)^2 \times 3 = 12\pi$. Thus, it would take 12 fillings of the smaller cylinder to fill the larger cylinder.

59. D
Plane Geometry

Key Math Concepts for the ACT, #85. Draw a picture of the triangle, and carefully apply your knowledge of the ratio of the lengths of the sides of a 30°-60°-90° triangle ($x : x\sqrt{3} : 2x$). So if the longer leg has a length of 12, the shorter leg has a length of

$$\frac{12}{\sqrt{3}} = \frac{12\sqrt{3}}{\sqrt{3} \times \sqrt{3}} = \frac{12\sqrt{3}}{3} = 4\sqrt{3}.$$

Thus, the hypotenuse is twice this, or $8\sqrt{3}$. So the perimeter is the sum of the three sides, or

$$4\sqrt{3} + 12 + 8\sqrt{3} = 12\sqrt{3} + 12.$$

60. J
Proportions and Probability

Key Math Concepts for the ACT, # 41. Remember the average formula on this one. The average formula states, $\text{Average} = \dfrac{\text{Sum of the terms}}{\text{Number of the terms}}$. So to find the total average, find the total sum and divide it by the total number of terms. If a team averages x points in n games, then it scored nx points in n games. In the final game of the season, it scored y points. So the total sum of points for the season is $nx + y$, and the total number of games is $n + 1$. So the team's average score for the entire season is $\dfrac{nx + y}{n + 1}$, (J).

READING TEST

Reading questions can be divided into four basic types: Detail questions, Inference questions, Global questions, Vocab-in-Context questions, Writer's View questions, and Function questions. As you review the answers and explanations, note which types you tend to answer correctly or incorrectly and tailor your studying to focus on areas where you need improvement.

PASSAGE I

1. C
Detail
The answer can be found in lines 31–36: "The real evils, indeed, of Emma's situation were the power of having rather too much her own way, and a disposition to think a little too well of herself; these were the disadvantages which threatened alloy to her many enjoyments."

2. G
Detail
Isabella's name is given in line 73.

3. B
Detail
The answer can be found in lines 20–21: "Between them it was more the intimacy of sisters."

4. F
Vocab-in-Context
As it is used in the sentence, *disposition* means "tendency" or "inclination." It would not make sense for Emma to have (G), control; (H), placement; or (J), transfer "to think a little too well of herself" (lines 33–34).

5. D
Detail
The answer can be found in lines 62–69: "She recalled her past kindness—the kindness, the affection of sixteen years—how she had taught her and…how she had devoted all her powers to attach and amuse her in health—and how she had nursed her through the various illnesses of childhood."

6. H
Inference
Miss Taylor will continue to be a part of Emma's life, but they will not be as close because Miss Taylor no longer lives with Emma and because Miss Taylor will be primarily concerned with her husband's, not Emma's, well-being.

7. C
Inference
Emma is self-centered, as evidenced by her description of her relationship with Miss Taylor. Among Miss Taylor's admirable qualities, Emma includes the fact that Miss Taylor was "interested in her, in every pleasure, every scheme of hers—one to whom she could speak every thought as it arose, and who had such an affection for her as could never find fault" (lines 80–84). Emma is also clearly headstrong. She is described as "having rather too much her own way" (lines 32–33).

8. G
Generalization
Emma's description of her friendship with Miss Taylor suggests that Emma most highly values devotion in her friends.

9. B
Detail
The description of Mr. Weston is in lines 53–56: "The marriage had every promise of happiness for her friend. Mr. Weston was a man of unexceptionable character, easy fortune, suitable age, and pleasant manners." None of the other choices match this description.

10. H
Inference
The answer to the question is in lines 28–31: "Emma doing just what she liked, highly esteeming Miss Taylor's judgment, but directed chiefly by her own."

PASSAGE II

11. B
Generalization
The passage presents the three main systems of memory and states that these systems are widely accepted—so eliminate (A)—but gives alternate theories about the way long-term memories are formed and possible flaws in the process. Although the passage mentions two early ideas about memory that were too simplistic, (C) and (D), this is not the main focus of the passage.

12. H
Inference
Described in paragraph 3, semantic memory holds facts and general knowledge, like the multiplication tables, choice (H). Ballet steps, (F), and riding a bicycle, (J), would be in procedural memory; a childhood memory, (G), would be in episodic.

13. B
Inference
All the information you need is in paragraph 3. Memories of one's personal life would be held in episodic memory; therefore, the man's episodic memory was affected. Eliminate (C) and (D). Long-term memories are "never lost," but they may become inaccessible; therefore, the author would most likely agree that the man's episodic memories had become inaccessible to him.

14. F
Function
While memory was once viewed as relatively simple and automatic with memories being held exactly as they were originally received, it is now believed that many factors alter the way memories are formed and retrieved (lines 69–81). Choices (G) and (J) contradict this. Choice (H) is too extreme.

15. C
Inference
In the last paragraph, the author states that assumptions and inferences can affect memory. A person might assume that if the ball hits a window, the window will break. Interference, (A), is when one unrelated memory alters another. The memory described in the question is not inaccessible, (B), but wrong. And most of the memory was still correct, not false, (D).

16. J
Detail
This Detail question requires very careful reading. Refresh your memory by looking at *episodic* in paragraph 3. It's in long-term memory and involves personal events closely identified with a time and place. Choices (F), (G), and (H) fit that idea closely. If you're unsure, look at the description of working (short-term) memory in paragraph 2. You'll see that it includes those things briefly remembered and then lost forever—like the face of a stranger passed on the street.

17. B
Inference
Paragraph 2 describes this change in terminology. The term *short-term memory* did not accurately describe all the functions of this category of memory. *Working memory* is more accurate since, although these memories degrade quickly—eliminating (A)—these memories can also be used and manipulated as described in the second paragraph. Choice (C) and (D) confuse information in other paragraphs.

18. H
Vocab-in-Context
Don't panic. All you have to do is look at the line where this term is defined for you. The term doesn't relate to any of the usual meanings of the word *icon*.

19. B
Detail
The second sentence in paragraph 3 states, "Memories recorded in long-term memory are never lost…" Although absolute statements are often too extreme to be correct in Reading, when the passage explicitly supports an absolute statement don't be afraid to choose it. You might choose A if you mistook *short-term* and *working* memory for two separate categories. Choice (C) is contradicted in paragraph 4, and (D) is contradicted at the end of paragraph 2 and again at the start of paragraph 5.

20. H
Detail
Paragraph 2 states that working memories decay rapidly, which means that they are quickly forgotten. Choices (F) and (G) relate to sensory memory. Choice (J) is characteristic of long-term memory.

PASSAGE III

21. B
Inference
In lines 11–13, Julia Margaret Cameron is described as "the first woman to have achieved eminence in photography." The other answer choices contradict information supplied in the passage.

22. F
Detail
The answer to this question can be found in lines 82–83: "Contemporary taste much prefers her portraits…" and in lines 88–89: "today her fame rests upon her portraits…"

23. D
Detail
The dates used in the passage tell you that this is a chronological account; the author begins with Cameron's birth in 1815, tells of her marriage and then her move to England in 1848, points out that she received her first photographic equipment in 1863, describes one of her photographs from 1864, and then concludes the paragraph with her death in 1874.

24. F
Vocab-in-Context
The dictionary definition of *cumbersome* is "difficult to handle because of weight or bulk." Choice (F) most closely fits this definition, and it is the only answer choice that makes sense within the context of the sentence.

25. B
Inference
Lines 55–56 describe how Cameron "devoted herself wholly to this art," which matches choice B. Choice (A) contradicts information from the passage, which suggests that Cameron led anything but a conventional life. Neither the money that Cameron earned as a photographer nor her religious beliefs are discussed in the passage, making (C) and (D) incorrect.

26. F
Generalization
Lines 60–63 say, "she produced a large body of work that stands up as one of the notable artistic achievements of the Victorian period." To say that she is "the greatest photographer who ever lived" goes beyond anything stated or implied in the passage. The third paragraph does not compare her importance as an artist during her lifetime to her importance today. The passage also does not state that she "revolutionized" any photographic methods.

27. C
Detail

The answer to this question can be found in lines 7–10: "photography, being a new medium outside the traditional academic framework, was wide open to women and offered them opportunities that the older fields did not…"

28. G
Detail

These titles refer to allegorical pictures, as described in lines 78–81: "Victorian critics were particularly impressed by her allegorical pictures, many of them based on the poems of her friend and neighbor Tennyson…"

29. D
Detail

The answer to this question can be found in lines 82–84: "Contemporary taste much prefers her portraits and finds her narrative scenes sentimental and sometimes in bad taste."

30. F
Inference

The author says that Cameron "achieved eminence" (line 12) in her field, that she "devoted herself wholly to this art" (lines 55–56), and that "no other woman photographer has ever enjoyed such success" (lines 74–75). Only (F) fits these descriptions.

PASSAGE IV

31. C
Detail

For details about the eye, look at paragraph 3. Only the cornea and stenopaic pupil are relevant, eliminating (A) and (D). But the cornea, choice (B), is helpful underwater, not on land.

32. G
Inference

The eye is covered in paragraph 3. The seal's cornea improves vision in the water (note the comparison to human underwater vision), but distorts light moving through the air. Another adaptation was then needed to *minimize* (line 53) distortion, but that doesn't mean distortion is completely eliminated, so the seal's vision in the air is distorted, (G).

33. D
Detail

The vibrissae are discussed only in the last paragraph. They sense wave disturbances made by nearby moving fish, so (D) is correct. Choice (B), by using the phrase "in the air," distorts information in the passage.

34. F
Detail

This is stated in the second paragraph, where the seal's hearing is discussed.

35. D
Detail

This appears in the first paragraph, which introduces the influences on the seal's adaptations. They include that the seal "does most of its fishing at night," that "noise levels are high," and that these factors are compounded by the seal's "two habitats."

36. H
Detail

Locating each of these claims in the passage, we find that (H) is *suggested* (line 68) and the subject of speculation, rather than stated as fact. All of the others are given in support of claims.

37. A
Inference

We find in the first paragraph that they live along the northern Atlantic and Pacific coasts. Since they live in both the land and water, the coastlines must be accessible. We can infer that the waters are cold rather than warm, eliminating (D). Choices (B) and (C) are too broad.

38. J
Detail
This feature is mentioned at the end of paragraph 2. It shouldn't be confused with echolocation, which is discussed in paragraph 4, but not connected with any particular sensory organ.

39. B
Function
The entire passage is about how the seal's sensory organs have adapted to life on land and in the water, making (B) the best choice. Generally, we are told about differences, not similarities, between the sensory organs of humans and harbor seals, eliminating (A). The relative success of human and seal adaptation to their environments isn't discussed, thus eliminating (C) and (D).

40. G
Detail
In paragraph 3, we see that human corneas refract light badly in water, and the seal's corneas perform well.

SCIENCE TEST

All Science questions will fall under one of the three SmartPoints: Figure questions, Pattern questions, and Scientific Reasoning questions.

PASSAGE I

1. B
Figure Interpretation
To answer this question, you have to examine the third column of the table, transmittance range. For a material to transmit light at a wavelength of 25 μm, its transmittance range—the range of wavelengths over which the material is transparent—must

include 25 μm. Only potassium bromide (0.3–29 μm) and cesium iodide (0.3–70 μm) have transmittance ranges that include 25 μm, so (B) is correct.

2. F
Figure Interpretation
The material that contradicts this hypothesis is going to have poor chemical resistance but a transmittance range less than 10 μm. Lithium fluoride, (F), fits the bill: Its chemical resistance is poor, and its transmittance range is less than 6 μm wide. Choices (G) and (J) are wrong because both flint glass and quartz have excellent chemical resistance. Choice (H) is out because cesium iodide has a transmittance range nearly 70 μm wide.

3. D
Scientific Reasoning
The correct answer is a pair of materials in which the refractive index of the first material is greater than that of the second. In (A), (B), and (C), the refractive index of the first material is less than that of the second. In (D), however, flint glass has a refractive index of 1.66 while calcium fluoride's refractive index is only 1.43. That makes (D) the correct answer.

4. J
Scientific Reasoning
The easiest way to answer this question is to use the first couple of materials and test each hypothesis on them. Choices (F) and (G) are incorrect because the transmittance range of lithium fluoride is wider than its useful prism range. Comparing the data on lithium fluoride and calcium fluoride rules out choice (H) because transmittance range does NOT increase as useful prism range decreases. In fact, looking down the rest of the table, you see that transmittance range seems to decrease as useful prism range decreases. Choice (J) is the only one left, and the data on lithium fluoride and calcium fluoride as well as all the other materials confirms that the transmittance range is always wider than, and includes within it, the useful prism range.

5. B

Figure Interpretation

According to the footnote to the table, quartz infused with lead oxide is flint glass. Comparison of the properties of pure quartz and flint glass shows that the transmittance range of flint glass is narrower than that of quartz but that its refractive index is greater. This supports (B).

PASSAGE II

6. H

Scientific Reasoning

Use the results of both experiments to answer this question. The answer choices all involve temperature, concentration, and solvent in different combinations. To determine whether osmotic pressure is dependent upon a variable, look for a pair of trials in which all conditions except for that variable are identical. In doing so, you see that temperature and concentration affect osmotic pressure, but solvent does not.

7. C

Figure Interpretation

Find methanol at 0.5 mol/L, which is in Table 2. The text above the table states that all the trials were conducted under the same temperature (298 K). Therefore, simply look across the row that you identified. The osmotic pressure is 12.23, (C).

8. G

Scientific Reasoning

To figure out whether or not the sucrose solution will diffuse across the membrane under the conditions described in the question, go back to the definition of osmotic pressure given in the introduction. Once the external pressure reaches the osmotic pressure, osmosis will not occur. In order for osmosis to occur, the external pressure must be less than the osmotic pressure of the solution. The solution in this question is a 0.1 mol/L aqueous sucrose solution at 298 K; those conditions correspond to an osmotic pressure of 2.45 atm.

Since the external pressure is 1 atm, which is less than the osmotic pressure, osmosis will occur. From the definition of osmosis in the passage, it is clear that the solution will diffuse from the side of the membrane with a lower concentration of dissolved material, in this case pure water, to the side with a higher concentration, in this case sucrose solution. Choice (G) is correct.

9. C

Figure Interpretation

To determine what the scientists investigated in Experiment 1, look at what they varied and what they measured. In Experiment 1, the scientists varied the concentration and the temperature of sucrose solutions, and they measured the osmotic pressure. Therefore, they were investigating the effect of concentration and temperature on osmotic pressure, (C). Watch out for (A): It states what was investigated in Experiment 2, not Experiment 1.

10. F

Patterns

The results in Table 2 indicate that osmotic pressure doesn't depend on the solvent, as discussed in the explanation to question 6. So Statement I is a valid conclusion, and (G) can be eliminated. Statement II is false. The results in Table 1 indicate that osmotic pressure is dependent on concentration as well as temperature. So (H) can be ruled out. Now consider Statement III. It is not a valid conclusion because osmotic pressure is the pressure required to prevent osmosis, so osmosis occurs only if the external pressure is less than the osmotic pressure.

11. D

Scientific Reasoning

To answer questions that ask about the design of an experiment, look at what the scientists are trying to measure. You're told that osmotic pressure is the pressure required to prevent osmosis. In order to measure the osmotic pressure of a solution, scientists need to be able to tell when osmosis begins. If you have two clear solutions with sucrose dissolved in one of them, how can you tell when there's any movement of solvent between the two of them? If the sucrose is dyed, the blue solution will become paler when osmosis starts, i.e., when solvent moves across the membrane to create an equilibrium. Therefore, (D) is correct.

PASSAGE III

12. J
Scientific Reasoning

Even if you do not know how many °C are equivalent to room temperature, you can eliminate all of the incorrect answer choices. Choices (F), (G), and (H) all reach a boiling point at low temperatures and, therefore, would all be gases at room temperature. Choice (J), at 36°C, is the only logical choice.

13. C
Patterns

To answer this question, you have to look for trends in each table and draw conclusions. This can be done by looking at the values in each category and seeing how they vary with respect to each other. If you look at Tables 1 and 2, you can see that there is a direct variation between boiling point and molecular weight: as one increases, the other increases. Therefore, Statement I is correct, Statement II is false, and you can eliminate (B) and (D). Now consider Statement III. To investigate the relationship between molecular structure and boiling point, you have to keep the third variable—molecular weight—constant. Look at the data for two compounds with different molecular structures but the same molecular weight: N_2 and CO match that description and their boiling points differ. Therefore, Statement III is correct, and (C) is the correct response.

14. G
Figure Interpretation

In order to answer this question, you need to establish where C_6H_{14} would fit in Table 1. It is clear from Table 1 that the boiling point increases as the molecular weight increases, so the boiling point of C_6H_{14} will be between the boiling points of molecules with greater and lesser molecular weights. The molecular weight of C_6H_{14} is 86 g/mol, so it will lie between those hydrocarbons with molecular weights of 72 g/mol and 114 g/mol. Therefore, its boiling point will be between 36°C and 126°C. Choice (G), with a value of 70°C, is the only choice that lies between these two boiling points.

15. A
Figure Interpretation

N_2, a non-polar molecule, and CO, a polar molecule, have identical molecular weights and their boiling points differ by only 4°C. SiH_4 (non-polar) and PH_3 (polar) have nearly identical molecular weights as well, but the difference between their boiling points is 27°C—much greater than the difference between the boiling points of N_2 and CO, which have lower molecular weights than SiH_4 and PH_3. The difference between the boiling points of polar and non-polar substances of similar molecular weight increases as molecular weight increases, so (A) is correct.

16. H
Figure Interpretation

If you refer to Table 2, you'll see that for polar substances, as the molar weight goes from 78 to 162, the boiling point goes from −55°C to 97°C. You know the molar weight has to be somewhere between 78 and 162, so F is clearly out, and G, 80, is too close to 78 to be the answer. You would expect the molar weight to be closer to 78 than 162, since 0 is closer to −55 than 97. Therefore, (J), 132, is out, and (H) is the answer.

PASSAGE IV

17. A
Scientific Reasoning

The question refers to Experiment 2 only, so the correct answer will involve sunlight. Table 2 shows that the average length of the leaves increased from 5.3 cm to 12.4 cm as the amount of sunlight increased from 0 to 3 hours per day. But as the amount of sunlight increased further, leaf size decreased. Therefore, (D) is incorrect. Neither humidity, (B), nor water, (C), is relevant to Experiment 2.

18. G
Figure Interpretation
Table 1 gives leaf widths at 35% and 55% humidity at 1.8 cm and 2.0 cm, respectively. The leaf width at 40% humidity would most likely be between those two figures. Choice (G) is the only choice within that range.

19. B
Scientific Reasoning
All the answer choices involve humidity and sunlight, which were investigated in Experiments 1 and 2, respectively. In Table 1, leaf length and width were greatest at 75% humidity. In Table 2, they were greatest at three hours per day of sunlight. Combining those two conditions, as in (B), would probably produce the largest leaves.

20. F
Scientific Reasoning
This question relates to the method of the study. Each experiment begins with a statement that five groups of seedlings were used. Therefore, (F) is correct. The other choices list variables that were manipulated.

21. D
Scientific Reasoning
Choice (D) is an assumption that underlies the design of all three experiments. If the seedlings were not equally capable of further growth, then changes in leaf size and density could not be reliably attributed to researcher-controlled changes in humidity, sunlight, and temperature. Choice (A) is wrong because all the seedlings were 2–3 cm tall. The seedlings' abilities to germinate, (B), or to produce flowers, (C), were not mentioned in the passage.

22. H
Scientific Reasoning
Each of the three experiments investigated a different factor related to leaf growth. To produce the most useful new data, researchers would probably vary a fourth condition. Soil mineral content would be an appropriate factor to examine. None of the other choices relate directly to the purpose of the experiments as expressed in paragraph 1 of the passage.

PASSAGE V

23. B
Figure Interpretation
According to the table, decreasing the cross-sectional area of a given wire always increases resistance, so (B) is correct. Choice (C) is wrong because resistivity, displayed in the second column, is constant for each material and thus cannot be responsible for variations in resistance for any given material. Gauge varies inversely with cross-sectional area, so (D) is incorrect.

24. G
Patterns
Because resistance varies inversely with cross-sectional area A, as discussed in the previous explanation, the correct answer to this question must place A in the denominator. The only choice that does so is (G).

25. D
Patterns
Compare the choices two at a time. The wires in A and B are made of the same material and have the same cross-sectional area; only their length is different. Doubling the length doubles the resistance, so (B) would have a higher resistance than (A). By similar reasoning, (D) would have a higher resistance than (C). The only difference between (B) and (D) is the material. Even though the research team didn't test wire with a 0.33 mm^2 cross-sectional area, Table

1 shows that tungsten wire has higher levels of resistance than aluminum wire across all factors.

26. J
Scientific Reasoning

The larger circle represents 10-gauge wire; its diameter is 2.59 mm. The smaller circle has a diameter of only 1.29 mm, but it represents 16-gauge wire, so Statement I is true, and you can eliminate (G) and (H) without even checking Statements II or III. To check Statement III, the table shows that the resistance of an iron (Fe) wire is much higher than that of an aluminum (Al) wire with the same length and cross-sectional area. The first sentence of paragraph 1 defined the resistance of a conductor as "the extent to which it opposes the flow of electricity." Since iron has a higher resistance than aluminum, iron must not conduct electricity as well. Therefore, Statement III is true, and (J) is correct.

27. D
Patterns

The data indicates that the resistivity of a material doesn't change when wire length changes. Therefore, the graph of resistivity versus length for tungsten (or any other) wire is a horizontal line.

PASSAGE VI

28. F
Scientific Reasoning

To answer this question, you have to refer to the examples presented by the scientists to find a point of agreement. Both use the example of giraffes to show how scarcity of food and the need to reach higher and higher branches led to the evolution of long necks; thus, they both agree that environment affects evolution.

29. C
Scientific Reasoning

This Principle question requires that you figure out how new evidence affects the two hypotheses. To answer it, all you have to consider are the hypotheses of the two scientists. Scientist 2 believes that characteristics acquired by an individual over a lifetime are passed on to its offspring, a theory that would be supported by this finding.

30. J
Scientific Reasoning

This question requires some reasoning. Scientist 2 states that all of the changes that occur in an individual's life can be passed on to offspring. Since he believes that any characteristic can undergo change, he must also believe that any characteristic can be inherited.

31. B
Scientific Reasoning

You don't need any information other than the hypothesis of Scientist 1 to answer this question. He believes that random mutations continually occur within a species as it propagates and that advantageous mutations, such as long necks on giraffes, help the species adapt to environmental changes, and thus become more prevalent within the species, which is what (B) states.

32. G
Scientific Reasoning

Here, you don't need any information other than the hypotheses of the two scientists. The crux of their disagreement is over how evolution occurs—whether through random mutations or through the inheritance of acquired characteristics.

33. B
Scientific Reasoning

Recall that Scientist 2 states that evolution occurs through the inheritance of acquired characteristics. In order to account for humans possessing nerve endings now that were not present before the discovery of fire, Scientist 2 would have to believe that new nerve endings could be acquired during a single lifetime. Choice (B) directly contradicts this idea and would therefore refute the hypothesis.

34. F
Scientific Reasoning

Recall that Scientist 1 explains that evolution occurs as a result of random mutation, while Scientist 2 credits the inheritance of acquired characteristics. Choice (G) can then be eliminated, since it is related to the explanation of the wrong scientist. Choice (H) would actually refute Scientist 1's hypothesis, and (J) is irrelevant. Only (F) provides a valid explanation for the increase in average height based on the random mutations described by Scientist 1.

PASSAGE VII

35. D
Figure Interpretation

In Experiment 1, the researchers vary what is fed to the cows by giving them meat from scrapie-free sheep and from scrapie-infected sheep. The cows are later examined for signs of BSE. One common type of wrong answer choice for Experiment questions are choices, such as (B) for this question, that include factors that are outside the parameters of the experiment.

36. F
Figure Interpretation

In Experiment 2, the researchers vary what is injected into cows' brains. Any answer choice that discusses ingestion as a focus of this experiment is wrong. This eliminates (G), (H), and (J). Often, wrong answer choices for Experiment questions, such as (G) for this question, will include the appropriate information from the wrong experiment.

37. B
Scientific Reasoning

By examining the method used in a given experiment, one can determine the assumptions the researchers made in carrying out the experiment and the sources of error. Often, an error enters the experiment because of the assumptions researchers make. In Experiments 1 and 2, the researchers examined the brains of cows a year and a half after the cows were fed scrapie-infected sheep meat or were injected with scrapie-infected sheep brains. If a year and a half is not a sufficient amount of time for BSE to develop, some of the cows that were counted as not infected might have developed BSE if they had been given more time.

38. H
Scientific Reasoning

To answer this question, you need to determine how to test whether BSE can be transmitted via scrapie-infected goats. To test this, one would compare the effects of feeding cows scrapie-free goat meat with the effects of feeding cows scrapie-infected goat meat and compare the effects of injecting cows with scrapie-free goat brains with the effects of injecting them with scrapie-infected goat brains.

39. A
Scientific Reasoning

Remember that control groups are used as standards of comparison. The control group used in Experiment 1 is the group that is fed scrapie-free sheep meat. If the same proportion of Group A developed BSE as that of Group B, then the researchers would not have any evidence to support the hypothesis that the ingestion of scrapie-infected sheep meat causes BSE.

40. G
Scientific Reasoning

Since the proportion of the group of cows that ate scrapie-infected sheep meat and developed BSE was greater than the proportion of the group that were injected with scrapie-infected sheep brains and developed BSE, one can conclude that a cow that eats scrapie-infected sheep meat is more likely to develop BSE than a cow that is injected with scrapie-infected sheep brains. Mere exposure to scrapie-infected sheep, as opposed to ingestion of it, is never studied in either experiment, so conclusion I can be eliminated.

WRITING TEST

MODEL ESSAY

Below is an example of what a high-scoring essay might look like. Notice the author states her position clearly in the introductory paragraph and supports that position with evidence in the following paragraphs. This essay also uses transitions, some advanced vocabulary, and an effective "hook" to draw in the reader.

When people think about what students should learn in high school, they often focus on "the three Rs": reading, writing, and arithmetic. It's true that in an increasingly competitive global economy, those skills are more important than ever. However, in our society's rush to make sure students are keeping up through required standardized testing and increased computer education, are we forgetting another important aspect of education? Are we forgetting to teach our students how to think creatively and express themselves artistically? I think that requiring all high school students to take music or visual arts classes would benefit our country's students in several ways.

Learning about art and music actually helps students do better in other subjects. People often forget that studying art or music isn't just about putting paint to canvas or lips to trumpet. There is a lot of background information that students learn as well. When students study music they also have to learn a lot of history: who was the composer, where was he or she from, what was happening politically and socially during the time the music was composed, and how does the work compare historically to music by other composers. The same holds true for the visual arts; students can learn a lot from art history, not just about the artist but also about different cultures and time periods. Studies have shown that students who take music classes do better at math, maybe because these classes emphasize dividing up measures of music and counting out times.

With so much focus on standardized test scores and grade point averages, schools today emphasize individual academic performance and overlook the teaching of teamwork skills. Through playing in my high school's band, I have learned that even though it is important for me to practice so that I can play my best (and maybe move up a chair), what really matters is how we sound as a group. My bandmates and I push each other to succeed, and we get together outside of school to practice for big games and competitions. Band is also where I have made most of my friends. Participation in the arts is a great way for students to build social skills and create school spirit. It teaches students to help one another so that going to school isn't just about getting good grades for one's own benefit.

Learning about art or music is also helpful to students because it teaches them how to think creatively. When you take a photograph or paint a portrait you have to look at things in a new way, and you must try to synthesize your perception into a medium that other people can relate to. Between all the pressure to do well academically and all the social pressure teenagers face to fit in, being a teenager can be really stressful. Art and music can allow students to express their feelings in a positive, constructive way. Such classes can give students who aren't good at traditional academic subjects like math or science a chance to shine.

In conclusion, I think requiring all high school students to take music or visual arts classes would help students not only academically but socially and emotionally as well. Studying the arts actually helps students succeed in traditional subject areas, builds their confidence and social skills, and gives them the opportunity to learn to think creatively, all skills that will help them once they reach the workforce.

You can evaluate your essay and the model essay based on the following criteria, covered in the Scoring section of Inside the ACT Writing Test:

- Does the author answer the question?

- Is the author's position clearly stated?

- Does the body of the essay support and develop the position taken?

- Are there at least two supporting paragraphs?

- Is the relevance of each supporting paragraph clear?

- Does the writer address the other side of the argument?

- Is the essay organized, with a clear introduction, middle, and end?

- Does the author start a new paragraph for each new idea?

- Is each sentence in a paragraph relevant to the point made in that paragraph?

- Are transitions clear?

- Is the essay easy to read? Is it engaging?

- Are sentences varied?

- Is vocabulary used effectively? Is college-level vocabulary used?

Practice Test Two

ACT Practice Test Two
ANSWER SHEET

ENGLISH TEST

1. Ⓐ Ⓑ Ⓒ Ⓓ   11. Ⓐ Ⓑ Ⓒ Ⓓ   21. Ⓐ Ⓑ Ⓒ Ⓓ   31. Ⓐ Ⓑ Ⓒ Ⓓ   41. Ⓐ Ⓑ Ⓒ Ⓓ   51. Ⓐ Ⓑ Ⓒ Ⓓ   61. Ⓐ Ⓑ Ⓒ Ⓓ   71. Ⓐ Ⓑ Ⓒ Ⓓ
2. Ⓕ Ⓖ Ⓗ Ⓙ   12. Ⓕ Ⓖ Ⓗ Ⓙ   22. Ⓕ Ⓖ Ⓗ Ⓙ   32. Ⓕ Ⓖ Ⓗ Ⓙ   42. Ⓕ Ⓖ Ⓗ Ⓙ   52. Ⓕ Ⓖ Ⓗ Ⓙ   62. Ⓕ Ⓖ Ⓗ Ⓙ   72. Ⓕ Ⓖ Ⓗ Ⓙ
3. Ⓐ Ⓑ Ⓒ Ⓓ   13. Ⓐ Ⓑ Ⓒ Ⓓ   23. Ⓐ Ⓑ Ⓒ Ⓓ   33. Ⓐ Ⓑ Ⓒ Ⓓ   43. Ⓐ Ⓑ Ⓒ Ⓓ   53. Ⓐ Ⓑ Ⓒ Ⓓ   63. Ⓐ Ⓑ Ⓒ Ⓓ   73. Ⓐ Ⓑ Ⓒ Ⓓ
4. Ⓕ Ⓖ Ⓗ Ⓙ   14. Ⓕ Ⓖ Ⓗ Ⓙ   24. Ⓕ Ⓖ Ⓗ Ⓙ   34. Ⓕ Ⓖ Ⓗ Ⓙ   44. Ⓕ Ⓖ Ⓗ Ⓙ   54. Ⓕ Ⓖ Ⓗ Ⓙ   64. Ⓕ Ⓖ Ⓗ Ⓙ   74. Ⓕ Ⓖ Ⓗ Ⓙ
5. Ⓐ Ⓑ Ⓒ Ⓓ   15. Ⓐ Ⓑ Ⓒ Ⓓ   25. Ⓐ Ⓑ Ⓒ Ⓓ   35. Ⓐ Ⓑ Ⓒ Ⓓ   45. Ⓐ Ⓑ Ⓒ Ⓓ   55. Ⓐ Ⓑ Ⓒ Ⓓ   65. Ⓐ Ⓑ Ⓒ Ⓓ   75. Ⓐ Ⓑ Ⓒ Ⓓ
6. Ⓕ Ⓖ Ⓗ Ⓙ   16. Ⓕ Ⓖ Ⓗ Ⓙ   26. Ⓕ Ⓖ Ⓗ Ⓙ   36. Ⓕ Ⓖ Ⓗ Ⓙ   46. Ⓕ Ⓖ Ⓗ Ⓙ   56. Ⓕ Ⓖ Ⓗ Ⓙ   66. Ⓕ Ⓖ Ⓗ Ⓙ
7. Ⓐ Ⓑ Ⓒ Ⓓ   17. Ⓐ Ⓑ Ⓒ Ⓓ   27. Ⓐ Ⓑ Ⓒ Ⓓ   37. Ⓐ Ⓑ Ⓒ Ⓓ   47. Ⓐ Ⓑ Ⓒ Ⓓ   57. Ⓐ Ⓑ Ⓒ Ⓓ   67. Ⓐ Ⓑ Ⓒ Ⓓ
8. Ⓕ Ⓖ Ⓗ Ⓙ   18. Ⓕ Ⓖ Ⓗ Ⓙ   28. Ⓕ Ⓖ Ⓗ Ⓙ   38. Ⓕ Ⓖ Ⓗ Ⓙ   48. Ⓕ Ⓖ Ⓗ Ⓙ   58. Ⓕ Ⓖ Ⓗ Ⓙ   68. Ⓕ Ⓖ Ⓗ Ⓙ
9. Ⓐ Ⓑ Ⓒ Ⓓ   19. Ⓐ Ⓑ Ⓒ Ⓓ   29. Ⓐ Ⓑ Ⓒ Ⓓ   39. Ⓐ Ⓑ Ⓒ Ⓓ   49. Ⓐ Ⓑ Ⓒ Ⓓ   59. Ⓐ Ⓑ Ⓒ Ⓓ   69. Ⓐ Ⓑ Ⓒ Ⓓ
10. Ⓕ Ⓖ Ⓗ Ⓙ   20. Ⓕ Ⓖ Ⓗ Ⓙ   30. Ⓕ Ⓖ Ⓗ Ⓙ   40. Ⓕ Ⓖ Ⓗ Ⓙ   50. Ⓕ Ⓖ Ⓗ Ⓙ   60. Ⓕ Ⓖ Ⓗ Ⓙ   70. Ⓕ Ⓖ Ⓗ Ⓙ

MATH TEST

1. Ⓐ Ⓑ Ⓒ Ⓓ Ⓔ   11. Ⓐ Ⓑ Ⓒ Ⓓ Ⓔ   21. Ⓐ Ⓑ Ⓒ Ⓓ Ⓔ   31. Ⓐ Ⓑ Ⓒ Ⓓ Ⓔ   41. Ⓐ Ⓑ Ⓒ Ⓓ Ⓔ   51. Ⓐ Ⓑ Ⓒ Ⓓ Ⓔ
2. Ⓐ Ⓑ Ⓒ Ⓓ Ⓔ   12. Ⓕ Ⓖ Ⓗ Ⓙ Ⓚ   22. Ⓕ Ⓖ Ⓗ Ⓙ Ⓚ   32. Ⓕ Ⓖ Ⓗ Ⓙ Ⓚ   42. Ⓕ Ⓖ Ⓗ Ⓙ Ⓚ   52. Ⓕ Ⓖ Ⓗ Ⓙ Ⓚ
3. Ⓐ Ⓑ Ⓒ Ⓓ Ⓔ   13. Ⓐ Ⓑ Ⓒ Ⓓ Ⓔ   23. Ⓐ Ⓑ Ⓒ Ⓓ Ⓔ   33. Ⓐ Ⓑ Ⓒ Ⓓ Ⓔ   43. Ⓐ Ⓑ Ⓒ Ⓓ Ⓔ   53. Ⓐ Ⓑ Ⓒ Ⓓ Ⓔ
4. Ⓕ Ⓖ Ⓗ Ⓙ Ⓚ   14. Ⓕ Ⓖ Ⓗ Ⓙ Ⓚ   24. Ⓕ Ⓖ Ⓗ Ⓙ Ⓚ   34. Ⓕ Ⓖ Ⓗ Ⓙ Ⓚ   44. Ⓕ Ⓖ Ⓗ Ⓙ Ⓚ   54. Ⓕ Ⓖ Ⓗ Ⓙ Ⓚ
5. Ⓐ Ⓑ Ⓒ Ⓓ Ⓔ   15. Ⓐ Ⓑ Ⓒ Ⓓ Ⓔ   25. Ⓐ Ⓑ Ⓒ Ⓓ Ⓔ   35. Ⓐ Ⓑ Ⓒ Ⓓ Ⓔ   45. Ⓐ Ⓑ Ⓒ Ⓓ Ⓔ   55. Ⓐ Ⓑ Ⓒ Ⓓ Ⓔ
6. Ⓕ Ⓖ Ⓗ Ⓙ Ⓚ   16. Ⓕ Ⓖ Ⓗ Ⓙ Ⓚ   26. Ⓕ Ⓖ Ⓗ Ⓙ Ⓚ   36. Ⓕ Ⓖ Ⓗ Ⓙ Ⓚ   46. Ⓕ Ⓖ Ⓗ Ⓙ Ⓚ   56. Ⓕ Ⓖ Ⓗ Ⓙ Ⓚ
7. Ⓐ Ⓑ Ⓒ Ⓓ Ⓔ   17. Ⓐ Ⓑ Ⓒ Ⓓ Ⓔ   27. Ⓐ Ⓑ Ⓒ Ⓓ Ⓔ   37. Ⓐ Ⓑ Ⓒ Ⓓ Ⓔ   47. Ⓐ Ⓑ Ⓒ Ⓓ Ⓔ   57. Ⓐ Ⓑ Ⓒ Ⓓ Ⓔ
8. Ⓕ Ⓖ Ⓗ Ⓙ Ⓚ   18. Ⓕ Ⓖ Ⓗ Ⓙ Ⓚ   28. Ⓕ Ⓖ Ⓗ Ⓙ Ⓚ   38. Ⓕ Ⓖ Ⓗ Ⓙ Ⓚ   48. Ⓕ Ⓖ Ⓗ Ⓙ Ⓚ   58. Ⓕ Ⓖ Ⓗ Ⓙ Ⓚ
9. Ⓐ Ⓑ Ⓒ Ⓓ Ⓔ   19. Ⓐ Ⓑ Ⓒ Ⓓ Ⓔ   29. Ⓐ Ⓑ Ⓒ Ⓓ Ⓔ   39. Ⓐ Ⓑ Ⓒ Ⓓ Ⓔ   49. Ⓐ Ⓑ Ⓒ Ⓓ Ⓔ   59. Ⓐ Ⓑ Ⓒ Ⓓ Ⓔ
10. Ⓕ Ⓖ Ⓗ Ⓙ Ⓚ   20. Ⓕ Ⓖ Ⓗ Ⓙ Ⓚ   30. Ⓕ Ⓖ Ⓗ Ⓙ Ⓚ   40. Ⓕ Ⓖ Ⓗ Ⓙ Ⓚ   50. Ⓕ Ⓖ Ⓗ Ⓙ Ⓚ   60. Ⓕ Ⓖ Ⓗ Ⓙ Ⓚ

READING TEST

1. Ⓐ Ⓑ Ⓒ Ⓓ   6. Ⓕ Ⓖ Ⓗ Ⓙ   11. Ⓐ Ⓑ Ⓒ Ⓓ   16. Ⓕ Ⓖ Ⓗ Ⓙ   21. Ⓐ Ⓑ Ⓒ Ⓓ   26. Ⓕ Ⓖ Ⓗ Ⓙ   31. Ⓐ Ⓑ Ⓒ Ⓓ   36. Ⓕ Ⓖ Ⓗ Ⓙ
2. Ⓕ Ⓖ Ⓗ Ⓙ   7. Ⓐ Ⓑ Ⓒ Ⓓ   12. Ⓕ Ⓖ Ⓗ Ⓙ   17. Ⓐ Ⓑ Ⓒ Ⓓ   22. Ⓕ Ⓖ Ⓗ Ⓙ   27. Ⓐ Ⓑ Ⓒ Ⓓ   32. Ⓕ Ⓖ Ⓗ Ⓙ   37. Ⓐ Ⓑ Ⓒ Ⓓ
3. Ⓐ Ⓑ Ⓒ Ⓓ   8. Ⓕ Ⓖ Ⓗ Ⓙ   13. Ⓐ Ⓑ Ⓒ Ⓓ   18. Ⓕ Ⓖ Ⓗ Ⓙ   23. Ⓐ Ⓑ Ⓒ Ⓓ   28. Ⓕ Ⓖ Ⓗ Ⓙ   33. Ⓐ Ⓑ Ⓒ Ⓓ   38. Ⓕ Ⓖ Ⓗ Ⓙ
4. Ⓕ Ⓖ Ⓗ Ⓙ   9. Ⓐ Ⓑ Ⓒ Ⓓ   14. Ⓕ Ⓖ Ⓗ Ⓙ   19. Ⓐ Ⓑ Ⓒ Ⓓ   24. Ⓕ Ⓖ Ⓗ Ⓙ   29. Ⓐ Ⓑ Ⓒ Ⓓ   34. Ⓕ Ⓖ Ⓗ Ⓙ   39. Ⓐ Ⓑ Ⓒ Ⓓ
5. Ⓐ Ⓑ Ⓒ Ⓓ   10. Ⓕ Ⓖ Ⓗ Ⓙ   15. Ⓐ Ⓑ Ⓒ Ⓓ   20. Ⓕ Ⓖ Ⓗ Ⓙ   25. Ⓐ Ⓑ Ⓒ Ⓓ   30. Ⓕ Ⓖ Ⓗ Ⓙ   35. Ⓐ Ⓑ Ⓒ Ⓓ   40. Ⓕ Ⓖ Ⓗ Ⓙ

SCIENCE TEST

1. Ⓐ Ⓑ Ⓒ Ⓓ   6. Ⓕ Ⓖ Ⓗ Ⓙ   11. Ⓐ Ⓑ Ⓒ Ⓓ   16. Ⓕ Ⓖ Ⓗ Ⓙ   21. Ⓐ Ⓑ Ⓒ Ⓓ   26. Ⓕ Ⓖ Ⓗ Ⓙ   31. Ⓐ Ⓑ Ⓒ Ⓓ   36. Ⓕ Ⓖ Ⓗ Ⓙ
2. Ⓕ Ⓖ Ⓗ Ⓙ   7. Ⓐ Ⓑ Ⓒ Ⓓ   12. Ⓕ Ⓖ Ⓗ Ⓙ   17. Ⓐ Ⓑ Ⓒ Ⓓ   22. Ⓕ Ⓖ Ⓗ Ⓙ   27. Ⓐ Ⓑ Ⓒ Ⓓ   32. Ⓕ Ⓖ Ⓗ Ⓙ   37. Ⓐ Ⓑ Ⓒ Ⓓ
3. Ⓐ Ⓑ Ⓒ Ⓓ   8. Ⓕ Ⓖ Ⓗ Ⓙ   13. Ⓐ Ⓑ Ⓒ Ⓓ   18. Ⓕ Ⓖ Ⓗ Ⓙ   23. Ⓐ Ⓑ Ⓒ Ⓓ   28. Ⓕ Ⓖ Ⓗ Ⓙ   33. Ⓐ Ⓑ Ⓒ Ⓓ   38. Ⓕ Ⓖ Ⓗ Ⓙ
4. Ⓕ Ⓖ Ⓗ Ⓙ   9. Ⓐ Ⓑ Ⓒ Ⓓ   14. Ⓕ Ⓖ Ⓗ Ⓙ   19. Ⓐ Ⓑ Ⓒ Ⓓ   24. Ⓕ Ⓖ Ⓗ Ⓙ   29. Ⓐ Ⓑ Ⓒ Ⓓ   34. Ⓕ Ⓖ Ⓗ Ⓙ   39. Ⓐ Ⓑ Ⓒ Ⓓ
5. Ⓐ Ⓑ Ⓒ Ⓓ   10. Ⓕ Ⓖ Ⓗ Ⓙ   15. Ⓐ Ⓑ Ⓒ Ⓓ   20. Ⓕ Ⓖ Ⓗ Ⓙ   25. Ⓐ Ⓑ Ⓒ Ⓓ   30. Ⓕ Ⓖ Ⓗ Ⓙ   35. Ⓐ Ⓑ Ⓒ Ⓓ   40. Ⓕ Ⓖ Ⓗ Ⓙ

ENGLISH TEST

45 Minutes—75 Questions

Directions: In the following five passages, certain words and phrases are underlined and numbered. In the right-hand column are alternatives for each underlined portion. Select the one that best conveys the idea, creates the most grammatically correct sentence, or is the most consistent with the style and tone of the passage. If you decide that the original version is best, select NO CHANGE. You may also find questions that ask about the entire passage or a section of the passage. These questions will correspond to small numbered boxes in the text. For these questions, decide which choice best accomplishes the purpose set out in the question stem. After you've selected the best choice, fill in the corresponding oval in your Answer Grid. For some questions, you'll need to read the context in order to answer correctly. Be sure to read until you have enough information to determine the correct answer choice.

You will also find questions about a section of the passage or about the passage as a whole. These questions do not refer to an underlined portion of the passage, but rather are identified by a number or numbers in a box.

For each question, choose the alternative you consider best and fill in the corresponding oval on your answer document. Read each passage through once before you begin to answer the questions that accompany it. For many of the questions, you must read several sentences beyond the question to determine the answer. Be sure that you have read enough ahead each time you choose an alternative.

PASSAGE I

DUKE ELLINGTON, A JAZZ GREAT

[1]

By the time Duke Ellington published his autobiography, *Music is My Mistress,* in 1973 he had traveled to
₁
dozens of countries and every continent. "I pay rent in New York City," he answered when asked of his residence.

1. A. NO CHANGE
   B. 1973. He had
   C. 1973, it had
   D. 1973, he had

[2]

 In the 1920s, though, Ellington pays more than rent
₂
in New York; he paid his dues on the bandstand. Having moved to Harlem from Washington, D.C., in 1923, Ellington

2. F. NO CHANGE
   G. paid
   H. has to pay
   J. pay

established: his own band and achieved critical recognition with a polished sound and appearance. The
first New York review of the Ellingtonians in 1923
commented, "The boys look neat in dress suits and labor
hard but not in vain at their music." As Ellington made
a name for himself as a leader arranger and pianist,
his Harlem Renaissance compositions and recordings
highlighted two enduring characteristics of the man.
First, Ellington lived for jazz. Second, Harlem sustained
it, physically and spiritually.

[3]

Ellington himself admitted he was not a very
good pianist. As a teenager in Washington. He missed
more piano

lessons then he took with his teacher, Mrs. Clinkscales,
and spent more time going to dances than practicing the
the piano.

Mrs. Clinkscales was really the name of his piano
teacher! In the clubs,

3. A. NO CHANGE
   B. established the following: his own
   C. established his own
   D. took the time and effort to establish his own

4. F. NO CHANGE
   G. leader arranger, and pianist,
   H. leader, arranger, and pianist
   J. leader, arranger, and pianist,

5. A. NO CHANGE
   B. him,
   C. them,
   D. itself,

6. F. NO CHANGE
   G. good pianist as a teenager
   H. good pianist, a teenager
   J. good pianist, as a teenager

7. A. NO CHANGE
   B. lessons then he had taken
   C. lessons; he took
   D. lessons than he took

8. F. NO CHANGE
   G. That was really the name of his piano teacher: Mrs. Clinkscales!
   H. Mrs. Clinkscales was really the name of his piano teacher.
   J. OMIT the underlined portion.

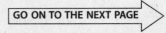
GO ON TO THE NEXT PAGE

<u>therefore</u>, Ellington and his friends eventually caught
9
word of New York and the opportunities

<u>that awaited and were there for</u> young musicians. El-
10
lington wrote, "Harlem, to our minds, did indeed have

the world's most glamorous atmosphere. We had to go

there."

<u>He left Washington with drummer Sonny Greer.</u> Before
11
they could even unpack in Harlem, though, they found

themselves penniless. Not until Ellington was lucky

enough to find fifteen dollars on the street could he

return to Washington and recollect himself.

[4]

Ellington eventually did return to Harlem, and he

achieved great success as the bandleader at the Cotton

Club from 1927 to 1932. Located in the heart of Harlem

at 142nd Street and Lenox Avenue, <u>he played at the</u>
12
<u>Cotton Club, which was frequented</u> by top entertainers
12
and rich patrons. Harlem's nightlife, "cut out of a very

luxurious, royal-blue bolt of velvet," was an inspirational

backdrop, and Ellington composed, arranged, and

recorded prolifically to the rave of excited critical ac-

claim. "Black and Tan Fantasy," "Hot and Bothered," and

"Rockin' in Rhythm" were Ellington's early hits during

this period.

9. A. NO CHANGE
   B. however
   C. despite
   D. then

10. F. NO CHANGE
    G. awaiting and being there for
    H. that awaited
    J. that were there for

11. A. NO CHANGE
    B. With drummer Sonny Greer, it was
       Washington that he left.
    C. Leaving Washington, he, Ellington, left
       with drummer Sonny Greer.
    D. OMIT the underlined portion.

12. F. NO CHANGE
    G. he played at the Cotton Club, a club
       that was frequented
    H. the Cotton Club, which was frequented
    J. the Cotton Club was frequented

GO ON TO THE NEXT PAGE ▷

[13] They exhibited his unique ability to compose music that animated both dancers in search of a good time and improvising musicians in search of good music. Before long, the once fumbling pianist from Washington, D.C., became the undisputed leader of hot jazz in decadent Harlem. [14]

13. The purpose of including the names of Ellington's songs is to:
    A. provide some details about Ellington's early music.
    B. contradict an earlier point that Ellington did not create his own music.
    C. illustrate the complexity of Ellington's music.
    D. discuss the atmosphere at the Cotton Club.

14. The purpose of paragraph 4, as it relates to the previous paragraphs, is primarily to:
    F. demonstrate how accomplished Ellington had become.
    G. suggest that Ellington did not like living in New York.
    H. remind us how difficult it is to be a musician.
    J. make us skeptical of Ellington's abilities.

Question 15 asks about the preceding passage as a whole.

15. The writer wishes to insert the following detail into the essay:

    The combination of fun and seriousness in his music led to critical acclaim and wide mass appeal.

    The sentence would most logically be inserted into paragraph:
    A. 1, after the last sentence.
    B. 3, before the first sentence.
    C. 4, after the first sentence.
    D. 4, before the last sentence.

GO ON TO THE NEXT PAGE

PASSAGE II

COLORING AS SELF-DEFENSE IN ANIMALS

The following paragraphs may or may not be in the most logical order. Each paragraph is numbered in brackets, and question 29 will ask you to choose the appropriate order.

[1]

Some animals change <u>its</u> coloring with the seasons. The
16
ptarmigan sheds its brown plumage

16. F. NO CHANGE
    G. their
    H. it's
    J. there

<u>in winter, replacing</u> it with white feathers. The stoat,
17
a member of the

17. A. NO CHANGE
    B. winter and replacing
    C. winter: replacing
    D. winter replacing

<u>weasel family is known</u> as the *ermine* in winter because
18
its brown fur changes to white. The chameleon is per-

haps the most versatile of all animals

18. F. NO CHANGE
    G. weasel family known
    H. weasel family, which is known
    J. weasel family, is known

<u>having changed</u> their protective coloration. The
19
chameleon changes its color in just a few minutes to

whatever surface it happens to be sitting on.

19. A. NO CHANGE
    B. who changes
    C. that change
    D. that changed

[2]

While animals like the chameleon <u>use their</u>
20
<u>coloring</u> as a way of hiding from predators, the skunk
20
uses its distinctive white stripe as a way of standing out

from its surroundings. Far from placing it in

20. F. NO CHANGE
    G. their use coloring
    H. use coloring their
    J. coloring their use

GO ON TO THE NEXT PAGE

danger; the skunk's visibility actually protects it. By
21
distinguishing itself from other

21. A. NO CHANGE
B. danger, the skunk's
C. danger; the skunks'
D. danger, it is the skunk's

animals. The skunk warns its predators to avoid its infa-
22
mous stink. Think about it:

22. F. NO CHANGE
G. animals, therefore, the
H. animals because
J. animals, the

the question is would your appetite be whetted by the
23
skunk's odor?
23

23. A. NO CHANGE
B. would your appetite be whetted by the
skunk's odor?
C. the question is as follows, would your
appetite be whetted by the skunk's
odor?
D. the question is would your appetite be
whetted by the odor of the skunk?

[3]

Researchers have been investigating how animal
24
species have come to use coloring as a means of protecting themselves. One study has shown that certain
animals have glands that release special hormones,
resulting in the change of skin or fur color. Therefore,
25
not all the animals that camouflage themselves have
these glands.

24. F. NO CHANGE
G. investigated
H. were investigating
J. investigate

25. A. NO CHANGE
B. Nevertheless,
C. However,
D. Finally,

The topic remains and endures as one of the many mys-
26
teries of the natural world.

26. F. NO CHANGE
G. remaining and enduring as
H. remains and endures
J. remains

GO ON TO THE NEXT PAGE

[4]

Animals have a variety of ways of protecting themselves from enemies. Some animals adapt in shape and color to their environment. The tree frog, for example, blends perfectly into its surroundings. When it sits motionless, <u>a background of leaves completely hides the tree frog.</u>
27

27

<u>This camouflage enables the tree frog to hide from other</u>
28
<u>animals that would be interested in eating the tree frog.</u>
28

27. A. NO CHANGE
B. the tree frog is completely hidden in a background of leaves.
C. completely hidden is the tree frog in a background of leaves.
D. a background of leaves and the tree frog are completely hidden.

28. F. NO CHANGE
G. This camouflage enables the tree frog to hide from predators.
H. This camouflage enables the tree frog to hide from other animals interested in eating the tree frog.
J. OMIT the underlined portion.

Questions 29–30 ask about the preceding passage as a whole.

29. What would be the most logical order of paragraphs for this essay?
A. 3, 1, 4, 2
B. 1, 2, 4, 3
C. 4, 1, 2, 3
D. 2, 1, 3, 4

30. Suppose the author had been asked to write an essay on how animals use their colorings to protect themselves in the wild. Would this essay meet the requirement?
F. Yes, because the author covers several aspects of how animals use their colorings to protect themselves.
G. Yes, because the author thoroughly investigates how one animal protects itself with its colorings.
H. No, because the author does not consider animals that exist in the wild.
J. No, because the author does not include information from research studies.

GO ON TO THE NEXT PAGE

PASSAGE III

THE HISTORY OF CHOCOLATE

The word *chocolate* is used to describe a variety of

<u>foods made</u> from the beans of the cacao tree. The first
   31

people known to have made chocolate were the

<u>Aztecs, a people who used</u> cacao seeds to make a bit-
      32

ter but tasty drink. However, it was not until Hernan

Cortez's exploration of Mexico in

<u>1519. That</u> Europeans first learned of chocolate.
  33

     Cortez came to the New World in search of gold,

but his interest was also fired by the Aztecs' strange

drink. When Cortez returned to Spain, his ship's cargo

<u>included and held</u> three chests of cacao beans. It was
    34

from these beans that Europe experienced its first taste

of what

<u>seemed to be</u> a very unusual beverage. The drink soon
  35

became popular among those people wealthy enough to

afford it.

31. **A.** NO CHANGE
    B. foods, which are made
    C. foods and made
    D. foods and are

32. **F.** NO CHANGE
    G. Aztecs, and they used
    H. Aztecs a people that use
    J. Aztecs, who used

33. **A.** NO CHANGE
    B. 1519 that
    C. 1519, that
    D. 1519:

34. **F.** NO CHANGE
    G. included, held
    H. included
    J. including and holding

35. **A.** NO CHANGE
    B. seems to be
    C. seemingly is
    D. seemed being

GO ON TO THE NEXT PAGE →

<u>Over the next century cafes specializing</u> in chocolate
36
drinks began to appear throughout Europe. [37]

Of course, chocolate is very popular today. People
all over the world enjoy <u>chocolate bars chocolate sprin
kles and even chocolate soda.</u>
38

<u>In fact,</u> Asia has cultivated the delicacy of chocolate-
39
covered ants! People enjoy this food as a snack at the
movies or sporting events. The chocolate ant phenomenon has yet to take over America,
<u>but enjoy their chocolate Americans do</u> nonetheless.
40

Many chocolate lovers around the world were
ecstatic to hear that chocolate may actually be good for
you. Researchers

36. F. NO CHANGE
     G. Over the next century cafes specialize
     H. Over the next century, cafes specializing
     J. Over the next century, there were cafes
         specializing

37. The author is considering the addition of
     another sentence here that briefly describes
     one of the first European cafes to serve a
     chocolate drink. This addition would:
     A. weaken the author's argument.
     B. provide some interesting details.
     C. contradict the topic of the paragraph.
     D. highlight the author's opinion of
         chocolate.

38. F. NO CHANGE
     G. chocolate, bars, chocolate, sprinkles,
         and even chocolate soda.
     H. chocolate bars chocolate sprinkles—
         even chocolate soda.
     J. chocolate bars, chocolate sprinkles, and
         even chocolate soda.

39. A. NO CHANGE
     B. Unfortunately
     C. In spite of this
     D. The truth is

40. F. NO CHANGE
     G. but Americans enjoy their chocolate
     H. but enjoy their chocolate is what
         Americans do
     J. but Americans do enjoy their chocolate

GO ON TO THE NEXT PAGE

say: chocolate contains a chemical that could prevent
41
cancer and heart disease. New research measures the

amount of catechins, the chemical thought to be behind

the benefits, in different types of chocolate.

The substance is also found in tea. The studies show
42
that chocolate is very high in catechins. The research is

likely to be welcomed

by those with a sweet tooth, although dentists
43

may less be pleased.
44

41. A. NO CHANGE
    B. have said the following: chocolate contains
    C. say that chocolate contains
    D. say: chocolate contained

42. F. NO CHANGE
    G. Another place where the substance is found is tea.
    H. Also, tea contains the substance.
    J. OMIT the underlined portion.

43. A. NO CHANGE
    B. with them
    C. by us
    D. to those

44. F. NO CHANGE
    G. pleased less they will be.
    H. may be pleased less.
    J. may be less pleased.

Question 45 asks about the preceding passage as a whole.

45. Suppose the author had been given the assignment of writing about culinary trends in history. Would this essay satisfy the requirement?

    A. Yes, because the essay discusses many culinary trends in history.
    B. Yes, because the essay shows how chocolate has been used over time.
    C. No, because the essay focuses too much on chocolate in present times.
    D. No, because the essay only covers chocolate.

GO ON TO THE NEXT PAGE

PASSAGE IV

THE MILITARY UNIFORM OF THE FUTURE

[1]

Scientists, in programs <u>administers by</u> the United States
46
Army, are experimenting to develop the military uni-

form of the future. As imagined, it

<u>would be light as silk, bulletproof, and able to</u> rapidly
47
change at the molecular level to adapt to biological or

chemical threats. In response to a detected anthrax

threat, for example, it would become an impermeable

shield. The pant leg of a

<u>soldier who's</u> leg had been broken
48

<u>would have been</u> able to morph into a
49

<u>splint, or, even form</u> an artificial muscle. Nanosensors
50
would transmit vital signs back to a medical team or

monitor the breath for increased nitric oxide, a sign of

stress.

[2]

The especially promising Invisible Soldier program

aims to make the long-held dream of human invisibility

a reality by using

46. F. NO CHANGE
    G. administering by
    H. administered by
    J. administers with

47. A. NO CHANGE
    B. would: be light as silk, bulletproof, and able to
    C. would be light as silk bulletproof and able to
    D. light as silk, bulletproof, and was able to

48. F. NO CHANGE
    G. soldier whose
    H. soldier, who's
    J. soldier that's

49. A. NO CHANGE
    B. would be
    C. will have been
    D. is

50. F. NO CHANGE
    G. splint or even form
    H. splint, or even, form
    J. splint or, even, form

GO ON TO THE NEXT PAGE ⇨

technology. To create a covering capable of
        51

concealing a soldier and making him invisible from
                         52
most wavelengths of visible light. 53 54

51. A. NO CHANGE
    B. technology to create
    C. technology, which were creating
    D. technology; create

52. F. NO CHANGE
    G. making a soldier invisible and
       concealing him
    H. concealing a soldier making that soldier
       invisible
    J. concealing a soldier

53. The writer's description of the U.S. Army's
    Invisible Soldier program seems to indicate
    that the army's opinion of the program is:
    A. skeptical.
    B. curious.
    C. enthusiastic.
    D. detailed.

54. What is the purpose of this paragraph, as it
    relates to the rest of the essay?
    F. To highlight one of the successes of the
       scientists' programs
    G. To predict the future of U.S. military
       uniforms
    H. To outline what will follow in the
       essay
    J. To introduce a specific example of the
       uniform of the future

[3]

A solution proposed in the early stages near the
                                      55
beginning of the program's development would construct
        55
a suit or cape from fabric linked to sensors that can

detect the coloring and pattern of the background. The

sensors would then send varying intensities of electrical

current to the appropriate areas of the fabric,

55. A. NO CHANGE
    B. beginning and the early stages of
    C. early stages of
    D. OMIT the underlined portion.

GO ON TO THE NEXT PAGE

<u>they</u> would be impregnated with chemicals sensitive to
  56
electricity. The coveralls would change colors continu-

ally as the soldier moved.

[4]

The problem with this solution from a military

standpoint, <u>you know, is</u>
            57

<u>power: the fact that the suit</u> would require a continuous
            58
flow of electricity means that a soldier would have to

carry a large number of batteries, which would hardly

contribute to ease of movement and camouflage.

[5]

[1] To address this problem, army researchers have

developed a new kind of color-changing pixel, known as

the intererometric modulator or i-mod. [2] The research-

ers hope that a flexible suit made of i-mod pixels could

completely blend into any background. [3] In addition to

matching a background, the pixels could also be set to show

other colors, for example, a camouflage mode that would

render a soldier effectively invisible in the forest and a flash

mode that would enhance a soldier's visibility in a rescue

situation. [4] Changing the distance between the mirrors

changes the color of the light that they reflect. [5] Each i-

mod pixel is made up of a pair of tiny mirrors. 59

56. F. NO CHANGE
    G. that
    H. it
    J. which

57. A. NO CHANGE
    B. is, like,
    C. however, is
    D. therefore, is

58. F. NO CHANGE
    G. power; the fact that the suit
    H. power the fact that the suit
    J. power the fact that, the suit

59. Which of the following sequences would
    make paragraph 5 most logical?
    A. 2, 4, 5, 3, 1
    B. 2, 3, 1, 5, 4
    C. 1, 4, 5, 2, 3
    D. 1, 5, 4, 2, 3

GO ON TO THE NEXT PAGE

Question 60 asks about the preceding passage as a whole.

60. The writer wishes to insert the following material into the passage:

When H.G. Wells wrote *The Invisible Man*, there was no interest in camouflaging soldiers; the British army was garbed in bright red uniforms. Since that time, governments have learned the value of making soldiers difficult to see, first by using camouflage fabrics, and today by envisioning something even more effective that would change color to match the terrain.

The new material would most logically be placed in paragraph:

F. 2.

G. 3.

H. 4.

J. 5.

GO ON TO THE NEXT PAGE

PASSAGE V

CALIFORNIA: A STATE BUILT ON DREAMS

It lasted fewer than 10 years, but when it was over, the

United States had been radically and forever changed.

The population had exploded on the West Coast of

the country, <u>fortunes had been made and those same</u>
                                         61
<u>fortunes were lost,</u> and a new state had entered the
         61
union—a state that would become a state of mind for all

61. A. NO CHANGE
    B. fortunes had been made and lost,
    C. fortunes, which had been made, were
       then lost,
    D. made and lost were fortunes,

<u>Americans: California.</u>
         62

62. F. NO CHANGE
    G. Americans, and that place was called
       California.
    H. Americans, California.
    J. Americans. California.

The United States <u>acquiring</u> the territory that
                       63
would later become California during the Mexican War
(1846–1848). One of the many settlers who traveled to
the new territory was

63. A. NO CHANGE
    B. has acquired
    C. is acquiring
    D. acquired

<u>John Sutter who was a shopkeeper</u> from Switzerland
                 64
who had left behind his wife, his children, and his debts,
in search of a new life.

64. F. NO CHANGE
    G. John Sutter, a shopkeeper
    H. John Sutter; a shopkeeper
    J. John Sutter, who was a shopkeeper

GO ON TO THE NEXT PAGE

<u>Hired he did</u> a carpenter named James Marshall to build
65
a sawmill for him on the American River in the foothills

of the Sierra Nevada mountains.

65. A. NO CHANGE
    B. He hired
    C. Hiring
    D. He did hire

On January 24, 1848, <u>while inspecting the mill's</u>
66
<u>runoff into the river,</u> Marshall saw two shiny objects
66
below the surface of the water. He took the nuggets to

Sutter, who was annoyed by the discovery; Sutter didn't

want

66. F. NO CHANGE
    G. (he was inspecting the mill's runoff into
       the river)
    H. inspecting the mill's runoff into the
       river all the while
    J. OMIT the underlined portion.

<u>them</u> mill workers distracted by gold fever.
67

67. A. NO CHANGE
    B. this
    C. his
    D. there

<u>Keeping the discovery</u> quiet for a while, but then he
68
couldn't resist bragging about it. Word got out, and

workers began quitting their jobs and heading into the

hills to look for the source of the gold that had washed

down the river.

[69] Thousands of people poured into California in

search of fortune and glory.

68. F. NO CHANGE
    G. The discovery he was keeping
    H. He kept the discovery
    J. Keeps he the discovery

69. Which of the following would provide the
    best transition here, guiding the reader from
    the topic of the previous paragraph to the
    new topic of this paragraph?
    A. Sutter and Marshall did not make a
       profit.
    B. The gold rush had officially begun.
    C. Can you image how a small discovery
       led to such a large state?
    D. Most of the "gold" turned out to be a
       hoax.

GO ON TO THE NEXT PAGE ⟹

This is similar to recent stock market increases. During the two years after Marshall's discovery, more than 90,000 people made their way to California, looking for gold. In fact, so many people moved West in just
70

singularly one of those years, 1849, that all the prospectors, regardless of when they arrived, became known as
71
Forty-niners. By 1850, so many people had moved to the California territory that the United States Congress was forced to declare it a new state. In 1854, the population had increased by another 300,000 people. In fact, 1
72
out of every 90 people then living in the United States was living in California.

Even after all of the gold had been taken from the ground, California remained a magical place in the American imagination. The 31st state had become a place that lives could change, fortunes could be made,
73
and dreams could come true. For many

people, and California is still such a place.
74

70. F. NO CHANGE
    G. The rush for gold was similar to recent stock market increases.
    H. This was similar to recent stock market increases.
    J. OMIT the underlined portion.

71. A. NO CHANGE
    B. one
    C. one and only one
    D. singular

72. F. NO CHANGE
    G. In spite of this,
    H. Believe it or not,
    J. Therefore,

73. A. NO CHANGE
    B. where
    C. through which
    D. in

74. F. NO CHANGE
    G. Forty-niners, California
    H. people and California
    J. people, California

GO ON TO THE NEXT PAGE

Question 75 asks about the preceding passage as a whole.

75. Suppose the writer had been assigned to write a brief essay detailing the life of a Forty-niner during the California gold rush. Would this essay successfully fulfill the assignment?

A. Yes, because the essay tells about the lives of John Sutter and James Marshall.

B. No, because the essay covers a historical rather than biographical perspective of the gold rush.

C. Yes, because one can imagine the life of a Forty-niner from the details provided in the essay.

D. No, because the essay does not discuss Forty-niners.

IF YOU FINISH BEFORE TIME IS CALLED, YOU MAY CHECK YOUR WORK ON THIS SECTION ONLY. DO NOT TURN TO ANY OTHER SECTION IN THE TEST. **STOP**

MATH TEST

60 Minutes—60 Questions

Directions: Solve each problem, choose the correct answer, and then fill in the corresponding oval on your answer document.

Do not linger over problems that take too much time. Solve as many as you can, then return to the others in the time you have left for this test.

You are permitted to use a calculator on this test. You may use your calculator for any problems you choose, but some of the problems may best be done without using a calculator.

1. The regular price for a certain bicycle is $125.00. If that price is reduced by 20%, what is the new price?

   A. $100.00

   B. $105.00

   C. $112.50

   D. $120.00

   E. $122.50

2. If $x = -5$, then $2x^2 - 6x + 5 = ?$

   F. −15

   G. 15

   H. 25

   J. 85

   K. 135

3. How many distinct prime factors does the number 36 have?

   A. 2

   B. 3

   C. 4

   D. 5

   E. 6

4. In the following figure, what is the value of x ?

   F. 105°

   G. 115°

   H. 135°

   J. 245°

   K. 255°

5. What is the average of $\frac{1}{20}$ and $\frac{1}{30}$?

   A. $\frac{1}{25}$

   B. $\frac{1}{24}$

   C. $\frac{2}{25}$

   D. $\frac{1}{12}$

   E. $\frac{1}{6}$

GO ON TO THE NEXT PAGE ⟹

6. The toll for driving a segment of a certain freeway is $1.50 plus 25 cents for each mile traveled. Joy paid a $25 toll for driving a segment of the freeway. How many miles did she travel?

    F. 10
    G. 75
    H. 94
    J. 96
    K. 100

7. For all x, $3x^2 \times 5x^3 = ?$

    A. $8x^5$
    B. $8x^6$
    C. $15x^5$
    D. $15x^6$
    E. $15x^8$

8. How many units apart are the points $P(-1, -2)$ and $Q(2, 2)$ in the standard (x, y) coordinate plane?

    F. 2
    G. 3
    H. 4
    J. 5
    K. 6

9. In a group of 25 students, 16 are female. What percentage of the group is female?

    A. 16%
    B. 40%
    C. 60%
    D. 64%
    E. 75%

10. For how many integer values of x will $\dfrac{7}{x}$ be greater than $\dfrac{1}{4}$ and less than $\dfrac{1}{3}$?

    F. 6
    G. 7
    H. 12
    J. 28
    K. Infinitely many

11. Which of the following is a polynomial factor of $6x^2 - 13x + 6$?

    A. $2x + 3$
    B. $3x - 2$
    C. $3x + 2$
    D. $6x - 2$
    E. $6x + 2$

12. What is the value of a if $\dfrac{1}{a} + \dfrac{2}{a} + \dfrac{3}{a} + \dfrac{4}{a} = 5$?

    F. $\dfrac{1}{2}$
    G. 2
    H. 4
    J. $12\dfrac{1}{2}$
    K. 50

GO ON TO THE NEXT PAGE

13. In the following figure, $\overline{AD}$, $\overline{BE}$, and $\overline{CF}$ all intersect at point G. If the measure of $\angle AGB$ is 40° and the measure of $\angle CGE$ is 105°, what is the measure of $\angle AGF$?

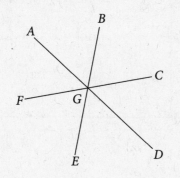

   A. 35°

   B. 45°

   C. 55°

   D. 65°

   E. 75°

14. Which of the following is the solution statement for the inequality $-3 < 4x - 5$?

   F. $x > -2$

   G. $x > \dfrac{1}{2}$

   H. $x < -2$

   J. $x < \dfrac{1}{2}$

   K. $x < 2$

15. In the following figure, BD bisects $\angle ABC$. The measure of $\angle ABC$ is 100° and the measure of $\angle BAD$ is 60°. What is the measure of $\angle BDC$?

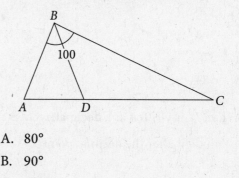

   A. 80°

   B. 90°

   C. 100°

   D. 110°

   E. 120°

16. If $x + 2y - 3 = xy$, where x and y are positive, then which of the following equations expresses y in terms of x?

   F. $y = \dfrac{3 - x}{2 - x}$

   G. $y = \dfrac{3 - x}{x - 2}$

   H. $y = \dfrac{x - 3}{2 - x}$

   J. $y = \dfrac{x - 2}{x - 3}$

   K. $y = \dfrac{6 - x}{x - 2}$

17. In a group of 50 students, 28 speak English and 37 speak Spanish. If everyone in the group speaks at least one of the two languages, how many speak both English and Spanish?

   A. 11

   B. 12

   C. 13

   D. 14

   E. 15

GO ON TO THE NEXT PAGE ⟶

18. A car travels 288 miles in 6 hours. At that rate, how many miles will it travel in 8 hours?

    F. 216
    G. 360
    H. 368
    J. 376
    K. 384

19. When $\dfrac{4}{11}$ is written as a decimal, what is the 100th digit after the decimal point?

    A. 3
    B. 4
    C. 5
    D. 6
    E. 7

20. What is the solution for x in the system of the following equations?

    $$3x + 4y = 31$$
    $$3x - 4y = -1$$

    F. 4
    G. 5
    H. 6
    J. 9
    K. 10

21. In the standard (x, y) coordinate plane, points P and Q have coordinates $(2, 3)$ and $(12, -15)$, respectively. What are the coordinates of the midpoint of $\overline{PQ}$?

    A. $(6, -12)$
    B. $(6, -9)$
    C. $(6, -6)$
    D. $(7, -9)$
    E. $(7, -6)$

22. In the following figure, $\angle B$ is a right angle, and the measure of $\angle C$ is θ. What is the value of $\cos \theta$?

    F. $\dfrac{3}{4}$
    G. $\dfrac{3}{5}$
    H. $\dfrac{4}{5}$
    J. $\dfrac{5}{4}$
    K. $\dfrac{4}{3}$

23. In the following figure, the circle centered at P is tangent to the circle centered at Q. Point Q is on the circumference of circle P. If the circumference of circle P is 6 inches, what is the circumference, in inches, of circle Q?

    A. 12
    B. 24
    C. 36
    D. 12π
    E. 36π

GO ON TO THE NEXT PAGE

24. If $f(x) = x^3 - x^2 - x$, what is the value of $f(-3)$?

    F. −39

    G. −33

    H. −21

    J. −15

    K. 0

25. If the lengths, in inches, of all three sides of a triangle are integers, and one side is 7 inches long, what is the least possible perimeter of the triangle, in inches?

    A. 9

    B. 10

    C. 15

    D. 21

    E. 24

26. What is the complete factorization of $2x + 3x^2 + x^3$?

    F. $x(x^2 + 2)$

    G. $x(x - 2)(x + 3)$

    H. $x(x - 1)(x + 2)$

    J. $x(x + 1)(x + 2)$

    K. $x(x + 2)(x + 3)$

27. If $xyz \neq 0$, which of the following is equivalent to $\dfrac{x^2 y^3 z^4}{\left(xyz^2\right)^2}$?

    A. $\dfrac{1}{y}$

    B. $\dfrac{1}{z}$

    C. y

    D. $\dfrac{x}{yz}$

    E. xyz

28. As a decimal, what is the sum of $\dfrac{2}{3}$ and $\dfrac{1}{12}$?

    F. 0.2

    G. 0.5

    H. 0.75

    J. 0.833

    K. 0.875

29. The formula for converting a Fahrenheit temperature reading to Celsius is $C = \dfrac{5}{9}(F - 32)$, where C is the reading in degrees Celsius and F is the reading in degrees Fahrenheit. Which of the following is the Fahrenheit equivalent to a reading of 95° Celsius?

    A. 35°F

    B. 53°F

    C. 63°F

    D. 203°F

    E. 207°F

30. A jar contains 4 green marbles, 5 red marbles, and 11 white marbles. If 1 marble is chosen at random, what is the probability that it will be green?

    F. $\dfrac{1}{3}$

    G. $\dfrac{1}{4}$

    H. $\dfrac{1}{5}$

    J. $\dfrac{1}{16}$

    K. $\dfrac{5}{15}$

GO ON TO THE NEXT PAGE

31. What is the average of the expressions $2x + 5$, $5x - 6$, and $-4x + 2$?

    A. $x + \dfrac{1}{3}$

    B. $x + 1$

    C. $3x + \dfrac{1}{3}$

    D. $3x + 3$

    E. $3x + 3\dfrac{1}{3}$

32. The line that passes through the points $(1, 1)$ and $(2, 16)$ in the standard (x, y) coordinate plane is parallel to the line that passes through the points $(-10, -5)$ and $(a, 25)$. What is the value of a?

    F. -8

    G. 3

    H. 5

    J. 15

    K. 20

33. In the following figure, $\overline{QS}$ and $\overline{PT}$ are parallel, and the lengths of $\overline{QR}$ and $\overline{PQ}$, in units, are as marked. If the perimeter of $\triangle QRS$ is 11 units, how many units long is the perimeter of $\triangle PRT$?

    A. 22

    B. 33

    C. 66

    D. 88

    E. 99

34. The figure shown belongs in which of the following classifications?

    I.   Polygon
    II. Quadrilateral
    III. Rectangle
    IV. Trapezoid

    F. I only

    G. II only

    H. IV only

    J. I, II, and III only

    K. I, II, and IV only

35. If one solution to the equation $2x^2 + (a - 4)$ $x - 2a = 0$ is $x = -3$, what is the value of a?

    A. 0

    B. 2

    C. 4

    D. 6

    E. 12

36. A menu offers 4 choices for the first course, 5 choices for the second course, and 3 choices for dessert. How many different meals, consisting of a first course, a second course, and a dessert, can one choose from this menu?

    F. 12

    G. 24

    H. 30

    J. 36

    K. 60

GO ON TO THE NEXT PAGE ⟶

37. If an integer is divisible by 6 and by 9, then the integer must be evenly divisible by which of the following?

      I. 12

      II. 18

      III. 36

A. I only

B. II only

C. I and II only

D. I, II, and III

E. None

38. For all $x \neq 0$, $\dfrac{x^2 + x^2 + x^2}{x^2} = ?$

F. 3

G. $3x$

H. x^2

J. x^3

K. x^4

39. Joan has q quarters, d dimes, n nickels, and no other coins in her pocket. Which of the following represents the total number of coins in Joan's pocket?

A. $q + d + n$

B. $5q + 2d + n$

C. $0.25q + 0.10d + 0.05n$

D. $(25 + 10 + 5)(q + d + n)$

E. $25q + 10d + 5n$

40. Which of the following graphs represents the solutions for x of the inequality $5x - 2(1 - x) \geq 4(x + 1)$?

41. In the standard (x, y) coordinate plane, line m is perpendicular to the line containing the points $(5, 6)$ and $(6, 10)$. What is the slope of line m?

A. -4

B. $-\dfrac{1}{4}$

C. $\dfrac{1}{4}$

D. 4

E. 8

GO ON TO THE NEXT PAGE

42. In the right triangle below, sin θ = ?

12 in   13 in

5 in

F. $\dfrac{5}{13}$

G. $\dfrac{5}{12}$

H. $\dfrac{12}{13}$

J. $\dfrac{13}{12}$

K. $\dfrac{13}{5}$

43. If $9^{2x-1} = 3^{3x+3}$, then $x = ?$

A. -4

B. $-\dfrac{7}{4}$

C. $-\dfrac{10}{7}$

D. 2

E. 5

44. From 1970 through 1980, the population of City Q increased by 20%. From 1980 through 1990, the population increased by 30%. What was the combined percent increase for the period 1970–1990?

F. 25%

G. 26%

H. 36%

J. 50%

K. 56%

45. Martin's average score after four tests is 89. What score on the fifth test would bring Martin's average up to exactly 90?

A. 90

B. 91

C. 92

D. 93

E. 94

46. Which of the following is an equation for the circle in the standard (x, y) coordinate plane that has its center at $(-1, -1)$ and passes through the point $(7, 5)$?

F. $(x - 1)^2 + (y - 1)^2 = 10$

G. $(x + 1)^2 + (y + 1)^2 = 10$

H. $(x - 1)^2 + (y - 1)^2 = 12$

J. $(x - 1)^2 + (y - 1)^2 = 100$

K. $(x + 1)^2 + (y + 1)^2 = 100$

47. Which of the following is an equation for the graph in the following standard (x, y) coordinate plane?

A. $y = -2x + 1$

B. $y = x + 1$

C. $y = x + 2$

D. $y = 2x + 1$

E. $y = 2x + 2$

GO ON TO THE NEXT PAGE

48. What is $\frac{1}{4}$% of 16?

    F. 0.004

    G. 0.04

    H. 0.4

    J. 4

    K. 64

49. For all s, $(s + 4)(s - 4) + (2s + 2)(s - 2) = ?$

    A. $s^2 - 2s - 20$

    B. $3s^2 - 12$

    C. $3s^2 - 2s - 20$

    D. $3s^2 + 2s - 20$

    E. $5s^2 - 2s - 20$

50. Which of the following is an equation of the parabola graphed in the following (x, y) coordinate plane?

    F. $y = \dfrac{x^2}{3} - 3$

    G. $y = \dfrac{x^2 - 3}{3}$

    H. $y = \dfrac{x^2}{3} + 3$

    J. $y = \dfrac{x^2 + 3}{3}$

    K. $y = 3x^2 - 3$

51. In the following figure, $\sin a = \dfrac{4}{5}$. What is $\cos b$?

    A. $\dfrac{3}{4}$

    B. $\dfrac{3}{5}$

    C. $\dfrac{4}{5}$

    D. $\dfrac{5}{4}$

    E. $\dfrac{4}{3}$

52. For all $x \neq 0$, $\dfrac{x^2 + x^2 + x^2}{x} = ?$

    F. $3x$

    G. x^3

    H. x^5

    J. x^7

    K. $2x^2 + x$

53. One can determine a student's score S on a certain test by dividing the number of wrong answers (w) by 4 and subtracting the result from the number of right answers (r). This relation is expressed by which of the following formulas?

    A. $S = \dfrac{r - w}{4}$

    B. $S = r - \dfrac{w}{4}$

    C. $S = \dfrac{r}{4} - w$

    D. $S = 4r - w$

    E. $S = r - 4w$

GO ON TO THE NEXT PAGE

54. What is the volume, in cubic inches, of the cylinder shown in the following figure?

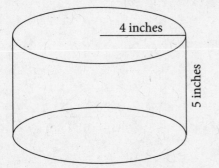

F. 20π

G. 40π

H. 60π

J. 80π

K. 100π

55. In the following figure, $\overline{AB}$ is perpendicular to BC. The lengths of $\overline{AB}$ and $\overline{BC}$, in inches, are given in terms of x. Which of the following represents the area of $\triangle ABC$, in square inches, for all $x > 1$?

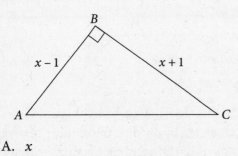

A. x

B. $2x$

C. x^2

D. $x^2 - 1$

E. $\dfrac{x^2 - 1}{2}$

56. In 1990, the population of Town A was 9,400 and the population of Town B was 7,600. Starting then, each year the population of Town A decreased by 100, and the population of Town B increased by 100. In what year were the two populations equal?

F. 1998

G. 1999

H. 2000

J. 2008

K. 2009

57. In a certain club, the average age of the male members is 35 and the average age of the female members is 25. If 20% of the members are male, what is the average age of all the club members?

A. 26

B. 27

C. 28

D. 29

E. 30

GO ON TO THE NEXT PAGE

58. To determine the height h of a tree, Roger stands b feet from the base of the tree and measures the angle of elevation to be θ, as shown in the following figure. Which of the following relates h and b?

  F. $\sin\theta = \dfrac{h}{b}$

  G. $\sin\theta = \dfrac{b}{h}$

  H. $\sin\theta = \dfrac{b}{\sqrt{b^2 + h^2}}$

  J. $\sin\theta = \dfrac{h}{\sqrt{b^2 + h^2}}$

  K. $\sin\theta = \dfrac{\sqrt{b^2 + h^2}}{b}$

59. The formula for the lateral surface area S of a right circular cone is $S = \pi r\sqrt{r^2 + h^2}$, where r is the radius of the base and h is the altitude. What is the lateral surface area, in square feet, of a right circular cone with base radius 3 feet and altitude 4 feet?

  A. $3\pi\sqrt{5}$

  B. $3\pi\sqrt{7}$

  C. 15π

  D. 21π

  E. $\dfrac{75\pi}{2}$

60. In the following figure, line t crosses parallel lines m and n. Which of the following statements must be true?

  F. $a = b$

  G. $a = d$

  H. $b = e$

  J. $c = g$

  K. $d = g$

READING TEST

35 Minutes—40 Questions

Directions: There are four passages in this test. Each passage is followed by several questions. After reading a passage, choose the best answer to each question and fill in the corresponding oval on your answer document. You may refer to the passages as often as necessary.

PASSAGE I

PROSE FICTION

This passage is adapted from Bleak House, *by Charles Dickens, which was first published in 1853. In this excerpt, Esther recounts some of her childhood experiences.*

I can remember, when I was a very little girl indeed, I used to say to my doll when we were alone together, "Now, Dolly, I am not
Line clever, you know very well, and you must be
(5) patient with me, like a dear!"

…My dear old doll! I was such a shy little thing that I seldom dared to open my lips, and never dared to open my heart, to anybody else. It almost makes me cry
(10) to think what a relief it used to be to me when I came home from school of a day to run upstairs to my room and say, "Oh, you dear faithful Dolly, I knew you would be expecting me!" and then to sit down on
(15) the floor, leaning on the elbow of her great chair, and tell her all I had noticed since we parted…

I was brought up, from my earliest remembrance—like some of the princesses
(20) in the fairy stories, only I was not charming—by my godmother. At least, I only knew her as such. She was a good, good woman! She went to church three times every Sunday, and to morning prayers on
(25) Wednesdays and Fridays, and to lectures whenever there were lectures, and never missed. She was handsome; and if she had ever smiled, would have been (I used to think) like an angel—but she never smiled.

(30) She was always grave and strict. She was so very good herself, I thought, that the badness of other people made her frown all her life…It made me very sorry to consider how good she was and how unworthy of
(35) her I was, and I used ardently to hope that I might have a better heart; and I talked it over very often with the dear old doll, but I never loved my godmother as I ought to have loved her and as I felt I must have
(40) loved her if I had been a better girl…

I had never heard my mama spoken of…
I had never been shown my mama's grave.
I had never been told where it was…

Although there were seven girls at
(45) the neighboring school where I was a day boarder, and although they called me little Esther Summerson, I knew none of them at home. All of them were older than I, to be sure (I was the youngest there by a good
(50) deal), but there seemed to be some other separation between us besides that, and besides their being far more clever than I was and knowing much more than I did. One of them in the first week of my going to
(55) the school (I remember it very well) invited me home to a little party, to my great joy. But my godmother wrote a stiff letter declining for me, and I never went. I never went out at all.

(60) It was my birthday. There were holidays at school on other birthdays—none on mine. There were rejoicings at home on other birthdays, as I knew from what I heard the

GO ON TO THE NEXT PAGE

girls relate to one another—there were none
(65) on mine. My birthday was the most melancholy
day at home in the whole year…

Dinner was over, and my godmother
and I were sitting at the table before the
fire. The clock ticked, the fire clicked; not
(70) another sound had been heard in the room
or in the house for I don't know how long.
I happened to look timidly up from my
stitching, across the table at my godmother,
and I saw in her face, looking gloomily at me,
(75) "It would have been far better, little Esther,
that you had had no birthday, that you had
never been born!"

I broke out crying and sobbing, and I
said, "Oh, dear godmother, tell me, pray do
(80) tell me, did Mama die on my birthday?"

"No," she returned. "Ask me no more,
child!"

…I put up my trembling little hand to
clasp hers or to beg her pardon with what
(85) earnestness I might, but withdrew it as
she looked at me, and laid it on my fluttering
heart. She…said slowly in a cold, low
voice—I see her knitted brow and pointed
finger—"The time will come—and soon
(90) enough—when you will understand this
better and will feel it too…I have forgiven
her"—but her face did not relent—"the
wrong she did to me, and I say no more of
it, though it was greater than you will ever
(95) know…Forget your mother and leave all
other people to forget her…Now, go!"

…I went up to my room, and crept to
bed, and laid my doll's cheek against mine
wet with tears, and holding that solitary
(100) friend upon my bosom, cried myself to
sleep. Imperfect as my understanding of my
sorrow was, I knew that I had brought no
joy at any time to anybody's heart and that
I was to no one upon earth what Dolly was
(105) to me.

Dear, dear, to think how much time we
passed alone together afterwards, and how
often I repeated to the doll the story of my
birthday and confided to her that I would

(110) try as hard as ever I could to repair the fault
I had been born with…I hope it is not self-
indulgent to shed these tears as I think of it.

1. According to the passage, Esther only
remembers:

A. being brought up by her parents for a
short time.

B. being brought up by her mother for a
short time.

C. being brought up by her godmother for
a short time.

D. being brought up by her godmother.

2. It is most likely that Esther thought of her doll
as:

F. only an amusing plaything.

G. her only friend and confidante.

H. a princess in a fairy tale.

J. a beautiful toy that was too fragile to
touch.

3. As it is used in the passage, *stiff* (line 57) most
closely means:

A. difficult to bend.

B. rigidly formal.

C. unchanging.

D. not moving easily or freely.

4. Which of the following most likely contributed to Esther's belief that she had been born
with a fault (lines 110–111)?

F. She is not very clever.

G. Her birthday was never celebrated.

H. She did not have any friends at school.

J. Her mother died in childbirth.

GO ON TO THE NEXT PAGE

5. Esther's godmother's words, actions, and facial expression as described in paragraph 10 (lines 83–96) suggest that she:

   A. had a change of heart about celebrating Esther's birthday.

   B. did not know what had happened to Esther's mother.

   C. continued to resent Esther's mother.

   D. had truly forgiven Esther's mother.

6. According to the passage, Esther's childhood could be most accurately characterized as:

   F. an adventure.

   G. a time of loneliness and confusion.

   H. a period of dedication to education and self-improvement.

   J. a period of attempting to become more like her godmother.

7. From Esther's statement, "I was to no one upon earth what Dolly was to me" (lines 104–105), it is reasonable to infer that Esther:

   A. believed that her godmother loved her.

   B. believed that she would be able to become friends with the girls at school.

   C. believed that no one loved her.

   D. believed that her mother was alive.

8. In the passage, it is implied that all of the following contributed to separating Esther from the other girls at her school EXCEPT:

   F. the other girls were older than Esther.

   G. Esther's godmother did not allow Esther to socialize with the other girls outside of school.

   H. Esther believed that the other girls were much smarter.

   J. Esther was self-indulgent.

9. According to the passage, one reason that Esther thinks of her godmother as a "good, good woman" (lines 22–23) is:

   A. that when she smiles, she looks like an angel.

   B. that she forgave Esther's mother.

   C. that she frequently attends church services.

   D. that she gave Esther a doll.

10. In the passage, Esther describes herself as a child as:

    F. self-indulgent and not very clever.

    G. shy and not very clever.

    H. shy and faithful.

    J. self-indulgent and faithful.

GO ON TO THE NEXT PAGE

PASSAGE II

SOCIAL SCIENCE

This passage is excerpted from "The Return of the Big Cats," by Mac Margolis, Newsweek, December 11, 2000, © 2000 by Newsweek, Inc. All rights reserved. Reprinted by permission.

Marcos Nunes is not likely to forget his first holiday in Brazil's Pantanal wilderness. One afternoon last October he was coaxing his
Line horse through a lonely tuft of woods when
(5) he suddenly found himself staring down a fully grown spotted jaguar. He held his breath while the painted cat and her cub paraded silkily through the grove, not 10 meters away…"Thank you," he wrote later
(10) in a hotel visitor's log, "for the wonderful fright!"

As Nunes and other ecotourists are discovering, these big, beautiful animals, once at the brink of extinction, are now
(15) staging a comeback. Exactly how dramatic a comeback is difficult to say because jaguars—*Panthera onca*, the largest feline in the New World—are solitary, secretive, nocturnal predators. Each cat needs to
(20) prowl at least 35 square kilometers by itself. Brazil's Pantanal, vast wetlands that spill over a 140,000-square-kilometer swath of South America the size of Germany, gives them plenty of room to roam. Nevertheless,
(25) scientists who have been tagging jaguars with radio transmitters for two decades have in recent years been reporting a big increase in sightings. Hotels, campgrounds, and bed-and-breakfasts have sprung up to
(30) accommodate the half-million tourists a year (twice the number of five years ago) bent on sampling the Pantanal's wildlife, of which the great cats must be the most magnificent example.
(35) Most sightings come from local cattle herders—but their jaguar stories have a very different ring. One day last September, ranch hand Abel Monteiro was tending cattle near the Rio Vermelho, in the southern Pantanal,
(40) when, he says, a snarling jaguar leaped from the scrub and killed his two bloodhounds. Monteiro barely had time to grab his .38 revolver and kill the angry cat. Leonelson Ramos da Silva says last May he and a group
(45) of field hands had to throw flaming sticks all night to keep a prowling jaguar from invading their forest camp…The Brazilian interior, famous for its generous spirit and cowboy *bonhomie*, is now the scene of a
(50) political cat fight between the scientists, environmentalists, and ecotourists who want to protect the jaguars and the embattled ranchers who want to protect themselves and their livelihood.
(55) The ranchers, to be sure, have enough headaches coping with the harsh, sodden landscape without jaguars attacking their herds and threatening their livelihoods. Hard data on cattle losses due to jaguars in
(60) the Pantanal are nonexistent, but there are stories. In 1995, Joo Julio Dittmar bought a 6,200-hectare strip of ideal breeding ground, only to lose 152 of his 600 calves to jaguars, he claims. Ranchers chafe at laws that forbid
(65) them to kill the jaguars. "This is a question of democracy," says Dittmar. "We ranchers ought to be allowed to control our own environment."

Man and jaguar have been sparring for
(70) territory ever since 18th-century settlers, traders, and herdsmen began to move into this sparsely populated serto, or back lands. By the 1960s, the Pantanal was a vast, soggy canvas, white with gleaming herds of Nelore
(75) cattle. Game hunters were bagging 15,000 jaguars a year in the nearby Amazon Basin (no figures exist on the Pantanal) as the worldwide trade in pelts reached $30 million a year. As the jaguars grew scarce, their

GO ON TO THE NEXT PAGE ▷

(80) chief food staple, the capybaras—a meter-
long rodent, the world's largest—overran
farmers' fields and spread trichomoniasis,
a livestock disease that renders cows sterile.

Then in 1967, Brazil outlawed jaguar
(85) hunting, and a world ban on selling pelts
followed in 1973. Weather patterns also
shifted radically—due most likely to global
warming—and drove annual floods to
near-Biblical proportions. The waters are
(90) only now retreating from some inundated
pasturelands. As the Pantanal herds shrank
from 6 million to about 3.5 million head,
the jaguars advanced. Along the way they
developed a taste for the bovine intruders.

(95)   The ranchers' fear of the big cats is
partly cultural. The ancient Inca and Maya
believed that jaguars possessed supernatural
powers. In Brazil, the most treacherous
enemy is said to be *o amigo da onca*, a
(100) friend to the jaguar…

Some people believe there may be a way
for ranchers and jaguars to coexist. Sports
hunters on "green safaris" might shoot
jaguars with immobilizing drugs, allowing
(105) scientists to fit the cats with radio collars.
Fees would help sustain jaguar research and
compensate ranchers for livestock losses.
(Many environmentalists, though, fear
fraudulent claims.) Scientists are setting up
(110) workshops to teach ranchers how to protect
their herds with modern husbandry, pasture
management, and such gadgets as blinking
lights and electric fences.

Like many rural folk, however, the
(115) wetland ranchers tend to bristle at bureaucrats
and foreigners telling them what to do.
When the scholars go home and the greens
log off, the *pantaneiros* will still be there—
left on their own to deal with the jaguars as
(120) they see fit.

11. As it is used in the passage, *canvas* (line 74)
most closely means:

A. a survey of public opinion.

B. a background.

C. a coarse cotton fabric.

D. a painting.

12. According to the passage, one result of the
decline of the jaguar population during the
1960s was:

F. the increase in the population of the
settlers.

G. an increase in Brazil's ecotourist
business.

H. an increase in the price of a jaguar pelt.

J. an increase in the population of their
most common source of food, the
capybaras.

13. According to the passage, it is difficult to
determine the extent of the jaguar's comeback
because:

A. the area they inhabit is so large.

B. the stories that the local ranchers tell
about jaguars contradict the conclusions
reached by scientists.

C. jaguars are solitary, nocturnal animals
that can have a territory of 35 square
kilometers.

D. scientists have only used radio transmitters to track the movements of the
jaguar population.

GO ON TO THE NEXT PAGE ⟹

14. The information about ecotourism in the first and second paragraphs of the passage (lines 1–34) suggests that:

    F. the jaguars are seen as a threat to the safety of tourists.

    G. the jaguars are important to the success of Brazil's growing ecotourism industry.

    H. the growth of the ecotourism industry is threatening the habitat of the jaguars.

    J. it is common for ecotourists to spot one or more jaguars.

15. According to the passage, which of the following is NOT a method for protecting cattle herds that scientists are teaching ranchers?

    A. "Green safaris"

    B. Pasture management

    C. The use of blinking lights and electric fences

    D. Modern husbandry

16. It is most likely that the author of the passage included the jaguar stories of three ranchers (lines 35–47, 61–68) in order to:

    F. express more sympathy toward the ranchers than toward the environmentalists and scientists.

    G. illustrate the dangers and economic losses that the jaguars currently pose to ranchers.

    H. show the violent nature of the ranchers.

    J. provide a complete picture of the Pantanal landscape.

17. From information in the passage, it is most reasonable to infer that the cattle herds "shrank from 6 million to about 3.5 million head" (lines 91–92) because:

    A. the jaguars had killed so many cattle.

    B. environmentalists and scientists worked to convert pastureland into refuges for the jaguars.

    C. many cows had become sterile from trichomoniasis, and annual floods submerged much of the pastureland used by ranchers.

    D. the cattle could not tolerate the increase in the average temperature caused by global warming.

18. The main conclusion reached about the future of the relationship between the people and the jaguars in the Pantanal is that:

    F. the increase in ecotourism will ensure the continued growth in the jaguar population.

    G. the ranchers themselves will ultimately determine how they will cope with the jaguars.

    H. the jaguar population will continue to fluctuate with the number of tourists coming into the Pantanal.

    J. the scientists' new ranching methods will make it easy for the ranchers and jaguars to coexist.

19. According to the passage, which of the following groups want to protect the jaguar?

    I. Ecotourists
    II. Environmentalists
    III. Scientists

    A. I and II only

    B. I and III only

    C. II and III only

    D. I, II, and III

GO ON TO THE NEXT PAGE

20. According to the passage, there is no accurate data available on:

F. the number of cattle killed by jaguars.

G. the number of ranchers attacked by jaguars.

H. the growth rate of ecotourism in Brazil.

J. the percentage of the Pantanal wetlands inhabited by jaguars.

PASSAGE III

HUMANITIES

This passage is excerpted from Music Through the Ages Revised Edition, *© 1987 by Marion Bauer and Ethel R. Peyser, edited by Elizabeth E. Rogers, copyright © 1932 by Marion Bauer and Ethel R. Peyser, renewed copyright © 1960 by Ethel R. Peyser. Reprinted by permission of G. P. Putnam's Sons, a division of Penguin Group (USA), Inc.*

Greek instruments can be classified into two general categories—string and pipe, or lyre and aulos. Our knowledge of them comes
Line from representations on monuments, vases,
(5) statues, and friezes and from the testimony of Greek authors. The lyre was the national instrument and included a wide variety of types. In its most antique form, the chelys, it is traced back to the age of fable and
(10) allegedly owed its invention to Hermes. Easy to carry, this small lyre became the favorite instrument of the home, amateurs, and women, a popular accompaniment for drinking songs and love songs as well as
(15) more noble kinds of poetry...Professional Homeric singers used a kithara, a larger, more powerful instrument, which probably came from Egypt. The kithara had a flat wooden sound box and an upper horizontal
(20) bar supported by two curving arms. Within this frame were stretched strings of equal length, at first but three or four in number. Fastened to the performer by means of a sling, the kithara was played with both
(25) hands. We are not sure in just what manner the instrument was used to accompany the epics. It may have been employed for a pitch-fixing prelude and for interludes, or it may have paralleled or decorated the vocal
(30) melody in more or less free fashion.
...Two types of tuning were used: the dynamic, or pitch method, naming the degrees "according to function"; and the

GO ON TO THE NEXT PAGE →

thetic, or tablature, naming them "according
(35) to position" on the instrument.

As early as the eighth century B.C.,
lyres of five strings appeared. Terpander
(fl. c. 675 B.C.), one of the first innovators,
is said to have increased the number
(40) of strings to seven. He is also supposed to
have completed the octave and created the
Mixolydian scale. Aristoxenos claimed that
the poetess Sappho, in the seventh century
B.C., in addition to introducing a mode in
(45) which Dorian and Lydian characteristics
were blended, initiated use of the plectrum
or pick. At the time of Sophocles (495–406
B.C.), the lyre had eleven strings.

Another harplike instrument was the
(50) magadis, whose tone was described as
trumpetlike. Of foreign importation, it had
twenty strings, which, by means of frets,
played octaves. As some of the strings were
tuned in quartertones, it was an instrument
(55) associated with the enharmonic mode.
Smaller versions, the pectis and the barbitos,
were also tuned in quartertones. Greek men
and boys had a style of singing in octaves
that was called magadizing, after the octave-
(60) playing instruments.

The kithara was identified with Apollo
and the Apollonian cult, representing the
intellectual and idealistic side of Greek art.
The aulos or reed pipe was the instrument of
(65) Dionysians, who represented the unbridled,
sensual and passionate aspect of Greek
culture.

Although translated as "flute,"
the aulos is more like our oboe. Usually found
(70) in double form, the pipes set at an angle,
the aulos was imputed to have a far more
exciting effect than that produced by the
subdued lyre. About 600 B.C., the aulos
was chosen as the official instrument of
(75) the Delphian and Pythian festivals. It was
also used in performances of the Dionysian
dithyramb as well as a supplement of the
chorus in classic Greek tragedy and comedy.

There was a complete family of auloi
(80) covering the same range as human voices.
One authority names three species of
simple pipes and five varieties of double
pipes. (The double pipe was the professional
instrument.) An early specimen
(85) was supposed to have been tuned to the
chromatic tetrachord D, C sharp, B flat, A—
a fact that points to Oriental origin. Elegiac
songs called aulodia were composed in
this mode to be accompanied by an aulos.
(90) Although the first wooden pipes had only
three or four finger holes, the number later
increased so that the Dorian, Phrygian and
Lydian modes might be performed on a
single pair. Pictures of auletes show them
(95) with a bandage or phorbeia over their faces;
this might have been necessary to hold the
two pipes in place, to modulate the tone or,
perhaps, to aid in storing air in the cheeks
for the purpose of sustained performance.

21. The passage suggests that the aulos was con-
    sidered "the instrument of the Dionysians"
    (lines 64–65) because:

    A. it expressed the excitement and passion
       of that aspect of Greek culture.

    B. it was chosen as the official instrument
       of the Delphian and Pythian festivals.

    C. it represented the intellectual and ideal-
       istic side of Greek art.

    D. it was invented around the time that the
       Dionysian cult originated.

22. The statement that the chelys can be "traced
    back to the age of fable" (line 9) implies that
    the chelys:

    F. was invented by storytellers.

    G. was used to accompany the epics.

    H. probably existed in legend only.

    J. was a particularly ancient instrument.

GO ON TO THE NEXT PAGE ▷

23. The main purpose of the passage is to describe the:

    A. use of the lyre in different musical settings.

    B. connection between the ancient Greek arts of music and drama.

    C. references to music in ancient Greek literature.

    D. origin and development of various Greek instruments.

24. According to the passage, the kithara was:

    F. most likely of Greek origin.

    G. played with one hand.

    H. used by professional musicians.

    J. less powerful than a chelys.

25. Which of the following is NOT cited as a change that occurred to the lyre between the eighth and fifth centuries B.C.?

    A. Musicians began to use a plectrum.

    B. Lyres featured increasing numbers of strings.

    C. Musicians began to use different scales and modes.

    D. Lyres were used to accompany dramatic productions.

26. It can be inferred from the passage that the chromatic tetrachord D, C sharp, B flat, A (line 86) was:

    F. not appropriate for elegiac songs.

    G. only used by professional musicians.

    H. impossible on the first wooden pipes.

    J. present in ancient Oriental music.

27. According to the passage, the most ancient form of the lyre was called a:

    A. magadis.

    B. kithara.

    C. chelys.

    D. barbitos.

28. According to the passage, one of Sappho's contributions to ancient Greek music was that she:

    F. completed the octave and created the Mixolydian scale.

    G. introduced a mode blending Dorian and Lydian characteristics.

    H. incorporated poetry into recitals of lyre music.

    J. helped increase the number of strings on the lyre.

29. According to the passage, which of the following is/are characteristic of the aulos?

    I. It was used in performances of the Dionysian dithyramb.

    II. It sounded more exciting than the lyre.

    III. It resembles the modern-day flute more than it does the oboe.

    A. I only

    B. I and II only

    C. II and III only

    D. I, II, and III

30. Which of the following does the passage suggest is true about our knowledge of ancient Greek instruments?

    F. Our knowledge is dependent on secondary sources.

    G. Little is known about how instruments were tuned.

    H. Very few pictures of ancient Greek instruments have survived.

    J. More is known about string instruments than about pipe instruments.

GO ON TO THE NEXT PAGE

PASSAGE IV

NATURAL SCIENCE

This passage is an excerpt from "The Solar Incon-
stant," by John Horgan, Scientific American, *Septem-*
ber 1988, © 1988 by Scientific American. Reprinted
by permission of Scientific American.

Astronomers noted more than 150 years
ago that sunspots wax and wane in number
in an 11-year cycle. Ever since, people have
Line speculated that the solar cycle might exert
(5) some influence on the Earth's weather. In
this century, for example, scientists have
linked the solar cycle to droughts in the
American Midwest. Until recently, however,
none of these correlations has held up under
(10) close scrutiny.

One problem is that sunspots themselves
are so poorly understood. Observations have
revealed that the swirly smudges represent
areas of intense magnetic activity where
(15) the sun's radiative energy has been blocked
and that they are considerably cooler than
bright regions of the sun. Scientists have not
been able, however, to determine just how
sunspots are created or what effect they have
(20) on the solar constant (a misnomer that refers
to the sun's total radiance at any instant).

The latter question, at least, now seems
to have been resolved by data from the
Solar Maximum Mission satellite, which has
(25) monitored the solar constant since 1980, the
peak of the last solar cycle. As the number
of sunspots decreased through 1986, the
satellite recorded a gradual dimming of the
sun. Over the past year, as sunspots have
(30) proliferated, the sun has brightened. The
data suggest that the sun is 0.1 percent more
luminous at the peak of the solar cycle,
when the number of sunspots is greatest,
than at its nadir, according to Richard C.
(35) Willson of the Jet Propulsion Laboratory
and Hugh S. Hudson of the University of
California at San Diego.

The data show that sunspots do not
themselves make the sun shine brighter.
(40) Quite the contrary. When a sunspot appears,
it initially causes the sun to dim slightly,
but then after a period of weeks or months
islands of brilliance called faculas usually
emerge near the sunspot and more than
(45) compensate for its dimming effect. Willson
says faculas may represent regions where
energy that initially was blocked beneath a
sunspot has finally breached the surface.

Does the subtle fluctuation in the
(50) solar constant manifest itself in the Earth's
weather? Some recent reports offer statistical
evidence that it does, albeit rather indirectly.
The link seems to be mediated by a phenomenon
known as the quasi-biennial oscillation
(55) (QBO), a 180-degree shift in the direction of
stratospheric winds above the Tropics that
occurs about every two years.

Karin Labitzke of the Free University of
Berlin and Harry van Loon of the National
(60) Center for Atmospheric Research in Boulder,
Colorado, were the first to uncover
the QBO link. They gathered temperature and
air-pressure readings from various latitudes
and altitudes over the past three solar cycles.
(65) They found no correlation between the
solar cycle and their data until they sorted
the data into two categories: those gathered
during the QBO's west phase (when the
stratospheric winds blow west) and those
(70) gathered during its east phase. A remarkable
correlation appeared: temperatures and
pressures coincident with the QBO's west
phase rose and fell in accordance with the
solar cycle.

(75) Building on this finding, Brian A.
Tinsley of the National Science Foundation
discovered a statistical correlation between
the solar cycle and the position of storms in
the North Atlantic. The latitude of storms

GO ON TO THE NEXT PAGE ▶

(80) during the west phase of the QBO, Tinsley found, varied with the solar cycle: storms occurring toward the peak of a solar cycle traveled at latitudes about six degrees nearer the Equator than storms during the cycle's

(85) nadir.

Labitzke, van Loon, and Tinsley acknowledge that their findings are still rather mysterious. Why does the solar cycle seem to exert more of an influence

(90) during the west phase of the QBO than it does during the east phase? How does the 0.1 percent variance in solar radiation trigger the much larger changes—up to six degrees Celsius in polar regions—observed

(95) by Labitzke and van Loon? Van Loon says simply, "We can't explain it."

John A. Eddy of the National Center for Atmospheric Research, nonetheless, thinks these QBO findings as well as the

(100) *Solar Maximum Mission* data "look like breakthroughs" in the search for a link between the solar cycle and weather. With further research, for example, into how the oceans damp the effects of solar flux, these

(105) findings may lead to models that have some predictive value. The next few years may be particularly rich in solar flux.

31. According to the passage, the main source of information about the effect of sunspots on the solar constant is provided by:

   A. studies of droughts in the Midwest.

   B. data from the *Solar Maximum Mission* satellite.

   C. temperature and air pressure readings taken in Colorado.

   D. discussions between various eminent astronomers.

32. As it is used in the passage, the term *solar constant* refers to:

   F. magnetic activity.

   G. the sun's total radiance.

   H. the sun's surface temperature.

   J. wind direction.

33. The main purpose of this passage is to:

   A. explain why scientists have failed to find any direct correlation between sunspots and the Earth's weather.

   B. describe a possible correlation between the solar cycle and the Earth's weather.

   C. describe the solar cycle and its relation to the solar constant.

   D. prove conclusively that sunspots dramatically influence the Earth's weather.

34. As it is used in line 30, the word *proliferated* means:

   F. grown in size.

   G. brightened.

   H. decreased in number.

   J. increased in number.

35. Which of the following explains why the sun appears brighter during periods of sunspot activity?

   A. Energy that has been blocked is finally released.

   B. The sun shines brighter when sunspots first appear.

   C. Magnetic activity increases the sun's temperature.

   D. Air pressure in the Earth's atmosphere falls.

GO ON TO THE NEXT PAGE

36. The shift in the direction of stratospheric winds that occurs every two years is known as:

    F. a facula.

    G. the solar flux.

    H. North Atlantic storms.

    J. the quasi-biennial oscillation.

37. Which of the following best summarizes the main point of the last paragraph?

    A. Scientists will soon be in a position to accurately predict the Earth's weather.

    B. Many findings of the *Solar Maximum Mission* cannot yet be explained.

    C. The relationship between the solar cycle and the Earth's weather may become clear with further research.

    D. Scientists disagree as to whether studying sunspots will ever have any practical value.

38. According to the passage, changes in the solar cycle may influence the Earth's weather in which of the following ways?

    I.   Changing the direction of stratospheric winds

    II. Altering temperature and pressure levels

    III. Influencing the latitude of storms

    F. I only

    G. I and II only

    H. II and III only

    J. I, II, and III

39. From the information in the first paragraph, it may be inferred that scientists now consider a correlation between the solar cycle and droughts in the American Midwest to be:

    A. probable.

    B. unlikely.

    C. confusing.

    D. useful.

40. According to the passage, which of the following statements best describes the current understanding of the relationship between sunspot activity and solar luminosity?

    F. At the peak of sunspot activity, the solar constant decreases in magnitude.

    G. At the peak of sunspot activity, the solar constant increases in magnitude.

    H. At the low point of sunspot activity, the sun is 0.1 percent brighter than it is at the peak of such activity.

    J. Scientists have yet to demonstrate a relationship between the two phenomena.

SCIENCE TEST

35 Minutes—40 Questions

Directions: There are seven passages in this test. Each passage is followed by several questions. After reading a passage, choose the best answer to each question and fill in the corresponding oval on your answer document. You may refer to the passages as often as necessary. You are NOT permitted to use a calculator on this test.

PASSAGE I

Acid-base indicators are used to determine changes in pH. The pH is a quantitative measure of the hydrogen ion concentration of a solution. For any solution, the pH ranges from 0 to 14. An acid-base indicator is a weak acid or base that is sensitive to the hydrogen ion concentration and changes color at a known pH. At any other pH, the acid-base indicator is clear.

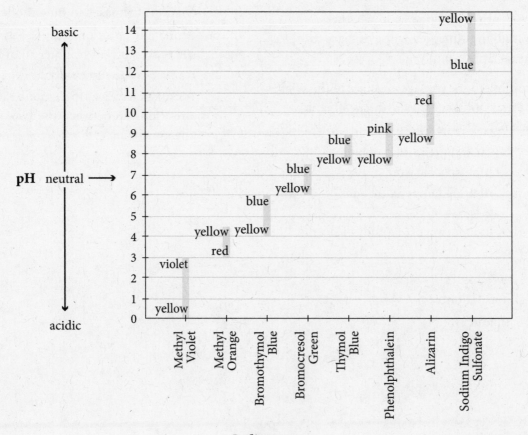

Indicators

GO ON TO THE NEXT PAGE

1. Which indicators undergo a color change in the region from pH 8 to pH 12?

   A. Bromocresol green, bromothymol blue, and thymol blue

   B. Thymol blue, phenolphthalein, and alizarin

   C. Phenolphthalein, alizarin, and sodium indigo sulfonate

   D. Phenolphthalein and bromothymol blue

2. Which of the following indicators undergoes a red-to-yellow or yellow-to-red color change?

      I. Alizarin
     II. Thymol blue
    III. Methyl orange

   F. I only

   G. II only

   H. I and III only

   J. I, II, and III

3. A chemist is running an experiment in a solution that becomes basic upon completion. According to the diagram, the reaction is complete when:

   A. the addition of bromocresol green results in a blue color.

   B. any indicator turns violet.

   C. a white solid appears.

   D. the addition of bromothymol blue results in a blue color.

4. Which of the following hypotheses is consistent with the information in the passage and the diagram?

   F. Color changes for any given acid-base indicator occur in a solution with a pH less than 7.

   G. Color changes for any given acid-base indicator occur in a solution with a pH greater than 7.

   H. Color changes for acid-base indicators always occur within the same pH range.

   J. Color changes for acid-base indicators vary within the pH range.

5. Compared to bromothymol blue, phenolphthalein undergoes a color change at:

   A. a higher pH.

   B. a lower pH.

   C. the same pH.

   D. Cannot be determined from the data provided.

GO ON TO THE NEXT PAGE

PASSAGE II

The Brazilian tree frog (*Hyla faber*) exchanges gases through both its skin and lungs. The exchange rate depends on the temperature of the frog's environment. A series of experiments was performed to investigate this dependence.

EXPERIMENT 1

Fifty frogs were placed in a controlled atmosphere that, with the exception of temperature, was designed to simulate their native habitat. The temperature was varied from 5°C to 25°C, and equilibrium was attained before each successive temperature change. The amount of oxygen absorbed by the frogs' lungs and skin per hour was measured, and the results for all the frogs were averaged. The results are shown in Table 1.

Table 1

Temperature (°C)	Moles O_2 absorbed/hr	
	Skin	Lungs
5	15.4	8.3
10	22.7	35.1
15	43.6	64.9
20	42.1	73.5
25	40.4	78.7

EXPERIMENT 2

The same frogs were placed under the same conditions as in Experiment 1. For this experiment, the amount of carbon dioxide eliminated through the skin and lungs was measured. The results are averaged and given in Table 2.

Table 2

Temperature (°C)	Moles O_2 absorbed/hr	
	Skin	Lungs
5	18.9	2.1
10	43.8	12.7
15	79.2	21.3
20	91.6	21.9
25	96.5	21.4

6. The results of Experiment 1 suggest that the total amount of O_2 absorbed per hour is:

   F. affected by the temperature.

   G. independent of the temperature.

   H. an indication of how healthy a Brazilian tree frog is.

   J. always less than the total amount of CO_2 eliminated per hour.

7. According to Experiment 2, the total amount of CO_2 eliminated per hour at 17°C is closest to:

   A. 21 mol/hr.

   B. 85 mol/hr.

   C. 106 mol/hr.

   D. 115 mol/hr.

8. Ectotherms are animals whose bodily functions are affected by the temperature of their environment. Which of the following results supports the conclusion that *Hyla fabers* is an ectotherm?

   F. The oxygen absorbed at 25°C

   G. The carbon dioxide released by the lungs

   H. The oxygen absorbed over the entire temperature range

   J. The results do not support this conclusion.

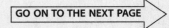

GO ON TO THE NEXT PAGE

9. According to the results of Experiment 2, which of the following plots best represents the amount of carbon dioxide eliminated through the skin and lungs as a function of temperature?

A.

B.

C.

D.

10. On the basis of the experimental results, one could conclude that as temperature increases:

F. O_2 absorbed by the lungs increases and CO_2 released by the skin decreases.

G. O_2 absorbed by the lungs increases and CO_2 released by the skin increases.

H. O_2 absorbed by the lungs decreases and CO_2 released by the lungs increases.

J. O_2 absorbed by the lungs decreases and CO_2 released by the lungs decreases.

11. According to the results of these experiments, as the temperature rises above 15°C, which of the following phenomena can be observed?

A. The Brazilian tree frog's ability to absorb oxygen through the skin decreases, as does its ability to release carbon dioxide through the lungs.

B. The Brazilian tree frog's ability to absorb oxygen through the skin decreases, while its ability to release carbon dioxide through the lungs remains about the same.

C. The Brazilian tree frog's ability to absorb oxygen through the skin remains about the same, as does its ability to release carbon dioxide through the lungs.

D. The Brazilian tree frog's ability to absorb oxygen through the skin increases, while its ability to release carbon dioxide through the lungs remains about the same.

PASSAGE III

A scientist wants to use a certain organic reagent to develop a means of extracting valuable elements from radioactive nuclear power plant effluent. Using the organic reagent, she measured extraction curves for six different elements: tungsten (W), molybdenum (Mo), ytterbium (Yb), erbium (Er), thulium (Tm), and europium (Eu).

12. At which pH level is the organic reagent most effective in extracting molybdenum?

    F. 3
    G. 4
    H. 5
    J. 6

13. The engineers who run a power plant that ejects waste with high levels of erbium and tungsten isotopes would like to extract as much of both elements as possible. Assuming a single-step extraction, this could be accomplished by using the organic reagent at a pH of:

    A. less than 1.5 or greater than 5.5.
    B. 4.
    C. 4.6.
    D. It is impossible to extract large amounts of both elements using the reagent at any pH.

14. Based on the data given, which of the following conclusions can be drawn about the effect of pH on the percentage extracted?

    F. The percentage of an element extracted increases as pH increases.
    G. The percentage of an element extracted decreases as pH increases.
    H. The percentage of an element extracted is independent of pH.
    J. The effect of pH is different for different elements.

15. The researcher was able to extract 45% of the thulium from the plant's effluent. The pH level of the organic reagent was most likely between:

    A. 4 and 5.
    B. 5 and 6.
    C. 6 and 7.
    D. 7 and 8.

16. If erbium is among the elements being extracted by the organic reagent at a certain pH, which of the following cannot be among the other elements being extracted?

    F. Europium
    G. Thulium
    H. Molybdenum
    J. Ytterbium

GO ON TO THE NEXT PAGE →

PASSAGE IV

While the focus (point of origin) of most earthquakes lies less than 20 km below the Earth's surface, certain unusual seismographic readings indicate that some activity originates at considerably greater depths. Below, two scientists discuss the possible causes of deep-focus earthquakes.

SCIENTIST 1

Surface earthquakes occur when rock in the Earth's crust fractures to relieve stress. However, below 50 km, rock is under too much pressure to fracture normally. Deep-focus earthquakes are caused by the pressure of fluids trapped in the Earth's tectonic plates. As a plate is forced down into the mantle by convection, increases in temperature and pressure cause changes in the crystalline structure of minerals such as serpentine. In adopting a denser configuration, the crystals dehydrate, releasing water. Other sources of fluid include water trapped in pockets of deep-sea trenches and carried down with the plates. Laboratory work has shown that fluids trapped in rock pores can cause rock to fail at lower shear stresses. In fact, at the Rocky Mountain Arsenal, the injection of fluid wastes into the ground accidentally induced a series of shallow-focus earthquakes.

SCIENTIST 2

Deep-focus earthquakes cannot result from normal fractures because rock becomes ductile at the temperatures and pressures that exist at depths greater than 50 km. Furthermore, mantle rock below 300 km is probably totally dehydrated because of the extreme pressure. Therefore, trapped fluids could not cause quakes below that depth. A better explanation is that deep-focus quakes result from the slippage that occurs when rock in a descending tectonic plate undergoes a phase change in its crystalline structure along a thin plane parallel to a stress. Just such a phase change and resultant slippage can be produced

in the laboratory by compressing a slab of calcium magnesium silicate. The pattern of deep-quake activity supports this theory. In most seismic zones, the recorded incidence of deep-focus earthquakes corresponds to the depths at which phase changes are predicted to occur in mantle rock. For example, little or no phase change is thought to occur at 400 km, and indeed, earthquake activity at this level is negligible. Between 400 and 680 km, activity once again increases. Although seismologists initially believed that earthquakes could be generated at depths as low as 1,080 or 1,200 km, no foci have been confirmed below 700 km. No phase changes are predicted for mantle rock below 680 km.

17. Scientists 1 and 2 agree on which point?

   A. Deep-earthquake activity does not occur below 400 km.
   B. Fluid allows tectonic plates to slip past one another.
   C. Water can penetrate mantle rock.
   D. Rock below 50 km will not fracture normally.

18. Which of the following is evidence that would support Scientists 1's hypothesis?

   F. The discovery that water can be extracted from mantle-like rock at temperatures and pressures similar to those found below 300 km
   G. Seismographic indications that earthquakes occur 300 km below the surface of the Earth
   H. The discovery that phase changes occur in the mantle rock at depths of 1,080 km
   J. An earthquake underneath Los Angeles that was shown to have been caused by water trapped in sewer lines

GO ON TO THE NEXT PAGE

19. Both scientists assume that:

    A. deep-focus earthquakes are more common than surface earthquakes.

    B. trapped fluids cause surface earthquakes.

    C. the Earth's crust is composed of mobile tectonic plates.

    D. deep-focus earthquakes cannot be felt on the Earth's crust without special recording devices.

20. To best refute Scientist 2's hypothesis, Scientist 1 might:

    F. find evidence of other sources of underground water.

    G. record a deep-focus earthquake below 680 km.

    H. find a substance that doesn't undergo phase changes even at depths equivalent to 680 km.

    J. show that rock becomes ductile at depths of less than 50 km.

21. According to Scientist 1, the earthquake at Rocky Mountain Arsenal occurred because:

    A. serpentine or other minerals dehydrated and released water.

    B. fluid wastes injected into the ground compressed a thin slab of calcium magnesium silicate.

    C. fluid wastes injected into the ground flooded pockets of a deep-sea trench.

    D. fluid wastes injected into the ground lowered the shear stress failure point of the rock.

22. Scientist 2's hypothesis would be strengthened by evidence showing that:

    F. water evaporates at high temperatures and pressures.

    G. deep-focus earthquakes can occur at 680 km.

    H. stress has the same effect on mantle rock that it has on calcium magnesium silicate.

    J. water pockets exist at depths below 300 km.

23. According to Scientist 2, phase changes in the crystalline structure of a descending tectonic plate:

    A. occur only at the Earth's surface.

    B. are not possible.

    C. cause certain minerals to release water, which exerts pressure within the plate.

    D. cause slippage that directly results in an earthquake.

GO ON TO THE NEXT PAGE

PASSAGE V

Astronomers want to know the effects of atmospheric conditions on the impact of an asteroid-to-Earth collision. The most common hypothesis is that the presence of moisture in the Earth's atmosphere significantly reduces the hazardous effects of such a collision. One researcher has decided to create a laboratory model of the Earth. The researcher has the ability to control the amount of moisture surrounding the model. The researcher has also created models of asteroids at various sizes. The researcher will use a collision indicator (see table below) based on the Torino Scale to measure the results of two experiments.

Collision Indicator	
Torino Scale Collision Rating	**Impact Effect**
0 to 0.9	A collision capable of little destruction
1 to 3.9	A collision capable of localized destruction
4 to 6.9	A collision capable of regional destruction
7 to 10	A collision capable of global catastrophe

EXPERIMENT 1

The researcher simulated collisions on the Earth model with asteroid models equivalent to mass ranging from 1,000 kg to 1,000,000 kg. The controlled moisture level of the model Earth's atmosphere was 86%. The effects of the collisions were recorded and rated according to the collision indicator.

EXPERIMENT 2

The researcher simulated collisions on the Earth model with asteroid models equivalent to the same mass as in Experiment 1. The controlled moisture level of the model Earth's atmosphere in this experiment was 12%. The effects of the collisions were recorded and rated according to the collision indicator. The results of both experiments are shown in the graph.

24. How was the experimental design of Experiment 1 different from that of Experiment 2?

F. The impacts of more asteroids were measured.

G. The impacts of larger asteroids were measured.

H. There was more moisture in the atmosphere.

J. There was a different collision indicator.

25. If the atmospheric moisture in Experiment 2 was increased to 50%, the collision rating for an asteroid with a mass of 400,000 kg would most likely be between:

A. 2 and 3.

B. 4.5 and 5.5.

C. 6 and 7.

D. 9 and 10.

GO ON TO THE NEXT PAGE ⟶

26. Based on the experimental results, one can generalize that an increase of moisture in the atmosphere would:

    F. decrease the impact of an asteroid-to-Earth collision, regardless of the size of the asteroid.

    G. decrease the impact of an asteroid-to-Earth collision with asteroids under 700,000 kg.

    H. increase the impact of an asteroid-to-Earth collision, regardless of the size of the asteroid.

    J. increase the impact of an asteroid-to-Earth collision with asteroids under 700,000 kg.

27. In a simulated asteroid-to-Earth collision, a 400,000 kg asteroid received a collision rating of 4. The amount of moisture in the atmosphere was most likely closest to:

    A. 0%.

    B. 12%.

    C. 86%.

    D. 100%.

28. According to the researcher's model, a 100,000 kg asteroid colliding in an atmosphere with a moisture level of 12% would be likely to have the same impact as an asteroid colliding in an atmosphere with a moisture level of 86% with a size closest to which of the following?

    F. 50,000 kg

    G. 120,000 kg

    H. 270,000 kg

    J. 490,000 kg

29. To be minimally capable of regional destruction, an asteroid entering an atmosphere with a moisture level of 86% would have to be roughly what percent larger than an asteroid capable of the same level of destruction entering an atmosphere with a moisture level of 12%?

    A. 20%

    B. 70%

    C. 150%

    D. 220%

GO ON TO THE NEXT PAGE

PASSAGE VI

The electrical conductivity of a material determines how it will react to various temperature conditions in a consumer product. Product researchers need to know how a material will react in order to determine its safety for consumer use. The electrical conductivity of two different samples of a platinum dithiolate compound was measured from 10 K to 275 K. The results and general conductivity versus temperature plots for conductors and semiconductors are shown here.

30. For Sample HST-52, which of the following describes its behavior when the temperature is dropped from 200 K to 100 K?

    F. The sample remains a semiconductor.

    G. The sample remains a conductor.

    H. The sample undergoes a conductor to semiconductor transition.

    J. The sample undergoes a semiconductor to conductor transition.

31. In a material exhibiting conductor-like behavior, the conductivity:

    A. increases as the temperature increases.

    B. decreases as the temperature increases.

    C. decreases as the temperature decreases.

    D. remains the same at all temperatures.

GO ON TO THE NEXT PAGE

32. A newly developed material has a semiconductor to conductor transition at about 10 K as the temperature increases. Its conductivity versus temperature plot would resemble which of the following?

    F.

    G.

    H.

    J.

33. An industrial firm wishes to use HST-52 as a semiconductor in an assembly line component. The experimental results indicate that:

    A. HST-52 is not a semiconductor; a new material will have to be chosen.

    B. HST-52 is suitable for the planned application.

    C. HST-52 is too brittle to be used in this manner.

    D. HST-52 will be usable only if the assembly line is maintained at less than 150 K.

34. The temperature at which a compound's conductivity-versus-temperature plot declines most quickly is known as its "optimal conductor" temperature. Which of the following could be the optimal conductor temperature for Sample HST-52?

    F. 20 K

    G. 80 K

    H. 160 K

    J. 180 K

PASSAGE VII

Siamese cats have a genotype for dark fur, but the enzymes that produce the dark coloring function best at temperatures below the cat's normal body temperature. A Siamese cat usually has darker fur on its ears, nose, paws, and tail, because these parts have a lower temperature than the rest of its body. If a Siamese cat spends more than one hour a day for six consecutive days outdoors (an "outdoor" cat) during very cold weather, darker fur grows in other places on its body. If a Siamese cat does not spend this amount of time outdoors, it is an "indoor" cat. The amount of dark fur on its body remains constant throughout the year.

35. According to the graph, if the average temperature outdoors drops from 2°C to 0°C over the course of a month, what will most likely happen to the fur of an outdoor Siamese cat during the same time period? Over that time, the percentage of the cat's body covered in dark fur will:

    A. increase.

    B. decrease.

    C. remain the same.

    D. increase, then decrease.

36. A particular Siamese cat goes outdoors a total of three hours per week during the coldest part of the year. One could predict that the percentage of its body covered by dark fur would be closest to:

    F. 0%.

    G. 10%.

    H. 40%.

    J. 60%.

37. According to the graph, what is the most likely temperature outside if outdoor Siamese cats have 45% of their bodies covered in dark fur?

    A. 0°C

    B. 3°C

    C. 6°C

    D. 9°C

38. If a Siamese cat that lived indoors was lost and later found with dark fur over 30% of its body, which of the following could be inferred about the period during which it was missing:

    I. It was living in an area where temperatures fell below 5°C.

    II. It spent more time outdoors than indoors.

    III. It was missing for at least six days.

    F. I and II only

    G. I and III only

    H. II and III only

    J. I, II, and III

GO ON TO THE NEXT PAGE

39. If a Siamese cat has dark fur over 10% of its body, which of the following must be true about the cat?

   A. It lives indoors.

   B. It lives in an area where the temperature outdoors is usually 7°C or higher.

   C. It either lives indoors or it lives in an area where the temperature outdoors is usually 7°C or higher.

   D. None of the above

40. If a researcher wants to find out how fur color is affected by the amount of time a Siamese cat spends outside in cold weather, which experiment would be the most helpful?

   F. The indoor cats in the original experiment should be used as the control group, and their fur color should be compared to a group of Siamese cats spending six hours or more a day outside in cold weather for six consecutive days.

   G. A new group of Siamese cats should be formed and kept outside two or more hours a day at varying temperatures. Their fur color at different outdoor temperatures should be compared to the outdoor cats already charted.

   H. Siamese cats should be split into two groups, one group spending only one hour per day outside for six consecutive days in cold weather and the other group spending at least two hours a day outside for six consecutive days in the same weather.

   J. No new experiment is needed. The data already gathered shows that the more time a Siamese cat spends outside in cold weather, the darker its fur will be.

WRITING TEST

30 Minutes—1 Question

Directions: This is a test of your writing skills. You will have thirty (30) minutes to write an essay in English. Before you begin planning and writing your essay, read the writing prompt carefully to understand exactly what you are being asked to do. Your essay will be evaluated on the evidence it provides of your ability to express judgments by taking a position on the issue in the writing prompt; to maintain a focus on the topic throughout the essay; to develop a position by using logical reasoning and by supporting your ideas; to organize ideas in a logical way; and to use language clearly and effectively according to the conventions of standard written English.

You may use the unlined pages in this test booklet to plan your essay. These pages will not be scored. *You must write your essay in pencil on the lined pages in the answer folder.* Your writing on those lined pages will be scored. You may not need all the lined pages, but to ensure you have enough room to finish, do NOT skip lines. You may write corrections or additions neatly between the lines of your essay, but do NOT write in the margins of the lined pages. *Illegible essays cannot be scored, so you must write (or print) clearly.*

If you finish before time is called, you may review your work. Lay your pencil down immediately when time is called.

DO NOT OPEN THIS BOOKLET UNTIL TOLD TO DO SO.

ACT WRITING TEST PROMPT

School athletics has become increasingly competitive in recent years, as professional athletes are drafted at younger ages and the money and fame that professional athletes enjoy have risen to astronomical levels. Some students and school administrators believe that all student athletes should be required to maintain a minimum grade point average or be barred from playing, to ensure that they still get a good education. Others believe this requirement would be unfair because athletics and academics are unrelated and because such a rule would make it too difficult for coaches to do their jobs. In your opinion, should student athletes be required to maintain a minimum grade point average?

In your essay, take a position on this question. You may write about either one of the two points of view given, or you may present a different point of view on this question. Use specific reasons and examples to support your position.

Use this space to *plan* your essay. Your work here will not be graded. Write your essay on the lined pages that follow.

_____

_____

_____

_____

_____

_____

_____

_____

_____

_____

_____

_____

_____

_____

_____

_____

_____

_____

_____

_____

_____

_____

_____

_____

_____

Practice Test Two
ANSWER KEY

ENGLISH TEST

1. D	11. A	21. B	31. A	41. C	51. B	61. B	71. B
2. G	12. J	22. J	32. J	42. J	52. J	62. F	72. F
3. C	13. A	23. B	33. B	43. A	53. C	63. D	73. B
4. J	14. F	24. F	34. H	44. J	54. J	64. G	74. J
5. B	15. D	25. C	35. A	45. D	55. C	65. B	75. B
6. G	16. G	26. J	36. H	46. H	56. J	66. F	
7. D	17. A	27. B	37. B	47. A	57. C	67. C	
8. J	18. J	28. G	38. J	48. G	58. F	68. H	
9. B	19. C	29. C	39. A	49. B	59. D	69. B	
10. H	20. F	30. F	40. G	50. G	60. F	70. J	

MATH TEST

1. A	9. D	17. E	25. C	33. B	41. B	49. C	57. B
2. J	10. F	18. K	26. J	34. K	42. H	50. F	58. J
3. A	11. B	19. D	27. C	35. D	43. E	51. C	59. C
4. G	12. G	20. G	28. H	36. K	44. K	52. F	60. J
5. B	13. D	21. E	29. D	37. B	45. E	53. B	
6. H	14. G	22. H	30. H	38. F	46. K	54. J	
7. C	15. D	23. A	31. A	39. A	47. E	55. E	
8. J	16. F	24. G	32. F	40. K	48. G	56. G	

READING TEST

1. D	6. G	11. B	16. G	21. A	26. J	31. B	36. J
2. G	7. C	12. J	17. C	22. J	27. C	32. G	37. C
3. B	8. J	13. C	18. G	23. D	28. G	33. B	38. H
4. G	9. C	14. G	19. D	24. H	29. B	34. J	39. A
5. C	10. G	15. A	20. F	25. D	30. F	35. A	40. G

SCIENCE TEST

1. B	6. F	11. B	16. J	21. D	26. G	31. B	36. G
2. H	7. C	12. F	17. D	22. H	27. C	32. H	37. B
3. A	8. H	13. D	18. F	23. D	28. H	33. D	38. G
4. J	9. B	14. J	19. C	24. H	29. B	34. J	39. C
5. A	10. G	15. B	20. G	25. B	30. H	35. C	40. H

ANSWERS AND EXPLANATIONS

ENGLISH TEST

PASSAGE I

1. D
Punctuation
A comma is needed to set off the introductory phrase, so (A) cannot be correct. Choice (B) creates a sentence fragment, and the pronoun *it* in (C) does not match the subject of the sentence—Duke Ellington.

2. G
Verb Tenses
The whole passage is in past tense, and there is no reason why this verb should not be in past tense as well. Also, the part of the sentence on the other side of the semicolon gives you a big clue by using *paid*.

3. C
Punctuation
The colon is used incorrectly in the original sentence, and (B) does not solve the problem. Choice (D) is unnecessarily wordy.

4. J
Punctuation
Commas are needed between items in a series, so eliminate (F) and (G). A comma is also needed to set off the introductory phrase, so eliminate choice (H).

5. B
Word Choice
In order to figure out the appropriate pronoun, identify the noun to which the pronoun refers. The only possible corresponding noun is *Ellington*; therefore, (B) is the correct answer.

6. G
Sentence Sense
"As a teenager in Washington" is not a complete sentence. Choice (H) does not make sense, and (J) is incorrect because the comma is unnecessary.

7. D
Word Choice
The word *then* should be *than*—(D) is the choice that makes this correction.

8. J
Wordiness
Even though the piano teacher's name is mentioned in the preceding sentence, more information about her name is unnecessary to make the sentence relevant to the passage.

9. B
Connections
There is a contrast between Ellington's not being a good pianist and his hearing about the opportunities for musicians in New York. The correct contrast is established by (B).

10. H
Wordiness
Awaited and *were there for* mean the same thing, so one part of the underlined portion should be deleted—that eliminates (F) and (G). Choice (J) is also unnecessarily wordy.

11. A
Sentence Sense
The sentence is logical in the flow of the paragraph, so eliminate (D). The paragraph discusses Ellington's move to Harlem, and the *they* in the next sentence indicates Ellington wasn't alone. Choice (A) is the simplest and most correct way to phrase the sentence.

12. J
Word Choice
The subject of the sentence is the Cotton Club, so choices with the pronoun *he*—(F) and (G)—should be eliminated. Choice (H) creates a sentence fragment.

13. A
Writing Strategy
This list of songs follows a description of Ellington's early musical career, so (A) is correct. The songs do not contradict anything, so eliminate (B). The names of the songs themselves do not illustrate complexity; therefore, (C) is incorrect. This part of the paragraph is no longer about the Cotton Club, so eliminate (D).

14. F
Writing Strategy
The last paragraph of the essay lists the accomplishments of Ellington. Choice (F) is the only answer choice that makes sense.

15. D
Organization
Paragraph 4 is the only paragraph that covers elements of Ellington's music. The logical place for the insertion is before the last sentence of the essay where his musical ability is discussed.

PASSAGE II

16. G
Word Choice
The subject is *animals*, so a plural pronoun is needed. Choice (F) is a singular pronoun, (H) is a contraction, and (J) uses *there* instead of *their*.

17. A
Punctuation
The comma is needed to set off the second clause from the first, so eliminate (B) and (D). Choice (C) incorrectly uses a colon.

18. J
Punctuation
The phrase "a member of the weasel family" is a nonessential clause and should be set off by commas. Eliminate (G) and (H) because they create sentence fragments.

19. C
Verb Tenses
"Having changed" is the incorrect verb tense. Ermines are nonhuman, so (B) is incorrect; (C) uses *that* correctly. The whole passage is in present tense, so eliminate (D) because it is in past tense.

20. F
Sentence Sense
Choose the most logical order of the words. Choice (F) is the choice that makes the most sense.

21. B
Punctuation
"Far from placing it in danger" is an introductory phrase and should be set off by a comma. Eliminate (A) and (C). Choice (D) is unnecessarily wordy and doesn't make sense with the rest of the sentence.

22. J
Wordiness
"By distinguishing itself from other animals" is a sentence fragment. These words make sense as an introductory phrase and should therefore be set off by a comma. Choice (J) is the only choice that accomplishes this concisely.

23. B
Wordiness
The unnecessary phrase "the question is" should be eliminated. Choice (B) is the simplest and most correct way to phrase the question.

24. F
Verb Tenses
The investigating has occurred in the past, and it is still occurring. The tense of the answer choice should be present perfect. Choices (G) and (H) only refer to the past, and (J) refers only to the present.

25. C
Connections
The previous sentence speaks of special glands, but this sentence says that some animals do not have these glands. This is a contrast, and *however* sets it up best.

26. J
Wordiness
Remains and *endures as* are the same thing, so the correct choice will eliminate one of them. Choice (J) does just that.

27. B
Word Choice
The pronoun *it* refers to the tree frog, not a background of leaves. Choice (B) fixes this modifier error by placing "the tree frog" after the modifying phrase.

28. G
Wordiness
The information pertains to the paragraph's topic, so eliminate (J). Choice (G) is a simple and logical way of rephrasing all of the excess words.

29. C
Organization
Paragraph 4 begins with an introduction, and paragraph 3 ends with a conclusion. Choice (C) is the only choice that features this correct order.

30. F
Writing Strategy
The author covers a range of topics in the area and uses several animals as examples. All of the other answer choices are incorrect because they contradict things that the author does in the essay.

PASSAGE III

31. A
Wordiness
The other answer choices are unnecessarily wordy.

32. J
Wordiness
The other answer choices are unnecessarily wordy.

33. B
Sentence Sense
The sentences on both sides of the period are fragments. The best way to fix this mistake is to simply combine the sentences as choice (B) does.

34. H
Wordiness
Included and *held* relay the same information. Choice (H) deletes one of the unnecessary words.

35. A
Verb Tenses
The drink was unusual to the people who never experienced it before. In other words, the verb form should be past tense. Eliminate (B) and (C). Choice (D) does not make sense, so eliminate it.

36. H
Sentence Sense
"Over the next century" is an introductory phrase and should be set off by a comma. Choices (H) and (J) add the comma, but (J) also adds unnecessary words.

37. B
Writing Strategy
This description would provide some "color" to the essay. It would not weaken or contradict anything, so eliminate (A) and (C). It would not say anything

about the author's opinion of chocolate either, so eliminate (D).

38. J
Punctuation

Commas are needed between items in a series. Choice (G) is incorrect because there are too many commas.

39. A
Connections

The sentence provides an example of the uses of chocolate worldwide. Choices (B) and (C) set up an unwarranted contrast. Choice (D) is not a good transition between the two sentences.

40. G
Sentence Sense

The word *do* is unnecessary in the sentence, especially with the presence of *nonetheless*. Choice (G) is the most concise statement of the information.

41. C
Punctuation

The colon is not used properly here, so eliminate (A), (B), and (D).

42. J
Wordiness

Tea has nothing to do with the topic, so the sentence should be eliminated.

43. A
Word Choice

The research will be welcomed *by* people, not *to* or *with* them. Therefore, eliminate choices (B) and (D). "Us with a sweet tooth" does not make sense, so choice A is the correct answer.

44. J
Wordiness

Choices (F) and (G) do not make any sense at all. Between (H) and (J), the latter is the best style.

45. D
Writing Strategy

This essay is about only chocolate, and it does not cover any other culinary trends in history. Therefore, it would not meet the requirement.

PASSAGE IV

46. H
Word Choice

Here, the verb is being used as part of a modifying phrase. Choice (H) is idiomatically correct.

47. A
Punctuation

Commas are needed in a series, so eliminate (C). A colon is not appropriate; eliminate (B). Choice (D) incorrectly switches to the past tense.

48. G
Word Choice

The form needed is the possessive of *who*, so (G) is correct.

49. B
Verb Tenses

This sentence is part of a list of proposed "uniform of the future" developments. The other sentences in that list use the verbs *would be*, *would become*, and *would transmit*; the correct form is (B).

50. G
Punctuation

No commas are needed in a list of only two items.

51. B
Sentence Sense

Be wary of sentences that begin with *to*; they are often fragments like the one here. Choice (B) is the best and most concise way to combine the two parts of the sentence.

52. J
Wordiness
Two words in the underlined portion of the sentence have closely related meanings: *concealing* means "keeping from being observed" or "hiding," and *invisible* means "hidden" or "impossible to see." Because these words convey the same idea, this is a simple redundancy that can be fixed by eliminating one of the two words. Therefore, we can eliminate (F), (G), and (H) and select (J) as the answer.

53. C
Writing Strategy
To determine the U.S. Army's opinion of the Invisible Soldier program, look at the words used to introduce and describe it: the army has dreamed of such a program and invested in it. So the army attitude is positive; we can eliminate the negative word *skeptical* in (A) and the neutral words *curious* and *detailed* in (B) and (D), leaving *enthusiastic*, (C).

54. J
Writing Strategy
In context, this paragraph offers a specific example of the more general issues raised in paragraph 1.

55. C
Wordiness
Although the underlined segment is necessary, having *beginning* and *early stages* is redundant. Choice (C) is the most concise way to rephrase this.

56. J
Sentence Sense
As written, this is a run-on sentence, so eliminate (F). To correct it, the new clause should be made subordinate by replacing the pronoun with a relative pronoun, so eliminate (H). The correct form, since it follows a comma, is *which* rather than *that*, so eliminate (G).

57. C
Word Choice
The passage has a formal, technical tone. It would, therefore, be inappropriate for the author to use the highly informal expressions "you know, is" or "is, like" eliminate (A) and (B). The choice "however, is" is appropriate since this paragraph contrasts with the preceding one. Choice (D) would be appropriate if this paragraph drew a conclusion based on the prior paragraph, but it doesn't.

58. F
Punctuation
A colon is correct punctuation here because the material that follows it is an explanation of what precedes it.

59. D
Organization
Only sentence 2 and sentence 1 are choices for a first sentence. To put the sentences in logical order, first look for a good transition from paragraph 4, which discusses a problem. Sentence 1 explicitly refers to addressing the problem, so it's the better choice. Eliminate (A) and (B). The second sentence should follow logically from sentence 1's description of the new color-changing pixel, and our choices are sentences 4 and 5. Sentence 4 in (C) refers to mirrors, which we haven't encountered before in the passage, rather than pixels, so we can eliminate this choice. That leaves us with (D), sentence 5, which refers to the pixels introduced in the first sentence.

60. F
Organization
To answer this question, we need an idea of the purpose of each paragraph. Paragraph 1 introduces the "uniform of the future," paragraph 2 the Invisible Soldier program, paragraph 3 the program's early-stage solution, paragraph 4 a problem with that solution, and paragraph 5 a new advance that may solve that problem. The new sentences to be inserted do not discuss a problem with such

a program. We can therefore eliminate (G), (H), and (J). The material properly belongs in paragraph 2, (F), because it introduces camouflage generally.

PASSAGE V

61. B
Sentence Sense

Choices (A) and (C) are too wordy, and (D) does not continue the verb tense established in the series.

62. F
Punctuation

The colon is used here to dramatically introduce California. The commas in (G) and (H) do not do this well, and the separate sentence in (J) does not work either.

63. D
Verb Tenses

This paragraph is in the past tense, so the introductory sentence should be in the past tense as well.

64. G
Punctuation

This is a long nonessential clause that should be set off by a comma—eliminate (F) and (H). Choice (J) is incorrect because it unnecessarily adds more words.

65. B
Sentence Sense

The word order is incorrect in (A). Choice (C) creates a sentence fragment, and *did* in (D) is unnecessary.

66. F
Wordiness

The information is pertinent to the topic, and (F) is the clearest way to express it.

67. C
Word Choice

The only choice that works here is (C), which uses the correct possessive form. *Their* would have also

worked, but it does not appear as one of the answer choices.

68. H
Sentence Sense

Choice (F) is a sentence fragment. Choice (G) and (J) are very awkward.

69. B
Writing Strategy

The last sentence of the previous paragraph talks about how workers began to quit their jobs to join the gold rush. The first sentence of this paragraph magnifies this point. Choice (B) is the only logical transition.

70. J
Wordiness

This information is not pertinent to the gold rush back in 1849.

71. B
Wordiness

Singularly and *one* are redundant. Choice (C) is too wordy, and (D) is incorrect within the context of the sentence.

72. F
Connections

This sentence is a more specific detail that illustrates the preceding sentence. Choice (F) is the best transition between the two sentences.

73. B
Word Choice

Choice (A) makes it sound as though lives are changing the place rather than the other way around. Choice (C) does not make sense, and (D) is grammatically incorrect.

74. J

Sentence Sense

Choices (F) and (H) do not make sense because of the word *and*. Choice (G) is incorrect because the sentence is talking about people today, not the Forty-niners.

75. B

Writing Strategy

Though the Forty-niners are mentioned, the focus of the essay is on the history of the California gold rush. Therefore, the essay would not meet the requirements of the assignment.

MATH TEST

Answer explanations for the Math test refer to 100 Key Math Concepts for the ACT, found inside Part 1.

1. A

Proportions and Probability

100 Key Math Concepts for the ACT, #33. To reduce a number by 20%, you could take 20% of the original number and subtract the result, or you could just take 80% of the original number:

New price = 80% of original price
$$= (0.80)(\$125)$$
$$= \$100$$

2. J

Variable Manipulation

100 Key Math Concepts for the ACT, #52. Plug in $x = -5$ and see what you get:

$$2x^2 - 6x + 5 = 2(-5)^2 - 6(-5) + 5$$
$$= 2 \times 25 - (-30) + 5$$
$$= 50 + 30 + 5$$
$$= 85$$

3. A

Number Properties

100 Key Math Concepts for the ACT, #11. The prime factorization of 36 is $2 \times 2 \times 3 \times 3$. That factorization includes two distinct prime factors, 2 and 3.

4. G

Plane Geometry

100 Key Math Concepts for the ACT, #81. The exterior angles of a triangle (or any polygon, for that matter) add up to 360°:

$$x + 85 + 160 = 360$$
$$x = 115$$

5. B

Number Properties

100 Key Math Concepts for the ACT, #41, #22. Don't jump to hasty conclusions—don't just average the denominators. Do it right—add the fractions and divide by 2:

$$\text{Average of two numbers} = \frac{\text{Sum}}{2}$$

$$\frac{\frac{1}{20} + \frac{1}{30}}{2} = \frac{\frac{3}{60} + \frac{2}{60}}{2} = \frac{\frac{5}{60}}{2} = \frac{\frac{1}{12}}{2} = \frac{1}{12} \times \frac{1}{2} = \frac{1}{24}$$

6. H

Variable Manipulation

100 Key Math Concepts for the ACT, #39. Everyone pays $1.50, and the rest of the toll is based on the number of miles traveled. Subtract $1.50 from Joy's toll to see how much is based on distance traveled: $25.00 − $1.50 = $23.50. Then divide that amount by 25 cents per mile:

$$\frac{\$23.50}{\$0.25 \, \text{per mile}} = 94 \, \text{mile}$$

7. C
Operations

100 Key Math Concepts for the ACT, #47, #55. Multiply the coefficients and add the exponents:

$$3x^2 \times 5x^3 = 3 \times 5 \times x^2 + x^3 = 15x^5$$

8. J
Coordinate Geometry

100 Key Math Concepts for the ACT, #71. You could use the distance formula, but it's easier here to think about a right triangle. One leg is the difference between the xs, which is 3, and the other leg is the difference between the ys, which is 4, so you're looking at a 3-4-5 triangle, and the hypotenuse, which is the distance from P to Q, is 5.

9. D
Proportions and Probability

100 Key Math Concepts for the ACT, #32. Percent times whole equals part:

$$(\text{Percent}) \times 25 = 16$$
$$\text{Percent} = \frac{16}{25} = 0.64 = 64\%$$

10. F
Proportions and Probability

100 Key Math Concepts for the ACT, #28. For $\frac{7}{x}$ to be greater than $\frac{1}{4}$, the denominator x has to be less than 4 times the numerator, or 28. And for $\frac{7}{x}$ to be less than $\frac{1}{3}$, the denominator x has to be greater than 3 times the numerator, or 21. Thus, x could be any of the integers 22 through 27, of which there are 6.

11. B
Variable Manipulation

100 Key Math Concepts for the ACT, #61. To factor $6x^2 - 13x + 6$, you need a pair of binomials whose "first" terms will give you a product of $6x^2$ and whose "last" terms will give you a product of 6. And

since the middle term of the result is negative, the two last terms must both be negative. You know that one of the factors is among the answer choices, so you can use them in your trial-and-error effort to factor. You know you're looking for a factor with a minus sign in it, so the answer's either choice (B) or (D).

Try choice (B) first: Its first term is $3x$, so the other factor's first term would have to be $2x$ (to get that $6x^2$ in the product). (B)'s last term is -2, so the other factor's last term would have to be -3. Check to see if $(3x - 2)(2x - 3)$ works:

$$(3x - 2)(2x - 3) = (3x \times 2x) + [3x\,(-3)] + [(-2)(2x)] + [(-2)(-3)]$$
$$= 6x^2 - 9x - 4x + 6$$
$$= 6x^2 - 13x + 6$$

It works. There's no need to check choice (D).

12. G
Variable Manipulation

100 Key Math Concepts for the ACT, #22. The four fractions on the left side of the equation are all ready to be added, because they already have a common denominator: a.

$$\frac{1}{a} + \frac{2}{a} + \frac{3}{a} + \frac{4}{a} = 5$$
$$\frac{1+2+3+4}{a} = 5$$
$$\frac{10}{a} = 5$$
$$10 = 5a$$
$$a = 2$$

13. D
Plane Geometry

100 Key Math Concepts for the ACT, #78. $\angle CGE$ and $\angle BGF$ are vertical angles, since $\angle BGF$ measures $105°$. If you subtract $\angle AGB$ from $\angle BGF$, you're left with $\angle AGF$, the angle you're looking for. So $\angle AGF$ measures $105° - 40°$, or $65°$.

14. G
Variable Manipulation

100 Key Math Concepts for the ACT, #69. You solve an inequality much the way you solve an equation: Do the same things to both sides until you've isolated what you're solving for. (Just remember to flip the sign if you ever multiply or divide both sides by a negative number.) Here, you want to isolate x:

$$-3 < 4x - 5$$
$$2 < 4x$$
$$\frac{2}{4} < x$$
$$x > \frac{1}{2}$$

15. D
Plane Geometry

100 Key Math Concepts for the ACT, #80, #81. Because BD bisects $\angle ABC$, the measure of $\angle ABD$ is 50°. Now you know two of the three angles of $\triangle ABD$, so the third angle measures $180° - 60° - 50° = 70°$.

$\angle BDC$, the angle you're looking for, is supplementary to the 70° angle, so $\angle BDC$ measures $180° - 70° = 110°$.

16. F
Variable Manipulation

100 Key Math Concepts for the ACT, #64, #58. To express y in terms of x, isolate y:

$$x + 2y - 3 = xy$$
$$2y - xy = -x + 3$$
$$y(2 - x) = 3 - x$$
$$y = \frac{3 - x}{2 - x}$$

17. E
Proportions and Probability

100 Key Math Concepts for the ACT, #31. If you add the number of English-speakers and the number of Spanish-speakers, you get $28 + 37 = 65$. But there are only 50 students, so $65 - 50 = 15$ of them are being counted twice—because those 15 speak both languages.

18. K
Proportions and Probability

100 Key Math Concepts for the ACT, #39. Set up a proportion:

$$\frac{288 \text{ miles}}{6 \text{ hours}} = \frac{x \text{ miles}}{8 \text{ hours}}$$
$$6x = 288 \times 8$$
$$6x = 2{,}304$$
$$x = 384$$

19. D
Number Properties

100 Key Math Concepts for the ACT, #30. To convert a fraction to a decimal, you divide the denominator into the numerator. Clearly, you don't have time to take the division out to 100 places after the decimal point. There must be a pattern you can take advantage of. Start dividing and continue just until you see what the pattern is:

$$11\overline{)4.000000\ldots} = .363636\ldots$$

The 1st, 3rd, 5th, etc. digits are 3; and the 2nd, 4th, etc. digits are 6. In other words, every odd-numbered digit is a 3 and every even-numbered digit is a 6. The 100th digit is an even-numbered digit, so it's a 6.

20. G
Variable Manipulations

100 Key Math Concepts for the ACT, #67. Since it's x you're looking for, eliminate y. Fortunately, the equations are all ready for you—just add them and the $+ 4y$ cancels with the $- 4y$:

$$3x + 4y = 31$$
$$3x - 4y = -1$$
$$6x = 30$$
$$x = 5$$

21. E
Coordinate Geometry

100 Key Math Concepts for the ACT, #71. The coordinates of the midpoint are the averages of the coordinates of the endpoints. The average of the x's is $\frac{2+12}{2} = 7$, and the average of the y's is $\frac{3+(-15)}{2} = -6$, so the coordinates of the midpoint are $(7, -6)$.

22. H
Trigonometry

100 Key Math Concepts for the ACT, #96. Cosine is "adjacent over hypotenuse." Here, the leg adjacent to θ is 4 and the hypotenuse is 5, so $\cos\theta = \frac{4}{5}$.

23. A
Plane Geometry

100 Key Math Concepts for the ACT, #89. The center of Q is on P's circumference, and the radius of circle Q is twice the radius of circle P. You could use the circumference of circle P to find the radius of circle P, then double that radius to get the radius of circle Q, and finally use that radius to calculate the circumference of circle Q. It's much easier and faster, however, if you realize that "double the radius means double the circumference." If the circumference of circle P is 6, then the circumference of circle Q is twice that, or 12.

24. G
Variable Manipulation

100 Key Math Concepts for the ACT, #52. This looks like a functions question, but in fact it's just a "plug-in-the-number-and-see-what-you-get" question:

$$f(x) = x^3 - x^2 - x$$
$$f(-3) = (-3)^3 - (-3)^2 - (-3)$$
$$= -27 - 9 + 3$$
$$= -33$$

25. C
Plane Geometry

100 Key Math Concepts for the ACT, #3. If the two unknown side lengths are integers, and the sum of the two lengths has to be greater than 7, then the least amount the two unknown sides could add up to would be 8, which would make the perimeter $7 + 8 = 15$.

26. J
Variable Manipulation

100 Key Math Concepts for the ACT, #61. First factor out an x from each term, then factor what's left:

$$2x + 3x^2 + x^3 = x(2 + 3x + x^2)$$
$$= x(x^2 + 3x + 2)$$
$$= x(x + 1)(x + 2)$$

27. C
Operations

100 Key Math Concepts for the ACT, #62, #47, #48. Get rid of the parentheses in the denominator, and then cancel factors the numerator and denominator have in common:

$$\frac{x^2y^3z^4}{(xyz^2)^2} = \frac{x^2y^3z^4}{x^2y^2z^4} = \frac{x^2}{x^2} \cdot \frac{y^3}{y^2} \cdot \frac{z^4}{z^4} = y$$

28. H
Number Properties

100 Key Math Concepts for the ACT, #22, #29. Normally you would have a choice: either convert the fractions to decimals first and then add, or add the fractions first and then convert the sum to a decimal. In this case, however, both fractions would convert to endlessly repeating decimals, which might be a bit unwieldy when adding. In this case, it seems to make sense to add first, then convert:

$$\frac{2}{3} + \frac{1}{12} = \frac{8}{12} + \frac{1}{12} = \frac{9}{12} = \frac{3}{4} = 0.75$$

29. D
Variable Manipulation

100 Key Math Concepts for the ACT, #63. This looks like a physics question, but in fact it's just a

"plug-in-the-number-and-see-what-you-get" question. Be sure you plug 95 in for C (not F):

$$C = \frac{5}{9}(F - 32)$$

$$95 = \frac{5}{9}(F - 32)$$

$$\frac{9}{5} \times 95 = F - 32$$

$$F - 32 = 171$$

$$F = 171 + 32 = 203$$

30. H
Proportions and Probability

100 Key Math Concepts for the ACT, #46. Probability equals the number of favorable outcomes divided by the total number of possible outcomes. In this problem, a favorable outcome is choosing a green marble—that's 4. The "total number of possible outcomes" is the total number of marbles, or 20:

$$\text{Probability} = \frac{\text{Favorable outcomes}}{\text{Total number of possible outcomes}}$$

$$= \frac{4}{20}$$

$$= \frac{1}{5}$$

31. A
Number Properties

100 Key Math Concepts for the ACT, #54, #41. To find the average of three numbers—even if they're algebraic expressions—add them and divide by 3:

$$\text{Average} = \frac{\text{Sum of terms}}{\text{Number of terms}}$$

$$= \frac{(2x + 5) + (5x - 6) + (-4x + 2)}{3}$$

$$= \frac{3x + 1}{3}$$

$$= x + \frac{1}{3}$$

32. F
Coordinate Geometry

100 Key Math Concepts for the ACT, #72. Parallel lines have the same slope. Use the first pair of points to figure out the slope:

$$\text{Slope} = \frac{y_2 - y_1}{x_2 - x_1} = \frac{16 - 1}{2 - 1} = 15$$

Then use the slope to figure out the missing coordinate in the second pair of points:

$$\text{Slope} = \frac{y_2 - y_1}{x_2 - x_1}$$

$$15 = \frac{(25 - (-5))}{a - (-10)}$$

$$15 = \frac{30}{a + 10}$$

$$15a + 150 = 30$$

$$15a = -120$$

$$a = -8$$

33. B
Plane Geometry

100 Key Math Concepts for the ACT, #82. When parallel lines make a big triangle and a little triangle as they do here, the triangles are similar (because they have the same angle measurements). Side $\overline{PR}$ is three times the length of $\overline{QR}$, so each side of the big triangle is three times the length of the corresponding side of the smaller triangle, and therefore the ratio of the perimeters is also 3:1. So the perimeter of $\triangle PRT$ is 3 times 11, or 33.

34. K
Plane Geometry

100 Key Math Concepts for the ACT, #86. It is a polygon because it's composed of straight line segments. It is a quadrilateral because it has four sides. It is not a rectangle because opposite sides are not equal. It is a trapezoid because it has one pair of parallel sides.

35. D
Variable Manipulation
100 Key Math Concepts for the ACT, #52, #63.

Plug in $x = -3$ and solve for a:

$$2x^2 + (a - 4)x - 2a = 0$$
$$2(-3)^2 + (a - 4)(-3) - 2a = 0$$
$$18 - 3a + 12 - 2a = 0$$
$$30 - 5a = 0$$
$$-5a = -30$$
$$a = 6$$

36. K
Proportions and Probability
100 Key Math Concepts for the ACT, #45. The total number of combinations of a first course, second course, and dessert is equal to the product of the three numbers:

$$\text{Total possibilities} = 4 \times 5 \times 3 = 60$$

37. B
Number Properties
100 Key Math Concepts for the ACT, #11, #14. An integer that's divisible by 6 has at least one 2 and one 3 in its prime factorization. An integer that's divisible by 9 has at least two 3s in its prime factorization. Therefore, an integer that's divisible by both 6 and 9 has at least one 2 and two 3s in its prime factorization. That means it's divisible by 2, 3, $2 \times 3 = 6$, $3 \times 3 = 9$, and $2 \times 3 \times 3 = 18$. It's not necessarily divisible by 12 or 36, each of which includes two 2s in its prime factorization. You could also do this one by Picking Numbers. Think of a common multiple of 6 and 9 and use it to eliminate some options. 6 $\times$ 9 = 54 is an obvious common multiple—and it's not divisible by 12 or 36, but it is divisible by 18. The *least* common multiple of 6 and 9 is 18, which is also divisible by 18. It looks like every common multiple of 6 and 9 is also a multiple of 18.

38. F
Variable Manipulation
100 Key Math Concepts for the ACT, #62.

$$\frac{x^2 + x^2 + x^2}{x^2} = \frac{3x^2}{x^2} = 3$$

39. A
Variable Manipulation
100 Key Math Concepts for the ACT, #65. Read carefully. This question's a lot easier than you might think. It's asking for the total number of coins, not the total value. q quarters, d dimes, and n nickels add up to a total of $q + d + n$ coins.

40. K
Variable Manipulation
100 Key Math Concepts for the ACT, #69, #70. You solve an inequality much the way you solve an equation: Do the same things to both sides until you've isolated what you're solving for. (Just remember to flip the sign if you ever multiply or divide both sides by a negative number.)

$$5x - 2(1 - x) \geq 4(x + 1)$$
$$5x - 2 + 2x \geq 4x + 4$$
$$5x + 2x - 4x \geq 4 + 2$$
$$3x \geq 6$$
$$x \geq 2$$

The "greater-than-or-equal-to" symbol is graphed as a solid circle.

41. B
Coordinate Geometry
100 Key Math Concepts for the ACT, #72. First find the slope of the line that contains the given points:

$$\text{Slope} = \frac{y_2 - y_1}{x_2 - x_1} = \frac{10 - 6}{6 - 5} = 4$$

Line m is perpendicular to the above line, so the slope of m is the negative reciprocal of 4, or $-\frac{1}{4}$

42. H
Trigonometry
100 Key Math Concepts for the ACT, #96. Sine is "opposite over hypotenuse." Here, the leg opposite θ is 12 and the hypotenuse is 13, so:

$$\sin \theta = \frac{12}{13}$$

43. E
Operations
100 Key Math Concepts for the ACT, #48, #63. Express the left side of the equation so that both sides have the same base:

$$9^{2x-1} = 3^{3x+3}$$
$$(3^2)^{2x-1} = 3^{3x+3}$$
$$3^{4x-2} = 3^{3x+3}$$

Now that the bases are the same, just set the exponents equal:

$$4x - 2 = 3x + 3$$
$$4x - 3x = 3 + 2$$
$$x = 5$$

44. K
Proportions and Probability
100 Key Math Concepts for the ACT, #35. Be careful with combined percent increase. You cannot just add the two percents, because they're generally percents of different wholes. In this instance, the 20% increase is based on the 1970 population, but the 30% increase is based on the larger 1980 population. If you just added 20% and 30% to get 50%, you fell into the test maker's trap.

The best way to do a problem like this one is to pick a number for the original whole and just see what happens. As usual, the best number to pick is 100. (That may be a small number for the population of a city, but verisimilitude is not important—all that matters is the math.)

If the 1970 population was 100, then a 20% increase would put the 1980 population at 120. Now, to figure the 30% increase, multiply 120 by 130%:

New # = (Original #) + (30% of Original #)
New # = 130% of Original #
$$x = 1.3(120)$$
$$= 156$$

Since the population went from 100 to 156, that's a 56% increase.

45. E
Number Properties
100 Key Math Concepts for the ACT, #44. The best way to deal with changing averages is to go by way of the sums. Use the old average to figure out the total of the first four scores:

Sum of first 4 scores = 4 × 89 = 356
And use the new average to figure out the total he needs after the fifth score:

Sum of five scores = 5 × 90 = 450
To get his sum up from 356 to 450, Martin needs to score 450 − 356 = 94.

46. K
Coordinate Geometry
100 Key Math Concepts for the ACT, #75. If you find the distance from the center to the given point on the circle, you'll have the radius. The difference between the x's is 8, and the difference between the y's is 6. If 8 and 6 are the lengths of the legs of a right triangle, then the hypotenuse is 10. The radius, then, is 10. Now you can plug the radius and the coordinates of the center point into the general form of the equation of a circle:

$$(x - h)^2 + (y - k)^2 = r^2$$
$$(x + 1)^2 + (y + 1)^2 = 10^2$$
$$(x + 1)^2 + (y + 1)^2 = 100$$

47. E
Coordinate Geometry
100 Key Math Concepts for the ACT, #72, #73, #74. In addition to picking coordinates from the line and plugging them into the answer choices, use the points where the line crosses the axes—(−1,0) and (0,2)—to find the slope:

$$\text{Slope} = \frac{y_2 - y_1}{x_2 - x_1} = \frac{2 - 0}{0 - (-1)} = 2$$

The y-intercept is 2. Now plug $m = 2$ and $b = 2$ into the slope-intercept equation form:

$$y = mx + b$$
$$y = 2x + 2$$

48. G
Proportions and Probability

100 Key Math Concepts for the ACT, #32. Be careful. The question is not asking, "What is $\frac{1}{4}$ of 16?" It's asking, "What is $\frac{1}{4}$% of 16?" One-fourth of 1% is 0.25%, or 0.0025:

$$\frac{1}{4}\% \text{ of } 16 = 0.0025 \times 16 = 0.04$$

49. C
Variable Manipulation

100 Key Math Concepts for the ACT, #56. Use FOIL to get rid of the parentheses, and then combine like terms:

$$(s+4)(s-4)+(2s+2)(s-2) = (s^2-16)+(2s^2-2s-4)$$
$$= s^2+2s^2-2s-16-4$$
$$= 3s^2-2s-20$$

50. F
Coordinate Geometry

100 Key Math Concepts for the ACT, #76, #52. The easiest way to find the equation of a given parabola is to take a point or two from the graph and plug the coordinates into the answer choices, eliminating the choices that don't work. Start with a point with coordinates that are easy to work with. Here, you could start with (3, 0). Plug $x = 3$ and $y = 0$ into each answer choice, and you'll find that only F works.

51. C
Trigonometry

100 Key Math Concepts for the ACT, #96. Since $\sin a = \frac{4}{5}$, you could think of this as a 3-4-5 triangle:

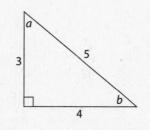

Cosine is "adjacent over hypotenuse." Here, the leg adjacent to b is 4, and the hypotenuse is 5, so $b = \frac{4}{5}$. (Notice that the sine of one acute angle in a right triangle is equal to the cosine of the other acute angle.)

52. F
Variable Manipulation

100 Key Math Concepts for the ACT, #53, #62. Add the like terms in the numerator and then divide by the denominator:

$$\frac{x^2+x^2+x^2}{x} = \frac{3x^2}{x} = 3x$$

If you weren't careful, you might have confused this with problem 38 and missed the change in the denominator.

53. B
Variable Manipulation

100 Key Math Concepts for the ACT, #65. When you divide w by 4, you get $\frac{w}{4}$. When you subtract that result from r, you get $r - \frac{w}{4}$.

54. J
Plane Geometry

100 Key Math Concepts for the ACT, #95. The formula for the volume of a cylinder is $V = \pi r^2 h$, where r is the radius of the circular base and h is the height. Here $r = 4$ and $h = 5$, so:

$$\text{Volume} = \pi r^2 h$$
$$= \pi(4)^2(5)$$

$$= \pi(16)(5)$$
$$= 80\pi$$

55. E
Plane Geometry

100 Key Math Concepts for the ACT, #83, #56. With a right triangle, you can use the two legs as the base and the height to figure out the area. Here, the leg lengths are expressed algebraically. Just plug the two expressions in for b and h in the triangle area formula:

$$\text{Area} = \frac{1}{2}(x-1)(x+1) = \frac{1}{2}(x^2 - 1) = \frac{x^2 - 1}{2}$$

56. G
Proportions and Probability

100 Key Math Concepts for the ACT, #39. The difference between the populations in 1990 was 9,400 − 7,600 = 1,800. Each year, as the larger population goes down by 100 and the smaller population goes up by 100, the difference decreases by 200. Thus, it will take 1,800 ÷ 200 = 9 years to erase the difference.

57. B
Number Properties

The overall average is not simply the average of the two average ages. Because there are a lot more women than men, women carry more weight, and the overall average will be closer to 25 than 35. Pick particular numbers for the females and males, say 4 females and 1 male. The ages of the 4 females total 4 times 25, or 100, and the age of the 1 male totals 35. The average, then, is (100 + 35) divided by 5, or 27.

58. J
Trigonometry

100 Key Math Concepts for the ACT #96, #84. The height h of the tree is the leg opposite θ. The distance b from the base of the tree is the leg adjacent to θ. "Opposite over adjacent" is tangent, but all the answer choices are in terms of the sine. Sine is "opposite over hypotenuse," so you're going to have to figure out the hypotenuse. Use the Pythagorean theorem:

$$(\text{hypotenuse})^2 = (\text{leg}_1)^2 + (\text{leg}_2)^2$$
$$(\text{hypotenuse})^2 = b^2 + h^2$$
$$\text{hypotenuse} = \sqrt{b^2 + h^2}$$

Now, to get the sine, put the opposite h over the hypotenuse $\sqrt{b^2 + h^2}$: $\sin\theta = \dfrac{h}{\sqrt{b^2 + h^2}}$

59. C
Variable Manipulation

100 Key Math Concepts for the ACT, #52. This looks like a solid geometry question, but in fact it's just a "plug-in-the-numbers" question:

$$S = \pi r \sqrt{r^2 + h^2} = \pi(3)\sqrt{3^2 + 4^2} = 3\pi\sqrt{9 + 16}$$
$$= 3\pi\sqrt{25} = 3\pi \times 5 = 15\pi$$

60. J
Plane Geometry

100 Key Math Concepts for the ACT, #79. When a transversal crosses parallel lines, all the resulting acute angles are equal and all the resulting obtuse angles are equal. (You can generally tell at sight which angles are equal.) In this problem's figure, $a = c = e = g$ and $b = d = f = h$. Only (J) is true: c and g are both obtuse. In all the other choices, you'll find an obtuse and an acute angle.

READING TEST

Reading questions can be divided into four basic types: Detail questions, Inference questions, Global questions, Vocab-in-Context questions, Writer's View questions, and Function questions. As you review the answers and explanations, note which types you tend to answer correctly or incorrectly and tailor your studying to focus on areas where you need improvement.

PASSAGE I

1. D
Detail
Lines 18–21 provide the answer: "I was brought up, from my earliest remembrance...by my god-mother."

2. G
Inference
From the description of Dolly in the first two paragraphs, it is clear that Esther viewed her doll as her only friend. "I was such a shy little thing that I seldom dared to open my lips, and never dared to open my heart, to anybody else" (lines 6–9). This idea is repeated in lines 97–101: "I went up to my room, and crept to bed, and laid my doll's cheek against mine wet with tears, and holding that solitary friend upon my bosom, cried myself to sleep."

3. B
Vocab-in-Context
In this case, *stiff* is used to describe the tone of the letter that Esther's godmother wrote to decline the invitation to another student's birthday party. Choice (B), "rigidly formal," is the most appropriate definition in this context.

4. G
Inference
This is a Global question. Esther mentions that her birthday was never celebrated and the pivotal scene in the passage happens on her birthday. In lines 3–4, Esther tells her doll that she is not very clever, but that is not the focus of the passage. In lines 54–57, she mentions being invited to a friend's home for a party so (H) is not correct. In lines 79–82, we find out that Esther's mother did not die on her birthday, so choice (J) is not correct.

5. C
Inference
Although Esther's godmother says that she has forgiven Esther's mother, her facial expression directly contradicts this. "I see her knitted brow and pointed finger...her face did not relent..." (lines 88–92).

6. G
Detail
Esther is clearly lonely, as evidenced by her description of Dolly as her only friend and her explanation that there is a separation dividing her from the other girls at school. The birthday scene with her godmother also shows that Esther is quite confused about her own family past.

7. C
Inference
Her confrontation with her godmother gives Esther further reason to believe that no one loves her. The phrase before the cited line also points to choice (C) as the best answer: "I knew that I had brought no joy at any time to anybody's heart" (lines 102–103).

8. J
Detail
Choices (F), (G), and (H) are all mentioned in paragraph 5 (lines 44–59). At the end of the passage, Esther says, "I hope it is not self-indulgent to shed these tears as I think of it" (lines 111–112).

9. C
Detail
Esther's evidence that her godmother is a "good, good woman" is explained in lines 22–27: "She went to church three times every Sunday, and to morning prayers on Wednesdays and Fridays, and to lectures whenever there were lectures, and never missed."

10. G
Detail
In the first paragraph, Esther says, "Now, Dolly, I am not clever..." (lines 3–4). In the second paragraph,

Esther describes herself as "such a shy little thing" (lines 6–7).

PASSAGE II

11. B
Vocab-in-Context
In the phrase "the Pantanal was a vast, soggy canvas, white with gleaming herds of Nelore cattle" (lines 73–75), *canvas* is used to mean "a background." None of the other choices makes sense.

12. J
Detail
The answer to this question can be found in lines 79–82: "As the jaguars grew scarce, their chief food staple, the capybaras—a meter-long rodent, the world's largest—overran farmers' fields…"

13. C
Detail
The answer to this question can be found in lines 15–20: "Exactly how dramatic a comeback is difficult to say because jaguars—*Panthera onca*, the largest feline in the New World—are solitary, secretive, nocturnal predators. Each cat needs to prowl at least 35 square kilometers by itself."

14. G
Inference
The last sentence of the second paragraph provides the answer. "Hotels, campgrounds, and bed-and-breakfasts have sprung up to accommodate the half-million tourists a year…bent on sampling the Pantanal's wildlife, of which the great cats must be the most magnificent example" (lines 28–34). Tourists want to see the jaguars, and not having the jaguars might negatively affect the booming ecotourist business.

15. A
Detail
The "green safari" example is mentioned as a way for "scientists to fit the cats with radio collars" (lines 103–105). The other three examples provided are listed in lines 110–114 as methods the scientists are teaching the ranchers.

16. G
Generalization
In lines 59–60, the author says, "Hard data on cattle losses due to jaguars in the Pantanal are nonexistent…" One reason for providing anecdotal information, then, is to tell the story of the hardships faced by the ranchers due to the jaguars. The author does not suggest that he empathizes with the ranchers more than the jaguars—in fact, he refers to the jaguars as "magnificent." The only example that shows rancher violence is Abel Monteiro shooting an attacking jaguar who had killed his two dogs (lines 43–47), an act of self-defense. The landscape of the Pantanal is not the focus of these two paragraphs, so choice (J) can be eliminated.

17. C
Inference
The passage explains that because of the decrease in the jaguar population, the capybara population increased. These rodents "spread trichomoniasis, a livestock disease that renders cows sterile" (lines 82–83). Lines 86–91 describe the effect of weather patterns and floods on the ranchers' land. "Weather patterns also shifted radically—due most likely to global warming—and drove annual floods to near-Biblical proportions. The waters are only now retreating from some inundated pasturelands."

18. G
Detail
The last sentence of the passage reads, "When the scholars go home and the greens log off, the *pantaneiros* will still be there—left on their own to deal with the jaguars as they see fit" (lines 117–120).

19. D

Detail

Evidence is given throughout the passage that all three groups support protecting the jaguars. It is most concisely stated in lines 49–53: "a political cat fight between the scientists, environmentalists, and ecotourists who want to protect the jaguars and the embattled ranchers…"

20. F

Detail

The answer to this question can be found in lines 59–61: "Hard data on cattle losses due to jaguars in the Pantanal are nonexistent, but there are stories."

PASSAGE III

21. A

Inference

This question asks you why the aulos was considered "the instrument of the Dionysians." In the fifth paragraph, you find out that the Dionysians "represented the unbridled, sensual and passionate aspect of Greek culture" (lines 65–67). The passage also says that the aulos had a "far more exciting effect" (lines 71–72) than the lyre. The suggestion here is clearly that the aulos must have been able to express the unbridled passion and excitement of the Dionysians, making choice (A) the best answer. Choice (B) is out because the fact that the aulos was chosen as the official instrument of the Delphian and Pythian festivals doesn't explain why it was the instrument of the Dionysians. Choice (C) contradicts the passage. The kithara, not the aulos, represented the intellectual, idealistic side of Greek art. Finally, the author never says when the Dionysian cult originated, so choice (D) is also out.

22. J

Detail

All the author means by saying that the chelys can be "traced back to the age of fable" is that it is an ancient instrument. The chelys was an actual, not an imaginary, instrument, so choice (H) is wrong. Choice (G) is out because the kithara was used to accompany the epics, not the chelys.

23. D

Generalization

Choice (D) is the only answer choice that adequately covers the entire passage. Choice (A) focuses only on the lyre. The connection between Greek music and drama, choice (B), is mentioned only in passing, as are the references to music in ancient Greek literature, choice (C). The passage is really all about the "origin and development of various Greek instruments," choice (D).

24. H

Detail

The first thing the author says about the kithara is that it was used by "professional Homeric singers" (lines 15–16). The kithara, according to the author, probably came from Egypt, so choice (F) is wrong. Choice (G) and (J) contradict information in the paragraph to the effect that the kithara was more powerful than the chelys and was played with both hands.

25. D

Detail

Skim through the third paragraph to find the changes that occurred to the lyre between the eighth and fifth centuries B.C. Musicians began to use a plectrum in the seventh century B.C., choice (A), lyres featured an increasing number of strings, choice (B), during this period, and musicians also began to use different scales and modes, choice (C). That leaves choice (D). Nothing in the paragraph indicates that lyres were used to accompany dramatic productions.

26. J

Inference

The final paragraph says that "an early specimen" of the aulos was tuned to the chromatic tetrachord, "a fact that points to Oriental origin" (line 87). From this, you can infer that the chromatic tetrachord must have been used in ancient Oriental music, choice (J). Choice (F) is contradicted by the author's assertion that elegiac songs were composed in the mode of the chromatic tetrachord. There is no evidence to support either choice (G) or (H).

27. C
Detail

In the fourth sentence of the first paragraph (lines 8–10), the author indicates that the chelys is the most antique form of the lyre.

28. G
Detail

Sappho did two things that we know about from lines 44–47. She introduced a mode "in which Dorian and Lydian characteristics were blended," and she "initiated the use of the plectrum."

29. B
Detail

All of the details you need to answer this question are in the sixth paragraph (lines 68–78). The first sentence states that the aulos is more like our oboe than our flute, so III is false. This means choices (C) and (D) can be eliminated. The second sentence of the paragraph confirms that the aulos sounded more exciting than the lyre (II). Since choice (B) is the only remaining answer choice that includes II, you know it has to be the best answer.

30. F
Generalization

Greek instruments are discussed as a whole at the very beginning of the passage. The author says that our knowledge of Greek instruments comes from "representations on monuments, vases, statues, and friezes and from the testimony of Greek authors" (lines 4–6). These are all "secondary sources" of information about the instruments, so choice (F) is the best answer. Choice (G) is wrong because quite a bit is known about the tuning of the instruments, as represented in the second paragraph. Choice (H) is contradicted by the same sentence that supports choice (F). Finally, there is no evidence to suggest that more is known about one type of instrument than the other, choice (J).

PASSAGE IV

31. B
Detail

Lines 17–20 state that "Scientists have not been able, however, to determine just how sunspots are created or what effect they have on the solar constant…" This is followed by the statement that the question might be answered with "data from the *Solar Maximum Mission* satellite, which has monitored the solar constant since 1980." (lines 23–25)

32. G
Vocab-in-Context

The definition of *solar constant* is given in lines 20–21: "a misnomer that refers to the sun's total radiance at any instant."

33. B
Generalization

The second sentence of the passage says, "people have speculated that the solar cycle might exert some influence on the Earth's weather" (lines 3–5). The concluding paragraph suggests that the findings discussed in the passage point to "a link between the solar cycle and weather" (lines 101–102).

34. J
Vocab-in-Context

From the sentence alone, it may be difficult to determine the answer. But the preceding sentence clarifies that *proliferated* means "increased in number."

35. A
Detail

The answer to this question can be found in lines 40–48: "When a sunspot appears, it initially causes the sun to dim slightly, but then after a period of weeks or months islands of brilliance called faculas usually emerge near the sunspot and more than compensate for its dimming effect. Willson says faculas may represent regions where energy that initially was blocked beneath a sunspot has finally breached the surface."

36. J
Detail

The answer to this question is found in lines 54–57: "the quasi-biennial oscillation (QBO), a 180-degree shift in the direction of stratospheric winds above the Tropics that occurs about every two years."

37. C
Generalization

The last paragraph quotes a scientist as believing that there will be "breakthroughs" (line 101) in our understanding of the relationship between the solar cycle and the weather.

38. H
Detail

As described in the passage, the QBO changes directions every two years independently of the solar cycle. Lines 71–74 state that: "temperatures and pressures coincident with the QBO's west phase rose and fell in accordance with the solar cycle." Lines 79–81 state that: "The latitude of storms during the west phase of the QBO…varied with the solar cycle…"

39. A
Inference

Lines 8–10 read: "Until recently, however, none of these correlations has held up under close scrutiny." This suggests that recently they have begun to hold up under scrutiny.

40. G
Detail

The answer to this question can be found in lines 30–33: "The data suggest that the sun is 0.1 percent more luminous at the peak of the solar cycle, when the number of sunspots is greatest…"

SCIENCE TEST

All Science questions will fall under one of the three SmartPoints: Figure questions, Pattern questions, and Scientific Reasoning questions.

PASSAGE I

1. B
Figure Interpretation

Look at the y-axis of the graph between the region of pH 8 and pH 12 and then scan across at that level. The indicators that undergo color change at this pH range are thymol blue, phenolphthalein, and alizarin. These indicators correspond to choice (B).

2. H
Figure Interpretation

Looking carefully at the graph, you can see that methyl orange changes from red to yellow between pH 3 and pH 5, and alizarin changes from yellow to red between pH 9 and pH 11. Thymol blue undergoes a yellow to blue color change, so it is not correct.

3. A
Patterns

In order to determine when the reaction is complete and the solution is basic, the chemist should select an indicator that turns color when the pH has risen into the region of basicity (above 7). When bromocresol green inches above the pH of 7, it turns blue, so choice (A) is correct.

4. J
Scientific Reasoning

This question requires you to make a broad conclusion about acid-base indicators. Choices (F) and (G) are incorrect because there are plenty of indicators that change colors above or below pH 7. Choice (H) is incorrect because different indicators change colors at different pH levels, which explains why choice (J) is correct.

5. A
Figure Interpretation

Compare the two indicators on the graph and you'll find that phenolphthalein undergoes a color change at a higher pH than bromothymol blue.

PASSAGE II

6. F
Figure Interpretation

The quickest way to answer the question is to eliminate the wrong answer choices. A look at Table 1 rules out choice (G) because the total amount of oxygen absorbed is clearly affected by temperature. Choice (H) is wrong because frog health is never an issue. The very mention of CO_2 makes choice (J) incorrect—Experiment 1 was only concerned with oxygen.

7. C
Patterns

There is no data for 17°C, so an estimate is necessary. The total (skin plus lungs) amount of carbon dioxide released per hour was about 100 mol/hr at 15°C and about 110 mol/hr at 20°C. The only choice that falls between these is choice (C).

8. H
Scientific Reasoning

To show that *Hyla faber* is an ectotherm, one must find evidence demonstrating that changes in temperature cause changes in gas exchange. Table 1 demonstrates that as temperature increases, *Hyla faber's* oxygen absorption increases, so (H) is correct.

Choice (F) is not good evidence because data for only one temperature does not give an idea of how temperature changes affect gas exchange. Choice (G) is incorrect because the amount of carbon dioxide eliminated by the lungs is the same for 15°C, 20°C, and 25°C, which makes it look as though changes in temperature have little effect on gas exchange in the frog.

9. B
Figure Interpretation

The amount of carbon dioxide eliminated by the skin increases over the range of temperatures; the increase levels off at the highest temperature. Carbon dioxide release by the lungs increases a bit over the lower temperatures and then levels off almost completely. The curve for skin release has to be much higher on the graph than the curve for lung release because the skin eliminated more carbon dioxide at each temperature than did the lungs. Choice (B) is the only graph that fits these patterns.

10. G
Patterns

When the answer choices all look similar like in this problem, find the differences between them and rule out the ones that cannot be correct. You can eliminate choice (H) and (J) right away because the results show that as temperature increases, O_2 absorbed by the lungs increases. Choice (F) is not correct either—as temperature increases, CO_2 released by the skin increases, which is stated by choice (G).

11. B
Figure Interpretation

Here again, you want to be careful and refer to the answer choices as you review the tables to observe what happens as the temperature rises above 15°C. Since each of the answer choices refers to the tree frog's ability to absorb oxygen through the skin, start there. From Table 1, you can see that the skin's oxygen absorption rate goes down, so choices (C) and (D) are out. Now you need to refer to Table 2 to see what happens to the rate at which carbon dioxide is released from the lungs. It appears to remain about the same, so the correct answer is choice (B).

PASSAGE III

12. F
Figure Interpretation

A good way to approach this question would be to draw a vertical line on the graph from 100% extraction of molybdenum (Mo) to the x-axis. This line lands closest to the pH of 3. Therefore, choice (F) is correct.

13. D
Figure Interpretation

To answer this question, you need to look at the extraction curves for both erbium and tungsten and observe how they change with pH. For tungsten, the percentage extracted decreases from 100% to 0% as the pH increases from 1 to 2. The percentage of erbium extracted increases from 0% to 100% as the pH increases from 4 to 6. There is no overlap between the two ranges. "A single-step extraction" could not remove both at the same time.

14. J
Figure Interpretation

In the graph, there are two types of slopes: one in which the percentage of an element extracted increases as the pH increases, and one in which the percentage of an element extracted decreases with increasing pH. Since there are two types of slopes, choice (J) is the correct response. Choice (F) or (G) would be correct if the question pertained to a specific element, but the question asks you to consider the graph as a whole. If the percentage of an element extracted was independent of pH, you would expect to see the same percentage extracted at every pH. In other words, the graph for each element would be a horizontal line. This is not the case, so choice (H) is incorrect.

15. B
Figure Interpretation

Draw a line on the graph from 45% to the line for thulium (Tm). Then draw a vertical line from that point to the x-axis. You should land on the x-axis between 5 and 6.

16. J
Figure Interpretation

To answer this question, refer to the extraction curve for erbium. Erbium begins to be extracted when the pH level of the organic reagent is 4 or greater, and by a pH of 6, all of it is being extracted. Ytterbium, choice (J), does not begin to be extracted until pH reaches approximately 9.

PASSAGE IV

17. D
Scientific Reasoning

Scientist 1 states that "below 50 km, rock is under too much pressure to fracture normally." Scientist 2 gives the fact that "rock becomes ductile at the temperatures and pressures that exist at depths greater than 50 km" as the reason that "deep-focus earthquakes cannot result from normal fractures."

18. F
Scientific Reasoning

Scientist 1's theory is invalid unless water can be shown to exist in mantle rock at the level of deep-focus earthquakes. If researchers could subject mantle-like rock to those temperatures and pressures, and then extract water from it, choice (F), their experimental results would support the hypothesis of Scientist 1.

19. C
Scientific Reasoning

Both scientists believe that the Earth's crust (surface layer) is composed of mobile tectonic plates. In describing the plates as being "forced down into the mantle," Scientist 1 implies that they are normally in the crust, and Scientist 2 makes reference to "a descending tectonic plate." The introductory paragraph says that "most" earthquakes originate less than 20 km below the Earth's surface, so choice A is wrong. Neither scientist assumes that surface quakes are caused by trapped fluids, choice (B); both state that such quakes are caused by normal fractures in the Earth's crust. Neither scientist discusses how deep-focus earthquakes are detected, so choice (D) is not an assumption made by either scientist.

20. G
Scientific Reasoning
Scientist 2 believes that deep-focus quakes are the result of slippage caused by phase changes. Scientist 2 would, therefore, not expect deep quakes to occur below 680 km where, according to the last sentence of the passage, "no phase changes are predicted." Recording a quake with an origin below that depth would send Scientist 2 back to the drawing board, or at least in search of deeper phase changes.

21. D
Scientific Reasoning
The final sentence of Scientist 1's paragraph mentions that when fluids were injected into the ground at the Rocky Mountain Arsenal, the unintended result was "a series of shallow-focus earthquakes." The opening words *in fact* signal that this final sentence is meant to illustrate the previous sentence, which refers to experiments in which trapped fluids caused rock to fail at lower than normal shear stresses. The implication is that the quakes at the arsenal occurred because the fluid wastes lowered the shear stress failure point of the rock, choice (D). Dehydration, choice (A), is an important part of the hypothesis of Scientist 1 but is not specifically mentioned where Scientist 1 discusses the Rocky Mountain Arsenal. The slab of calcium magnesium silicate, choice (B), belongs in Scientist 2's paragraph. Choice (C) confuses the Rocky Mountain

Arsenal incident with the deep-sea trenches that are mentioned in the previous two sentences.

22. H
Scientific Reasoning
Scientist 2 claims that the slippage involved in deep-focus quakes results from phase changes. To support this contention, she cites laboratory work that produced similar phase changes and slippage in a slab of calcium magnesium silicate. But neither scientist says that mantle rock is composed of calcium magnesium silicate. If the slippery slab is to serve as evidence for Scientist 2's theory, it must at least be similar to mantle rock, so choice (H) is correct. Choice (F) might help refute Scientist 1's viewpoint, but would not strengthen Scientist 2's theory. Choices (G) and (J) would tend to weaken Scientist 2's theory.

23. D
Scientific Reasoning
Phase changes are fundamental to the arguments of both scientists, and both agree that they occur deep beneath the Earth's surface, so you can eliminate choices choice (A) and (B). The release of water from minerals is part of the explanation of Scientist 1, so choice (C) is out as well. Only choice (D) agrees with the logic of Scientist 2.

PASSAGE V

24. H
Figure Interpretation
The one variable that changes is the amount of moisture. Choice (G) cannot be correct because Experiment 2 says that the researcher used models equivalent to the same mass as in Experiment 1. There is no evidence for choice (F) or (J).

25. B
Scientific Reasoning
The moisture in Experiment 1 is 86%, and the moisture in Experiment 2 is 12%. If the moisture was changed to 50%, the collision rating would fall

between the lines of the two experiments on the graphs. At 400,000 kg, the collision rating would be between 4.5 and 5.5.

26. G
Scientific Reasoning

The collision ratings for Experiment 1, with a high percentage of moisture in the atmosphere, were mostly lower than those in Experiment 2. Therefore, an increase in moisture would decrease the impact of a collision. Eliminate choices H and J. However, for asteroids over 700,000 kg, the lines on the graph meet—the presence of moisture loses its effect. Choice (G) is correct.

27. C
Figure Interpretation

Feel free to draw on the graph (you can write on your test booklet during the ACT). Draw a line from 4 on the x-axis straight up. Draw a line from 4 on the y-axis straight across. Those two lines meet on the line for Experiment 1. The moisture level for Experiment 1 was 86%, so choice (C) is correct.

28. H
Figure Interpretation

Again, it might help to draw on the graph to answer this question. Draw a vertical line up from 1 (100,000 kg) on the horizontal scale to see where it hits the curve representing Experiment 2. Then draw a horizontal line from this curve to the curve representing Experiment 1, and draw from that point down to the horizontal scale once again. You'll see that the size is closest to choice (H), 270,000 kg.

29. B
Figure Interpretation

To be minimally capable of regional destruction, an asteroid must have a collision rating of 4, so draw a horizontal line over from 4 on the vertical scale. If you do so, you'll see that size of an asteroid capable of such destruction goes from roughly 250,000 kg at a 12% moisture level to about 400,000 kg at an

86% moisture level. 400,000 is roughly 70% larger than 250,000, so choice (B) is the correct answer.

PASSAGE VI

30. H
Figure Interpretation

Following HST-52 from right to left across the first figure (because the temperature is decreasing), conductivity increases and temperature decreases—just like the conductivity of a conductor—until 160 K, at which point HST-52's conductivity starts to decrease with decreasing temperature, like a semiconductor. With decreasing temperature, the sample undergoes a conductor to semiconductor transition, choice (H).

31. B
Patterns

The plot for conductor-like behavior indicates that as the temperature increases, its conductivity decreases. Choices (A) and (C) describe the behavior of semiconductors, not conductors. Choice (D) is incorrect: If the conductivity of conductors were the same at all temperatures, the plot of conductivity versus temperature for conductors would be a horizontal line.

32. H
Patterns

A material that has a semiconductor to conductor transition at 10 K will show a brief increase and then, starting at 10 K, a steady decrease as the temperature increases. Choice (H) is the plot that shows this brief increase at low temperatures and then the decrease as the temperature rises.

33. D
Scientific Reasoning

The figure shows that HST-52 displays semiconductor behavior only up to about 150 K. Therefore, HST-52 will be usable as a semiconductor only at temperatures below about 150 K, choice (D). Choice (A) is wrong because HST-52 is a semiconductor at certain temperatures, and (B) is wrong because HST-52 is not a semiconductor at all temperatures. The brittleness of HST-52 is never discussed in the passage, so choice (C) should be eliminated from the outset.

34. J
Patterns
You are looking for the temperature at which the downward slope for Sample HST-52 is the steepest. This is somewhat difficult to determine, but this much is clear: The slope does not begin to go down until the temperature rises above 160 K. Thus, the only answer that could make sense is choice (J), 180 K.

PASSAGE VII

35. C
Figure Interpretation
The graph shows no difference in the percentage of body covered in dark fur for outdoor temperatures less than or equal to 2°C, making choice (C) correct. The phrase "According to the graph" should remind you to extract data directly from the graph. Based on the passage alone, you might incorrectly assume that since the temperature drops over that month the percentage of body covered in dark fur would increase as in choice (A). The graph shows, however, that this is only true for outdoor temperatures between 2°C and 7°C.

36. G
Scientific Reasoning
The key to this question is determining whether the cat in question is an outdoor or indoor cat. This cat goes outdoors a total of three hours per week, whereas an outdoor cat would spend at least six hours outdoors per week. Therefore, this cat is an indoor cat, and the percentage of dark fur on its body would remain just above 10%.

37. B
Figure Interpretation
You can draw a line from 45% dark fur across to the solid line representing outdoor cats. If you draw a line from that intersection straight down to the x-axis, you will hit 3°C.

38. G
Patterns
If the cat grew dark fur over 30% of its body, it must have been an outdoor cat as defined in the passage, and according to the graph, been exposed to temperature below 5°C (Statement I). To be an outdoor cat, a cat does not have to spend more time outdoors than indoors (Statement II), but it has to spend time outdoors for six consecutive days (Statement III).

39. C
Patterns
If a Siamese cat does not have dark fur over more than 10% of its body, then it must *either* be an indoor cat *or* live in an area where it is not regularly exposed to temperatures below 7°C.

40. H
Scientific Reasoning
Choice (F) is wrong because the indoor cats will not help us, since they don't go outside. Choice (G) is not a good choice because the outdoor cats of the original experiment cannot be used as a control group: The time they spent outside was not monitored—we only know that they spent more than one hour outside a day. Choice (J) is incorrect because the data already gathered only shows that outdoor cats turn darker in cold weather than indoor cats and doesn't provide any information about how varying the amount of time outdoors affects fur color. The correct answer is (H). A completely new experiment would have to be set up.

WRITING TEST

MODEL ESSAY

Below is an example of what a high-scoring essay might look like. Notice the author states her position clearly in the introductory paragraph and supports that position with evidence in the following paragraphs. This essay also uses transitions, some advanced vocabulary, and an effective "hook" to draw in the reader.

While some people believe academics and athletics are not related, I think it is important to hold student athletes responsible for earning a minimum grade point average. We live in a sports-obsessed world, where professional athletes receive multi-million dollar contracts and where highly paid athletes are becoming younger and younger. For example, LeBron James, still in high school, obtained a lucrative endorsement deal with Nike and was a highly sought-after NBA draft pick. Sadly, when teams are recruiting young athletes, the last thing they often look at is grades. It is also unfortunate that, feeling the pressure from alumni and fans to have successful teams, schools are often willing to overlook poor grades in their high-performing athletes. With so much money and fame at stake, and with so many institutions turning a blind eye, is it any wonder that many young athletes will sacrifice anything to get ahead, even their academic performance? Requiring student athletes to maintain a minimum grade point average is important for several reasons.

As an educational institution, a school's number-one priority should be the education of its students. The school does its student athletes a disservice when it doesn't push them to do their best at academics and learn as much as they can. It is unfair to hold other students, who may not be lucky enough to have the same natural athletic abilities, to a higher academic standard than athletes, and devalues any effort they make to get good grades by showing them in effect that what really matters in life is how good you are at sports. Also, since sports place so many demands on students' time and energy, what incentive do athletes have to take the extra time to keep up with schoolwork if they aren't required to do so?

When a school does not require student athletes to achieve a specified grade point average, it sets them up for failure later in life. The hard truth is that there are not enough jobs in professional sports for every student athlete. If students don't get drafted to play sports once they finish school, or if they do get chosen and then get injured and can no longer play the sport as well or at all, they only will have their grades and grade point average to show for their time in school. If their grades aren't good, they will have difficulty finding a job and starting a new career.

I am not trying to say that high-school sports are bad, or that they don't offer benefits to students involved in them. Not only do those students get in shape, but they also get to be on a team and feel like a part of something important. I think, however, that when schools treat academics as secondary they are taking the focus off all the positive things students get by participating in sports. When students think their athletic performance is their best chance for a post-high school career, they no longer think about accomplishments like learning discipline and improving self-esteem. They only focus on winning at all costs. Schools encourage this by making athletic performance more important than academics. If students know that they have a high enough grade point average to succeed if their sport doesn't become their career, maybe sports can go back to being fun again.

Participating in sports is a great thing for students to do. It builds self-confidence, fosters school spirit, and teaches determination. However, high schoolers should be students first. Requiring student athletes to maintain a certain grade point average would ensure that students get the education they need whether or not they go on to play professional sports. Schools' number-one priority should be making sure that all of their students, whether they are athletes or not, have the education required to succeed in life.

You can evaluate your essay and the model essay based on the following criteria, covered in the Scoring section of Inside the ACT Writing Test:

- Does the author answer the question?

- Is the author's position clearly stated?

- Does the body of the essay support and develop the position taken?

- Are there at least two supporting paragraphs?

- Is the relevance of each supporting paragraph clear?

- Does the writer address the other side of the argument?

- Is the essay organized, with a clear introduction, middle, and end?

- Does the author start a new paragraph for each new idea?

- Is each sentence in a paragraph relevant to the point made in that paragraph?

- Are transitions clear?

- Is the essay easy to read? Is it engaging?

- Are sentences varied?

- Is vocabulary used effectively? Is college-level vocabulary used?

Practice Test Three

ACT Practice Test Three
ANSWER SHEET

ENGLISH TEST

1. Ⓐ Ⓑ Ⓒ Ⓓ 11. Ⓐ Ⓑ Ⓒ Ⓓ 21. Ⓐ Ⓑ Ⓒ Ⓓ 31. Ⓐ Ⓑ Ⓒ Ⓓ 41. Ⓐ Ⓑ Ⓒ Ⓓ 51. Ⓐ Ⓑ Ⓒ Ⓓ 61. Ⓐ Ⓑ Ⓒ Ⓓ 71. Ⓐ Ⓑ Ⓒ Ⓓ
2. Ⓕ Ⓖ Ⓗ Ⓙ 12. Ⓕ Ⓖ Ⓗ Ⓙ 22. Ⓕ Ⓖ Ⓗ Ⓙ 32. Ⓕ Ⓖ Ⓗ Ⓙ 42. Ⓕ Ⓖ Ⓗ Ⓙ 52. Ⓕ Ⓖ Ⓗ Ⓙ 62. Ⓕ Ⓖ Ⓗ Ⓙ 72. Ⓕ Ⓖ Ⓗ Ⓙ
3. Ⓐ Ⓑ Ⓒ Ⓓ 13. Ⓐ Ⓑ Ⓒ Ⓓ 23. Ⓐ Ⓑ Ⓒ Ⓓ 33. Ⓐ Ⓑ Ⓒ Ⓓ 43. Ⓐ Ⓑ Ⓒ Ⓓ 53. Ⓐ Ⓑ Ⓒ Ⓓ 63. Ⓐ Ⓑ Ⓒ Ⓓ 73. Ⓐ Ⓑ Ⓒ Ⓓ
4. Ⓕ Ⓖ Ⓗ Ⓙ 14. Ⓕ Ⓖ Ⓗ Ⓙ 24. Ⓕ Ⓖ Ⓗ Ⓙ 34. Ⓕ Ⓖ Ⓗ Ⓙ 44. Ⓕ Ⓖ Ⓗ Ⓙ 54. Ⓕ Ⓖ Ⓗ Ⓙ 64. Ⓕ Ⓖ Ⓗ Ⓙ 74. Ⓕ Ⓖ Ⓗ Ⓙ
5. Ⓐ Ⓑ Ⓒ Ⓓ 15. Ⓐ Ⓑ Ⓒ Ⓓ 25. Ⓐ Ⓑ Ⓒ Ⓓ 35. Ⓐ Ⓑ Ⓒ Ⓓ 45. Ⓐ Ⓑ Ⓒ Ⓓ 55. Ⓐ Ⓑ Ⓒ Ⓓ 65. Ⓐ Ⓑ Ⓒ Ⓓ 75. Ⓐ Ⓑ Ⓒ Ⓓ
6. Ⓕ Ⓖ Ⓗ Ⓙ 16. Ⓕ Ⓖ Ⓗ Ⓙ 26. Ⓕ Ⓖ Ⓗ Ⓙ 36. Ⓕ Ⓖ Ⓗ Ⓙ 46. Ⓕ Ⓖ Ⓗ Ⓙ 56. Ⓕ Ⓖ Ⓗ Ⓙ 66. Ⓕ Ⓖ Ⓗ Ⓙ
7. Ⓐ Ⓑ Ⓒ Ⓓ 17. Ⓐ Ⓑ Ⓒ Ⓓ 27. Ⓐ Ⓑ Ⓒ Ⓓ 37. Ⓐ Ⓑ Ⓒ Ⓓ 47. Ⓐ Ⓑ Ⓒ Ⓓ 57. Ⓐ Ⓑ Ⓒ Ⓓ 67. Ⓐ Ⓑ Ⓒ Ⓓ
8. Ⓕ Ⓖ Ⓗ Ⓙ 18. Ⓕ Ⓖ Ⓗ Ⓙ 28. Ⓕ Ⓖ Ⓗ Ⓙ 38. Ⓕ Ⓖ Ⓗ Ⓙ 48. Ⓕ Ⓖ Ⓗ Ⓙ 58. Ⓕ Ⓖ Ⓗ Ⓙ 68. Ⓕ Ⓖ Ⓗ Ⓙ
9. Ⓐ Ⓑ Ⓒ Ⓓ 19. Ⓐ Ⓑ Ⓒ Ⓓ 29. Ⓐ Ⓑ Ⓒ Ⓓ 39. Ⓐ Ⓑ Ⓒ Ⓓ 49. Ⓐ Ⓑ Ⓒ Ⓓ 59. Ⓐ Ⓑ Ⓒ Ⓓ 69. Ⓐ Ⓑ Ⓒ Ⓓ
10. Ⓕ Ⓖ Ⓗ Ⓙ 20. Ⓕ Ⓖ Ⓗ Ⓙ 30. Ⓕ Ⓖ Ⓗ Ⓙ 40. Ⓕ Ⓖ Ⓗ Ⓙ 50. Ⓕ Ⓖ Ⓗ Ⓙ 60. Ⓕ Ⓖ Ⓗ Ⓙ 70. Ⓕ Ⓖ Ⓗ Ⓙ

MATH TEST

1. Ⓐ Ⓑ Ⓒ Ⓓ Ⓔ 11. Ⓐ Ⓑ Ⓒ Ⓓ Ⓔ 21. Ⓐ Ⓑ Ⓒ Ⓓ Ⓔ 31. Ⓐ Ⓑ Ⓒ Ⓓ Ⓔ 41. Ⓐ Ⓑ Ⓒ Ⓓ Ⓔ 51. Ⓐ Ⓑ Ⓒ Ⓓ Ⓔ
2. Ⓐ Ⓑ Ⓒ Ⓓ Ⓔ 12. Ⓕ Ⓖ Ⓗ Ⓙ Ⓚ 22. Ⓕ Ⓖ Ⓗ Ⓙ Ⓚ 32. Ⓕ Ⓖ Ⓗ Ⓙ Ⓚ 42. Ⓕ Ⓖ Ⓗ Ⓙ Ⓚ 52. Ⓕ Ⓖ Ⓗ Ⓙ Ⓚ
3. Ⓐ Ⓑ Ⓒ Ⓓ Ⓔ 13. Ⓐ Ⓑ Ⓒ Ⓓ Ⓔ 23. Ⓐ Ⓑ Ⓒ Ⓓ Ⓔ 33. Ⓐ Ⓑ Ⓒ Ⓓ Ⓔ 43. Ⓐ Ⓑ Ⓒ Ⓓ Ⓔ 53. Ⓐ Ⓑ Ⓒ Ⓓ Ⓔ
4. Ⓕ Ⓖ Ⓗ Ⓙ Ⓚ 14. Ⓕ Ⓖ Ⓗ Ⓙ Ⓚ 24. Ⓕ Ⓖ Ⓗ Ⓙ Ⓚ 34. Ⓕ Ⓖ Ⓗ Ⓙ Ⓚ 44. Ⓕ Ⓖ Ⓗ Ⓙ Ⓚ 54. Ⓕ Ⓖ Ⓗ Ⓙ Ⓚ
5. Ⓐ Ⓑ Ⓒ Ⓓ Ⓔ 15. Ⓐ Ⓑ Ⓒ Ⓓ Ⓔ 25. Ⓐ Ⓑ Ⓒ Ⓓ Ⓔ 35. Ⓐ Ⓑ Ⓒ Ⓓ Ⓔ 45. Ⓐ Ⓑ Ⓒ Ⓓ Ⓔ 55. Ⓐ Ⓑ Ⓒ Ⓓ Ⓔ
6. Ⓕ Ⓖ Ⓗ Ⓙ Ⓚ 16. Ⓕ Ⓖ Ⓗ Ⓙ Ⓚ 26. Ⓕ Ⓖ Ⓗ Ⓙ Ⓚ 36. Ⓕ Ⓖ Ⓗ Ⓙ Ⓚ 46. Ⓕ Ⓖ Ⓗ Ⓙ Ⓚ 56. Ⓕ Ⓖ Ⓗ Ⓙ Ⓚ
7. Ⓐ Ⓑ Ⓒ Ⓓ Ⓔ 17. Ⓐ Ⓑ Ⓒ Ⓓ Ⓔ 27. Ⓐ Ⓑ Ⓒ Ⓓ Ⓔ 37. Ⓐ Ⓑ Ⓒ Ⓓ Ⓔ 47. Ⓐ Ⓑ Ⓒ Ⓓ Ⓔ 57. Ⓐ Ⓑ Ⓒ Ⓓ Ⓔ
8. Ⓕ Ⓖ Ⓗ Ⓙ Ⓚ 18. Ⓕ Ⓖ Ⓗ Ⓙ Ⓚ 28. Ⓕ Ⓖ Ⓗ Ⓙ Ⓚ 38. Ⓕ Ⓖ Ⓗ Ⓙ Ⓚ 48. Ⓕ Ⓖ Ⓗ Ⓙ Ⓚ 58. Ⓕ Ⓖ Ⓗ Ⓙ Ⓚ
9. Ⓐ Ⓑ Ⓒ Ⓓ Ⓔ 19. Ⓐ Ⓑ Ⓒ Ⓓ Ⓔ 29. Ⓐ Ⓑ Ⓒ Ⓓ Ⓔ 39. Ⓐ Ⓑ Ⓒ Ⓓ Ⓔ 49. Ⓐ Ⓑ Ⓒ Ⓓ Ⓔ 59. Ⓐ Ⓑ Ⓒ Ⓓ Ⓔ
10. Ⓕ Ⓖ Ⓗ Ⓙ Ⓚ 20. Ⓕ Ⓖ Ⓗ Ⓙ Ⓚ 30. Ⓕ Ⓖ Ⓗ Ⓙ Ⓚ 40. Ⓕ Ⓖ Ⓗ Ⓙ Ⓚ 50. Ⓕ Ⓖ Ⓗ Ⓙ Ⓚ 60. Ⓕ Ⓖ Ⓗ Ⓙ Ⓚ

READING TEST

1. Ⓐ Ⓑ Ⓒ Ⓓ 6. Ⓕ Ⓖ Ⓗ Ⓙ 11. Ⓐ Ⓑ Ⓒ Ⓓ 16. Ⓕ Ⓖ Ⓗ Ⓙ 21. Ⓐ Ⓑ Ⓒ Ⓓ 26. Ⓕ Ⓖ Ⓗ Ⓙ 31. Ⓐ Ⓑ Ⓒ Ⓓ 36. Ⓕ Ⓖ Ⓗ Ⓙ
2. Ⓕ Ⓖ Ⓗ Ⓙ 7. Ⓐ Ⓑ Ⓒ Ⓓ 12. Ⓕ Ⓖ Ⓗ Ⓙ 17. Ⓐ Ⓑ Ⓒ Ⓓ 22. Ⓕ Ⓖ Ⓗ Ⓙ 27. Ⓐ Ⓑ Ⓒ Ⓓ 32. Ⓕ Ⓖ Ⓗ Ⓙ 37. Ⓐ Ⓑ Ⓒ Ⓓ
3. Ⓐ Ⓑ Ⓒ Ⓓ 8. Ⓕ Ⓖ Ⓗ Ⓙ 13. Ⓐ Ⓑ Ⓒ Ⓓ 18. Ⓕ Ⓖ Ⓗ Ⓙ 23. Ⓐ Ⓑ Ⓒ Ⓓ 28. Ⓕ Ⓖ Ⓗ Ⓙ 33. Ⓐ Ⓑ Ⓒ Ⓓ 38. Ⓕ Ⓖ Ⓗ Ⓙ
4. Ⓕ Ⓖ Ⓗ Ⓙ 9. Ⓐ Ⓑ Ⓒ Ⓓ 14. Ⓕ Ⓖ Ⓗ Ⓙ 19. Ⓐ Ⓑ Ⓒ Ⓓ 24. Ⓕ Ⓖ Ⓗ Ⓙ 29. Ⓐ Ⓑ Ⓒ Ⓓ 34. Ⓕ Ⓖ Ⓗ Ⓙ 39. Ⓐ Ⓑ Ⓒ Ⓓ
5. Ⓐ Ⓑ Ⓒ Ⓓ 10. Ⓕ Ⓖ Ⓗ Ⓙ 15. Ⓐ Ⓑ Ⓒ Ⓓ 20. Ⓕ Ⓖ Ⓗ Ⓙ 25. Ⓐ Ⓑ Ⓒ Ⓓ 30. Ⓕ Ⓖ Ⓗ Ⓙ 35. Ⓐ Ⓑ Ⓒ Ⓓ 40. Ⓕ Ⓖ Ⓗ Ⓙ

SCIENCE TEST

1. Ⓐ Ⓑ Ⓒ Ⓓ 6. Ⓕ Ⓖ Ⓗ Ⓙ 11. Ⓐ Ⓑ Ⓒ Ⓓ 16. Ⓕ Ⓖ Ⓗ Ⓙ 21. Ⓐ Ⓑ Ⓒ Ⓓ 26. Ⓕ Ⓖ Ⓗ Ⓙ 31. Ⓐ Ⓑ Ⓒ Ⓓ 36. Ⓕ Ⓖ Ⓗ Ⓙ
2. Ⓕ Ⓖ Ⓗ Ⓙ 7. Ⓐ Ⓑ Ⓒ Ⓓ 12. Ⓕ Ⓖ Ⓗ Ⓙ 17. Ⓐ Ⓑ Ⓒ Ⓓ 22. Ⓕ Ⓖ Ⓗ Ⓙ 27. Ⓐ Ⓑ Ⓒ Ⓓ 32. Ⓕ Ⓖ Ⓗ Ⓙ 37. Ⓐ Ⓑ Ⓒ Ⓓ
3. Ⓐ Ⓑ Ⓒ Ⓓ 8. Ⓕ Ⓖ Ⓗ Ⓙ 13. Ⓐ Ⓑ Ⓒ Ⓓ 18. Ⓕ Ⓖ Ⓗ Ⓙ 23. Ⓐ Ⓑ Ⓒ Ⓓ 28. Ⓕ Ⓖ Ⓗ Ⓙ 33. Ⓐ Ⓑ Ⓒ Ⓓ 38. Ⓕ Ⓖ Ⓗ Ⓙ
4. Ⓕ Ⓖ Ⓗ Ⓙ 9. Ⓐ Ⓑ Ⓒ Ⓓ 14. Ⓕ Ⓖ Ⓗ Ⓙ 19. Ⓐ Ⓑ Ⓒ Ⓓ 24. Ⓕ Ⓖ Ⓗ Ⓙ 29. Ⓐ Ⓑ Ⓒ Ⓓ 34. Ⓕ Ⓖ Ⓗ Ⓙ 39. Ⓐ Ⓑ Ⓒ Ⓓ
5. Ⓐ Ⓑ Ⓒ Ⓓ 10. Ⓕ Ⓖ Ⓗ Ⓙ 15. Ⓐ Ⓑ Ⓒ Ⓓ 20. Ⓕ Ⓖ Ⓗ Ⓙ 25. Ⓐ Ⓑ Ⓒ Ⓓ 30. Ⓕ Ⓖ Ⓗ Ⓙ 35. Ⓐ Ⓑ Ⓒ Ⓓ 40. Ⓕ Ⓖ Ⓗ Ⓙ

ENGLISH TEST

45 Minutes—75 Questions

Directions: In the following five passages, certain words and phrases are underlined and numbered. In the right-hand column are alternatives for each underlined portion. Select the one that best conveys the idea, creates the most grammatically correct sentence, or is the most consistent with the style and tone of the passage. If you decide that the original version is best, select NO CHANGE. You may also find questions that ask about the entire passage or a section of the passage. These questions will correspond to small numbered boxes in the text. For these questions, decide which choice best accomplishes the purpose set out in the question stem. After you've selected the best choice, fill in the corresponding oval in your Answer Grid. For some questions, you'll need to read the context in order to answer correctly. Be sure to read until you have enough information to determine the correct answer choice.

You will also find questions about a section of the passage or about the passage as a whole. These questions do not refer to an underlined portion of the passage, but rather are identified by a number or numbers in a box.

For each question, choose the alternative you consider best and fill in the corresponding oval on your answer document. Read each passage through once before you begin to answer the questions that accompany it. For many of the questions, you must read several sentences beyond the question to determine the answer. Be sure that you have read enough ahead each time you choose an alternative.

PASSAGE I

A SWIMMING CHANGE

[1]

Until three years ago, I had never considered myself to be athletically talented. I have never been able to hit, catch, throw, or kick a ball with any degree of confidence or accuracy. For years, physical <u>education being</u>
1
often the worst part of the school day for me. Units on tennis, touch football, volleyball, and basketball were torturous. I not only dreaded fumbling a pass,

<u>so</u> I also feared being hit in the face by a ball. However,
2
at the beginning of my freshman year of high school, my attitude toward sports changed.

1. A. NO CHANGE
   B. education, was
   C. education was
   D. education,

2. F. NO CHANGE
   G. and
   H. but
   J. though

GO ON TO THE NEXT PAGE ⟶

[2]

Somehow, my good friend Gretchen convinced me

to join <u>our schools</u> swim team.
     3

<u>Knowing that I enjoyed swimming, over the course of</u>
                              4
<u>two summers, it was with Gretchen that I practically</u>
                              4
<u>had lived at the pool.</u> My mother had
          4

3. A. NO CHANGE
   B. our schools'
   C. our school's
   D. ours school

4. F. NO CHANGE
   G. Because we had spent two summers
       practically living at the pool, it was
       Gretchen who knew that swimming was
       enjoyed by me.
   H. Having practically lived at the pool over
       two summers, the two of us, Gretchen
       knew it was swimming that I enjoyed.
   J. Gretchen knew I enjoyed swimming, as
       we had spent two summers practically
       living at the pool.

<u>insisted</u> that I take swimming lessons every summer
     5
since I was seven, so I was entirely comfortable in the

water. I was also eager to start my high school experience

with a new challenge and a new way to think of myself.

[3]

Of course, I had no idea what I was getting into

when Gretchen and I showed up for the first day of

practice. The team was made up of twenty young

<u>women, most of these swimmers</u> had been participating
                    6
in the community swim team for years. I couldn't do a

flip turn at the end of of the lane without getting water

up my nose. In contrast, most of the other swimmers,

who

5. Of the four choices, which is the only one
   that does NOT indicate that the narrator's
   mother decided that the narrator must take
   swimming lessons?
   A. NO CHANGE
   B. suggested
   C. required
   D. demanded

6. F. NO CHANGE
   G. women, the majority of them
   H. women most of them
   J. women, most of whom

GO ON TO THE NEXT PAGE

had been swimming competitively, since elementary school, were able to gracefully somersault and begin the
<u>7</u>
next lap. By the end of the first hour of practice, I was

exhausted and waterlogged.

[4]

However, I had no intention of <u>giving up, which</u>
<u>8</u>
<u>would mean quitting.</u> I came back the next day and the
<u>8</u>
next day for practice. Things

<u>begun</u> to get serious in the second week, when we
<u>9</u>
started the regular schedule of four early morning and

five afternoon practices. Our coach,

<u>whom</u> had led the team to several state championships,
<u>10</u>
demanded dedication from everyone on the team. The

hard work

<u>eventually paid off. By</u> the end of the first month, I had
<u>11</u>
discovered that I was good at the butterfly,

7. A. NO CHANGE
   B. had been swimming competitively since elementary school,
   C. had been swimming, competitively since elementary school,
   D. had been swimming competitively since elementary school

8. F. NO CHANGE
   G. giving up and resigning myself to failure.
   H. giving up and quitting what I had set out to do.
   J. giving up.

9. A. NO CHANGE
   B. had been begun
   C. had began
   D. began

10. F. NO CHANGE
    G. for whom
    H. who
    J. which

11. A. NO CHANGE
    B. eventually paid off, so, as a result
    C. paid off eventually, however, by
    D. paid off, eventually, by

GO ON TO THE NEXT PAGE ▷

a relatively new stroke that was first introduced in the
                                                    12
1930s. I rarely won individual races, but I made a solid
12
member of our

team's medley relay.
13

[5]

After that intimidating first season, I continued

swimming. I even will have earned a varsity letter last
                          14
year. Now I'm hoping to earn a spot in the state compe-

tition my senior year. [15]

12. Assuming each of the following creates a true statement, which provides the information most relevant to the narrator's experience on the swim team?

    F. NO CHANGE

    G. a difficult stroke that interested few other members of our team.

    H. which is faster than the backstroke but somewhat slower than the crawl.

    J. which is still sometimes called the dolphin because it incorporates a two-stroke dolphin kick.

13. A. NO CHANGE

    B. team's medley relay (it consists of four swimmers).

    C. team's medley relay, which the person swimming backstroke always begins.

    D. team.

14. F. NO CHANGE

    G. would have earned

    H. earned

    J. earn

15. If inserted here, which of the following would be the most appropriate sentence to conclude the essay?

    A. My coach continues to schedule demanding practices, but I have come to enjoy the early morning swims.

    B. For someone who thought she didn't have any athletic talent, I have come a long way.

    C. Gretchen is also still on the team, but she does not swim the medley relay.

    D. I've always enjoyed swimming, so I'm not all that surprised by my success as an athlete.

PASSAGE II

EXPLORING DUBUQUE'S AQUARIUM

[1]

One lazy day last summer, my parents decided that my younger sister and I needed a break from our vacation from academics. They took us to the National Mississippi River Museum and Aquarium in Dubuque, Iowa. I was prepared to be bored by this family educational trip. However, from the first moment I walked through the museum's doors, I was captivated; by all that there was
16
to learn about life in the Mississippi.

[2]

[1] A large tank stocked with fish and turtles was there to greet us as we walked into the main hall. [2]
17
There were also animals I had never before glimpsed, such as a fish called the long-nosed gar. [3] I was amazed by this fish in particular. [4] Its long, tubular shape and distinctive rod-shaped nose that made it ap-
18
pear like something that lived in the dark depths of the ocean. [5] This first of five freshwater aquariums offered a close-up view of
familiar animals that I had seen before, such as ducks. [20]
19

16. F. NO CHANGE
    G. captivated, by
    H. captivated by,
    J. captivated by

17. A. NO CHANGE
    B. is there
    C. are there
    D. were there

18. F. NO CHANGE
    G. nose, which
    H. nose, and this
    J. nose

19. A. NO CHANGE
    B. animals that were familiar sights to me,
    C. familiar animals to which I was no stranger,
    D. familiar animals,

20. To make paragraph 2 coherent and logical, the best placement of sentence 5 is:
    F. where it is now.
    G. before sentence 1.
    H. after sentence 1.
    J. after sentence 2.

GO ON TO THE NEXT PAGE

[3]

In the next aquarium, I <u>see</u> a catfish bigger than I
                        21
had ever imagined this species could be. According to

the posted information, this specimen weighed more

than 100 pounds. With its long whiskers and slow, lazy

movements, this catfish looked like the grandfather of

all the other fish in the tank.

21. A. NO CHANGE
    B. had been seeing
    C. saw
    D. spot

[4]

<u>I couldn't decide which I liked better, the catfish</u>
                                    22
<u>or the long-nosed gar.</u> The next floor-to-ceiling tank,
      22
which represented the ecosystem of the Mississippi

bayou, held an animal I had never seen: an alligator. At

first, I had a hard time spotting the creature—it blended

in almost completely with a half-submerged log.

22. Which sentence most effectively connects
    this paragraph to the preceding paragraph?

    F. NO CHANGE
    G. Although the catfish was impressive, it
       was not the biggest animal on display in
       the museum.
    H. After seeing the catfish, I was interested
       in exhibits that were a bit more hands-
       on.
    J. Until my visit to the museum, I had
       never really considered what the Missis-
       sippi River was like south of my home.

23 Suddenly, though, it

23. At this point, the writer is considering
    removing the following phrase:

    it blended in almost completely with a half-
    submerged log.

    The primary effect of removing this phrase
    would be:

    A. a smoother transition between
       sentences.
    B. a greater contrast between images.
    C. the loss of descriptive information.
    D. an increased level of suspense.

GO ON TO THE NEXT PAGE

slides into the water and aims itself right at the glass
24
separating me from its ferocious claws and skin-tearing

teeth. I had a

slightly moment of panic before I remembered that, try
25
as it might, this alligator would never successfully hunt

tourists like me. As

much of the on-lookers squealed in delight as the alligator
26
moved through the tank, I noticed his companion. Far off

in a corner slept an enormous snapping turtle. I could im-

agine no better roommate for the alligator than this hook-

beaked turtle with rough ridges running along its shell.

[5]

Despite my initial expectations, I happily spent

the entire day soaking up information about creatures

that live in the Mississippi River. In one section of the

museum, I held a crayfish. 27 Later, I had the opportu-

nity to touch the cool, sleek skin of a stingray, which can

be found where the Mississippi empties into the Gulf of

Mexico.

24. F. NO CHANGE
    G. slides into the water to aim
    H. slid into the water and aiming
    J. slid into the water and aimed

25. A. NO CHANGE
    B. momentarily slight
    C. moment of slight
    D. momentarily of slight

26. F. NO CHANGE
    G. a large amount
    H. the many
    J. many

27. The writer would like to insert a sentence
    describing the appearance of the crayfish
    at this point. Which sentence would best
    accomplish the writer's goal?

    A. Also known as crawdads, crayfish are
       close relatives of the lobsters that live in
       freshwater.

    B. At an average length of about three
       inches, the crayfish looks like a
       miniature lobster, complete with small
       but effective front pincers.

    C. Although they are found throughout the
       United States, crayfish populations are
       densest in Kentucky and Mississippi.

    D. At first, I was a bit nervous to touch the
       small creature, but then I relaxed and
       enjoyed the opportunity to look at it so
       closely.

GO ON TO THE NEXT PAGE

[6]

After seeing <u>all, I could inside the museum,</u> I wan-
    28
dered outside, only to find even more exhibits.

28. F. NO CHANGE
    G. all I could inside the museum,
    H. all, I could inside the museum
    J. all I could inside the museum

<u>Having just enough time, it was that I was able</u> to see
                 29
the otters and watch a riverboat launching, but it was

closing time before I was able to see the most impressive

thing the museum had to offer. A football-field-sized

steamboat from the 1930s is open to

<u>tourists. And operates</u> as a "Boat and Breakfast" that
       30
hosts overnight guests. I'm hoping that my family will

plan another educational trip to Dubuque soon so I can

experience life on a steamboat.

29. A. NO CHANGE
    B. It was that I had just enough time, so I
        was able
    C. Having just enough time, it was possible
    D. I had just enough time

30. F. NO CHANGE
    G. tourists and that operates
    H. tourists, it operates
    J. tourists and operates

PASSAGE III

THE MYSTERY DINER

The paragraphs in this essay may or may not follow the most logical order. Each paragraph
is numbered, and question 45 will ask you to determine the best placement of paragraph 6.

[1]

Although secret identities and elaborate disguises are

typically associated with the world of spies and villains,

<u>it has</u> other uses. For six years, Ruth
 31

31. A. NO CHANGE
    B. it does have
    C. they do have
    D. and they have

GO ON TO THE NEXT PAGE

Reichl the restaurant critic for the *New York Times,* used
32
aliases and costumes as a regular part of her job.

[2]

Dining is big business in New York City, from the neighborhood noodle shops and diners to the upscale steak houses and four-star French restaurants.

33 Many of the more than one million people who read the *Times* each day

look to it for advice on where to eat. A positive review
34
from the *Times*

could have brought a restaurant unimagined suc-
35
cess and month-long waiting lists for reservations. A

32. F. NO CHANGE

G. Reichl, the restaurant critic, for the *New York Times,*

H. Reichl, the restaurant critic for the *New York Times,*

J. Reichl the restaurant critic for the *New York Times*

33. Should the following sentence be inserted into the passage at this point?

The legendary French restaurant Le Bernardin received a four-star rating from the *Times* shortly after opening in 1986, an honor it has maintained ever since.

A. Yes, because the added sentence emphasizes how important a positive review from the *Times* can be.

B. Yes, because the specific information helps the reader develop a clearer picture of the type of restaurant reviewed by the *Times.*

C. No, because it is unclear whether Reichl was responsible for reviewing this specific restaurant.

D. No, because the specific information about one restaurant leads the reader away from the main topic of the essay.

34. F. NO CHANGE

G. look with

H. look by

J. looking to

35. A. NO CHANGE

B. can bring

C. will have brought

D. will be bringing

GO ON TO THE NEXT PAGE ▷

negative review, on the other hand, can undermine a

restaurant's popularity and seriously cut into its profits.

Obviously,

restaurant owners and workers have a lot at stake when
      36
the restaurant critic for the *Times* walks in the door.

Waiters and chefs often pull out all of the stops to impress the writer

that the meal can make or break a restaurant.
  37

[3]

Reichl was acutely aware that she received special
                                      38
treatment once restaurant staff recognized her. She
  38
would be graciously greeted and led to the best table

in the restaurant, offered dishes prepared specially by

the head chef, and given multiple courses of amazing

desserts. In other words, the dining experience of the

restaurant critic was nothing like that of the commonly
                                                  39
ordinary person walking in from the street.
  39

[4]

To remedy this, Reichl decided a solution would be
                                        40
to become, for short periods of time, someone else.
  40

36. F. NO CHANGE
     G. restaurant owners and workers;
     H. restaurant, owners and workers
     J. restaurant owners, and workers

37. A. NO CHANGE
     B. who's
     C. whose
     D. which

38. F. NO CHANGE
     G. special treatment was received by her
     H. she was the recipient of special
         treatment
     J. she was in the position of receiving
         special treatment

39. A. NO CHANGE
     B. common, representative, and average
     C. typical
     D. extravagant

40. F. NO CHANGE
     G. she created a solution to the problem by
         becoming
     H. Reichl decided to become
     J. Reichl found a way to fix the problem,
         which involved becoming

Transforming herself into different personas, Reichl used
                                    41
wigs, special makeup, and carefully selected clothing,
                                    41
such as an attractive blonde named Chloe, a redhead

named Brenda, and an older woman named Betty. 42

41. A. NO CHANGE

B. With wigs, special makeup, and carefully selected clothing, Reichl transformed herself into different personas,

C. Transformed with wigs, special makeup, and carefully selected clothing, Reichl's different personas,

D. Reichl used wigs, special makeup, and carefully selected clothing, that transformed herself into different personas,

42. Which of the following true statements would make the most effective and logical conclusion for paragraph 4?

F. Reichl found that she could quickly disguise herself as Betty, but it took more time to become Chloe.

G. Her true identity hidden, Reichl would then dine at a restaurant she was currently evaluating.

H. After six years at the *Times,* Reichl moved on to become the editor of *Gourmet* magazine.

J. The former restaurant critic for the *Times* did not always agree with Reichl's methods or her selection of restaurants to review.

[5]

Sometimes, Reichl developed a different view about

the quality when she was not treated like a very impor-

tant person of a restaurant. Indeed, the difference be-
                    43
tween the treatment she received as herself and as one

43. For the sake of logic and coherence, the underlined portion should be placed:

A. where it is now.

B. after the word *developed.*

C. after the word *view.*

D. after the word *quality.*

GO ON TO THE NEXT PAGE ⟩

of her characters was occasionally so great that Reichl would revise her initial impression of a restaurant and write a more negative review. 44

[6]

By becoming an average customer, Reichl encouraged even the most expensive and popular restaurants to improve how they treated all of their customers. After all, waiters could never be certain when they were serving the powerful restaurant critic for the *New York Times*.

44. Would deleting the word *occasionally* from the previous sentence change the meaning of the sentence?

F. Yes, because without this word, the reader would not understand that Reichl had different experiences when she dined in disguise.

G. Yes, because without this word, the reader would think that Reichl always changed her impression of restaurants when she received different treatment because she was not recognized.

H. No, because this word repeats an idea that is already presented in the sentence.

J. No, because this word is used only to show emphasis, and it does not contribute to the meaning of the sentence.

Question 45 asks about the preceding passage as a whole.

45. To make the passage flow logically and smoothly, the best place for paragraph 6 is:

A. where it is now.

B. after paragraph 1.

C. after paragraph 3.

D. after paragraph 4.

GO ON TO THE NEXT PAGE

PASSAGE IV

THE BENEFITS OF A SQUARE-FOOT GARDEN

[1]

[1] I used to start every spring with great hopes for my backyard vegetable garden. [2] After the last freeze in late March or early April, I devoted an entire weekend to preparing the soil in the garden. [3] I thinned out the rows that had too many plants and spent hours tugging out each weed that threatened to rob my little plants of the nutrients they needed to thrive. [4] Once spring truly arrived, I marked out my rows and scattered the packets of seeds that I hoped, would develop into prize-winning vegetables. [5] In the first few weeks of the season, I was almost always in the garden. 47

[2]

Despite my best intentions, my garden never lived up to the vision I had for it. After I had devoted several weekends to watering and weeding, the garden always started to become more of a

burden less of a hobby. By July, the garden was usually in disarray, and I didn't have the energy or time to save it.

46. F. NO CHANGE
    G. hoped, would,
    H. hoped would,
    J. hoped would

47. To make paragraph 1 more logical and coherent, sentence 3 should be placed:
    A. where it is now.
    B. before sentence 1.
    C. after sentence 1.
    D. after sentence 4.

48. F. NO CHANGE
    G. burden:
    H. burden and
    J. burden, but,

GO ON TO THE NEXT PAGE

<u>July and August are always the hottest parts of the year.</u>
49

49. A. NO CHANGE
    B. The hottest months are July and August.
    C. (July, along with August, provides the hottest temperatures of the year.)
    D. OMIT the underlined portion.

[3]

This past year, <u>however,</u> my garden was finally the
                 50
success I had imagined it could be. Instead of planning the traditional garden of closely planted

50. Of the following choices, which would be the LEAST acceptable substitution for the underlined word?
    F. on the other hand
    G. indeed
    H. though
    J. in contrast

<u>rows that is modeled after large-scale farming,</u> I tried a
                 51
new technique. My new approach is called square-foot gardening.

51. A. NO CHANGE
    B. rows, which is modeled after large-scale farming,
    C. rows, which is based on the techniques for large-scale farming,
    D. rows,

[4]

<u>A square-foot garden is designed for efficiency.</u>
52

52. Which sentence most effectively links the topic of paragraph 3 to the topic of paragraph 4?
    F. NO CHANGE
    G. The technique of square-foot gardening was pioneered by Mel Bartholomew.
    H. One of the benefits of a square-foot garden is that it is less expensive to maintain than a traditional garden.
    J. My neighbor, who always has a beautiful garden, introduced me to the concept of square-foot gardening, and I have been grateful ever since.

GO ON TO THE NEXT PAGE

In a <u>traditionally</u> garden, you scatter a packet of seeds
53
down a row. When the plants emerge,

53. A. NO CHANGE
B. conventionally
C. traditional
D. tradition

<u>they spend</u> hours thinning each row by pulling out at
54
least half of what was planted. In a square-foot garden,

you plant each seed individually, so there is never a need

for thinning

54. F. NO CHANGE
G. he spends
H. people spend
J. you spend

<u>in the garden.</u> You create the garden plan 1 square foot
55
at a time, until you have a block of 16 squares. Sturdy

pieces of lumber

55. A. NO CHANGE
B. out the garden
C. in that garden
D. OMIT the underlined portion.

<u>which could make</u> effective borders for each square.
56
Walking paths that are at least 2 feet wide separate each

16-square-foot garden. The design is clean and simple,

and it eliminates the problem of getting to the rows in

the middle of a large garden. In fact,

56. F. NO CHANGE
G. that make
H. make
J. OMIT the underlined portion.

<u>you can do</u> all the weeding, watering, and harvesting
57
from the walking paths.

57. A. NO CHANGE
B. you could have done
C. one can do
D. one is able to do

[5]

In addition to being easier to weed and water, a

square-foot garden takes up much less space than a

regular garden. I was able to grow

<u>an increased number of more</u> vegetables in two square-
58
foot gardens, which took up a total of 32 square feet,

than I ever had grown in my traditional garden, which

took up 84 square feet. Preparing the soil for the smaller

58. F. NO CHANGE
G. a larger quantity of more
H. an increased, bigger quantity
J. more

GO ON TO THE NEXT PAGE

space only required a few hours instead of a whole weekend. There was so much less weeding to do that the task never felt overwhelming. One season of using the square garden techniques <u>were all</u> it took for me
^{59}
to convert to a completely new outlook on backyard gardening.

59. A. NO CHANGE
    B. were just what
    C. was all
    D. could be

Question 60 asks about the preceding passage as a whole.

60. If the writer had intended to write an essay detailing how to plan, prepare, and care for a square garden, would this essay meet the writer's goal?

    F. No, because the writer relies on generalities rather than specifics when describing her square garden.

    G. No, because the writer focuses on comparing two different types of gardens instead of explaining how to begin and care for one type of garden.

    H. Yes, because the writer states specific measurements for her square garden.

    J. Yes, because the writer maintains that square gardens are superior to traditional gardens.

GO ON TO THE NEXT PAGE ⟹

PASSAGE V

THE IMPORTANCE OF MAINTAINING YOUR CAR

[1]

Most new car owners glance briefly at the owner's manual before depositing it in the glove compartment of their new automobile. Owners may dig out their manuals when something goes <u>wrong, such as a flat tire or a flashing engine light</u> but few car owners take the
₆₁
time to learn the basics about maintaining their new purchase. This is truly unfortunate, as a few simple and routine steps

61. A. NO CHANGE
    B. wrong; such as a flat tire or a flashing engine light
    C. wrong, such as a flat tire, or a flashing engine light
    D. wrong, such as a flat tire or a flashing engine light,

<u>improves the long-term performance of an automobile and decreases</u> the possibility of a traffic accident.
₆₂

[2]

One of the easiest and most overlooked maintenance steps is caring for a car's wiper blades. Most people don't

62. F. NO CHANGE
    G. improve the long-term performance of an automobile and decreases
    H. improve the long-term performance of an automobile and decrease
    J. improves the long-term performance of an automobile and decrease

<u>notice a problem</u> until the blades fail to clear the windshield during a rainstorm or heavy snowfall. When a driver's
₆₃

63. A. NO CHANGE
    B. notice a problem that causes trouble
    C. recognize that their wiper blades are the source of a problem
    D. realize that their blades are failing and will become a problem

<u>vision being</u> obscured, an accident is more likely to happen. Replacing the
₆₄

64. F. NO CHANGE
    G. vision, has been
    H. vision is
    J. vision,

GO ON TO THE NEXT PAGE →

<u>set</u> blades at a time each year greatly reduces this risk.
65

In addition, frequently refilling the windshield washer

fluid reservoir guarantees that there will always be

enough fluid to wash away grime that accumulates on

the windshield.

[3]

Much of car maintenance focuses on preventing

problems before they occur. For example, checking the

levels of coolant, oil, brake fluid, and transmission fluid

can avert serious malfunctions. <u>In general,</u> these fluids
66

should be checked monthly and refilled whenever the

need is indicated.

[4]

<u>Cars are becoming more sophisticated every year,</u>
67

<u>but car owners without any expertise in mechanics can</u>
67

<u>still perform much of the basic upkeep of their vehicle.</u>
67

You should change the oil in most cars every 3,000 to

7,000 miles. This task requires a willingness to get a bit

dirty,

<u>so</u> you don't have to be a mechanic to change a car's oil.
68

Before you get started, read the oil change

65. The underlined word would be most logically placed:

A. where it is now.

B. before the word *time*.

C. before the word *year*.

D. before the word *risk*.

66. F. NO CHANGE

G. For generally,

H. With usual

J. By typically,

67. Which sentence is the most effective way to begin paragraph 4?

A. NO CHANGE

B. Changing the oil and oil filter regularly is another key to keeping your car's engine performing at its best.

C. An entire industry now focuses on providing regular car maintenance, such as changing the oil and rotating the tires.

D. Even if you haven't read your car owner's manual, you probably know that your car needs a tune-up every so often.

68. F. NO CHANGE

G. but

H. for

J. because

GO ON TO THE NEXT PAGE

section, in your owner's manual and collect all of the
69
tools you will need. You

won't need many tools, but you will definitely need a car
70
jack. Never get under a car that is supported only by car
70

jacks: you do not want to risk being crushed by a car.
71
After you've secured the car, changing the oil is as

straightforward as sliding under the car with a drain

pan to catch the oil and a wrench to loosen the oil drain

plug. Then follow the instructions for changing the oil

filter, and fill the oil pan to the recommended level with

fresh oil. [72]

[5]

These simple steps to maintaining the health of a

car can be done by just about anyone. However, success-

fully changing a car's oil does not turn a car owner into a

repair expert. More complicated tasks, such as adjusting

a carburetor or installing new brake pads, should be

69. A. NO CHANGE
    B. section, in your owner's manual,
    C. section in your owner's manual;
    D. section in your owner's manual,

70. In paragraph 4, the writer wants to provide
    an explanation of how to change the oil
    in an automobile. Which of the following
    would most logically fit the writer's
    intention for this paragraph?

    F. NO CHANGE
    G. need to get under the car to open the
       oil drain, so use car jacks to raise
       the car and sturdy car jack stands to
       support it.
    H. may find it helpful to watch someone
       else change the oil before you try to
       perform the job on your own.
    J. only need to follow a few basic steps in
       order to successfully change your car's
       oil.

71. A. NO CHANGE
    B. jacks, you
    C. jacks you
    D. jacks you,

72. Paragraph 4 of the essay uses the second
    person (you, your). Revising this paragraph
    to remove the second-person pronouns
    would have the primary effect of:

    F. disrupting the logical flow of the essay.
    G. making paragraph 4 more consistent
       with the voice used in the rest of the
       essay.
    J. underscoring the direct advice given to
       the reader.
    K. lightening the essay's formal tone.

GO ON TO THE NEXT PAGE →

<u>performed by a qualified</u> auto mechanic.
 73

73. A. NO CHANGE
B. professionally completed by a qualified
C. performed by a certifiably qualified
D. undertaken by qualifying

Questions 74–75 ask about the preceding passage as a whole.

74. After reading back through the essay, the writer decided that the following sentence contains important information:

> The owner's manual provides instructions on how to test the levels of these different fluids used to lubricate and cool the engine.

Logically, this sentence should be placed:

F. after the last sentence of paragraph 2.
G. before the first sentence of paragraph 3.
H. after the last sentence of paragraph 3.
J. after the last sentence of paragraph 4.

75. If the writer had intended to write an essay persuading readers to familiarize themselves with the basic safety features and maintenance needs of their cars, would this essay meet the writer's goal?

A. Yes, because the essay repeatedly encourages readers to refer to the owner's manual for their car.
B. Yes, because the essay lists many basic maintenance steps that owners can independently accomplish.
C. No, because the essay encourages readers to go beyond learning about the features of their car and actually perform some of the basic upkeep.
D. No, because the essay does not discuss a car's safety features in any detail.

MATH TEST

60 Minutes—60 Questions

Directions: Solve each problem, choose the correct answer, and then fill in the corresponding oval on your answer document.

Do not linger over problems that take too much time. Solve as many as you can, then return to the others in the time you have left for this test.

You are permitted to use a calculator on this test. You may use your calculator for any problems you choose, but some of the problems may best be done without using a calculator.

1. Tanya used $3\frac{3}{8}$ yards of fabric to make her dress, and she used $1\frac{1}{3}$ yards of fabric to make her jacket. What was the total amount, in yards, that Tanya used for the complete outfit of dress and jacket?

   A. $4\frac{1}{8}$

   B. $4\frac{1}{6}$

   C. $4\frac{4}{11}$

   D. $4\frac{1}{2}$

   E. $4\frac{17}{24}$

2. $5x^3y^5 \times 6y^2 \times 2xy$ is equivalent to:

   F. $13x^3y^7$.

   G. $13x^4y^8$.

   H. $60x^3y^7$.

   J. $60x^3y^{10}$.

   K. $60x^4y^8$.

3. Brandon puts 6% of his $36,000 yearly salary into savings, in 12 equal monthly installments. Jacqui deposits $200 every month into savings. At the end of one full year, what is the difference, in dollars, between the amount of money that Jacqui saved and the amount of money that Brandon saved?

   A. 20

   B. 24

   C. 240

   D. 1,960

   E. 2,800

4. Mikhail has received bowling scores of 190, 200, 145, and 180 so far in the state bowling tournament. What score must he receive on the fifth game to earn an average score of 180 for his five games?

   F. 179

   G. 180

   H. 185

   J. 200

   K. Mikhail cannot earn an average of 180.

GO ON TO THE NEXT PAGE

5. For steel to be considered stainless steel, it must have a minimum of 10.5% chromium in the metal alloy. If there are 262.5 pounds of chromium available, what is the maximum amount of stainless steel, in pounds, that can be manufactured?

    A. 27.56
    B. 252
    C. 262.5
    D. 2,500
    E. 25,000

6. A homeowner wants to put a wallpaper border on the top edge of all the walls of his kitchen. The kitchen measures 6.5 meters by 4 meters. What is the required length, in meters, of the border?

    F. 8
    G. 10.5
    H. 13
    J. 21
    K. 26

7. Which expression below is equivalent to $w(x - (y + z))$?

    A. $wx - wy - wz$
    B. $wx - wy + wz$
    C. $wx - y + z$
    D. $wx - y - z$
    E. $wxy + wxz$

8. If $6n - 4 = 3n + 24$, $n = ?$

    F. 28
    G. $\dfrac{28}{3}$
    H. $\dfrac{28}{9}$
    J. $\dfrac{20}{9}$
    K. $\dfrac{3}{28}$

9. What two numbers should be placed in the blanks below so that the difference between successive entries is the same?
    26,_____,_____, 53

    A. 36, 43
    B. 35, 44
    C. 34, 45
    D. 33, 46
    E. 30, 49

10. What is the real number value of $m^3 + \sqrt{12m}$ when $5m^2 = 45$?

    F. 5
    G. 27
    H. 33
    J. 38.09
    K. 739.39

11. The radius of a sphere is $3\dfrac{3}{5}$ meters. What is the volume of the sphere, to the nearest cubic meter? Use the formula $V = \dfrac{4}{3}\pi r^3$.

    A. 42
    B. 45
    C. 157
    D. 195
    E. 3,429

GO ON TO THE NEXT PAGE ⇒

12. There are 10 peanuts, 6 cashews, and 8 almonds in a bag of mixed nuts. If a nut is chosen at random from the bag, what is the probability that the nut is NOT a peanut?

   F. $\dfrac{5}{12}$

   G. $\dfrac{7}{12}$

   H. $\dfrac{5}{7}$

   J. 10

   K. 14

13. The number of people in the electronics store is shown in the matrix below.

Adolescents	Adults	Senior Citizens
75	100	30

   The ratio of people from each age group who will purchase a product to the number of people in that age group in the store is shown in the following matrix:

Adolescents	0.20
Adults	0.35
Senior Citizens	0.10

   Based on the matrices, how many people will make purchases?

   A. 15

   B. 41

   C. 53

   D. 133

   E. 205

Use the following table to answer questions 14 and 15:

The table below shows the genres of radio music, broken down by the medium (AM, FM, or satellite) on which they are aired. In addition, the table shows the number of hours in which there is a live disc jockey.

Genre	Medium	# of Hours Where There Is a Live Disc Jockey
Classical	AM	6
	FM	3
	Satellite	12
Country	AM	24
	FM	7
	Satellite	16
News	AM	24
	FM	24
	Satellite	24
Pop	AM	14
	Satellite	15
Rock	AM	12
	Satellite	24

14. What is the average number of hours, rounded to the nearest hour, that the country genre has a live disc jockey?

   F. 3

   G. 7

   H. 14

   J. 16

   K. 24

GO ON TO THE NEXT PAGE

15. The time of day in which there is a live disc jockey does not matter, as long as there is a live disc jockey for the number of hours listed in the table. Assume that a disc jockey can switch from any genre and medium to another with the flip of a switch. Based on the table, what is the minimum number of disc jockeys needed to cover all genres and mediums, if each works an eight-hour shift?

A. 5

B. 13

C. 24

D. 25

E. 195

16. In the following table, every row, column, and diagonal must have equivalent sums. What is the value of the lower left cell in order for this to be true?

m	$-4m$	$3m$
$2m$	0	$-2m$
	$4m$	$-m$

F. $-4m$

G. $-3m$

H. -3

J. 0

K. m

17. The following standard coordinate plane is shown, with the four quadrants labeled. Point R, denoted by $R(x, y)$ is graphed on this plane, such that $x \neq 0$ and $y \neq 0$.

If the product xy is a positive number, then point R is located in:

A. quadrant I only.

B. quadrant II only.

C. quadrant III only.

D. quadrant I or IV only.

E. quadrant I or III only.

18. The cafeteria offers 7 different sandwiches, 3 different soups, and 4 different drink choices on the luncheon menu. How many distinct meals are available if a meal consists of 1 sandwich, 1 soup, and 1 drink?

F. 7

G. 14

H. 21

J. 84

K. Cannot be determined from the given information.

19. At the university, there are 5 females for every 3 males. If there are 6,000 male students, how many students are female?

A. 10,000

B. 12,000

C. 16,000

D. 18,000

E. 30,000

GO ON TO THE NEXT PAGE ⟹

20. What is the length, in inches, of the diagonal of a rectangle whose dimensions are 16 inches by 30 inches?

    F. 25

    G. 23

    H. 34

    J. 578

    K. 1,156

21. Which of the following expressions is NOT equivalent to $5n + 1$, if $n > 0$?

    A. $\dfrac{1}{5n+1}$

    B. $5(n + 2) - 9$

    C. $\dfrac{1}{\dfrac{1}{5n+1}}$

    D. $\dfrac{5n^2 + n}{n}$

    E. $\dfrac{25n^2 - 1}{5n - 1}$

22. Which of the following equations is equivalent to $3x + 2y = 16$?

    F. $y = -\dfrac{3}{2}x + 16$

    G. $y = -\dfrac{2}{3}x + 8$

    H. $y = \dfrac{3}{2}x + 8$

    J. $y = -\dfrac{3}{2}x + 8$

    K. $y = -\dfrac{2}{3}x + 8$

23. A solution to the equation $x^2 - 20x + 75 = 0$ is:

    A. –15.

    B. –5.

    C. 0.

    D. 3.

    E. 5.

24. Given the following right triangle ΔLMN, what is the value of $\cos N$?

    F. $\dfrac{5}{13}$

    G. $\dfrac{5}{12}$

    H. $\dfrac{12}{13}$

    J. $\dfrac{13}{12}$

    K. $\dfrac{13}{5}$

GO ON TO THE NEXT PAGE

25. In the following circle, chord *AB* passes through the center of circle *O*. If the radius *OC* is perpendicular to chord *AB* and has length of 7 centimeters, what is the length of chord *BC*, to the nearest tenth of a centimeter?

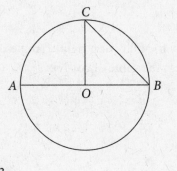

   A. 5.3

   B. 7.0

   C. 9.9

   D. 12.1

   E. 14.0

26. To convert a temperature in degrees Celsius to degrees Fahrenheit, the formula is $F = \frac{9}{5}C + 32$, where *C* is the degrees in Celsius. What temperature, to the nearest degree Celsius, equals a temperature of 86 degrees Fahrenheit?

   F. 30

   G. 54

   H. 80

   J. 86

   K. 187

27. The Olympic-sized pool is 50 meters long, 25 meters wide, and holds 14,375 cubic meters of water. If the pool is the same depth in all parts, about how many meters deep is the water in the pool?

   A. Less than 9

   B. Between 9 and 10

   C. Between 10 and 11

   D. Between 11 and 12

   E. More than 12

28. In the following right triangle $\triangle DEF$, the measure of segment *DE* is 42 inches, and the tangent of angle *D* is $\frac{5}{8}$. What is the length of segment *EF*, to the nearest tenth of an inch?

   F. 26.3

   G. 42.625

   H. 49.6

   J. 67.2

   K. 210.0

GO ON TO THE NEXT PAGE ⟹

29. The following bar graph shows the number of people at the spring prom, according to their grade level at the high school. According to the graph, what fraction of the people at the prom were sophomores?

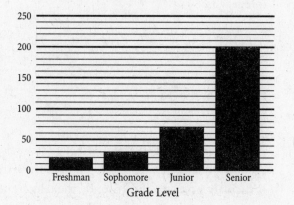

Number of Prom Attendees, by Grade Level

A. $\dfrac{1}{16}$

B. $\dfrac{3}{32}$

C. $\dfrac{3}{29}$

D. $\dfrac{3}{20}$

E. $\dfrac{3}{10}$

30. In the following segment shown, point X is the midpoint of segment WZ. If the measure of WY is 26 cm and the measure of WZ is 44 cm, what is the length, in centimeters, of segment XY?

F. 4

G. 13

H. 18

J. 22

K. 70

31. What is the x-coordinate of the intersection point, in the (x, y) coordinate system, of the lines $2x + 3y = 8$ and $5x + y = 7$?

A. −1

B. $\dfrac{15}{7}$

C. 1

D. 2

E. 3

32. For all pairs of real numbers a and b, where $a = 2b - 8$, $b = ?$

F. $a + 4$

G. $2a - 8$

H. $2a + 8$

J. $\dfrac{a - 8}{2}$

K. $\dfrac{a + 8}{2}$

33. What is the area, in square millimeters, of the parallelogram $RSUT$ shown?

A. 30

B. 39

C. 54

D. 168

E. 182

GO ON TO THE NEXT PAGE

34. If $x = -(y + 3)$, then $(x + y)^3 = ?$

    F. −27

    G. −9

    H. 9

    J. 27

    K. Cannot be determined from the given information.

35. The following is a partial map of Centerville, showing 80 square miles: a total of 8 miles of Main Street and a total of 10 miles of Front Street. There is a fire station at the corner of Main and Front Streets, shown as point *F*. The town wants to build a new fire station exactly halfway between the hospital, at *H,* and the school, at *S*. What would be the driving directions to get from the current fire station to the new fire station, by way of Main and Elm streets? All streets and avenues shown intersect at right angles.

    A. 2.5 miles east, 4 miles north

    B. 2.5 miles west, 4 miles north

    C. 2.5 miles east, 6 miles south

    D. 5.5 miles west, 4 miles south

    E. 5.5 miles west, 6 miles south

36. There are two consecutive odd integers. The difference between four times the larger and twice the smaller is 36. If *x* represents the smaller integer, which of the following equations can be used to determine the smaller integer?

    F. $4x - 2x = 36$

    G. $4(x + 1) - 2x = 36$

    H. $4(x + 2) - 2x = 36$

    J. $(x + 3) - 2x = 36$

    K. $36 - 4x = 2x$

37. A 15-foot supporting wire is attached to a telephone pole 12 feet from the ground. The wire is then anchored to the ground. The telephone pole stands perpendicular to the ground. How far, in feet, is the anchor of the supporting wire from the base of the telephone pole?

    A. 3

    B. 6

    C. 9

    D. 12

    E. 15

38. In the following figure, the sides of the square are tangent to the inner circle. If the area of the circle is 100π square units, what is the unit length of a side of the square?

    F. 400

    G. 100

    H. 20

    J. 10

    K. π

GO ON TO THE NEXT PAGE

39. The rectangles *ABCD* and *EFGH* shown are similar. Using the given information, what is the length of side *EH*, to the nearest tenth of an inch?

    A. 0.8
    B. 1.3
    C. 5.3
    D. 7.0
    E. 8.0

40. In the parallelogram *VWXY* shown, points *U, V, Y,* and *Z* form a straight line. Given the angle measures as shown in the figure, what is the measure of angle ∠*WYX* ?

    F. 25°
    G. 30°
    H. 50°
    J. 100°
    K. 150°

41. In the following figure, all interior angles are 90°, and all dimension lengths are given in centimeters. What is the perimeter of this figure, in centimeters?

    A. 40
    B. 61
    C. 82
    D. 122
    E. Cannot be determined from the given information.

42. In the mayoral election, $\frac{3}{4}$ of the eligible voters at one site cast a vote. Three-fifths of the votes at this site were for candidate Martinez. If there are 3,500 eligible voters at this site, how many of them voted for Martinez?

    F. 417
    G. 1,575
    H. 2,100
    J. 2,625
    K. 4,725

43. Given that *a* and *b* are positive integers, and the greatest common factor of a^4b^2 and a^3b is 54, what is a possible value for *b*?

    A. 2
    B. 3
    C. 6
    D. 9
    E. 27

GO ON TO THE NEXT PAGE

44. If 40% of x is 70, then what is 160% of x?

    F.   28
    G.   45
    H.   112
    J.   175
    K.   280

45. Point M (2,3) and point N (6,5) are points on the coordinate plane. What is the length of the segment MN?

    A. $\sqrt{2}$ units
    B. $2\sqrt{3}$ units
    C. $2\sqrt{5}$ units
    D.   6 units
    E.   20 units

46. The ratio of the sides of two squares is 5:7. What is the ratio of the perimeters of these squares?

    F.   1:2
    G.   1:12
    H.   1:35
    J.   5:7
    K.   25:49

47. What is the equation of a circle in the coordinate plane with center (–2, 3) and radius of 9 units?

    A. $(x - 2)^2 + (y + 3)^2 = 9$
    B. $(x + 2)^2 + (y - 3)^2 = 9$
    C. $(x - 2)^2 + (y + 3)^2 = 81$
    D. $(x + 2)^2 + (y - 3)^2 = 3$
    E. $(x + 2)^2 + (y - 3)^2 = 81$

48. In the complex number system, $i^2 = -1$.
    Given that $\dfrac{3}{5 - i}$ is a complex number, what is the result of $\dfrac{3}{5 - i} \times \dfrac{5 + i}{5 + i}$?

    F. $\dfrac{3}{5 + i}$
    G. $\dfrac{15 + 3i}{24}$
    H. $\dfrac{15 + 3i}{26}$
    J. $\dfrac{15 + i}{26}$
    K. $\dfrac{15 + i}{24}$

49. The following figures show regular polygons and the sum of the degrees of the angles in each polygon. Based on these figures, what is the number of degrees in an n-sided regular polygon?

    A. $60n$
    B. $180n$
    C. $180(n - 2)$
    D. $20n^2$
    E.   Cannot be determined from the information given.

GO ON TO THE NEXT PAGE

50. Fifty high school students were polled to see if they owned a cell phone and an mp3 player. A total of 35 of the students own a cell phone, and a total of 18 of the students own an mp3 player. What is the minimum number of students who own both a cell phone and an mp3 player?

F. 0

G. 3

H. 17

J. 32

K. 53

51. What is the solution set of all real numbers n such that $-4n + 3 > -4n + 1$?

A. All real numbers

B. All positive numbers

C. All negative numbers

D. All numbers such that $n > -\dfrac{1}{2}$

E. All numbers such that $n < -\dfrac{1}{2}$

52. If 3 people all shake hands with each other, there are a total of 3 handshakes. If 4 people all shake hands with each other, there are a total of 6 handshakes. How many total handshakes will there be if 5 people all shake hands with each other?

F. 7

G. 9

H. 10

J. 11

K. 12

53. The following chart shows the percentages of the county budget expenses by category. The remainder of the budget will be placed in the category Miscellaneous. If this data is to be put into a circle graph, what will be the degree measure of the Miscellaneous wedge, rounded to the nearest degree?

Budget Category	Percentage of Budget
Salaries	23
Road Repair	5
Employee Benefits	22
Building Mainte-nance/Utilities	18

A. 32

B. 58

C. 68

D. 115

E. 245

54. If $\tan \theta = -\dfrac{4}{3}$, and $\dfrac{\pi}{2} < \theta < \pi$, then $\sin \theta = ?$

F. $-\dfrac{4}{5}$

G. $-\dfrac{3}{4}$

H. $-\dfrac{3}{5}$

J. $\dfrac{3}{5}$

K. $\dfrac{4}{5}$

GO ON TO THE NEXT PAGE

55. Which of the following systems of inequalities is represented by the shaded region on the coordinate plane below?

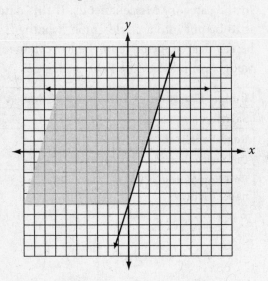

A. $y < 6$ and $y > 3x - 5$

B. $x < 6$ and $y > 3x - 5$

C. $y < 6$ and $y < 3x - 5$

D. $x < 6$ and $y < -3x - 5$

E. $y < 6$ and $y > \dfrac{1}{3}x - 5$

56. If $f(x) = 2(x + 7)$, then $f(x + c) = ?$

F. $2x + 2c + 7$

G. $2x + c + 7$

H. $2x + c + 14$

J. $2x + 2c + 14$

K. $2(x + 7) + c$

57. Which graph represents the solution set for the equation $y = \dfrac{2x^2 - 8}{x - 2}$?

A.

B.

C.

D.

E.

 GO ON TO THE NEXT PAGE

58. What are the coordinates of Q', the reflection of the point $Q(r,s)$ after a reflection over the y-axis?

    F. $(-r,s)$

    G. $(-r,-s)$

    H. $(s,-r)$

    J. $(r,-s)$

    K. $(-s,r)$

59. If $g = 4q + 3$ and $h = 2q - 8$, what is g in terms of h ?

    A. $g = \dfrac{h+8}{2}$

    B. $g = \dfrac{4h+11}{2}$

    C. $2h + 19$

    D. $2h + 11$

    E. $h = \dfrac{g-3}{4}$

60. Find the $\cos(75°)$ knowing that $\cos(75°) = \cos(30° + 45°)$. Use the formula $\cos(\alpha + \beta) = \cos(\alpha)\cos(\beta) - \sin(\alpha)\sin(\beta)$ and the following table of values:

θ	$\sin \theta$	$\cos \theta$	$\tan \theta$
30°	$\dfrac{1}{2}$	$\dfrac{\sqrt{3}}{2}$	$\dfrac{\sqrt{3}}{3}$
45°	$\dfrac{\sqrt{2}}{2}$	$\dfrac{\sqrt{2}}{2}$	1
60°	$\dfrac{\sqrt{3}}{2}$	$\dfrac{1}{2}$	$\sqrt{3}$

    F. $\dfrac{\sqrt{3} - \sqrt{2}}{4}$

    G. $\dfrac{\sqrt{3} - \sqrt{2}}{2}$

    H. $\dfrac{\sqrt{6} - \sqrt{2}}{4}$

    J. $\dfrac{\sqrt{6} - \sqrt{2}}{2}$

    K. $\dfrac{3 - \sqrt{2}}{4}$

READING TEST

35 Minutes—40 Questions

Directions: There are four passages in this test. Each passage is followed by several questions. After reading a passage, choose the best answer to each question and fill in the corresponding oval on your answer document. You may refer to the passages as often as necessary.

PASSAGE I

PROSE FICTION

This excerpt from a short story describes a conversation between a woman and her husband, who is a twin.

Emily couldn't help but grin broadly after answering the phone. She frequently called us "two peas in a pod," but I'd always felt
Line like any time we were mentioned outside
(5) of my presence he was "Bruce" and I was "Bruce's twin brother." Because of this, I wasn't surprised to hear my wife giggling uncontrollably and see her twirling the phone cord around her finger while talking
(10) to him. Despite the fact she was speaking to someone genetically identical to me, I couldn't help but wonder if she had ever responded so enthusiastically to one of my stories.
(15)   "Okay, I'll tell him. Talk to you soon." After Emily hung up, I watched her take a deep, almost wistful breath before walking over to me.
      "Bruce seems well," I said, trying to
(20) sound casual. "He told me about the new job and everything. What did you guys talk about?"
      "Not much." Emily replied. She walked behind my chair and patted my shoulder
(25) before sitting on the couch and opening her magazine. It didn't appear as if she were really reading. She seemed to stop and start, pausing and reflecting about something unrelated to the smiling celebrities featured
(30) in the article.
      "It's funny to think that he knows some of these people," she said, pointing at her magazine.

I looked at the gleaming teeth and
(35) chiseled features of the actors, and then looked over at a picture of Bruce and me resting on the mantel. Looking closely at the photo always made my stomach turn; as with every picture of us, there was an
(40) unmistakable vitality in Bruce's face that wasn't present in mine. It were as if I were wearing a "Bruce" costume; I was trying to mimic one of his trademark smiles, but I always seemed to produce a different failed
(45) attempt.
      "You all right?" Emily asked, noticing my expression.
      I grabbed the picture from the mantel and brought it to her. She looked at it and
(50) looked up at me quizzically.
      "Can you tell which one is me?" I asked.
      She looked back at the picture and pushed her lip out as she looked from one face to the next. After about five seconds she
(55) pointed to my face, then turned and looked at me confidently.
      "How could you tell?" I asked.
      "Well, it wasn't very hard," she responded. "You are my husband, and I love
(60) the way you smile. Bruce looks exactly the same in every picture, it looks practiced, but for you it always seems like you're thinking about something, even concentrating, to make sure you smile right."
(65)   "Really?" I was surprised by how much thought she had put into this.
      She took the picture and put it back on the mantel. I could still see the perfection in

GO ON TO THE NEXT PAGE →

Bruce's smile and hesitation in mine, but at
(70) least Emily found a way to compliment my
insecurities.

Emily went back to perusing her
magazine.

"At least you ended up with a Fairholm,"
(75) I said, "even if it wasn't the famous one."

"Oh, was I supposed to pursue the
famous one?" she shot back.

She closed her magazine and put it
down on the coffee table. There wasn't an
(80) argument coming, but I saw her disappointment.
The problem was not that she actually
would have married my brother before me;
it was the simple fact that I couldn't help but
believe that to be the case. I saw myself as
(85) second to him and always had. With embarrassing
relatives, people will always point
out that one can't choose his or her family,
but when you're a twin, it's not the association
that you fear, it's the comparison.
(90) "Do you want to be where he is?" she
inquired, with an empty tone.

"This is exactly where I want to be,"
I replied. "I just never know how to explain
to people that I'm an insurance adjuster,
(95) not a Hollywood agent. They always want
to know how it happened when we had the
same upbringing and education. They look
at me as if I did something wrong."

"Do you ever call him?" she asked.
(100) "I figure he's busy, and he calls enough,"
I said.

She cradled her chin in her hand, and
looked at me in mild disbelief. "You realize
that by not calling and turning down his
(105) invitations to visit you make him feel
rejected, right?"

"Come on, Emily. He's surrounded
by famous people, he doesn't need my
approval."
(110) "Maybe not," she sighed, "but his favorite
stories to tell me aren't about Hollywood,
they're about you two growing up."

"Well, he was popular then, too," I said,
shrugging.

(115) "He doesn't look at it that way," she
responded. "He would give up a lot to have
your approval, Dave. He wants to be your
brother, not a competitor."

"It's okay, Emily. I'll call him soon, but I
(120) think that he'll be okay either way."

1. Dave would probably agree with which of the
   following statements regarding his relationship with Bruce?

   A. They would be better off not talking at
      all.

   B. Their phone conversations are vital to
      their relationship.

   C. Their bond as twins is stronger due to
      Emily's effort.

   D. Their competition makes it harder for
      them to get along.

2. Emily is best described as:

   F. aloof and ineffectual.

   G. needling and meddlesome.

   H. caring and diplomatic.

   J. pained and inconsolable.

3. Which of the following statements does
   NOT describe a feeling Dave has toward his
   brother?

   A. He is jealous of the reaction his brother
      gets from Emily during their phone
      conversation.

   B. He believes he would be better suited
      for his brother's type of work.

   C. He is resentful of his brother's superior
      social skills.

   D. He is skeptical of his brother's desire for
      his approval.

GO ON TO THE NEXT PAGE ⟩

4. The primary focus of the first paragraph is:

   F. Emily's attempt to make her husband jealous.

   G. Emily's desire for the brothers to resolve their differences.

   H. Dave's hope to distance himself from his twin brother.

   J. Dave's feelings of inferiority to his twin brother.

5. Lines 99–120 ("Do you ever…either way") suggest that Dave does not contact Bruce because Dave:

   A. believes that Bruce has great need for him but does not want to admit to Emily that she is right.

   B. feels guilty about being distant toward Bruce and worries that he will have to explain himself.

   C. wants to prove to Emily that he is not impressed by Bruce's high profile job.

   D. still harbors resentment over Bruce getting preferential treatment during their childhood.

6. According to the passage, when Dave looks at the photograph, he sees:

   F. his brother being cruel to him.

   G. two indistinguishable faces.

   H. a comparison unfavorable to him.

   J. his wife paying more attention to Bruce.

7. Which of the following best summarizes Dave's feelings when he asks Emily to pick him out in the picture?

   A. Dave is confident that Emily will prefer his image to Bruce's.

   B. Dave is insecure; he feels the picture compares him unfavorably to Bruce.

   C. Dave is worried, because he thinks Emily will want to talk more about Bruce after seeing a picture of him.

   D. Dave is angry because he did not want to talk about the picture in the first place.

8. It can be logically deduced from the passage that Dave and Bruce:

   F. tell Emily different sounding stories about their shared childhood.

   G. are frequently at odds regarding their different professions.

   H. have often fought over Emily's attention.

   J. were much closer shortly before Bruce moved.

9. It can be inferred from the passage that both Emily and Dave conclude that when pictures are taken of the brothers:

   A. Bruce looks much better than Dave.

   B. Dave appears angry at Bruce.

   C. pictures of Bruce are more consistent than those of Dave.

   D. Dave's expression makes a greater impression on the viewer than Bruce's.

GO ON TO THE NEXT PAGE ⇨

10. According to the passage, the reason Emily tells Dave about the content of Bruce's stories is because Emily:

    F. wants to convince Dave that Bruce does not see himself as better than Dave.

    G. wishes to hear Dave's version of the stories.

    H. sees this as a way to make Dave more impressed with his brother.

    J. thinks that this will make Dave sympathetic to Bruce's loneliness.

PASSAGE II

SOCIAL SCIENCE

This passage discusses the relationship between the media and public opinion.

Large-scale media would likely be traced back to ancient tribes sharing information about the edibility of berries or the
Line aggressiveness of animals. Despite constant
(5) evolution, the information most sought after is that regarding personal safety, personal opportunity, and the triumphs and misdeeds of others—the larger the persona and more laudatory or despicable the act,
(10) the better. When a story is of continued national interest, however, the focus shifts even further from facts and more to theater. To step back and compose an objective plot of goings on is a distant possibility, but
(15) establishing the hero or villain of the day is paramount. Ultimately, the public's desire to have cold, dry, and correct facts is virtually nonexistent.

Current newscasts exacerbate this by
(20) delivering an assault on the senses with meaningless graphics and theatrical music; meanwhile, the monotone newscaster reads, verbatim from a teleprompter, often using phrases identical to those on other
(25) networks. Additionally, the viewer has

probably already read the same story on the Internet earlier. When television was limited to three networks, rather than ubiquitous news-only channels, the newscaster
(30) was a national figure, audience members would eagerly await information that was new to them, and would expect a relatively thorough explanation of any complicated goings on. For example, to this day many
(35) people, in explaining the Watergate scandal to those too young to know of it, use Walter Cronkite's delineation as the basis for their understanding.

The objective, trustworthy anchorperson
(40) has also given way to vociferous demagogues promising truth but delivering oversimplified, bias-driven sound bites. The idea of allowing individuals to draw their own conclusions is notably absent; in fact, many
(45) personalities mock those with opinions differing from those presented. The availability of neutral online sources mitigates this slightly, but not to any large degree. While the actual article may be impartial,
(50) electronic periodicals will still sensationalize headlines in order to attract casual readers, and those very headlines sway many readers to certain opinions before the article is even read. For example, if a headline mentions
(55) an "enraged public," the reader is far more likely to both read and take umbrage with the information than he or she would if the article mentioned a subject that "irked locals."

(60) In truth, though, the public is as desirous for dry and objective facts as finicky children are for brussels sprouts. The personalities willing to shrug off accountability in favor of wild accusations and
(65) bombastic slogans captivate a large demographic, while one would be generous by saying that objective fact-based programs occupy even a niche market. This not only damages the general accuracy of so-called
(70) "news," but further polarizes the public. People now have the option to receive their

GO ON TO THE NEXT PAGE ⟶

news from hosts with a variety of political leanings, and one almost invariably chooses to watch the personality closest to one's own (75) personal opinions. This is more harmful than convenient, because it allows viewers to simply parrot information they are given, eliminating any thought or scrutiny. It is this intellectual laziness that aids in (80) distancing the general public from factual information: as a growing number become resigned to accept whatever their favorite host tells them, the more freedom networks have in passing sensationalist entertainment (85) as news. It boils down to the unfortunate truth that most are far more likely to accept inaccurate information as fact rather than question the legitimacy of something that seems to fit with opinions a particular (90) audience member holds.

Those who make the news also obfuscate objective facts. A legion of employees is designated solely for the purpose of making the decisions of political figures sound (95) flawless. Oftentimes, important decisions are made, and throughout a lengthy press conference, not a single factual implication is discussed. The meeting becomes nothing more than an opportunity for political (100) employees to test their infallible sounding slogans, while the media dissects the semantics rather than the facts. Semantics, however, are all the media is presented with.

Despite all these methods of prevarication, (105) people still are better informed than they were in the past. Public knowledge of events often occurs minutes after the fact, rather than days or weeks. The populace has a strong desire for news in general, (110) and amid all the unscrupulous presentation methods, facts do exist. However, the profitability of news has made presentation premium, not trustworthiness. Complicating matters further is the populace's impatience; (115) the standard consumer would rather be presented with a minute and potentially inaccurate statement—one that may or may not be retracted the following day—than

suffer through a lengthy treatise comprised (120) of all the known facts and nuances of a particular event. The desire to know still exists, however; it just happens to be overshadowed by the public's desire for personal consensus and the media's desire to reel in (125) the public.

11. One of the primary points the author attempts to make regarding the current news media is that:

A. the media passes off made-up stories as facts.

B. the news anchors are not as opinionated as they were in decades past.

C. the media focuses more on presentation than substance.

D. the media goes directly against what news audiences truly desire to see.

12. The author makes what claim about impartial news stories?

F. They no longer exist.

G. They can be sensationalized in ways other than article content.

H. They often have headlines that correctly reflect the emotional level of the story.

J. They all have headlines that attempt to make the reader feel involved in the story.

13. The author brings up Walter Cronkite's coverage of Watergate in order to assert that:

A. Walter Cronkite was a particularly adept newsperson.

B. a previous standard for news rightly included clarification of complex issues.

C. current newscasters are far more forgettable than those before them.

D. the expanding number of television channels has made individual newscasters less famous.

GO ON TO THE NEXT PAGE →

14. By stating that "personal consensus" is of great importance to the public (lines 123–124), the author is probably suggesting that members of the public:

   F. do not want information that contradicts their own beliefs.

   G. work hard to find the source closest to truth, despite the difficulties present.

   H. wish to resolve any moral conflicts they may have with practices in news reporting.

   J. have difficulty finding news sources reflecting their personal views.

15. According to the passage, what type of news stories are sensationalized the most?

   A. Those with a fairly clear chain of events

   B. Those that stay in the public's consciousness for long periods of time

   C. Those that clearly support one political view

   D. Those with the most scandalous information

16. As used in line 14 (paragraph 1), the word *distant* most nearly means:

   F. separated.

   G. different.

   H. reserved.

   J. unlikely.

17. Based on the passage, which of the following headlines would the author be most likely to criticize?

   A. Earthquake Rocks Small Community, Arouses Questions Regarding Preparedness

   B. New Tax Protested by Idaho Farmers

   C. Parents Across Country Outraged at Offensive Song

   D. Governor Describes Proposed Legislation as "Monstrous"

18. The author asserts that individuals will often accept potentially inaccurate information because they:

   F. believe that most newscasters are honest.

   G. have no way to research correct facts.

   H. are forced to translate the guarded words of political employees.

   J. have similar political beliefs to specific media personalities.

19. In the fourth paragraph, the phrase "even a niche market" (line 68) expresses the author's feeling that:

   A. media companies are influenced greatly by public demand.

   B. cable television networks are unwilling to present objective facts.

   C. factual news media should look into better marketing practices.

   D. factual news would be profitable with greater exposure.

20. The author argues that in searching for a news source, audience members are most likely to choose the source that:

   F. features the most entertaining newscaster.

   G. validates the audience member's opinion.

   H. presents the shortest and simplest explanation for goings on.

   J. focuses on big stories rather than local ones.

GO ON TO THE NEXT PAGE

PASSAGE III

HUMANITIES

This passage explores the relationship between the immigrant experience and one person's career choice.

My grandfather was born in a turbulent time in Russia. His non-communist lineage made him unwelcome, before he had left the
Line womb. His father, an officer in the Russian
(5) army, was considered an enemy of the communist Bolsheviks, so my grandfather lived less than a year in what was his native Moscow, and spent most of his younger years moving across Asia. Despite this, he
(10) had pride in being Russian, associated with Russians throughout his life, and would frequently quiz me on Russian history. This all in tribute to a country that ended up under different rule during the time his
(15) mother was pregnant with him.

As a child, exiled to Siberia, my grandfather heard his father tell of the greatness that existed within the country that had forced the family into exile. It was known
(20) that, first with his parents, and later as an adult, my grandfather was going to have to seek a new place to call home. Despite this foregone conclusion, Russia was still romanticized, and my grandfather learned
(25) to treat the country with reverence. This was in contrast to the sentiments found in other recently exiled Russians, who would not simply lament the actions taken by the country, but disparage all eight million
(30) square miles. In my family's search for a place to settle, attempting to forge a consistent identity was nearly impossible, as no one knew if the next location would hold for a month, let alone a year, all hoped for an
(35) unattainable "new Moscow."

The first elongated refuge was found, ironically, in China, which would later have its own communist revolution. After several years of relative stability, the revolution

(40) precipitated the move to the United States. Upon arrival in San Francisco, my grandfather, along with my grandmother and their young son, my father, found other Russian immigrants who were also new to the
(45) country. "*Ya amerikanets*" people would say, and despite the fact that they were recent immigrants who associated primarily with those of shared ethnicity and circumstance, they would play the role they desired, and
(50) repeat "*ya amerikanets*"—"I am American." They would share many stories about their native land, but did not repeat "*ya russkiy*," because being Russian went without saying.

While it was clear that this would be
(55) the last country my grandfather would reside in, and that he wished to become more American, it was perhaps the most confusing of times. It was less of a problem in acclimating to an adopted
(60) setting; the problem was dealing with a permanent setting at all. The only consistency throughout the first thirty years of my grandfather's life was the knowledge that every "home" was temporary, and now this
(65) was no longer the case. I often wonder if his successful career in the real estate business had anything to do with what must have been a rare transformation of circumstance.

Not only was my grandfather interested
(70) in real estate, he was ardent about the importance of ownership, a naturally discordant view to that of the then Soviet Union, and thus selling homes became a purpose in addition to an occupation.

(75) Part of his success in real estate was owed to strategic compromise. Considering American sentiments regarding Russia during the Cold War, there were times that he was sure he lost certain house sales due
(80) to his last name and accent. However, to those willing to listen, he found advantages informing people that he was an exiled

GO ON TO THE NEXT PAGE ⟶

Russian, and ardently disagreed with
the communist government. He would
(85) also point out his pride in being a new
American, and allow a potential buyer to
degrade Russia without blinking.

Fortunately, the 1950s were a time of
settling across the country, and this made
(90) real estate a very lucrative profession. It
wasn't just this that attracted my grandfather,
though; he also saw it as an opportunity
to give tiny parts of the country to
other people, returning the favor, in a way.

(95) Yet, it always seemed that something
vital still rested in the opposite hemisphere.
Once communism fell, he began
returning to Russia yearly, and while he and
my grandmother never showed the family
(100) pictures from Russia the way they would
from the various cruise ships they traveled
on, it could be deduced that returning to
Russia was analogous to an adopted child
traveling to meet his or her birth-parents:
(105) the journey is one of personal necessity
rather than pleasure, and the encounter
is one that elucidates one's very existence.
In selling real estate, my grandfather had
worked to make this unnecessary. I believe
(110) that he wished for people to keep those
houses, and pass them down to later generations,
giving the space a sort of familial
permanence, rather than a fleeting stay.

For most, the thought of real estate
(115) agents conjures up images of smiling
advertisements on benches and buses, and
the skill of selling something so important.
Many are wary of salespeople in general,
questioning the practice of convincing
(120) people something is in their best interest
when the salesperson stands to personally
benefit. My grandfather did financially
benefit from sales, but there was more to
it; his realization of the American dream
(125) only made him want to be a part of others
reaching for the same thing, whether their
native home was around the block or
thousands of miles away.

21. One of the main points the author attempts to
convey in the passage is that:

A. immigrants would often rather live in
their native land.

B. American-born people tend not to be
able to understand how displacement
affects immigrants.

C. immigrants that acclimate well to
America still may have indelible ties to
their native land.

D. immigrants are often shocked by the
stability offered to them in America.

22. Based on the first three paragraphs, which of
the following best describes the movements of
the author's grandfather, prior to his emigra-
tion to America?

F. He grew up primarily in Siberia and
then moved to China during the
Russian revolution.

G. He grew up in Moscow, was exiled as
an adult, and rapidly moved through
Asia.

H. He was born in Moscow, moved rapidly
through Asia, and settled for a while in
communist China.

J. He was born in Moscow, exiled to
Siberia with his family, and moved
frequently before settling for a
somewhat longer period in China.

23. The author's grandfather's "purpose" (line 73)
and desire to return "the favor" (line 94) are
best described as:

A. providing others with a sense of pride
in being American.

B. shedding light on injustices carried out
by other countries.

C. facilitating a stable situation for others.

D. providing well for his family.

GO ON TO THE NEXT PAGE

24. Which of the following actions contradicts a general attitude held by the author's grandfather?

   F. "He would also point out his pride in being a new American, and allow a potential buyer to degrade Russia without blinking" (lines 84–87).

   G. "They would share many stories about their native land, but did not repeat "*ya russkiy*," because being Russian went without saying" (lines 51–53).

   H. "He was ardent about the importance of ownership, a naturally discordant view to that of the then Soviet Union" (lines 70–72).

   J. "Once communism fell, he began returning to Russia yearly" (lines 97–98).

25. The author classifies a "new Moscow" as "unattainable" (line 35) because:

   A. the family believed Moscow to be the most desirable city in the world.

   B. it was unlikely that communism would fall shortly after the revolution.

   C. cities in other countries are entirely unlike those in Russia.

   D. it would not be possible to find a new home that could still be considered a native home.

26. When the author refers to Russians playing "the role" (line 49), he most likely means that the Russians were:

   F. convincing themselves that they were ready to acclimate.

   G. joking with each other.

   H. naïve to the way Americans tend to act with each other.

   J. still hopeful that they would see Russia again.

27. The "strategic compromise" applied by the author's grandfather (line 76) would most likely involve:

   A. agreeing with the potential buyer, no matter what.

   B. ignoring offensive statements.

   C. acting as American as possible.

   D. taking America's side in international disputes.

28. According to the passage, the grandfather's trip back to his native Russia provided him with:

   F. a greater understanding of the inner workings of his native land.

   G. greater motivation to sell homes in America.

   H. a greater sense of personal understanding.

   J. a necessary visit with estranged family members.

29. According to the first paragraph, the author's grandfather's birth happened:

   A. during the communist revolution.

   B. under communist rule.

   C. prior to the communist revolution.

   D. after the fall of communism.

30. When the author states that his grandfather "worked to make this unnecessary" (line 109), he is suggesting that his grandfather's occupation could potentially:

   F. help his grandfather feel more connected to America through his success.

   G. oversee a transaction that could give others a sense belonging.

   H. sell houses that would allow other recent immigrants stability.

   J. help others realize the American dream.

GO ON TO THE NEXT PAGE

PASSAGE IV

NATURAL SCIENCE

This passage discusses the degree to which rattlesnakes pose a threat to humans.

In both recorded and oral history, the rattlesnakes
are categorized as malevolent beings.
Their lance-shaped heads and angular brow-lines
Line make them look the perfect villain,
(5) and their venom cements this classification.
Publicized reports of bite victims seem to
prove their nefarious nature.

Unlike mammalian predators such as
bears, rattlesnakes do not have the reputation
(10) of an animal deserving human respect.
One imagines the rattlesnake hiding in our
backyards, waiting to strike.

In recent long-term studies, however,
the social behavior of rattlesnakes has been
(15) found to be quite different than many would
expect. Herpetologists, scientists who study
snakes, had long suspected a more complex
and thoughtful existence for the reptiles,
and now have hard information to back up
(20) their theories. When examined, the sinister
opportunist lurking in the shadows better
resembles a mild-mannered domestic.
Unlike the nonvenomous kingsnake, rattlesnakes
are entirely noncannibalistic, and
(25) tend to spend their entire lives with a single
mate. The mating ritual in which two males
will extend almost half of their bodies off
the ground to wrestle is not lethal, and, once
bested, a rattlesnake peacefully retreats to
(30) find a new den of eligible mates. Female
rattlesnakes give birth to live young, and
rattlesnakes often share their dens, even
hibernating with tortoises without incident.

Sadly, it seems that only those with an
(35) existing fascination with snakes are aware of
this socially functional rattlesnake. Another
discovery that made little stir in the public
consciousness is an experiment in which
herpetologists tracked snakes with radio
(40) transmitters, and saw their behavior when

humans entered their habitat. While a few
snakes did hold their ground and rattle,
most saw or sensed a disturbance (snakes
cannot hear) and immediately headed in
(45) the opposite direction. Many of the snakes
that were handled by herpetologists did not
coil or strike. This is not to say that a snake
will not bite a human if disturbed, but the
tendency is to retreat first and give warning
(50) second, before striking becomes a possibility.

Describing a more docile nature does
not imply that rattlesnakes would make
good pets for children, but considering the
aggressiveness often displayed by a South
(55) American pit viper, the fer-de-lance, one
familiar with both would have far fewer
trepidations in passing by a rattlesnake. For
one thing, rattlesnakes do coil and rattle,
giving humans an opportunity to move
(60) away, while fer-de-lances will often strike
at passersby without warning. Furthermore,
when it comes down to statistics,
American hospitals report an average of
7,000 snakebite patients a year; generally
(65) more than half are actually from nonvenomous
snakes thought by victims to be
venomous. On average, fewer than six people
die of snake envenomation annually, and
the vast majority of the serious bites are due
(70) to either handling the snake or stepping on
it; most people bitten by snakes they were
not engaging end up with very mild bites.
Compare this with an average of over one
million hospital visits for dog bites and
(75) twenty annual deaths at the jaws of man's
best friend. With such miniscule statistics
regarding snakebites, it is curious why they
are still viewed as unfathomably dangerous,
when bees, lightning—and yes, dogs—are
(80) responsible for far more human fatalities.
The fer-de-lance, however, is responsible for
thousands of annual deaths in Central and
South America.

GO ON TO THE NEXT PAGE ▷

If one is looking for proof that rattlesnakes
(85) do not intend to harm humans, one
should consider perhaps the most stunning
evidence regarding bite behavior. Over
half of the bites rattlesnakes administer to
humans are "dry," meaning the rattlesnake
(90) purposely does not release venom. While I
will not posit that this is due to rattlesnakes
possessing awareness for the well-being of
their non-food-source bite victim, there is
a great deal of thought present. The snake
(95) acknowledges that venom is needed for
immobilizing and digesting prey (venom
is actually saliva), producing venom takes
time, and the human is not a food source.
Therefore, if the snake is not surprised or
(100) fearing death, the damage of a rattlesnake
bite will likely be far less severe than if the
snake used all its venom. This has been
known for some time, but, in many cases, it
is probably better for humans to believe that
(105) the snakes are more liberal with venom than
they are, simply because a frightened and
cornered rattlesnake is very dangerous.

Unfortunately, some people take the
traditional view of the rattlesnake and use
(110) it as an excuse to harm the animals. People
in various areas use the fearsome reputation
of rattlesnakes, along with the more docile
reality, for profit. Rattlesnake roundups are
held, where people collect snakes
(115) beforehand and join in a festival celebrating their
conquest. The events are billed as both
entertainment and as making surrounding
residential areas safer for children; however,
the vast majority of snakes are collected
(120) from uninhabited areas, and people are
frequently bitten at the festivals while
handling the snakes for the audience. Eventually,
the snakes are killed to make clothing
or trophies, and these events are estimated
(125) to be responsible for 100,000 rattlesnake
deaths annually, in comparison to fewer
than six human deaths from rattlesnakes.

Behavior like this provides a better
reason for *crotalid* mythology. With

(130) statistics categorically showing a low level of
danger from rattlesnakes to humans, and an
extremely high level vice versa, it would be
a wonder to see what human-related folklore
would be like if rattlesnakes were able to
(135) speak or write.

31. In relation to the entire passage, the phrase
"the sinister opportunist lurking in the shadows better resembles a mild-mannered domestic" (lines 20–22) most likely implies that:

A. adult rattlesnakes are considerably less
aggressive than juveniles.

B. recent studies regarding rattlesnakes
found few incidents of aggressive
behavior.

C. rattlesnakes are more similar to
mammals than once thought.

D. rattlesnakes are entirely predictable in
behavior.

32. The passage implies that the rattlesnake's fearsome reputation can be beneficial because:

F. it influences people to avoid or move
away from rattlesnakes.

G. it protects the lives of rattlesnakes.

H. it inspires medical advancement in
treating snakebites, despite a low
mortality rate.

J. adventurous people may seek rattlesnakes as pets.

33. What evidence does the passage give regarding the social ability of rattlesnakes?

A. Rattlesnakes are aware of the uses of
their venom.

B. Wrestling between males establishes a
social hierarchy.

C. Rattlesnakes can share their habitat
with other species.

D. Rattlesnakes rarely eat other snakes.

GO ON TO THE NEXT PAGE

34. The statement "it would be a wonder to see what human-related folklore would be like if rattlesnakes were able to speak or write" (lines 132–135) means that:

    F. humans and rattlesnakes both present great risks to each other's safety.

    G. humans and rattlesnakes behave in many similar ways.

    H. humans are a much greater threat to rattlesnakes than rattlesnakes are to humans.

    J. humans have traditionally assigned human emotions to rattlesnakes in folklore.

35. According to the passage, what is the correlation between human behavior and serious rattlesnake bites?

    A. There is no statistical relationship.

    B. Humans that move in quick motions attract strikes.

    C. Humans that actively seek interaction with snakes are less likely to receive a "dry" bite.

    D. Rattlesnakes deliver a variable amount of venom based on how threatening humans act.

36. What is suggested by lines 51–53 when the author states that the new evidence "does not imply that rattlesnakes would make good pets for children"?

    F. Only professional herpetologists should keep rattlesnakes.

    G. Dogs can also be dangerous pets.

    H. Nonaggressive behavior does not make a venomous animal harmless.

    J. Rattlesnakes in the wild are more docile than those in captivity.

37. The passage states that the relative likelihood of a human being killed by a rattlesnake bite is:

    A. greater than that of a dog bite.

    B. less than that of a bee sting.

    C. equal to that of a lightning strike.

    D. comparable to that of the South American fer-de-lance.

38. Which of the following correctly categorizes a rattlesnake's strategy in venom usage?

    F. The larger the prey or predator, the more venom is used.

    G. Even when threatened, a rattlesnake reserves venom to use on prey.

    H. Rattlesnakes are aware that they will wound larger animals.

    J. Rattlesnakes would rather use venom solely for prey.

39. The author states rattlesnake roundups use contradictory logic because:

    A. children are rarely bitten by rattlesnakes.

    B. the rattlesnakes that bite people at roundups would have been far less likely to bite someone in their natural habitat.

    C. organizers use erroneous statistics to make the rattlesnakes seem more dangerous and the events more impressive.

    D. many that go to the events are unaware of how many snakes are killed.

GO ON TO THE NEXT PAGE ▷

40. As used in line 129, the term *crotalid* is most likely:

   F. an unfavorable characterization of humans.

   G. a scientific word meaning "rattlesnakes."

   H. a word describing a herpetologist that specializes in rattlesnakes.

   J. a general word for a group unfairly accused of wrongdoing.

SCIENCE TEST

35 Minutes—40 Questions

Directions: There are seven passages in this test. Each passage is followed by several questions. After reading a passage, choose the best answer to each question and fill in the corresponding oval on your answer document. You may refer to the passages as often as necessary. You are NOT permitted to use a calculator on this test.

PASSAGE I

Glaciers are large masses of ice that move slowly over the Earth's surface due to the force of gravity and changes in elevation. Glacial *calving* occurs when one edge of a glacier borders a body of water. A calving glacier's *terminus* (the lower edge) periodically produces icebergs as they break away from the glacier and into the water.

STUDY 1

A computer was used to create a model of a typical calving glacier. It was hypothesized that a primary factor determining the calving rate is the glacier's velocity at its terminus. Figure 1 shows the calving rate, in meters per year, and length of the computer-generated glacier over a period of 2,000 years.

Figure 1

GO ON TO THE NEXT PAGE ⟹

STUDY 2

Four calving glaciers (A–D) were studied over a period of 10 years. The average velocity at the terminus of each glacier was recorded for years 1–5 and again for years 6–10. The calving rate of each glacier was estimated for the same time periods. The results are recorded in Table 1.

Table 1

Glacier	Years 1–5		Years 6–10	
	Average velocity (m/yr)	Calving rate (m/yr)	Average velocity (m/yr)	Calving rate (m/yr)
A	72	72	63	64
B	51	52	45	47
C	98	106	256	312
D	160	189	53	54

STUDY 3

Meteorologists reported unusually high average temperatures in the regions of Glacier C and Glacier D during the same ten-year period examined in Study 2. It was hypothesized that the high temperatures were responsible for the relatively rapid variations in velocity and calving rates evident for Glacier C and Glacier D in Table 1.

1. If the glacier model used in Study 1 is typical of all calving glaciers, the scientists would draw which of the following conclusions about the relationship between glacier length and calving rate?

   A. As calving rate decreases, glacier length always increases.

   B. As glacier length decreases, calving rate always decreases.

   C. A sharp increase in calving rate results in a sharp decrease in glacier length.

   D. A sharp increase in calving rate results in a sharp increase in glacier length.

2. The meteorologists in Study 3 hypothesized that the faster the calving rate, the faster the sea level at a calving glacier's terminus would rise. If this hypothesis is correct, which of the following glaciers resulted in the fastest rise in sea level during years 6–10?

   F. Glacier A

   G. Glacier B

   H. Glacier C

   J. Glacier D

3. Based on the results of Study 2, a calving glacier traveling at a velocity of 80 m/yr would most likely have a calving rate:

   A. between 72 m/yr and 106 m/yr.

   B. between 106 m/yr and 189 m/yr.

   C. between 189 m/yr and 312 m/yr.

   D. over 312 m/yr.

4. Which of the following statements best describes the behavior of the glaciers observed during Study 2?

   F. All of the glaciers observed traveled faster during the first five years than during the last five years.

   G. All of the glaciers observed traveled faster during the last five years than during the first five years.

   H. The calving rate is always less than the average velocity for all of the glaciers observed.

   J. The calving rate is always greater than or equal to the average velocity for all of the glaciers observed.

GO ON TO THE NEXT PAGE

5. Which of the following graphs best represents the relationship between the calving rate and the average velocity of the glaciers observed in Study 2 for years 6–10?

A.

B.

C.

D.

6. If the hypothesis made by the meteorologists in Study 3 is correct, the glacier modeled in Study 1 most likely experienced unusually high temperatures at approximately what time during the simulated 2,000-year study?

F. 500 years

G. 1,000 years

H. 1,500 years

J. 2,000 years

GO ON TO THE NEXT PAGE

PASSAGE II

Allergic rhinitis refers to a person's nasal reaction to small airborne particles called *allergens*. Table 1 shows the specific allergen, its type, and the approximate number of reported cases of allergic symptoms for a population of 1,000 people living in northern Kentucky during a single year.

Table 1

Month	Allergen type — Specific allergen	Pollen — Trees	Pollen — Grass	Pollen — Weeds	Mold — Alternaria	Mold — Cladosporium	Mold — Aspergillus
January					✿	✿	✿
February					✿	✿	✿
March		✿✿			✿	✿	✿
April		✿✿✿✿			✿	✿	✿
May		✿✿✿	✿✿✿		✿	✿	✿
June			✿✿✿✿		✿	✿	✿
July			✿✿	✿	✿✿	✿	✿
August				✿✿✿	✿✿✿✿	✿✿✿	✿✿✿✿
September				✿✿	✿✿✿	✿✿✿✿	✿✿✿✿
October				✿✿	✿✿✿	✿✿✿	✿✿✿
November					✿✿	✿	✿
December					✿	✿	✿

Note: Each ✿ equals 100 reported cases of allergic rhinitis.

Weekly tree pollen and total mold spore concentrations were measured in grains per cubic meter (gr/m³) for samples of air taken in southern Iowa for eight weeks. The pollen and mold spore counts are shown in Figures 1 and 2, respectively.

Figure 1

Figure 2

GO ON TO THE NEXT PAGE ⇒

7. Based on Figure 1, the tree pollen count on March 2 was closest to:

   A. 75 gr/m³.

   B. 150 gr/m³.

   C. 1,500 gr/m³.

   D. 1,900 gr/m³.

8. According to Figure 2, the mold spore count in the weeks after November 5:

   F. increased.

   G. decreased.

   H. varied between 1,000 gr/m³ and 2,000 gr/m³.

   J. remained above 2,000 gr/m³.

9. Based on the data in Figure 1, the tree pollen count increased the most between which two dates?

   A. February 9 to February 16

   B. February 23 to March 2

   C. March 2 to March 9

   D. October 29 to November 5

10. According to Figure 1, which of the following conclusions about the tree pollen count is most valid?

    F. The tree pollen count was highest on March 9.

    G. The tree pollen count was highest on March 16.

    H. The tree pollen count was lowest on February 23.

    J. The tree pollen count was lowest on March 16.

11. Based on Table 1, most of the cases of allergic rhinitis in May in northern Kentucky were caused by which of the following allergens?

    A. Tree and grass pollen

    B. Grass and weed pollen

    C. Alternaria

    D. Aspergillus

PASSAGE III

Simple harmonic motion (SHM) is motion that is *periodic*, or repetitive, and can be described by a frequency of oscillation. Students performed three experiments to study SHM.

EXPERIMENT 1

The students assembled the pendulum shown in Diagram 1. The mass at the end of the arm was raised to a small height, h, and released. The frequency of oscillation was measured in oscillations per second, or Hertz (Hz), and the process was repeated for several different arm lengths. The results are shown in Figure 1.

Diagram 1

Figure 1

GO ON TO THE NEXT PAGE ⟶

EXPERIMENT 2

A spring was suspended vertically from a hook, and a mass was connected to the bottom of the spring, as shown in Diagram 2. The mass was pulled downward a short distance and released, and the frequency of the resulting oscillation was measured. The procedure was repeated with four different springs and four different masses, and the results are shown in Figure 2.

Diagram 2

Figure 2

EXPERIMENT 3

Using the apparatus from Experiment 2, the mass-spring system was allowed to come to rest, and the *equilibrium length* of the spring was measured. The same four masses and four springs were used, and the results are shown in Figure 3.

Figure 3

12. In Experiment 3, for which of the following masses would Spring B, Spring C, and Spring D have closest to the same equilibrium lengths?

    F. 100 g

    G. 270 g

    H. 500 g

    J. 1,000 g

13. A student has hypothesized that as the length of the arm of a pendulum increases, the oscillation frequency of the pendulum during SHM will decrease. Do the results of Experiment 1 support her hypothesis?

    A. Yes; the oscillation frequency of the pendulum observed in Experiment 1 decreased as the arm length increased.

    B. Yes; although the longest pendulum arm resulted in the highest oscillation frequency, the frequency decreased with increasing arm length for the other three lengths tested.

    C. No; the oscillation frequency of the pendulum observed in Experiment 1 increased as the arm length increased.

    D. No; although the longest pendulum arm resulted in the lowest oscillation frequency, the frequency increased with increasing arm length for the other three lengths tested.

14. Based on the results of Experiment 2, if an engineer needs a spring that oscillates most slowly after being stretched and released, which of the following springs should be chosen?

    F. Spring A
    G. Spring B
    H. Spring C
    J. Spring D

15. Based on the results of Experiment 3, if a 700 g mass was suspended from Spring A, at what equilibrium length would the system come to rest?

    A. Less than 20 cm
    B. Between 20 cm and 30 cm
    C. Between 30 cm and 50 cm
    D. Greater than 50 cm

16. The students tested a fifth spring, Spring E, in the same manner as in Experiment 2. With a 100 g mass suspended from Spring E, the oscillation frequency was 1.4 Hz. Based on the results of Experiment 2, which of the following correctly lists the five springs by their oscillation frequency with a 100 g mass suspended from *fastest* to *slowest*?

    F. Spring E, Spring B, Spring C, Spring A, Spring D

    G. Spring D, Spring A, Spring C, Spring B, Spring E

    H. Spring A, Spring B, Spring C, Spring E, Spring D

    J. Spring D, Spring E, Spring C, Spring B, Spring A

GO ON TO THE NEXT PAGE ⟶

17. Experiment 1 was repeated using a larger pendulum mass. Which of the following figures best expresses the comparison between the results found using the larger pendulum mass and using the original mass?

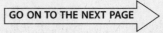

PASSAGE IV

An *alloy* is a uniform mixture of two or more metals. When the melting point of an alloy is lower than the melting point of any of its metal components, the alloy is referred to as a *eutectic* system. Figure 1 is a *phase diagram* that illustrates the states of matter of the gold-silicon (Au-Si) eutectic system over a range of temperatures and alloy compositions. For the Au-Si system, 0% Si means pure Au, and 100% Si means pure Si.

Note: (Au) and (Si) represent the solid forms of gold and silicon, respectively.

Figure 1

18. According to Figure 1, at what temperature will Au begin to boil?

    F. 363°C

    G. 1,063°C

    H. 1,412°C

    J. The boiling point of Au is not included on the figure.

19. Based on Figure 1, an alloy that is atomically 50% Si and 50% Au will be in what state at a temperature of 600°C?

    A. Completely liquid

    B. Liquid with some amount of solid Si

    C. Liquid with some amount of solid Au

    D. Completely solid

20. A *solder* is a metallic material designed specifically to have a very low melting point. To make a solder out of a Au-Si alloy, what atomic percentages of Au and Si would be most appropriate?

    F. 0% Si, 100% Au

    G. 19.5% Si, 80.5% Au

    H. 80.5% Si, 19.5% Au

    J. 100% Si, 0% Au

GO ON TO THE NEXT PAGE

21. Based on the information in Figure 1, one could generalize that for Au-Si alloy compositions containing atomically less than 10% Si, the temperature at which the alloy becomes completely liquid decreases with:

   A. increasing Si atomic percentage.

   B. decreasing Si atomic percentage.

   C. increasing Au atomic percentage.

   D. neither increasing nor decreasing Si atomic percentage. The melting point is constant for all alloy compositions.

22. A liquid Au-Si alloy of unknown composition is gradually cooled from an initial temperature of 1,500°C. Solid particles are observed to begin forming as the temperature drops to 1,200°C. The particles must consist of which material, and what must be the approximate atomic composition of the alloy?

   F. The particles are Au, and the atomic composition of the alloy is 10% Si, 90% Au.

   G. The particles are Au, and the atomic composition of the alloy is 19.5% Si, 80.5% Au.

   H. The particles are Si, and the atomic composition of the alloy is 73% Si, 27% Au.

   J. The particles are Si, and the atomic composition of the alloy is 90% Si, 10% Au.

GO ON TO THE NEXT PAGE

PASSAGE V

A person requires a certain percentage of oxygen in the blood for proper respiratory function. The amount of oxygen in the air varies enough with altitude that people normally accustomed to breathing near sea level may experience respiratory problems at significantly higher altitudes. Table 1 shows the average percentage of oxygen saturation in the blood, as well as the blood concentrations of three enzymes, GST, ECH, and CR, for three populations of high altitude (ha) dwellers and three populations of sea level (sl) dwellers. Enzyme concentrations are given in arbitrary units (a.u.). Figure 1 shows average oxygen partial pressure and average temperature at various altitudes.

Table 1

Population	Altitude range (m)	Oxygen saturation (%)	Enzyme concentration (a.u.)		
			GST	ECH	CR
ha 1	3,500–4,000	98.1	121.0	89.2	48.8
ha 2	3,300–3,700	99.0	108.3	93.5	45.6
ha 3	3,900–4,200	97.9	111.6	91.9	52.3
sl 1	0–300	98.5	86.7	57.1	44.9
sl 2	0–150	99.2	79.8	65.8	53.1
sl 3	0–200	98.7	82.5	61.4	47.0

Figure 1

GO ON TO THE NEXT PAGE

23. Based on the data in Table 1, one would conclude that the blood of high altitude dwellers contains a higher concentration of:

    A. CR than ECH.

    B. CR than GST.

    C. ECH than GST.

    D. GST than CR.

24. Based on the information given, one would expect that, compared to the high altitude dwellers, the sea level dwellers:

    F. have blood with a lower percentage oxygen saturation.

    G. have blood with a lower GST concentration.

    H. can tolerate lower oxygen partial pressures.

    J. can tolerate lower temperatures.

25. According to Figure 1, an atmospheric sample found at an oxygen partial pressure of 110 mm Hg was most likely found at a temperature of about:

    A. –8.1°C.

    B. 0°C.

    C. –5.4°C.

    D. –12.5°C.

26. ECH is an enzyme that improves the efficiency of cellular energy production. Assume that people with higher ECH concentrations in the blood can function normally at higher altitudes without any respiratory difficulties. Based on Table 1, people from which population can function normally at the highest altitude?

    F. sl 1

    G. sl 2

    H. ha 2

    J. ha 3

27. Assume that a person's blood oxygen saturation percentage is determined only by the oxygen partial pressure at the location at which they live and the efficiency of the person's respiratory system at incorporating oxygen into the blood. Which of the following pieces of information supports the hypothesis that people from population ha 2 can incorporate oxygen into their blood more efficiently than people from population sl 1?

    A. Population ha 2 lives where the oxygen partial pressure is lower than that of where population sl 1 lives, yet population ha 2 has a higher blood oxygen saturation percentage than does population ha 1.

    B. Population ha 2 lives where the oxygen partial pressure is higher than that of where population sl 1 lives, yet population ha 2 has a lower blood oxygen saturation percentage than does population ha 1.

    C. Population ha 2 has a higher CR concentration than does population sl 1.

    D. Population ha 2 has an unusually high GST concentration.

GO ON TO THE NEXT PAGE

PASSAGE VI

Two students explain why lakes freeze from the surface downward. They also discuss the phenomena of the melting of ice under the blades of an ice skater's skates.

STUDENT 1

Water freezes first at the surface of lakes because the freezing point of water decreases with increasing pressure. Under the surface, *hydrostatic pressure* causes the freezing point of water to be slightly lower than it is at the surface. Thus, as the air temperature drops, it reaches the freezing point of water at the surface before reaching that of the water beneath it. Only as the temperature becomes even colder will the layer of ice at the surface become thicker.

Pressure is defined as *force* divided by the *surface area* over which the force is exerted. An ice skater exerts the entire force of her body weight over the tiny surface area of two very thin blades. This results in a very large pressure, which quickly melts a small amount of ice directly under the blades.

STUDENT 2

Water freezes first at the surface of lakes because the density of ice is less than that of liquid water. Unlike most liquids, the volume of a given mass of water expands upon freezing, and the density therefore decreases. As a result, the *buoyant force* of water acting upward is greater than the force of gravity exerted downward by any mass of ice, and all ice particles float to the surface upon freezing.

Ice melts under an ice skater's skates because of friction. The energy used to overcome the force of friction is converted to heat, which melts the ice under the skates. The greater the weight of the skater, the greater the force of friction, and the faster the ice melts.

28. According to Student 1, which of the following quantities is *greater* for water molecules beneath a lake's surface than for water molecules at the surface?

    F. Temperature
    G. Density
    H. Buoyant force
    J. Hydrostatic pressure

29. When two ice skaters, wearing identical skates, skated across a frozen lake at the same speed, the ice under the blades of Skater B was found to melt faster than the ice under the blades of Skater A. What conclusion would each student draw about which skater is heavier?

    A. Both Student 1 and Student 2 would conclude that Skater A is heavier.
    B. Both Student 1 and Student 2 would conclude that Skater B is heavier.
    C. Student 1 would conclude that Skater A is heavier; Student 2 would conclude that Skater B is heavier.
    D. Student 1 would conclude that Skater B is heavier; Student 2 would conclude that Skater A is heavier.

30. Which student(s), if either, would predict that ice will melt under the blades of an ice skater who is NOT moving?

    F. Student 1 only
    G. Student 2 only
    H. Both Student 1 and Student 2
    J. Neither Student 1 nor Student 2

GO ON TO THE NEXT PAGE ➡

31. A beaker of ethanol is found to freeze from the bottom upward, instead of from the surface downward. Student 2 would most likely argue that the density of frozen ethanol is:

    A. greater than the density of water.

    B. less than the density of ice.

    C. greater than the density of liquid ethanol.

    D. less than the density of liquid ethanol.

32. A toy boat was placed on the surface of a small pool of water, and the boat was gradually filled with sand. After a certain amount of sand had been added, the boat began to sink. Based on Student 2's explanation, the boat began to sink because:

    F. hydrostatic pressure became greater than the buoyant force of the water on the boat.

    G. atmospheric pressure became greater than the buoyant force of the water on the boat.

    H. the force of gravity of the boat on the water became greater than the buoyant force of the water on the boat.

    J. the force of gravity of the boat on the water became less than the buoyant force of the water on the boat.

33. According to Student 2, if friction between the ice and the blades of an ice skater's skates is reduced, which of the following quantities simultaneously decreases at the point where the blades and the ice are in contact?

    A. Pressure exerted by the blades on the ice

    B. Heat produced

    C. Force of gravity of the blades on the ice

    D. Freezing point of water

34. Based on Student 2's explanation, the reason a hot air balloon is able to rise above the ground is that the balloon and the air inside it are:

    F. less dense than the air outside the balloon.

    G. more dense than the air outside the balloon.

    H. at a higher pressure than the air outside the balloon.

    J. less buoyant than the air outside the balloon.

PASSAGE VII

In many communities, chemicals containing fluoride ions (F⁻) are added to the drinking water supply to help prevent tooth decay. Use of F⁻ is controversial because studies have linked F⁻ with bone disease. Students performed two experiments to measure F⁻ levels.

EXPERIMENT I

Five solutions, each containing a different amount of Na_2SiF_6 (sodium silicofluoride) in H_2O were prepared. Five identical *electrodynamic cells* were filled with equal volumes of each of the five solutions, and a sixth identical cell was filled with a *blank* solution (one containing no added Na_2SiF_6). The cells were activated to measure the electrical *conductivity* for each. The conductivities were then corrected by subtracting the conductivity of the blank solution from each value (see Table 1 and Figure 1).

Table 1

Concentration of F⁻ (mg/L*)	Measured conductivity (μS/cm**)	Corrected conductivity (μS/cm**)
0.0	15.96	0.00
0.1	16.13	0.17
0.5	16.80	0.084
1.0	17.63	1.67
2.0	19.30	3.34
4.0	22.64	6.68
*mg/L is milligrams per liter. **μS/cm is microsiemens per centimer.		

Figure 1

GO ON TO THE NEXT PAGE ⟩
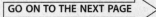

EXPERIMENT 2

A water sample was taken directly from the drinking water supply of one community. An electrodynamic cell identical to those used in Experiment 1 was filled with water from this sample, and the cell was activated. The procedure was repeated for water samples from several communities, and the conductivities were measured (Table 2).

Table 2

Community	Measured conductivity (μS/cm)	Concentration of F$^-$ (mg/L)
Newtown	22.31	3.8
Springfield	16.46	0.3
Lakewood	18.63	1.6
Reading	19.47	2.1

35. Based on the results of Experiment 1, if the concentration of F$^-$ in a solution is doubled, then the corrected conductivity of the solution will approximately:

    A. remain the same.

    B. halve.

    C. double.

    D. quadruple.

36. A sample was also taken from the drinking water supply of the community of Bluewater in Experiment 2, and its conductivity was measured to be 20.69 μS/cm. Which of the following correctly lists the drinking water supplies of Newtown, Lakewood, and Bluewater in *increasing* order of F$^-$ concentration?

    F. Lakewood, Newtown, Bluewater

    G. Bluewater, Newtown, Lakewood

    H. Newtown, Bluewater, Lakewood

    J. Lakewood, Bluewater, Newtown

37. Based on the results of Experiment 1, if a solution with a concentration of 3.0 mg/L F$^-$ had been tested, the corrected conductivity would have been closest to which of the following values?

    A. 1.3 μS/cm

    B. 3.3 μS/cm

    C. 5.0 μS/cm

    D. 6.5 μS/cm

38. If Experiments 1 and 2 were repeated to measure the concentration of chloride ions (Cl$^-$) in drinking water, then which of the following changes in procedure would be necessary?

    F. The solutions in Experiment 1 should be prepared by adding different concentrations of NaCl (or another chemical containing Cl$^-$) to H_2O.

    G. The conductivity of the blank solution should be added to the measured conductivities.

    H. The electrodynamic cells should be set to measure resistivity instead of conductivity.

    J. Both NaCl and Na_2SiF_6 should be added to all of the samples.

39. Based on the results of Experiments 1 and 2, if the measured conductivities for the samples tested in Experiment 2 were compared with their corrected conductivities, the measured conductivities would be:

    A. lower for all of the samples tested.

    B. higher for all of the samples tested.

    C. lower for some of the samples tested, higher for others.

    D. the same for all of the samples tested.

GO ON TO THE NEXT PAGE ⟹

40. The presence of other negative ions, such as
Cl $^-$, results in an increase in the electrical
conductivity of a solution. If all of the samples
tested in Experiment 2 contained trace concentrations of Cl $^-$, how would the measurements have been affected? Compared to the
actual F$^-$ concentrations, the F$^-$ concentrations
apparently measured would be:

F. higher.

G. lower.

H. the same.

J. higher for some of the samples, lower
for others.

WRITING TEST

30 Minutes—1 Question

Directions: This is a test of your writing skills. You will have thirty (30) minutes to write an essay in English. Before you begin planning and writing your essay, read the writing prompt carefully to understand exactly what you are being asked to do. Your essay will be evaluated on the evidence it provides of your ability to express judgments by taking a position on the issue in the writing prompt; to maintain a focus on the topic throughout the essay; to develop a position by using logical reasoning and by supporting your ideas; to organize ideas in a logical way; and to use language clearly and effectively according to the conventions of standard written English.

You may use the unlined pages in this test booklet to plan your essay. These pages will not be scored. *You must write your essay in pencil on the lined pages in the answer folder.* Your writing on those lined pages will be scored. You may not need all the lined pages, but to ensure you have enough room to finish, do NOT skip lines. You may write corrections or additions neatly between the lines of your essay, but do NOT write in the margins of the lined pages. *Illegible essays cannot be scored, so you must write (or print) clearly.*

If you finish before time is called, you may review your work. Lay your pencil down immediately when time is called.

DO NOT OPEN THIS BOOKLET UNTIL TOLD TO DO SO.

ACT WRITING TEST PROMPT

In some cities, laws have been proposed that would restrict licensed drivers under 18 to driving alone or with an adult in the car. Parents and lawmakers who favor such laws point to the high incidence of car accidents with 16- and 17-year-old drivers, and claim that not allowing teenagers under 18 to ride together will help newer drivers to focus on driving safely. Teenagers and parents who are against the restriction argue that teenagers riding together isn't necessarily the cause of accidents and that more comprehensive driver training is a better way to reduce accidents. In your opinion, should cities pass laws that ban teenagers from riding in a car that is driven by a person under 18?

In your essay, take a position on this question. You may write about either one of the two points of view given, or you may present a different point of view on this question. Use specific reasons and examples to support your position.

Use this space to *plan* your essay. Your work here will not be graded. Write your essay on the lined pages that follow.

Practice Test Three
ANSWER KEY

ENGLISH TEST

1. C	11. A	21. C	31. C	41. B	51. D	61. D	71. A
2. H	12. G	22. G	32. H	42. G	52. F	62. H	72. G
3. C	13. A	23. C	33. D	43. D	53. C	63. A	73. A
4. J	14. H	24. J	34. F	44. G	54. J	64. H	74. H
5. B	15. B	25. C	35. B	45. A	55. D	65. B	75. D
6. J	16. J	26. J	36. F	46. J	56. H	66. F	
7. B	17. A	27. B	37. C	47. D	57. A	67. B	
8. J	18. J	28. G	38. F	48. H	58. J	68. G	
9. D	19. D	29. D	39. C	49. D	59. C	69. D	
10. H	20. H	30. J	40. H	50. G	60. G	70. G	

MATH TEST

1. E	9. B	17. E	25. C	33. D	41. D	49. C	57. B
2. K	10. H	18. J	26. F	34. F	42. G	50. G	58. F
3. C	11. D	19. A	27. D	35. E	43. A	51. A	59. C
4. H	12. G	20. H	28. F	36. H	44. K	52. H	60. H
5. D	13. C	21. A	29. B	37. C	45. C	53. D	
6. J	14. J	22. J	30. F	38. H	46. J	54. K	
7. A	15. D	23. E	31. C	39. C	47. E	55. A	
8. G	16. G	24. H	32. K	40. J	48. H	56. J	

READING TEST

1. D	6. H	11. C	16. J	21. C	26. F	31. B	36. H
2. H	7. B	12. G	17. C	22. J	27. B	32. F	37. B
3. B	8. F	13. B	18. J	23. C	28. H	33. C	38. J
4. J	9. C	14. F	19. A	24. F	29. B	34. H	39. B
5. D	10. F	15. B	20. G	25. D	30. G	35. C	40. G

SCIENCE TEST

1. C	6. H	11. A	16. J	21. A	26. H	31. C	36. J
2. H	7. C	12. G	17. C	22. H	27. A	32. H	37. C
3. A	8. H	13. A	18. J	23. D	28. J	33. B	38. F
4. J	9. B	14. F	19. B	24. G	29. B	34. F	39. B
5. B	10. F	15. C	20. G	25. C	30. F	35. C	40. F

ANSWERS AND EXPLANATIONS

ENGLISH TEST

PASSAGE I

1. C
Word Choice
Choice (C) forms a complete sentence by using the simple past tense *was*. Choice (A) creates a sentence fragment; an *-ing* verb needs a helping verb, such as *was* or *is*, to be the main verb in a sentence. Choice (B) incorrectly uses a comma to separate the subject from the main verb. Choice (D) omits the verb entirely, creating a sentence fragment.

2. H
Word Choice
The phrase *not only* in the beginning of the sentence is your clue to the correct answer. Logically, the phrase *not only* is always followed by *but also*. The other choices neither complete the idiom correctly nor convey the necessary contrast between the ideas in the two clauses.

3. C
Punctuation
Add an apostrophe and an *s* to a singular noun to show possession. The narrator and Gretchen attend one school, so (C) is correct. Choice (A) omits the apostrophe needed to show that the *swim team* belongs to the *school*. Choice (B) incorrectly treats *school* as a plural, placing the apostrophe after the *s*. Choice (D) incorrectly uses *ours* and does not make *school* possessive.

4. J
Wordiness
The test makers value simple and direct prose, so change passive constructions such as "it was with Gretchen that I " when you're given the opportunity. As is often the case on the English test of the

ACT, the shortest choice—(J)—is correct. In addition to being verbose, choice (F) contains a sentence structure error: It is not clear who knows that the writer enjoyed swimming. Choices (G) and (H) are both also verbose.

5. B
Writing Strategy
Slow down and carefully read the Nonstandard-Format questions. You just may see a question such as this that tests vocabulary. Choice (B) indicates that the narrator's mother recommended swimming lessons but did not decide that the narrator *must* take them. Choices (A), (C), and (D) all indicate that the mother's mind was made up.

6. J
Sentence Sense
If a sentence seems to have too many ideas, then it is probably a run-on. By itself, a comma cannot separate two clauses that could be independent sentences, as in (F). Choice (G) replaces *swimmers* with a pronoun but does not correct the run-on. Similarly, (H) removes the comma but does not address the problem of two complete thoughts that are incorrectly joined. Choice (J) solves the problem by using *whom*, which turns the second half of the sentence into a dependent clause that describes the *women*.

7. B
Punctuation
This sentence contains a parenthetical phrase. If you omitted "who had been swimming competitively since elementary school," you would still have a complete sentence. Like all parenthetical phrases, this needs to be set off from the rest of the sentence. A comma is used at the beginning of the phrase, so a comma must also be used at the end of the phrase. This makes (D) incorrect. Choices

(A) and (C) insert unnecessary commas within the parenthetical phrase.

8. J
Wordiness

When in doubt, take it out. *Giving up,* by definition, means "quitting" or "failing." Choices (F), (G), and (H) create redundancies.

9. D
Verb Tense

Trust your ear. *Begin* is an irregular verb; the simple past tense *began* can be used by itself, but the past participle *begun* cannot. Instead, *begun* always appears with *has*, *have*, or *had*, as in "I *have begun* to prepare for the ACT." Choice (D) correctly uses the simple past tense *began*. Choice (B) creates another verb usage error by inserting *been*. Choice (C) incorrectly uses *began* with *had*.

10. H
Word Choice

Don't panic if you see a question that tests the use of *who* and *whom*. The pronoun *who* serves as a subject, just like the pronouns *he* and *she* replace subjects. The pronoun *whom* serves as an object, just like the pronouns *him* and *her* replace objects. Here, *coach* is the subject of the sentence, so *who*, (H), is correct. Never refer to a person as *which*, (J).

11. A
Wordiness

Don't force a change where one isn't needed. The correct answer for some of the underlined portions will be NO CHANGE. The sentence "The hard work eventually paid off " is correct and concise as it is written. Choice (B) is verbose, and (C) and (D) create run-on sentences.

12. G
Writing Strategy

Start by asking yourself, "Does this stuff belong here?" The question asks for a sentence that is relevant to the narrator's experience on the swim team. Only (G) is connected to the narrator and the swim team; the sentence explains that the narrator was one of the only swimmers on the team to be interested in the butterfly. The history of the stroke, (F), the relative speed of the stroke, (H), and an alternative name for the stroke, (J), are not as related to the narrator's personal experience.

13. A
Writing Strategy

The shortest answer is often, but not always, correct. Don't omit portions that add relevant information to the sentence. The sentence is about the narrator's swimming, so her participation in the medley relay is relevant. Choices (B) and (C) add descriptions of the medley relay that are not relevant to the topic.

14. H
Verb Tense

The four choices offer different tenses of the same verb. The clue *last year* indicates that the narrator earned the varsity letter in the past. Choice (H), the simple past tense, is correct. Neither the future tense, (F), nor the present tense, (J), makes sense with the clue *last year*. Choice (G) would only make sense if something had prevented the narrator from earning the varsity letter.

15. B
Writing Strategy

Keep the main point of the passage in mind. Before beginning high school, the narrator had never thought of herself as an athlete. Then she joined the swim team and became successful at the sport. Choice (B) is most relevant to the central ideas of the passage. Choices (A) and (C) focus too narrowly on details in the passage, while (D) contradicts the main point of the passage.

PASSAGE II

16. J
Punctuation

Don't assume that a comma or semicolon is needed just because a sentence is long. Read the sentence aloud to yourself, and you should be able to hear that a comma is not needed in the underlined portion. A semicolon would only be correct if the second half of the sentence expressed a complete thought, as in (F). Choices (G) and (H) both use an unnecessary comma.

17. A
Word Choice

When a verb is underlined, check to see if it agrees with its noun. Watch out for descriptive phrases that separate a verb from its noun. Here, the verb *was* agrees with the singular noun *tank*. NO CHANGE is needed. Choice (B) uses the present tense, but the surrounding sentences use the past tense. Choices (C) and (D) incorrectly use a verb in the plural form.

18. J
Sentence Sense

When the word *that* or *which* is underlined, watch out for an incomplete sentence. As it is written, this is a sentence fragment; a complete verb is missing. Removing *that*, as in (J), turns *made* into the main verb of a complete and correct sentence. Choice (G) does not address the sentence fragment error, and (H) also fails to provide a clear and appropriate sentence.

19. D
Wordiness

If you are *familiar* with a type of animal, then you have almost certainly *seen it before*. Choice D creates a concise sentence that does not lose any of the original meaning. The other choices are redundant. Choice (B) repeats *sights* when *view* has already been used, and (C) uses the unnecessarily repetitive phrase "to which I was no stranger."

20. H
Organization

Scan the paragraph for connecting words and phrases that you can use as clues to determine the most logical order of sentences. In sentence 5, the word *first* suggests that the sentence should be placed close to the beginning of the paragraph. Sentence 2 says, "There were *also* animals I had never before glimpsed," which indicates that a preceding sentence discusses animals the writer had glimpsed. Sentence 5, which describes the writer's view of familiar animals, most logically belongs immediately after sentence 1.

21. C
Verb Tenses

If an underlined verb agrees with its noun, then determine whether the verb's tense makes sense in the context of the passage. The surrounding verbs are in the past tense, so this sentence should use the simple past tense *saw*, (C). Choices (A) and (D) use the present tense, and (B) illogically uses the past progressive "had been seeing."

22. G
Connections

An effective first sentence for a paragraph will introduce the topic of the paragraph and connect that topic to ideas that have come before. Paragraph 3 focuses on the catfish, while paragraph 4 describes the large alligator and snapping turtle in the bayou tank. Choice (G) is an effective connection between these paragraphs, referring to the catfish and introducing the idea that there were even bigger animals on display. Neither (F) nor (H) lead into the topic of paragraph 4. Choice (J) doesn't provide a transition from the discussion of the catfish in paragraph 3.

23. C
Writing Strategy

The phrase in question provides a visual image; deleting the phrase would mean losing a description, (C). The removal of the phrase would not affect the transition between sentences, (A). Contrary to (B), the contrast between images would be decreased. The level of suspense may be somewhat decreased by the loss of the description, but it would not be increased, (D).

24. J
Verb Tenses

The verbs *slides* and *aims* agree with the singular subject *it*, but they are in the wrong tense. The rest of the paragraph describes actions that took place in the past. For the sentence to make sense in context, these verbs should also be in the past tense, (J). Choices (F) and (G) use present-tense verbs. Choice (H) creates a logically incomplete sentence.

25. C
Sentence Sense

If something sounds awkward or unusual, there is probably an error. Most words that end in -*ly* are adverbs; they are used to modify verbs, adjectives, or other adverbs. Adverbs cannot be used to describe nouns, such as *moment,* (A). Choice (C) correctly uses the adjective *slight* to modify *panic*. The sentences formed by (B) and (D) don't make sense.

26. J
Idioms

The phrase "much of the onlookers" probably sounds strange to you. That's because *much* is used with noncountable things or concepts (as in "there isn't much time") or quantities (as in "there isn't much pizza left"). You could count the number of *onlookers*, so *many*, (J), is correct. Choices (G) and (H) also create idiomatic errors.

27. B
Writing Strategy

The question tells you that the writer's goal is to describe the appearance of the crayfish, so eliminate any sentences that do not have details about how crayfish look, (C). Choice (A) suggests that crayfish look like lobsters, and (D) describes the

crayfish as small. Neither of these sentences offers the descriptive detail that is given in (B).

28. G
Punctuation

Trust your ear. You naturally pause when a comma or semicolon is needed in a sentence. A pause between *all* and *I* just doesn't sound right; that's because the full introductory phrase "After seeing all I could inside the museum" should not be interrupted. A comma should not separate a verb (*seeing*) from its object (*museum*). This eliminates (F) and (H). A comma is needed between an introductory phrase and the complete thought that follows, making (G) correct and (J) incorrect.

29. D
Wordiness

Say it simply. The shortest answer here is correct: it turns the passive construction "it was that" in (A) and (B) into the active "I had." Choice (C) is unnecessarily wordy.

30. J
Sentence Sense

A sentence must have a subject and verb and express a complete thought. The sentence that begins "And operates" does not have a subject. Removing the period, (J), creates a grammatically correct sentence. Choice (G) is awkwardly worded. Choice (H) creates a run-on sentence; a coordinating conjunction such as *and* needs to be used along with a comma to link two complete thoughts.

PASSAGE III

31. C
Pronouns

When a pronoun is underlined, check to see that it agrees in number with the noun it replaces or refers to. In this sentence, the underlined pronoun refers back to the plural "secret identities and elaborate disguises." Choice (C) uses the correct plural pronoun *they*. Choices (A) and (B) create pronoun agreement errors by using the singular pronoun *it*. Choice (D) creates a sentence fragment.

32. H
Punctuation
Many English questions will focus on the correct use of commas. Commas should be used to separate an appositive or descriptive phrase from the main part of the sentence. The phrase "the restaurant critic for the *New York Times*" describes the noun *Ruth Reichl*, so the phrase should be set off with commas, (H). Choices (F) and (J) fail to use both necessary commas. On the other hand, (G) incorrectly inserts a third comma.

33. D
Writing Strategy
Only add sentences that are directly connected to the topic of a paragraph. Paragraph 2 discusses the importance of a *Times* review to restaurants in New York City. The suggested sentence provides a specific detail about one restaurant without explaining how the review from the *Times* affected business. Choice (D) best explains why the sentence should not be added.

34. F
Idioms
Trust your ear. We look *to* someone or something for advice. No change is needed. Choice (G) suggests that the paper is looking along *with* its readers, while (H) suggests that the readers are looking near the newspaper. Choice (J) uses an *-ing* verb without a helping verb, which creates a sentence fragment.

35. B
Verb Tenses
Verbs must make sense in the context of the passage. The next sentence says that a negative review "can undermine" a restaurant. Because the two sentences discuss possible results of a review, the underlined verb in this sentence should be in the

same tense—"can bring," (B). Choice (A) illogically uses the conditional in the past tense, while (C) and (D) do not use the conditional at all.

36. F
Punctuation
The subject of the sentence is "restaurant owners and workers," and the verb is *have*. There isn't a descriptive phrase or clause separating the subject and verb, so no comma is needed. A semicolon should be used to connect two complete thoughts, (G). Choice (H) incorrectly treats *restaurant* as the first item in a list; instead, *restaurant* identifies the type of *owners* and *workers*.

37. C
Pronouns
To whom does the meal belong? It belongs to the *writer,* so the possessive pronoun *whose* is correct. *Who's* is always a contraction for *who is* or *who has,* (B). Choices (A) and (D) introduce sentence structure errors.

38. F
Wordiness
The shortest answer is often correct. The sentence is concise and direct as it is written. Each of the other choices adds unnecessary words to the underlined portion.

39. C
Wordiness
On the ACT, there's no need to say the same thing twice. *Common, ordinary, representative*, and *average* all have very similar meanings; (A) and (B) use redundant language. Choice (C) makes the sentence concise by using only *typical*. Choice (D) uses a word that does not make sense in the context of the sentence.

40. H
Wordiness

If you have *decided* to do something to solve a problem, you have found a *solution*—there's no need to use both words. Choice (H) eliminates the redundancy and verbosity errors of the other choices.

41. B
Sentence Sense

As a rule, modifying words, phrases, and clauses should be as close as possible to the things or actions they describe. For instance, the list beginning "such as an attractive blonde named Chloe" describes the *different personas*. Therefore, *different personas* should come right before the list. This eliminates (A). Choice (B) correctly uses an introductory phrase and makes *Reichl* the subject of the sentence. Choice (C) is a sentence fragment; a complete verb is missing. Choice (D) inserts an unnecessary comma between *clothing* and *that*, and the pronoun *herself* is incorrect in context.

42. G
Writing Strategy

The most logical and effective sentence will be connected to the main topic of the paragraph and make a transition to the following sentence. Paragraph 4 describes how Reichl turned herself into different characters, and paragraph 5 describes the result of reviewing a restaurant while in disguise. The best link between these ideas is (G). Choice (F) is a narrow detail that does not connect the two paragraphs, while (H) and (J) move completely away from the topic of Reichl's disguises.

43. D
Organization

Sometimes it helps to rephrase a question in your own words. For example, how this question could be rewritten: "What does the phrase *of a restaurant* describe?" Reichl focuses on the quality of a restaurant, so the best placement is (D). The phrase does not describe *developed*, *view*, or *person*.

44. G
Sentence Sense

The word *occasionally* means "sometimes"; its placement in this sentence indicates that Reichl was sometimes treated very differently when she was in disguise, and sometimes she wasn't. Removing the word *occasionally* would indicate that Reichl always or typically had a different experience as one of her personas, (G).

45. A
Organization

Paragraph 6 describes the effect of Reichl's use of disguises when she reviewed restaurants. Logically, this effect should follow the explanation of why and how Ruth dined as different people, the topics of paragraphs 3 and 4. Paragraph 6 should remain where it is.

PASSAGE IV

46. J
Punctuation

Trust your ear. A comma indicates a short pause, which you won't hear when you read this part of the sentence aloud. No comma is needed, (J). A comma can be used to separate a descriptive phrase from the rest of the sentence, (F) and (H), but neither "would develop into prize-winning vegetables" nor "develop into prize-winning vegetables" is a descriptive phrase. Choice (G) incorrectly treats the underlined portion of the sentence as part of a list.

47. D
Organization

The paragraph describes events in chronological order, from the last freeze of the year to the time that spring *truly arrived*. Sentence 3 describes thinning out the plants and pulling weeds so the new plants would grow; it would only make sense to do this *after* the seeds have been planted and have started to grow. Sentence 4 is about planting seeds, so sentence 3 must come after sentence 4, (D).

48. H
Connections
When you read this sentence aloud, you should be able to hear a short pause between *burden* and *less*. This pause indicates that the conjunction *and* is needed to separate the two descriptions, (H). Choice (G) is wrong because a colon is used to introduce a brief definition, explanation, or list. Choice (J) uses the inappropriate conjunction *but*, which doesn't make sense in context.

49. D
Wordiness
When "OMIT the underlined portion" is an option, consider whether the underlined portion is relevant to the topic of the sentence or paragraph. Paragraph 2 is about the writer's failure to maintain her garden, not about the weather in July and August. Choice (D) is correct.

50. G
Connections
Always read the questions carefully! This one asks for the choice that would NOT work in the sentence. In other words, three of the answer choices would make sense in the sentence. The first sentence of paragraph 3 contrasts with paragraph 2, so the contrasting transitions in (F), (H), and (J) are all possible substitutions for the underlined word. *Indeed*, (G), is a word used to show emphasis, not contrast.

51. D
Wordiness
The shortest answer is often correct. Choices (A), (B), and (C) all refer to large-scale farming, which is only loosely related to the topic of gardening. Choice (D) keeps the sentence focused on the topic of paragraph 3.

52. F
Connections
Before you answer this question, read enough of paragraph 4 to identify its main idea. Paragraph 3 introduces the topic of square-foot gardening, and paragraph 4 describes several of its advantages. The best link between these ideas is the original sentence, (F). Paragraph 4 doesn't mention the history of square-foot gardening or the writer's neighbor, so (G) and (J) don't make sense. Choice (H) is a detail about square-foot gardening, but it does not function as a topic sentence for the paragraph.

53. C
Sentence Sense
If an underlined word ends in *-ly*, you can be pretty sure that it is an adverb. Remember that adverbs can be used to describe verbs, adjectives, and other adverbs, but not nouns. The word *garden* is a noun, so (A) and (B) are incorrect. The adjective *traditional*, (C), is correct. The phrase *tradition garden*, (D), does not make sense.

54. J
Word Choice
Who spends hours thinning each row? From this sentence, it's unclear: you have no idea who *they* are. Other sentences in paragraph 4 use the pronoun *you*, so it makes sense to use *you* here.

55. D
Wordiness
"OMIT the underlined portion" is an option, so check to see if the information is irrelevant to the topic or repetitive. This sentence begins with the phrase "In a square-foot garden," so it is unnecessary to repeat "in the garden." Choice (D) is correct.

56. H
Sentence Sense
"OMIT the underlined portion" isn't always the correct answer. As it is written, the sentence does not express a complete thought. To correct the error, remove *which could* so that *make* becomes the main verb of the sentence. Choices (G) and (J) create sentence fragments.

57. A
Word Choice

Don't look too hard for an error—many of the English questions will require NO CHANGE. The present tense and the pronoun *you* are used throughout paragraph 4, so this sentence is correct as it is written.

58. J
Wordiness

Remember that the ACT values economy. If you can express an underlined portion in fewer words without changing or losing the original meaning, then the shortest answer is probably correct. The only choice that does not use redundant language is (J).

59. C
Word Choice

The verb in this sentence is separated from its singular subject "one season" by the phrase "of using the square garden techniques." Choice (C) corrects the subject-verb agreement error of the original sentence. Incorrect choices use the plural form of the verb (A) and (B) or the future tense (D), which does not make sense in the context of the sentence.

60. G
Writing Strategy

This question asks about the passage as a whole, so take a moment to think about the main idea of the passage. Paragraphs 1 and 2 describe the writer's failed attempts at a traditional garden, while paragraphs 3, 4, and 5 focus on the writer's success with a square-foot garden. The essay is not instructive; instead, it compares two types of gardens, (G).

PASSAGE V

61. D
Punctuation

When a coordinating conjunction such as *but* or *and* combines two independent clauses (complete thoughts), a comma must come before it. In this sentence, a comma should be inserted after *light*,

(D). Choice (C) incorrectly places a comma in a compound and fails to add one before the coordinating conjunction, and (B) incorrectly uses a semicolon between an independent and a dependent clause. You'll likely see at least one semicolon question on the ACT, so remember that a semicolon is used to separate two complete thoughts or to separate items in a series or list when one or more of those items already contains commas.

62. H
Word Choice

The answer choices present different forms of the verbs *improves* and *decreases*, so you know the issue is subject-verb agreement. The two underlined verbs need to agree with the plural subject *steps*; only (H) puts both *improve* and *decrease* in the correct form.

63. A
Wordiness

The simplest way to say something is often the most correct way to say something. The original sentence is the most concise and correct version. Choice (B) is redundant, using both *problem* and *trouble*. Choices (C) and (D) are both unnecessarily wordy in comparison to (A), which expresses the same meaning.

64. H
Sentence Sense

An *-ing* verb needs a helping verb to function as the main verb in a clause or sentence. Changing *being* to *is*, as in (H), corrects the sentence structure error. Choice (G) inserts an incorrect comma between *vision* and *has been*, while (J) creates a new sentence structure error by omitting the verb *being*.

65. B
Sentence Sense

Something that is *set* is established or predetermined. For the sentence to make sense, *set* should describe *time*; the wiper blades should be replaced at an *established* time each year. Choice (B) is correct.

It does not make sense for the *blades,* (A), the *year,* (C), or the *risk,* (D) to be *set*, or established.

66. F
Word Choice

Trust your ear. With some idiom questions, you have to rely on your ear to hear what sounds correct. *In general* is an introductory phrase used to mean "usually" or "typically." Choice (F) provides the correct idiom for this context. The other choices contain idioms that are not typical of spoken English and do not fit this context.

67. B
Writing Strategies

To pick the best first sentence for paragraph 4, you must be able to identify the main idea of the paragraph. If you scan a few sentences of paragraph 4 before you answer the question, you'll see that the topic of the paragraph is changing a car's oil and oil filter. Only (B) introduces this topic. Choice (A) is too general, while (C) and (D) refer to car maintenance procedures that are not discussed in paragraph 4.

68. G
Connections

The connecting word *so* is underlined, so consider the relationship between the two parts of the sentence. There is a slight contrast—the first part of the sentence explains what you *do* need, while the second part identifies what you *don't* need. The contrasting conjunction *but,* (G), makes the most sense in context. The other choices indicate a cause-and-effect relationship that is not present in the sentence.

69. D
Punctuation

Information that is key to the main idea of a sentence should not be set off by commas. Here, it's important to know that the section is "in your owner's manual," so commas are incorrect. Choice (D) is correct. Choice (C) incorrectly uses a semicolon; a complete thought is not expressed by "and collect all of the tools you need."

70. G
Writing Strategy

Carefully read the question so that you understand the writer's purpose. If the writer wants to explain how to change oil, then the sentence should explain at least one specific step in the process. Choice (G) provides the most detailed information about how to go about changing oil.

71. A
Punctuation

Use a semicolon to introduce or emphasize what follows. The warning "you do not want to risk being crushed by a car" is certainly worthy of emphasis, so the sentence is correct as it is written. The other choices create run-ons, as the sentence expresses two complete thoughts; additionally, Choice (D) incorrectly separates a subject noun from its verb with a comma.

72. G
Writing Strategy

Paragraph 4 uses the informal *you* and *your,* while the rest of the essay uses the more formal third person. Therefore, eliminating the second-person pronouns from paragraph 4 would make the paragraph match the tone and voice of the rest of the essay, (G). Choices (H) and (J) are opposite answers: eliminating *you* and *your* would make the advice less direct and would make the essay more formal.

73. A
Wordiness

Watch out for redundant language! A "qualified mechanic" will do a *professional* job, just as a "qualified mechanic" is likely *certified*; (B) and (C) use repetitive language. Choice (D) introduces a sentence structure error. The best version of the underlined portion is (A).

74. H
Writing Strategy

Knowing the general topic of each paragraph will help you quickly answer a question like this one. The sentence refers to "these different fluids," so look for a part of the passage that discusses fluids. The second and third sentences of paragraph 3 refer to different fluids (*coolant, oil, brake fluid*, and *transmission fluid*), so the most logical placement for the sentence is at the end of paragraph 3 (H). Paragraph 2 and paragraph 4 each only refer to one fluid, so (F) and (J) are incorrect.

75. D
Writing Strategy

Use your Reading Comp skills to answer this question. Does the main idea of the passage fit with this purpose? Not really, as the passage focuses solely on basic maintenance that car owners can do themselves. The passage doesn't discuss the need to learn about a car's safety features. Choice (D) is correct.

MATH TEST

Answer explanations for the Math test refer to 100 Key Math Concepts for the ACT, found inside Part 1.

1. E
Operations

100 Key Math Concepts for the ACT, #22. To determine the total amount of fabric used, add the mixed numbers. To add mixed numbers, add the whole number parts, and then add the fractions. The whole number parts add to 4. To add the fractions, find the least common denominator of 8 and 3, which is 24. Convert each fraction to an equivalent fraction with a denominator of 24: $\frac{3 \times 3}{8 \times 3} = \frac{9}{24}$ and $\frac{1 \times 8}{3 \times 8} = \frac{8}{24}$.

Now, add the numerators, and keep the denominator: $\frac{9}{24} + \frac{8}{24} + \frac{17}{24}$. The total fabric used is $4\frac{17}{24}$. If you chose (B), you found a common denominator, but you forgot to multiply the numerators by the same factor that you had multiplied the denominators by. A common error when adding fractions would result in (C). This fraction was obtained by the incorrect procedure of adding the numerators, and then adding the denominators.

2. K
Operations

100 Key Math Concepts for the ACT #47, #55. To simplify this expression, first multiply the numerical coefficients to get $5 \times 6 \times 2 = 60$. To multiply the variable terms, keep the base of the variable and add the exponents. Remember that x denotes x^1. Multiply the x variable terms: $x^3 \times x = x^{3+1} = x^4$. Multiply the y variable terms: $y^5 \times y^2 \times y = y^{5+2+1} = y^8$. The resultant expression is $60x^4y^8$.

If your answer was (J), you fell into the common trap of multiplying the exponents instead of the correct method of adding the exponents. If your answer was either (F) and (G), you added the numerical coefficients instead of multiplying. If your answer was (H), you did not include the exponents of 1 for the single terms of x and y.

3. C
Proportions and Probability

100 Key Math Concepts for the ACT, #32. First, find the amount each person saves yearly. Brandon saves 6% of his $36,000 salary, or $0.06 \times 36,000 = \$2,160$ each year. Jacqui saves $200 every month, or $12 \times 200 = \$2,400$ each year. The difference, in dollars, of their savings is therefore $2,400 - 2,160 = \$240$.

Choice (A) reflects the *monthly* difference in their savings. If you chose (D), you incorrectly found the difference between Brandon's yearly savings and Jacqui's *monthly* savings. Choice (E) indicates Brandon's monthly *salary* minus Jacqui's monthly savings.

4. H
Proportions and Probability

100 Key Math Concepts for the ACT, #41, #43, #44. An average is found by taking the total sum of the terms and dividing it by the total number of terms. Therefore, the sum = (average) × (number of terms). For Mikhail to have an average for the five games of 180, the sum = 180 × 5 = 900. The first four scores total 190 + 200 + 145 + 180 = 715. Therefore, his score for the fifth game must be 900 − 715 = 185.

Choice (F) is just the average of the first four scores. Choice (G) is the average of the first four scores added and averaged with 180.

5. D
Proportions and Probability

100 Key Math Concepts for the ACT, #32. The amount of chromium is a part of the whole alloy. Use the formula Part = Percent × Whole. There are 262.5 pounds of chromium available, which must reflect at least 10.5% of the whole. Let w represent the whole amount of alloy that can be manufactured and write the algebraic equation: $262.5 = 10.5\%w$ or $262.5 = 0.105w$. Divide both sides of the equation by 0.105: $w = \dfrac{262.5}{0.105}$ pounds of steel.

Choice A represents 10.5% of 262.5. If you chose (B), you simply subtracted 10.5 from 262.5, without regard to the percent or the whole amount. Choice (C) is simply the amount of chromium. If you chose (E), you set up the problem correctly but incorrectly converted 10.5% to the decimal 0.0105.

6. J
Plane Geometry

100 Key Math Concepts for the ACT, #86. A wallpaper border is a strip that surrounds the perimeter of the kitchen. The perimeter of a rectangle = 2(length + width). The kitchen has a length of 6.5 meters and a width of 4 meters, so the amount of border needed is 2(6.5 + 4) = 2(10.5) = 21 meters.

Choice (G) is a common mistake made when calculating perimeter. This answer would result from just adding the two dimensions and not multiplying by 2. Choice (K) is the area, not the perimeter, of the kitchen.

7. A
Operations

100 Key Math Concepts for the ACT, #7. To find an equivalent for the given expression, use the distributive property. First, evaluate the inner parentheses according to the order of operations, or PEMDAS. Distribute the negative sign to $(y + z)$ to get $w(x − y − z)$. Next, distribute the variable w to all terms in parentheses to get $wx − wy − wz$.

Choice (B) fails to distribute the negative sign to the z term. Choices (C) and (D) only distribute the w to the first term. Choice (E) incorrectly distributes wx to the $(y + z)$ term.

8. G
Variable Manipulation

100 Key Math Concepts for the ACT, #63. This is an equation with a variable on both sides. To solve, work to get the n terms isolated on one side of the equation and the numerical terms on the other side. Subtract $3n$ from both sides to get $6n − 3n − 4 = 3n − 3n + 24$. Combine like terms: $3n − 4 = 24$. Now, add 4 to both sides: $3n − 4 + 4 = 24 + 4$, or $3n = 28$. Finally, divide both

sides by 3: $n = \dfrac{28}{3}$. Choice (F) reflects a common trap: forgetting to divide by 3. If you chose (H) or (J) you incorrectly added 6n and 3n and possibly subtracted 4 from 24 instead of adding 4. Dividing incorrectly at the last step would have led you to (K).

9. B
Patterns, Logic, and Data

100 Key Math Concepts for the ACT, #63, #65. In this arithmetic sequence, you can think of the terms as 26, 26 + s, 26 + s + s, and 26 + s + s + s. In this example, s represents the difference between successive terms. The final term is 53, so set up an algebraic equation: 26 + s + s + s = 53. Solve this equation for s, by first combining like terms: 26 + 3s = 53. Subtract 26 from both sides to get 26 − 26 + 3s = 53 − 26, or 3s = 27. Divide both sides by 3 to find that s, the difference between terms, is 9. Therefore, the terms are 26, 26 + 9, 26 + 9 + 9, 53, or 26, 35, 44, 53.

Answer choice D results from taking 53 − 26, dividing by 4, adding this value to each term, and rounding. In all of the incorrect answer choices, there is a common difference between second—first and then fourth—third, but it is different than the difference between the third and the second terms.

10. H
Variable Manipulation

100 Key Math Concepts for the ACT, #52, #63. First, solve the equation $5m^2 = 45$ for m. Once a value is obtained for m, substitute this into the expression to evaluate and find the answer. To solve the equation, divide both sides of the equation by 5 to get $m^2 = 9$. Take the square root of each side to get $m = 3$, or $m = -3$. Now, evaluate the expression. Because the expression contains the radical $\sqrt{12m}$, and the

expression must be a real number, reject the value of $m = -3$. When a radicand, the expression under the radical sign, is negative, the number does not have a value in the set of real numbers. Substitute 3 for m in the expression:

$$(3)^3 + \sqrt{12(3)} = 27 + \sqrt{36} = 27 + 6 = 33$$

If you chose (G), you just found the value of m^3. You might have selected answer choice J if you interpreted the 12m under the radical sign as the number 12^3 instead of 12×3. If you chose (K), you probably failed to take the square root of 9 when solving the equation and used the value of 9 for m.

11. D
Plane Geometry

100 Key Math Concepts for the ACT, #29, #95. First, convert the mixed number radius to a decimal: $3\dfrac{3}{5} = 3.6$. Substitute 3.6 into the formula to get $V = \dfrac{4}{3} \times \pi \times (3.6)^3$. Use the π key on your calculator. If your calculator has fractional capability and follows the correct order of operations, type the entry in as listed above. Otherwise, first find 3.6 to the third power. Multiply the result by 4, and then divide by 3. Finally, multiply by π. In either case, the result is approximately 195.43, or 195 to the nearest cubic meter.

If you chose (A) or (B), you multiplied the radius by 3, instead of taking the radius to the third power. For (C) and (A), you incorrectly converted $3\dfrac{3}{5}$ to 3.35, a common trap. If you arrived at (E), you first multiplied $\dfrac{4}{3} \times \pi \times (3.6)$, and then raised this value to the third power.

12. G
Proportions and Probabilty

100 Key Math Concepts for the ACT, #46. Probability is a ratio that compares the number of favorable, or desired, outcomes to the total number of outcomes. Probability is always a number between 0 and 1, and is never greater than 1. In this question, the favorable outcome is the number of nuts that are NOT peanuts, or $6 + 8 = 14$. The total number of outcomes is $10 + 6 + 8 = 24$. The probability that the nut is NOT a peanut is $\frac{14}{24} = \frac{7}{12}$, in lowest terms. Choice (F) is the probability that the nut IS a peanut. Choice (H) is the ratio that compares peanuts to other nuts.

13. C
Patterns, Logic, and Data

100 Key Math Concepts for the ACT, #32. The matrices outline the corresponding number of people in the store to the ratio, written as a decimal, of the number of people making purchases, *with reference to their age group*. A ratio written as a decimal is essentially a percentage. So following the correspondence yields $75 \times 0.20 = 15$ adolescent purchases, $100 \times 0.35 = 35$ adult purchases, and $30 \times 0.10 = 3$ senior-citizen purchases. This is a total of $15 + 35 + 3 = 53$ people making purchases.

Choice (A) represents the adolescent purchases. If you chose (B), you took the total number of people in the store, 205, and multiplied by the ratio for adolescents, 0.20. Choice (D) adds the total number of people, 205, multiplies by the sum of the ratios, 0.65, and then rounds. Choice (E) is the total number of people in the store, not the total number of purchases.

14. J
Patterns, Logic, and Data

100 Key Math Concepts for the ACT, #41. To find an average, calculate the sum of the data and then divide by the total number of data items. According to the table, the number of hours that the country genre has a live disc jockey is 24, 7, and 16. $24 + 7 + 16 = 47$. Divide: $47 \div 3 = 15.67$, which is 16 to the nearest hour.

Choice (F) is the number of *entries*, not hours, for the country genre. Choice (G) is the average number of hours for the classical genre. Choice (K) is the average number of hours for the news genre.

15. D
Patterns, Logic, and Data

100 Key Math Concepts for the ACT, #20. To find an average, calculate the sum of the numbers, then divide by the total number of items. According to the table, the numbers of hours for which the country genre has a live disc jockey are 24, 7, and 16. $24 + 7 + 16 = 47$. Divide: $47 \div 3 = 15.67$, which is closest to 16, (D).

A common trap would be (C) because the answer would round down to 24 disc jockeys, but this would fall short of the requirement to fulfill all of the hours.

Choice (E) reflects the total number of hours needed. Choice (A) is the number of 24-hour segments that require a live disc jockey.

16. G
Patterns, Logic, and Data

100 Key Math Concepts for the ACT, #5, #53. To find the missing value, add the monomials in the first row: $m + -4m + 3m = 0$. This first row sums to zero. To be sure, check the rightmost column: $3m + -2m + -m = 0$. Every row, column, and diagonal must sum to 0. The first column must therefore be $m + 2m + \square = 0$, or $3m + \square = 0$. Isolate the missing term on one side of the equation by subtracting $3m$ from both sides: $\square = -3m$.

If your choice was (H), you ignored the m variable in the term. If your choice was (F), (J), or (K), you may have just looked at the first column and the last row and found a value that would work with those, without considering the other rows, columns, and diagonals.

17. E
Number Properties

100 Key Math Concepts for the ACT, #6. The algebraic expression xy means to multiply the point's x value by its y value. If the product is positive, then the x and y factors are either both positive or both negative, according to the rules for multiplying signed numbers. Positive x-coordinates are to the right of the origin. Positive y-coordinates are above the origin. In quadrant I, both coordinates are positive, and in quadrant III, both coordinates are negative. In quadrant II, the x-coordinate is negative (to the left of the origin) and the y-coordinate is positive (above the origin). In quadrant IV, the x-coordinate is positive (to the right of the origin), and the y-coordinate is negative (below the origin).

18. J
Patterns, Logic, and Data

100 Key Math Concepts for the ACT, #45. The number of distinct lunches is determined by the fundamental counting principle. The counting principle directs you to multiply the different choices together to find the total number of combinations: $7 \times 3 \times 4 = 84$. If you consider just the sandwiches and soups alone, each sandwich can be paired with one of three soups, so there would be $7 \times 3 = 21$ different alternatives. These 21 alternatives would then become $21 \times 4 = 84$ different meals, because each of these 21 meals could be combined with four different drink choices.

A common trap answer is (G), where the numbers are added together, instead of multiplied. Choice (F) is the number of sandwiches available, not the number of distinct meals. Choice (H) reflects the number of distinct choices of just sandwich and soup.

19. A
Proportions and Probability

100 Key Math Concepts for the ACT, #36, #38. The question describes a comparison of the number of female to male students. This is a ratio—the ratio of female to male students is 5 to 3, or $\frac{5}{3}$. Let n represent the number of female students. Set up the proportion $\frac{5}{3} = \frac{n}{6,000}$ and cross multiply to get $3n = 5 \times 6,000$, or $3n = 30,000$. Divide both sides by 3 to get $n = 10,000$ females.

If you chose answer choice B, you may have used rounding and incorrectly considered the ratio to be twice as many females as males. Choice (C) represents the total number of students at the university. If you chose (D) or (E), you may have stopped after multiplying 6,000 by 3 or by 5, respectively.

20. H
Plane Geometry

100 Key Math Concepts for the ACT, #84, #86. Draw a diagram of a rectangle:

Because a rectangle has four right angles, you can treat the diagonal, QS, as the hypotenuse of a right triangle with legs of 16 and 30 inches. Use the Pythagorean theorem to solve for the length of the hypotenuse. If c represents the length of the hypotenuse and a and b represent the length of the legs, then $a^2 + b^2 = c^2$. Substitute into the formula:

$$c^2 = 16^2 + 30^2$$
$$c^2 = 256 + 900$$
$$c^2 = 1,156$$

Take the square root of both sides of the equation to find that $c = 34$ inches.

If you chose (F), you used 30 inches for c (the hypotenuse) in the formula, and then solved for one of the legs. Choice (G) adds the two dimensions and divides by 2. If you chose (J), you incorrectly divided by 2 instead of taking the square root; for (K), you added the squares but did not take the square root of the sum.

21. A
Variable Manipulation

100 Key Math Concepts for the ACT, #62. Choice (A) is not equivalent to $5n + 1$—it is the reciprocal. If you chose (B), you may have incorrectly simplified by not multiplying 5×2. The expression simplifies as $5n + 10 - 9$, or $5n + 1$. Choice (C) is also equivalent to $5n + 1$—when you divide fractions, you multiply by the reciprocal of the denominator, and

$$\frac{1}{1} \div \frac{1}{5n+1} = \frac{1}{1} \times \frac{5n+1}{1} = 5n + 1.$$

If you chose either (D) or (E), you may have thought that they could not be equivalent because they have a squared variable. But when (D) is factored and simplified, you can see it is equivalent: $\frac{n(5n+1)}{n} = 5n + 1$. The same is true for (E): $\frac{(5n+1)(5n-1)}{5n-1} = 5n + 1$.

22. J
Variable Manipulation

100 Key Math Concepts for the ACT, #64. Each of the answer choices is in the form $y = \ldots$, so solve for y in terms of x. Isolate y on one side of the equation. First, subtract $3x$ from both sides: $3x - 3x + 2y = -3x + 16$. Combine like terms to get $2y = -3x + 16$. Now, divide all terms on both sides by 2: $y = -\frac{3}{2}x + 8$.

In answer choice (F), the numeric term 16 is not divided by 2. Answer choices (G) and (K) have the reciprocal of the coefficient of x. In (H), $3x$ was added to both sides of the equation instead of subtracted, to get the incorrect term of $+\frac{3}{2}x$.

23. E
Variable Manipulation

100 Key Math Concepts for the ACT, #61, #66. To solve a quadratic equation, first factor the trinomial in the form $ax^2 + bx + c$. Since the c term is positive and the b term is negative, the factors will be $(x - \#)(x - \#)$. Look for factors of 75 that when added together will equal 20, the b coefficient. Some factor possibilities for 75 are 1 and 75, 3 and 25, and 5 and 15. Only the factors 5 and 15 will add to 20. The equation, after factoring, becomes $(x - 5)(x - 15) = 0$. The solutions are the values of x that result in either of the factors equaling 0: $x = 5$ or $x = 15$.

The common error traps are (A) or (B) where you might have quickly looked at the factors and thought the answers were either −5 or −15. If you chose (D), you may have thought the only factors of 75 were 3 and 25, and therefore chose 3 as a solution. If you chose (C), you may have ignored the term of 75 and found a solution of 0.

24. H
Trigonometry

100 Key Math Concepts for the ACT, #96. The cosine (cos) ratio is the ratio of the side adjacent to angle N to the hypotenuse of the right triangle. The $\cos N = \frac{12}{13}$.

Choice (F) is the sine (sin) ratio of angle N. Choice (G) is the tangent (tan) ratio of angle N. Choice (J) is the secant (sec), or the reciprocal of the cos to angle N. Choice (K) is the cosecant (csc), or the reciprocal of the sin to angle N.

25. C
Plane Geometry

100 Key Math Concepts for the ACT, #85. Since chord AB passes through the center, it is a diameter of the circle, and segment OB is a radius, equal to 7 cm. Because OC is perpendicular to AB, a right angle is

formed. To find the length of chord *CB*, note that it is the hypotenuse of right triangle Δ*COB*, with legs that each measure 7 cm. Because the legs have the same measure, this is a special right triangle, the 45°-45°-90° right triangle, and the sides are in the ratio of $n : n : n\sqrt{2}$. Chord *BC* is therefore $7\sqrt{2} \approx 9.899$, or 9.9 to the nearest tenth of a centimeter. Alternately, you could have used the Pythagorean theorem, $a^2 + b^2 = c^2$, where $a = b = 7$:

$$7^2 + 7^2 = c^2$$
$$49 + 49 = c^2$$
$$c = \sqrt{98} \approx 9.9 \text{ cm}$$

If your answer was (A), you used the Pythagorean theorem but evaluated 7^2 as 7×2, instead of 7×7. This is a common trap. Choice (B) is the length of the legs, not the hypotenuse. Choice (D) is $7\sqrt{3}$. Choice (E) is the length of the diameter of the circle.

26. F
Variable Manipulation

100 Key Math Concepts for the ACT, #63. Substitute the value of 86 into the formula for *F*, the degrees in Fahrenheit, to get $86 = \frac{9}{5}C + 32$. Subtract 32 from both sides:

$$86 - 32 = \frac{9}{5}C + 32 - 32$$
$$54 = \frac{9}{5}C$$

Now, multiply both sides by the reciprocal of $\frac{9}{5}$ to isolate *C*:

$$\frac{5}{9} \times 54 = \frac{5}{9} \times \frac{9}{5} \times C$$
$$30 = C$$

If you chose (G), you forgot to multiply by the reciprocal to get rid of the fraction on the right side of

the equation. Choice (H) incorrectly multiplies 86 by $\frac{5}{9}$ first, then adds 32. Choice (J) is the degrees in Fahrenheit. Choice (K) would be the degrees in Fahrenheit of 86 degrees Celsius.

27. D
Plane Geometry

100 Key Math Concepts for the ACT, #94. A swimming pool that is the same depth in all parts is a rectangular solid. The amount of water in the pool is the volume of the water. Use the formula $V = lwh$, and substitute in the volume, length, and width given in the problem. $14,375 = 50 \times 25 \times h$, or $14,375 = 1,250h$. Divide both sides of the equation by 1,250, to get $11.5 = h$. The depth is between 11 and 12 meters.

28. F
Trigonometry

100 Key Math Concepts for the ACT, #96. The tangent is the ratio of the side opposite to the given angle over the side adjacent to the given angle. Segment *EF* is the side opposite to angle *D*, so call this side *m*. Segment *DE*, the adjacent side to angle *D*, equals 42 inches. Set up the equation:

$$\frac{5}{8} = \frac{m}{42}$$
$$(42)(5) = 8m$$
$$210 = 8m$$
$$m = 26.3$$

If you chose (G), you added 42 and $\frac{5}{8}$. Choice (H) reflects the length of side *DF*, the hypotenuse of the right triangle. Choice (J) incorrectly uses 42 as the opposite side and side *EF* as the adjacent side.

29. B
Proportions and Probability

100 Key Math Concepts for the ACT, #36. The fraction of the people who were sophomores would be the ratio of the number of sophomores to the

total number of people at the prom. There were 30 sophomores and a total of $20 + 30 + 70 + 200 = 320$ people at the prom. The fraction is $\frac{30}{320} = \frac{3}{32}$.

Choice (A) is the fraction of the attendees who were freshmen. Choice (C) is the ratio of sophomores to those who are NOT sophomores. Choice (D) is the ratio of sophomores to seniors. Choice (E) is a common trap—it compares the number of sophomores to 100, instead of to the total number of students in attendance.

30. F
Number Properties

100 Key Math Concepts for the ACT, #5. This problem requires you to understand that the sum of the parts of a segment is equal to the whole segment. It is given that X is the midpoint of segment WZ. Because the length of $WZ = 44$ cm, the length of WX is one-half of this, or 22 cm. From the relative positions of the points in the segment, $WX + XY = WY$, or alternately, $WY - WX = XY$. It is given that $WY = 26$ and calculated that WX is 22. Therefore, $XY = 26 - 22$, or 4 centimeters.

If you chose (K), you just added the two numbers given in the problem. Choice (J) is the length of one-half of segment WZ, or the length of WX. If your answer was choice (H), you subtracted the two numbers given in the problem. Choice (G) is one-half of segment WY.

31. C
Variable Manipulation

100 Key Math Concepts for the ACT, #67. Find the point of intersection of two lines by solving the system of equations. Use the elimination method, by lining up the equations by like terms:

$$5x + y = 7$$
$$2x + 3y = 8$$

The problem asks for the x-coordinate, so look at the equations, and multiply one of them so that when the equations are combined, the y values are eliminated. If you multiply all terms in the top

equation by -3, when you combine them, the y values will be eliminated:

$$-3(5x + y = 7) \Rightarrow -15x - 3y = -21$$
$$2x + 3y = 8 \Rightarrow 2x + 3y = 8$$

Combine like terms in the resulting equations: $(-15x + 2x) + (-3y + 3y) = -21 + 8$, or $-13x = -13$. Now, divide both sides of this simpler equation by -13 to get $x = 1$.

If you chose (A), you probably divided the negative numbers incorrectly to get -1. Choice (B) may have resulted from only multiplying the y by -3 and not multiplying the terms of $5x$ and 7, and getting the result of $7x = 15$, or $x = \frac{15}{7}$. Choice (D) is the y-coordinate of the intersection of the two lines.

32. K
Variable Manipulation

100 Key Math Concepts for the ACT, #64. To solve the equation for b, isolate b on one side of the equation. First, add 8 to both sides of the equation: $a + 8 = 2b - 8 + 8$, or $a + 8 = 2b$. Now, divide both sides by 2 to get $b = \frac{a + 8}{2}$.

If your answer was (F), you forgot to divide a by 2. In (G), you exchanged the variable a for the variable b, instead of solving for b. Choice (H) is similar to (G), but the subtraction was changed to addition. In (J), you may have subtracted 8 from both sides instead of adding 8.

33. D
Plane Geometry

100 Key Math Concepts for the ACT, #87. The area of a parallelogram is $A = bh$, where height h is the length of the perpendicular segment to one of the sides of the parallelogram. In the figure, segment RT, of length $9 + 5$, or 14 mm, is the base and the dotted segment, of length 12 mm, is the height. The area is $14 \times 12 = 168$ mm^2.

Answer choice A is the area of the little triangle at the top, not the parallelogram. If you chose (B), you added the given numbers, without recognizing that the problem is asking for area. Choice (C) is the perimeter of the parallelogram. Choice (E) reflects a common error, where you multiplied the sides together, instead of the base times the height.

34. F

Variable Manipulation

100 Key Math Concepts for the ACT, #52, #63. The problem asks for you to evaluate $(x + y)^3$, so manipulate the given equation to isolate $x + y$ on one side of the equation. Once you have this value, cube it to find the answer to the problem. For the given equation $x = -(y + 3)$, first distribute the negative sign on the right-hand side to get $x = -y - 3$. Now add y to both sides of the equation: $x + y = -y + y - 3$. Combine like terms to arrive at $x + y = -3$. Now substitute -3 for $(x + y)$ in the expression to get $(-3)^3 = -3 \times -3 \times -3 = -27$.

Choice (G) is a common trap: evaluating $(-3)^3$ as $-3 \times 3 = -9$. Choices (H) and (J) result from not applying integer multiplication rules for negative numbers.

35. E

Plane Geometry

100 Key Math Concepts for the ACT, #86. Because all streets and avenues shown intersect at right angles, the map is a rectangle in which opposite sides have the same measures. To find the location halfway from H and S, first think of the corner of Oak and 10th to be the origin, or (0, 0). Just as in coordinate geometry, the first ordered pair represents the east-west direction, and the second ordered pair represents the north-south direction. The distance from the origin at Oak Street to the school is 5 miles east. The distance from the origin at 10th

Avenue to the hospital is 8 miles north. The new station will be halfway between these coordinates, or $\frac{5}{2} = 2.5$ miles east of the origin and $\frac{8}{2} = 4$ miles north of the origin.

To drive from F to the new fire station, you would have to drive $8 - 2.5 = 5.5$ miles west on Main Street, and then $10 - 4 = 6$ miles south on Elm Street (the first 2 miles south to get to 2nd Avenue, and then the 4 more miles south to be halfway from the hospital and the school). Choice (A) is the directions of the new fire station starting from the origin at Oak and 10th. Choice (B) is the directions of the new fire station starting from the school. Choice (C) is the directions from the corner of Main and Oak to the new station. If you answered (D), you forgot to add in the 2 miles on Elm Street to get from Main to 2nd Avenue.

36. H

Variable Manipulation

100 Key Math Concepts for the ACT, #65. Consecutive integers are integers that differ by 1, such as 3, 4, 5…Consecutive odd integers are odd integers that differ by 2, such as 7, 9, 11, 13…Because the answer choices use the variable x, let x represent the smaller of the consecutive odd integers, so $(x + 2)$ would be the larger of the integers. Four times the larger is represented by $4(x + 2)$, and twice the smaller by $2x$. The key word *difference* means to subtract the smaller from the larger, and the key word *is* means "equals." The equation is $4(x + 2) - 2x = 36$.

Choice (F) represents four times a number, minus twice the same number. Even though (G) and (J) are odd integers, they differ by an odd number, which would make the next number even. Choice (K) is an equation for the difference between 36 and four times the smaller integer.

37. C

Plane Geometry

100 Key Math Concepts for the ACT, #84. The question states that the telephone pole is perpendicular to

the ground and a wire is attached to the pole. This will result in a right triangle. It helps to draw a quick figure to represent the situation. The thicker side of the triangle represents the telephone pole, and the hypotenuse is the wire:

To find out how far the anchor of the supporting wire is from the base of the telephone pole, solve for the length of the missing leg. Use the Pythagorean theorem, which is $a^2 + b^2 = hypotenuse^2$. Let b represent the missing leg, and substitute in the given values to get $12^2 + b^2 = 15^2$, or $144 + b^2 = 225$. Subtract 144 from both sides: $b^2 = 81$. To solve for b, take the square root of both sides: $\sqrt{b^2} = \sqrt{81}$, so $b = 9$ or -9. A length cannot be negative, so the length is 9 ft.

Choice (A) subtracts 15 – 12 to get 3. If you chose (B), you may have thought that 15^2 meant 15×2 and calculated 30 – 24 = 6. Choice (D) is the length up the pole, and choice E is the length of the wire.

38. H
Plane Geometry

100 Key Math Concepts for the ACT, #91. The area of a circle is $A = \pi r^2$, where r is the radius of the circle. Use the equation $100\pi = \pi r^2$, and solve for r by dividing both sides by π: $100 = r^2$. If you take the square root of both sides, then $r = 10$ or -10. Reject the –10 value, because a radius length cannot be negative. The radius of the circle is 10, so

the diameter of the circle, which is the same as the length of a side of the square, is $2 \times 10 = 20$ units.

Choice (F) is the area of the square. Choice (G) is r^2. Choosing (J) is a common error that mistakes the radius of the circle for the side of the square.

39. C
Proportions and Probability

100 Key Math Concepts for the ACT, #36, #38. When figures are similar, the side lengths are in proportion. Let x represent the missing side length, and set up the proportion of shorter side to longer side: $\frac{3}{8} = \frac{2}{x}$.

Cross-multiply to get $3x = 16$. Divide both sides by 3 to get $x = 16 \div 3 \approx 5.3$, to the nearest tenth of an inch.

If you chose (A) or (B), you set up the proportion incorrectly—make sure to match up the long sides and the short sides on the same side of the fraction. Choice (D) is the most common error made with similar figures, by assuming that since 3 – 1 = 2, the missing side would be 8 – 1 = 7. Similar figures have sides that are in proportion, which is not an additive relationship.

40. J
Plane Geometry

100 Key Math Concepts for the ACT, #79. The figure shown is a parallelogram. Extend the top side out to make a parallel line to line *UZ*. Line *WY* is a transversal to the parallel lines, forming alternate interior angles, $\angle XWY$ and $\angle WYV$, which have the same measures of 50°. Line *WV* is another transversal line to the parallel lines, forming alternate interior angles $\angle UVW$ and $\angle VWX$. Because they have the same measure, $\angle VWX = 150°$. In addition, $\angle VWX$ and $\angle VYX$ have the same measure—they are opposite angles in a parallelogram. Now $\angle VYX - \angle WYV = \angle WYX$, or 150 – 50 = 100°.

If your answer was (H), you incorrectly thought that ∠WYX had the same measure as ∠XWY. Choice (K) is the measure of ∠VYX, not ∠WYX.

41. D
Plane Geometry

100 Key Math Concepts for the ACT, #86. The key to solving this problem is to simplify the drawing, knowing that you are looking for the perimeter. This figure, for perimeter purposes, can be thought of as a rectangle—just lower all the bottom pieces and move all left pieces to the right and you have a rectangle, with side lengths of 40 centimeters, and top/bottom lengths of 12 + 5 + 4 = 21 centimeters:

The perimeter is two times the length plus two times the width, or 2(40) + 2(21) = 80 + 42 = 122 centimeters.

Choice (A) is the measure of the length. Choice (B) is just the measure of two sides of the figure (just the numbers that are shown).

42. G
Proportions and Probability

100 Key Math Concepts for the ACT, #29, #65. Convert the fractions into decimal equivalents, and remember that the key word *of* means to multiply. Because $\frac{3}{4}$ of the 3,500 eligible voters cast a vote, this is 0.75 × 3,500 = 2,625 votes that were cast at the

site. Three-fifths of these votes were for Martinez, or 0.6 × 2,625 = 1,575 votes for Martinez.

If you answered (F), you followed the correct procedure, but incorrectly converted the fractions. Choice (H) is $\frac{3}{5}$ of all the eligible voters. Choice (J) is $\frac{3}{4}$ of the eligible voters. Answer (K) is the sum of (H) and (J).

43. A
Number Properties

100 Key Math Concepts for the ACT, #15, #52. To find the greatest common factor, find all factor pieces that the two expressions have in common. In this case, the factors in common are a, a, a, and b, or a^3b. It is given that the greatest common factor is 54, so think of a cubic number that is a factor of 54. The first cubic numbers are 1^3 (1), 2^3 (8), and 3^3 (27). Twenty-seven is a factor of 54: 27 × 2 = 54, so a possible value for b is 2.

Choice (B) is the value of the variable a. Choice (C), 6, is a factor of 54, but that leaves the value of 9 for a, and 9 is not a perfect cube. The same reasoning would eliminate (D). Choice (E) is the value of a^3.

44. K
Proportions and Probability

100 Key Math Concepts for the ACT, #32. To tackle this problem, break it up into its parts. First, find the value of x, given that 40% of x is 70. The key word *of* means to multiply. Write this as the equation 0.40x = 70; divide both sides by 0.40 to get x = 175. Now find 160% of x, or 1.60 × 175 = 280.

Choice (F) is 40% of 70. Choice (G) is 160% of 28, the incorrect value from (F). Choice (H) is 160% of 70. A common trap is (J), which is the value of the variable x.

45. C
Coordinate Geometry

100 Key Math Concepts for the ACT, #49, #71. To find the length of segment *MN*, use the distance

formula: $d = \sqrt{(x_2 - x_1)^2 + (y_2 - y_1)^2}$. Substitute in the point values:

$$d = \sqrt{(6-2)^2 + (5-3)^2}$$
$$d = \sqrt{4^2 + 2^2}$$
$$d = \sqrt{20} = \sqrt{4} \times \sqrt{5} = 2\sqrt{5}$$

If you chose answer choice A, you may have used the distance formula incorrectly, using $(y_1 - x_1)$ and $(y_2 - x_2)$ instead of finding the difference between the x- and y-coordinates. Choice (B) multiplies by 2 instead of raising to the second power in the formula. Choice (D) is just the sum of the differences between the x- and y-coordinates. If your answer was (E), you forgot to take the square root of 20, as indicated by the distance formula.

46. J
Plane Geometry

100 Key Math Concepts for the ACT, #36, #86. If the sides are in the ratio of 5:7, the perimeter will also be in this exact same ratio. When finding a perimeter, you add up the sides. Perimeter is measured in single units, just as is the side length. Therefore, the ratio will not change. If you are unsure about this fact, assign values and actually calculate the perimeters. Consider the smaller square to have sides 5s in length and the larger square to have sides 7s in length. The smaller square has a perimeter of $4 \times 5s = 20s$, and the larger $4 \times 7s = 28s$. The ratio 20s:28s is equivalent to 5:7, after dividing both terms of the ratio by 4s.

If you chose (F), you may have thought you needed to subtract $7 - 5 = 2$, to get the (incorrect) ratio 1:2. Likewise, (G) adds $7 + 5 = 12$. Choice (H) multiplies $7 \times 5 = 35$. Choice (K) confuses area and perimeter—the ratio of the *areas* is 25 : 49.

47. E
Plane Geometry

100 Key Math Concepts for the ACT, #75. The equation of a circle, when given the coordinates of the center (h, k) and the radius (r), is obtained by $(x - h)^2 + (y - k)^2 = r^2$. Substitute in the given values to get

$(x - (-2))^2 + (y - 3)^2 = 9^2$. This simplifies to $(x + 2)^2 + (y - 3)^2 = 81$.

There are two common traps when finding the equation of a circle. One trap is to forget to square the radius, as in (B). The other common trap is adding h and k to x and y, instead of subtracting, as in (C). Choice (A) is both of these traps together. Choice (D) incorrectly takes the square root of the radius, instead of squaring the radius.

48. H
Variable Manipulation

100 Key Math Concepts for the ACT, #5, #23. In the complex number system, i^2 is defined to be equal to -1, as you are told in the question stem. Use the distributive property to multiply the fraction:

$$\frac{3}{5-i} \times \frac{5+i}{5+i} = \frac{(3 \times 5) + 3i}{5^2 + 5i - 5i - i^2} =$$

$$\frac{15 + 3i}{25 - (-1)} = \frac{15 + 3i}{26}$$

If your answer was (F), you may have cancelled incorrectly to simplify. Choice (G) reflects a common error when multiplying complex numbers—$25 - i^2$ was incorrectly interpreted to be $25 - 1 = 24$. In (J), the 3 in the numerator was not distributed to the i term. Choice (K) is the result of two errors—the common error described in (G) and the error in (J).

49. C
Plane Geometry

100 Key Math Concepts for the ACT, #88. One way to solve this problem is to make a table. Each time the number of sides goes up by 1, the sum of the angles goes up by 180°. Make a third column in the table to discover a relationship.

Number of Sides	Sum of the Angles	
3	180°	180° × 1
4	360°	180° × 2
5	540°	180° × 3
6	720°	180° × 4

Notice that to find the sum of the angles, you can multiply 180 times 2 less than the number of sides of the polygon. This is (C).

If you chose (A), you may have just considered the triangle and assumed that the relationship was 60n. If your answer was (B), you may have noticed that the number of degrees rose by 180°, but this did not consider the sides of the polygons. Choice (D) is a relationship that works for the three-sided and six-sided polygons, but not the other two.

50. G
Patterns, Data, and Logic

100 Key Math Concepts for the ACT, #31. This problem is a method of logical thinking. The key to solving this problem is to first assume that there are no students who have both a cell phone and an mp3 player. If this were the case, then there would be 35 + 18 = 53 students polled. The problem states that 50 students were polled, so therefore at least 3 students have both electronic devices. This is the minimum number of students who own both.

If you chose (F), you may have ignored the fact that 50 students were polled. Choice (H) is the difference between the number of cell phone owners and mp3 owners. Choice (J) is a possible number of students who own *only* a cell phone. Choice (K) is the sum of 35 and 18.

51. A
Variable Manipulation

100 Key Math Concepts for the ACT, #69. To solve this inequality, attempt to get the variable on one side of the inequality by adding 4n to both sides: $-4n + 4n + 3 > -4n + 4n + 1$. Combine like terms to get 3 > 1. This inequality is always true for the set of real numbers.

If you chose answer (B) or (C), you may have thought that the term $-4n$ would limit the set of solutions. If your answer was (D) or (E), you may have mistakenly added $-4n$ to both sides and added 3 to both sides to get $-8n > 4$, and then solved for n.

52. H
Patterns, Data, and Logic

100 Key Math Concepts for the ACT, #36. This question tests your problem-solving strategies. Make this question easier to visualize by naming the five people:

A B C D E

Now you only need to identify the number of different combinations.

AB, AC, AD, AE

BC, BD, BE

CD, CE

DE

There are 10 distinct combinations, meaning 10 total handshakes.

If you chose (F), you may have seen that 4 people have 2 more handshakes than people and assumed this was the pattern for more people. If you chose (G), you may have thought that the pattern in handshakes was multiples of 3. The key is to have a clear way to visualize information.

53. D
Proportions and Probability

100 Key Math Concepts for the ACT, #36, #38. First, determine the percentage in the category Miscellaneous. The total percentage must sum to 100%, so the percentage for Miscellaneous is 100 − 23 − 5 − 22 − 18 = 32%. To find the number of degrees in a circle graph that corresponds with 32%, set up the ratio, where x represents the number of degrees for the Miscellaneous category. Recall that there are 360° in a circle: $\frac{32}{100} = \frac{x}{360}$. Cross-multiply to get 32 × 360 = 100x, or 11,520 = 100x. Divide both sides by 100 to get x = 115°, rounded to the nearest degree.

Choice (A) is a common trap that represents the percentage, not the number of degrees in a circle graph. If your answer was (B), you thought that there were 180° in a circle.. Choice (C) is the percentage of categories that are *not* Miscellaneous, and (E) is the number of degrees that are *not* Miscellaneous.

54. K
Trigonometry

100 Key Math Concepts for the ACT, #85, #96. The information $\frac{\pi}{2} < \theta < \pi$ tells you that the angle is in quadrant II of the coordinate plane. In quadrant II, the sin values are positive. So the answer must be positive. Eliminate (F), (G), and (H). You are given the value of tan θ, which is the ratio of the opposite side to the adjacent side of a right triangle. Sketch this triangle, using leg lengths of 4 and 3:

This is a special right triangle, the 3-4-5 Pythagorean triple, so the hypotenuse is 5 units in length. The sin of an angle is the ratio of the length of the opposite side to the length of the hypotenuse, or $\frac{4}{5}$. If you chose (F), you may have ignored the fact that the angle is in quadrant II and thought that the sin value would be negative. Choice (G) is the cotangent of the angle. Choices (H) and (J) are cosine values for the angle for quadrants II and I, respectively.

55. A
Coordinate Geometry

100 Key Math Concepts for the ACT, #73, #74. Look at the graphed boundary lines for the inequalities. Find the equation for these boundary lines and then determine if the shading represents less than or greater than these boundary lines. The horizontal line has a slope of 0 and a y-intercept (where the line crosses the y-axis) of 6, so the equation of this boundary line is $y = 6$. It is shaded below this line, so the inequality is $y < 6$. The slanted line has a slope with a change in y values of 3 and a change in x values of 1, so the slope is $\frac{3}{1} = 3$. The y-intercept is –5. The line is increasing, so the slope is positive. The shading is greater than, or above, this boundary line, so the inequality is $y > 3x - 5$. If you chose (B), you fell into a common trap of interpreting the horizontal boundary line equation to be $x < 6$. Choice (C) is another common error, thinking that the shading represents less than, or below, the slanted line. Choice (D) interprets the slope as –3. Negative slopes decrease, or slant downwards, when going from left to right. Choice (E) represents a slope of $\frac{1}{3}$, not the correct slope of 3. A slope of $\frac{1}{3}$ would mean for every change of 1 in the y values, the x values would change by 3.

56. J
Variable Manipulation

100 Key Math Concepts for the ACT, #52. The question asks you to evaluate the function f(x), replacing x with (x + c). Replace any instance of x in the function definition with x + c. This means that 2(x +

7) will be $2(x + c + 7)$. Use the distributive property and multiply each term in parentheses by 2 to get $2x + 2c + 2 \times 7$, or $2x + 2c + 14$.

In (F), the 2 was not distributed to the constant term 7. Choice (G) only multiplies the 2 by the first term in the parentheses. In (H) and (K), the c term was just added onto the end of the function definition, instead of replacing the x with $(x + c)$.

57. B
Coordinate Geometry

100 Key Math Concepts for the ACT, #62, #73, #74. First, simplify the equation by simplifying the fraction on the right-hand side. Factor the numerator and then cancel the $(x - 2)$ factor from the numerator and denominator:

$$\frac{2x^2 - 8}{x - 2} = \frac{2(x^2 - 4)}{x - 2} = \frac{2(x + 2)(x - 2)}{x - 2} = 2(x + 2)$$

The simplified equation is $y = 2(x + 2)$, or $y = 2x + 4$. This equation is now in slope-intercept form, where the y-intercept is 4 and the slope is $\frac{2}{1}$. Choice (B) is the correct graph that has a slope of 2 and crosses the y-axis at 4.

If you ignored the denominator in the given equation, then you would have incorrectly chosen (A), the graph of the quadratic $y = 2x^2 - 8$.

Choice (C) is the graph of the equation $y = \frac{1}{2}x + 4$. If this was your choice, you may have misinterpreted the slope of a line. Choice (D) is the graph of a quadratic function, not the correct linear function. You cannot assume a function is a quadratic just because you see a variable that is squared; you must first try to simplify the equation. Choice (E) is the graph of the linear function $y = -2x + 4$.

58. F
Coordinate Geometry

This problem tests your knowledge of line reflections in the coordinate plane.

When you reflect a point or a figure over the y-axis, the x-coordinate of each point is the opposite sign and the y-coordinate stays the same. The reflection of the point $Q(r,s)$ after a reflection over the y-axis is therefore $Q'(-r,s)$.

Choice (G) would be the result of a reflection over the y-axis, followed by a reflection over the x-axis. Choice (H) is incorrect—the x- and y- coordinates were switched. Choice (J) is a common trap that represents a reflection over the x-axis.

59. C
Variable Manipulation

100 Key Math Concepts for the ACT, #64. The problem is asking what is the value of g in terms of h. The two given equations do not show a direct relationship between g and h, so you must solve for q in the second equation to get q in terms of h, and then substitute this value in for q in the first equation. To solve for q in the second equation, isolate q by first adding 8 to both sides of the equation: $h + 8 = 2q - 8 + 8$, or $h + 8 = 2q$. Divide both sides by 2 to get $\frac{h + 8}{2} = q$. Use this value of q in the first equation: $g = 4q + 3$ becomes $g = \frac{4(h + 8)}{2} + 3$.

Factor out a 2 from the numerator and the denominator of the first term to get $g = 2(h + 8) + 3$. Multiply the terms in parentheses by 2, or $g = 2h + 16 + 3$, or $g = 2h + 19$.

Choice (A) is the value of q in terms of h from the second equation. In (B), the constant term 3 in the first equation was incorrectly added to the numerator of the transformed first equation, and the 4 was not distributed to both terms of h and 8. In (D), the

2 was factored out correctly, but the remaining 2 was not distributed to the constant term of 8. Choice (E) is the value of q, not h, in terms of g from the first equation.

60. H
Trigonometry

100 Key Math Concepts for the ACT, #52, #98. In this problem, you are asked to use the formula $\cos(\alpha + \beta) = \cos(\alpha)\cos(\beta) - \sin(\alpha)\sin(\beta)$ and the table of values to find the value of $\cos(75°) = \cos(30° + 45°)$. Substitute in 30° for α and 45° for β to get: $\cos(30°)\cos(45°) - \sin(30°)\sin(45°)$. Now use the table to replace each sin or cos with the corresponding values in the table: $\frac{\sqrt{3}}{2} \times \frac{\sqrt{2}}{2} - \frac{1}{2} \times \frac{\sqrt{2}}{2}$. Using order of operations, multiply and then subtract the numerators and keep the denominator: $\frac{\sqrt{6}}{4} - \frac{\sqrt{2}}{4} = \frac{\sqrt{6} - \sqrt{2}}{4}$. Alternately, you could use your calculator to find the value of the $\cos(75°) \approx 0.2588$, and then test each answer choice to find the answer closest to this value. Choice (H) will be the only value to equal the $\cos(75°)$.

If you chose (F) or (K), you probably used the wrong values in the table. In (G), you used the wrong values in the table and also forgot to multiply the denominators, resulting in a denominator of 2 instead of 4. Choice (J) is the common trap—you correctly used the table but did not multiply the denominators to get a denominator of 4.

READING TEST

Reading questions can be divided into four basic types: Detail questions, Inference questions, Global questions, Vocab-in-Context questions, Writer's View questions, and Function questions. As you review the answers and explanations, note which types you tend to answer correctly or incorrectly and tailor your studying to focus on areas where you need improvement.

PASSAGE I

1. D
Inference

The question is asking about Dave's opinion specifically. Throughout the passage, Dave describes the problems with comparison between twins, and many of his comments to Emily are also focused on comparing himself to his twin. Choice (D) is correct because it mentions this competition and implies that it makes their relationship more difficult. Choice (A) is extreme, (B) implies that their relationship is stronger than it is, and (C) is not supported by the text because Emily doesn't seem to be able to convince Dave to make more of an effort.

2. H
Detail

Emily has a good relationship with both brothers; she has an enjoyable conversation with Bruce and works to make Dave feel better. Also, she wants the brothers to be closer than they are. Because it reflects these details, (H) is the correct answer. Choice (F) is the opposite; Emily is very attentive, and (G) and (J) are both extreme and negative distortions of Emily's desire to help relations between the brothers.

3. B
Detail

This question is asking you to identify which answer choice is NOT represented in the passage, so the first step is to eliminate choices that ARE contained in the passage. In the first paragraph, Dave is envious of the reaction his wife has when talking to Bruce, eliminating (A). The paragraph about Dave's reaction to the picture captures his negative feelings regarding the difference in their popularity, eliminating (C). The final conversation shows Dave as doubtful of Bruce's need for his approval, eliminating (D). This leaves (B), which is not found in the passage and is therefore the correct answer.

4. J
Function
The first paragraph starts with a description of Emily on the phone, but the focus quickly shifts to Dave's reaction. It then moves to Dave making some points about his brother's popularity and questioning if his own wife ever reacted so favorably to him. Choice (J) summarizes this well. Choices (F) and (H) are not found in the passage, and (G) occurs much later.

5. D
Inference
Emily attempts to make Dave believe that he is important to Bruce, but Dave still feels he is in Bruce's shadow. It is unclear whether or not Dave entirely believes Emily, but when she brings up Bruce's desire to talk about the brothers' childhood, Dave's response suggests that he does not want to talk about it because it again reminds him of how Bruce has always been the more popular of the two. This makes (D) the correct answer. Choice (A) is out-of-scope; the passage does not suggest that Dave does anything to spite Emily. Choice (B) is incorrect because Dave does not feel guilty; he sees Bruce's success as proof that it doesn't matter whether he calls Bruce or not. Choice (C) is out-of-scope; Dave's reasons for not calling Bruce have to do with his feelings toward his brother, not any feelings related to Emily.

6. H
Detail
In lines 39–42, Dave explicitly talks about how Bruce's image has positive aspects (vitality) that his image lacks. This is a perfect match for (H), which restates this generally. Choices (F) and (J) are not found in the passage, and (G) is contradicted by the fact that both Dave and Emily can tell the difference between the twins.

7. B
Inference
Dave is uncomfortable at this point, because Emily is clearly thinking about Bruce. The previous paragraph describes the picture as a source of insecurity for Dave, suggesting that he is nervous and seeking reassurance that Emily is with him for reasons other than his connection to Bruce. Only (B) describes these feelings. Choice (A) is the opposite of what Dave is feeling, and neither (C) nor (D) can be deduced from the information in the passage.

8. F
Inference
With an open-ended question like this, the answer choices must be individually tested. Choice (F) can be logically deduced, especially from the last exchange: Emily mentions that Bruce tells her stories about their childhood, and when Dave makes a comment about Bruce's popularity, Emily responds that "[Bruce] doesn't look at it that way" (line 115). This suggests that there is a difference between each brother's childhood stories. Choice (G) is too extreme and better describes the reaction other people have to the different professions of Bruce and Dave. Choice (H) is also too extreme: Dave feels competitive with Bruce, but that does not imply that they have fought. Choice (J) is not supported by the text; their childhood is the only time when it is stated that they spent time together.

9. C
Detail
Dave and Emily have different opinions regarding the picture. Dave is displeased with his image, while Emily professes to like his smile. However, Dave describes Bruce's smile as *trademark* (line 43), and Emily says that Bruce looks "exactly the same" (lines 60–61) in every picture. This makes (C) correct. Choices (A) and (D) depict opinions that are strictly Dave's and Emily's, respectively, and (B) is not supported by the passage at all.

10. F
Inference
Emily follows her comment about Bruce's stories by dismissing Dave's comment about Bruce's popularity, saying that Bruce "doesn't look at it that way" (line 115). This is in reaction to Dave's frequent comments suggesting that Bruce has been more successful socially and Dave's implication that Bruce feels superior to Dave. This matches (F), which correctly restates this idea. Choice (G) is not supported by the passage; (H) is opposite because Emily wants Dave to focus less on his brother's successes; and (J) is extreme, since Bruce wants more attention from his brother but is not necessarily lonely.

PASSAGE II

11. C
Generalization
The author is critical of the media throughout the passage and focuses mostly on ways in which the current media is not concerned enough with factual accuracy. Choice (C) matches this nicely. Choice (A) is too extreme; the author talks about distorting facts, not making them up. Choice (B) contradicts paragraph 2, which characterizes some news personalities as *demagogues* with biased views. Choice (D) contradicts paragraph 4; the public's desire for this type of news is one of the reasons for its existence.

12. G
Inference
In paragraph 3, the author mentions how impartial stories can sway the opinions of readers through headlines rather than content. Choices (H) and (J) both mention headlines, but (H) makes the opposite point, and (J) is far too specific, using the example as a basis for a point that the author does not explicitly make. Choice (F) is contradicted by the passage. Choice (G) is general, but correct: the headline is another method used to sensationalize the story, as illustrated by the example of the "enraged public" (line 55) versus the "irked locals" (lines 58–59).

13. B
Function
The sentence preceding the Walter Cronkite example states that audience members expected to have complicated events explained to them; the Cronkite example follows this logic. Choice (B) matches this perfectly. Choice (A) may be inferred, but it is not the point the author is making—the author's concern is the treatment of the news, not specific news personalities. This reasoning also eliminates (C). Choice (D) is never mentioned in or suggested by the passage.

14. F
Inference
In order to research this statement, it is a good idea to look back at paragraph 3 because it discusses the public. "Personal consensus" applies to the author's point about people looking for news reported with a political opinion similar to their own. Choice (F) matches this. Choices (G) and (J) are both contradicted by information given in paragraph 3. Choice (H) is not supported by the passage and contradicts the author's main point.

15. B
Detail
In paragraph 1, the author states that in stories of "continued national interest" (lines 10–11), the focus shifts from facts to *theater* (line 12). Choice (B) is the best match. Choices (A), (C), and (D) are not explicitly mentioned as more or less likely to be sensationalized.

16. J
Vocab-in-Context
The sentence describes objective reporting as a "distant possibility." Questions like this are made easier if you pick a word that means the same thing in context. In this case, you can predict *improbable* or something similar. This matches (J) perfectly. Choices (F), (G), and (H) do not address the likelihood of objective reporting.

17. C
Writer's View
The author is most likely to criticize a headline that sensationalizes or makes a value judgment, and the end of paragraph 3 gives an example. Choices (A), (B), and (D) are all basically factual and specific. Choice (C) is correct because it uses a very inclusive group, like the example in paragraph 3 does, makes a value judgment by calling the song offensive, and uses emotional language.

18. J
Detail
The fourth paragraph focuses on the flaws of the public and states that individuals who agree with certain politically biased hosts are unlikely to question the validity of the "facts" presented. This matches (J) perfectly. Choices (F) and (G) are not explicitly stated by the author. Choice (H) describes accuracy problems for the media, not the public.

19. A
Detail
The author makes the point that fact-based news only captures a small minority of the news audience. Also, the beginning of paragraph 4 states that the public is not interested in dry facts. Choice (A) can be inferred because the media companies are providing the type of programs that the public seems to want. Choice (B) is extreme—in fact, it could be inferred that if the greater public was interested in objective facts, the media (including cable) would provide programs of that sort. Choices (C) and (D) cannot be deduced from the passage; the author seems to believe that factual news will not draw a large audience no matter what.

20. G
Inference
Because this question deals with the audience, paragraph 4 is a good place to look. The author states that audience members look for hosts who share their political opinions. Choice (G) is a general restatement of this idea, so it is correct. Choice (F) is not stated in the passage. Choice (H) distorts a

detail from the last paragraph; audience members prefer short to lengthy, but there is no statement about audience members gravitating toward the shortest or most simple stories. Choice (J) misuses the detail about headlines from paragraph 3.

PASSAGE III

21. C
Generalization
The author frequently describes his grandfather's actions and describes their relationship to his heritage. Choice (C) fits this, as the other Russians in paragraph 3 are also characterized as being naturally tied to Russia. Choice (A) distorts the grandfather's later visits to Russia; the passage does not imply that immigrants would prefer to be elsewhere. Choice (B) cites the opinions of American-born people, while the passage does not focus on those opinions. Choice (D) refers only to the grandfather, who was perpetually displaced; his story is addressed as being unique.

22. J
Inference
The three specific locations mentioned are Moscow, Siberia, and China, in that order. Also, the author mentions that China was the longest stay. Choices (F), (G), and (H) all have errors: (F) puts the Russian revolution in the wrong time period, (G) says he was exiled from Russia as an adult, and (H) says he settled in communist China, when he left during the revolution.

23. C
Inference
These line references both have to do with his work in real estate. You can deduce that he sees real estate as providing stability for people, something he did not have earlier in his life. Choice (C) matches this very well. Choice (A) is part of his sales strategy, not his purpose. Choices (B) and (D) are never discussed as tasks he specifically attempts.

24. F
Detail
The grandfather is proud to be Russian, and deeply influenced by his heritage, but is also proud to do his job and be a successful American. Choice (F) contradicts the grandfather's attitude, because while he criticizes the government, he loves the country itself. Choice (G) suggests an unspoken pride between Russians, which is in line with the grandfather's characterization. Choices (H) and (J) both fit because he is critical of the communist government but still reverent regarding the country.

25. D
Inference
The passage deals heavily with displacement, and its implications, along with its effects on people. Since Moscow was where the family was originally from, you can deduce that the answer will have something to do with belonging. Choice (D) fits this classification well; Moscow is the family's native home, and all feel tied to Russia but are searching for places to live outside of Russia. Choices (A) and (C) are not implied at all in the passage. Choice (B) may be factually true but does not apply to the desires of the family.

26. F
Vocab-in-Context
This selection refers to Russians saying, "I am American" in Russian. It is contrasted with points about the fact that they are speaking Russian with other Russians, therefore suggesting that "playing the role" must mean becoming more accustomed to their new country. Choice (F) matches this perfectly. Choices (G) and (H) cannot be deduced from the information given, and (J) may be true, but does not apply to "playing the role."

27. B
Inference
"Strategic compromise" applies to the grandfather's desire to sell homes, in spite of the current stigma against Russians. The tactics mentioned by the author are informing the customer he was exiled and disagreed with the current Russian government, and not responding to negative remarks regarding the entire country of Russia. Choice (B) fits this final part, as negative statements about Russia as a whole would offend the grandfather. Choices (A) and (D) are too extreme and specific. Choice (C) is not mentioned.

28. H
Inference
According to the passage, this sort of trip "elucidates one's very existence" (line 107). This is the only result given; the rest of the details apply to the emotional strain involved. Choice (H) is the only choice that applies to this. Choices (F) and (G) are not even implied by the text, and (J) applies to the adoption analogy rather than the grandfather.

29. B
Detail
The last sentence in the first paragraph states that the country came under new rule during the time his mother was pregnant with him. He was therefore born after the revolution and under communist rule. Choice (B) is correct. The other choices contradict that factual sentence.

30. G
Inference
The need to rediscover a lost native land is what would be made unnecessary so the correct answer would have to describe the opposite situation. Choice (G) fits this very well; having a sense of belonging would alleviate the need to search for it. Choice (F) is incorrect because the grandfather embodies the feelings he is potentially making unnecessary. Choice (H) describes people that may still desire to revisit their roots. Choice (J) describes a totally unrelated achievement possible in real estate.

PASSAGE IV

31. B
Inference

The passage is most concerned with discrediting the myth that rattlesnakes are aggressive and very dangerous, and the selection refers to exactly that: the "sinister opportunist" is the myth, while the "mild-mannered domestic" is closer to fact. Choice (B) can be deduced from this. Choice (A) is incorrect, as juvenile snakes are not even mentioned. Choice (C) misuses the detail about rattlesnakes giving live birth, which is not treated as a recent discovery. Choice (D) is too extreme; the author describes rattlesnakes as fairly docile but not entirely predictable.

32. F
Inference

At the end of paragraph 6, the author states that the reputation is good because a frightened and cornered rattlesnake is dangerous. Choice (F) fits this because if people did not avoid or move away from rattlesnakes, there would be more dangerous interaction between humans and snakes. Choices (G) and (J) are contradicted by the passage; in rattlesnake roundups, their reputation costs the snakes their lives, and the author, who is aware of their docile nature, would certainly never believe a rattlesnake should be a pet. Choice (H) misuses the detail about snakebite deaths.

33. C
Detail

The passage gives quite a few examples of the social behavior of rattlesnakes, so be prepared to find a restated fact among the answer choices. Choice (C) fits this nicely, because the second paragraph states that rattlesnakes have been known to hibernate with tortoises. Choice (A) is not a social behavior. Choice (B) goes beyond the text; the wrestling is used to claim a mate, but the losing snake will leave, rather than take a place within a hierarchy. Choice (D) also misuses a detail; rattlesnakes are described

as "entirely noncannibalistic" (line 24), meaning they never eat other snakes.

34. H
Inference

The mythology referred to is that of the heartless, aggressive rattlesnake. This relates to rattlesnake roundups (line 113) to which the author clearly objects, so it would follow that the author sees this particular human behavior as heartless and aggressive. Choice (H) matches this perfectly, and the statistical comparison in paragraph 7 supports this. Choice (F) contradicts the author's belief that rattlesnakes are not as dangerous as commonly thought. Choices (G) and (J) do not relate to the point the author is making.

35. C
Detail

The sixth paragraph states that serious bites can usually be traced to people that either handle or step on snakes, in contrast to those who were not engaging the snakes. Choice (C) fits this nicely, specifically focusing on those handling snakes, an example of individuals purposefully seeking interaction. Choice (A) is incorrect because a relationship is mentioned. Choice (B) is not mentioned in the text. Choice (D) is a distortion, because rattlesnakes deliver venom based on how threatened they feel, not necessarily based on how threatening humans act.

36. H
Inference

The selection's sentence starts with describing the docile behavior of rattlesnakes, as a follow-up to scientific findings in the previous paragraph. The implication is that snakes, while not as dangerous as often thought, can still be dangerous. Choice (H) matches this perfectly. Choice (F) is outside the scope of the passage; there is no mention of herpetologists keeping snakes. Choice (G) misuses a later detail; the author is not comparing the rattlesnake as a pet to dogs. Choice (J) states a comparison that is never made.

37. B
Detail

In paragraph 5, the author lists various statistics and states that dogs, bees, and lightning are all responsible for more annual deaths than rattlesnakes and that the fer-de-lance is responsible for substantially more. Choice (B) is the only answer that fits; every other choice is contradicted by the facts given.

38. J
Detail

In paragraph 6, the author explains that the rattlesnake knows that it needs its venom for food, and goes on to state that the only situation in which a rattlesnake would release all of its venom is when it feels threatened. Choice (J) fits with this; the rattlesnake wishes to conserve its venom, specifically for prey. Choice (F) is incorrect because humans are large in comparison and receive mostly "dry" bites. Choice (G) contradicts the statement about rattlesnakes potentially using all their venom if threatened. Choice (H) contradicts the statement that rattlesnakes are not aware of the well-being of nonfood sources.

39. B
Inference

The author examines two pieces of contradictory logic. The first is that the organizers use the reputation of the rattlesnake to promote interest but rely on the more docile nature of the snakes. The second is the fact that most of the snakes are taken from areas without people and put into contact with people, thus making for a more dangerous situation. Choice (B) matches the second piece of information. Choice (A) is not stated as fact in the text. Choice (C) brings up erroneous statistics, when really it is the rattlesnake's erroneous reputation that is used. Choice (D) is not mentioned in the passage.

40. G
Vocab-in-Context

The answer lies in the last sentence, which speculates on the status of humans in rattlesnake folklore "if rattlesnakes were able to speak or write." This makes it clear that *crotalid* must have something to do with actual rattlesnakes. Choice (G) is the only choice that fits because the sentence is mocking the way that humans have characterized rattlesnakes within human mythology. Choices (F), (H), and (J) all are incorrect because they mention groups that are not specifically rattlesnakes.

SCIENCE TEST

All Science questions will fall under one of the three SmartPoints: Figure questions, Pattern questions, and Scientific Reasoning questions.

PASSAGE I

The first passage requires a little basic understanding of the scientific method and a lot of figure interpretation. You don't need to grasp all of the details of the passage or the diagrams, but do take note of obvious trends or extremes in the given data. For example, the large changes in the data in Figure 1 at around 1,500 years are particularly worth noting.

1. C
Patterns

Be careful of extreme language, such as the use of *always* in (A) and (B). While the general trend is that decreasing glacier length corresponds to decreasing calving rate, the opposite is true at the sharp peak in calving rate at around 1,500 years, which (C) correctly describes.

2. H
Figure Interpretation

This question asks you to find the glacier with the largest calving rate for years 6–10 in Table 1. Make sure you are looking in the right place, which in this case is the far right column of Table 1.

3. A
Patterns

This question requires a little deeper understanding of the data presented in Table 1. For all four glaciers during both time periods, the calving rate is slightly greater than or equal to the average velocity. To predict the calving rate of a glacier with a velocity of 80 m/yr, you must look for glaciers traveling at similar velocities. The closest values come from glaciers A and C during years 1–5, which had velocities of 72 m/yr and 98 m/yr, respectively. The corresponding calving rates for these two glaciers are 72 m/yr and 106 m/yr. The correct answer should fall within this range, as described by (A).

4. J
Figure Interpretation

With open-ended questions like this one, a simple process of elimination is usually most efficient. Comparison of each choice with the data in Table 1 reveals that only choice J accurately reflects the "behavior of the glaciers."

5. B
Figure Interpretation

Don't be too concerned with the strange scale of the horizontal axis of each choice. The values on the axis correspond exactly to the calving rates for years 6–10 given in Table 1. Simply find the graph that correctly plots the four points given by the data in the last two columns of Table 1.

6. H
Scientific Reasoning

The meteorologists in Study 3 hypothesized that high temperatures cause rapid variations in velocity and calving rate. Figure 1 shows a rapid change in calving rate at around 1,500 years. If the hypothesis is true, then the glacier modeled in Study 1 experienced a rapid change in temperature approximately 1,500 years ago, and (H) is correct.

PASSAGE II

This passage consists almost entirely of Table 1 and Figures 1 and 2, with very little descriptive language. Fortunately, the more complicated the diagram, the more likely the questions referring to that diagram will be straightforward. In other words, don't waste too much time trying to interpret Table 1 right away. As it turns out, only one question requires you to refer to Table 1.

7. C
Figure Interpretation

Sometimes, you will be asked to simply read information directly from a graph. If you are careful to refer to the right part of the right graph, you will find correct answers to these kinds of questions very quickly. The bar for March 2 on Figure 1 rises to approximately 1,500 gr/m^3, as in (C).

8. H
Patterns

You are asked to describe a trend in the data in Figure 1 beyond the high value given for November 5. After this value, the data maintains no discernible trend, but does stay within a relatively small range of values, as is correctly described in (H).

9. B
Figure Interpretation

Be careful to answer the correct question. "Increased the most" doesn't necessarily mean the count increased to its largest value, which is the trap set in (C). Choice (D) is also a trap, set for those who refer to the wrong figure.

10. F
Figure Interpretation

This question asks about the tree pollen count, so you should refer to Figure 1. Process of elimination reveals that only (F) correctly reflects the data shown in the figure.

11. A
Figure Interpretation
You are finally asked to refer to the rather complicated Table 1. Find the row for the month of May, and look for the corresponding column(s) containing the most reported cases of allergic rhinitis. In this case, that means the most ❀ symbols. Tree and grass pollen account for six of the nine total ❀ symbols in the May row, which indeed constitute most of the cases.

PASSAGE III
When a passage includes multiple experiments designed to study the same topic, look for key similarities and differences between the experiments. In Experiment 1, oscillation frequency of a pendulum is measured, and the only variable is the length of the pendulum arm. In Experiment 2, the oscillation frequencies of several springs are measured, and there are two variables: the spring and the suspended mass. Experiment 3 involves the same springs as does Experiment 2 but measures equilibrium length instead of oscillation frequency.

12. G
Figure Interpretation
Notice that in Figure 3, the lines plotted for Springs B, C, and D intersect at approximately the same mass. The exact mass value is not completely clear from the figure, but it is definitely larger than (F) and smaller than (H), which leaves (G) as the only possibility.

13. A
Figure Interpretation
According to Figure 1, oscillation frequency does indeed decrease with increasing arm length, so you can eliminate (C) and (D). The second part of (B) is simply false, which leaves only (A).

14. F
Scientific Reasoning
This question requires a couple of steps of logic. First, you must realize what *slowly* means in terms of oscillation frequency. Recall from the passage that oscillation frequency is measured in "oscillations per second." The faster the spring oscillates, the more oscillations it will complete per second. Therefore, you are looking for the spring with the lowest value for oscillation frequency, which is Spring A.

15. C
Figure Interpretation
Refer to the line plotted for Spring A in Figure 3. On that line, a mass of 700 g corresponds to an equilibrium length of just less than 40 cm. Only (C) includes this estimate.

16. J
Patterns
According to Figure 2, an oscillation frequency of 1.4 Hz at a mass of 100 g would be represented by a data point that would fall in between the frequency values for Spring C and Spring D at that mass. Only (H) and (J) place Spring E correctly between Springs C and D, and (J) correctly lists the springs in order of *decreasing* oscillation frequency.

17. C
Scientific Reasoning
The effects of mass are not mentioned in Experiment 1. Only the pendulum arm length affects the oscillation frequency, so the plots for the original mass and the larger mass should be identical, as in (C).

PASSAGE IV
This passage is based almost entirely on Figure 1, which contains a great deal of information and deserves a few moments of your attention before attacking the questions. As always, it is important to understand what is represented on each axis. In this case, the vertical axis is straightforward, but

the horizontal axis is a bit unconventional. The last sentence in the passage should help you to grasp that the horizontal axis represents the composition of the alloy, where the value (0–100%) is the atomic percentage of Si in the alloy. The farther to the right on the figure, the more Si and less Au there are in the alloy. The lines on the graph separate the different phases of the alloy, from completely solid at the bottom of the graph to completely liquid at the top. Play close attention to any notes included to help describe a figure. The note in this case tells you that parentheses around an element indicate that element's solid state.

18. J
Figure Interpretation
Be careful to not confuse melting point with boiling point. Only the melting points are shown in Figure 1, so (J) is correct.

19. B
Figure Interpretation
Draw a vertical line from the 50% mark on the horizontal axis and a horizontal line from the 600°C mark on the vertical axis. These lines intersect in the region of the diagram labeled "liquid + (Si)," which the note tells you means liquid plus Si in its solid state.

20. G
Patterns
The lowest melting point is indicated by the section of the graph labeled "liquid" that reaches the farthest down on the graph. An arrow on the graph labels this point the "eutectic point" and gives the exact alloy composition there, which is reproduced correctly in (G).

21. A
Scientific Reasoning
The question asks you to look at compositions with less than 10% Si, which means you can draw a vertical line from the 10% mark on the horizontal axis

and ignore everything to the right of that line. In the portion of the graph to the left of this line, the temperature required for the alloy to become completely liquid decreases with increasing Si atomic percentage. Choice (D) is a trap set for those drawn to the wrong line on the figure. The horizontal line at a temperature of 363°C indicates the temperature at which the alloy becomes completely solid, not liquid.

22. H
Figure Interpretation
Draw a horizontal line from 1,200°C on the y-axis to where it intersects the plot. Draw a line down from that point to the x-axis. It intersects somewhere between 70 and 80% Si. According to the figure, solid Si particles would also begin to form at this temperature. Choice (H) encompasses this information and is correct.

PASSAGE V
Don't be intimidated by unfamiliar language like the biological terms in this passage. Remember that no advanced scientific knowledge is assumed. As usual, here the important task is to be able to locate the appropriate information from the given figures. Note the trends in both figures, namely the decreases in temperature and oxygen partial pressure with increasing altitude in Figure 1 and the elevated GST and ECH concentrations of the high altitude dwellers in Table 1.

23. D
Figure Interpretation
Make sure you refer to the correct part of Table 1 for the enzyme concentration values of populations ha 1, ha 2, and ha 3. The table shows that for all three high altitude populations, GST levels are highest, CR levels are lowest, and ECH levels are intermediate. Only (D) does not violate this relationship.

24. G
Figure Interpretation
The process of elimination works best here. Choice (F) is not universally true; the oxygen saturation percentages are pretty similar for high altitude and sea level dwellers. Neither Table 1 nor Figure 1 shows a comparison between high or low altitude populations and temperature or partial oxygen pressure, so (H) and (J) cannot be correct. Only (G) is directly supported by the values in the table.

25. C
Figure Interpretation
The answer to this question comes directly from Figure 1, but you must be careful to not confuse the two data sets. You can draw a horizontal line from 110 mm Hg on the left vertical axis until it intersects with the oxygen partial pressure data (squares). That intersection happens at about 3,200 m. To find the temperature at this altitude, draw a horizontal line from the temperature plot (circles) at 3,200 m to the right axis. It intersects at between –5°C and –10°C, meaning it must be (C). Accidentally reversing the two data sets likely results in selecting answer trap (A).

26. H
Figure Interpretation
You are asked to find the highest ECH concentration for any of the six populations, which occurs for population ha 2.

27. A
Scientific Reasoning
Only choices A and C agree with the information in Table 1. You can eliminate choice C, though, because nothing in the passage or data suggests that CR concentration has anything to do with efficiency at incorporating oxygen into the blood.

PASSAGE VI
On passages that present two conflicting viewpoints, make sure you read the first passage and answer the questions associated with it before reading the second passage and answering the remaining questions. Note the fundamental similarities and differences between the two viewpoints. In this case, Student 1 attributes the fact that lakes freeze from the surface downward to the effects of pressure, while Student 2 credits a change in density. Both students are able to apply their explanations to the ice skating situation as well. You are not asked to determine the validity of either viewpoint, but instead to follow each argument separately and be able to apply each student's reasoning.

28. J
Scientific Reasoning
Recall that Student 1 credits pressure for the freezing phenomenon. Choices (G) and (H) reflect elements of the viewpoint of Student 2 and can therefore be eliminated. If (F) were true, the temperature and pressure effects would work against each other, so only (J) makes sense.

29. B
Scientific Reasoning
According to Student 1, pressure causes the ice to melt, and pressure increases with increasing weight. Student 2 states that friction causes the ice to melt and that the force of friction increases with increasing weight. Therefore, the students would agree that ice would melt faster under the heavier skater, as in (B).

30. F
Scientific Reasoning
In the explanation of Student 2, ice melts when heat is generated as the skater overcomes the force of friction by *moving* across the ice. If the skater is not moving, then, no heat should be generated. Student 1, though, explains that ice melts due to pressure, which is present whether or not the skater is moving, making (F) correct.

31. C
Scientific Reasoning

Student 2 explains that less dense materials float above more dense materials. Since the frozen ethanol remains below the liquid ethanol, (C) must be true.

32. H
Scientific Reasoning

You can eliminate (F) and (G) due to the mention of pressure in both, which is a concept only Student 1 contemplates. Student 2 describes floating as the case in which the buoyant force exceeds the force of gravity, so the sinking boat is evidence of the opposite situation described in (H).

33. B
Scientific Reasoning

Eliminate (A) because only Student 1 considers pressure, and eliminate (D) because the only possible support for this explanation also comes from Student 1. Eliminate (C) because the force of gravity will only change as the mass of the skater changes. Student 2 states that heat is produced by overcoming friction, so less friction would mean less heat, as in (B).

34. F
Scientific Reasoning

Recall that the viewpoint of Student 2 focuses on a difference in *density*, and eliminate (H). Choices (G) and (J) both actually mean the same thing, but the term *buoyant* is included in choice J to entice the unwary test taker. In either case, the balloon would remain on the ground. The less dense balloon described in (F) would indeed rise above the ground.

PASSAGE VII

The first paragraph of this research summary passage explains that the experiments were conducted to study F^- concentrations in water. Experiment 1 tested solutions prepared by the students to have specific F^- concentrations, and the solutions' electrical conductivities were measured. Table 1 shows a direct relationship between F^- concentration and conductivity, and Figure 1 further emphasizes the linearity of this relationship. Be careful to notice the difference between *measured* and *corrected* conductivities and that it is the corrected conductivities that are plotted in Figure 1. Don't worry if you don't recognize the units given for conductivity; knowledge of these units is not required to answer the questions.

Experiment 2 tested solutions taken from various communities' drinking water supplies. The direct relationship between F^- concentration and conductivity seen in Experiment 1 is confirmed.

35. C
Patterns

Either Table 1 or Figure 1 can provide the answer here. Table 1 contains numerical examples of cases where the F^- concentration is indeed doubled (from 0.5 mg/L to 1 mg/L, for example) and gives the corresponding change in conductivity. Taking care to look in the *corrected* conductivity column, you can see that 2 times the concentration results in 2 times the corrected conductivity. Likewise, Figure 1 makes it clear that relationship between the two quantities is linear, which means that any multiplication of the concentration results in the same multiplication of the conductivity.

36. J
Figure Interpretation

Compare the new conductivity value to those given in Table 2, specifically those for Newtown and Lakewood, and recall the direct relationship between conductivity and F^- concentration. Noticing that Bluewater's conductivity value lies between the values for Newtown and Lakewood allows you to eliminate (F) and (G). Taking care to list the towns in order of *increasing* F^- leads you to (J).

37. C
Patterns

Refer to Table 1 to see where a value of 3.0 mg/L would fit in. This new concentration is between the 2.0 mg/L and 4.0 mg/L values given in the table, so the corrected conductivity should lie between 3.34 μS/cm and 6.68 μS/cm. Choices (B) and (D) are too close to the extremes of this range, but (C) is exactly in the middle as it should be. Alternatively, you could read the corrected conductivity for a concentration of 3.0 mg/L directly from Figure 1.

38. F
Scientific Reasoning

Questions that ask you to change the procedure of an experiment usually require you to review the original experiment before answering. In this case, the description of Experiment 1 tells you that F^- is added in the form of dissolved Na_2SiF_6. To study Cl^- concentrations, the students must use a chemical that contains Cl^- when preparing the solutions, as in (F).

39. B
Scientific Reasoning

Experimental data is not required to answer this question. The last sentence of the description of Experiment 1 explains that the corrected conductivity is calculated by *subtracting* the measured conductivity of the blank solution. This always results in the corrected conductivity being less than the measured conductivity, as in (B).

40. F
Scientific Reasoning

You are told that Cl^- results in an increase in conductivity, and the data shows that F^- results in an increase in conductivity. Therefore, in a solution containing both F^- and Cl^-, it would be impossible to distinguish the contributions to conductivity from each ion given only conductivity measurements. Conductivity would be increased by the presence of Cl^-, and the apparent values for F^- concentration would be falsely high, as in (F). If you miss this point, you could at least eliminate choice J since the question asks only about the case where *all* of the samples have Cl^- concentrations. The effect of the Cl^- should not be different for different solutions.

WRITING TEST

MODEL ESSAY

Below is an example of what a high-scoring essay might look like. Notice the author states her position clearly in the introductory paragraph and supports that position with evidence in the following paragraphs. The essay also uses transitions, some advanced vocabulary, and an effective "hook" to draw in the reader.

The elevated rate of automobile accidents that occur when teenaged drivers are behind the wheel has driven some parents and legislators to lobby for laws that would ban drivers under 18 from driving with other teenagers in the car. Those who support these laws believe that driving alone or with an adult would minimize distraction for new drivers, helping them to drive more safely. Others disagree, pointing to the lack of evidence that groups of teenagers riding together are actually the cause of these accidents.

Everyone benefits from having more safe drivers on the road, but efforts to curb the freedoms of drivers under 18 are misguided and unfair. For example, elderly drivers may have impaired vision or motor skills, but are not subject to additional restrictions based only on their age. Male drivers are more prone to car accidents than female drivers, but one can only imagine the outcry if a restriction on the driving privileges of all men were proposed! A driver's license should provide the same responsibilities and freedoms to each person who receives one. If we don't believe that 16-year-olds are as capable of operating a car safely as 18-year-olds, we should not issue them driver's licenses at all.

If we want to promote safe driving, there are more evenhanded methods of doing so. In our state, all drivers who take their license exam must have completed 40 hours of classroom training, regardless of age. These classes are an effective way to ensure that everyone who takes the driver's exam has the same base level of knowledge about traffic laws, operation of a motor vehicle, and the importance of driving safely. This information is important for all new drivers. A requirement for licensed drivers to take a refresher course every five years could help to ensure that more drivers remain aware of new laws and safety issues.

Proponents of this law claim that preventing teenagers from riding in cars together will help to lower the number of accidents. However, no studies have been released that can isolate the presence of other teenagers in the car as a cause of accidents. Having a conversation with a friend in the passenger seat could certainly be distracting, but talking on a cell phone, or listening to loud music, might be equally or even more distracting—and again, all of these distractions can occur when an older person is driving, as well.

Safety and responsibility are important for drivers of all ages. The proposed laws target younger drivers unfairly, and there is no evidence that they would prevent accidents. Measures that attempt to promote safe driving should be aimed at all drivers, not the small percentage of them who are under 18 years old.

You can evaluate your essay and the model essay based on the following criteria, covered in the Scoring section of Inside the ACT Writing Test:

- Does the author answer the question?
- Is the author's position clearly stated?
- Does the body of the essay support and develop the position taken?
- Are there at least two supporting paragraphs?
- Is the relevance of each supporting paragraph clear?
- Does the writer address the other side of the argument?
- Is the essay organized, with a clear introduction, middle, and end?
- Does the author start a new paragraph for each new idea?
- Is each sentence in a paragraph relevant to the point made in that paragraph?
- Are transitions clear?
- Is the essay easy to read? Is it engaging?
- Are sentences varied?
- Is vocabulary used effectively? Is college-level vocabulary used?

Compute Your Score

1. **Figure out your score in each subject test.** Refer to the answer keys to figure out the number right in each test. Enter the results in the chart:

		TEST 1	TEST 2	TEST 3
RAW SCORES	English:			
	Math:			
	Reading:			
	Science:			

2. **Find your Practice Test scores.** Find your raw score on each subject test in the following table. The score on the far left column indicates your estimated scaled score if this were an actual ACT.

SCALED SCORE	RAW SCORES			
	English	**Mathematics**	**Reading**	**Science**
36	75	60	40	40
35	74	60	40	40
34	73	59	39	39
33	72	58	39	39
32	71	57	38	38
31	70	55–56	37	37
30	69	53–54	36	36
29	68	50–52	35	35
28	67	48–49	34	34
27	65–66	45–47	33	33
26	63–64	43–44	32	32
25	61–62	40–42	31	30–31
24	58–60	38–39	30	28–29
23	56–57	35–37	29	26–27
22	53–55	33–34	28	24–25
21	49–52	31–32	27	21–23
20	46–48	28–30	25–26	19–20
19	44–45	26–27	23–24	17–18
18	41–43	23–25	21–22	16
17	39–40	20–22	19–20	15
16	36–38	17–19	17–18	14
15	34–35	15–16	15–16	13
14	30–33	13–14	13–14	12
13	28–29	11–12	12–13	11
12	25–27	9–10	10–11	10
11	23–24	8	9	9
10	20–22	7	8	8
9	17–19	6	7	7
8	14–16	5	6	6
7	12–13	4	5	5
6	9–11	3	4	4
5	7–8	2	3	3
4	4–6	1	2	2
3	3	1	1	1
2	2	0	0	0
1	1	0	0	0

	TEST 1	TEST 2	TEST 3
SCALED SCORES English:			
Math:			
Reading:			
Science:			

3. **Find your estimated Composite score.** To calculate your estimated Composite score, simply add together your scaled scores on each subject test and divide by four.

COMPOSITE SCORE

TEST 1	TEST 2	TEST 3